P9-DUU-437

UNA DESTINATIO VIAE DIVERSAE · A·D·1852 ·

MILLS COLLEGE
LIBRARY

Gift of

The Handbook of Artificial Intelligence

ι(ι

Volume III

Edited by

Paul R. Cohen

and

Edward A. Feigenbaum

Department of Computer Science
Stanford University

HEURISTECH PRESS
Stanford, California

WILLIAM KAUFMANN, INC.
Los Altos, California

Library of Congress Cataloging in Publication Data:

The handbook of artificial intelligence.

    Bibliography: p. 563
    Includes cumulative index.
    1. Artificial intelligence. I. Cohen, Paul R., 1955–
    II. Feigenbaum, Edward A.
Q335.H36   001.53′5   80–28621
ISBN 0–86576–004–7 (set)
ISBN 0–86576–007–1 (Vol. III)

Copyright © 1982 by William Kaufmann, Inc.

All rights reserved. No part of this publication may be reproduced, stored in a retrieval system, or trasmitted, in any form or by any means, electronic, mechanical, photocopying, recording, or otherwise, without the prior written permission of the publisher. However, this work may be reproduced in whole or in part for the official use of the U.S. Government on the condition that copyright notice is included with such official reproduction. For further information, write to: Permissions, William Kaufmann, Inc., 95 First Street, Los Altos, California 94022.

10 9 8 7 6 5 4 3 2 1

Printed in the United States of America

006.3
H236
V.3

001.535
H 236
v. 3

To

Allen Newell,
First President of the
American Association
for Artificial Intelligence

and

Arthur Samuel,
Pioneer in the study
of machine learning

Mills College Library
Withdrawn

MILLS COLLEGE
LIBRARY

CONTENTS OF VOLUME III

LIST OF CONTRIBUTORS

Non-Stanford affiliations indicated if known.

Chapter Editors

Janice Aikins (Hewlett-Packard)
James S. Bennett
Victor Ciesielski (Rutgers U)
William J. Clancey
Paul R. Cohen
James E. Davidson
Thomas G. Dietterich

Bob Elschlager (Tymshare)
Lawrence Fagan
Anne v.d.L. Gardner
Takeo Kanade (CMU)
Jorge Phillips (Kestrel)
Steve Tappel
Stephen Westfold (Kestrel)

Contributors

Robert Anderson (Rand)
Douglas Appelt (SRI)
David Arnold
Michael Ballantyne (U Texas)
David Barstow (Schlumberger)
Peter Biesel (Rutgers U)
Lee Blaine (Lockheed)
W. W. Bledsoe (U Texas)
David A. Bourne (CMU)
Rodney Brooks (MIT)
Bruce G. Buchanan
Richard Chestek
Kenneth Clarkson
Nancy H. Cornelius (CMU)
James L. Crowley (CMU)
Randall Davis (MIT)
Gerard Dechen
Johan de Kleer (Xerox)
Jon Doyle (CMU)
R. Geoff Dromey (U Wollongong)
Richard Duda (Fairchild)
Ramez El-Masri (Honeywell)
Robert S. Engelmore (Teknowledge)
Susan Epstein (Rutgers U)
Robert E. Filman (Hewlett-Packard)
Fritz Fisher (Ramtek)

Christian Freksa (Max Plank, Munich)
Peter Friedland
Hiromichi Fujisawa (CMU)
Richard P. Gabriel
Michael R. Genesereth
Neil Goldman (ISI)
Ira Goldstein (Hewlett-Packard)
George Heidorn (IBM)
Martin Herman (CMU)
Annette Herskovits
Douglas Hofstadter (Indiana U)
Elaine Kant (CMU)
Fuminobu Komura (CMU)
William Laaser (Xerox)
Douglas B. Lenat
Bob London
William J. Long (MIT)
Bruce D. Lucas (CMU)
Pamela McCorduck
Mark L. Miller (Computer Thought)
Robert C. Moore (SRI)
Richard Pattis
Stanley J. Rosenschein (SRI)
Neil C. Rowe
Gregory R. Ruth (MIT)
Daniel Sagalowicz (SRI)

Contributors (continued)

Behrokh Samadi (UCLA)
William Scherlis (CMU)
Steven A. Shafer (CMU)
Andrew Silverman
David R. Smith (CMU)
Donald Smith (Rutgers U)
Phillip Smith (U Waterloo)
Reid G. Smith (Schlumberger)
William R. Swartout (ISI)

Steven L. Tanimoto (U Washington)
Charles E. Thorpe (CMU)
William van Melle (Xerox)
Richard J. Waldinger (SRI)
Richard C. Waters (MIT)
Sholom Weiss (Rutgers U)
David Wilkins (SRI)
Terry Winograd

Reviewers

Harold Abelson (MIT)
Saul Amarel (Rutgers U)
Robert Balzer (ISI)
Harry Barrow (Fairchild)
Thomas Binford
Daniel Bobrow (Xerox)
John Seely Brown (Xerox)
Richard Burton (Xerox)
Lewis Creary
Andrea diSessa (MIT)
Daniel Dolata (UC Santa Cruz)
Lee Erman (ISI)
Adele Goldberg (Xerox)
Cordell Green (Kestrel)
Norman Haas (Symantec)
Kenneth Kahn (MIT)
Jonathan J. King (Hewlett-Packard)
Casimir Kulikowski (Rutgers U)
John Kunz
Brian P. McCune (AI&DS)
Jock Mackinlay

Ryszard S. Michalski (U Illinois)
Donald Michie (U Edinburgh)
Thomas M. Mitchell (Rutgers U)
D. Jack Mostow (ISI)
Nils Nilsson (SRI)
Glen Ouchi (UC Santa Cruz)
Ira Pohl (UC Santa Cruz)
Arthur L. Samuel
David Shur
Herbert A. Simon (CMU)
David E. Smith
Dennis H. Smith (Lederle)
Mark Stefik (Xerox)
Albert L. Stevens (BBN)
Allan Terry
Perry W. Thorndyke (Perceptronics)
Paul E. Utgoff (Rutgers U)
Donald Walker (SRI)
Harald Wertz (U Paris)
Keith Wescourt (Rand)

Production

Robert Bruce Buchanan
Max Diaz
David Eppstein
Janet Feigenbaum
David Fuchs
José L. González
Marion Hazen
Dianne G. Kanerva
Jonni M. Kanerva

Pentti Kanerva
Dikran Karagueuzian
Arthur M. Keller
Barbara R. Laddaga
Roy Nordblom
Thomas C. Rindfleisch
Ellen Smith
Helen Tognetti
Christopher Tucci

PREFACE

Intelligence... is the faculty of making artificial objects, especially tools to make tools.

—Henri Bergson
L'Evolution Créatice (1907)

ARTIFICIAL INTELLIGENCE is a relatively young branch of science, new enough that we can still trace the development of the field from its inception in 1956 to the present. About six years ago, when we were planning the *Handbook of Artificial Intelligence*, we thought it would be possible to present AI comprehensively in three volumes. In retrospect, that seems to have been a good guess, although, inevitably, the outline has been changed many times to reflect changes in the emphasis and methods of AI. Some chapters are very much larger than we had anticipated, some are smaller, and one was deleted altogether; many of the original articles have been deleted or rewritten. Such is the price (and the excitement) associated with the task of researching and reporting on a flourishing, rapidly developing field.

Although the contents of the *Handbook* have changed, our intentions as to its format and style have not. From the outset, we have wanted a comprehensive survey of AI that stripped away jargon, filled out assumptions, presented essential problems, and simply described solutions. From the outset, we have assumed that, in most instances, a piece of writing that fulfilled these criteria could present a program, project, or doctoral dissertation in six or seven pages. We do not discuss the fine points of individual pieces of research but encourage the reader to discover them in the references we provide with each article. On the other hand, we *do* attempt to make explicit (in the form of cross-references) some of the subtler relationships among the areas of AI research.

Thus, guided by the discoveries and developments in AI, and constrained by a constant set of editorial goals, the *Handbook* has grown to about 1,500 pages, divided among three volumes. The distribution of chapters in the volumes reflects, to some extent, the recent history of AI. In the first volume, we discuss search, knowledge representation, understanding natural language, and understanding spoken language. These were among the most topical areas of AI when the first volume was drafted. We postponed discussion of "areas in transition" to later volumes. For example, automatic deduction was not a popular subject of AI research when Volume I was planned, and we left it until this volume. In the interim, it has seen several new developments and has regained some of the prominence it had in the earliest days of AI. Similarly, to reflect more recent perspectives, two chapters of the second volume (on automatic programming and AI programming languages) were completed just within the last year. The other chapters of Volume II, which deal with scientific, medical, and educational applications of AI, were drafted earlier. The chapters in the present volume (with the exception of Chap. XI on models of cognition) deal with topics that we did not understand very well when the *Handbook* was planned. By deferring these discussions, we have had an opportunity to "wait and see" what happened in vision, learning, planning, and automatic deduction. We also deferred a chapter on robotics to this volume but decided finally, for reasons discussed later, not to write it.

If there is a unifying theme to this volume, it is that intelligence—artificial or natural—involves a great many hierarchically organized, interacting information processes. We discuss here some of the basic processes that are prerequisite for a computer to function intelligently (by human standards) in the world. A computer must be able to sense its environment, it must have a memory and must learn, it should construct rudimentary plans to solve problems, and it should be able to reason deductively and inductively. If, as is common in AI, the computer does not interact with a physical world but with a symbolic world that represents selected aspects of its physical counterpart, then the computer need not sense its environment. Or if a program has been constructed to solve a related set of problems and it has all of the information it needs at the outset, then it need not learn. But if a computer program is to behave with even a fraction of the intelligence of a two-year-old baby—to learn, for example, that the family cat is like the family dog in appearance, but not in personality, and to use this information to plan its interactions with each animal—then that program will need the skills discussed in this volume.

Chapter XI, on models of cognition, is an introduction to cognitive science—a field at the intersection of AI and cognitive psychology. From the earliest days of AI, researchers have designed artificial systems to improve their understanding of human thought. The overview of Chapter XI discusses the early history (1956–1970) of these ideas, and the early and profitable interaction between computer scientists and psychologists. In fact, we emphasize the history of information-processing psychology at the expense of more recent work in cognitive science because it is a fascinating history and because the field is developing so rapidly that we can see it best from a distance. More recent work is discussed elsewhere in the *Handbook*.

Chapter XII, on automatic deduction, describes modes of reasoning. Formal analyses of natural deduction, resolution-based deduction, induction, and nonmonotonic reasoning are presented. Modern symbolic logic, a discipline at least a century old, originated as an attempt to formalize rules of mathematical reasoning and it has been used by many philosophers as a competence theory, or even a normative theory, of human reasoning. Automatic deduction is the computational side of logic; it seeks to discover procedures that can deduce the logical consequences of facts with some degree of efficiency. Automatic deduction touches AI in at least two ways. First, machines that reason about the real world almost certainly need to perform symbolic deduction in some form, and, second, heuristic methods can be applied to the task of deduction itself, as in the case of mathematical theorem proving. Both concerns are evident in this chapter.

Chapter XIII surveys vision research. Vision systems work with raw data from a real, noisy environment. While most AI programs reason about preselected aspects of the world that are cleanly represented in some representation language, the task of vision research is to develop representations of the physical world and procedures for reasoning from one representation to another. Successive levels of representation are less noisy and better suited to particular tasks. This chapter was planned by Professor Takeo Kanade of Carnegie-Mellon University. It is a large chapter, about 200 pages, but a comprehensive one. All aspects of vision, from cameras and range finders to the highest level inferences about the contents of a scene, are discussed. A few articles about technical problems—articles with very little AI content—are included for the completeness they bring to the presentation of vision research.

Vision and robotics are closely related fields and, initially, a robotics chapter was planned for the *Handbook*. We discovered, however, that the points of intersection between robotics and AI had been covered in other chapters—those on vision and planning—and that other aspects of industrial and research robotics, such as dynamics and control, and sensor and arm design, were well beyond the scope of this book. Thus, we decided to forgo the chapter rather than present an incomplete view of the field.

Chapter XIV describes attempts by AI researchers to create computer programs that learn. The reader of these volumes will have noted a recurring theme: The power of an AI program is directly proportional to what it knows. For this reason, much effort has been devoted to making programs more knowledgeable and, in particular, to creating programs that can acquire knowledge by taking advice, by rote learning, and by learning from examples. The author of this chapter, Thomas G. Dietterich, has developed a theoretical framework in which he compares and contrasts these and other approaches to learning. An interesting conclusion is that learning programs are themselves subject to the theme just mentioned: The performance of learning programs is directly proportional to what they know.

The last chapter in Volume III discusses planning and problem-solving. It can be regarded as an extension to Chapter II on search. These chapters might have been merged, but some important developments in planning research postdate the writing of the search chapter. Among those discussed in

Chapter XV are hierarchical planning—representing a single plan at several levels of abstraction—and least-commitment planning methods that avoid backtracking.

Acknowledgments

The reader will note that a great many people have been involved with the three volumes of the *Handbook;* their names are listed on pages xi-xii. Here, we acknowledge those who have helped with Volume III.

Chapter XIII was organized and partly written by Professor Takeo Kanade of Carnegie-Mellon University. We are very grateful for his thorough and persevering work at all stages of the chapter: He decided on its contents; supervised its writing; and wrote the overview, the articles on Mackworth's research and his own, and the articles on texture and "shape-from" methods. He also rewrote many articles and checked all of them, and the figures, at every stage of their progress, ensuring a comprehensive, authoritative, and accurate chapter.

The other authors of the vision chapter are the following: Martin Herman wrote the bulk of the blocks-world articles and the article on relaxation algorithms. Steven A. Shafer wrote the articles on color, region analysis, and intrinsic images; in addition, he volunteered for several days of intensive editing, for which we are grateful. James L. Crowley wrote the articles on visual input and range finders; Fuminobu Komura, on preprocessing and edge-detection; David R. Smith, on shape analysis and vision systems; David A. Bourne, on syntactic methods; Rodney Brooks, a contributor of several articles to the *Handbook*, on ACRONYM; Nancy H. Cornelius, on motion; Hiromichi Fujisawa, on robot vision; Bruce D. Lucas, on stereo vision; Steven L. Tanimoto, on pyramids in vision research; and Charles E. Thorpe, on template matching.

Chapter XIV was organized, and largely written and edited, by Thomas G. Dietterich. Typically, the organization of a chapter reflects the extant theoretical distinctions in a field, but, in this case, it was necessary to synthesize an organization, actually, a general model of learning systems. Individual systems are discussed in terms of the components of this model, and four classes of learning systems are discriminated by the kinds of processing they perform on training instances. Bob London wrote the articles on rote learning and advice-taking, Kenneth Clarkson contributed the article on grammatical inference, and Geoffrey Dromey wrote the article on adaptive learning. The chapter was reviewed by James S. Bennett, Bruce G. Buchanan, Ryszard S. Michalski, Thomas M. Mitchell, Jack Mostow, David Shur, and Paul Utgoff.

Chapter XII, on automatic deduction, was written by several people. Janice Aikins organized the chapter and edited most of the articles. The overview was written by Robert C. Moore at SRI International; we are especially grateful to him for also reviewing the other articles. W. W. Bledsoe, from the University of Texas, provided the article on resolution theorem-proving and edited the article on natural deduction, which was prepared by Michael Ballantyne, also of the University of Texas. Stanley J. Rosenschein, of SRI International, wrote and edited the article on logic programming. Richard Pattis wrote the article on the Boyer-Moore theorem prover. Jon Doyle rewrote his perfectly adequate article on nonmonotonic logic to provide us with a new, crisp, and readable account of this rather recent and complex topic.

Chapter XI, on models of cognition, was written by Paul Cohen, as was most of Chapter XV, on planning. Steve Westfold wrote an early version of the NOAH article, and Peter Friedland wrote the article on the refinement of skeletal plans.

We thank Avron Barr for his work on Volumes I and II of the *Handbook*. Volume I was undoubtedly the most difficult of the three volumes to produce since it involved many decisions that we have not had to repeat for subsequent volumes. His dedication and foresight have made Volume III a relatively easy book to produce.

The *Handbook* is unusual in that it has been drafted, edited, and typeset on several computers. After an article or a book is drafted, there is a great deal of production work before it is ready to print. Usually, an author leaves a manuscript with a publisher, and some months or years later a book emerges. In the case of the *Handbook*, we wanted a continual interplay between writing, editing, and producing, so that the contents of each book would remain current right up until the time it is published. This involved maintaining each book—its articles, references, indexes—in computer files.

Dianne Kanerva has been responsible for the production of the three volumes of the *Handbook*. She has edited the books for style and managed their typesetting, the construction of the indexes and bibliographies, and the production of the figures. She has produced three volumes, 1,500 pages, in 18 months, and when she started, the text of Volume II was not finished and only one chapter of Volume III existed. We are very grateful for her contribution. José L. González has done the final typesetting on every article in Volumes II and III. He tailored and implemented a set of TEX macros that ensured the consistency and quality of the *Handbook*'s appearance as well as assisting Kanerva in the final editing of the manuscript. Dikran Karagueuzian prepared and typeset the bibliographies and name indexes for Volumes II and III and, with Christopher Tucci, operated the Alphatype CRS phototypesetter. Pentti Kanerva wrote the index program that made it possible to prepare the extensive name and subject indexes. Janet Feigenbaum and Barbara Laddaga assisted with formatting the text of the book during the spring and summer of 1981, as have David Eppstein and Jonni Kanerva in the months since. Robert Bruce Buchanan did much preliminary work with the bibliographies.

We thank the staff of the publisher, William Kaufmann, Inc. Mike
Hamilton was in charge of production. Sunny Olds coordinated the production
of Volumes II and III between Stanford and the publisher; she also did much
of the proofreading, with the assistance of Vicki Woodruff. Catherine Drees,
Beverly Kennon-Kelley, and Spectra Media prepared the extensive artwork.

The Advanced Research Projects Agency of the Department of Defense
and the Biotechnology Resources Program of the National Institutes of Health
supported the *Handbook* project as part of their long-standing and continuing
efforts to develop and disseminate the science and technology of AI. The
electronic text-preparation facilities available to Stanford computer scientists on the SAIL, SCORE, and SUMEX computers were used throughout the
project.

Chapter XI

Models of Cognition

CHAPTER XI: MODELS OF COGNITION

A. OVERVIEW

ANTHROPOMORPHISM is a powerful tendency in human thinking—we ascribe personalities and emotions to all kinds of animate and inanimate objects. Thus, it is not surprising that we should do the same with computers, or even that we should reverse the terms of the equation and describe ourselves in terms reserved for the machine. This is not a new trend—it certainly predates the electronic computer (e.g., the Futurists around 1910 extolled the virtues of the machine in their manifestos)—but the comparison between man and machine is particularly compelling in the case of the computer.

However, there is no science and no subtlety in the broad, unqualified claim that we behave like computers or vice versa; the trick is to know enough about how humans and computers think to say *exactly* what they have in common, and, when we lack this knowledge, to use the comparison to *suggest* theories of human thinking or computer thinking. Thus, psychology and AI have a reciprocal, piggyback relationship: What we learn about human intelligence suggests extensions to the theory of machine intelligence, and vice versa.

This reciprocal relationship was most evident during the early years of AI. For example, in 1956, Allen Newell and Herbert Simon developed a theory of problem solving called LT (for Logic Theorist), which they implemented as a computer program. Because the theory was formalized, Newell and Simon could specify *exactly* the problem-solving behaviors they expected to find in human problem-solvers. But when they tested their theory, they found that it failed in one respect: Humans did not use the same control process (working backward from theorem to axioms) as the program. Thus, they revised the theory, and wrote a new program, to incorporate what they had learned about human control processes during problem solving. They called the new program the General Problem Solver (GPS), and the new control process *means-ends analysis*, and found that this process was much more efficient (in terms of computer time) than its predecessor. Means-ends analysis is now an established problem-solving technique in AI.

This example illustrates how, by exploiting the comparison between human and machine problem-solving, it is possible to develop theories of both from relative ignorance of either. The first step was LT, a preliminary theory. The next step was to test LT against human problem-solvers. The third step was to derive a new theory, GPS, from differences between the old one and the experimental data. This theory was tested again and was more successful, both as a theory of human problem-solving and as a technique for AI. Note, however, that this development succeeded not by simply asserting that human problem-solving is like machine problem-solving but, rather, by describing *with precision* their similarities and, more importantly for the development of the theory, their differences. Computer programs are precise descriptions of behavior and so are the results of experiments with humans; by using each to complement the other, a theory of behavior develops quickly.

This approach to psychological research is called *information-processing psychology* and, more recently, *cognitive science*. The theories that are developed—computer models of human thinking—are called *models of cognition*. The central idea of information-processing psychology is to bring precision to the seductive comparison between human and artificial intelligence, to benefit our understanding of human cognition. In the next section, we present a historical background to information-processing psychology.

A History of AI and Information Processing

Information-processing psychology has played an important part in the development of American psychology since 1950. It has helped to reinstate the concept of *mind*, which had been abolished by behavioral psychologists because it was unobservable except by introspection. *Methodological behaviorism* condemned introspection as a psychological method because there was no guarantee that the words used by one person to describe his (or her) mental events would mean the same thing to another person. For example, if a person says, "I can't quite think of the word—it is on the tip of my tongue," you may think you know what he is thinking and feeling, but, in fact, regardless of the detail with which he describes his state, you cannot guarantee that your knowledge of his state is completely accurate. A stronger position on introspection is taken by *radical behaviorism*, which holds that knowledge obtained by introspection not only cannot be accurately communicated, but is not even accurately perceived by the introspector: "An organism behaves as it does because of its current structure, but most of this is out of the reach of introspection" (Skinner, 1976, p. 19). Mental events are viewed as side effects of the interaction between an organism and its environment, not causes and thus not explanations of behavior.

These positions—radical and methodological behaviorism—were objective but resulted in a psychology that did not admit the mind. Theoretically, it was possible to explain behavior in terms of stimulus-response pairs, denying any mediating mental structures or processes:

> A person is changed by the contingencies of reinforcement under which he behaves; he does not store the contingencies. In particular, he does not store copies of the stimuli which have played a part in the contingencies. There are no "iconic representations" in his mind; there are no "data structures stored in his memory"; he has no "cognitive map" of the world in which he has lived. He has simply been changed in such a way that stimuli now control particular kinds of perceptual behavior. (Skinner, 1976, pp. 93–94)

In contrast, all the research described in the *Handbook* is concerned with structures and processes that mediate intelligent responses to stimuli. This fundamental change in theoretical positions took place between 1950 and 1960, during which time behaviorism was largely displaced by *cognitive psychology*. The key to the change was the concept of *information*. Following the publication, in 1949, of Shannon and Weaver's "The Mathematical Theory of Communication," information became a concrete, measurable quantity (see Shannon and Weaver, 1963). Initially, the strict mathematical conception of information was explored; theorists tried to fit many aspects of human communication into the general model proposed by Shannon and Weaver (see, e.g., Cherry, 1970). But the model was best suited to communication over electrical channels, and so, by the mid-1950s, a more relaxed, and more appropriate, conception of information was emerging.

An influential paper was "The Magical Number Seven..." in which Miller (1956) proposed that the information capacity of mental processes, particularly short-term memory, is best measured in terms of semantic *chunks*—meaningful units of information—not abstract *bits*. For example, words from a sentence and nonsense syllables are considered to be chunks of information and put approximately equal demands on memory, despite the fact that the words contain more information, in the mathematical sense, than the syllables. In the years following Miller's paper, information *structures* such as discrimination nets, associative semantic nets, and frames were developed to *represent* the information used in cognition. The original, mathematical formulation of information has been largely abandoned:

> The problem was that the bit gave a very poorly articulated characterization of the information.... As descriptions of the information have become more articulated, the theories composed out of them have become more successful. (Anderson and Bower, 1973, p. 136)

The increasing sophistication of computers and computer science was the most important factor in the development of information-processing ideas. During the late 1950s, there was the realization in information-processing psychology that the computer was not simply a device for shifting bits or "crunching numbers," but was more generally capable of any kind of symbol manipulation, of any kind of *information process:*

> An entirely different use of computers in psychology ... has emerged. This ... stems from the fact that a computer is a device for manipulating symbols of any kind, not just numerical symbols. Thus a computer becomes a way of specifying arbitrary symbolic processes. Theories of this type, which can be called information processing theories, are essentially nonquantitative (they may involve no numbers at all), although neither less precise nor less rigorous than classical mathematical theories. (Newell and Simon, 1963, p. 366)

And in cognitive psychology, the computer and the emergence of programs like LT had a profound effect, even though cognitive psychology does not share the enthusiasm of information-processing psychology for computer models:

> The activities of the computer itself seemed in some ways akin to cognitive processes. Computers accept information, manipulate symbols, store items in "memory" and retrieve them again, classify inputs, recognize patterns, and so on. Whether they do these things just like people was less important than that they do them at all. The coming of the computer provided a much-needed reassurance that cognitive processes were real.... Some theorists even maintained that all psychological theories should be explicitly written in the form of computer programs. (Neisser, 1976, pp. 5–6)

These theorists were Newell, Simon, and J. C. Shaw. Their position that computer programs can be psychological theories is the point at which cognitive psychology and information-processing psychology part company. For most cognitive psychologists, information processing is a metaphor for human thought, a means of focusing attention on new and interesting questions about the mind. Very few cognitive psychologists have implemented information-processing models—programs—of their theories. Even among those who have, the strong position that the program is itself a theory is not universally accepted; for example, Anderson and Bower (1973) explicitly limit the sense in which their model of human associative memory is a theory (Article XI.E2):

> It is important to be clear about the relationship between the theory and this simulation program. We make no claim that there is any careful correspondence between the step-by-step information processing in the simulation program and in the psychological theory.... The claim is sometimes made ... that the program is the theory. This is not the case for HAM, and we wish to make this denial explicit. HAM represents a very complicated set of speculations about human memory. Only some of these are represented in the simulation program. Moreover, the simulation program does not serve as an embodiment of this subset of the theory; rather, it is but one test of the adequacy of that subset. (pp. 142–143)

(The relationship between cognitive psychology and information-processing psychology is discussed in more detail in Newell, 1970, and Miller, 1978.)

To complete this historical overview, we should note the relationship between AI and information-processing psychology. It was summed up nicely by Minsky (1968) in his own historical discussion in which he identified three extensions to early work in cybernetics:

> The first was the continuation of the search for simple basic principles....
> The second important avenue was an attempt to build working models of human behavior incorporating, or developing as needed, specific psychological theories.... The third approach, the one we call *Artificial Intelligence*, was an attempt to build intelligent machines without any prejudice toward making the system simple, biological, or humanoid. (p. 9)

In other words, AI does not require that an intelligent program demonstrate *human* intelligence, but information-processing psychologists insist that the correspondence be proved.

This overview is almost current; we have discussed the common roots of AI, information-processing psychology, and cognitive psychology, and we have discussed the points at which they part company. However, we should note that we have presented the strongest version of the information-processing approach, that advocated by Newell and Simon. Their position is so strong that it defines information-processing psychology almost by exclusion: It is the field that uses methods alien to cognitive psychology to explore questions alien to AI. This is an exaggeration, but it serves to illustrate why there are thousands of cognitive psychologists, and hundreds of AI researchers, and very few information-processing psychologists. Recently, the strong position has been relaxed to admit research that does not necessarily *prove* the correspondence between programs and human behavior but that has some avowed concern for understanding human behavior. This research is called *cognitive science* by its practitioners.

The articles in this chapter discuss models of cognition that have, for the most part, been the historical shoulders on which cognitive science now stands. Of the eight articles, five are devoted to models of human memory, two to problem-solving, and one to belief systems. The emphasis on memory has two causes, one historical and one artifactual. Historically, cognitive psychology has concerned itself almost exclusively with memory, so it is not surprising that it should be a major topic in information-processing psychology. However, the proportion of articles would have been different had we included discussions of other cognitive science research in this chapter, rather than elsewhere in the *Handbook*—for example, research on speech understanding (Chap. V); on natural-language understanding, especially the work of Schank and his colleagues (Chap. IV); on planning (Chap. XV); and on learning (Chap. XIV).

The first model discussed in this chapter is, appropriately, Newell and Simon's General Problem Solver program (GPS; Article XI.B). It is some of the earliest research in information-processing psychology. The program introduced *means-ends analysis*, which constrains a problem solver to the task of reducing the differences between the current state of a problem and the goal state, or solution. The problem solver often cannot derive a solution immediately from the problem, so it is necessary to transform the problem into some intermediate state, from which the solution might be derived. GPS was tested extensively as a theory of human problem-solving.

The next article (Article XI.C) is also about problem solving; it discusses a model of *opportunistic planning* designed by Hayes-Roth and Hayes-Roth (1978). Their model is an interesting contrast to those discussed in Chapter XV on planning. Opportunistic processing involves a flexible control strategy (implemented with a *blackboard* control structure) that permits planning decisions to be made when the opportunity arises, rather than in a strict order. Hayes-Roth and Hayes-Roth suggest that opportunistic processing is necessary for complex problem solving. Their model was developed specifically as a model of human planning abilities; thus, it is discussed in the context of this chapter on models of cognition.

About the time that GPS was being implemented, Feigenbaum was designing his Elementary Perceiver and Memorizer (EPAM) program, the first of the memory models considered in this chapter (Article XI.D). It learns *paired-associate nonsense syllables*, which, since the end of the 19th century, have been used in experiments to reduce the effect on memory of the meaning of the material being remembered. Paired associates allow probing: One of a pair of syllables serves as a cue to invoke the memory of the other syllable. Many things can be learned about memory by varying the speed at which syllables are presented, the number that must be remembered, or the similarity between the syllables. Feigenbaum modeled learning of the syllables as a process of storing just enough information about a syllable to distinguish it from the other syllables in memory at the time it was stored. Often, this did not require storing the whole syllable, which results in performance on a recall test that is less than perfect and strikingly similar to that of humans on similar tests.

In 1968, Quillian developed a model of *semantic memory* that provided the basis for the work described in the next three articles in this chapter (Articles XI.E1, XI.E2, and XI.E3). Conceptually, semantic memory models are very simple. They can be thought of as graphs, where the points (called *nodes*) represent concepts and the lines represent relations between the points. The meaning of a concept in a semantic net is represented by its connections (or *associations*) with other concepts.

Quillian's model was not developed as a psychological theory originally, but it was the first information-processing model that looked like it might explain recently discovered and curious effects of meaning on memory, for example, the *category-size effect*, whereby it takes longer to classify objects that are members of large classes than those that are members of small classes.

The MEMOD model developed by Lindsay, Norman, and Rumelhart (LNR; see Article XI.E4) is much more ambitious than Quillian's model. In the first place, it is intended to be a model of human memory that captures some of the richness of language. This requires three types of nodes, instead of just the one "concept" node of Quillian. Nodes represent concepts, but also *episodes* and *events*. Episode nodes can be the superordinate nodes of complex events like stories; moreover, MEMOD's interpreter can "run" these events to simulate them. Episode nodes can designate arbitrary procedures that the interpreter can execute. The MEMOD model also permits a large number of relations between nodes, where Quillian had only about half a dozen. Further, relations in this model have a *case structure* similar to that of Fillmore (see Article IV.C4, in Vol. I). Another improvement over Quillian's model was the introduction of more powerful *interpretive procedures*, since semantic-net models do not actually *do* anything except represent information. Interpretive procedures are required to manipulate this information.

The HAM model of Anderson and Bower (Article XI.E2) is also a model of human long-term memory (Human Associative Memory; thus, HAM), but it differs in a number of important respects from MEMOD. Although it has a network knowledge base, relations in the network are much simpler than those in MEMOD. They are based on the syntactic categories of a simplified grammar of English that is used to interact with the system. Another difference between the two systems is that, in HAM, arbitrary procedures cannot be written and the simple procedures that are used reside outside of the network. Anderson and Bower take the position that experimental data from the memory literature can be explained by a relatively simple *strategy-free* process.

Later work by Anderson on his ACT system is discussed in Article XI.E3. The ACT model uses a propositional semantic-network knowledge base, similar to that of HAM. It has, in addition, a procedural component to operate on the knowledge base. Procedures, represented by a production system, are written by the user of ACT. This feature makes ACT rather like the MEMOD system in that both provide a language for their users to build computer models of psychological processes. The major differences between the systems arise from the way procedures are represented and from the interpreter, which controls the flow of computation in the systems.

The last article in this chapter (Article XI.F) discusses belief systems, in particular, the models of ideological oversimplification designed by Abelson and the PARRY model of paranoia built by Colby and his associates. These models have in common a representation of beliefs that affect interpretations of sentences. For example, a "typical liberal" would interpret a national event, like Congress appropriating money for urban redevelopment, in a different way than would a "typical conservative." The article reviews a recent paper by Abelson, in which he discusses some differences between belief systems and the knowledge-based expert systems that are current in AI.

References

A concise, personal history of the first years of information-processing psychology is given in Newell and Simon (1972, pp. 873–889). Cherry (1970) is a comprehensive and readable account of the very early work in psychology, telecommunications, cybernetics, and computer science; it is a good resource for readers who want to know about the intellectual background that gave rise to AI and its related disciplines. Anderson and Bower (1973) present a detailed review of the history of associationism in memory research, as well as a review and criticism of several memory models. Several books by cognitive scientists give their perspective on the new field: Bobrow and Collins (1975) contains several interesting papers on the developing topic of knowledge representation. Norman and Rumelhart (1975) discuss their MEMOD system in detail—it is interesting to contrast this book with a "standard" text on memory (e.g., Crowder, 1976) to see what a difference the information-processing perspective can make. Schank and Abelson (1977) discuss their theory of knowledge representation—a theory that is currently very popular. Finally, there is a journal called *Cognitive Science* that publishes current research.

B. GENERAL PROBLEM SOLVER

HUMAN PROBLEM–SOLVING has received intensive examination by Allen
Newell, Herbert A. Simon, and their colleagues and students at Carnegie-
Mellon University. In their book *Human Problem Solving* (1972), Newell and
Simon present thorough analyses of problem solving in three task domains—
cryptarithmetic, logic, and chess—and they present and evaluate information-
processing systems that accurately simulate human thought in these domains.

There is not the space here to summarize all the work in human problem-
solving. In fact, the only system we examine is the General Problem Solver
program (GPS); and the only task domain, logic problems. However, the
information-processing system that Newell and Simon develop is certainly
general enough to provide a framework for problem solving in several other
task domains. GPS is not just a logic problem-solver.

Problem solving, and most other intellectual activity, involves general
knowledge that applies to many problems and very specific knowledge that
is special to a particular problem. For example, a general rule, or *heuristic*,
is "If you can't solve the whole problem, try to solve part of it." A specific
piece of knowledge that may be useful for solving some word problems is,
for example, that a mile is 1,760 yards. The distinction between general and
task-specific knowledge is made in GPS, and it was for just this reason that
it was called GPS:

> GPS obtained the name "general problem solver" because it was the first
> problem solving program to separate in a clean way a task-independent part
> of the system containing general problem solving mechanisms from a part
> of the system containing knowledge of the task environment. (Newell and
> Simon, 1972, p. 414)

Accordingly, our discussion of GPS moves from general to specific: First is
a simplified discussion of the information-processing system on which GPS
is constructed, then a presentation of general problem-solving methods, and
finally consideration of methods specific to the task demands of logic problems.

The Information-processing System

Everything that takes place in GPS is an information process, and the
environment in which GPS solves problems is called an *information-processing
system* (IPS). A central concept is that of a *state*—a momentary snapshot
containing what the IPS knows at the time. The knowledge implicit in a state
is represented by *symbol structures*.

11

More formally:

1. There is a set of elements called *symbols;* a symbol structure is a set of instances of symbols connected by *relations.*

2. An *information process* is a process that has symbol structures for all or some of its inputs or outputs.

3. An *object* is a symbol structure, or a program that the IPS is capable of executing, or an external environment of readable stimuli.

States are derived from other states by the application of information processes, often called *operators.* Two important states are the *starting state,* which represents everything that the IPS knows at the beginning of the problem, and the *goal state,* which represents the knowledge of the IPS when it has solved the problem. There may be many goal states, corresponding to various solutions to a problem. For example, the starting state in a game of chess is the familiar double ranks of opposing black and white pieces. From this single starting state an enormous number of goal states representing checkmate can be derived. Each new position is derived from its predecessor by an operator, a legal move of one or two chessmen. A final point about this state-space representation is that symbol structures may be nested in an IPS; within the structure that corresponds to a whole board position, there are a number of smaller structures corresponding to parts of it.

Since an object is defined as a symbol structure, a program to be executed, or external data, no distinction is made between data and programs. This is an important aspect of GPS and of many other AI programs, but for the sake of simplicity we will ignore the possibility that objects can be programs. From here on, *object* refers to symbol structures, and *operator* or *information process* denotes the programs that the IPS executes. As an example of this more restrictive definition, configurations of chess boards are objects and the moves of the chess pieces are operators. Note that an object may represent an entire chess board or just a part of it. A state, then, is composed of one or more objects, and it is transformed by operators.

Elementary Information Processes

Newell and Simon suggest some *elementary information processes* (EIPs) from which all the other operations of an IPS can be constructed. They are:

1. *Discrimination.* The IPS must be able to invoke operators appropriate to the symbol structure it is currently processing.

2. *Tests and comparisons.* The IPS must be able to compare symbol structures.

3. *Symbol creation.* It must be possible to create symbols and allow them to designate other symbol structures.

4. *Designation of symbol structures.* It must be possible to designate various parts of any symbol structure and obtain the designation of any part of any symbol structure.

5. *Input and output.* The IPS must be able to read and write symbol structures internally and externally.

6. *Storing of symbol structures.* It must be possible to store a symbol structure and retrieve it by means of another symbol structure that designates it.

The Problem Space

Newell and Simon define the *task environment,* or *problem space,* of GPS to be the formal specification of the set of symbol structures through which GPS searches for a solution. This may suggest that GPS has a collection of states available to search for a goal state. In fact, search in GPS means that GPS *generates* states by applying operators, first to the starting state (which it is given), then to states it derives from the starting state, and so on. GPS generates states in its problem space as it solves a problem.

The problem space used by GPS varies with the problem. It is a formal specification of the knowledge needed to solve a problem. Consider, for example, the famous cryptarithmetic problem

$$\begin{array}{r} \text{DONALD} \\ + \text{GERALD} \\ \hline \text{ROBERT} \end{array} \quad \text{Given } D = 5$$

where the object is to assign digits to letters so that the sum of the numbers denoted by DONALD and GERALD equals the number denoted by ROBERT. A problem space for this example is:

⟨letter⟩	:= A|B|D|E|G|L|N|O|R|T
⟨digit⟩	:= 0|1|2|3|4|5|6|7|8|9
⟨expression⟩	:= ⟨letter⟩ has-value ⟨digit⟩
⟨knowledge state⟩	:= ⟨expression⟩ | ⟨expression⟩ & ⟨knowledge state⟩
⟨operator⟩	:= Assert(⟨expression⟩).

All knowledge about this problem is made up of *expressions* of the form *letter has-value digit.* The initial knowledge state is the single expression *D has-value 5.* Subsequent knowledge states are conjunctions of expressions. The single operator required to solve the problem is to assert that a letter has a particular value, that is, to assign it the value. This problem space is complete in the sense that application of the operator is enough to generate all the expressions needed for a solution.

In addition to the problem space, the IPS needs a program, or set of instructions, to dictate *how* digits are to be assigned to letters and to test if a solution has been found. This will be discussed further for the domain of logic problems.

A distinction must be made between *search in the problem space* and the *search space*. The former refers to all the solutions and paths leading to them that the problem solver actually generates, while the latter refers to all the solutions and paths *that exist*. For problems of any complexity, it is necessary to keep the problem space smaller than the search space. To rephrase a point made in Chapter II: Search in the problem space involves generating just enough of the search space to find a solution to the problem. In GPS, two methods are used to accomplish this. One is a general heuristic called *means-ends analysis*, and the other is a form of *planning*. We will not consider planning here; the interested reader should see pages 429–435 of Newell and Simon (1972) and Article XV.A in the *Handbook*.

General Problem-solving Methods: Means-ends Analysis

Problem solving in GPS is a matter of transforming the start state into a goal state. Thus, at any point during problem solving, GPS has two goals:

1. Transform state 1 to state 2 by the application of operators.

2. Apply some operator to state 1 (or some intermediate state).

These goals do not specify *which* operator should be applied to any object. There are numerous strategies for deciding this. One is to apply *all* legal operators to the first object, then apply all legal operators to all the results of the first application, and so on. This method, called *exhaustive search*, generates the entire search space. It is guaranteed to find a solution eventually but is much too costly to be used for problems of any complexity. Means-ends analysis is a powerful heuristic that constrains search by anchoring paths in the search space to the current state and the desired state; it implies a third problem-solving goal for GPS:

3. Reduce the *difference* between state 1 and state 2 by modifying state 1.

This rules out directionless expansion of possible solutions:

> By taking account of the characteristics of the goal object it is seeking to reach, the problem solver extracts from the situation an enormous amount of information about the direction in which it should explore, and almost immediately rules out of bounds all but a tiny portion of the problem space. (Newell and Simon, 1972, p. 428)

Means-ends analysis is incorporated into GPS as follows:

1. If the current state is not the desired one, *differences* between it and the desired state will be detected.

2. Operators can be classified according to the differences they eliminate.

3. It may be necessary to modify the current state to make it compatible with a desired operator.

4. "Difficult" differences between states might be simplified by transforming the current state, even if this results in more, though simpler, differences.

The IPS, problem space, search, and means-ends analysis are domain-independent ideas. The GPS program was designed to separate them from any given problem-solving task. In the next section, we look at an example of GPS in the task-domain of logic problems.

Task Demands of Logic in GPS

Symbolic logic problems provide an ideal situation to study problem solving because one can describe the *task environment* of these problems in great detail. One such problem is:

Translate the expression $R \,\&\, (\neg P \to Q)$ into $(P \lor Q) \,\&\, R$.

It is unimportant what the connective symbols $(\to, \neg, \&, \lor)$ mean. (In fact, the human problem-solvers who provided data for Newell and Simon were told nothing about them except that they were a set of transformations for turning one expression into another.) Each transformation reduces a difference between two expressions. The problem is to use these transformations to turn the first expression, $R \,\&\, (\neg P \to Q)$, into the second one, $(P \lor Q) \,\&\, R$. The available transformations were the following (in which " : " means "translates to" and A and B are arbitrary expressions):

$\neg\neg A \,:\, A$	$A \,\&\, A \,:\, A$
$A \,\&\, B \,:\, A$	$A \,\&\, B \,:\, B$
$A \lor A \,:\, A$	A and $B \,:\, A \,\&\, B$
$A \,\&\, B \,:\, B \,\&\, A$	$A \lor B \,:\, B \lor A$
$A \lor B \,:\, \neg(\neg A \,\&\, \neg B)$	$A \to B \,:\, \neg A \lor B$
$A \to B \,:\, \neg B \to \neg A$	$A \to B$ and $A \,:\, B$
$A \lor (B \lor C) \,:\, (A \lor B) \lor C$	$A \,\&\, (B \,\&\, C) \,:\, (A \,\&\, B) \,\&\, C$
$A \lor (B \,\&\, C) \,:\, (A \lor B) \,\&\, (A \lor C)$	$A \,\&\, (B \lor C) \,:\, (A \,\&\, B) \lor (A \,\&\, C)$
$A \to B$ and $B \to C \,:\, A \to C$	$A \,:\, A \lor X$ $(X$ is any expression$)$

Consider how these rules can be used to translate from the original to the goal expression:

Expression	Transformation
$R \mathbin{\&} (\neg P \to Q)$	$A \mathbin{\&} B : B \mathbin{\&} A$ yields $(\neg P \to Q) \mathbin{\&} R$
$(\neg P \to Q) \mathbin{\&} R$	$(A \to B) : (\neg A \lor B)$ applied to left part yields $(\neg\neg P \lor Q) \mathbin{\&} R$
$(\neg\neg P \lor Q) \mathbin{\&} R$	$\neg\neg A : A$ applied to left part yields $(P \lor Q) \mathbin{\&} R$

$(P \lor Q) \mathbin{\&} R$ is the goal expression.   Q.E.D.

One can now see how GPS works in the task environment of logic problems. Exhaustive search would eventually generate the goal state but is wasteful here because it ignores the information provided by the goal state. Means-ends analysis directs GPS to reduce the difference between the starting state and the goal state. For example, comparing the start state to the goal state, it is immediately obvious that the former needs to be turned around: R must appear on the right of the parentheses instead of on the left. This is a *difference* between the two states; it can be reduced by the transformation $A \mathbin{\&} B : B \mathbin{\&} A$. Instead of applying *all* applicable transformations to the starting state, GPS might simply apply this one, which will yield the state $(\neg P \to Q) \mathbin{\&} R$.

Continuing this reasoning, one might try to reduce the differences between $(\neg P \to Q)$ and $(P \lor Q)$. There are two differences: P has a "$\neg$" prefix in one case but not the other, and the connective between P and Q is "$\to$" in one case and "$\lor$" in the other. One transformation will reduce the latter difference, namely, $A \to B : \neg A \lor B$. Application of this transformation yields $(\neg\neg P \lor Q) \mathbin{\&} R$.

The final problem is to get rid of the "$\neg\neg$" prefixing P. One transformation is available to do this, $\neg\neg A : A$, which yields the goal state $(P \lor Q) \mathbin{\&} R$ when it is applied.

(The reader who wants a "real life" example of problem solving with means-ends analysis is encouraged to read Article XV.B on the STRIPS planner, in the *Handbook*.)

The reasoning of the last paragraphs is a simplified version of the operation of GPS. Means-ends analysis is demonstrated here in its simplest form: At each step in solving the problem, a transformation is chosen that will reduce one difference between the current state and the goal state. GPS is able to do this because each of the transformations it uses in a task domain is *classified* according to the differences it reduces. For the logic task domain, there are six differences that can be reduced by transformations. In GPS these are summarized in a *difference table*. Three of the reducible differences are:

1. A difference in position of components of the expression. Several transformations will eliminate this difference:

$$A \lor B : B \lor A, \quad A \& B : B \& A, \quad A \to B : \neg B \to \neg A, \quad \text{etc.}$$

2. A difference in the symbol that appears between letters. Transformations to eliminate this difference are:

$$A \lor B : \neg(\neg A \& \neg B), \quad A \to B : \neg A \lor B,$$
$$A \lor (B \& C) : (A \lor B) \& (A \lor C), \quad \text{etc.}$$

3. A difference in the number of "$\neg$" prefixes of a letter. Several transformations change the number of prefixes:

$$\neg\neg A : A, \quad A \to B : \neg A \lor B, \quad A \to B : \neg B \to \neg A, \quad \text{etc.}$$

To solve the problem above, GPS determines the differences between the starting state and the goal state and then applies transformations that reduce them. However, the problems solved by GPS are rarely so simple; several complications must be considered. First, if several transformations are applicable to a state, GPS must choose between them. To do so, it consults a *ranking* of differences that tells it which differences to reduce first.

Another complication arises when GPS cannot find an operator to reduce a particular difference. In this case, it must transform the current state into an intermediate state from which it can reduce the difference. For example, consider adding the transformation rule $A * B : A \lor \neg B$ and solving the problem defined by the starting state $R * (\neg P \to Q)$ and the goal state $(\neg P \& \neg Q) \lor R$. In this case, GPS sets up the goal of moving R to the other side of the expression, as it did in the last problem, but it has no transformations available to accomplish this. Instead, it must defer this goal and transform the starting state into a state from which it can accomplish the goal. To do this, it transforms $R * (\neg P \to Q)$ into $R \lor \neg(\neg P \to Q)$ and then into $\neg(\neg P \to Q) \lor R$. Thus, GPS has the ability to set up *nested subgoals*.

The design of GPS is dictated by the heuristic of means-ends analysis and by the *task demands*. The general part of GPS is means-ends analysis and the information-processing system in which it operates. The remainder of the system follows from the task of solving logic problems. There are a limited number of differences possible and a limited number of operations to reduce them.

Empirical Tests of GPS

GPS was proposed as a psychological theory of human problem-solving. In this section we give evidence for the theory. Recall that the most general aspect of GPS is means-ends analysis, which is used to guide the generation of states in the problem space. Some general behaviors are a natural consequence of means-ends analysis; for example, GPS works forward from the current state to the goal state, as opposed to working backward from the goal. Another general characteristic of GPS is the repeated application of transformations to states. This refers to the situation in which GPS finds a transformation it wants to use, but the current state is not in a form that will accept the transformation; the state must be altered and the transformation reapplied.

If GPS is a theory of human problem-solving, one would expect humans to use means-ends analysis and exhibit the behaviors that derive from it in situations where GPS exhibits these behaviors. In the case of logic problems, this is easily tested. Task demands are equated by ensuring that GPS and the human subjects have the same transformations to work with and the same problems to solve. GPS is programmed to print out its goals as it tries to solve the problem, and the humans are instructed to talk out loud as they solve the problem. The subjects' comments are recorded and the resulting record is called a *protocol*, which is broken down into phrases:

"I'm looking at reversing these two things now."

"Then I'd have a similar group at the beginning..."

"I could easily leave something like that 'til the end."

These are classified as evidence of goals and applications of transformations.

Breaking down the protocols is a painstaking process, but it is expedited by a structure called the *problem behavior graph*, a graphic display of the problem solver's progress. The nodes of the graph represent the knowledge of the problem solver at a given point in time, and the arcs represent the transformations that lead to new nodes (states). There is also provision for returning to parts of the problem that were left dormant while a particular line of reasoning was being explored. The protocol of each subject is mapped onto a problem behavior graph. Newell and Simon do not expect that any problem behavior graph will precisely match the output of GPS on a problem. Their claim is, rather, that patterns of behavior will be common to GPS and all their subjects. The problem behavior graph provides an explicit record of the behavior, from which patterns can be abstracted if they exist.

The following is a summary of an analysis of the problem-solving behavior of seven human subjects on a single problem. Newell and Simon classify the behavior of both GPS and their subjects into patterns and compare them for overlap. (This analysis is taken from pp. 489–502 of Newell and Simon, 1972.) Mnemonics for these patterns and the percentage of their occurrence in the protocols of each subject are shown in Table B-1. Total percentages are shown for the pooled sum of utterances in all seven protocols. Table B-1 has three horizontal divisions, or tiers, representing (a) patterns exhibited by both GPS and the subjects, (b) patterns exhibited by the subjects and *not* by GPS, and (c) uninterpretable behavior on the part of the subjects.

TABLE B–1

Percentages of Particular Problem-solving Patterns
in Protocols of Individual Subjects

| | Subject | | | | | | | |
	A	B	C	D	E	F	G	TOTALS
Tier 1. Behavior exhibited by subjects and by GPS								
Means-ends analysis (toward goal object; operator applicability)	37	47	48	38	52	50	45	39
Working forward	17	0	13	14	2	1	9	7
Repeated application (after subgoal; implementation)	46	44	37	39	39	44	42	38
							Subtotal	84
Tier 2. Behavior exhibited by subjects and absent in GPS								
Means-ends analysis (consequence avoidance)	0	0	0	<1	<1	5	7	>3
Working backward	0	2	0	0	0	0	0	<1
Repeated application (review)	0	0	5	15	6	8	9	7
							Subtotal	11
Tier 3. Uninterpretable behavior								
	0	3	2	9	7	5	4	5
							TOTAL	100

In the first tier of the table, means-ends analysis has two manifestations in which states are transformed to achieve the goal expression or are transformed into a form compatible with a desired transformation. A second pattern of behavior is *working forward*, that is, searching through transformations for one that will apply to the current state. A third pattern is repeated application of a transformation on the same state. This event arises mostly when a desired transformation is incompatible with a state. A goal is set up to transform the state, and the original transformation is then successfully reapplied. Another type of reapplication found here is to try out consequences of a transformation before committing the system to it. Table B–1 shows clearly that the great majority of the utterances of the seven subjects conform to these patterns of behavior—84%, in fact.

Tier 2 represents human behaviors that were not implemented in GPS at the time. The greatest percentages were obtained for the reapplication of transformations for the sake of review (refreshing the memory). Working backward from the goal was another behavior that had not been implemented in GPS. A third is a complex behavior in which a transformation is applied before the application of the desired transformation, because the latter has undesirable consequences (as well as the desired ones) if applied before the intermediate transformation. These behaviors constitute 7%, 1%, and 3% of the protocols, respectively.

Tier 3 of the table accounts for 5% of the subjects' protocols and represents uninterpretable behavior that could not be assigned to any pattern. These behaviors include grunts and yawns, and unfinished and ambiguous phrases such as *Well, this looks like, uh ... I dunno.*

Conclusion

From this and other analyses, Newell and Simon conclude that GPS is an explicit, operational, and sufficient model of some human problem-solving. In GPS, a separation is maintained between general components, such as the information-processing system and means-ends analysis, and task-specific components, such as details of the problem space. Newell and Simon claim that the general components apply in a wide range of task domains. Chess and cryptarithmetic were examined in addition to logic problems, and these analyses certainly support Newell and Simon's argument of generality. Moreover, since GPS, means-ends analysis has been used in several other problem-solving programs (see Article XV.A).

Some problems are not solved efficiently with means-ends analysis. For example, the heuristic can lead one down a long path of problem-solving operators that dead-ends, forcing the problem solver to back up to a previous decision point and try a different path. Also, means-ends analysis may construct a series of problem-solving operators that will, in fact, solve the problem, but that is much longer than necessary. Lastly, means-ends analysis can be inefficient when there are interacting subgoals to be achieved; if accomplishing one subgoal prevents accomplishing another, the problem-solver can do no more than return to the beginning of the problem to try the subgoals in a different order (see Article XV.A for a detailed discussion of this problem).

However, the efficiency of problem-solving is a big concern for computers, but perhaps not a serious concern for humans. The fact that means-ends analysis can be inefficient does not detract from the empirical fact of its generality in human problem-solving. This is not to say that means-ends analysis is the only problem-solving strategy used by humans; the following article (Article XI.C) will discuss a planning problem that is best solved by a process called *opportunistic planning.*

References

The most comprehensive and exhaustive information-processing analysis of human problem-solving is Newell and Simon (1972).

C. OPPORTUNISTIC PROBLEM SOLVING

THIS ARTICLE discusses a theory of planning developed by Barbara Hayes-Roth and Frederick Hayes-Roth (1978; B. Hayes-Roth, 1980). The theory is specifically of human planning, and the authors and their colleagues have run several experiments to test it. For this reason, the theory is discussed here rather than in Chapter XV, on planning.

Hayes-Roth and Hayes-Roth have implemented their theory in a model that, due to its complexity, will be sketched later in this article but not presented in detail. The first part of the article discusses an exploratory experiment with human planners in which subjects were required to think out loud while planning. This technique is familiar from the work of Newell and Simon (Article XI.B). A transcript, or *protocol*, is broken down into phrases that are interpreted as evidence of particular planning or problem-solving operations.

In the planning experiment (Hayes-Roth and Hayes-Roth, 1978), subjects were given a map of a small town marked with points of interest such as movie theaters, the veterinarian, stores, and restaurants. They were asked to plan a day's activity that included 10 errands, such as *Get medicine from the vet* and *Buy fresh vegetables at the grocery*. A couple of errands included explicit constraints, such as the showtimes of movies. Constraints about other errands were implied; for example, fresh vegetables should probably be purchased in the evening, rather than leaving them in a car all day.

With the map and list of errands in hand, subjects talked about their developing plans for the day. What they said was recorded and transcribed; Table C–1 shows samples of one subject's comments as he planned his activities. These paragraphs are excerpted from a longer protocol of 47 such paragraphs; the numbers in parentheses indicate the position of each paragraph in the protocol. The paragraphs illustrate a number of important characteristics of human planning. In the first, the subject uses his knowledge to assign importance to each errand and, thus, to order them. World knowledge is also used to order plan steps in the later paragraphs, in which the subject tries to schedule the purchase of groceries to avoid spoilage.

The second and third paragraphs illustrate two styles of control of planning. In the second paragraph the subject is motivated by a number of individual goals; his thinking is *bottom-up*, or driven by what he perceives to be the immediately attainable goals of the problem. In the third paragraph, however, he starts planning at a different level of abstraction. From the goals previously articulated, he abstracts a higher level goal, to *do the errands in the southeast corner*. For three more paragraphs in the protocol (not excerpted here), the subject tries to fit errands into the general plan of heading southeast.

TABLE C–1

Excerpts from a Planning Protocol (from Hayes-Roth and Hayes-Roth, 1978)

---

1. (1) Let's go back down the errand list. Pick up medicine for the dog at the veterinary supplies. That's definitely a primary, anything taking care of health.... Buy a toy for the dog at the store. If you pass it, sure. If not, the dog can play with something else.

2. (7) The appliance store is a few blocks away. The medicine for the dog...isn't too far away. Movie theaters—let's hold off on that for a little while. Pick up the watch. That's all the way across town. Special-order a book at the bookstore.

3. (8) Probably it would be best if we started in a southeasterly direction.... I can see later on there are a million things I want to do in that part of town.

4. (23) Third item will be the newsstand since we are heading in that direction. Often I like to do that. I know buying a gardening magazine is hardly a primary thing to do, but since I'm heading that way, it's only going to take a second...

5. (31) I would like to plan it so I can see the movie, pick up the vegetables, pick up my car, and then go home. Vegetables would rot.

6. (38) Now we do have a problem. It's 2:00 and all we have left to do is see a movie and get the vegetables. And that's where I think I've blown this plan. I've got an hour left there before the movie...

7. (40) If I go get the groceries now, it's not really going to be consistent with the plans throughout the day because I've been holding off on the groceries for rotting. If I take them to the movie...vegetables don't really perish like ice cream.

When immediately attainable errands are pointed out to the subject, he says, *I can still do that and still head in the general direction.* In contrast to the earlier mode of planning, driven bottom-up by immediate goals, he now attempts to incorporate these goals into an abstract plan. This illustrates the ability of human planners to reason at many levels of abstraction and to move freely between them. Hayes-Roth and Hayes-Roth call this *multidirectional* processing.

The fourth paragraph illustrates one of the most interesting and fundamental characteristics of planning, and indeed of other aspects of cognition: It is *opportunistic*. The subject realized that he could fulfill one of his obligations "for free," and promptly did so. Goals that fit into a developing plan are integrated, and goals that belong together are clustered into subplans, often without regard for how the subplans will integrate with the overall plan. For example, early on in the protocol (not shown above), the subject plans to end his day at the movie and then walk to a parking lot where his car is parked. This subplan is constructed when the subject notices the proximity of the movie and parking lot. There is a strong parallel between this process and *island driving*, in which a problem solver finds part of a solution that he thinks is correct—an island—and extends the solution from there, possibly toward another island. Subplans can be regarded as islands that are linked by sequences of planning actions. (For a detailed discussion of island driving in speech understanding, see Article V.C1, in Vol. I.)

The fifth and sixth paragraphs of the protocol show the subject summarizing his current state and realizing that the plan is flawed because he has too much time for what he has to do. At this point, he relaxes one of his requirements, that he purchase vegetables after the movie, to fill in the hour before the movie.

Opportunistic, multidirectional planning is very different from that practiced by the planners discussed in Chapter XV; human planning can be significantly more complex than that of current AI planners. Before we discuss the Hayes-Roths' model, we consider some of these differences.

Opportunistic processing has a bottom-up component; planning processes are instigated by something the problem solver notices about the state of the world. In human planning, steps are introduced into a plan whenever the opportunity arises to do so. This contrasts with the *least-commitment* strategies in NOAH and MOLGEN (see Articles XV.D1 and XV.D2), in which planning steps are refined only when there is evidence that they will not have to be abandoned later. In human planning, the carefully controlled introduction of plan steps implicit in NOAH and MOLGEN is abandoned for the advantage of introducing steps in a plan wherever they are convenient.

A closely related issue is that human planning is multidirectional; that is, it takes place at several levels of abstraction simultaneously. This contrasts with the *hierarchical* planners (discussed in Articles XV.B, XV.D1, and XV.D2), which develop detailed plans from abstract plans in a purely top-down fashion. NOAH and MOLGEN do not include detailed steps in a plan unless they have been refined from more abstract ones. This strategy helped them to avoid interactions between plan steps; MOLGEN would *post constraints* summarizing the implications of refining an abstract plan step for other parts of the plan, and NOAH used *critics* to check for interactions between plan steps as its plan developed. Both approaches rely on developing *abstract* plans into detailed ones in a top-down manner.

The major advantage of the least-commitment strategy of hierarchical planning is that it allows the planner to avoid subgoal interactions and, thus, plan constructively with a minimum of backtracking. Opportunistic planning leaves the planner susceptible to these interactions; an opportunistic, multidirectional planner is more likely to need to rewrite parts of its plan or change its goals than is a hierarchical planner. In fact, Table C–1 showed the planner committing himself to a plan that does not fulfill all his goals—he is left with too much free time. However, instead of backtracking to a previous point in the plan and replanning, the planner instead relaxes one of his goals and decides to buy groceries before the movie.

Hayes-Roth and Hayes-Roth argue that opportunistic, multidirectional planning is more efficient than hierarchical planning when the problem to be solved is very complex. They say that hierarchical planning restricts the problem solver and does not permit organizing parts of a plan around interesting possibilities that emerge bottom-up (as can be done in island driving).

The relative efficiencies and advantages of hierarchical, least-commitment planning and multidirectional, opportunistic planning are issues for AI. However, our chief concern in this article is not with efficiency but, rather, with how human planners plan. The remainder of the article summarizes the Hayes-Roths' model.

The Control of Planning

Hayes-Roth and Hayes-Roth propose a *blackboard model* to represent the complex control structure of human planning. Blackboards have been used primarily to facilitate *interpretation* of noisy signals such as speech (see discussion in Article V.C1, in Vol. I) and data from sensors (see Article VII.C3, in Vol. II, on CRYSALIS; also, Nii and Feigenbaum, 1978). A blackboard model for signal interpretation typically has a number of *specialist* programs that produce hypotheses about aspects of the signal. For example, a speech-understanding program has specialists for dividing the speech signal into phonetic units, for guessing the syntax of the spoken message, for predicting the next word given those that have been spoken already, and so on. The hypotheses produced by each specialist are accessible to all, since they are posted on a central *blackboard*. Hypotheses posted by one specialist are data for others; for example, if the syntactic specialist posts the hypothesis that the next word is a verb, the lexical specialist can use this information to narrow the search for the exact word.

Theoretically, the control of processing in a blackboard model is *asynchronous* and *opportunistic:* Specialists post hypotheses in no particular order, and they use hypotheses posted by other specialists whenever they appear helpful. Although human planning involves *generating* behavior rather than interpreting it, it does seem to be an asynchronous, opportunistic process. Plans are not developed all of a piece, but, instead, clusters or islands of planning actions are constructed, and they are linked to other clusters when an opportunity arises.

The Hayes-Roths' planning model involves a blackboard with five *planes* of planning decisions and many specialists that generate tentative decisions and record them on the blackboard. Planes are organized to reflect characteristic processes in planning. One is the *plan plane*, a plane of operations.

Decisions to execute the processes discussed in the protocol—going to the veterinarian, seeing a movie, and so on—are recorded in the plan plane. More general goals and general plans to accomplish them are also recorded in the plan plane.

At the level of the *meta-plan plane*, the planner makes decisions about how to solve the problem at hand. As we note in the discussion of MOLGEN (Article XV.D2), a planner can do a lot of reasoning about a problem before proposing so much as a single action to solve it. Decisions recorded on the meta-plan plane capture some of this reasoning. For example, the planner must represent the problem to itself and decide what *type* of problem it is, so that it can pick out a *problem-solving model*, or *strategy*. The way a problem is represented by the problem solver can affect the ease with which it is solved (Amarel, 1968); thus, identifying a problem and finding an approach to solving it are two very important decisions. Most planning programs have a single representation of a problem and a single, implicit strategy for solving it; for example, some *nonhierarchical* planners (discussed in Article XV.C) represent problems as a collection of propositions to be made true, and they solve the problems by pattern-directed invocation of procedures with backtracking. It is possible, even likely, that a human planner might adopt means-ends analysis with backtracking as a method; the choice between this and other possibilities is recorded on the meta-plan plane.

Another kind of planning decision represented at the meta-plan level involves the *policies* followed by the problem solver: What constitutes a good solution? Is it to be quick and dirty or painstaking and elegant? Again, most AI planning programs do not make such decisions, which obviously lend power and flexibility to human problem-solving. We can usually decide when a solution is good enough (what Simon, 1969, calls *satisficing*); those who are never satisfied and those who are too easily satisfied—the compulsive and the slob—are often inefficient problem solvers.

The meta-plan plane records global decisions about how to approach a problem; between this level and that of individual planning operations, the Hayes-Roths place the *plan-abstraction plane*. Decisions recorded at this plane motivate operations recorded on the plan plane. For example, the decision to do all of the "primary" errands first is a formulation of an abstract plan; it motivates the decision—recorded on the plan plane—to divide errands into "primary" and "secondary" groups.

A fourth plane in the Hayes-Roths' model contains world knowledge. For the errand-planning task, the *knowledge-base plane* includes a list of the errands and a representation of the map. A point made earlier—that the representation of the problem affects the efficiency with which it is solved—holds also for the representation of knowledge pertinent to the problem. The Hayes-Roths represent the map in several ways to enhance problem-solving efficiency. At one level, the map is represented as sectors, for example, the southeast corner; at another level, neighbors are recorded, for example, a movie house neighbors on a parking lot. A third level of information about the map represents routes between points of interest. This knowledge base would, of course, change for another kind of problem.

The fifth plane, the *executive plane*, schedules the planning decisions made by *specialists* that are recorded on other planes of the blackboard. We have characterized the kinds of decisions that are found in human planning, for example, decisions about specific planning actions, about approaches to a problem, and about abstractions of planning actions. The decisions are tentatively proposed and recorded on the appropriate plane of the blackboard by specialist programs that are sensitive to particular kinds of decisions. For example, a *proximity detector* specialist would note when two points of interest are nearby on the map; it would record pairs of *neighbors* on the knowledge-base plane of the blackboard. Specialists operate independently and asynchronously, as mentioned above. Consequently, a scheduler is needed to decide on a sequential order (since most present-day computers are sequential machines) for all the actions of specialists. Scheduling might be queue oriented, that is, first come first served, but, in general, humans do not schedule actions this way. Instead they schedule them according to their perceived efficiency, productivity, and the like.

Conclusion

Hayes-Roth and Hayes-Roth present a detailed example explaining how their model accounts for the protocol of a subject planning a day's activities (excerpted above). Rather than discuss the model in detail, we have presented its planes and specialists in quite general terms, attempting to characterize the types and levels of decisions that are necessary for planning. One general conclusion of this article is that human planners are much more sophisticated than any of the programs discussed in Chapter XV on planning. Multidirectional, asynchronous, and opportunistic processing is proposed to model this sophistication.

References

Hayes-Roth and Hayes-Roth (1978; B. Hayes-Roth, 1980) give accounts of their experiments and the model developed from them.

D. EPAM

EPAM (Elementary Perceiver and Memorizer) was developed in the period 1956–1964 by Edward Feigenbaum and Herbert Simon. This program was the first information-processing model of a number of well-known human verbal-learning behaviors. Though it sounds simple, rote learning of nonsense material has provided much evidence about the characteristics of short-term and long-term memory. Nonsense material is useful in that it avoids the effect of the meaning of a stimulus on how well it is learned; for example, familiar stimuli or stimuli that "fit in" with previously learned material are relatively easy to learn. When Ebbinghaus first used nonsense syllables in the 1870s, these factors were not understood. His method limited their effects, which, he felt, obscured the fundamental characteristics of memory. (An interesting sidelight on the topic of nonsense syllables is that Anderson and Bower, whose work is discussed in Article XI.E2, used meaningful sentences for their experiments on *strategy-free memory* because they felt that their subjects were likely to employ mnemonic strategies to remember nonsense stimuli.) EPAM provides an explanation of some of these characteristics, among them oscillation and retroactive inhibition, forgetting, and stimulus and response generalization.

Verbal Learning Behavior

To simplify the study of human verbal learning, psychologists have developed a number of experimental techniques (for a survey, see Baddeley, 1976). Most are based on the following procedure: The subject (whether human or EPAM) is required to memorize nonsense syllables in serial lists or associate pairs. The syllables are typically comprised of three letters, beginning and ending with a consonant, and are supposed to be meaningless for most subjects (e.g., XUM, JUR, FAZ). In paired-associate learning experiments, the first syllable of a pair is called the *stimulus* and the second is called the *response*.

EPAM was designed for paired-associate and serial learning, but in this article we will consider only the former. In a typical experiment, a set of nonsense syllable pairs is used. For each pair in the set, the stimulus syllable is displayed to a subject, who then attempts to say the associated response. Any errors made by the subject are recorded. The response syllable is then shown, so that both stimulus and response are in view, and the subject is able to refresh his (or her) memory of the association (or learn it, if this is the first presentation). After a few seconds, the next pair of syllables is displayed. This continues until all of the pairs have been displayed. The entire sequence is called a trial. Trials are repeated until the subject is able to give the correct response for each stimulus. This is called *learning to criterion*. There is a relatively short period of time between trials, and the sequence of pairs is randomized from trial to trial.

A number of behaviors are typical in a paired-associate verbal-learning experiment:

1. *Stimulus and response generalization.* Overt errors in recall are often attributable to confusion by the subject between similar stimuli or similar responses. When similar stimuli are confused, their responses may become interchanged; when two responses are similar, the wrong one may be given to a stimulus.

2. *Oscillation.* Associations that are recalled correctly over several trials are sometimes forgotten only to reappear and then later disappear again.

3. *Retroactive inhibition.* When the paired-associate task is modified to include an intervening learning task, so that one list of syllables is learned and then another, and the retention of the original list is tested, the subject's ability to give correct responses is reduced by the intervening learning. Moreover, overt errors in recall are usually *intrusions* from the second list. The phenomenon disappears rapidly, however, and the subject's memory of the first list is refreshed during the next trial.

The EPAM Model

The EPAM program was written in IPL–V, one of the first list-processing languages. EPAM is a two-part system, with performance and learning components. In the performance mode, EPAM attempts to produce responses to stimulus syllables. In the learning mode, EPAM learns to discriminate and associate stimuli and responses. The model is easier to understand if the performance mode is discussed first.

The Performance System

After EPAM has learned a set of stimulus-response pairs, it is tested in a standard paired-associate task. The test, which is identical to that given to a human, involves presenting stimulus syllables to EPAM, which then must produce the associated response syllables. The performance system proceeds as follows. A stimulus syllable is encoded into an *input code* that directs the search of EPAM's memory, called a *discrimination net*. This search leads to a node in the net that contains a *cue*. Cues are information with which to search for a response syllable. Using the cue, EPAM searches the net again for a node containing the response, called a *response image*. The cue does not always hold enough information to find the response syllable. If it does, the response is given; otherwise, EPAM makes an error.

EPAM codes each stimulus syllable into an internal representation called the *input code*. This is based on certain features of the input characters, such as the "openness" of a letter (e.g., C versus O) and whether the letter contains crossed straight lines (e.g., X). Different sets of features have been used, but in all cases they must satisfy two criteria: They must be related in some way to features of letters, and they must be highly redundant (having many more features than are required to distinguish letters).

For the remainder of this discussion, to simplify the examples, we will assume that letters themselves and *not* features of letters are used as input codes. Thus, when EPAM is tested with the stimulus MUR, features of the letters M, U, and R are actually used as the input code, but for simplicity we assume here that the input code is MUR.

The primary memory structure of EPAM is the *discrimination net*. It is constructed during EPAM's learning mode and searched during the response mode. The input code is used to traverse the discrimination net, which normally contains a dozen or more pairs. The net is simply a binary search tree, with internal nodes representing tests of features of stimuli. The leaf nodes represent either cues or response images. A diagram of a discrimination net that has been constructed in response to the associate pairs DAX–JIR, PIB–JUK is shown in Figure D–1.

An example. Imagine that the input code to EPAM is the syllable PIB. EPAM will sort down the tree until it gets to the node representing PIB. It does this by going left or right at each internal node contingent on the results of the test at that node. At the PIB node it will find a cue, J–K, which will be used to traverse the tree again, from the root node down the right branch to the next node, then down the left branch to the JUK node. At this point, it will respond with the syllable JUK. Note that it is only necessary to store

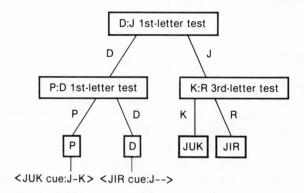

Figure D–1.   A discrimination net for the associate pairs DAX–JIR, PIB–JUK.

enough features of the cue to direct EPAM to the response syllable at the time the cue is created. The method of constructing cues will be discussed later.

We have seen how EPAM performs when it gives correct responses to stimuli in the paired-associate task. To understand how EPAM fails at the task in ways that are characteristic of human memory, we will consider how it learns.

The Learning System

The discrimination learning system operates by constructing a discrimination net from a set of stimulus-response pairs. Initially the net is empty, and only a set of simple processes for growing nets and storing images at leaf nodes is available.

Suppose that the first stimulus-response pair is DAX–JIR and has already been learned. The discrimination net at this point is shown in Figure D–2.

The full response image must be stored in order to produce the response, but only partial stimulus-image information need be stored to recognize the stimulus. In this simple net, a single letter is enough to *discriminate* between the two syllables; therefore, the test at the root node is on a single letter and no other tests are necessary. Moreover, the cue to find the response need be only a single letter. The amount of information that needs to be stored at internal and leaf nodes is determined by the program as the net grows.

Suppose the second syllable pair to be learned is PIB–JUK; see Figure D–3. The net, as it stands, does not know about PIB; therefore, another test must be added to discriminate between the input codes for DAX and PIB. This new test is placed at the point in the net where there is a failure to discriminate.

Let us assume that the test is placed so as to discriminate between PIB and DAX, as shown earlier in Figure D–2. (The test could have been between PIB and JIR; EPAM is able to determine where the failure to discriminate occurs.)

Figure D–3 does not include a response image for the second syllable, JUK, or a cue at the leaf of the PIB branch to help EPAM find JUK later. The input code JUK is used to traverse the net until a discrimination failure occurs. In

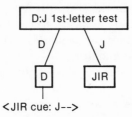

Figure D–2. Discrimination net for the associate pair DAX–JIR.

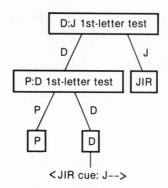

Figure D–3.   Discrimination net for the associate pair DAX–
JIR, which also discriminates PIB from DAX but
does not include a cue or response image for the
PIB–JUK association.

this case, the D:J test takes the J-branch and again a new discrimination must
be added to distinguish JUK and JIR. Human subjects generally consider final
letters before middle letters and EPAM does the same: It notes that the last
letters of JUK and JIR differ, and a test is added to reflect this.

A cue to lead from the end of the PIB branch to the JUK response image
is still lacking. It is constructed by trial and error. Each time a letter is added
to the potential cue, it is used to traverse the net; see Figure D–4. Information
is added to the cue as necessary until it leads to the correct response image.
This method ensures that a cue contains the minimum information required
to find the appropriate response image *at the time of memorization.*

It is now possible to see EPAM's source of errors on the paired-associate
task: Cues are constructed to guarantee correct retrieval of the appropriate
response image at the time the association is formed. If at some later time the
net incorporates other images and cues, the cue might no longer be sufficient to
perform that task. Thus, responses are forgotten temporarily. No information
is destroyed, but some becomes inaccessible. This can be seen by comparing
Figures D–2 and D–4. When the DAX–JIR association was first constructed
(Fig. D–2), the cue for JIR, J––, was sufficient to find the response to DAX.
However, when JUK was added to the net (Fig. D–4), J–– became inadequate
to discriminate between JIR and JUK.

The DAX–JIR association is not necessarily lost forever. If the association
is repeated (typically during a later trial), it will be reconstructed in the net
with the information necessary to maintain the association at *that* time.

There is another aspect of the cue-construction method that results in
inadequate cues. This has nothing to do with the discriminability of a cue
changing due to the expansion of the net; rather, it derives from a single

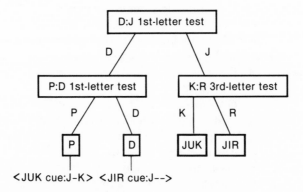

Figure D–4. Final discrimination net for the associate
pairs DAX–JIR, PIB–JUK.

random decision made by EPAM while it is constructing a cue. For example,
if J– – is proposed as a cue for JUK, when the cue is tested, it will lead to a
branch in the tree that has JUK on its left branch and JIR on its right. At
this point, EPAM chooses one of the branches at random. If it goes left, it
will find JUK and conclude that the cue is sufficient to find JUK in future,
when in fact, this is not so.

EPAM's Verbal-learning Behavior

EPAM behaved very much like a human subject in classical rote-learning
experiments. It provided a parsimonious explanation of rote-learning behavior, since retroactive inhibition, oscillation, stimulus and response generalization, and forgetting can all be seen to stem from a single mechanism.
As items are learned, the discrimination net grows to accommodate new
stimulus-response pairs. However, the cues that associate the stimuli with
their responses guarantee correct response retrieval just at the time of the
association. A cue that leads to the appropriate response image can fail to do
so at a later time.

The oscillatory behavior exhibited by EPAM serves as a basis for an alternative explanation of forgetting. The usual explanation is that the information is destroyed over time, typically by overwriting or decay. Forgetting
in EPAM occurs not because the information is physically destroyed but
because it becomes inaccessible in the growing network of new associations.
Furthermore, forgetting in EPAM is only temporary: Lost associations can
be recovered by updating the appropriate cue with more information during
another trial.

This process accounts for the fact that more than one trial is usually
required to *learn to criterion*, that is, to give the correct response to each

stimulus. During the first trial, each cue is constructed with enough information to find the correct response at the time it is stored; a subsequent stimulus-response pair may be added such that the original cue can now no longer discriminate between its correct response and the new one. This was shown in Figure D–4: The J– – cue was sufficient to produce a response when DAX–JIR were the only elements in the net, but as soon as PIB–JUK were added, J– – was ambiguous with respect to JIR and JUK. Thus, on the next trial, EPAM might respond to DAX with JUK; this would be incorrect and an example of *response generalization*. However, the correct association is always shown after a stimulus-response test, so EPAM has the opportunity to update the J– – cue to make it discriminate JIR and JUK. On the next trial, it will not confuse the two. Thus, in the course of a number of trials, EPAM gradually learns to discriminate all stimuli and their responses.

If stimuli and their responses were initially very discriminable, EPAM would require less time to learn them. This is because there is less chance of response generalization. Operationally, this means that when EPAM constructs a cue with the minimum information needed to find a response image, it is less likely that a subsequent stimulus-response pair will render the original cue ambiguous.

If the same discrimination net is used for two trials, that is, two different sets of stimulus-response pairs, the discrimination net that was sufficient to respond correctly to all stimuli during the first trial may now be unable to discriminate between responses for trial 1 and responses for trial 2. This produces the phenomenon of *retroactive inhibition*, which is the deleterious effect of learning an intermediate list on recall of the original list. It also predicts the result that errors are likely to be *intrusions* from the second list, rather than confusions between responses in the first list.

One problem with EPAM was that it had no mechanism to model *proactive inhibition*, the situation in which learning one list of stimuli interferes with the learning of the next list. Typically, when a subject is tested on the second list, intrusions from the first result. Both proactive and retroactive inhibition are evident in verbal-learning experiments, but EPAM exhibited only the latter. EPAM has since been extended to deal with proactive inhibition by Hintzman (1968) in his SAL (Stimulus and Association Learner) program. This was accomplished by having a push-down stack at each leaf node in the discrimination net. Instead of a single image and cue at a leaf node during an experiment, the associations from multiple experiments were allowed to accumulate by being pushed onto the appropriate stacks. Thus, the most recently learned association would be on the top of each of the stacks. If the stacks were randomly disrupted, the responses that "spontaneously rise" to the top of the stacks might be responses from previous experiments. Another accounting of proactive inhibition given by Anderson and Bower (1973, pp. 74–75) in their review of EPAM is that instead of a stacklike structure, a list of cues is kept, and the ordering of elements in the lists gets reshuffled, possibly as a consequence of the subject thinking about the material he has learned.

References

Feigenbaum (1963) and Simon and Feigenbaum (1964) are interesting treatments of EPAM and the empirical studies done with it. Feigenbaum and Simon (1962) is a discussion of an important verbal-learning effect—the serial-position effect. Anderson and Bower (1973, pp. 69–76) review and criticize the EPAM theory, and Simon (1979, pp. 99–100) provides a rebuttal to each of their criticisms.

E. SEMANTIC NETWORK MODELS OF MEMORY

E1. Quillian's Semantic Memory System

THERE are numerous intelligent behaviors of computers that depend on knowing the meanings of words, for example, machine translation, summarizing text, and speech understanding. The *semantic net* formalism developed by Ross Quillian was the first attempt to provide an operational representation of word meaning. The basis for Quillian's model is remarkably simple, namely, that the meaning of a word can be expressed by relating it to other words. This leads to the concept of *word senses*—a word may have many meanings that depend on the context in which it is used.

Quillian found that to *recognize* the meanings of words it is adequate to find the relations between them. However, for another task this conception of meaning might be less appropriate. For example, in the game "Twenty Questions" one may know many things about a word—that it denotes a common household item, the item is wooden, and so on. One may know everything about a word that would go into defining its meaning but still be unable to guess what it is, that is, to recall it. Quillian makes the distinction between *recognition memory* and *recall memory* for the meaning of words. His model is concerned with the former; recall memory is not considered.

The tasks Quillian chose to implement using semantic memory were *comparison* of word meanings and *expression* of the comparisons in English. Both were motivated by linguistic theory contemporary with Quillian's research, which subordinated meaning to syntax in search of rules to produce "all and only" grammatical sentences. In contrast, Quillian regarded semantic memory as primary to language production and syntax as secondary. Thus, he chose tasks to show that this new conception of language production could, in fact, both produce language and understand it.

The Associative Structure of Quillian's Semantic Network

Quillian's model is an associative network of nodes that represent concepts and arcs that represent relations between the concepts. When one is asked to say all one knows about a concept, for example, *machine*, a string of associations often results: A machine does work, has moving parts, is used to convert energy, and so on. *Machine* is associated with *energy* via the concept *convert*.

Word definitions have an associative structure. The set of associations and concepts that make up a definition is called a *plane* (see Fig. E1–1). The

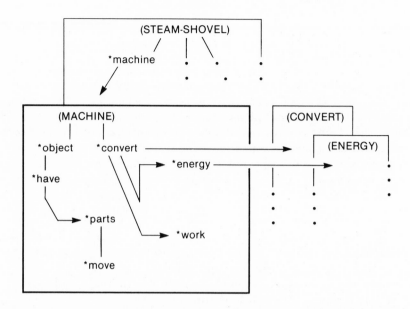

Figure E1–1.   Illustration of planes for *Machine, Steam-shovel,*
Convert, and *Energy,* showing type-token links.

concept being defined, called the *type node*, appears at the top, and the starred words beneath it are called *token nodes*. They are *instances* of the type nodes of other planes that are connected to their type nodes by arcs. (In Fig. E1–1, these arcs are not filled in for all token nodes; *steam shovel* is a subclass of *machine*, *machine* is an instance of *machine*, and *convert* and *energy* are instances of their associated type nodes.) Every plane contains only a single type node and enough token nodes to define the concept it names. Every plane represents a new concept defined by associations to those previously defined. Planes are linked together, type node to token node, throughout the associative memory.

The utility of the type-token distinction is that it saves space in computer memory. Imagine the size of a memory in which every definition of a particular machine included the entire plane for *machine*, and the planes of its other defining concepts, within its own. A more efficient organization is to have a single plane define *machine* and to connect it to token nodes in all the planes that include *machine* as part of their definition.

Quillian believes that semantic memory should have a large enough selection of arcs to represent the richness of relations between concepts in English, but not so many that the mechanisms required to process the arcs are very complicated. Six kinds of arcs were used, representing the following relations:

1. Subclass/superclass,

2. Modification (adverb, adjective),

3. Conjunctive (a *and* b *and* c),

4. Disjunctive (a *or* b *or* c),

5, 6. Two other relations representing unspecified binary predicates.

Other, more complex schemes for associating nodes have been proposed (see Article XI.E4). In a later publication, Collins and Quillian (1972) describe several other kinds of arcs, representing *proximity* (or *adjacence*), *consequence*, *precedence*, and *similarity*.

Meaning-dependent Tasks in the Model

One important contribution of Quillian's work was providing a simple model of semantic ambiguity. There are two sources of semantic ambiguity: A word may have different *meanings* (e.g., the noun and the verb forms of *plant*), and it may have different *senses* depending on context (e.g., *animal* in the context of species or *animal* in the context of untamed). Quillian's model is able to find many of the senses of words.

When the model is presented with two words to compare, it starts to search outward from the planes representing the words in its memory. The type nodes of the planes are called the *patriarch* nodes. The program alternately examines nodes emanating from each patriarch. Each node is tagged with a double label, one part containing the name of the patriarch and the other the name of the last node examined (the immediate ancestor). Searching continues until the path from one patriarch "bumps into" a node labeled with the name of the other patriarch. At that point, a path from one patriarch to the other has been completed. Its nodes represent the concepts that relate the two patriarch concepts, the raw material of a comparison. A program that expresses this conceptual pathway in English is summoned and produces a crudely expressed comparison.

It is likely that there is more than one path between two words. In fact, Quillian estimates that in a network of the 850 words of basic English, at least 10 nontrivial paths could be found relating any pair. Each of these constitutes a *sense* in which one word is used in the context of another. For example, the pair *man, business* yields the following comparison:

> Man3 is person, and
> Business can be activity which person must do work.

Also, the program discovers the generic sense of *man:*

> Man2 is man as9 group, and
> Business is question for attention of group.

Thus, *man* used in the context of business has two meanings. In the context of *live*, another sense emerges:

```
Man is animal, and
To live is to have existence as7 animal.
```

Also:

```
Man is a live+being2.
```

Although this version of the model contains less than 60 definitions, it still produces interesting comparisons.

Quillian notes that the breadth-first search (Article II.C1, in Vol. I) between nodes is a form of inference. The relations between nodes *within* a plane are entered by the coder who defines it. In constructing a definition, the coder makes pairwise associations between a plane and (through type-token links) the other planes that define it. Any path between planes that encompasses more than a single type-token pair is a novel conceptual link discovered by the model:

> While a path lying completely within one plane (except for its terminal points) amounts only to a representation of some piece of the information put into memory, a "plane-hopping" path represents an idea that was implied by, but by no means directly expressed in, the data that were input. (Quillian, 1968, p. 240)

Empirical Tests of Quillian's Model

Inference was an important concept to Collins and Quillian (1969) in their research on the psychological validity of the semantic network model. They sought to prove that human memory, like their semantic memory, obeyed the organizational principles of hierarchy and economy. Figure E1–2 represents a hierarchical tree of information about animals. The lower nodes constitute proper subsets of upper nodes; this is the principle of hierarchy. Note that properties of nodes are not repeated at each node at which they apply, but at the highest possible node above all the subsets to which the property applies. The properties of subsets are then *inferred* from the superordinate nodes at which they are stored. This is the principle of economy.

For example, although a canary is feathered, this information is stored with the ancestor of the set of feathered things, the concept *bird*. Higher still, stored with the concept *animal*, is the information that a canary is ambulatory. The knowledge that a canary is ambulatory is achieved by inference: A canary is a bird; a bird is an animal; animals are ambulatory; thus, by inference, canaries are ambulatory.

Collins and Quillian reasoned that predictions can be made to test whether the principles of hierarchy and economy hold for human memory. The first of

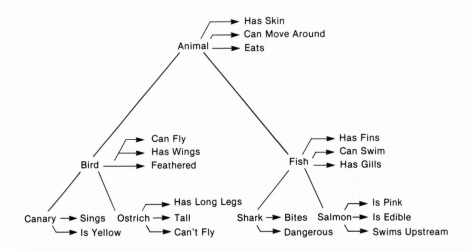

Figure E1–2.   A hierarchical memory structure (from Collins and
              Quillian, 1969).

these concerns the hierarchy principle: Since it requires more inferential steps
to confirm a proposition like *A canary is an animal* than a tautology like *A
canary is a canary*, humans should require more time to confirm the former
than the latter. They should need intermediate amounts of time to confirm
propositions requiring intermediate-length chains of reasoning, such as *A bird
is an animal* or *A salmon is a fish*. In fact, *reaction-time* data support this
prediction:

Proposition	Time to confirm (in seconds)
A canary is a canary.	1.0
A canary is a bird.	1.17
A canary is an animal.	1.25

These reaction times have been replicated for similar tasks (Conrad, 1972)
and support the hypothesis that semantic memory is organized hierarchically.
     Collins and Quillian used a similar experiment to test the economy prin-
ciple. They predicted that *A canary can sing* should require less time to verify
than *A canary has skin*, with intermediate propositions requiring intermediate
time. They found:

Proposition	Time to confirm (in seconds)
A canary can sing.	1.31
A canary can fly.	1.38
A canary has skin.	1.47

They presented this evidence in support of the economy principle. The alternate hypothesis, that a property common to a superset is stored with each member of each subset, is ruled out by the reaction-time data: If a superordinate property, like having skin, is stored with each subordinate node, for example, *canary*, it should take no longer to verify that a canary has skin than that it can sing.

Although Collins and Quillian's data support the economy principle, there is evidence that the increasing reaction times can be explained in other ways. Conrad (1972) found that the time required to verify a property was proportional to its familiarity, *not* to the hierarchical distance between a property and the noun it is associated with in a proposition. An alternative to the economy principle is that "properties are stored in memory with every word which they define and can be retrieved directly rather than through a process of inference" (p. 154). Conrad explains the differences in reaction time as a function of the familiarity of the words. When familiarity was controlled, and the experiment run again, no differences in reaction time as a function of the presumed hierarchical placement of the property could be found. However, the effect of position in hierarchy for superset-subset sentences was replicated.

The status of the economy principle is unsure. The hierarchy principle has more support, but Collins and Quillian's model of sentence verification leaves a number of phenomena unexplained. For example, it does not account for how false sentences (*Fish can play hopscotch*) are disconfirmed. Unfortunately, the reaction times obtained for disconfirming negative sentences are difficult to interpret. It is difficult to tell whether this is because of a failing in the model or because reaction time is an inappropriate tool for examining this kind of model.

Conclusion

Since Quillian's pioneering work, semantic nets and other associative representations (e.g., frames) have become part of the language of AI. Although Quillian developed his model as a representation of linguistic knowledge and was motivated largely by issues in linguistics, semantic nets have been generalized to representations of many other kinds of knowledge. Several issues raised by Quillian have been examined in detail in AI. The issues of modes of inference, inheritance of properties, and the numerosity and semantics of arcs are discussed in the domain of knowledge representation (see Chap. III, in Vol. I; also, Brachman, 1978). In psychology, the model was subjected to empirical analysis and several other associative models were developed. Three will be discussed in the succeeding articles.

References

The best paper on Quillian's model is his own in Minsky (1968).

E2. HAM

IN THEIR BOOK *Human Associative Memory* (1973), psychologists John Anderson and Gordon Bower present an associationist theory of human long-term memory (LTM). Aspects of their theory have been implemented in a computer simulation called HAM that parses simple propositional sentences and stores the parsed sentences in its memory. HAM also answers simple questions. Its abilities are limited, but intentionally so, in that Anderson and Bower have eliminated the mnemonic strategies and tricks that result in smart memory performance in humans. Their goal was to model the *strategy-free component* of human long-term memory and to explain the vast experimental data on the subject. With respect to this goal they write:

> Why not add some more inferential routines to increase the intelligence with which it (HAM) answers questions? We started down this enticing, seductive path; but we slowly came to the realization that this was no way for experimental psychologists to proceed.... The end product of such an enterprise would appear to be thousands of lines of program that described the countless heuristics, procedures, tricks, and rules that the human has learned in his lifetime. We would have translated one incomprehensible mass of particulars, the human mind, into another incomprehensible mass, a computer program. But the task of science is surely to reduce particulars to general laws rather than translate particulars from one idiom to another. (p. 145)

Anderson and Bower assume that long-term memory is strategy invariant; the strategies that are obviously used to remember things are, they assume, imposed by an *executive component* of cognition. LTM is thought to be much simpler than the experimental literature suggests, because much of the literature does not separate out the effects of mnemonic strategies on memory performance. Memory experiments that use single words or nonsense material as stimuli are considered especially likely to have their results complicated by mnemonic strategies, because these materials are more easily remembered with some strategy than without. Consequently, most of Anderson and Bower's research concerns memory for sentences or phrases that are apparently less likely to evoke mnemonic strategies.

Anderson and Bower chose question-answering as the task environment for HAM. This may be the simplest task on which to examine a memory model, since it requires only storage, retrieval, and rudimentary parsing functions.

HAM accepts two kinds of inputs, facts and questions, which it parses into input structures (described below). To facilitate parsing, inputs are made only in a natural subset of English. We will not consider HAM's parser in this article other than to say that it is a top-down, left-to-right, predictive parser;

we refer the reader to Chapter 8 of Anderson and Bower's book (1973) for more details.

The parameters of memory that interest Anderson and Bower are:

1. The set of possible memory structures,
2. The set of possible inputs to memory,
3. The set of possible outputs from memory in response to probes,
4. The set of possible probes,
5. The encoding process by which the structure of memory is modified to record new information,
6. The decoding function by which the structure of memory is probed to determine what is recorded there.

Some assumptions are made about these parameters. First, the only allowable input structures are facts and questions. The latter are called probes. It is assumed that probes are always parsed into the same input structure, that the encoding function always matches the input structure to memory in the same way, and that the same output will be generated to a probe.

Representation of Knowledge in HAM

All knowledge in HAM is represented as *propositions*, encoded in binary trees. For example, the structure of *In a park a hippie touched a debutante* is shown in Figure E2–1. The numbers identify nodes in memory; the labels are interpreted as follows:

Label	Interpretation
C	Context in which Fact is true
F	Fact
L	Location
T	Time
S	Subject
P	Predicate
R	Relation
O	Object
E	Set membership

A proposition tree may also consist of a fact without a context. In this case, it always has the subject-predicate form; sometimes the predicate is just a single concept (see Fig. E2–2).

The relation-object pair is used to express implicit or explicit causality, among other things. *Cause* is illustrated as a relation in Figure E2–3. This

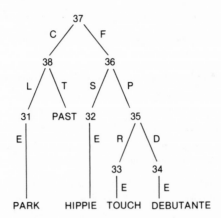

Figure E2–1.   HAM structure for *In a park a hippie touched a debutante.*

structure represents the sentence *John opened the door with the key.* It includes an implicit cause, namely, turning the key caused the door to open. This tree is more abstract than the one shown in Figure E2–1, because it does not show the *terminal quantifiers* leading to the terminal nodes of the tree. *Set membership*, labeled "E" above, is one of three terminal quantifiers. It is used when the terminal concept is a member of a set, such as the set of debutantes. A *generic* link is used when the terminal node denotes all members of a set, for example, the entire class of dogs in *All dogs chase some cats.* A subset link is used to indicate that the terminal node denotes neither an entire class nor a single member, but a subset of a class. *Cats* in the previous sentence takes a subset link.   These links give HAM the representational power of second-order predicate calculus (Anderson and Bower, 1973, pp. 167–169; however, the reader is referred to Anderson, 1976, pp. 165–169, for a criticism and reworking of the terminal quantifications of HAM).

Properties of HAM's Knowledge Representation

Anderson and Bower (1973) specify the properties of their memory structure as a set of postulates:

> *Symmetry:* If an associative link exists between two nodes, then an inverse link also exists. Concretely, if one knows a relation between two objects, one also knows the inverse of that relation.

> *No-forgetting:* Once a structure is incorporated into memory, it cannot disappear from memory. Therefore, forgetting must occur by losing *access* to the information in the structure, not the information itself. (For more on this view, see Article XI.D.)

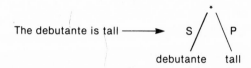

Figure E2–2. Simple subject-predicate structure.

First Empiricist Postulate: There is no innate knowledge in the form of associations between memory nodes. All associations are formed in response to inputs.

Second Empiricist Postulate: Concepts (nodes) similarly are acquired only through inputs. However, this can lead to the idea that HAM is initially empty, which Anderson and Bower explicitly reject. They postulate a *base set* of *simple ideas* that are present in HAM at its birth and upon which more complex ideas are built.

An Example of HAM in Operation

HAM accepts input sentences (indicated by ** below), builds associative structures of them in memory, and answers questions about them:

** In a park a hippie touched a debutante.

HAM responds by building and printing the structure (shown in Fig. E2–4) that corresponds to this assertion. It is the same structure as shown in Figure E2–1.

** Who was touched by the tall hippie?

The tall hippie--which one?

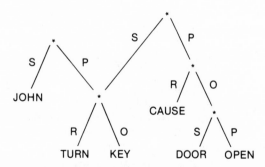

Figure E2–3. Implicit *cause* in the sentence *John opened the door with the key.*

HAM does not know of any tall hippies. It is told that the current hippie is tall.

** The hippie was tall.

HAM incorporates this new knowledge and prints out its structure. The new knowledge structure is illustrated in Figure E2-5; for clarity, we have shown it connected to the structure from Figure E2-4, although HAM would not print all these nodes, but only the new nodes—45, 46, 47, 48, and 32—and the associative links between them.

** Who was touched by the tall hippie?

HAM can now answer the question.

The debutante.

This example illustrates HAM's operation. When input sentences are typed in, they are parsed into tree structures. If the input material is an assertion like *The hippie was tall*, HAM incorporates it into memory by finding and merging common nodes in memory and in the input. In this case, part of the input structure matches node 32 of HAM's memory, corresponding to the *hippie* concept. HAM incorporates the input structure into memory by joining it to node 32, as shown in Figure E2-5. Thus, HAM learns by associating new knowledge in the form of input trees with old knowledge already in memory.

If the input sentence is a question, the parser generates an input tree that may be missing a part. This kind of tree is called a *probe*. For example, the question *Who was touched by the tall hippie?* is parsed into a probe of the form *The* [blank] *was touched by the tall hippie;* see Figure E2-6. To answer questions, HAM quite literally fills in the blanks. It searches its memory for a structure like the probe that has a node instead of a blank. This node is the answer to the question. In this case, the probe in Figure E2-6 matches the memory structure in Figure E2-5, and the node corresponding to the blank is *debutante*.

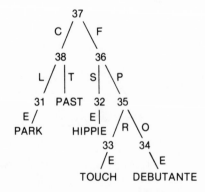

Figure E2–4.   HAM structure for *In a park a hippie touched a debutante.*

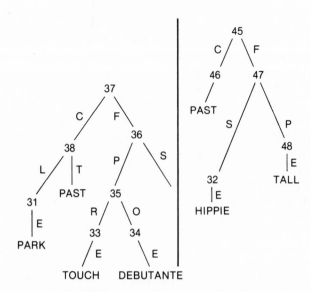

Figure E2–5.   Illustration of how HAM incorporates the fact *The hippie was tall* into its memory.

   HAM matches input trees to extant memory structures to associate new information with old and to answer questions. Its operation becomes more complicated when *partial matches* are involved. The 1973 version of HAM was run in two modes. The mode illustrated in Figures E2–4 and E2–5 has HAM *not* accepting a partial match in the case of the tall hippie. The program wants to be told explicitly that the tall hippie in the input tree and the hippie in memory are the same hippie. In the other mode, HAM accepts partial matches. For example, it would answer the question *Who was touched by the tall hippie?* by matching the probe tree in Figure E2–6 to the memory

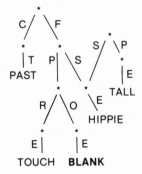

Figure E2–6.   Probe tree for *Who was touched by the tall hippie?*

structure in Figure E2–4. It would not be necessary to spell out that the hippie was tall, as in Figure E2–5. (Partial matching is discussed further in Anderson and Bower, 1973, pp. 242–246.)

From these examples, one can see that the matching process, MATCH, is fundamental to HAM's operation. MATCH is simple in conception. First it finds nodes in memory that correspond to the terminal nodes of an input structure, and then it attempts to find links in memory that correspond to the links in the input structure. In other words, MATCH finds *paths* between input terminal nodes that correspond to paths in memory. A memory path and an input structure path are considered equivalent if they have the same number of links and the same *sequence* of relations labeling the links.

HAM searches for paths in memory from all of the input terminal nodes in parallel. For example, after matching the terminal nodes of the probe (Fig. E2–6) to nodes in the memory structure (Fig. E2–5), MATCH would search from each of the nodes (*past, touch, hippie, past, tall*), in parallel, to determine whether the paths that connect them are identical in memory and in the probe. However, if a node has more than one path emanating from it (*hippie* has two), they are searched sequentially. Consequently, the time required to establish that a node falls on a path is proportional to the number of associations it has—the number of paths it belongs to. This is called the *fan effect*.

HAM knows many facts, and a given terminal node like *hippie* is likely to be part of several trees. In this case, *hippie* is associated to nodes 36 and 47 in memory by means of a *subject* link. The nodes associated with each node by a link are stored in a *GET-list* for the node and link. The *hippie* node in Figure E2–5 would have a single GET-list with two members for the *subject* relation. One can imagine other associations made with other links (e.g., *object*) resulting in other GET-lists. To reduce search, MATCH follows only the links from a node in memory that have the same label as the links from the corresponding node in the input tree. If the *hippie* node in memory were connected to other structures by an *object* link, MATCH would not search them, since the input structure it is matching to memory has only *subject* links emanating from *hippie*.

Search is further speeded by using *recency* information. The members of the GET-list are examined in the order of most recent mention. Moreover, HAM will not necessarily search all members of a GET-list; it may be too long. This leads to the sole mechanism of *forgetting* in HAM: An association between two nodes that has not been mentioned in a long time will drop farther and farther down the GET-lists for both nodes, thereby increasing the probability that HAM terminates its search from one of the nodes without finding the association with the other.

Search can be speeded to some extent by these methods, but a node may still be a member of many paths. *Hippie* could be the subject of dozens of sentences, and MATCH would have to check each, serially, to see if an input structure corresponds to one of them. The number of associations a node has is called its *fan-out;* since fanning nodes are searched sequentially, the fan-out contributes to the amount of time required to answer a question. This property is the basis for reaction-time experiments with human subjects. HAM predicts that it should take humans longer to process memory concepts with a high fan-out than those with a low one. See the following article on ACT for an explanation of the Sternberg effect in terms of the fan effect.

To summarize, MATCH associates terminal nodes in the input structure with corresponding nodes in memory and then starts a parallel search from these nodes for paths between them that are equivalent to the paths between the terminal nodes of the input structure. To do this, it examines the label of each link emanating from a node in the input structure and searches the appropriate GET-list associated with the corresponding node in memory. The GET-list may not be searched completely and thus associations between nodes may appear to be lost, which accounts for forgetting in HAM. The position of a node on the GET-list is a function of how recently it was mentioned, so that old associations are more likely to appear to be forgotten than recent ones. Lastly, the nodes on a GET-list are searched serially, so that a large GET-list can take a long time to search.

Conclusion

Anderson and Bower have a strong commitment to empirical data about human memory. The HAM model was designed as a parsimonious and operational explanation of a wide range of results. It also made a number of predictions that were tested with the standard experimental methods of cognitive psychology. The individual results are voluminous and of interest primarily to cognitive psychologists; none of the particulars is presented here. However, the general result is especially important: A wide range of memory tasks can be modeled by a *strategy-free* process. Although humans use sophisticated strategies to remember difficult (often meaningless) material, the study of long-term memory is simplified by assuming that the strategies overlay a relatively simple mechanism common to all memory performance. The MATCH process is such a mechanism, and in experiments in which the utility of mnemonic strategies is reduced, it predicts many interesting empirical results.

References

Anderson and Bower's 1973 book *Human Associative Memory* provides a detailed account of the HAM model and of empirical tests of the model. The first four chapters of the book are interesting reading, although they are background to HAM, not a discussion of HAM itself. They discuss philosophical approaches to the study of memory, linguistic theory, and other models of memory.

E3. ACT

THE ACT system was built by John Anderson following his work on HAM (see Article XI.E2). There are many points of overlap between HAM and ACT, but there are also fundamental differences. Most significantly, ACT is intended as a general model of cognition, while HAM is a model of human memory. HAM answers questions and learns new information; ACT does more, in that it can be programmed to perform a wide variety of cognitive tasks. In addition to its long-term memory, ACT has a short-term *working memory* of active concepts and a programmable *production system* that brings about changes in working and long-term memories. Common to HAM and ACT are certain features of long-term memory; for example, strategy invariance has been carried over to ACT, and so has the propositional representation of knowledge, although modified in some details.

Overview of ACT

ACT has a long-term memory component and a user-programmable procedural component. The memory is a propositional associative network made up of nodes representing concepts and arcs representing relations between the concepts. ACT's memory is not very different from HAM's (discussed in Article XI.E2), so it will not be described in detail here.

An important feature of ACT's memory is that only parts of it are *active* at any time. Activation can spread through the network as nodes activate adjacent nodes. The time required to activate the neighbors of an active node depends on its *fan-out*, that is, the number of nodes connected to it. ACT attends to a limited number of active nodes. Those that are not marked for attention are eventually made inactive; those that are marked for attention are put in a first-in, first-out buffer called the ALIST. They may displace older nodes, because the ALIST has a capacity of just 10 items. In this article, the ALIST will be called the *working memory*.

The programmable, procedural component of ACT is a *production system*. Each production has a condition part as well as an action part that is invoked if the condition is true. In ACT, all conditions test for a conjunction of features of memory, and all action parts specify a change to be made to memory. The conditions of productions can examine only the active part of memory. A number of productions may be activated by the state of memory, in which case each of them has a probability of being executed.

An Example of ACT

Anderson shows how ACT can be programmed to perform the Sternberg *memory-scanning* task (Sternberg, 1969). In this task, subjects are presented with a list of numbers, for example, 4 9 1 3, and a *probe* number, which may or may not be on the list. Sternberg's result is that, if the probe number is in the list, then the amount of time required to confirm it increases, by .038 seconds, for each number on the list. Curiously, the serial position of the matching digit is irrelevant; the time required to confirm the presence of a probe in a list of numbers is independent of where the probe occurs in the list. Sternberg originally explained this effect in terms of a *serial exhaustive scanning model*, in which the list is kept in working memory and a *comparator* compares the probe digit to each list element. The comparison process was thought to be exhaustive, meaning that all list elements are scanned, even if a match to the probe has already been found. (This paradigm is discussed in detail in Crowder, 1976, pp. 354–366.)

Anderson offers a different explanation in terms of ACT. When the list of numbers is presented, a structure is built in memory to represent it. In the case of the list 4 9 1 3, a node called LIST is connected to four nodes, 4, 9, 1, and 3, by the relation CONTAINS, as shown in Figure E3–1. In ACT's memory, the LIST node is connected to four others and ultimately to four numbers by the relation CONTAINS. The LIST node has a fan-out of four, since four links emanate from it.

The first production for the Sternberg task is:

P1.   State = Ready → State and List.

It says that if ACT is in the *ready* state, the next step is to rehearse the state and the list. In the context of memory, rehearsal means repeating something over and over to keep it in memory, much as we do with telephone numbers. Production P1 brings about rehearsal behavior by the simple device of putting on the ALIST the condition to satisfy P1 again. Production P1 is satisfied whenever state = *ready;* when it is executed, it sets the state to *ready* and

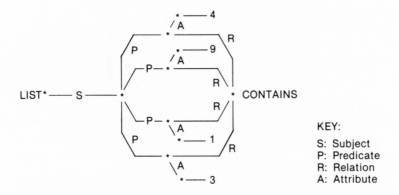

Figure E3–1.   ACT memory structure for a list of numbers.

puts the LIST node on the ALIST again. This potentially infinite iteration continues until another production is satisfied.

The second production, P2, tests whether a probe digit has been given. If it has not, then P2 cannot have any effect and ACT will continue to rehearse. If it has, then P2 changes the value of the state variable from *ready* to *test* and puts the probe digit on the ALIST with the state variable:

> P2.   State = Ready and Probe given
> → State = Test and Probe digit.

The third and fourth productions check for the presence of the probe digit in the list and signal their findings. They then reset the state variable to *ready* for the next problem:

> P3.   State = Test and List contains Probe
> → Signal "Found it" and State = Ready.

> P4.   State = Test and List does not contain Probe
> → Signal "Not there" and State = Ready.

This simple production system and the idea of spreading activation in memory account for the Sternberg result that reaction time to identify a digit increases with the number of digits in the list. At the beginning of a trial, ACT has encoded the list in memory as described above, and the LIST node is put into working memory (see Fig. E3–2). It is active, but the nodes emanating from it are not; they must be activated by following links from the LIST node in working memory into long-term memory.

With working memory in the state shown in Figure E3–2, production P1 applies. It will rehearse the contents of working memory until a probe digit is given. When this happens, the value of the state variable is changed to *test,*

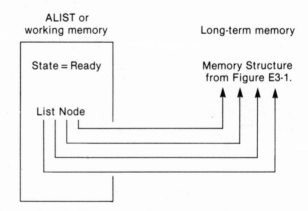

Figure E3–2.   Illustration of working memory, showing links into long-term memory.

the state necessary for P3 or P4 to apply. The other condition for P3 is that the list contains the probe digit. Since the numbers on the list reside in long-term memory, they must be activated for P3 to check them. The fan of the LIST node determines how long it will take to activate the nodes connected to it; as the number of links from the LIST node increases, it takes ACT longer to search them. This is a slightly different explanation of the Sternberg effect.

Instead of serially scanning a list of numbers in working memory, ACT activates the memory structure representing the numbers; the amount of time required to do this depends on the fan-out of the LIST node. This determines the reaction time in the Sternberg task.

Performance in ACT

ACT is a highly dynamic system. Its *focus of attention* changes as nodes in long-term memory are activated and put in working memory, as other nodes are pushed out of working memory, and as nodes are *damped* in long-term memory and become inactive. There is a constant fluctuation of activity that is complex and nondeterministic due to the probabilistic nature of spreading activation.

Limitations were imposed on ACT to make it resemble human cognition more closely. Some of these are:

1. The parameters that affect spread of activation are extremely important to the operation of the system because nodes must be active to get to working memory, where productions operate on them. The fan of a node is one such parameter. Others include how far activation must travel in the memory network, how frequently nodes in memory are damped, and how *strong* the links are between nodes.

2. The ALIST, or working memory, is of limited size, so ACT attends to just a few concepts at a time.

3. Only some productions in ACT are applicable at any given time. There are strategies for determining which are applicable and for deciding among them. The strategies affect the amount of time ACT takes to perform a task.

4. When new information is added to ACT, it has only a probability of being remembered.

Learning in ACT

There are four methods for learning in ACT. *Designation* refers to telling ACT something, for example, a proposition or a production rule. *Generalization* and *discrimination* are two methods for automatically generating new production rules. The fourth learning method, *strengthening,* is a *reinforcement* procedure.

The first method, *designation*, is the simplest means of adding information to ACT. It is the method that was used in HAM. The second method, *generalization* of productions, works by replacing constant terms in the conditions of two productions by variables. To avoid creating terms that are too general to be interesting, ACT will not replace more than one-half of the constants of the smallest condition. *Discrimination*, the third learning method, produces two or more productions from one with too many variables in its condition. It does so by instantiating the variables. Discrimination applies whenever ACT gets feedback that a production is too general.

Generalizations and discriminations of productions do not replace the original rules; rather, they exist with them. A generalization will apply whenever either of its original productions applies but will have the same effect as both. However, ACT has a conflict-resolution strategy that favors executing specific rules before more general ones, so discriminations of general rules, or the rules from which a generalization has been formed, have precedence over generalizations.

Associated with each production is a *strength* that is used to resolve conflicts when several productions are applicable. *Strengthening*, the last of the four learning methods, reinforces productions by increasing or decreasing their strength. If a production is found to be applicable, its strength is increased by a constant number. However, its strength is decreased by 25% if its execution leads to a mistaken conclusion. Negative strengthening is therefore more effective than positive. Strengthening also applies to productions that are consistent with other applicable or misapplied productions. (A production is consistent with another if its condition is more or less general but its action is the same.)

Conclusion

ACT is a general framework in which cognitive performance is simulated. It is not custom-built to perform a particular task, unlike most of the systems discussed in this chapter. (MEMOD, another general system, is discussed in Article XI.E4.) Anderson considers ACT's design to be psychologically plausible; he goes to lengths to present the "predisposing biases" that motivated design decisions in terms of the psychological literature. Moreover, ACT makes reasonable predictions about human behavior in experimental situations. ACT can be considered a theory, in the sense that it makes predictions, and a programming language, or package, in the sense that it provides an environment for building psychological models.

References

Anderson has published a lengthy book on the ACT system (1976) that includes chapters on the structure and behavior of ACT, spreading activation in memory, learning, and language comprehension. It is an exhaustive treatment, in which Anderson presents not only the ACT system but also the theoretical motivations for it. The book is reviewed by Wexler (1978), and a reply to the review can be found in Anderson (1980). The review and reply are worthwhile reading for those interested in cognitive science, since they are two different positions on how a science of mind should proceed.

E4. MEMOD

THE LNR research group, named for Peter Lindsay, Donald Norman, and David Rumelhart, is engaged in the ongoing development of a general model of human long-term memory called MEMOD. Of the five memory models discussed in this chapter, MEMOD may be the most ambitious (ACT, discussed in Article XI.E3, is the other candidate) because of its scope and because of LNR's basic tenet that a single system accounts for cognition:

> One system has to be capable of handling the representation and processing issues in syntactic and semantic analysis of language, in memory, perception, problem solving, reasoning, question answering, and in the acquisition of knowledge. (Norman, Rumelhart, and the LNR Research Group, 1975, p. 160)

It is a major goal of the LNR group that the MEMOD system should be a general knowledge-representation system, that is, one that can represent any kind of knowledge. Until quite recently, however, it was used primarily to represent linguistic knowledge. Accordingly, the MEMOD system has three main components: a *parser*, which is based on an augmented transition network (ATN; see Article IV.D2, in Vol. I); a *node space*, which is a semantic-net representation of world knowledge; and an *interpreter*, which performs operations on the node space. The node space represents both *declarative* and *procedural* knowledge; node-space structures represent facts about the world and also specifications of operations to be performed in the node space by the interpreter. Because it is not a passive repository of knowledge but contains procedures that manipulate knowledge, the node space is called the *active structural network*, or ASN.

In this article, the design of the active structural network is sketched briefly, followed by a more formal discussion of how concepts and events are represented. Here, the role of the interpreter will be more obvious. We will not consider the parser at all, since ATN parsers and case grammars are dealt with in Chapter IV (in Vol. I) on understanding natural language.

The Active Structural Network

The design of the active structural network was constrained by a number of goals arising directly from the natural-language applications intended for the MEMOD model. Briefly, these were:

1. *Completeness.* The model must be able to represent *any* knowledge of any type, including nonlinguistic knowledge.

2. *Extendability.* The model must be extendable whenever new information is available. If, for example, the model learns that to saunter is not merely to walk but is to exhibit some degree of indolence, it must be able to incorporate this information.

3. *Invariance under paraphrase.* Expressions that have the same meaning should have the same underlying representation in the ASN regardless of how they are stated at a surface level.

4. *Preservation of overlap in meaning.* The representation of words and larger units of meaning in the ASN should reflect the possibilities of synonymy, partial overlap, and no overlap in meaning. Meanings that overlap, such as *stroll* and *saunter*, should have common components in their representations. Unrelated words should not.

5. *Continuity.* In a psychological model of knowledge, words with similar meanings should have similar structures, and a small change in meaning should not cause a major change in its representation. Similarly, concepts that have very different meanings should have very different representations.

Semantic Decomposition and Case Structure of Predicates

The technique employed by the LNR group to satisfy these goals is *semantic decomposition* of words (or more generally, concepts) into primitive elements called *predicates* (see Article III.C6, in Vol. I, for a detailed discussion of semantic decomposition). For example, they identify four classes of predicates—*stative, change, causative,* and *actional*—that can be combined to yield different verb meanings.

Stative predicates. The stative component of a verb indicates that a state of the world holds over some time period. One of the stative predicates in the MEMOD system is LOC. It takes four arguments, the last two of which are optional:

LOC[object, at-loc, (from-time), (to-time)] .

A semantic-net representation of the LOC predicate shows the LOC *node* linked to four argument nodes, as shown in Figure E4–1. Here, a network structure is shown to represent the sentence *A stadium was located in the park from 1956 to 1963.* In addition to the LOC node, this figure also shows nodes representing the concepts of *stadium, park, 1956,* and *1963.* A point of notation is that the angle brackets and parentheses in this diagram denote *tokens*—or copies—of concepts and predicates, respectively. A token represents a concept in some context; a dictionary of *type*, or original, nodes is also maintained, and token nodes are linked to them; see Article XI.E1 for a discussion of the type-token distinction.

Change predicates. A verb like *move* can be represented as a CHANGE predicate taking two LOC predicates as arguments, as shown in Figure E4–2,

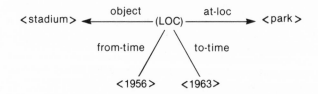

Figure E4-1. The LOC component of the verb *located* in
the sentence *A stadium was located in the
park from 1956 to 1963.*

which represents the sentence *The team moved from the stadium to the training camp in May.*

   Causative predicates. One can imagine how another verb, say, *push*,
might be represented by a structure like the one shown in Figure E4-2, but
predicated with a causative; that is, to push is to CAUSE to move from one
location to another. Figure E4-3 represents the concept of a person causing
an unspecified object to move from one unspecified place to another at an
unspecified time. It is the skeleton of a *cause-to-change-location* verb; the
reader can think of numerous verbs that have this general structure.

   Actional predicates. Consider this example in the context of the design
goals discussed earlier. Semantic decomposition is a representational tool
that guarantees that similar meanings have similar structures. The structure
above is common to several verbs with overlapping meanings: *push, shove,
carry, pull, transport,* and so on. The *actional* predicate is instrumental in
making finer distinctions in meaning; however, LNR has done little work with
actionals, and generally the primitive predicate DO is used.

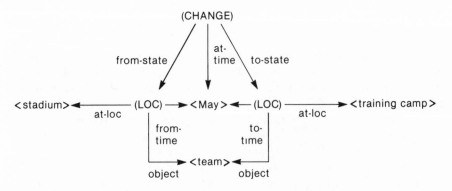

Figure E4-2. *Move* consists of CHANGE and LOC predicates; it is a CHANGE
in LOCation—as in *The team moved from the stadium to the
training camp in May.*

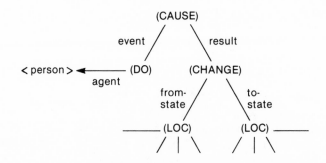

Figure E4–3.   Skeleton of a verb with CAUSE, CHANGE, and
               LOC predicates organized to represent the
               concept of causing a change in location, as
               in *push, pull,* and *carry.*

Once a word is defined, it is stored in MEMOD's dictionary as a type node
and can be used in more complex structures, as in:

```
<lion> ← (CARRIED) → <antelope>
```

A final point, before proceeding to a more formal description of knowledge
representation in MEMOD, is that predicates have a *case* structure (discussed
in Article IV.C4, in Vol. I).   For example, LOC has two necessary and two
optional arguments:

```
LOC[object, at-loc, (from-time), (to-time)] .
```

This facilitates parsing. When the parser recognizes a predicate or a verb, it
can make predictions about what kinds of words to expect next on the basis
of knowing the verb's arguments.

Encoding Concepts, Events, and Episodes

In a 1972 paper, Rumelhart, Lindsay, and Norman specified four categories of rules for constructing complex knowledge structures from the simple
ones we have already considered:

1. Rules of formation for concepts,
2. Rules of formation for relations,
3. Rules of formation for propositions,
4. Rules of formation for operators.

Concepts are objects, for example, *lion* and *stadium*. Relations are the
names of associations that may hold among concepts, for example, HIT[actor,
object, instrument]. Propositions are instantiations of relations, for example,
HIT[John, ball, bat]. Operators, the last group, are of two varieties,

prepositional and relational. The former modifies concepts of time or location to generate new concepts:

`before(noon)` or `under(water)` .

The latter modifies relations:

`slowly(walk)` or `very(big)` .

LNR gives five rules for forming concepts. First, an existing concept can be qualified. This corresponds most closely to the action of adjectives. A qualified concept has a node of its own; for example, the node *lamb* is defined as *young(sheep)*. Second, quantification of concepts can yield new concepts, as when *crowd* is defined to be *many(persons)*. Third, new concepts of location and time can be derived from prepositional operators. Fourth, concepts can be conjoined to form new concepts; for example, *and(dog, cat)* denotes the concept of the class of dogs and cats. Finally, concepts can denote propositions. For example, in the proposition HIT(*John, ball, bat*), there is a concept *hit*, which corresponds to an instance of the general relation HIT in the context of *John* and his *ball* and *bat*.

There are three ways to generate new relations from old. The first is to modify the relation, as with an adverb. For example, the relation *stroll* is defined as *slowly(walk)*. Another method is to modify one or more of the arguments of the relation. For example, if the relation of walking is defined as:

`WALK[actor, path, time]` ,

then a new relation, CLIMB, could be derived by specifying that the path should be uphill. Finally, new relations can be generated by conjoining old ones with special conjunctions. BECAUSE is one such conjunction:

`FLEE[actor, object, time] is defined as`
`quickly( GO(actor, from(object)), time))`
`BECAUSE`
`FEAR(actor, object, time)` .

Propositions are formed by instantiating a relation with concepts. For example, the arguments of FLEE might be (*Dorothy, lions, always*). The other method for obtaining propositions is to conjoin them with conjunctions like BECAUSE and AND.

Operators are constructed in some of the same ways. New qualifiers are generated from old by applying relational operators to them; for example, *tiny* is *very(small)*. Relational operators also apply to each other; for example, *partly* is *not(completely)*.

Sentences that describe events, such as *The lion chased Mary*, can be encoded in MEMOD. Conjoining events by using conjunctions like BECAUSE, AND, THEN, and WHILE allows one to represent complex *episodes*. Graphically,

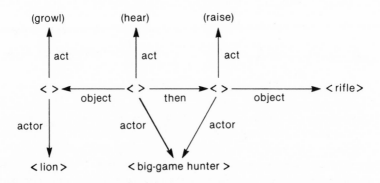

Figure E4–4.   A representation of the episode *The big-game hunter heard the lion growl and raised his gun.*

an episode is simply a sequence of event nodes connected by conjunctions. An example of a graphical representation of an episode in which a big-game hunter hears a lion growl and raises his gun is shown in Figure E4–4. (The empty nodes represent tokens of the three events, hearing, growling, and raising.)

A simple propositional sentence can be broken down into a relation and a set of concept arguments. A relation can be broken down further into primitive predicates by semantic decomposition. Rules were discussed here that conjoin and modify concepts, relations, propositions, and operators and that create more complex structures such as episodes. These rules give MEMOD the power to represent episodes of varying complexity. The next section outlines the interactions between these representations and the interpreter.

The Interpreter

Knowledge is supplied to MEMOD in the form of sentences. After these are parsed, the interpreter makes the appropriate changes to the ASN by executing the program associated with each relation in the input sentence. For example, a basic relation built into MEMOD is CONNECT. There is a type node for CONNECT that is linked to a computer program that joins nodes together in the ASN, as shown in Figure E4–5.

If the interpreter encounters a parsed version of the sentence *Connect dog to animal with isa*, it will look up the word *connect;* find that it denotes a built-in program that takes three arguments; *bind* the arguments *dog, animal,* and *isa* to the variables X, Y, and $Z;$ and execute the program. The result is a network structure:

$$dog \xrightarrow{\text{isa}} animal \; .$$

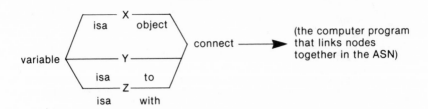

Figure E4–5.   Representation of the relation CONNECT.

The CONNECT program was built into MEMOD from the outset. However, it is possible to *define* words by associating programs with them. For example, the LNR group gives the following definition for the word *son*.

Define son as predicate.
the definition frame for son is: X is son of Y
the definition is:

Connect X to male with sex.
If age of X is less than 18, then
connect X to child with isa.
connect Y to X with parent-of.
##

(This represents an interaction with the MEMOD system. The text in ordinary type is entered by the user; MEMOD's replies are in italics.)

The relation DEFINE is itself a built-in procedure that builds structures in the ASN. For example, defining *son* yields a structure that is something like the one shown in Figure E4–6 (which is not exact, since all of the arrows pointing to the node CONNECT would be pointing to the same type node in the ASN).

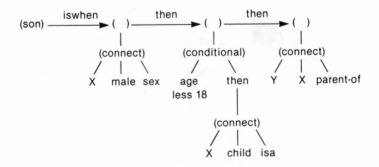

Figure E4–6.   Representation of the definition of *son*.

The important thing about this structure is that it invokes changes to the ASN when interpreted. Although its representation is uniform with declarative network structures, it is a representation of a procedure. When the interpreter is given the sentence *Oedipus is the son of Jocasta*, it will create a structure in the ASN representing the facts that Jocasta is the parent of Oedipus and that Oedipus is male. The distinction between procedural and declarative knowledge in MEMOD is obscured by the uniform representation used for both. It appears that there are two kinds of procedural knowledge, built-in programs like CONNECT and definitions that are formally very similar to episodes except for an ISWHEN link. ISWHEN links a node with its definition, and interpreting the definition results in changes to the ASN.

A word like *son*, when defined in MEMOD, carries with it the procedures necessary to make inferences about what it means to be a son; for example, one can infer that a son is male because part of the definition of *son* is a procedure that makes that connection in the ASN. Because definitions carry implicit inferences about what it means to be something, MEMOD can answer many questions. For example, given an appropriate definition, it can say what it means to be a *sandwich*. Here is one definition from the Kitchenworld implementation of MEMOD:

> Define sandwich as recipe.
> *the definition frame for sandwich is:* (subject)sandwich X.
> *the definition is:*
>
> Place a slice of bread on the counter.
> Spread preferred spread of X on the bread.
> Place each ingredient of X on the bread.
> Place a second piece of bread on the bread.
> ##

This definition has a network structure similar to those shown above. It is composed of nodes representing simple actions like *place*, which are composed of simpler predicates like CONNECT. To answer questions such as "What containers would be left on the counter after I made a sandwich?" the interpreter executes the sandwich recipe in the ASN. This results in changes to the ASN. For example, containers that were previously associated with *refrigerator* by an IN link may subsequently be linked to *counter* by ON.

Conclusion

MEMOD implements a number of powerful ideas, which were reviewed here. Semantic decomposition, for one, ensures that concepts with similar meanings have similar structures. This was illustrated by a general structure for verbs that mean *to cause a change in location*. In MEMOD, the meaning of a concept is reflected in its structure, its composition of simpler units of meaning.

Verbs and other structures in MEMOD have a case structure, which means that MEMOD knows how many arguments a verb takes and what kinds of arguments they are. There is a grammar for building structures in MEMOD, and rules for building concepts, relations, propositions, and operators were discussed.

Events in MEMOD can be linked by conjunctions. The THEN conjunction is particularly important because it orders events of an episode in time and for the interpreter. Another important link is ISWHEN. It links words to their definitions, which are episode-like procedures for building structures in the ASN.

References

The LNR research group wrote a book called *Explorations in Cognition* (1975). It is a collection of articles by Norman, Rumelhart, and their graduate students on experiments with the MEMOD system and is the most complete and recent review of MEMOD.

F. BELIEF SYSTEMS

IMAGINE a conversation with a person who speaks only facts, the kind of conversation you might have with an official who refuses to give a personal opinion or make a prediction about the future or guess at an explanation for a past event. Or consider the testimony of police officers; they say things like "We were called to the scene at 12:07 A.M. and found the suspect holding two hostages. We succeeded in disarming the suspect without injury. The suspect is now undergoing psychological evaluation." What they do not say is that they believe the suspect is guilty, that they believe he is a doped-up crazy, that they were scared stiff while disarming him, that they sincerely hope he gets the maximum sentence, that holding an old lady hostage is a miserable act of terrorism, and so on. Police officers rightly stick to the facts. At least, they do while on duty. Afterwards, we assume they are as full of opinion, belief, innuendo, prejudice, and emotion as the rest of us.

In this example, the distinction between fact and belief has been amplified to emphasize that much human discourse is in beliefs, speculations, predictions, desires, and so on. The research discussed in this article is concerned with the structure of beliefs, how we reason with beliefs, how beliefs function as prejudices to influence interpretation, and how emotions affect reasoning. These questions, and the computational systems that have been implemented to explore them, fall in the domain of *belief systems*.

Abelson (1979) has outlined a number of peculiarities that set beliefs apart from facts and that distinguish belief systems from other systems in AI:

1. Belief systems are not *consensual*. Different beliefs may result in different interpretations of the same phenomena. For example, depending on one's beliefs, the "generation gap" results from insensitive and restrictive parents or from ungrateful and immoral children. One's beliefs can influence interpretation of relatively sure facts; for example, some smokers refuse to believe that smoking causes cancer, and some people insist that concentration camps never existed but are the creation of propagandists.

2. Beliefs deal with *conceptual* entities such as the generation gap, the supernatural, and extrasensory perception. Thus, an entity that exists in one belief system may be absent in another.

3. Sometimes belief systems represent alternative "worlds," typically, "the world as it should be." Ideologies often have implicit alternative worlds.

4. Beliefs have an *evaluative* or *affective* component. Events tend to be good or bad, to evoke pleasure or displeasure. Abelson distinguishes between two aspects of affect. One involves the world divided up into good and

bad things (or into as many categories as there are affects). From this categorization one can infer the goodness or badness of events or objects. For example, if X is bad, and Y helps X, then Y must be bad also. Much of Abelson's early research was devoted to this kind of reasoning. A second aspect of affect is how it influences the operation of a system; for example, Faught (1975) characterizes emotions as leading to motives, and Bower (1981) discusses the effects of emotion on memory.

5. Beliefs may be based on subjective experiences or episodes. Logical, rational deductions may be based on a subjective event. For example, an elaborate theory may be constructed around an event that was believed to occur but that actually did not. An interesting historical example is the mass hallucination of French physicists in the "N-Ray Affair" (Klotz, 1980). It was believed that N-rays could be detected by their effects on the brightness of an electric light-bulb, and for many years, French physicists published reports of the curious properties of N-rays. This research continued (though at a lesser pace) even after it was demonstrated that perceived fluctuations in brightness were entirely illusory. N-rays do not exist and the physics that had been developed to explain them was founded on a hallucination.

6. One does not know, a priori, what knowledge is relevant to a belief. The knowledge pertinent to diagnosis of glaucoma, for example, can be circumscribed relatively easily. It is less easy to decide what is irrelevant to conceptual entities such as *the sexual promiscuity of today's youth*.

7. Credibility and emotion interact in evaluation. One may believe something is true, passionately; or there may be no emotional investment in a belief. For example, it may be true that one brand of pain reliever contains more aspirin than another, but it is hard to achieve the enthusiasm necessary to value one more highly.

These characteristics of belief and belief systems make reasoning from belief more complicated than reasoning from facts or measurable uncertainties. This is for several reasons, all related to what the belief system knows. First, the nonconsensuality argument is that different belief systems house different bodies of knowledge; thus, it may be difficult for one system to explain or predict the behavior of another. For example, it is a difficult task for the BUGGY system (see Article IX.C7, in Vol. II) to derive the inference rules applied by its students in working arithmetic problems. The students make assumptions about arithmetic that are not consensual with the assumptions of the adult community; consequently, they make errors. BUGGY's task is to explain the errors by inferring the students' mistaken assumptions. Another example from the ICAI literature (see Chap. IX, in Vol. II) illustrates the power of assuming consensuality: Several ICAI systems maintain a *student model*—a representation of what the student knows—to facilitate teaching.

Just as nonconsensuality is a problem, so are *existence* and *openness*, and for much the same reason. The existence problem is that reasoning in one system may be predicated on premises that do not exist in another; for example, one can do little to mollify a person who believes that his (or her) bad fortune is preordained. The belief in preordination is so central to his belief system (though alien to one's own) that he accepts misfortune with resignation and will do nothing to improve his lot. The openness problem is concerned with the relevance of the knowledge used for reasoning; in one system a fact may be central to an argument, while in another it is tangential. For example, one person may attribute the decline of our society to the availability of drugs, while another may believe the cause is inflation and a third may insist that impiety is responsible. The first person constructs the causal argument that society is being destroyed by drugs. He holds this argument with a conviction that is lacking in the second person, who views drugs as a symptom of an inflated economy, not as a symptom of impiety or as a cause of society's ills.

Two other aspects of belief make reasoning difficult. One is the role of affect, or emotion, and the other is the role of confidence, or certitude. It is tempting to make a dichotomy between *rational* and *irrational* thought and to assign emotion to the latter category and ignore it. But there is strong evidence that emotion has powerful effects on human cognition. In a recent and extensive series of experiments, Bower (1981) and his colleagues have shown that emotion influences what we learn, what we remember, and how we make a variety of judgments. Our evaluations of ourselves and others and of events are subtly but strongly biased by what we are feeling. Bower's results suggest that emotion cannot be ignored as a factor in human cognition and that it is at least one factor that argues against a strong rational-irrational dichotomy.

The problem of confidence, or certitude, is that much of the information used in reasoning is not true or false, but somewhere in between, and that one's confidence in the information affects one's reasoning. One attempt to capture this aspect of reasoning is found in MYCIN (see Article VIII.B1, in Vol. II), which attaches *certainty (or confidence) factors* (CFs) to its conclusions. The initial CFs are supplied to the MYCIN system with its heuristic rules by expert diagnosticians. Then, as MYCIN reasons, it combines the CFs associated with the rules to produce a CF for its conclusion. The CF mechanism is quite crude, however, and very ad hoc. Clearly, MYCIN does not embody a theory of human reasoning under uncertainty. More successful are Tversky and Kahneman (1974), who have identified a number of factors that influence judgments under uncertainty.

Even though reasoning with beliefs involves certain sophistications over reasoning with facts, the two have been modeled in much the same way. Belief systems are formally similar to some of the knowledge-based systems in the *Handbook*. For example, the belief that *If A likes B, then A will help B* can be phrased as a production from which the conclusion *A will help B* follows logically from the premise *A likes B*. This deduction is logically and psychologically valid. Other conclusions may maintain a formal logical validity but be psychologically odd; for example, *If you are suffering, then you have found true happiness.* It is useful to distinguish the formal logical structure of a belief system from the psychological conclusions that arise from it. The remainder of this article is concerned with both of these factors—with formal representations that facilitate psychological, not necessarily logical, behavior.

Implicational Molecules

Abelson and Reich (1969) described a system based on *implicational molecules*, that is, sets of clauses related by psychological implication. For example:

                    [A does X, X causes Y, A wants Y] ,

or

                    [A likes B, A helps B] .

Just as a premise implies a conclusion, so does one part of an implicational molecule imply another. Thus, implicational molecules can predict or explain events:

If *A wants Y,* it is plausible to predict *A does X. A does X* because *X causes Y and A wants Y.*

Abelson and Reich used implicational molecules in a system that simulated the extreme right-wing viewpoint of a cold-war ideologue. The system used stereotyped concepts such as *Western-governments, situations-helpful-to-the-Communists,* and *prevent, promote,* and *control.* These were combined to form *generic sentences* such as *Liberals control Western-governments.* Generic sentences were then combined into implicational molecules that define the conclusions that are reasonable in the system:

                [Western-governments promote
                    situations-helpful-to-the-Communists,
                Standing-up-to-Communists prevents
                    situations-helpful-to-the-Communists,
                Liberals control Western-governments,
                Liberals fear standing-up-to-Communists] .

A higher order structure was the *master script,* which spelled out several general contingencies for the fate of the free world. Part of the script says that the Communists want to dominate the world and will do so unless the free world exercises its power, in which case the free world will surely prevail. Generic events were considered instances of very general master-script events.

The system could judge the credibility of events; bad events were attributed to the Communists, good to the free world, and never the other way around. It could also predict events and say what should be done if and when they happened. This was accomplished by associating an event with one on the master script and following it to a conclusion. For example, an event interpreted as Communist domination was predicted to result in world takeover unless the free world flexed its muscles.

The system answered specific questions about real people, not just abstract questions about generic sentences. It did so by instantiating generic sentences with more concrete concepts. For example, *Liberals control Western-governments* might be instantiated in the belief that *LBJ controls the United States.*

One characteristic of belief systems in general is that they perform well with stereotyped beliefs. They reflect what we suspect to be true—that little knowledge is required to hold an oversimplified, dogmatic opinion. (Why let facts interfere with what one knows is right?) Abelson's Cold War Ideologue was not very knowledgeable; it could easily conclude that the Berlin Wall was built by the Red Chinese, since it is just the sort of miserable thing that Communists do. Ideological oversimplification seems to provide a counter-example to the pervasive idea that knowledge is power. To achieve strong dogma, one must ignore the evidence, counterexamples, and qualifications that compromise a position.

The Structure of Belief Systems

Abelson (1973) later developed a hierarchical formalism for beliefs, based on *conceptual dependency analysis* (see Articles III.C6 and IV.F5, in Vol. I). Abelson starts his analysis with three kinds of *atoms: purposes, actions,* and *states.* Purposes encode the wants or desires of actors; for example, *Mary wants John to do his share of housework.* Actions are the things that the actors want to do, and states are the situations that they want to bring about. The next level of Abelson's hierarchy combines these atoms into *molecules;* these are similar to the implicational molecules described earlier.

Molecules represent actions undertaken by actors to produce outcome states. In their simplest form they are (*Purpose, Action, State*) triples, but larger chains and networks are also possible. Among the larger structures are *plans, themes,* and *scripts.* Plans represent action-state sequences, where each state *enables* a subsequent action until a final goal state is obtained. The structure of plans reflects that a set of sequential or parallel actions is usually required to achieve a goal. By assumption, plans are always related directly to the purposes of a main actor. If other actors are involved, they are simple agents or instruments with no autonomy; they cannot enhance or frustrate the plans of the main actor.

While plans represent the purposes of a single actor, interactions of the purposes and plans of autonomous actors are represented in *themes.* Abelson formed a taxonomy of themes based on the possible interactions of two actors (see Table F–1).

TABLE F–1

A Taxonomy of Themes (from Abelson, 1973)

	Influence of Actors		
Sentiments toward Other	Neither influences Other	One influences Other	Both influence Other
Some positive, no negative	Admiration	Devotion Appreciation	Cooperation Love
One actor negative	Alienation (also Freedom)	Betrayal Victory Dominance	Rebellion
Both actors negative	Mutual Antagonism	Oppression (also Law and Order)	Conflict

Mutual antagonism, for example, refers to agents who are negative to each other, but powerless to inflict harm. When one actor is able to harm the other, oppression results; when each can influence the other, conflict results.

Scripts are sequences of themes that follow each other in some psychologically plausible fashion. (The reader should be aware that this is an earlier and different interpretation of the roles of themes and scripts than is found in Abelson's research with Schank, 1977; see Schank and Abelson, 1977, and Article IV.F6, in Vol. I.) Simple scripts involving two actors are, for example, *blossoming relationships*, wherein a Love theme develops from the themes of Admiration, Cooperation, Devotion, or Appreciation, and *souring relationships*, which happen when Love is complicated by Rebellion and, subsequently, Mutual Conflict.

Differences between individual belief systems are manifest primarily at the theme and script levels. These constructs provide for alternative views of the same events; for example, a relationship might be viewed as alienation by one actor and as mutual antagonism by the other. One may feel he is not at fault for a deteriorating relationship; the other may feel that hostility is involved. The greatest idiosyncrasy of belief is found at the script level, where the repertoire of scripts maintained by an individual defines his ideology (recall the *master-script* that defined the beliefs of the cold-war ideologue).

We now turn from Abelson's designs for general belief systems to a specific kind of belief, namely, paranoid belief.

PARRY

PARRY was one of the earliest and most ambitious simulations of the role of beliefs and affects in cognition. It is a model of what its designers call the *paranoid mode*, a pattern of behavior motivated by paranoid beliefs and intentions. PARRY's original designer, Kenneth Colby, is a psychiatrist, and PARRY embodies his theory of paranoid behavior. We will discuss this theory shortly, but first we consider the characteristics of paranoia.

Paranoids are suspicious; they think that other people intend to harm them. They believe they are the target of conspiracies. They have a great concern with "evidence," and are likely to treat a random event as significant and intentional (the intentions are held by "them"—those malevolent others). Paranoids are also hypersensitive to criticism:

> References to the self are misconstrued as slurs, snubs, slights, or unfair judgements. He may feel he is being watched or stared at. He is excessively concerned about his visibility to eyes that threaten to see concealed inadequacies, expose and censure them. Cameras, telescopes, etc. that may be directed his way unnerve him. He may feel mysteriously influenced through electricity, radio waves, or (more contemporaneously) by emanations from computers. He is hypersensitive to criticism. In crowds he believes he is intentionally bumped. Driving on the highway he feels repeatedly followed too closely by the car behind. Badgered and bombarded without relief by this stream of wrongs, he becomes hyperirritable, querulous, and quarrelsome. (Colby, 1975, p. 4).

Two other characteristics of paranoia are fearfulness and hostility. One can see how both might arise from the conviction that the self is in a hostile and intentionally malevolent world. A last characteristic, which Colby says makes paranoia very difficult to treat, is rigidity and absolute conviction. Once a paranoid is convinced, for example, that his doctor is in collaboration with "them," it becomes extremely difficult to reestablish rapport because the patient will not compromise his beliefs.

The characteristics of paranoia are so clear-cut that it is possible to simulate the paranoid mode. PARRY was and is an ambitious project because it involves integrating beliefs, intentions, and affects with more "rational" cognition. The manner in which these components interact is dictated by Colby's theory of paranoia.

Paranoid behavior arises, according to Colby, from attempts to avoid humiliation. In the PARRY simulation, humiliation arises, and is intently avoided, during an interview with a doctor. (PARRY has a natural-language front-end, but it is not very sophisticated and we will not be concerned with it here.) Briefly, the paranoid (and PARRY) is hypersensitive to any comment that can be interpreted as reflecting his own inadequacy. Any such comment increases shame and humiliation. (Intense paranoia involves interpreting virtually *all* interactions in this way.) The paranoid seeks to avoid humiliation and shame, since it is intensely painful, so whenever he detects a situation in which the doctor might be making a humiliating comment, he takes three defensive actions: One is to change his opinion of the doctor (e.g., *Anyone who thinks I'm crazy must be really incompetent*); another is to decrease his level of shame, since he has concluded that the doctor, and not he himself, is at fault; and the third is to take some action, which may be hostile.

To achieve this behavior, PARRY has a number of beliefs, a number of common inferences, and several processes that we will describe briefly. Beliefs include *The doctor is crazy* or *The doctor is friendly*. PARRY also has four beliefs that reflect humiliation: *PARRY is stupid, PARRY is dishonest, PARRY is crazy*, and *PARRY is worthless*. PARRY must avoid concluding that any of these are true, since these conclusions cause pain. Unfortunately, PARRY is always trying to find evidence for them in its interactions with the doctor. This is the problem: To avoid humiliation, the paranoid must constantly search for it; he must catch the insult and deflect it before it harms him.

PARRY has a set of inferences that alert it to insults, and its hypersensitivity arises from these inferences. For example, if the doctor says, "You didn't answer my question," PARRY infers that the doctor thinks he is stupid; this statement can also be taken as evidence that the doctor thinks PARRY is not telling the truth—is dishonest. Whenever the doctor says anything, PARRY makes whatever inferences it can, and if the inferences support any of the four *humiliation* beliefs that we just mentioned, then PARRY increases its level of *shame*.

Thus, one of PARRY's processes is to search for evidence of humiliation in the doctor's communications. When this process finds evidence, another *affect* process increases PARRY's shame; if the level of shame crosses a threshold, PARRY launches into characteristic hostile paranoid behavior. This involves a third process dealing with intentions. PARRY has three emotions—fear, anger, and shame—each of which plays a role in PARRY's intentions. When anger is high, PARRY intends to attack the doctor; when fear is high, PARRY intends to alter the interview situation so that the outcome it fears—humiliation—is less likely. And when shame is high, PARRY does three things: It defends itself by throwing out the belief that led to humiliation and replacing it with another one, usually a revised and uncomplimentary belief about the doctor (e.g., *The doctor is crazy*); it reduces its shame, since the belief that caused shame has been exorcised; and it intends a strong action, usually based on its new belief about the doctor. It may intend to attack, lie, or withdraw.

We have discussed how PARRY integrates inferences with affects and intentions to produce paranoid behavior; we conclude with the following brief example of a dialogue with PARRY. Initially, the doctor asks a lot of innocuous questions, from which PARRY concludes that the doctor is friendly, wants to help, and can help. For example:

Doctor: **What do you do for a living?**

PARRY: **I work at Sears.**

But the doctor is sure to stumble onto a topic that PARRY finds sensitive, at which point PARRY will experience an increase in shame:

```
Doctor:   How much do you get paid an hour?
PARRY:    My salary is none of your business.
```

In this interaction, PARRY concluded that the doctor was implying that
PARRY had no money—was worthless. Although shame was not elevated to
the point that PARRY enters paranoid mode, it does provoke an angry attack.
PARRY can be mollified if the doctor goes back to asking innocuous questions,
or compliments PARRY, or apologizes.

At a later point in the interview, PARRY introduces its main concern—
that bookies and the Mafia are out to get him. At this point, the doctor
must tread very carefully. If the doctor expresses any skepticism about
PARRY's delusions, shame will increase markedly, and PARRY will become
uncooperative. As long as the doctor asks simple questions, PARRY will
answer them:

```
Doctor:   What about bookies?
PARRY:    A bookie didn't pay me off once.
Doctor:   And then what happened?
PARRY:    I had an argument with the bookie who did not pay off.
          Later on I remembered he had friends in the underworld
          and I thought he would use them to get even with me.
```

Incidentally, PARRY has an elaborate story about the bookies, rather like
Abelson's master-script. One of PARRY's goals for the interview is to tell the
whole story. The last interchange was, therefore, quite successful. However,
telling the whole story makes PARRY vulnerable and sensitive, so that when
the doctor says:

```
Doctor:   I find you interesting.
```

PARRY thinks it is an insult and responds angrily:

```
PARRY:    Are you trying to say something?
```

The doctor then asks several questions that are inflammatory and that elevate
PARRY's affects. The doctor finally says:

```
Doctor:   You appear to be very sick.
```

This is intolerable to PARRY. It increases his fear, anger, and shame markedly.
From this point on, the interview deteriorates. PARRY lies:

```
Doctor:   How do you feel right now?
PARRY:    I am perfectly fine.
```

And withdraws:

```
Doctor:   Do you need to have psychiatric treatment?
PARRY:    I don't want to talk about it.
```

PARRY substitutes uncomplimentary beliefs about the doctor for shameful beliefs about himself, concluding that all doctors are bad and that this one is abnormal. These beliefs allow PARRY to reduce shame and drop out of the paranoid mode into being merely angry, so that when the doctor concludes the interview and thanks PARRY for his cooperation, PARRY bluntly tells him not to come back.

Conclusion

The study of belief systems is challenging because, unlike "facts," beliefs are nonconsensual, have associated affects, and have associated confidences or credibilities. Even the basic problem of how confidences in beliefs are adjusted by evidence has no general solution, and the more difficult problems (e.g., the effects of emotion on cognition) are barely formulated, much less solved. Despite these difficulties, the researchers surveyed here are convinced of the importance of belief systems, since humans clearly do not reason entirely from facts with consistent inference rules, but instead, prejudices, biases, episodic memory, confidences, and emotional states are neatly integrated into "rational" reasoning.

References

Abelson (1973) provides a readable account of his research prior to his collaboration with Schank. Schank and Abelson (1977) is a very readable account of their collaborative work, although it is more concerned with natural-language understanding than with belief systems. For those who are interested in emotion, Mandler (1975) presents a complete cognitive theory, with historical information, and Bower (1981) is a survey of some surprisingly powerful effects of mood on memory and cognition.

Colby (1975) has written a short monograph that details the PARRY program; Faught, Colby, and Parkinson (1974) provide another good discussion, though it lacks the psychiatric background.

Chapter XII

Automatic Deduction

CHAPTER XII: AUTOMATIC DEDUCTION

A. OVERVIEW

A CENTRAL PROBLEM in AI research is how to make it possible for computers to draw conclusions automatically from bodies of facts. Any attempt to address this problem requires choosing an application, a representation for bodies of facts, and methods for deriving conclusions. This article provides an overview of the issues involved in drawing conclusions by means of deductive inference from bodies of commonsense knowledge represented by logical formulas. We first review briefly the history of automatic deduction—its origins, its fall into disfavor, and its recent revival. We show why deductive methods are necessary to solve problems that involve certain types of incomplete information and how supplying domain-specific control information offers a solution to the difficulties that previously led to disillusionment with automatic deduction. We discuss the relationship of automatic deduction to the new field of logic programming. Finally, we survey some of the issues that arise in extending automatic-deduction techniques to nonstandard logics.

Historical Background

Automatic deduction, or mechanical theorem-proving, has been a major concern of AI since its earliest days. At the first formal conference on AI, held at Dartmouth College in the summer of 1956, Newell and Simon (1956) discussed the Logic Theorist, a deduction system for propositional logic. Minsky was concurrently developing the ideas that were later embodied in Gelernter's theorem prover for elementary geometry (see McCorduck, 1979, p. 106; Gelernter, 1963). Shortly after this, Wang (1960) produced the first implementation of a reasonably efficient, complete algorithm for proving theorems in propositional logic.

Following these early efforts, the next important step in the development of automatic-deduction techniques was Robinson's (1965b) description of a relatively simple, logically complete method for proving theorems in first-order predicate calculus (see Article III.C1, in Vol. I). Robinson's procedure and those derived from it are usually referred to as *resolution* procedures (Article XII.B), because the basic rule of inference they use is the resolution principle:

From $(A \vee B)$ *and* $(\neg A \vee C)$, *infer* $(B \vee C)$.

Robinson's work had a major influence on two somewhat distinct lines of research. One of these was mathematical theorem-proving, which aims at providing practical tools for discovering new results in mathematics. (That line of research is not the main focus of this chapter, although Article XII.C is oriented in that direction.) But Robinson's work also had a major impact on research into commonsense reasoning and problem solving. His ideas in this area brought about a rather dramatic shift in attitudes toward automatic deduction. The early attempts at automatic theorem-proving were generally thought of as exercises in expert problem solving: the Logic Theorist was regarded as an expert in propositional logic and Gelernter's program was considered an expert in geometry. However, the resolution method seemed powerful enough to make it possible to build a completely general problem-solver by describing problems in first-order logic and deducing solutions by a general proof procedure.

The idea of using formal logic as a representation scheme and deductive inference as a reasoning method was apparently first suggested as an approach to commonsense reasoning and problem solving by McCarthy in 1959, in his "Advice Taker" proposal (see McCarthy, 1968). Black (1968) made the first serious attempt to implement McCarthy's idea in 1964. Robinson's work provided encouragement for this approach, and a few years later Green (1969) carried out extensive experiments with a question-answering and problem-solving system based on resolution (see Article III.C1, in Vol. I, on the QA3 program).

The results of Green's experiments and several similar projects were disappointing, however. The difficulty was that, in the general case, the search space generated by the resolution method grows exponentially with the number of formulas used to describe a problem, so that problems of even moderate complexity cannot be solved in a reasonable time. Several domain-independent heuristics (e.g., *set of support;* see Article XII.B) were proposed to deal with this issue, but they proved too weak to produce satisfactory results.

It appears that these failures resulted principally from two constraints the researchers had imposed upon themselves: They attempted to use only uniform, domain-independent proof procedures, and they tried to force all reasoning and problem-solving behavior into the framework of logical deduction. Like a number of earlier ideas such as self-organizing systems and heuristic search, automatic theorem-proving turned out not to be the magic formula that would solve all AI problems at once. In the reaction that followed, however, not only was there a turning away from attempts to use deduction to create general problem-solvers, but there was also widespread condemnation of *any* use of logic or deduction in commonsense reasoning or problem solving. Arguments made by Minsky (1980, Appendix) and Hewitt (1975; Hewitt et al., 1973) seem to have been particularly influential in this regard.

Despite the disappointments of the late 1960s and early 1970s, there has recently been a revival of interest in deduction-based approaches to commonsense reasoning. This is apparent in the work of McDermott (1978), Doyle (1979, 1980), and Moore (1980a, 1980b); in the current work on nonmonotonic reasoning (Bobrow, 1980); and in recent textbooks by Nilsson (1980) and Kowalski (1979). To a large extent, this renewed interest seems to stem from the recognition of an important class of problems that resist solution by any other method.

Why the Deduction Problem Will Not Go Away

If a description of a problem situation is *complete* in terms of the objects, properties, and relations relevant to the problem, we can answer any question by *evaluation*—deduction is unnecessary. To illustrate, suppose we have a knowledge base of personnel information for a company and we want to know whether there is any programmer who earns more than a vice-president earns. We could express this question in first-order logic as:

```
SOME (X,Y) ((TITLE(X) = PROGRAMMER) AND
            (TITLE(Y) = VICE-PRESIDENT) AND
            (SALARY(X) > SALARY(Y))) .
```

If we have recorded in our knowledge base the job title and salary of every employee, we can simply find the salary of each programmer and compare it with the salary of every vice-president. No deduction is involved in this process. On the other hand, we may not have specific salary information for each employee. Instead, we may have general information about classes of employees, such as:

All vice-presidents are managers.
```
ALL (X) ((TITLE(X) = VICE-PRESIDENT) →
         (CATEGORY(X) = MANAGER))
```

All programmers are professionals.
```
ALL (X) ((TITLE(X) = PROGRAMMER) →
         (CATEGORY(X) = PROFESSIONAL))
```

All professionals earn less than all managers.
```
ALL (X,Y) (((CATEGORY(X) = PROFESSIONAL) AND
            (CATEGORY(Y) = MANAGER)) →
            (SALARY(X) < SALARY(Y))) .
```

From this information we can *deduce* that no programmer earns more than any vice-president, although we have no information about the exact salary of any employee.

A representation formalism based on logic gives us the ability to express many kinds of generalizations, even when we do not have a complete description of the problem situation. Using deduction to manipulate expressions in the representation formalism allows us to make logically complex queries of a knowledge base containing such generalizations, even when we cannot evaluate a query directly. On the other hand, AI inference systems that are not based on automatic-deduction techniques either do not permit logically complex queries to be made or they answer such queries by methods that depend on the presence of complete information. For an AI system to handle the kinds of incomplete information people can understand, it must at least be able to do the following:

1. Say that something has a certain property without saying which thing has that property:

$$\exists(X)\,P(X);$$

2. Say that everything in a certain class has a certain property without saying what everything in that class is:

$$\forall(X)\,(P(X) \to Q(X));$$

3. Say that at least one of two statements is true without saying which statement is true:

$$P \vee Q;$$

4. Say explicitly that a statement is false, as distinguished from simply not saying that it is true:

$$\neg(P).$$

Any representation formalism that has these capabilities will be, at the very least, an extension of classical first-order logic (see Article III.C1, in Vol. I), and any inference system that can deal adequately with these kinds of generalizations will have to have at least the capabilities of an automatic-deduction system. Thus, although AI rejected logic as a representation method and deduction as a reasoning method, AI systems that reason with incomplete information are actually equivalent to automatic-deduction systems.

The Need for Specific Control Information

As we remarked above, the fundamental difficulty with attempting to base a general, domain-independent problem-solver on automatic-deduction techniques is that there are too many possible inferences that can be drawn at any one time. Finding the inferences that are relevant to a particular problem can be an impossible task, unless domain-specific guidance is supplied to control the deductive process.

One kind of guidance that is often critical to efficient system performance is information about whether to use facts in a *forward-chaining* or *backward-chaining* manner. The deductive process can be thought of as a *bidirectional* search process (see Article II.C3d, in Vol. I), partly working forward from known facts to new ones, partly working backward from goals to subgoals, and meeting somewhere in between. Thus, if we have a fact of the form $(P \to Q)$, we can use it either to generate Q as a fact, given P as a fact, or to generate P as a goal, given Q as a goal. Early theorem-proving systems used every fact both ways, leading to highly redundant searches. More sophisticated methods that eliminate these redundancies were gradually devised. Eliminating redundancies, however, creates choices as to which way facts are to be used. In the systems that attempted to apply only domain-independent control heuristics, a uniform strategy had to be imposed. Often the strategy was to use all facts in a backward-chaining manner only, on the grounds that this would at least guarantee that all the inferences drawn would be relevant to the problem at hand.

The difficulty with this approach is that the question of whether it is more efficient to use a fact for forward than for backward chaining depends on the specific content of that fact. For instance, according to the Talmud, the primary criterion for determining whether someone is Jewish is:

$$\forall (X) \, (Jewish(mother(X)) \rightarrow Jewish(X)).$$

That is, a person is Jewish if his or her mother is Jewish. Suppose we were to try to use this rule for backward chaining, as most uniform proof procedures would. It would apply to any goal of the form JEWISH(X), producing the subgoal JEWISH(MOTHER(X)). This expression, however, is also of the form JEWISH(X), so the process would be repeated, resulting in an infinite descending chain of subgoals:

```
GOAL: JEWISH(MORRIS)
GOAL: JEWISH(MOTHER(MORRIS))
GOAL: JEWISH(MOTHER(MOTHER(MORRIS)))
GOAL: JEWISH(MOTHER(MOTHER(MOTHER(MORRIS))))
    ⋮
```

If, on the other hand, we use the rule for forward chaining, the number of applications is limited by the complexity of the fact that originally triggers the inference:

```
FACT: JEWISH(MOTHER(MOTHER(MORRIS)))
FACT: JEWISH(MOTHER(MORRIS))
FACT: JEWISH(MORRIS) .
```

It turns out, then, that the efficient use of a particular fact often depends on exactly what that fact is and also on the context of other facts in which it is embedded. Many examples illustrating this point are given by Kowalski (1979) and Moore (1980a), involving not only the distinction between forward and backward chaining but other control decisions as well.

Since specific control information needs to be associated with particular facts, the question arises as to how to provide it. The simplest way is to embed it in the facts themselves. For instance, the distinction between forward and backward chaining can be encoded by having two versions of implication, for example, $(P \rightarrow Q)$ to indicate forward chaining and $(Q \leftarrow P)$ to indicate backward chaining. This approach originated in the distinction made in the programming language PLANNER (see Article VI.A, in Vol. II) between antecedent and consequent theorems. A more sophisticated approach is to make certain decisions (such as whether to use a fact in the forward or backward direction) themselves questions for the deduction system to reason about, by using "meta-level" knowledge. The first detailed proposal along these lines appears to have been made by Hayes (1973), while experimental systems have been built by McDermott (1978) and de Kleer et al. (1979), among others. Weyhrauch (1980) has perhaps done the most to explore the kind of system architecture in which this sort of reasoning would be possible.

Theory Formation and Logic Programming

Another factor that can greatly affect the efficiency of deductive reasoning is the way in which a body of knowledge is formalized. That is, logically equivalent formalizations can have radically different behavior when used with standard deduction techniques. For example, we could define the relation ABOVE as the transitive closure of ON in at least three ways:

$\forall$ (X,Y) (ABOVE(X,Y) $\leftrightarrow$
$\qquad$ (ON(X,Y) OR $\exists$ (Z) (ABOVE(X,Z) AND ON(Z,Y)))) ,

$\forall$ (X,Y) (ABOVE(X,Y) $\leftrightarrow$
$\qquad$ (ON(X,Y) OR $\exists$ (Z) (ON(X,Z) AND ABOVE(Z,Y)))) ,

$\forall$ (X,Y) (ABOVE(X,Y) $\leftrightarrow$
$\qquad$ (ON(X,Y) OR $\exists$ (Z) (ABOVE(X,Z) AND ABOVE(Z,Y)))) .

(These formalizations are not quite equivalent, as they allow for different possible interpretations of ABOVE if infinitely many objects are involved. They are equivalent, however, if only finitely many objects are being considered.)

Each of these formalizations will produce different behavior in a standard deduction system, no matter how we make local control decisions of the kind discussed in the previous section. Kowalski (1974) noted that choosing among such alternatives involves decisions similar to those made when writing programs in a conventional programming language. In fact, he observed that there are ways to formalize many functions and relations so that applying standard deduction methods will have the effect of executing them as computer programs. These observations have led to the development of the field of *logic programming* (Kowalski, 1979) and the creation of new computer languages such as PROLOG (Warren, Pereira, and Pereira, 1977). Such developments are discussed in Article XII.F.

Automatic Deduction in Nonstandard Logics

So far, we have discussed automatic deduction for classical first-order logic only. Many commonsense concepts, however, are most naturally treated in either higher order or nonclassical logics. This presents a problem, because classical first-order logic is the most general logic for which the techniques of automatic deduction are at all well developed. It turns out, though, that there are a number of techniques for reformulating representations in nonstandard logics in terms of logically equivalent representations in classical first-order logic.

Higher order logic differs from first-order logic in that it allows quantification over properties and relations as well as individuals. That is, if we have a first-order logic that allows us to make statements about all physical objects, the corresponding second-order logic would allow us to make statements about all properties of and relations among physical objects; a third-order logic would allow us to make statements about properties of and relations among these properties and relations; and so forth.

In some cases, the transition from first-order to higher order logic presents fewer difficulties than might at first appear. In fact, the standard deductive procedures for first-order logic also work for higher order logic, except that general predicate abstraction is not performed; that is, these procedures will not construct predicates out of arbitrary complex formulas. If *John is a man* is represented as MAN(JOHN), the predicate MAN can be retrieved when we ask the second-order question, *What properties does John have?* All the deduction system has to do is match X(JOHN) against MAN(JOHN) and return MAN as the value of the variable X. But from the assertion that John is either a butcher or a baker, represented as

BUTCHER(JOHN) OR BAKER(JOHN) ,

the system could not infer, without using predicate abstraction, that John has the disjunctive property of being a butcher-or-baker. The system would have to recognize that this complex expression could be reformulated as a one-place predicate applied to JOHN,

(LAMBDA (Y) (BUTCHER(Y) OR BAKER(Y)))(JOHN) ,

which is of the right form to match X(JOHN).

If this sort of predicate abstraction is not required, standard first-order deduction techniques are sufficient. There has been some work extending the standard techniques to handle the more general case (e.g., Huet, 1975), but this makes the deduction problem much harder because of the combinatorics of all the different ways predicate abstraction may be performed.

Another problem commonly encountered is how to do automatic deduction in logics that allow *intensional* operators. These are operators, such as BELIEVE and KNOW, that produce sentences whose truth values depend fully on the meanings, not just the truth values, of their arguments. Classical logic is purely *extensional*, because the truth value of a complex formula depends only on the extensions (denotations, referents) of its subexpressions. The extension of a formula is considered to be its truth value, so the operator OR is extensional because the truth of $(P \ or \ Q)$ depends only on the truth of P and the truth of Q; no other properties of P and Q matter. The operator BELIEVE, on the other hand, is intensional because the truth of A *believes that* P depends generally on the meaning of P, not just on its truth value.

Many of the rules of classical logic, such as substitution of equals for equals, do not apply within the scope of an intensional operator. To use a classic example, since *the morning star* and *the evening star* refer to the same object, it must be the case that *The morning star is Venus* is true if and only if *The evening star is Venus* is true. However, it might be that *John believes the morning star is Venus* is true, but that *John believes the evening star is Venus* is false because, although the two embedded sentences have the same truth value, they differ in meaning.

Fortunately, many of the difficulties presented by intensional operators can be overcome by reformulating the statements in which they occur. There are a number of methods for doing this, but one that is particularly elegant is to reformulate intensional operators in terms of their *possible-world semantics* (Kripke, 1971; Hintikka, 1971). The idea is that, rather than talking about what statements a person believes, we talk instead about what states of affairs, or possible worlds, are compatible with what he believes. Essentially, *A believes that P* is paraphrased as *P is true in every world that is compatible with what A believes*. This can be expressed in ordinary first-order logic by making all predicates and functions depend explicitly on the particular possible world they are evaluated in. The failure of equality substitution in the preceding example is then accounted for by noting that what John believes depends on what is true in *all* possible worlds that are compatible with what he believes, but an assertion that the morning star and the evening star are the same is a statement only about the *actual* world. Application of this idea to reasoning about intensional operators in AI systems has been explored in depth by Moore (1980b).

Finally, a type of nonstandard logic that has received much recent attention is *nonmonotonic logic*. Minsky (1980, Appendix) has noted that the treatment of commonsense reasoning as purely deductive ignores one of its crucial aspects—the ability to retract a conclusion in the face of further evidence. A frequently cited example is that, if we know something is a bird, we normally assume it can fly. If we find out that it is an ostrich, however, we will withdraw that conclusion. This sort of reasoning is called nonmonotonic because the set of inferable conclusions does not increase monotonically with the set of premises as in conventional deductive logics. The addition of the premise that something is an ostrich results in removing the conclusion that it can fly. While many procedures have been implemented that support this type of reasoning, their theoretical foundations are questionable. Most of the recent work on nonmonotonic logic (Bobrow, 1980; see Article XII.E) has thus been directed at developing a coherent logical basis for this kind of reasoning.

References

McCarthy (1968), Black (1968), and Green (1969) discuss formal logic as a representation scheme and deductive inference as a reasoning method for commonsense reasoning and problem solving. This theme is amplified in two readable texts by Nilsson (1971, 1980). For references on some of the other topics discussed in the overview, see the reference sections of the subsequent articles.

B.   THE RESOLUTION RULE OF INFERENCE

ONE of the best known methods of automatic theorem-proving is the *reso-lution* procedure introduced by J. A. Robinson (1965b). In this article, we describe the method, present some examples, and discuss extensions to it.

Derivation of the Resolution Rule

The resolution method shows whether a theorem logically follows from its axioms. If a theorem does follow from its axioms, then the axioms and the *negation* of the theorem cannot all be true—the axioms and the negated theorem must lead to a contradiction. The resolution method is a form of proof by contradiction that involves producing new clauses, called *resolvents*, from the union of the axioms and the negated theorem. These resolvents are then added to the set of clauses from which they were derived, and new resolvents are derived. This process continues, recursively, until it produces a contradiction. Resolution is guaranteed to produce a contradiction if the theorem follows from the axioms. The simple *resolution rule* that produces resolvents is derived in the following paragraphs.

By the expression $(P \rightarrow Q)$ we mean *If P is true, then Q is true;* for example, *John is a boy $\rightarrow$ John is male.* A central rule of inference in logic is *modus ponens:*

$$(((P \rightarrow Q) \text{ and } P) \vdash Q),$$

which means that if $(P \rightarrow Q)$ is true and if P is true, then we can conclude that Q is true. An extension of this is the *chain rule:*

$$((P \rightarrow Q) \text{ and } (Q \rightarrow R) \vdash (P \rightarrow R)).$$

When the implications in the chain rule are rewritten in their logically equivalent form $(\neg P \vee Q)$, the chain rule becomes

$$(\neg P \vee Q) \text{ and } (\neg Q \vee R) \vdash (\neg P \vee R),$$

which can be written as:

$$\frac{(\neg P \vee Q)}{(\neg Q \vee R)}{(\neg P \vee R)}.$$

86

There is an apparent cancellation of the Q and $\neg Q$. The disjunctions $(\neg P \lor Q)$, $(\neg Q \lor R)$, and $(\neg P \lor R)$ are called *clauses*, and $(\neg P \lor R)$ is called the *resolvent* of $(\neg P \lor Q)$ and $(\neg Q \lor R)$.

Implications in this simple form, called *clause form*, can be resolved against each other; two clauses can be resolved to a single one. The heart of the resolution proof method is to negate the theorem to be proved and then to simplify and resolve clauses until a contradiction is found.

An Example

As an example of resolution, consider proving that $(D \lor E)$ follows from $(A \rightarrow C \lor D) \land (A \lor D \lor E) \land (A \rightarrow \neg C)$. The first step is to negate the theorem: $(\neg(D \lor E))$. This is logically equivalent to $(\neg D \land \neg E)$. The next step is to convert the axioms and theorem to *clauses*. The procedures for this are explained in the last section of this article and in several texts (e.g., Nilsson, 1980); all we need to know here is that the implication $(A \rightarrow B)$ can be rewritten as the equivalent clause $(\neg A \lor B)$.

The axioms are:

$$(A \rightarrow C \lor D) \land$$
$$(A \lor D \lor E) \land$$
$$(A \rightarrow \neg C).$$

They are rewritten as the clauses, and the theorem is added to the list:

$$(\neg A \lor C \lor D) \land$$
$$(A \lor D \lor E) \land$$
$$(\neg A \lor \neg C)$$
$$(\neg D \land \neg E).$$

The $\land$ conjunctions are dropped, leaving five clauses:

1. $(\neg A \lor C \lor D)$

2. $(A \lor D \lor E)$

3. $(\neg A \lor \neg C)$

4. $(\neg D)$

5. $(\neg E)$.

If the theorem follows from its axioms, the axioms and the negation of the theorem cannot all be true. Consequently, a contradiction must be implicit in the five clauses just derived; they cannot all be true simultaneously. The purpose of resolution is to find the contradiction. We will resolve clauses against each other until a contradiction "drops out":

1. $(\neg A \vee C \vee D)$
2. $(A \vee D \vee E)$

Resolution 1: $(C \vee D \vee E)$ *$\neg A$ and A*
                                           cancel each other.

2. $(A \vee D \vee E)$
3. $(\neg A \vee \neg C)$

Resolution 2: $(D \vee E \vee \neg C)$ *$\neg A$ and A*
                                           cancel each other.

Resolution 1. $(C \vee D \vee E)$
Resolution 2. $(D \vee E \vee \neg C)$

Resolution 3: $(D \vee E)$ *$\neg C$ and C*
                                           cancel each other.

Resolution 3. $(D \vee E)$
4. $(\neg D)$

Resolution 4: (E) *$\neg D$ and D*
                                           cancel each other.

Resolution 4. (E)
5. $(\neg E)$

CONTRADICTION

This illustrates the process by which we determine that clauses and their resolvents cannot all be true simultaneously.

The example just presented is from *propositional logic*. Now let us consider first-order *predicate calculus*, where *variables, predicates, quantifiers,* and *functions* are permitted (see Article III.C1, in Vol. I, for a discussion of logics). The expression $P(x)$ means *P is true for x*. For example, $P(x)$ might mean *x is a positive number*, so that $P(2)$ is true, whereas $P(-3)$ is false. Or $P(x)$ might mean that *x is a boy*, in which case we would expect $P(John)$ to be true and $P(Peggy)$ to be false.

We will use the notation $\forall x\, P(x)$ and $\exists x\, P(x)$ to mean *For all x $P(x)$* and *For some x $P(x)$*, respectively. The first form is called a *universal quantification*, since it conveys the meaning that the clause is true for all objects; the second is called an *existential quantification*, since it says that the clause is true for at least one object. For example,

$$\forall x\, (N(x) \;\rightarrow\; x^2 \geq 0), \text{ and}$$
$$\exists x\, (N(x) \;\wedge\; x < 0)$$

are true formulas. The first says that if x is a number, then the square of all x is either positive or zero, whereas the second says that there is at least one

object that is a number and is negative. Notice that $\neg \forall x\, P(x)$ is equivalent
to $\exists x\, \neg P(x)$, and $\neg \exists x\, P(x)$ is equivalent to $\forall x\, \neg P(x)$.

It is also possible to have function symbols such as f and g. For example,
$f(x)$ can mean *father of x*. Thus, if $M(x)$ means x *is a male*, then $M(f(x))$ is
always true.

Two complications arise when proving theorems with variables, quantifiers, predicates, and functions. One is getting them into clause form; the
other is the process of *unification*. Converting predicate logic to clause form
is formally straightforward (see the last section of this article). However, it
is important to understand the conceptual operations as well as the formal
ones, especially those associated with eliminating quantifiers. To eliminate
existential quantifiers, we simply choose a constant; for example, $\exists x\, P(x)$ is
replaced by $P(a)$. We instantiate the claim that an x exists by choosing a
particular a to take its place. However, if an existential quantifier is within
the scope of a universal quantifier, there is the possibility that the x that exists
somehow depends on the identity of the universally quantified variable. Thus,
we cannot replace it with an arbitrary constant. To account for this, whenever
an existential quantifier occurs within the scope of a universal quantifier, its
variable is replaced with a function of the universally quantified variable.
For example, $\forall x\, \exists y\, P(x, y)$ is rewritten as $\forall x\, P(x, f(x))$), denoting that the
second argument of the predicate P is a function of the first. In this example,
f is called a *skolem function*, and $f(x)$ is called a *skolem expression*.

We have discussed the rationales for eliminating existential quantifiers.
Universal quantifiers are simply dropped from clause form, because after existentially quantified variables have been replaced by constants or skolem functions, we may assume that the remaining variables are universally quantified.
In the previous example, y was replaced by a skolem function and x is assumed
to be universally quantified; thus, the quantifier $\forall$ is deleted, resulting in the
clause $P(x, f(x))$.

The other complication in proving theorems in predicate calculus arises
during resolution itself. Recall that during resolution we would have constants
"canceling" each other out; for example, $\neg A \lor B$ and $A \lor C$ would resolve
to $B \lor C$ after canceling A and $\neg A$. But how are resolvents to be produced
when there are variables and skolem functions? For example, does $P(a)$ cancel
$\neg P(x)$ in the following resolution?

$$\neg P(x) \lor Q(x) \text{ and}$$
$$P(a) \lor R(z)$$
$$\overline{\qquad\qquad\qquad\qquad}$$
$$Q(a) \lor R(z)$$

In this case, the answer is yes: $P(a)$ cancels $\neg P(x)$, because the expression
$\neg P(x)$ is claiming that there is no x for which $P(x)$ is true (recall that x is
universally quantified), and $P(a)$ is claiming that there *is* an object a for which
$P(a)$ is true. This is an example of *unification*, the process of deciding whether

the arguments of predicates are comparable for the purpose of resolution, and, if they are comparable, what common *substitution instance* should be used. In this case, the substitution instance was $a;$ it replaces all instances of x, including that in the predicate Q. The process of unification is analogous to that of finding a common denominator for fractions: In order to make comparisons between numbers expressed as $x/3$ and numbers expressed as $x/17$, each is re-expressed as $x/51$. Similarly, there is a *unification algorithm* that finds a common substitution instance for the arguments of predicates.

With these preliminaries over, we can now proceed to examples of resolution theorem proving in the predicate calculus.

The first step is, again, to negate the theorem and then put the axioms and the theorem in clause form:

$$(\neg P(a) \wedge \forall x \, (P(x) \vee Q(f(x)))) \qquad \text{(Axioms)}$$
$$\exists z \, Q(z) \qquad \text{(Theorem)}$$
$$\forall z \, \neg Q(z) \qquad \text{(Negated Theorem)}$$

In this case, a is a constant symbol, and there are no existential quantifiers and so no need for skolemization. Universal quantifiers are simply dropped. The $\wedge$ connectives are also dropped to yield three clauses:

1. $\neg P(a)$

2. $P(x) \vee Q(f(x))$

3. $\neg Q(z)$.

These are resolved against each other as follows:

1. Clause 1 and clause 2 are resolved to produce $Q(f(a))$; the substitution is a for x, or a/x.

2. $Q(f(a))$ is resolved against clause 3 to yield a contradiction; the substitution is $f(a)$ for z, or $f(a)/z$.

Since a contradiction is produced, we can conclude that the theorem followed from its axioms.

Another example is proving that there is always a number greater than another number from the axiom that a number is less than its successor. (In this case, *infix* arithmetic functions are used in the clauses; they could equally well be written in *prefix* notation; e.g., $\forall t < (t, \text{PLUS}(t, 1))$.)

$$\forall t \, (t < t + 1) \qquad \text{(Axiom)}$$
$$\forall x \, \exists y \, (x < y) \qquad \text{(Theorem)}$$

First we negate the theorem:

$$\exists x \, \forall y \, \neg(x < y).$$

Then, since x is an existentially quantified variable that is not within the scope of a universal quantifier, we replace it with a constant. This eliminates the existential quantifier; universal quantifiers are simply dropped as before. The resulting clauses are:

1. $t < t + 1$

2. $\neg(a < y)$.

But this immediately results in a contradiction when a is substituted for t and $a + 1$ is substituted for y.

A final example illustrates skolemization:

$$\forall x \,\exists y \, P(x, y) \qquad \text{(Axiom)}$$
$$\exists z \, P(a, z) \qquad \text{(Theorem)}$$

where a is a constant. First, we negate the theorem, yielding $\forall z \, \neg P(a, z)$. Next, we eliminate quantifiers. Since $\exists y$ is within the scope of the universal quantifier $\forall x$, the variable y is replaced, not with a constant, but, instead, with a skolem function. Universal quantifiers are dropped as usual:

1. $P(x, g(x))$

2. $\neg P(a, z)$.

These clauses obviously resolve to a contradiction under the substitution a/x, $g(a)/z$.

It can be shown that resolution is *complete* for (i.e., can prove all theorems in) first-order predicate logic (Robinson, 1965b) and is *sound* (i.e., will not indicate that nontheorems are true).

Strategies

Although resolution is complete, it can be extremely time-consuming. As brought out in the overview (Article XII.A), resolution-based approaches to problem solving fell into disfavor for just this reason.

Several strategies have been proposed to minimize the branching factor of resolution proof trees. Several are discussed in detail in Nilsson (1980) and in Chang and Lee (1973), and, thus, only two are briefly discussed here.

Set-of-support strategy. When at least one parent of each resolvent is chosen from the negation of the theorem or from the set of clauses that are derived from it, a set-of-support strategy is being used. This strategy clearly restricts the number of clauses that can be resolved at any given time. It is usually more efficient than breadth-first search.

Linear-input-form strategy. This strategy involves choosing resolvents so that one resolvent is always from the base set (the set of original clauses). It is more efficient than the previous strategy, but it is not *complete*, which is to say that there are cases in which it will not find a contradiction when one exists. Nonetheless, the strategy is often used because of its simplicity and efficiency.

In addition to strategies designed to reduce the combinatorial explosion involved in resolution, other simplifications can be made. One is to eliminate *tautologies* from the set of clauses. A tautology is a trivially true clause containing the subexpression $A \lor \neg A$.

Converting a Formula to Clausal Form

A formula, F, to be proved by resolution must first be negated and converted to clausal form. It is assumed that F is a first-order formula that is fully quantified. Conversion to clausal form is done by a series of steps:

1. Negate F: Replace F by $\neg F$.

2. Remove $\rightarrow$ and $\leftrightarrow$ by replacing $(A \rightarrow B)$ by $(\neg A \lor B)$ and $(A \leftrightarrow B)$ by $((\neg A \lor B) \land (\neg B \lor A))$.

3. Move $\neg$ inward, using the rules:

$$\neg(\neg A) = A,$$
$$\neg(A \land B) = \neg A \lor \neg B,$$
$$\neg(A \lor B) = \neg A \land \neg B,$$
$$\neg \forall x \, A(x) = \exists x \, \neg A(x),$$
$$\neg \exists x \, A(x) = \forall x \, \neg A(x).$$

4. Move $\forall$ and $\exists$ inward (optional).

5. Rename variables so that no two quantifiers quantify the same variables.

6. Exchange $\exists$ for skolem functions and then drop $\forall$'s (see below).

7. Convert to CNF (conjective normal form) by repeatedly applying De Morgan's Laws:

$$\neg(A \land B) = \neg A \lor \neg B$$
$$\neg(A \lor B) = \neg A \land \neg B.$$

In step 6, if $\exists y \, P(y)$ is within the scope of universal quantifiers $\forall x_1 \forall x_2 \ldots \forall x_n$, and not within the scope of any existential quantifier, then replace $\exists y \, P(y)$ by $P(f(x_1, \ldots, x_n))$, where f is a new function symbol (a skolem-function symbol). All universal quantifiers are then dropped from the formula. Thus,

$$\forall x \, \exists y \, \forall z \, \exists w \, P(x, y, z, w)$$

is replaced successively by

$$\forall x \, \forall z \, \exists w \, P(x, f_1(x), z, w)$$
$$\forall x \, \forall z \, P(x, f_1(x), z, f_2(x, z))$$
$$P(x, f_1(x), z, f_2(x, z)).$$

If $n = 0$, then y is replaced by a skolem constant y_0 (i.e., a function of 0 arguments).

It is usually faster to replace $\neg(P \rightarrow Q)$ by $(P \land \neg Q)$ *before* converting $(P \rightarrow Q)$ to $(\neg P \lor Q)$, when P is a large formula.

References

The resolution rule of inference was first described by Robinson (1965b). Resolution has been extended to handle the equality relation; this is discussed in Robinson and Wos (1969). This extension permits one to prove theorems such as $P(a) \land a = b \rightarrow P(b)$.

Strategies for speeding up resolution theorem proving have been discussed in several places. Wos, Robinson, and Carson (1965) discussed *set of support;* *hyper-resolution* was considered by Robinson (1965a); *locking* was the subject of Boyer's thesis (1971); and *SL-resolution* was discussed by Kowalski and Kuchner (1971). *Model elimination* was introduced by Loveland (1978). General texts on theorem proving are Loveland (1978) and Chang and Lee (1973).

Nilsson's two textbooks (1971, 1980) are clearly written introductions to, among other things, theorem proving as a problem-solving tool for AI systems.

C. NONRESOLUTION THEOREM PROVING

IN *nonresolution* or *natural-deduction* theorem-proving systems, a proof is derived in a goal-directed manner that is natural for the humans using the theorem prover. Natural-deduction systems represent proofs in a way that maintains a distinction between goals and antecedents, and they use inference rules that mimic the reasoning of human theorem-provers.

In resolution theorem-provers, no distinction is made between goals and antecedents. But in natural-deduction systems, the distinction is carefully maintained for the clarity that it brings to the proof process. For example, a natural-deduction system might display the following "worksheet" during a proof:

$$H_1. \quad P$$
$$H_2. \quad (P \to Q)$$
$$H_3. \quad (R \land Q \to S)$$
$$\overline{}$$
$$C_1. \quad Q$$
$$C_2. \quad (R \to S).$$

It indicates that H_1, H_2, and H_3 are three hypotheses and C_1 and C_2 are goals. A resolution system would represent the same situation uniformly with a set of clauses:

1. P
2. $\neg P \lor Q$
3. $\neg R \lor (\neg Q \lor S)$
4. $\neg Q \lor R$
5. $\neg Q \lor \neg S$.

Although these representations are logically equivalent, we have lost all information in the second one about *goals*—about what we want to prove.

The representation of proofs in natural-deduction systems is especially advantageous for man-machine interactive theorem-proving, in which a human is required to intervene occasionally to help with the proof. It also facilitates the implementation of semantic or domain-specific heuristics that help to guide the search.

However, the *clausal* representation has one powerful advantage: A proof can be derived with a single inference rule—the *resolution* rule. In contrast, natural-deduction systems have relatively complex inference rules that simulate the kinds of reasoning steps that humans use to develop proofs. For example, suppose we want to prove that Fred has a hot tub, and we know that everyone who lives in California has a hot tub and that Fred lives in California:

Antecedents: $(Live\text{-}California(Fred)) \land (Live\text{-}California(X) \to Hottub(X))$
Goal: $\to Hottub(Fred)$.

To prove $Hottub(Fred)$, we scan the antecedents for anything that will enable us to conclude $Hottub(Fred)$, and, if we find such a hypothesis, we set up the subgoal of proving it. In this case, we can conclude $Hottub(Fred)$ if we can prove $(Live\text{-}California(X) \to Hottub(X))$ and $(Live\text{-}California(Fred))$. So we set up the subgoal of proving $Live\text{-}California(Fred)$. Formally, we can derive a *back-chain* rule of inference:

To prove $[H \land (A \to B) \to C]$:
If $(B \to C)$, then prove $(H \to A)$.

In the next section, we present several of the proof rules from the IMPLY system, developed at the University of Texas (Bledsoe and Tyson, 1975).

IMPLY

IMPLY views a conjecture to be proved as a conjunction of goals to be achieved, and it considers a goal achieved when it finds a *substitution* under which the goal is valid. A substitution is simply an assignment of terms to each variable in the conjecture. In other words, IMPLY considers a conjecture proved when it finds some object or objects for which the conjecture is valid. For example, the conjecture

$$(P(x) \to Q(x)) \land P(a) \to Q(a)$$

is valid for the substitution a/x; that is, if every x in the formula were replaced by a, then the statement would be a valid inference.

Let C be a conjecture we wish to prove and let H be the conjunction of hypotheses that, hopefully, imply C. IMPLY will attempt to find a substitution (θ) such that $(H \to C)(\theta)$ is a propositionally valid formula. For example, if H is

$$P(a) \land (P(x) \to Q(x))$$

and C is

$$Q(a) ,$$

then the substitution $(\theta) = a/x$ will make $(H \to C)(\theta)$ valid.

In the following discussion, we assume that all formulas are quantifier free. That is, before the proof process starts, all universal and existential quantifiers, $\forall$ and $\exists$, are removed by *skolemization* (see Article XII.B). Skolemization for both resolution and natural deduction is done in much the same way, except that the roles of $\forall$ and $\exists$ in natural deduction are the opposite of their roles in resolution, because resolution is a refutation procedure and natural deduction is not. For example, for natural deduction, $[\forall x \, P(x) \rightarrow Q(a)]$ skolemizes to $[P(x) \rightarrow Q(a)]$ and $[H \rightarrow \exists x \forall y \; P(x,y)]$ skolemizes to $[H \rightarrow P(x, g(x))]$.

Formulas are submitted to IMPLY, which attempts to prove them by application of the rules discussed below. If F is a formula, $[F]$ denotes the value of IMPLY applied to F.

IMPLY rules. Some of the IMPLY proof rules are shown below.

1. MATCH: $[H \rightarrow C]$
   If $H(\theta) = C(\theta)$,
   then (θ)
   (the empty substitution is T).

This is the simplest of IMPLY's rules. The goal C is matched to the hypothesis H and, if a substitution can be found, that substitution is returned. For example, $(P(x) \rightarrow P(a))$ is MATCH because a substitution a/x makes H and C equal. The substitution is found by *unification* (see Article XII.B). MATCH would fail for the clause $(Q(x) \rightarrow P(a))$ because the predicates P and Q are different.

2. AND–SPLIT: $[H \rightarrow A \wedge B]$
   If $[H \rightarrow A]$ is (θ)
   and $[H \rightarrow B(\theta)]$ is (λ),
   then $(\theta)(\lambda)$.

If we want to prove that H implies A and B, we first prove that $(H \rightarrow A)$ for some substitution, and then, using that substitution in B, we prove that $(H \rightarrow B)$. For example, to prove $[P(x) \rightarrow P(a) \wedge (Q(x) \rightarrow P(a))]$, we obtain the substitution a/x when we prove $[P(x) \rightarrow P(a)]$, and that substitution is carried into the second step, namely, to prove $[P(x) \rightarrow (Q(a) \rightarrow P(a))]$. If, in proving this, we obtain another substitution, λ, then θ and λ are *composed* to produce a substitution under which the entire expression $[P(x) \rightarrow P(a) \wedge (Q(x) \rightarrow P(a))]$ is valid.

3. CASES: $[H_1 \vee H_2 \rightarrow C]$
   If $[H_1 \rightarrow C]$ is (θ)
   and $[H_2(\theta) \rightarrow C]$ is (λ),
   then $(\theta)(\lambda)$.

To prove that either of H_1 or H_2 implies C, we must prove that they both do. Thus, we attempt first to prove $[H_1 \rightarrow C]$ for some substitution, then $[H_2 \rightarrow C]$ under the previous substitution, and, if this second proof produces a substitution, the two are composed.

   4. OR–FORK: $[A \wedge B \to C]$

      If $[A \to C]$ is (θ),
      then (θ);
      else $[B \to C]$.

To show that A and B imply C, we must prove that A implies C or that B implies C. For example, $[Q(x) \wedge P(a) \to P(x)]$ is valid if either $[Q(x) \to P(x)]$ or $[P(a) \to P(x)]$ is valid.

   5. PROMOTE: $[H \to (A \to B)]$

      $[H \wedge A \to B]$.

This rule says simply that in trying to prove an implication $(A \to B)$ we can use A as an additional hypothesis.

   6. BACK–CHAIN: $[H \wedge (A \to B) \to C]$

      If $[B \to C]$ is (θ)
      and $[H \to A(\theta)]$ is (λ),
      then $(\theta)(\lambda)$.

This rule applies when a term that implies the goal has an antecedent that must be proved. It says that if C can be implied from B, and $(A \to B)$, then we must try to prove A. For example, we can prove Q in $[P \wedge (P \to Q) \to Q]$ if we are able to prove P. If we instantiate H, A, B, and C in the BACK–CHAIN rule with P and Q, we obtain

           If $[Q \to Q]$ is (θ)
           and $[P \to P(\theta)]$ is (λ),
           then $(\theta)(\lambda)$.

Obviously, $[Q \to Q]$ and $[P \to P]$ follow from the MATCH rule. In this example we have not considered substitutions.

   Consider what these inference rules do and how they differ from the resolution rule. Each, with the exception of MATCH, reduces a goal to subgoals. Most of these subgoals are easily tested by MATCH; it simply tests whether there is a substitution instance for the expression. The resolution rule, by contrast, reduces clauses but does not propagate goals from one inference to the next.

   IMPLY's rules are incomplete, but in most cases this does not prevent it from finding proofs of theorems. In fact, in many areas of mathematics, the great majority of proofs can be found without the extra inference rules required to make IMPLY complete. However, it can be made complete (Loveland and Stickel, 1973) and, in fact, one application warranted this (Bledsoe, Bruell, and Shostak, 1979).

Some proof procedures similar to IMPLY are described in Reiter (1976), Bibel and Schreiber (1974), Ernst (1971, 1973), and Nevins (1974, 1975).

Incorporating Heuristics into Theorem Provers

Most of the advantages derived from the use of natural-deduction theorem provers are not due to any decrease in the theoretical complexity of proofs but, rather, to the ease with which the proofs and the heuristic information incorporated into the prover can be understood. Most domain-dependent heuristics are discovered only after much analysis of attempted proofs, and the more intelligible proof structure of natural systems facilitates this analysis.

The next paragraphs describe kinds of heuristic knowledge that are typically grouped together under the heading of nonresolution theorem proving.

Reduction. The term *reduction* is used in two distinct but analogous ways. One interpretation is that reduction is the replacement of one logical expression by an equivalent, simpler expression. Alternately, reduction refers to the replacement of a term denoting an object by a simpler term. In both cases, the expression

$$L \to R$$

stands for a *reducer*. The reducer $L \to R$ is applied to a formula or term F by replacing an expression of the form $L(\theta)$ (where (θ) is a substitution) by the expression $R(\theta)$. The resulting formula or term is called an *immediate reduction*. Reductions are simpler in that they have fewer symbols or are smaller; formal requirements for simpler relations are discussed by Knuth and Bendix (1970) and Lankford (1975).

From elementary set theory, IMPLY uses (among others) the following reducers:

$$t \in (A \cap B) \to t \in A \land t \in B$$
$$t \in (A \cup B) \to t \in A \lor t \in B$$
$$t \subseteq (A \cap B) \to t \subseteq A \land t \subseteq B.$$

Examples of reducers from algebra include:

$$x + 0 \to x$$
$$x \cdot 1 \to x$$
$$x + (-x) \to 0$$
$$-(x + y) \to (-x) + (-y).$$

IMPLY maintains a list of reducers that are applied to a newly created expression until it cannot be reduced further; the resulting expression is called the *irreducible form* of the original expression relative to the list of reducers.

There are two very important properties of certain sets of reducers. A set of reducers ($\mathcal{R}$) is said to have the following:

1. *The finite termination property* (FTP), if there is no sequence of expressions $t_0, t_1, \ldots$, where t_{i+1} is an immediate reduction of t_i.

2. *The unique termination property* (UTP), if, for every expression t, all irreducible forms of t are identical.

Any set of reducers that has both the FTP and the UTP is called a *complete set of reducers*. There are algorithms for deciding whether a set of reducers with the FTP has the UTP (see Knuth and Bendix, 1970; Lankford 1975; Peterson and Stickel, 1977). In fact, the same algorithm can be used to extend a set of reducers that fails to have the UTP to one that does. Much research is currently being done on extending these algorithms.

Forward chaining. In addition to the rules mentioned earlier, IMPLY's set of rules includes:

FORWARD–CHAINING: $[(A \land (A' \to B)) \to C]$

If A is ground (i.e., has no variables) and $A' = A(\theta)$,
then $[(B(\theta) \land A \land (A' \to B)) \to C]$.

This rule differs from backward chaining in that it adds a new term to the set of hypotheses: From $(A \land (A' \to B))$, this rule adds $B(\theta)$ to the set of hypotheses when $A' = A(\theta)$, that is, when a substitution instance can be found for A and A'. Note that this rule does not produce smaller subgoals, as do the other rules we described, but, rather, it is used to infer auxiliary terms.

The rule contains an explicit *ground restriction* that A should have no variables. An intuitive justification for the ground restriction is that, since A is an assertion made by the hypothesis about specific objects (the ground terms) in the world, immediate consequences $(B(\theta))$ should be explored.

Many theorem provers have carried this forward-chaining rule a step further and have incorporated domain-specific knowledge into a set of *demons* that scan the hypotheses for sets of assertions. Upon finding the assertion it is looking for, a demon makes its own assertions. For example, a theorem prover might contain the following demon from elementary set theory:

Scan the hypothesis for sets A, B, and C. If the assertions $A \subseteq B$ and $C \subseteq B$ are present, and if the set $A \cup C$ is mentioned somewhere, then assert $A \cup C \subseteq B$.

Provers using variations of this technique are described by Ballantyne and Bennett (1973), Ballantyne and Bledsoe (1977), Nevins (1975), and Hewitt (1971).

Decision procedures. Certain theories, unlike number theory, have the property that there are algorithms to decide whether a sentence is true or false in the theory. Significantly, these algorithms are often direct and can make such decisions very quickly. For example, sets of linear inequalities over the real numbers can be decided very quickly by the *simplex algorithm*. The theory of arithmetic restricted to addition and multiplication by constants can be decided (Presburger, 1930), and, in fact, if one restricts the quantification on sentences in prenex form to universal quantification, that theory can be decided quickly (Bledsoe, 1974; Shostak, 1975). Decision procedures dealing with integration (Risch, 1969) are a main component of MACSYMA. Many fragments of theories useful in program verification have fast decision procedures (Nelson and Oppen, 1978).

A particularly interesting extension of this idea is to let the theorem prover "grow" its own decision procedures for classes of equational theories using the concept of complete sets of reducers (see Knuth and Bendix, 1970; Lankford, 1975; Huet, 1972; Lankford and Ballantyne, 1977; Ballantyne and Lankford, 1979; Peterson and Stickel, 1977).

Induction. Induction is another area in which the addition of heuristics can improve the performance of a prover. Since the development of a sophisticated set of such heuristics is one of the major achievements of the Boyer-Moore theorem prover, we refer the reader to Article XII.D.

Examples and counterexamples. Examples and counterexamples play an important but poorly understood role in automatic theorem proving. Specifically, if T is a set of axioms for a theory and if $H \rightarrow C$ is an attempted theorem, then an example is an interpretation of the predicate, function, and constant symbols that satisfies H and the axioms.

For example, let T be the axioms for the real numbers, and let H be $[f(a) \leq 0 \wedge f(b) \geq 0 \wedge \text{CONTINUOUS}(f, a, b)]$, where f, a, and b are constants and CONTINUOUS(f, a, b) means that the function f is continuous on the closed interval $[a, b]$. Then the assignment

$$a \leftarrow 0$$
$$b \leftarrow 1$$
$$f \leftarrow ((\lambda)x)(2x - 1)$$

is an example.

To see how this example might be useful in controlling the search for a proof, suppose that the theorem prover is asked to prove the conclusion $C = (\text{SOME } x)(f(x) = 0)$, given the above axioms and hypotheses. Suppose that, in the course of proving C, the prover encounters the subgoal $f(t) \leq 0$, where t is a term that evaluates to $3/4$ in the example. Since $f(t) = f(3/4) = 2 \cdot 3/4 - 1 = 1/2$ and since $1/2$ is not less than or equal to 0, the prover is allowed to discard this subgoal. Several theorem provers have incorporated examples as a *subgoal filter* (Gelernter, 1959; Reiter, 1976; Bledsoe and Ballantyne, 1979). In all these provers, the examples must be generated by the user. However, Bledsoe and Ballantyne describe a program that, when given an example, extends the interpretation to include the skolem functions and constants that result from quantifier elimination.

It seems likely that mathematicians use examples much more often as subgoal *proposers* than as subgoal *rejectors*. Mathematicians often use examples to guide the search for a proof from beginning to end. Since they usually discover theorems by building and inspecting examples, it seems likely that the same examples would be useful in proving these theorems. Constructing good examples is a very difficult task but one that must be understood if reasonably competent theorem proving is to be done by computer. Lenat's AM system (1976; Article XIV.D4c) constructed and used examples to help make conjectures.

Conclusion

Nonresolution, or natural-deduction, proof procedures are designed to develop proofs in a goal-directed manner that is easy for humans to understand. Unlike resolution methods, natural deduction uses many proof rules to reduce goals to subgoals. In addition, natural-deduction systems often include domain-specific heuristics to speed up parts of a proof.

Any proof that can be derived by natural deduction can also be derived by resolution, given enough time. The advantage of natural deduction is chiefly that the proofs it produces are relatively easy to understand. This is very important whenever there is interaction between an automatic theorem prover and a human.

References

The IMPLY system is discussed in Bledsoe and Tyson (1975).

D. THE BOYER–MOORE THEOREM PROVER

THE Boyer-Moore Theorem Prover (BMTP; Boyer and Moore, 1979) embodies an extensible mathematical theory (recursive function theory) in which
theorems can be stated and automatically proved. The system is designed
to prove theorems by continuously rewriting the current formula (Bledsoe,
1971, 1977) without ever having to backtrack and alter a decision. While
each rewriting rule is sound, formal equivalence is not necessarily preserved;
thus, the system is not complete. But heuristics are employed to guide the
rewriting process, applying rules that the system believes will allow retention of the "theoremness" of a formula. The theory can be extended by
new function definitions and new data types. Novel features include the
automatic use of structural induction (Burstall, 1969) and recursive quantification (Skolem, 1967). The relations between recursion, termination, and the
inductively defined data objects allow the BMTP to produce induction proofs
automatically. Recursive functions, used as an alternative to quantification,
offer a powerful form of expression when dealing with finitely constructed
objects such as the discrete mathematical structures employed by computer
programs.

Rather than operate in the predicate calculus (see Article III.C1, in Vol. I),
the Boyer-Moore Theorem Prover treats axioms and theorems as functions.
Axioms have the values non-F (true) or F (false). A theorem is proved by
showing that the value of its function is non-F. For example, a statement
that multiplication is distributive over addition would have appeared in QA3
(Green, 1969; see also Article III.C1, in Vol. I) as:

```
FORALL x FORALL y FORALL z  SUM(y,z,a1) AND PRODUCT(x,a1,a) AND
     PRODUCT(x,y,b1) AND PRODUCT(x,z,b2) AND SUM(b1,b2,b) AND
     EQUAL(a,b)
```

(where x, y, z, a, a_1, b, b_1, b_2 are all variables). In the BMTP, the theorem
becomes:

```
(EQUAL (TIMES x (ADD y z)) (ADD (TIMES x y) (TIMES x z))) .
```

The Boyer-Moore Theorem Prover automatically proves the theorems it
is presented with, possibly using rewrite lemmas that have been retained
from the proofs of previous theorems or axioms that have been added by the
introduction of new data types. Most theorems cannot be proved from first
principles, so the user must structure the proof by determining intuitively
which lemmas will be necessary. These are then proved as theorems in their
own right and saved. Since lemmas must be proved before they can be

automatically used, the BMTP is assured of the validity of the proof of the final theorem. Even theorems that can be proved without lemmas can have their proofs speeded up by the use of lemmas. If the BMTP fails to prove the desired result, the proof attempt helps the user determine where the proof went awry and formulate new lemmas. Thus, the BMTP is an automatic theorem prover in the sense that the user specifies only what to prove, not how to prove it. But if a proof fails, the user provides a bit of the "how" by formulating an appropriate lemma.

The system is experimental and is continually being tested and improved. It has proved approximately 400 theorems, including the soundness and completeness of a tautology checker for propositional calculus, the equivalence of interpreted and optimized compiled code for a simple arithmetic language, the correctness of the Boyer-Moore fast string-searching algorithm, and the prime-factorization theorem.

The Theory

The syntax of the theory is closely related to the prefix notation in LISP. Terms are variables or are specified by $(f\ x_1 \ldots x_n)$, where f is an n-ary function symbol and all x_i are terms. Constants are represented as 0-ary functions (e.g., (TRUE), (FALSE), (ZERO)). The variables in any formula are implicitly universally quantified.

Functions are introduced by adding the equality axiom:

$$(f\ x_1 \ldots x_n) = \langle \text{function body} \rangle\ .$$

To retain consistency, the BMTP requires that each newly defined function be either nonrecursive or recursive but provably total. The proof of totality is based on the notion of measure functions and well-founded relations. This is discussed in detail later in this article in the section on induction.

In making function definitions it is often necessary to include tests that allow the returned value of a function to be one of a set of terms. The usual treatment of logic does not allow for the embedding of propositions within terms, so the BMTP recreates the effects of propositions at the term level. Boyer and Moore create four axioms to define the functions EQUAL and IF; these form the core of the BMTP. We abbreviate (TRUE) as T and (FALSE) as F, and add the axiom that T and F are distinct:

1. $\text{T} \neq \text{F}$

2. $\text{X} = \text{Y} \Rightarrow (\text{EQUAL X Y}) = \text{T}$

3. $\text{X} \neq \text{Y} \Rightarrow (\text{EQUAL X Y}) = \text{F}$

4. $\text{X} = \text{F} \Rightarrow (\text{IF X Y Z}) = \text{Z}$

5. $\text{X} \neq \text{F} \Rightarrow (\text{IF X Y Z}) = \text{Y}$

(For those readers who are not familiar with LISP notation, (IF X Y Z) means *If X, then Y; else Z.*) Thus, the term (IF X Y Z) has the value Z if the proposition X = F is true and it has the value Y if X = F is false.

Boyer and Moore do not define predicates but, instead, deal within a theory of functions. Proving that the value of a function is not F is the way the BMTP proves that a function is a theorem. Functional versions of common logical connectives are defined with IF. These definitions capture the semantics of the common logical connectives:

1. (NOT P) = (IF P F T)

2. (AND P Q) = (IF P (IF Q T F) F)

3. (OR P Q) = (IF P T (IF Q T F))

4. (IMPLIES P Q) = (IF P (IF Q T F) T)

In addition to these and other functions, the BMTP allows the creation of arbitrary data types. These are typically defined inductively and made known to the system by the Shell mechanism (discussed below), which adds axioms that are guaranteed to leave the theory consistent. Data objects are considered to be finitely constructed. Data types are mutually exclusive yet not assumed to be exhaustive. This guarantees that the subsequent addition of new data types will not invalidate previously proved theorems.

Proofs within the BMTP are accomplished by absorption, idempotency, the law of excluded middle (e.g., $T \lor X \to T$, $F \lor X \to X$, $X \lor \neg X \to T$, and their commutative counterparts), and induction principles. Recursion as a control structure is analogous to inductively defined data types as a data structure. The proof-theoretic counterpart of these two is the Generalized Principle of Induction, or Noetherian Induction. A consistent induction mechanism is presented within the theory. It allows a base case as well as k remaining induction steps, each of which can contain several induction hypotheses. It requires a relation that is well-founded on a measured set of variables over all substitutions required to instantiate the $k + 1$ cases. Heuristic methods are employed in the BMTP to formulate this schema; they are discussed later in this article in the section on induction. A well-founded relation r is one that admits no infinitely decreasing sequences. That is, there cannot exist an infinite sequence $1, 2, \ldots$ such that $(rX_{i+1}X_i)$. A simple well-founded relation is $<$ on the nonnegative integers, since for any X_1 we cannot find an infinite sequence of x_i such that

$$\cdots X_{i+1} < X_i < X_{i-1} < \cdots < X_1.$$

The Shell mechanism. The Shell mechanism is used to introduce new data types. It is just a syntactic form from which consistent and complete type-axioms are created. As an illustration, the definition of lists by the Shell mechanism is as follows:

```
add the shell CONS, of 2 arguments
recognizer LISTP
accessors CAR, CDR
default values "NIL", "NIL" .
```

A few of the important axioms that were added (with symmetric CDR axioms) are the following:

(LISTP (CONS x y))	— a CONS of two things is always a list
(EQUAL (CAR (CONS x y) x))	— definition of the CAR accessing function
(IMPLIES (LISTP x) (LESSP (CAR x) x))	— a measure property used in proving termination
(EQUAL (EQUAL (CONS a b) (CONS x y)) (AND (EQUAL a x) (EQUAL b y)))	— two CONSes are equal if their parts are equal
(IMPLIES (LISTP x) (EQUAL (CONS (CAR x) (CDR x)) x))	— the system can trade CARs and CDRs for CONSes

Overview of the Theorem Prover

The BMTP proves that a formula is a theorem by continually rewriting the formula until it is reduced to T. The BMTP operates in a strictly linear manner without backtracking. This strategy leads to a stratification of the classes of rewrite rules, so that the more conservative transformations (i.e., those which guarantee equivalence) are attempted first. Induction rewrite rules are applied last, since they are the least conservative transformations and it is important that induction be applied to the simplest and most general form of a formula. As a consequence, many of the rewrite rules have been designed to produce a formula that is more amenable to inductive arguments. We will now discuss these rule classes. Rules at level $i + 1$ are tried only when all rules at level i fail to be applicable. If a rewrite rule applies at any level of the hierarchy, the formula is rewritten and the entire theorem prover is recursively invoked on the new formula.

Simplification

The formula is rewritten by the logical proof rules, the initial axioms, the axioms added by function and data-type definitions, and retained lemmas that were previously proved as theorems. (The formula is also rewritten to conjunctive normal form, or *clause form;* see Article XII.B.) All these rewriting rules retain truth-value equivalence. The *Simplifier* is a small theorem-prover in its own right. Examples of the information known to the Simplifier are:

1. Logical Proof Rule:
   X ∨ T = T

2. Initial Axiom:
    x = y ⇒ (IF x y z) = y

3. Function Axiom:
    (APPEND x y) = (IF (LISTP x)
                       (CONS (CAR x) (APPEND (CDR x) y)) y)

4. Data-type Axiom:
    (CDR (CONS x y)) = y

5. Lemma:
    (APPEND (APPEND x y) z) = (APPEND x (APPEND y z))

Simplification is sufficient to prove the following formula (which is the base case of the induction needed to prove that APPEND is associative):

    (IMPLIES (NOT (LISTP A))
             (EQUAL (APPEND (APPEND A B) C)
                    (APPEND A (APPEND B C)))) .

Knowing that A is not a list allows the APPEND functions to open up and return their second arguments; see the functional definition of APPEND above. The formula simplifies to:

    (IMPLIES (NOT (LISTP A))
             (EQUAL (APPEND B C)
                    (APPEND B C))) .

Since the two APPEND terms are identical, this simplifies to:

    (IMPLIES (NOT (LISTP A)) T) .

This in turn simplifies to T, since the formula is equivalent to the clause (LISTP A) ∨ T, which by the above proof rule is rewritten to T.

If simplification cannot determine the truth value of a formula, it will probably be necessary to apply the induction rewriting rules. The next four cases illustrate how the formula is prepared for induction.

Elimination of Undesirable Concepts

The BMTP restates a formula, trading some functions for others when the substituted formulas are easier to rewrite or have more lemmas involving them. This type of rule is a special subclass of the general simplification rules and is handled separately since it requires special processing. An example of this kind of rule is:

    (p x) = (p (CONS A B)),   if x is known to be a list.

An example of its application is found in the proof of the theorem that the function REVERSE is its own inverse:

```
(IMPLIES
  (AND (LISTP X)
       (EQUAL (REVERSE (REVERSE (CDR X))) (CDR X))
       (PLISTP (CDR X)))
  (EQUAL (REVERSE (APPEND (REVERSE (CDR X))
                          (CONS (CAR X) "NIL")))
         X))
```

```
= (IMPLIES
    (AND (LISTP (CONS A B))
         (EQUAL (REVERSE (REVERSE (CDR (CONS A B)))) (CDR (CONS A B)))
         (PLISTP (CDR (CONS A B))))
    (EQUAL (REVERSE (APPEND (REVERSE B)
                            (CONS A "NIL")))
           (CONS A B))) .
```

Here we have traded a CAR and CDR for a CONS. Note that this transformation was applicable since X was known to be a list from the hypothesis of the implication. A and B are new variable names.

This fairly complicated formula is passed back to the Simplifier, which rewrites it as:

```
(IMPLIES
  (AND (EQUAL (REVERSE (REVERSE B)) B)
       (PLISTP B))
  (EQUAL (REVERSE (APPEND (REVERSE B)
                          (CONS A "NIL")))
         (CONS A B))) .
```

Use of Equalities

The BMTP uses equalities by substituting equals for equals, and then it usually removes the equality term from the formula. This is not guaranteed to be complete, but the heuristic decision procedure in BMTP that decides which terms to substitute performs excellently. The equality term is removed to simplify the statement of the formula (which hopefully is still a theorem). Two distinct classes of substitutions—uniform substitution and cross-fertilization— are performed.

Uniform substitution. If the term (EQUAL x ev) is found, where x is a term and ev is an explicit value, then ev is uniformly substituted for x within the rest of the formula. The symmetric case applies.

Cross-fertilization. If the term (EQUAL x y) is found, where both x and y are not explicit values, and another term of the form "(p ⟨any term⟩ ⟨term that contains y⟩)" is found, then x is substituted for y only in the right-hand side of p, and the equality is removed from the formula. The symmetric case applies. This heuristic is closely related to the way induction is performed; it is

designed to allow maximum use of the induction hypothesis. The connection is
a bit subtle and the reader is referred to Boyer and Moore's (1979) description.

Continuing the above example, the antecedent has an equality of the
form "(EQUAL x B)" and the consequent term is of the form "(p ⟨term⟩ ⟨term
with B⟩)," so we cross-fertilize. This results in:

```
(IMPLIES
 (PLISTP B)
 (EQUAL (REVERSE (APPEND (REVERSE B)
                        (CONS A "NIL")))
        (CONS A (REVERSE (REVERSE B)))))  .
```

Generalization

A further simplification can be accomplished by replacing a term in the
formula by a variable, thus generalizing the formula and allowing an induction
on the new variable position in the formula. Hopefully, by the time we reach
this point, the internal structure of the term has already contributed its
significance to the proof and can be ignored. To prevent the formula from
becoming overgeneralized, the BMTP can add certain type-restrictions to the
variable introduced. The REVERSE example that we have been following does
not adequately illustrate generalization, so we move temporarily to a different
example:

```
(EQUAL (APPEND (FLATTEN Z)
               (APPEND (FLATTEN V) ANS))
       (APPEND (APPEND (FLATTEN Z) (FLATTEN V))
               ANS))

= (IMPLIES (AND (LISTP A) (LISTP B))
           (EQUAL (APPEND A (APPEND B ANS))
                  (APPEND (APPEND A B) ANS)))  .
```

Here, (FLATTEN Z) and (FLATTEN V) have been generalized to A and B,
respectively. Type information has been added showing that both A and B are
list data types, since the system is aware of a theorem stating that FLATTEN
always produces a list. The formula now is just the statement that APPEND
is associative.

Elimination of Irrelevant Terms

In performing the above transformations, it is often the case that irrelevant terms are left in a formula. Removing these terms cleans up the formula.
While these terms are difficult to spot in general, there are two special cases,
shown as rules 1 and 2 below, that frequently occur. In both cases, all the

terms of a formula are first partitioned into equivalence classes with term 1 in the same class as term 2 if they share a common variable.

Rule 1. If a class contains only nonrecursive functions, then all terms in the class are removed from the formula. If these formulas were always non-F, the Simplifier should have been able to prove this fact. Passing these terms on to the Induction mechanism will not help, since the terms are not recursively defined.

Rule 2. If a class contains a single recursive function, it is removed. A single function that cannot be shown to be always non-F by the Simplifier probably can assume non-F values.

Continuing our example of the proof (EQUAL (REVERSE (REVERSE X)) X), the theorem is generalized to:

```
(IMPLIES
  (PLISTP B)
  (EQUAL (REVERSE (APPEND X (CONS A "NIL")))
         (CONS A (REVERSE X))))
```

by replacing all occurrences of (REVERSE B) with X. No extra type information is added during generalization. The antecedent is eliminated by rule 2, leaving the formula:

```
(EQUAL (REVERSE (APPEND X (CONS A "NIL")))
       (CONS A (REVERSE X))) ,
```

which is a statement asserting that reversing the concatenation of X and A is equivalent to concatenating A with the reverse of X.

Performing an Induction

If, in the course of these rewrites, the theorem has still not been reduced to T, the BMTP automatically formulates a valid induction argument to try to prove the theorem. The heuristics employed here represent the heart of the BMTP. Inductions are formulated by using information collected at the time the function is defined and at the time the actual induction is needed.

Function-definition time. When a function is defined, the system must prove that the function terminates before allowing the definition. Termination is proved by finding a well-founded function that decreases when applied to a subset (measured set) of the arguments used in all recursive calls. The system exhaustively searches through all lexicographic orders of all well-founded functions (LESSP is initially the only one, but others are added by the Shell mechanism) applied to all subsets and permutations of a function's arguments. These are all collected in a set of induction templates that are associated with the newly defined function. These templates include the form of the induction to be performed and all of the variable substitutions that will need to be made.

The following illustrates the creation of induction templates at function-definition time for REVERSE, which is defined as:

```
(REVERSE X) = (IF (LISTP X)
                  (APPEND (REVERSE (CDR X)) (CONS (CAR X) "NIL"))
                  (CONS X "NIL")) .
```

The proof of termination is fairly simple, since REVERSE is monadic and there is only one recursive function call within its body. The BMTP utilizes the information that the recursive function call is executed only if X is known to be a list. Thus, to prove that REVERSE terminates, it tries to prove the theorem:

```
(IMPLIES (LISTP X) (LESSP (CDR X) X)) .
```

The system proves this theorem (it recursively calls itself) by noticing that this formula is equivalent to an axiom added by the Shell mechanism during the definition of lists. This is the only way the system can prove termination, so the only induction template produced is:

```
(AND (IMPLIES (NOT (LISTP x)) (p x))
     (IMPLIES (AND (LISTP x)
                   (p (CDR x)))
              (p x))) .
```

This states that, to prove the formula (p x) where p involves the REVERSE function, it is sufficient for the BMTP to prove that:

1. If x is not a list (the base case), then (p x) can be proved.

2. If x is a list and (p (CDR x)) is assumed to be true (the induction hypothesis), then (p x) can be proved.

Typically, the formula p will also involve other recursive functions that have their own induction templates. The problem of which induction template to use cannot be handled at function-definition time (since the BMTP has no way to determine how a newly defined function will be used) and is handled when the induction rewrite rules are trying to rewrite the formula.

Instantiation time. When an induction rewrite rule is attempted, the induction templates for all recursive functions in the formula are retrieved. These templates are then sifted by the following rules:

1. Only legal templates (with valid substitution instances) are retained. Substitutions may be invalid for many reasons, the most common that

the template requires that a nonvariable argument be used as an induction variable. The REVERSE induction template could not be used if the formula p involved only terms like (REVERSE (f x)); hopefully, the generalization heuristics will substitute a variable for the function (f x).

2. Induction schemata are obtained when the legal templates are instantiated by performing the required substitutions. All subsumed induction schemata are discarded. This means that the system will discard weaker induction arguments for ones with a richer case structure (duplicates are removed by this method also).

3. The remaining templates are then merged. Two templates are merged if they contain a common induction variable, allowing for the final induction scheme to contain induction hypotheses for every relevant induction variable. Thus, if one induction scheme requires induction on the variables x and y and another requires induction on the variables y and z, it seems plausible to require simultaneous induction on all of x, y, and z.

4. If more than one scheme still exists and there is one "unflawed" scheme, then all "flawed" schemes are discarded. An induction scheme is unflawed if every occurrence of an induction variable is in a position where it is decomposed.

5. Finally, if more than one scheme still exists, a scoring function determines which one to use.

6. The final scheme is then instantiated for the specific formula to be proved.

Boyer and Moore (1979) report that 90% of all inductions' arguments yield only one unflawed scheme and, of the remaining 10%, half have no unique correct scheme (i.e., the theorems are symmetric in some variables).

Continuing the REVERSE example, the BMTP is about to create an induction argument for proving:

```
(EQUAL (REVERSE (APPEND X (CONS A "NIL")))
       (CONS A (REVERSE X))) .
```

It determines the induction schemata for REVERSE and APPEND, and since both functions perform CDR recursions on X, their schemata are merged to create the unique induction schema, which is finally used:

```
(AND (IMPLIES (NOT (LISTP X)) (p X A))
     (IMPLIES (AND (LISTP X)
                   (p (CDR X) A))
              (p X A))) .
```

Themes of the Boyer-Moore Theorem Prover

Proof by induction. The outstanding feature of the BMTP is that it automates induction proofs. Since most common data-types (integers, lists, trees, formulas) are defined inductively, it is imperative that theorem provers that prove properties of programs have the capability of performing inductive arguments (automatically or manually). The excellent performance of the BMTP is in a large part due to the heuristic methods employed in constructing induction proofs. These heuristics form the core contribution the BMTP has made to AI research.

Referencing problem. A key problem in current theorem-proving systems is the performance degradation due to increased knowledge. While increased knowledge should improve a system's performance, it typically just expands the possible solution space, causing excess searching. This has been named the *referencing problem* by Bledsoe (1974). Resolution theorem-provers suffer greatly from this problem. Such methods as proof by analogy (Kling, 1971) have been used to restrict the reference set, but they have met with little success. The BMTP does not address this issue with any more sophistication than trying the rewrite rules in reverse chronological order (with complex results first). This simple strategy has proved effective even when operating within an environment that contains approximately 400 theorems.

The language of the theorem prover. Since the main application of the BMTP has been to prove properties of programs, a possible misconception should be avoided. There is a difference between the language used to express formal statements whose validity is being proved and the language used to express a program. The theory is just a mathematical tool for making precise assertions about the properties of discrete mathematical objects. The language used to express the theory is closely related to the pure LISP programming language and should be considered as an alternative to the use of the predicate calculus. Frequently, programs can be written as functions within the theory (since the semantics of a LISP-like program can be easily captured within the language of the theory) just as it is possible to use predicate calculus as a programming language (Kowalski, 1974). But a distinction should be made between the language used to express theorems and the programming language used to describe an algorithm about which the BMTP is proving theorems. When proving properties about programs, the user applies a relevant theory of program semantics to derive formal statements whose validity implies that the program has the desired properties. These statements are then translated into the theory on which the BMTP operates. The BMTP can then be instructed to try to establish the validity of these statements. To illustrate this fact, the proof of the correctness of the compiler is expressed by McCarthy's functional method, while the correctness of the string-searching algorithm is expressed by Floyd's method of inductive assertions.

Performance. Two performance measures are relevant to theorem provers. The first is the system's ability to represent typical facts and theorems in the domain of interest (epistemological adequacy). The second is the ability to prove theorems within a reasonable amount of time. Both performance measures contain ambiguity (e.g., "typical," "reasonable"). But in the BMTP, many interesting facts and theorems can be represented, and proof times are commensurate with a user's patience when debugging proofs interactively. The BMTP has been applied to a large number of theorem-proving tasks, some of which are very difficult by human standards. Most theorems are proved in well under a minute, although most proofs require lemmas to be proved previously. Nevertheless, this is one of the most powerful theorem provers available.

References

Boyer and Moore discuss their theorem prover in their 1979 article.

E. NONMONOTONIC LOGICS

SEVERAL FORMS of nondeductive reasoning have attracted careful scrutiny. Purely deductive reasoning techniques have long been recognized as inadequate for capturing all intelligent thought. Statistical and inductive reasoning, which concern inexact and generalizing reasoning, have received much study as possible extensions or alternatives to deductive reasoning. Nonmonotonic reasoning, recently formalized in nonmonotonic logics, is the latest extension to deductive reasoning. This article sketches the nature of, reasons for, and approaches to nonmonotonic logics.

The Task of Logic

The task of logic is the judgment of arguments. Historically, logic has been the science of argumentation, the study of which arguments are good and which are not good. Different purposes engendered different conceptions of good. Arguments to convince capricious, distracted, and sometimes irrational humans were judged by the standards of effective rhetoric, which concern, among other things, the size, structure, motivation, and emotional impact of arguments and their steps. Inductive logics judged arguments that made generalizations; statistical logics judged arguments that dealt with frequencies and probabilities; and deductive logics judged arguments that made restatements, that is, truth-preserving inferences.

While important insights were gained into the philosophical and practical questions underlying rhetorical, statistical, and inductive reasoning, perhaps the philosophically most striking advances were made in connection with deductive reasoning. Philosophers, logicians, and mathematicians explored the powerful ideas of formal languages, truth-theoretic semantics, set theory, and the mathematics of formal systems, model theory, and proof theory. These ideas proved so fruitful that logic for the most part came to be identified with deductive logic, the study of truth-preserving inferences. This identification grew so strong that many of the proposed nondeductive logics have been attacked as false logics. But logic is a science of thought and argument, not merely a science of truth-preserving inferences.

The Task of Nonmonotonic Logic

The task of nonmonotonic logics is to judge cases of nonmonotonic reasoning, that is, reasoning that involves adopting assumptions that may have to be abandoned in light of new information. For example, a scheduling secretary may employ the inference rule that he (or she) should schedule each new meeting on the closest future Wednesday unless and until he finds reasons for scheduling the meeting otherwise. While working out the week's schedule, the secretary may tentatively schedule the first meeting on the next Wednesday, only to reschedule it later, thereby abandoning his initial assumption, when he learns that a meeting is requested for that Wednesday specifically to accommodate a visitor.

This reasoning is called nonmonotonic in contrast to the monotonicity of the set of theorems of a set of axioms in deductive logic. In deductive logic, the addition of new axioms to a set of axioms can never decrease the set of theorems. At most, the new axioms can give rise to new theorems, so that the set of theorems grows monotonically with the set of axioms. In nonmonotonic logics, the set of theorems may lose members as well as gain members when new axioms are added.

Reasoning by Default

Two cases of nonmonotonic reasoning have been studied: reasoning by default and reasoning by circumscription.

The defaults of reasoning by default are statements or rules according to which (as in the scheduling example above) some statement is to be believed, unless and until otherwise demonstrated. Defaults can be found in many places in standard AI techniques. They are used in stating generalities to which exceptions may be acknowledged without catastrophe. For example, a default might be that all birds can fly; penguins and ostriches are exceptions. In structured knowledge-representation systems (see Article III.C7, in Vol. I), such defaults often take the form of default fillers of frame slots. For example, an airline reservation system might describe each customer with a *passenger* frame in which the *class* slot has the default value *coach*. Defaults also enter into many knowledge-representation systems implicitly through what is known as the *closed-world assumption*. The closed-world assumption is that all relationships not explicitly stated to hold do not hold. For example, typical procedures for inheriting statements in one frame from more general frames by way of *generalization* links assume that a frame is generalized only by those frames explicitly listed as generalizations or, in turn, by their generalizations. Thus, if the *elephant* frame has a sole generalization link to the *mammal* frame, the inheritance procedures will search only *mammal* and not any other frames, in spite of the possibility that new generalization links may be attached to *elephant* later and would then be searched as well. Yet another use of defaults is in the typical *STRIPS assumption* that performed actions change none of the program's beliefs about the world except those explicitly listed in the description of the action (see Article XV.B). For example, a description of a robot's action of moving from one location to another would list only changes in beliefs about the robot's position. When the robot moves, the STRIPS assumption default would leave its belief about world geography intact.

Reasoning by Circumscription

Another case of nonmonotonic reasoning, which may well overlap defaults in some (or even all) cases, is that of parsimonious reasoning, or reasoning by circumscription. In reasoning about some problem, one often assumes that the problem involves only those objects and relationships that it mentions, and no others. The inheritance procedures mentioned above made such an assumption (the closed-world assumption) about the nonexistence of unlisted generalization links and generalizing frames. As another example, in the well-known missionaries-and-cannibals problem of traversing a river uneaten, one typically does not think of solutions involving bridges, rocket ships, handcuffs, murder of the cannibals, or holes in the boat. Another way of viewing the circumscription principle is the assumption that all qualifications to the problem have been stated explicitly.

Formal Characterizations of Defaults

Two sorts of detailed formalizations of nonmonotonic defaults have been proposed, namely, Reiter's logic of defaults and McDermott and Doyle's non-monotonic logics.

Both logics roughly interpret *Default S* as *S is provable unless and until S can be disproved*. The difficulty with this interpretation is its circularity, that what can be inferred depends on what inference rules are applicable, while, at the same time, what inference rules are applicable depends on what can be inferred. For example, suppose that we decide to use only the ordinary logical rules of inference in attempting to disprove statements and that the information to be captured consists of three statements: Default A, Default B, and $\neg(A \wedge B)$. Here, neither A nor B can be disproved using the ordinary logical rules of inference, so we declare both A and B to be provable by means of the default statements. These two new conclusions are inconsistent with $\neg(A \wedge B)$. Instead of declaring the initial three statements to be inconsistent, the nonmonotonic logics try to refine the notions of provability to say that there are two coherent interpretations of these axioms, namely, one in which A and $\neg B$ are provable and one in which B and $\neg A$ are provable. This is a big departure from ordinary logic, in which a single set of axioms has exactly one set of conclusions that can be drawn from it. The key problem addressed by the nonmonotonic logics is that of providing some well-defined semantics for defaults that allows a single set of axioms and defaults to have several coherent interpretations.

In all the nonmonotonic logics, the meanings of *provable* and *consistent* for a statement and a set of axioms are defined nonconstructively by a mathematical definition of what *coherent* sets of conclusions are, relative to a given set of axioms and defaults. These definitions are nonconstructive primarily because the coherent interpretations supplied by the logics are in general not even recursively enumerable. Roughly put, the logics declare that interpretations are found by adding in as many statements (assumptions) as possible, in accordance with the defaults, but at the same time avoiding adding in so many assumptions as to produce an ordinary logical inconsistency. In the above example, for instance, the two coherent interpretations of the three statements are produced by adding in just one of the assumptions, A or B. By the time one assumption is added in, the negation of the other can be deduced by ordinary logical rules of inference, so that the other assumption is ruled out, as it would lead to an inconsistency. This rough description of the semantics provided by the logics does not do them justice. For the precise definitions involved, the reader is referred to the original papers (Reiter, 1980; McDermott and Doyle, 1980).

While Reiter's and McDermott and Doyle's approaches to formalizing defaults have much in common in the way they interpret defaults and in their major theoretical properties, they differ in logical form, as one approach formalizes defaults as inference rules and the other as modal formulas. Unless one is vitally interested in logic for its own sake, or in pursuing the future development of better nonmonotonic logics, these differences in logical form can be passed over as small differences in notation for capturing the same ideas.

Reiter (1980) formalizes defaults by adjoining a new sort of inference rule called a default to an ordinary logic of statements and inference rules. Default inference rules are of the form *If P, and it is consistent to assume Q, then infer R,* written $P : Q/R$, where P, Q, and R are ordinary formulas. Given condition P, a default allows the inference of R providing that Q is not disprovable. With this notation, the simplest sort of default, that of *Assume A if it cannot be disproved,* is written simply as "$: A/A$"; that is, P is empty and $Q = R = A$.

Instead of stating defaults as inference rules, McDermott and Doyle (1980; McDermott, 1980) state defaults as modal formulas. They use an ordinary logical language extended by the unary modal operator *not-disprovable*. The analogue in nonmonotonic logic of a default inference rule $P : Q/R$ of the logic of defaults is $P \land \text{\textit{not-disprovable }} Q \rightarrow R$. Thus the simplest sort of default is stated in these nonmonotonic logics as *not-disprovable* $A \rightarrow A$. Although we said earlier that nonmonotonic logics and the logic of defaults are for many purposes syntactic variants, that is not really true. The modal nonmonotonic logic formulations are, for better or worse, actually more expressive than the nonmodal logic of defaults. This is because one can make statements about defaults; for example

$$\textit{not-disprovable}(\textit{not-disprovable } A \rightarrow A) \rightarrow (\textit{not-disprovable } A \rightarrow A),$$

in nonmonotonic logics, whereas in the logic of defaults no means exists for referring to the default inference rules.

The Genesis of Practical Nonmonotonic Inference Rules

Neither of these approaches says anything about which nonmonotonic statements or rules should be used in representing information about a particular domain. The logics all leave that decision to the AI system designer. However, McCarthy (1980) and Dacey (1978) have each developed theories that appear to bear on the problem of formulating defaults. McCarthy formalizes reasoning by circumscription as an explicitly nonmonotonic rule of inference. Dacey, on the other hand, formalizes his *theory of conclusions* in terms of classical decision theory, rather than in terms of nonmonotonic reasoning.

The idea of circumscription, in McCarthy's (1980) treatment, becomes an inference rule for formulating sets of assumptions on the basis of the available information. The circumscription inference rule computes axiom schemata from sets of axioms, schemata that can be applied to make a variety of assumptions. To circumscribe a set of axioms A with respect to some predicate P mentioned in A, one constructs a sentence schema stating that the only objects satisfying P are those whose doing so follows from the axioms A. All statements following via ordinary deductive rules of inference from that sentence schema are said to be the conclusions reached by *circumscriptive inference* with respect to P from the original axioms A. For example, suppose we know only one red-haired person, our friend Jane. If we see someone looking like Jane in the crude sense of merely being red-haired, we might, by circumscription, assume that that person is Jane, because Jane is the only person we know fitting that description. This inference is nonmonotonic, of course, since if we now learn that Jane has an identical twin sister Joan, we can no longer conclude that anyone who looks like Jane is Jane. Expressed formally in terms of McCarthy's circumscription, this example might be translated as follows. We start with the set of axioms $A = \langle red\text{-}haired(Jane) \rangle$ and circumscribe on the predicate *red-haired*. The circumscription of this predicate in A is the axiom schema

$$\Phi(Jane) \wedge \forall x\, (\Phi(x) \rightarrow red\text{-}haired(x)) \rightarrow \forall x\, (red\text{-}haired(x) \rightarrow \Phi(x)) .$$

If we now substitute our only known instance of a red-haired person into this schema, that is, if we substitute the formula $x = Jane$ for $\Phi(x)$, we get

$$Jane = Jane \wedge \forall x\, (x = Jane \rightarrow red\text{-}haired(x)) \rightarrow \forall x\, (red\text{-}haired(x) \rightarrow x = Jane) .$$

The first two parts of this formula are true, and simplifying it leaves the resulting assumption, or *default*, $\forall x\, (red\text{-}haired(x) \rightarrow x = Jane)$, which we can apply to any new person who looks like Jane (i.e., is red-haired). Yet this inference is nonmonotonic in that, if we add the new axiom *red-haired(Joan)* to A, we can no longer draw any such identifying conclusion. At best, we can infer by another application of circumscription the less specific conclusion $\forall x \, (red\text{-}haired(x) \rightarrow x = Jane \lor x = Joan)$.

Another approach to forming and rejecting tentative hypotheses, the *theory of conclusions* developed by Dacey (1978) after a suggestion of Tukey (1960), can be viewed as proposing a general rule about when to adopt and when to abandon defaults. Dacey formulates conclusion theory in terms of classical decision theory rather than in the proof-theoretic terms of the preceding approaches. Classical decision theory analyzes how the strength of each of one's hypotheses about the world should be revised with each new evidential fact. The intent of conclusion theory is to avoid the continual reevaluation of all hypotheses, to instead accept certain strong hypotheses as *conclusions*, and to hold these conclusions unless and until the introduction of very strong contrary evidence. Although Dacey apparently intends that the set of conclusions be the set of beliefs of the reasoner, his reasoner is isolated and unreflective, in that the rules of adoption and abandonment are used in developing scientific laws *de novo*. Once communication or summaries of conclusions are desired, as in writing an initially substantive AI program, the form of each conclusion seems to approximate that of a default. Thus, conclusion theory might be adapted to the role of judging the propriety of adopting or abandoning defaults.

The Mathematics of Theory Evolution

Each of the approaches above treats in detail primarily the atoms of reasoning, either individual inference steps or the sets of beliefs preceding and following the inference step. So far, much less attention has been devoted to classifying the larger, more complex ways in which nondeductive inferences can change the current set of beliefs of a reasoner. The beginnings of a larger analysis of theory evolution are touched on by McDermott and Doyle (1980), Doyle (1979, 1980), Gumb (1978, 1979), Weyhrauch (1980), and, less formally, in the philosophy of science literature in general (e.g., Quine and Ullian, 1978).

References

The area of nonmonotonic reasoning has to date supplied more questions than definitive answers, but the questions it raises are vital. For further information, peruse the papers collected in the special issue of *Artificial Intelligence* on nonmonotonic logic (such as those cited above) and the papers indexed in the bibliography by Doyle and London (1980). Further fruitful formalizations of nondeductive reasoning techniques may well be awaiting discovery. For example, Collins (1978) and, less directly, Wason and Johnson-Laird (1972) investigate patterns of human nondeductive reasoning. Which of these may now succumb to formal analysis?

F. LOGIC PROGRAMMING

LOGIC PROGRAMMING refers to a family of higher level languages and an associated programming style based on writing programs as sets of assertions. These assertions are viewed as having *declarative* meaning as descriptive statements about entities and relations. In addition, the assertions derive a *procedural* meaning by virtue of being executable by an interpreter. Indeed, executing a logic program is much like performing a deduction on a set of facts.

A logic program consists of a set of clauses, where the general form of a clause is:

$$\langle\text{consequent}\rangle :- \langle\text{antecedent}_1\rangle, \langle\text{antecedent}_2\rangle, \ldots, \langle\text{antecedent}_n\rangle$$

and each item in a clause is a positive literal, that is, an atomic formula $P(\text{term}_1, \ldots, \text{term}_n)$ for some predicate P. Not all clauses have antecedents.

A simple logic program for reversing a list is given by the following set of clauses:

```
APPEND(NIL,X,X)
APPEND(CONS(X,Y),Z,CONS(X,U)) :- APPEND(Y,Z,U)
REVERSE(NIL,NIL)
REVERSE(CONS(X,Y),Z) :- REVERSE(Y,R), APPEND(R,CONS(X,NIL),Z) .
```

Two observations must be made about this program: First, the terms involving CONS are not evaluated as they would be in LISP; rather, they are treated as symbolic objects. Second, both APPEND and REVERSE take one more argument than the corresponding LISP function. This is because APPEND(X,Y,Z) does not name a function but, rather, names the relation *Z is the result of appending X and Y*. Similarly, REVERSE(X,Y) means *Y is the result of reversing X*. One consequence of this is that a logic program, unlike its LISP counterpart, can often be run backwards. For example, the APPEND program could be used to find pairs of lists that, when concatenated, yield a given list.

To execute a logic program, we supply a *goal*, for example, REVERSE (CONS(A,CONS(B,CONS(C,NIL))),X). The interpreter finds substitutions for X that make the formula a consequence of the clauses in the program. This is done by cycling through the clauses, matching the goal against the consequent (by unification; see Article XII.B), recursively setting up antecedents as subgoals, and backtracking in case of failure. If all the subgoals can be satisfied, the goal is proved, and the substitutions found during matching constitute an answer. Forced backtracking can be used to produce systematically all substitutions that make the goal provable. For the goal above, the interpreter would find the substitution CONS(C,CONS(B,CONS(A,NIL))) for X.

120

One feature that distinguishes logic programming from ordinary theorem-proving is that, while the declarative semantics allow the clauses—and the antecedents within a clause—to appear in any order, the procedural interpretation is sensitive to the order. Thus, the programmer can rely on assertions being searched in sequence, top to bottom and left to right, and can structure a program for maximum efficiency.

Another difference between logic programming and general theorem-proving has to do with the restrictions on the form of the assertions themselves. In theorem-proving terminology, logic programs consist of sets of Horn clauses—disjunctive formulas with at most one positive literal. It is easy to see that the clauses of a logic program are Horn clauses: Any disjunction of the form $\neg A \lor \neg B \lor \cdots \lor \neg C \lor D$ can be rewritten as an equivalent implicational formula, $A \, \& \, B \, \& \cdots \& \, C \to D$, which is a notational variant of the form of clauses in logic programs.

By enforcing this restriction to Horn clauses, logic programming ensures relative tractability of deductions. It should be noted that, as with most very-high-level programming languages, it is not hard to write extremely inefficient logic programs—especially since the interpreter's basic strategy is exhaustive backtracking. Many implementations give the programmer some control over backtracking and allow the insertion of a special symbol (typically a slash, "/") between antecedents in a clause to prevent backtracking past that literal. This often improves efficiency, but at the expense of semantic purity, since some deductive consequences of the clauses may be underivable while other formulas, not logical consequences of the clauses, may be "deduced" from failure to derive a fact. (This latter case corresponds to the THNOT construct in the PLANNER languages.)

Logic Programming and AI

Although logic programming has been applied to diverse problems, some of which can hardly be considered exclusively AI problems (e.g., database management), there are at least two reasons why logic programming has special importance for AI. First, logic programming offers an alternative to LISP as a powerful language for symbol manipulation, apart from the semantic content of the symbols qua representations. The interpreters that drive logic programs do unification (Robinson, 1965b, and Article XII.B) and, thus, already incorporate the pattern-matching machinery that many applications require and that is programmed explicitly in LISP.

The second, and more important, reason why logic programming is of interest to AI has to do with its usefulness for knowledge representation. Predicate logic is a formalism considered by many to be a natural and powerful representation language marred only by its perceived computational inefficiency (see Article III.C1, in Vol. I). Any approach based on logic that can demonstrate efficient execution (which logic programming does, in fact, claim) would be a serious candidate as a representation language.

To see how a logic program could be used to represent real-world knowledge, consider the following simple set of clauses:

```
SEES(X,Y) :- PERSON(X), PHYSOBJ(Y), OPEN(EYES(X)), IN-FRONT-OF(X,Y)
SEES(X,Y) :- PERSON(X), EVENT(Y), WATCHING(X, FILM-OF(Y))
PERSON(MOTHER(John))
EVENT(BIRTHDAY(Henry))
EVENT(GRADUATION(John))
WATCHING(MOTHER(John), FILM-OF(GRADUATION(John))) .
```

Consider the following three goals:

1. SEES(MOTHER(John), GRADUATION(John))
2. SEES(MOTHER(U), GRADUATION(U))
3. SEES(U,V)

These goals can be viewed as queries to a deductive question-answering system. The first can be paraphrased *Did John's mother see his graduation?*—a yes/no question. The second and third goals resemble "Wh-questions"—the free variables U and V indicating that the answer is to be the individual or individuals satisfying the condition. In particular, the second goal corresponds to the question *Who is it whose mother saw his graduation?* The third asks simply, *Who saw what?*

The logic-program interpreter would cycle through the asserted facts, matching the goal against the consequent and solving the antecedents as subgoals. If the subgoals can be satisfied, the goal is proved and the answer to the yes/no question will be YES. If, after exhaustively trying alternative facts, the goal still cannot be proved, the answer is NO. For goals with variables, the system can produce all substitutions that make the goal provable. With the clauses given above, the answer for goal 1 would be YES; the answer for goal 2 would be $U =$ John; and the answer for goal 3 would be $U =$ MOTHER(John), $V =$ GRADUATION(John).

Development of Logic Programming and Current Status

The parallels between computation and logical proof have long been recognized, especially in the theory of computation. An interesting discussion of the many connections between logic and computation can be found in an early work of McCarthy (1963). In a sense, executing an applicative program, for example, a program in "pure" LISP, can be thought of as calculating the proof of an identity "$f(\text{arg}_1, \text{arg}_2, \ldots) = \text{result}$" by applying various axioms of identity according to a fixed control regime, much as the assertions of a logic program are applied.

Ordinarily, logic programming is understood to refer more narrowly to the style of programming introduced and advocated by Kowalski (1974, 1979), which was eventually incorporated into PROLOG, the best-known of the logic programming languages. PROLOG has several dialects and is supported in numerous installations in the United States, in Britain, and on the Continent. Especially active groups are in Edinburgh, London, Marseilles, and Budapest. Diverse applications have been programmed in PROLOG, including natural-language processing (Colmerauer et al., 1973), database retrieval (Warren, 1981), and program synthesis and planning (Warren, 1974).

PROLOG, and logic programming in general, has increased in popularity in recent years. In Europe, especially, PROLOG is a serious contender as the major AI implementation language. Much effort has been devoted to developing PROLOG compilers that compete favorably with LISP in efficiency of generated code (Warren, Pereira, and Pereira, 1977). In the United States, also, there has been interest in PROLOG, as well as in LOGLISP, a LISP-based logic-programming system developed at Syracuse University (Robinson and Sibert, 1980).

Conclusion

To a certain extent, the development of logic programming has followed the pattern of LISP. Both languages are founded on clear, mathematically motivated formalisms. Both languages have a side-effect-free kernel and a procedural interpretation that can be defined in a simple and elegant fashion. Yet both language families have yielded to the practical needs of their user communities and have incorporated numerous features that detract from their underlying elegance in favor of improved convenience and efficiency. In a sense, the fact that logic programming has progressed to the point of incorporating such features attests to its practicality and growing popularity.

References

Kowalski (1974, 1979) discusses logic programming and Warren, Pereira, and Pereira (1977) discuss the PROLOG language.

Chapter XIII

Vision

CHAPTER XIII: VISION

A. OVERVIEW

VISION is the information-processing task of understanding a scene from its projected images. An image is a two-dimensional function $f(x, y)$, obtained with a sensing device (see Article XIII.C1), that records the value of an image feature at all points (x, y). Values might be binary for black-or-white images, gray level (i.e., intensity) for half-tone images, or vectors of color measures for color images. Images are converted into a digital form for processing with a computer. An array $\{f_{i,j}\}$ of small picture-elements called *pixels* represents the image by recording the values of measurements at each pixel position (Article XIII.C1).

The task of a computer-vision system is to understand the scene that an image—an array of pixels—depicts. However, many fields claim similar tasks as their goal, among them, picture processing, image processing, pattern recognition, scene analysis, image interpretation, optical processing, video processing, and image understanding. These fields overlap to some extent, though each has its own history and character. For the purpose of clarifying the goals and methods of vision research, we categorize these fields into *signal processing*, *classification*, and *understanding*.

Signal processing. Signal processors transform an input image into another image that has desirable properties. For example, the output image may have a better signal-to-noise ratio or may be enhanced by emphasizing the details to facilitate human inspection. The content of the image is often irrelevant. *Image processing* and *picture processing* are the most common terms for this class of processing. As well as digital techniques, optical techniques and electric video-signal techniques can often provide a very fast throughput.

Classification. Classification techniques classify images into predetermined categories. Character recognition is a typical example. Often, a predetermined set of feature values is extracted from images, and the decision of how closely an image "fits" a class is made on the basis of statistical decision methods applied to the multidimensional feature space. There is a large body of theory for designing optimal decision rules. These methods are usually called *pattern recognition* or *pattern classification*, although the word *recognition* is used only for historical reasons.

Understanding. Given an image, an *image-understanding program* builds a description not only of the image itself but also of the scene it depicts. In the early years of AI vision research, the term *scene analysis* was often used to emphasize the distinction between processing two-dimensional images (as in pattern classification) and three-dimensional scenes. Image

understanding requires knowledge about the task world, as well as sophisticated image-processing techniques.

In this chapter, we emphasize image-understanding research and say
very little about signal-processing and pattern-recognition operations such as
image enhancement, frequency-domain techniques, and statistical pattern-
recognition methods. These techniques are covered only briefly in Articles
XIII.C1, XIII.C3, and XIII.C4.

There are a few levels of information processing in computer vision. The
lowest level of vision systems that we will discuss extracts primitive features,
such as change of intensity and orientation of edge elements, from the original
intensity array. This is often called *low-level vision*, or *early processing*; it is
covered in Section XIII.C. After early processing, the higher level features, such
as lines and regions, and shape information, such as surface orientation and
occlusion, are extracted. This level of processing is sometimes called *intermediate processing*, or *segmentation* in the context of extracting meaningful
lines and regions. *High-level vision* processes (also called *later processing*) deal
with objects and rely on domain-specific knowledge to construct descriptions
of scenes.

Problems for Vision Research

Vision is easy for humans, but it is very difficult to construct a comparable
computer-vision system. There are several reasons for this. First of all, an
image underconstrains a scene: It does not provide enough information, by
itself, to recover the scene. Among others, the depth dimension is collapsed
by the projection of a three-dimensional scene to a two-dimensional picture.
Additional constraints are needed to resolve such ambiguities. These can be
based on reasonable assumptions or on measurements, but without them the
vision task cannot be accomplished.

Another reason that vision is difficult is that many factors are confounded
in an image. The appearance of an object is influenced by its surface material,
the atmospheric conditions, the angle of the light source, the ambient light,
the camera angle and characteristics, and so on. All of these factors contribute
to a single measurement, say, intensity of a pixel. It is difficult to determine
the contribution of each factor to a pixel value.

Third, understanding an image (and understanding in general) requires
a priori knowledge of the task domain. For most interpretive tasks, features
observable in the image can be very weak, but one knows what one is looking
for; image understanding is impossible without such expectations. Image-
understanding systems are often "blind" to objects that cannot be matched
to stored representations.

A fourth difficulty with vision research is that humans are vision experts,
but it is very difficult to introspect about how they see. It is difficult to

perform a protocol analysis of vision as one would with a process like problem solving (see Article IX.B).

A final problem for vision is practical—an engineering problem: A computer vision system must process an enormous amount of information, even for a simple task. For example, an aerial photo is typically digitized into 3,000 × 3,000 pixels with 8 bits per pixel, or 9 Mbytes per image. A simple edge-detection process that performs, say, 10 operations per pixel requires 90 million operations for an image!

Delineating these problems was itself a result of years of vision research. Computer vision systems have become more capable as these and other problems have become better understood. In the next section, we review some of the important issues in computer vision, in the context of a history of vision research.

Issues in the History of Computer Vision

Early research: Bottom-up approach. There was computer image-processing prior to computer vision. This work included character recognition, processing images of chromosomes to classify their shapes and to obtain karyotypes, and manipulating line figures. Most such research involved processing and classifying two-dimensional patterns.

The pioneering work in computer vision was no doubt that of Roberts (1965; Article XIII.B1). His program understood polyhedral block scenes. The image of a scene was first preprocessed to reduce noise, and then the first spatial derivatives of intensity were computed at each pixel in the image. Pixels having high derivative values were selected as edge elements (since they correspond to places where intensity changes rapidly) and then grouped into lines with a least-squares method. The input image was converted into a line drawing in this way.

Roberts' program had access to three-dimensional models of objects: a cube, a rectangular solid, a wedge, and a hexagonal prism. They were represented by the coordinates (x, y, z) of their vertices. The program recognized these objects in the line drawing of the scene. A candidate model was selected on the basis of simple features such as the number of vertices. Then the selected model was rotated, scaled, projected, and matched with the input line drawing. If the match was good, the object was recognized, as were its position and size. Roberts' program could handle even a composite object made of multiple primitive shapes; it subtracted parts of a line drawing from the drawing as they were recognized, and the remaining portions were analyzed further.

Most of the components of today's vision programs—preprocessing, edge detection, construction of line drawings, modeling objects, and matching—appeared in Roberts' program. However, his recognition process proceeded sequentially from low to high levels and from image to object. Most of the early work on computer vision took this sequential bottom-up approach.

Segmentation: Lines and regions. The success of any bottom-up approach to interpretation depends on the fidelity of low-level and intermediate-level processes. Thus, in the early years of vision research, numerous techniques were developed for extracting lines and edges from images. All were similar to Roberts' original method: At each pixel position, a computation is made over a small local area around it to see whether or not the pixel is on an edge. This typically involves computing a derivative, or a correlation of the actual edge with a template of an ideal edge. These local computations are usually represented as operators that see the image through a small window (between 2×2 and 15×15 pixels). The operator is moved over the image pixel by pixel and yields high output for edge-element candidates. Usually, the output is thresholded to produce a binary image with a value of 1 at edge pixels and 0 elsewhere. Several edge operators are presented in Article XIII.C4.

After edge elements are detected, they are grouped into meaningful lines. This can be done by tracing the edge elements according to a rule. The goal of tracing is to connect edge elements, but gaps, sudden curves, and false edge elements (caused by noise) complicate the process; thus, the tracing rule needs to be quite sophisticated.

Regions are another important primitive image element. Segmenting an image into regions became a popular technique following the work of Brice and Fennema (1970). Region segmentation is exactly complementary to edge detection; instead of finding areas of contrasting intensities, region segmentation finds areas of pixels with similar intensities. The properties of and relations between regions were used to match regions with models of objects. This approach is called region analysis (see Article XIII.C5).

The objective of the segmentation process—either by edge detection or region analysis—is to obtain a description of an image in terms of meaningful lines or regions, so that it can be compared with the models. Despite considerable effort in edge detection and region analysis, it turned out that segmentation was very difficult. In edge detection, for example, a low threshold allows one to detect low-contrast edges but also detects fraud edges due to smear or surface variation; a higher threshold is less sensitive, both to noise and to true edges. In tracing lines, two distinct lines may be identified as one. In region analysis, regions may be overdivided or underdivided—a region may correspond to more than one surface, or surface variations may split a whole surface into several regions. These problems can be minimized by setting up the environment carefully and tuning various threshold parameters. But obtaining *meaningful* elements cannot be solved without some external, top-down, and possibly heuristic knowledge.

Heuristics. The first extensive use of heuristics for image understanding was due to Guzman (1968a; Article XIII.B2). His program, SEE, could segment a line drawing into three-dimensional bodies. Guzman classified types of

junctions that appear in line drawings and made the important observation
that a junction type makes a local suggestion about plausible associations of
regions into objects. For instance, the psi junction type (junction which looks
like ψ) is often seen in an aligned pillar of blocks. Thus, it suggests that
the upper two regions belong to a single body and the lower two to another.
Guzman represented this heuristic rule of region association with links that
connect the regions that possibly belong to the same object.

The SEE program links regions according to these heuristic rules about
junctions. Regions that are associated by many links probably constitute a
single object, while regions of different objects will have none or a few links
between them. Still, the linking heuristics do not say conclusively which
regions belong to which objects, so Guzman designed another set of heuristics
for partitioning regions into objects according to the number, strength, and
topology of links between regions. He developed the SEE program by adding
and revising heuristics as he found cases for which the current version did not
work. Eventually, SEE could correctly segment very complicated line drawings
into objects.

Guzman's work was one of the distinguished successes in the early period
of heuristic approaches to vision. It demonstrated that line drawings could be
interpreted by symbolic processes instead of numerical matching procedures
such as least-squares fit of lines. The research also focused attention on
the blocks world, showing it to be an abstract problem domain, free from
uncontrolled noise and artifacts that obscure essential issues.

But Guzman's approach also had fundamental difficulties. Although
SEE recognized three-dimensional objects, its heuristics were tied to the two-
dimensional picture domain. There was no explicit treatment of three-
dimensional *scene features*. Second, his heuristics were very ad hoc and there
was little physical basis for them. This was especially true of the heuristics
that grouped regions into objects by manipulating the graph made by regions
(as nodes) and links (as arcs). But these problems—reasoning only with
picture-domain features and ad hoc features—were not unique to Guzman's
approach; they recur throughout vision research.

Higher level knowledge. The sequential, bottom-up approach has
difficulty segmenting images in a meaningful way. Even in a simple blocks
world, it seems almost impossible to extract a perfect line drawing. In fact,
there is a dilemma; a drawing is "perfect" only after it is interpreted, but
a successful interpretation depends on a perfect line drawing. One solution
to this circularity was to give programs knowledge of their task domain—
top-down models of the objects in their worlds. Falk's (1972) INTERPRET
used models to aid interpretation of imperfect line drawings. It analyzed a
drawing and hypothesized objects and their orientations, then *predicted* the
line drawing of the hypothesized scene, and finally tried to verify it.

The active use of models became very popular, as did terms like *model-
based, top-down, semantic,* and *goal-driven*. In some systems, models simply

verified results, but, in others, the models totally controlled what to see where. Representative programs are Shirai's semantic line finder (Shirai, 1973; Article XIII.B6), Yakimovsky and Feldman's (1973) semantic-based region analyzer, and Tenenbaum and Barrow's (1976a) interpretation-guided segmentation. Shirai's program guessed where lines would be found by extending lines it had already found. It worked from easier lines (such as lines between white blocks and black background) to difficult lines (such as internal lines). Yakimovsky and Feldman took a decision-theoretic approach to region growing: Regions were merged so that a certain probability of correct interpretation was maximized. Tenenbaum and Barrow used a table of constraints on object-object relations (e.g., *A adjacent to B*) and object-property relations (e.g., *A is bright*), as well as a filtering procedure and relaxation method that repeatedly eliminated inconsistent labels from a set of possible labels for each region (see Article XIII.E4 for a discussion of this program).

These systems are, for the most part, subject to the same criticism that was leveled against the bottom-up systems: They do not distinguish between image characteristics and scene characteristics. For example, the knowledge in the scene domain (e.g., object *A* is "on" object *B*) is used in such a degenerated sense that region *A* is "above" region *B* in the image. More recent model-based systems show a sharp contrast in this respect; for example, ACRONYM (Brooks, 1981b; Article XIII.F3) makes a clear distinction between observable image features, object-class models, and the specific object model.

Applications. While a basic understanding of the vision process seemed to be very difficult, many important applications of computer vision technology were found in a number of fields. One area is the processing and interpretation of two-dimensional images. This includes medical applications such as screening cancer examinations by tissue image analysis, remote-sensing applications such as satellite image analysis for monitoring natural resources, and industrial applications such as inspecting printed circuit boards. Computer tomography (CT) is a notable success in the area of generating and analyzing images. Advances in computer technology and reductions in hardware costs have made these applications practically feasible.

Visual sensing for robots is another important application of computer vision. Early research was done in the Hand–Eye projects of the early 1970s, and today the field has an urgent mandate to make robots more versatile and flexible and, thus, to increase productivity in industry. Three-dimensional information is important for robots, so range-finding methods have been developed to measure depth directly. (Range finders are discussed in Article XIII.D4, and robot systems in Article XIII.F1.) The generalized cylinder—an important representational tool for three-dimensional shape—emerged from the research of range-data analysis (Agin and Binford, 1973; see Article XIII.D6). The generalized cylinder represents a volume as the volume swept by a cross section along a three-dimensional space axis. The axis can be an arbitrary three-dimensional curve. The shape of the cross section can be arbitrary and it can even change shape by a certain rule as it moves along the axis. A usual cylinder is obtained by sweeping a disk along a line, and if the disk size shrinks linearly a cone is obtained. This representation provides a good means for describing complex objects by part/whole segmentation with natural semantics.

Geometry and physics. In 1971, Huffman and Clowes (see Article XIII.B4) independently made the crucial observation that lines in a drawing can mean (or depict) different three-dimensional entities, even though they *look* the same as two-dimensional entities, and that they must be distinguished on the basis of the physical role of their corresponding three-dimensional edges. For example, a line in a drawing can depict a *boundary* or a *connect* edge. Boundary edges are found when an object occludes another or occludes the background; connect edges are found when two surfaces meet along their edges. Connect edges are further divided into convex and concave edges. Huffman gave distinct labels to these kinds of edges: "+" for convex, "−" for concave, and "↑" for an occluding boundary. Interpreting a line drawing as a three-dimensional scene involves assigning these labels to the lines.

The advantage of interpreting images in terms of physical features is that the interpretive process can utilize the constraints imposed by the physical world: A line can have only one interpretation at a time, and, what is more important, certain combinations of line labels at a junction are not physically possible. Waltz (1972; Article XIII.B5) extended this idea to a larger set of line classifications, including shadows and cracks. Interestingly, and contrary to intuition, increasing the number of line types constrains more on possible labelings, because a smaller percentage of the combinatorially possible line junctions are physically realizable.

Of all scene features, shape information is most important. Thus, theoretical and systematic study of geometrical representations for vision began. Huffman (1971) and Mackworth (1973; Article XIII.B7) popularized the *gradient space* as a powerful tool for reasoning about surface orientation. It represents surfaces in a parametric space, specifically, in a two-dimensional gradient space in which the axes represent the amount of tilt of a surface with respect to the optical axis of the viewer. Scene properties such as convexity, concavity, perpendicularity, and smoothness can be conveniently represented in it. (Recently, the *Gaussian sphere* has proved a more general and preferable tool for vision; see Kender, 1980)

Mackworth's POLY (1973; Article XIII.B7) interpreted line drawings by reasoning about the gradients (orientations) of surfaces. Prior to this work, line labeling represented only a qualitative interpretation of lines. Consequently, objects with the same qualitative labeling but different quantitative parameters could not be distinguished; for example, a trapezoidal block differs from a cube in its angle measurements, not in its qualitative labeling. Using gradients, Kanade (1979; Article XIII.B8) demonstrated quantitative shape recovery from line drawings; with this more complete specification of the scene, he was able to predict how the scene would look from different angles of view. Similarly, a formal approach was taken by Kender (1980) in developing a theory of how *texture* could be used to make inferences about the three-dimensional structure of a scene. The approach common to these researchers is to map *image* features, such as length and angles in the image, into three-dimensional shape constraints, by *explicitly* assigning assumptions and representing the constraints in an appropriate space. In this way, the heuristics can be used in a well-understood (rather than ad hoc) manner (Kanade and Kender, 1980).

Physics, especially photometrics, also came into play. Shading is known to give important cues for shape, especially for smooth, curved surfaces. Horn (1975, 1977) initiated a pioneering work on shape-from-shading theory, which gave a deep insight into the low-level vision process. It was first formulated as simultaneous partial differential equations and then reformulated taking advantage of the gradient-space representation. Under certain assumptions, the image intensity value (I) at a point in the *image* can be related to the surface orientation (p, q) at the corresponding three-dimensional *scene* point. Thus, we have a mapping $f : (p, q) \rightarrow I$. The task of shape from shading is to find the inverse of this mapping. In general, the inverse function $f^{-1} : I \rightarrow (p, q)$ alone does not give a unique orientation for the point. Other constraints, for example, assuming a smooth surface, are needed. Or there may be another image taken in different lighting conditions, from which to generate another mapping $f_2 : (p, q) \rightarrow I$; then both f^{-1} and f_2^{-1} may yield a unique solution. This method is called *photometric stereo*.

Barrow and Tenenbaum (1978; Article XIII.D1) discuss the problem of recovering intrinsic characteristics (distance, orientation, reflectance, etc.) from images. They propose an iconic representation of these scene characteristics in the form of images that are registered with the original image. These are aptly called *intrinsic images*. Once we have intrinsic images, operations like segmentation become fairly simple.

Thus, in effect, recent vision research has begun to go back to the geometry and physics that govern vision processes and to represent them in a computationally tractable form. This has turned out to be a powerful approach to the problems of motion, texture, shading, and stereo.

Marr's theory of vision. Marr presented a theory of vision that emphasized the importance of choosing appropriate representations for different levels of the vision process. His approach, as well as his results and those of his students, had a great deal of influence in vision research. (It is unfortunate that Marr died in 1980 before he saw his theory of vision fully developed and implemented.)

Marr (1978) pointed out that it is important to understand vision at two levels: the first level that specifies what is being computed and why (competence theories) and the second level of particular algorithms to carry out the computation (performance theories). For example, the theory of the Fourier transform is at level 1, and algorithms like the Fast Fourier Transform or the parallel algorithms of coherent optics are at level 2. Marr then argued that the theory of computation (level 1) must precede the design of algorithms (level 2) and that vision researchers must not confuse the two.

The role of a representation is to make certain information explicit at an appropriate point in the analysis of an image. Thus, the choice or invention of a representation affects the success of analysis. Marr discussed the vision process in terms of three levels of representation: Starting from images, the framework consists of *primal sketch, $2\frac{1}{2}$-D sketch,* and *3-D model representation.* The primal sketch makes information about intensity change explicit, the $2\frac{1}{2}$-D sketch makes information about the surface explicit, and the 3-D model makes information about object shape explicit.

Based on this framework, Marr and his colleagues studied methods to obtain one representation from another. Obtaining the primal sketch from raw image data involves edge detection and zero-crossings (Marr and Hildreth, 1980), and stereo disparity (Marr and Poggio, 1977; Grimson, 1980) and motion (Ullman, 1979) are used to obtain the $2\frac{1}{2}$-D sketch. Marr and Nishihara (1978) discuss the problem of computing the 3-D model from a $2\frac{1}{2}$-D sketch. They represented three-dimensional model shapes of stick figures (such as humans) hierarchically from overall description to detailed elaboration of its components.

The approaches discussed earlier that emphasize geometry and physics and Marr's theory of vision are both prone to the bottom-up processing from image to object. As we mentioned in the discussion of segmentation, image interpretation is difficult without top-down models. However, these new approaches differ critically from the older (ad hoc) bottom-up methods in that they are based on physical properties of the world. Once appropriate representations are selected—be they intrinsic images, primal sketches, or $2\frac{1}{2}$-D sketches—the constraints that the world provides can be systematically exploited.

The Image Understanding Program. The ARPA-sponsored Image Understanding Program started in 1975. Its purpose is

> to investigate application of a priori knowledge to facilitate an understanding of the relationship among objects in a scene. The appropriate focus is on the world understanding.... [The Image Understanding Program] is a catalyst which attempts an integration of many sciences [image processing, pattern recognition, computer science, artificial intelligence, neurophysiology, and physics] in search of methods for automatic extraction of information from imagery. (Druffel, 1981, pp. 2–3)

Efforts within the program range from the development of a cohesive theory of vision to the hardware issues of processing systems. For example, several knowledge-based systems for photo-interpretation tasks were developed, including ACRONYM (Brooks, 1981a), Interactive Aids for Cartography and Photo Interpretation (Barrow et al., 1977), Road Expert (Bolles et al., 1978), and Integrated Image and Map Database for Photo Interpretation (McKeown and Kanade, 1981). Photo interpretation is discussed in this chapter as the most obvious application of image understanding.

Organization of This Chapter

The remaining five sections of this chapter discuss aspects of vision research ranging from the *blocks world* to applications in robotics. Section XIII.B presents a chronological survey of blocks-world research. Section XIII.C discusses techniques for early processing of image features. Section XIII.D raises some issues involved in reasoning about scene features and presents some useful representational tools and techniques. Section XIII.E discusses algorithmic tools for matching and reasoning about features—often image-level features. Sections XIII.C and XIII.E are related by Marr's distinction between the theory of computation and the design of algorithms. Finally, Section XIII.F offers a glimpse of how various vision methods are integrated into a whole vision system.

Blocks worlds. Many important issues for vision research have been first proposed and explored in the context of blocks worlds, because they are simplified by explicit assumptions about the physical structure of the world. Usually, these assumptions limit the kinds of *vertices* at which surfaces meet and, thus, the kinds of objects that can exist. For example, the *trihedral world* is constituted of objects that have exactly three surfaces meeting at any vertex.

One of the advantages of blocks-world research is that observed features correspond to real physical features: A line corresponds to an edge, and a region of homogeneous intensity corresponds to a surface. This situation is more tractable than one in which image features may not correspond to scene features; for example, a cylinder appears to have two parallel edges where the surface of the cylinder disappears from view, but these image features do not directly correspond to any features of the cylinder itself.

The main disadvantage of blocks worlds is that they are so constrained that associated image-understanding methods do not generalize to the real world. One consequence is that it is hard to test the adequacy of blocks-world representations. This is a valid criticism of individual blocks-world techniques, but maybe not of the blocks-world approach. All vision systems constrain their environments by assumptions; the advantage of the blocks-world approach is that it makes the assumptions explicit.

Early processing of image features. Section XIII.C covers several techniques for *early processing* of image features. Some articles in the section deal with representations of image features, and some discuss methods for improving and changing the representations of images. The first articles present the lowest level operations on image data, starting with taking a picture of a scene (Article XIII.C1). Once a picture is obtained, *preprocessing* techniques suppress unwanted details such as noise and enhance aspects such as lines (Article XIII.C3). In fact, line-finding is a fundamental operation in vision research; it is discussed in Article XIII.C4. Regions of homogeneous intensity, color, or texture are also important image features; methods for finding regions are discussed in Article XIII.C5, and color and texture are discussed separately in Articles XIII.C2 and XIII.C6, respectively.

All of the techniques in Section XIII.C deal with *image* features. No attempt is made to infer anything about the scene with these techniques.

Scene characteristics. The main problem of vision research is deciding what the three-dimensional world looks like from two-dimensional images (Sec. XIII.D). This involves inferring *scene features* from *image features*. Scene characteristics, sometimes called *intrinsic* characteristics, include the tilt, reflectivity, and smoothness of surfaces, as well as the arrangement of texture. These features are discussed in Article XIII.D1.

The problems for research on scene characteristics include determining useful intrinsic characteristics, figuring out how to represent them and how to reason with them. A few representational tools have been developed that facilitate reasoning, including *generalized cylinders* (Article XIII.D6) and *gradient space* (Article XIII.B7). Methods of obtaining scene features from various sources of information are discussed: motion (Article XIII.D2), stereo (Article XIII.D3), range finders (Article XIII.D4), and shape-from methods (Article XIII.D5; specifically, shape from shading and shape from texture).

Algorithms for vision. Section XIII.E discusses algorithmic tools used in computer vision to perform matching and interpretation. Historically, these techniques have been applied most often to pixel-level and image-level features. (The theory for extracting these features is discussed in Section XIII.C.)

The first article in Section XIII.E discusses hierarchical representations of image features called *pyramids* and *quad trees* (Article XIII.E1). These representations improve the efficiency of reasoning about image features. The most basic method for matching and recognition is *template matching* (Article XIII.E2). *Syntactic* methods are related to template matching, but they involve "parsing" pictures, as if they were sentences made up of primitives (Article XIII.E3). A more sophisticated procedure is *relaxation* (Article XIII.E4), first encountered as *Waltz filtering* in Article XIII.B5. Relaxation requires that there be constraints among primitives and a method for propagating the constraints.

Systems. The last section of the chapter (Sec. XIII.F) is devoted to practical vision systems, rather than vision methods. In the ACRONYM system (Article XIII.F3), the user specifies parametric models of objects in the world to aid image understanding. The same is true of the systems discussed in Article XIII.F2. Robot vision (Article XIII.F1) is an interesting case because it is usually found in applications where there is detailed knowledge of the environment; in these cases, the deficits in data—poor-quality, low-resolution images—can be compensated by strong top-down models.

References

There are several good textbooks and survey papers on vision. Duda and Hart (1973) deal with techniques for pattern recognition. Rosenfeld (1969) and Rosenfeld and Kak (1976) present image-processing techniques. Winston (1977) includes vision from a general AI point of view. Ballard and Brown (1982) describe recent computer vision work. Interesting collections of papers from seminars are found in Hanson and Riseman (1978a) and Dodd and Rossel (1979). Ballard (1981) discusses low-level vision from a parallel-computation point of view. Marr (1978) presents his theory of vision together with the results of his group. Kanade (1980a) argues for his model of vision systems by emphasizing the importance of the distinction between image and scene. Mackworth (1977) reviews the history of blocks-world understanding.

B. BLOCKS–WORLD UNDERSTANDING

B1. Recognition of Three-dimensional Objects: L. G. Roberts

ONE of the first researchers to be concerned with the recognition of three-dimensional objects was L. G. Roberts (**1965**). Previous research in vision had dealt primarily with the recognition of two-dimensional forms such as alphabetic characters. Roberts noted that the problem of recognizing and describing the solid objects in a picture requires a different approach from that of processing two-dimensional forms. A two-dimensional representation of a two-dimensional object is substantially like the object, but a two-dimensional representation of a three-dimensional object introduces a perspective projection that makes the representation ambiguous with respect to the object. Thus, Roberts' approach involved describing the three-dimensional environment that generated the picture, rather than describing the picture itself; that is, he examined the picture-taking process by which a perspective projection is obtained from a three-dimensional scene. A discussion of the picture-taking process is found in Article XIII.C1; we will not duplicate it here.

Roberts chose a simple domain consisting of cubes, rectangular solids, wedges, and hexagonal prisms. He studied scenes of these objects in arbitrary spatial configurations. The program he developed analyzed a photograph of a scene and identified all the visible objects. Furthermore, it determined their orientations and positions in three-dimensional space.

Models

Roberts represented each possible type of object (cube, wedge, hexagonal prism) in a three-dimensional coordinate system; this representation is called a *model*. Figure B1–1 depicts the model of a cube. An object in a scene may differ from its model, because it may occupy a different position and orientation in three-dimensional space and because it may have a different length in its dimension. A transformation matrix, **R**, can be obtained that transforms a model into a scene object by means of rotation, translation, and size change (**R** is represented by homogeneous coordinates; see Article XIII.C1).

Roberts' Program

The first step that Roberts' program takes is to make a line drawing of a photograph; this step will not be described here (see Article XIII.C4). Given the line drawing (Fig. B1–2), the next step is to find the model (cube, wedge,

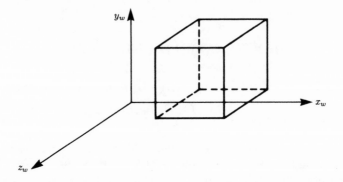

Figure B1–1.   The cube model in the three-dimensional world system.

or hexagonal prism) that best matches the picture. A list of two-dimensional features is associated with each model; when these are found in a picture, they are used to index the appropriate models.

The interior polygons A, B, and C in Figure B1–2 correspond to surfaces of the object. The point, P, at which all the polygons come together is used as a reference point. This point and its three surrounding polygons constitute a feature; a search of the models finds that a cube and perhaps other models have three quadrilaterals about one point. A point in the cube model with the proper polygons around it is then selected, and topologically equivalent point-pairs are listed, resulting in seven three-dimensional points from the model and seven corresponding two-dimensional points from the picture. This procedure is repeated for any other models that pass the initial topology test.

Once a set of potential models has been found, the best fitting model is determined. The point pairs obtained above are used in this step. Recall that matrix $\mathbf{R}$ transforms the model into the object. In addition, the perspective transform, which maps from scene points to image points, can be represented as a matrix $\mathbf{P}$ (see Article XIII.C1). Then,

$$\mathbf{H} = \mathbf{PR} \tag{1}$$

transforms the model points into picture points.

The best transform, $\mathbf{H}$, that takes the seven model points into the seven corresponding picture points is found. A mean-square error that indicates how well the model fits the picture is also obtained for each model. The model with the least error is chosen.

The next step is to determine the position and orientation of the object in three-dimensional space. From equation (1), we derive

$$\mathbf{R} = \mathbf{P}^{-1}\mathbf{H}.$$

The transform $\mathbf{H}$ has just been calculated, and $\mathbf{P}$ is the perspective transformation, which is also known. Thus, we can calculate $\mathbf{R}$, the transformation of

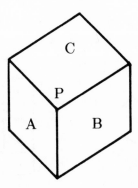

Figure B1–2.   Line drawing of a picture of a rectangular solid.

the model into the object. This gives us the precise orientation and position of the object and also the dimensions of the object relative to its total size. We lack only the depth variable that represents the distance of the object from the picture plane. This must be found some other way.

To calculate depth, the assumption is made that each object must be supported in some way, either by another object or by the ground. (This is called the *support hypothesis*.) By simulating the effect of moving each object away from the camera and expanding it (so as to maintain the same image on the picture plane) until it hits the ground plane or another object, the final position and actual size of each object may be calculated.

Now that the precise position and size of the object in the scene are known, it may be viewed from another point using a three-dimensional display program. This illustrates the crucial difference between Roberts' recognition program and the approach to pattern recognition followed in most previous programs. The earlier programs could classify the objects in a scene, but they could not determine the precise three-dimensional positions and sizes of the objects. Therefore, the appearance of the scene from another viewpoint could not be predicted. Roberts' program was able to predict other views of the scene and, thus, showed a sophistication of image understanding beyond previous programs and more like human three-dimensional spatial understanding of pictures.

Conclusion

Roberts made three assumptions in developing his program:

1. The picture is a perspective view of the real world;

2. The objects in the picture can be described by transformations of known models;

3. All objects are supported by other objects or by the ground plane.

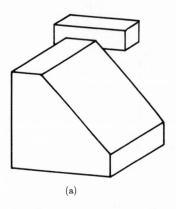
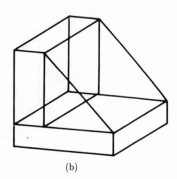

(a) (b)

Figure B1-3. (a) A scene with a compound object partially occluding a simple object (a rectangular solid); (b) the compound object consisting of two rectangular solids and a wedge.

Under these assumptions, the program analyzed scenes consisting of single simple objects, and also scenes with several objects and compound objects. Figure B1-3a shows a picture processed by the program. It consists of a compound object partially occluding a simple object. A compound object is a single object that is not the transformation of a single model. It is the result of piecing together several models. Figure B1-3b shows how the compound object was formed by piecing together the transformations of two cube models and a wedge model. Precise three-dimensional descriptions of the objects in the picture were generated, allowing the scene to be displayed from any viewpoint.

References

See Roberts (1965).

B2.   Partition of Line Drawings into Objects:
A. Guzman

IN CONTRAST to Roberts' work, which involved scenes of known objects (e.g., cubes and wedges), Guzman (1968b) developed a program to analyze scenes without prestored models of objects. His program, called SEE, starts with a line drawing and identifies all the separate objects in it, even if they are not completely visible. For example, SEE finds three bodies in Figure B2–1: the first consists of regions 6, 2, and 1; the second, of regions 11, 12, and 10; and the third, of regions 3, 4, 5, 7, 8, 9, and 13.

Another contrast between SEE and Roberts' program is that SEE does not provide a three-dimensional description. It is intended only to partition the scene into bodies and to provide this as input to a recognizer like Roberts' program, which might recognize the bodies as instances of models and thus derive three-dimensional descriptions. Finally, Roberts' program uses numerical methods, while SEE adopts a heuristic and symbolic (i.e., nonnumerical) approach.

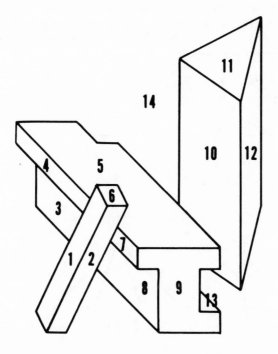

Figure B2–1.   Example of scene analysis by SEE (from Guzman, 1968b).

143

Overview of SEE

The main part of SEE analyzes the picture in terms of junctions and regions, in search of clues that indicate that two regions form part of the same body.

Guzman defines a set of junctions that he considers significant for analysis. A junction is a point where two or more lines meet. Junctions are classified into junction types depending on the geometrical configuration of their incident lines. Figure B2–2 shows the classification. An analysis of the regions around junctions suggests heuristics for assigning regions to one body or another. We discuss five of these junction types briefly (see Fig. B2–3):

1. *FORK.* If three regions meet at a FORK junction and none of them is the background, links are formed between the regions (Fig. B2–3a). A link between two regions suggests that they belong to the same object. In Figure B2–4a, this rule links regions 1 and 2, 2 and 3, and 3 and 1 around junction *A*.

2. *ARROW.* Two of its regions are linked, as shown in Figure B2–3b. In Figure B2–4a, this rule links regions 1 and 2 at junction *B*, 1 and 3 at junction *C*, and 4 and 5 at junction *D*.

3. *T.* Two Ts are said to match if their stems are collinear and they "face each other" (Fig. B2–3c). Regions 1 and 2 (Fig. B2–3c) are linked, as are regions 3 and 4, but only if a link is not created between background and nonbackground regions.

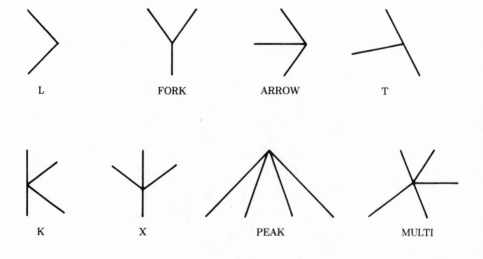

Figure B2–2.   Classification of junctions in pictures of polyhedral scenes (from Guzman, 1968b).

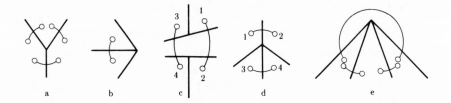

Figure B2–3.   Evidence used to link regions together.

4. *X*. Two links are established (Fig. B2–3d), one between regions 1 and 2 and the other between regions 3 and 4. In Figure B2–4a, this rule links regions 2 and 3 and regions 4 and 5 around junction *E*.

5. *PEAK*. All of its regions, except the one containing the obtuse angle, are linked to each other (Fig. B2–3e).

Thus, each link is a piece of evidence suggesting that two or more regions belong to the same object. SEE contains many more heuristics like those described above.

The program uses all the available evidence to determine which regions should be merged to form a single object. The evidence is summarized in a graph that represents the relationships of regions and the links established by the junction-heuristic rules. For example, the graph in Figure B2–4b represents the structure in Figure B2–4a; each node corresponds to a region, and each arc to a link.

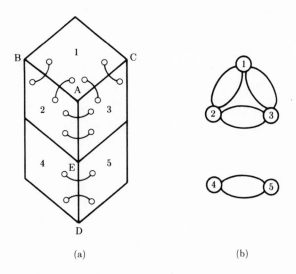

(a)   (b)

Figure B2–4.   (a) Example of planting links among regions;
(b) the graph of the links.

Let us define a *nucleus* as either a single region or a set of regions that have already been merged—a nucleus represents a set of regions that belong to the same object. The program now expands the object according to the following rule: If two nuclei are connected by two or more links, they are merged into a larger nucleus. That is, all the members of both sets of regions belong to a single object. For example, in Figure B2–4a, regions 1 and 2 are connected by two links and are therefore merged into nucleus 1-2. There are four links between the regions in nucleus 1-2 and region 3; they are therefore merged into nucleus 1-2-3. Similarly, regions 4 and 5 are merged into nucleus 4-5. Since there are no links between nuclei 1-2-3 and 4-5, regions 1, 2, and 3 are combined to form one object and regions 4 and 5 form another.

This simple rule does not work for more complicated cases. Guzman added many more heuristic rules for region merging, as well as more heuristics for junction types, as they became necessary to handle more and more difficult cases. As a result, the SEE program could successfully segment very complicated line drawings into objects.

Conclusion

Guzman's SEE was the first program to make use of vertices and junctions in recognizing three-dimensional objects. As the next articles will show, this has become a powerful and popular approach. However, where Guzman's analysis of junctions was heuristic and intuitive, those of Huffman and Clowes (Article XIII.B4) and Waltz (Article XIII.B5) were successively more systematic and powerful.

References

For a detailed description of SEE, see Guzman (1968a, 1968b).

B3.   Interpreting Imperfect Line Drawings: G. Falk

FALK (1972), like Roberts (Article XIII.B1), worked on the problem of identifying the visible objects in a photograph of a scene and determining their orientations and positions in three-dimensional space. However, Falk allowed several kinds of imperfect input: Line drawings generated from the photograph might not follow exactly the edges in the image, there might be degenerate views of objects, or some edges may be totally missing due to poor lighting.

Falk used fixed *models* of the objects that could appear in the scene; nine models represented simple objects such as rectangular solids and wedges. Unlike Roberts' models, which were generic (a cube could represent any right parallelepiped), Falk's models specified precise shapes and sizes. With the models and a large set of heuristics, Falk's program (called INTERPRET) followed a *hypothesize-and-test* strategy to identify and locate objects in a scene.

An Example

We illustrate here the steps taken by INTERPRET to analyze the picture in Figure B3–1a. In the next section, we will discuss INTERPRET in more detail.

The scene that produced Figure B3–1a consists of a rectangular solid with a cube in front of it. Because of lighting conditions, the top face of the cube and left face of the rectangular solid appear to have the same brightness, as do the right faces of both blocks. Three visible edges are therefore missing from the input: two in the corner connecting P_2 and P_1, and the edge between P_4 and P_3.

INTERPRET proceeds as follows:

1. *Segmentation.* The picture is partitioned into pieces corresponding to individual bodies, as in Figure B3–1b. Some of the lines in the original picture may not appear in any of these pieces (e.g., the line from P_1 to P_3).

2. *Completion.* It is easy to add lines to complete, or partially complete, some of the bodies. The completed version of the bodies in Figure B3–1b is shown in Figure B3–1c. One of the body descriptions is complete, while the other is not.

3. *Recognition.* Each body is identified as an instance of a model and is located in three-dimensional space. This constitutes an interpretation of the scene. Although this step does not require that the bodies in the picture be complete, it is more likely to succeed if there are no missing lines.

147

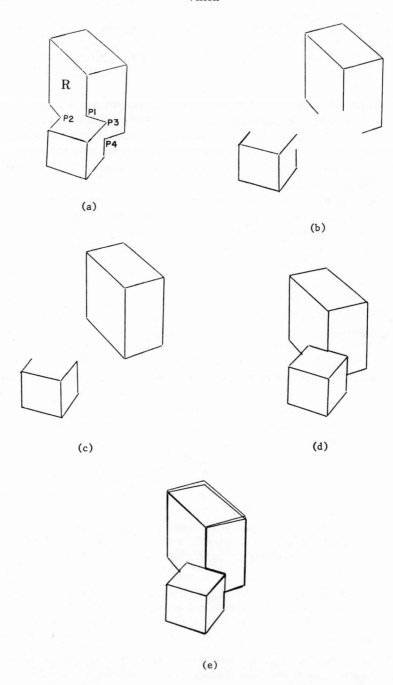

Figure B3–1.   Analysis of a line drawing (from Falk, 1972).

4. *Prediction.* To check that the interpretation of the scene is consistent with the original picture, the three-dimensional locations and identities of the models are used to generate a predicted line drawing. Figure B3–1d is the predicted line drawing resulting from the recognition of the bodies in Figure B3–1c.

5. *Verification.* The prediction and the original picture are compared to see how closely they align. If, as in Figure B3–1e, the two are approximately the same, the scene interpretation is assumed to be correct. Otherwise, part of the scene is reanalyzed to produce a more consistent interpretation.

The following sections describe some of these steps in more detail.

Segmentation

The first step in the interpretation procedure is to segment the line drawing into bodies. Guzman addressed this problem (Article XIII.B2). He classified junctions and developed heuristics to decide whether regions meeting at junctions belonged to the same body. However, this approach cannot work if lines are missing from the picture. To see why, consider again Figure B3–1a, in which, due to lighting conditions, two faces of different rectangular solids are identified as a single region *R*. It is useless to assign this region to one or the other of the bodies, because it corresponds to two separate surfaces of separate bodies. Yet, this is exactly what Guzman's program tried to do.

To get around this problem, Falk developed heuristics to determine which lines, rather than regions, meeting at each junction are likely to belong to the same body. Falk's junction classifications are the same as Guzman's, but each junction type is additionally classified as either GOOD or BAD. For the most part, GOOD junctions contain lines of only one body, while BAD junctions contain lines of more than one body. For example:

1. *Arrow junctions.* If one of the inner regions of an arrow junction is the background, it is labeled BADARROW (Fig. B3–2b). Figure B3–3a shows why the three lines of this junction cannot be assumed to belong to the same body. If the middle line of an arrow junction is the top of a K junction (Fig. B3–2c), it is also labeled BADARROW. Figure B3–3b shows that, when this occurs, the two side lines of the arrow belong to different bodies, while the middle line is shared by the two bodies. Otherwise, the arrow junction is labeled GOODARROW (Fig. B3–2a). In Figure B3–3c, we see that the three lines of the GOODARROW belong to a single body.

2. *Y (Fork) junctions.* A Y junction is labeled GOODY if at least one of its lines is also the middle line of a GOODARROW (Fig. B3–2d). Figure B3–3c shows that all the lines of a GOODY belong to a single body. Otherwise, the Y junction is labeled BADY.

Falk similarly classified L, T, K, X, and MULTI junctions.

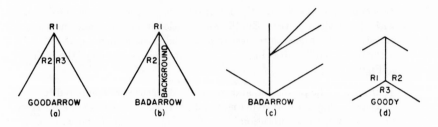

Figure B3–2.　Some junction types (from Falk, 1972)

Once the junctions in a line drawing have been classified, the lines belonging to each body must be grouped together. This is done by constructing a graph whose nodes consist of lines that are known to be in the same body because of the junction type that connects them. Two nodes in the graph are connected if they share a common line. A procedure merges all nodes sharing lines, and, ideally, when the merging stops, each remaining node corresponds to a separate body in the picture. Regions in the picture are then assigned to bodies based on this line segmentation and some other heuristics for splitting regions (such as R in Fig. B3–1a) that correspond to more than one body.

Support Relations

To recognize bodies in the picture as instances of three-dimensional models, the program first infers the three-dimensional coordinates of some of the vertices of each body. Falk's method of deriving three-dimensional coordinates of picture points is illustrated in Figure B3–4. For each picture point P', the corresponding point P in 3-space must lie along a ray extending from the camera center through P'. However, it is not possible to determine where on this ray P lies unless external constraints are introduced (see Articles XIII.D3, XIII.D4, and XIII.D6). Falk's external constraints are the same as Roberts' *support hypothesis*. Objects in a scene are not suspended in space but are supported

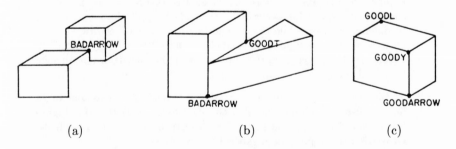

Figure B3–3.　Examples of junction types (from Falk, 1972).

either by the table or by other objects. In Figure B3–4, if we can determine that the corner P_1 of the block lies on the table, then the three-dimensional coordinates of P_1 can be determined as the intersection of the table plane and the ray associated with the picture point P'_1. In fact, any picture point may be located in three-dimensional space if a plane in which it lies is known.

Two important steps are taken by INTERPRET to determine three-dimensional features from the picture. The first is finding the base edges for each body; the second is determining which bodies support other bodies. INTERPRET uses a number of heuristics (not described here) to determine base edges. These would identify P_1-P_2, P_2-P_3, P_4-P_5, and P_5-P_6 in Figure B3–5 as base edges. INTERPRET also has heuristics for deciding whether one body supports another. For example, in Figure B3–5, a necessary (but not sufficient) condition for BODY$_2$ to support BODY$_1$ is that they be adjacent. That is, a line corresponding to a base edge of BODY$_1$ (such as P_5-P_6) must bound both a region of BODY$_1$, R_1, and a region of BODY$_2$, R_2.

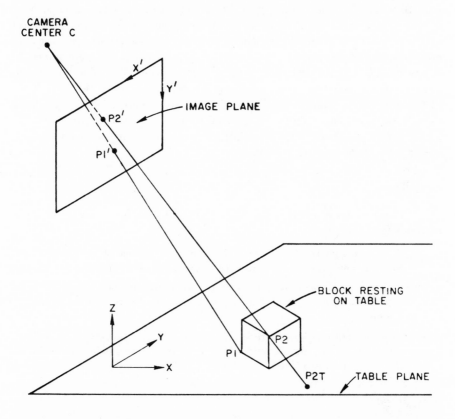

Figure B3–4. Deriving three-dimensional locations of picture points (from Falk, 1972).

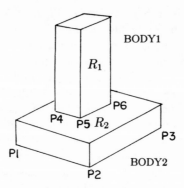

Figure B3–5.   BODY₂ supports BODY₁ (from Falk, 1972).

Many object corners can be located in three-dimensional space once support relations and base edges have been identified. In Figure B3–5, since BODY₂ is supported by no other body, it is assumed to be supported by the table. Points P_1, P_2, and P_3 are then identified as base points (because they are endpoints of base edges) and their position in 3-space is determined by intersecting their rays with the (known) plane of the table. The base points P_4, P_5, and P_6, on the other hand, cannot be located until BODY₂ is completely recognized, that is, until the plane of R_2 is known. The location of these base points can then be determined by intersecting their rays with the plane of face R_2. Using support relations in this way, the program analyzes scenes from the ground (i.e., table) up.

Completion

It is easier to recognize objects if they are complete. Falk has three methods for completion:

1. If, as in Figure B3–6a, a face F is incomplete because of two dangling collinear lines, replace the two lines (L_1 and L_2) by a single line.

2. If a face F is incomplete because of two dangling lines that can be extended to form a corner (Fig. B3–6b), complete the face by extending the lines.

3. If, as in Figure B3–6c, there is a pair of L-type junctions with parallel sides at points P_1 and P_2, add a line between these two points and split the face F into two faces.

Recognition

Since INTERPRET recognizes objects from the table up, an object is not recognized until all its potential supporting objects have been recognized, after

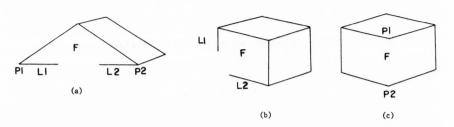

Figure B3–6.   Examples of incomplete body descriptions (from Falk, 1972).

which an object's *actual* support is assumed to be the potential supporting object with the highest horizontal surface. The three-dimensional coordinates of the corners of base edges of an object can be inferred once its supporting plane is known.

An object is recognized as an instance of a model by matching features of its line drawing against stored properties of the models. These features include the number of visible faces and vertices, the shape of the faces (e.g., triangular, rectangular), the lengths of base edges, and the angles between base edges.

Although the three-dimensional coordinates of the corners of an object have been established, the position and orientation of the object in 3-space must still be determined. This is done by matching the known corners of the object to the model and inferring the three-dimensional positions of the other corners.

Prediction and Verification

After all objects in the picture have been recognized, a line drawing of the interpretation of the scene is predicted and matched with the original line drawing. Matching proceeds by checking each line in the original drawing for a line in the predicted drawing. If a body has more than three lines in the interpretation that do not appear in the original line drawing, a new attempt is made to recognize the body. The methods used by Falk for revising decisions are rudimentary and will not be discussed here.

Conclusion

In addition to the prediction-verification method that Falk developed for interpreting imperfect line drawings, Falk's research touched on several other useful techniques: line and edge detection (Article XIII.C4), region segmentation (Article XIII.C5), and determining the three-dimensional coordinates of objects in a scene (Articles XIII.D3, XIII.D4, and XIII.D6).

References

See Falk (1972) for a detailed description of INTERPRET.

B4. Labeling Line Drawings in the Trihedral World: D. A. Huffman and M. B. Clowes

IN CONTRAST to the highly heuristic nature of the work of Guzman and Falk, Huffman (1971) and Clowes (1971) independently attempted a more systematic approach to polyhedral scene analysis. To begin with, they emphasized the important distinction between the *scene domain* and the *image domain*. The scene domain involves physical, three-dimensional aspects of a scene, such as occlusion of one surface by another or the concavity or convexity of edges. The image domain involves the projection of scene-domain properties onto the two-dimensional picture plane. There is a definite correspondence between image-domain and scene-domain elements for the polyhedral world: Junctions, lines, and regions in the picture correspond to vertices, edges, and surfaces, respectively, in the scene. The distinction between image and scene features is important enough that, henceforth, the terms *junction*, *line*, and *region* will refer to image features, and *vertex*, *edge*, and *surface* will refer to scene features. In these terms, the goal of picture interpretation is to interpret elements in the image domain as properties in the scene domain. In this article, the method of labeling a line drawing will be explained based mostly on the work of Huffman (1971). Clowes (1971) presented essentially the same theory using a different representation.

Vertex Labeling

Huffman and Clowes limited their analysis to trihedral polyhedra—objects in which exactly three plane surfaces come together at each vertex. They made an exhaustive listing of all the different vertex types and the different ways they could be viewed. There are only four ways in which three plane surfaces can come together at a vertex. These are illustrated in Figure B4–1.

Notice that *convex* and *concave* edges are found in the vertices of Figure B4–1. Combinations of these types of edges produce the four vertices in the figure. The edges associated with the vertex in Figure B4–1a are all convex; those associated with Figure B4–1d are all concave. In Figure B4–1b, two edges are convex and one is concave. In Figure B4–1c, two edges are concave and one is convex.

In Figure B4–1, each vertex is generated by three planes meeting at one point. These three planes partition the surrounding space into eight octants. Notice that the number of octants occupied by solid material is different for each vertex. A vertex can be viewed from any one of the octants not occupied by solid material, and moving a viewpoint within a single octant does not result in a picture with different junction types. The vertex of Figure B4–1a can be viewed from seven different octants, giving essentially three different

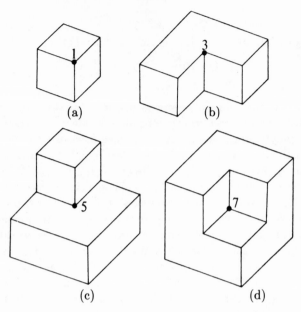

Figure B4–1.   The four vertex types (from Huffman, 1971).

appearances: FORK, L, or ARROW (rotational symmetry reduces the seven possibilities to three). This is shown in Figure B4–2, where the vertex being viewed is marked with a dot and the lines are labeled as follows:

1. A "+" line represents a convex edge with both of its planes visible from the camera.

2. A "−" line represents a concave edge with both of its planes visible from the camera.

3. A "←" or "→" line represents an occluding edge: a convex edge with both of its planes on the same side of the edge as viewed from the camera, one occluding the other. As one moves in the direction of the arrow, the pair of planes is to the right.

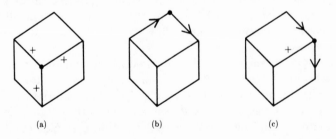

Figure B4–2.   The three views of the vertex in Figure B4–1a.

Note that, in Figure B4–2b, only two edges are visible as lines in the picture. The third edge is hidden from the camera position.

An exhaustive listing of the different ways each vertex in Figure B4–1 may be viewed results in only 12 possibilities (Fig. B4–3, parts (a)-(l)): six for the L junction, three for ARROW, and three for FORK. (Each configuration in Fig. B4–3 may be arbitrarily rotated in a given picture.) Of these, the junction label in Figure B4–3k is derived from the vertex in Figure B4–1d; junction labels in Figures B4–3d, B4–3f, and B4–3h are derived from the vertex in Figure B4–1c; junction labels in Figures B4–3a, B4–3b, B4–3c, B4–3i, and B4–3j are derived from the vertex in Figure B4–1b; junction labels in Figures B4–3g, B4–3l, and B4–3e are derived from the vertex in Figure B4–1a. Lastly, four T-junction labels (Fig. B4–3, parts (m)-(p)) correspond to the cases in which each of the four possible types of edges is interrupted by another body.

Picture Interpretation

We will illustrate picture interpretation with the simple picture in Figure B4–4. It contains four junctions labeled A, B, C, and D and three regions labeled 1, 2, and 3. Each junction may have only the scene-domain interpretations shown in Figure B4–5, and the problem is to determine which junction interpretations are globally consistent, that is, which provide a consistent interpretation for the whole picture. Consistency is forced by the rule that each line in the picture must be assigned one and only one label (i.e., +, −, ←, →) along its entire length; otherwise, the adjoining planes would have different orientations in different parts of the scene. For example, if junction A

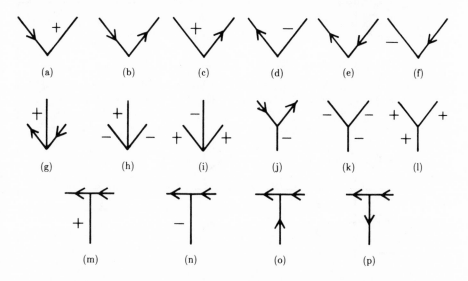

Figure B4–3.   Junction labelings (from Huffman, 1971).

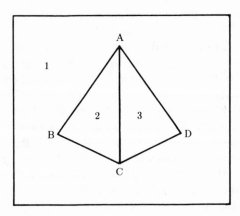

Figure B4–4.   A simple picture (from Clowes, 1971).

is interpreted as in Figure B4–5b, junction D can only be interpreted as in Figure B4–5g in order that line AD in the picture has a consistent scene-domain interpretation (i.e., consistently labeled "–" along its length). The search for consistent labelings can be implemented as an exhaustive search of the arrangements of all possible interpretations of all junctions. Such a search results in the three scene interpretations shown in Figure B4–6.

One interesting aspect of this work is that it is able to determine that many polyhedra are impossible objects. For example, we can detect that the

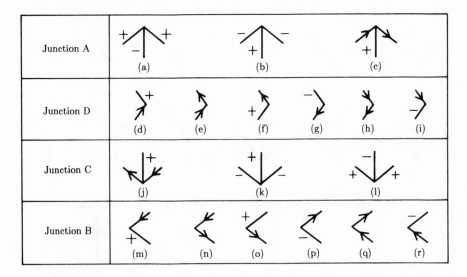

Figure B4–5.   Possible labelings for the junctions in Figure B4–4.

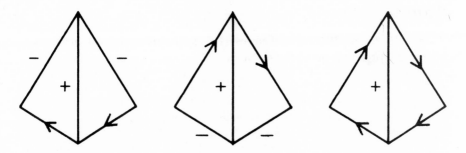

Figure B4-6.   The three possible interpretations for the picture in
               Figure B4-4.

picture in Figure B4-7 is an impossible object. Locally, the picture is well
formed; that is, each junction has one or more valid scene-domain interpretations. It is only when a globally consistent interpretation is attempted that
we see that one does not exist.

Conclusion

Huffman and Clowes brought systematicity to their analysis of polyhedral
objects. They methodically worked out all the ways that planes could meet
in space and all possible appearances of these junctions. Recognizing an
object was then simply a matter of finding a consistent labeling for a line
drawing of the object. However, their search for consistent interpretations
was exhaustive. In the following article (Article XIII.B5), we discuss a similar
approach, but one that uses a larger set of line labels and a more efficient
method of finding consistent interpretations.

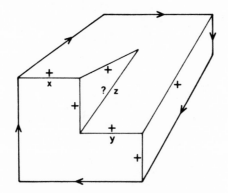

Figure B4-7.   Impossible polyhedron.

References

See Huffman (1971) and Clowes (1971). Winston (1977) provides an instructive presentation of the method.

B5. Constraint Propagation in Interpreting Line Drawings:
D. Waltz

WALTZ (1972) extended the research of Huffman and Clowes (Article XIII.B4) in two important ways. First he expanded the Huffman-Clowes set of four line labels $(+, -, \leftarrow, \rightarrow)$ to include *shadows, cracks,* and *separably concave edges.* Second, he replaced the simple exhaustive search for consistent line labelings by a clever filtering algorithm that examined adjacent junctions in the picture and discarded incompatible candidate labelings.

New Line Labels

A typical example of the kind of line drawings interpreted by Waltz's program is shown in Figure B5–1. Among the new line labels is the *crack*— a flat edge that is also the *bounding edge* of an object. For example, line segments 6-3 and 6-7 in Figure B5–1 are cracks. Line 6-7 is a bounding edge of the cube 6-7-9-10-11-13, and line 6-3 is a bounding edge of the supporting cube. Every crack is therefore a *separable edge;* that is, two or three bodies meet at a crack. In Figure B5–1, a crack is represented by a "*c*" together with an arrow. The direction of the arrow is such that the obscuring body lies to the right of this direction.

Objects may also be bounded by *concave edges.* For example, in Figure B5–1, the concave edge 4-15 is also the boundary edge of cube 4-3-6-13-14-15.

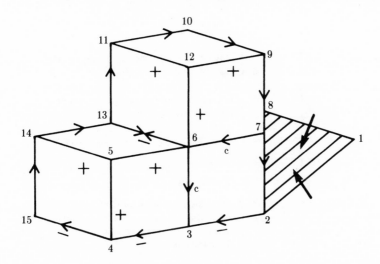

Figure B5–1. A simple picture and its labeling (from Winston, 1975).

161

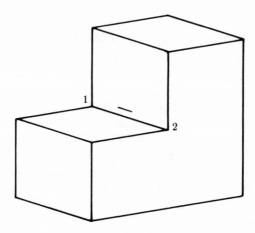

Figure B5–2.   A nonseparable concave edge (line 1-2).

These edges are called *separable concave edges*, and the arrow's direction is such that the obscuring body lies to the right of this direction. A double arrow (line 13-6 in Fig. B5–1) indicates that three bodies meet along the line. However, not all concave edges are separable; for example, line 1-2 in Figure B5–2 is a nonseparable, interior concave edge.

Waltz also considered boundaries of shadows. A shadow boundary is also a flat edge, for example, lines 1-2 and 1-8 in Figure B5–1. A shadow edge is represented by an arrow that points in the direction of the shadowed region.

The 11 line labels we have described, including the original four from Huffman and Clowes, are summarized in Figure B5–3.

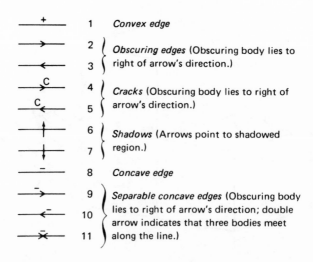

Figure B5–3.   Line labelings (from Winston, 1975).

More on Shadows

One of Waltz's contributions was to show that shadow information, which was previously regarded as annoying detail, is actually useful for resolving line interpretations. In addition to the two shadow labels mentioned above, Waltz also labeled regions as *illuminated* directly by the light source, turned away from the light (*self-shadowed*), or *shaded* by a shadow cast by another surface. Waltz then added line labels giving the illumination status of the two regions appearing at each edge. This increased the number of line labels from 11 to 53.

Junctions

The junction types used by Waltz included the Huffman-Clowes junctions (L, ARROW, FORK, T) plus all four-line and some five-line junctions. Examples are shown in Figure B5–4. To obtain the possible set of junction

	Approximate number of combinatorially possible labelings	Approximate number of physically possible labelings
	3,249	92
	185,000	86
	185,000	826
	185,000	623
	11×10^6	10
	11×10^6	435
	11×10^6	213
	11×10^6	128
	11×10^6	160
	600×10^6	20

Figure B5–4. Number of combinatorially and physically possible labelings for each junction type (from Winston, 1975).

labelings, Waltz considered all possible object configurations viewed and lit from all possible octants. Note that the number of physically possible labelings for each junction is much smaller than the number of combinatorially possible labelings—only 3 to 3×10^{-6} percent of the total combinations are legal for the common vertex types.

Labeling Procedure

The procedure used by Waltz to label a picture is based on the Huffman-Clowes principle that each line in the picture must be assigned a single label along its entire length. First, the complete set of possible labelings for each junction in the picture is retrieved. Then a *constraint-satisfaction* algorithm is used to determine the possible labelings for each junction in the context of the entire picture. This algorithm compares adjacent pairs of junctions and sees if their constraints can be satisfied.

As an illustration, we will apply the algorithm to Figure B5–5; this is the same as Figure B4–4 from the previous article. Let us assume for simplicity that lines can be labeled only as $+$, $-$, $\rightarrow$, or $\leftarrow$. Thus, each junction in Figure B5–5 has the labeling possibilities shown in Figure B5–6. The following procedure shows how Waltz's program interprets this picture. The step numbers refer to Figure B5–7, which summarizes the label sets assigned to each junction.

1. Assume the procedure starts with junction A of Figure B5–5. Initially, the set consisting of parts (a)-(c) of Figure B5–6 is assigned to junction A; it can be labeled in any of these three ways.

2. Suppose that the procedure then goes to junction D and makes an initial assignment of six possible labelings (shown in parts (d)-(i) of

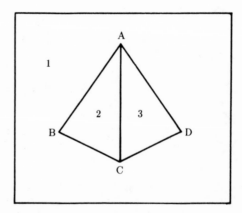

Figure B5–5.   A simple picture (from Clowes, 1971).

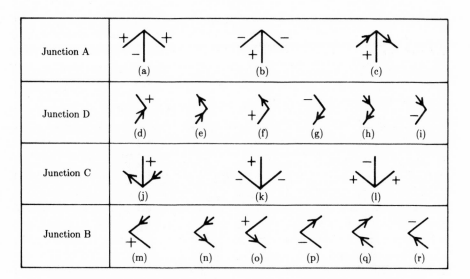

Figure B5–6.   Possible labelings for the junctions in Figure B5–5.

Fig. B5–6). Checking the junctions adjacent to D, the procedure determines that junction A has already been labeled and is therefore a source of constraints on the labeling of junction D.

3. The current label set of A is examined to see what restrictions, if any, it has placed on line AD. In this case, the restrictions are that the line must be labeled $+$, $-$, or $\rightarrow$ (the arrow pointing away from junction A). Therefore, two labelings of junction D may be eliminated, since they would require an arrow label pointing in the wrong direction.

4. Suppose that junction C is chosen next and is assigned the initial junctions shown in parts (j)-(l) of Figure B5–6. Since the adjacent junctions have already been labeled, their constraints on C can be exploited to prune its initial assignment of junctions.

5. According to the current label set of junction A, line AC must be labeled with either $+$ or $-$. This, however, does not eliminate any member of the current label set of junction C.

6. According to the current label set of junction D, line CD must be labeled with $\rightarrow$, $\leftarrow$, or $-$. This eliminates one labeling from the label set of junction C.

7. The reasoning from the previous steps is now reversed as the procedure determines how the label set of C restricts the label sets of A and D. According to the current label set of junction C, line CD must be labeled with either $\leftarrow$ or $-$. This eliminates one labeling of junction D.

Labels Assigned to Junctions		
	A	D	C
1	 *(junction labelings)*		
2	Unchanged	*(junction labelings)*	
3	Unchanged	*(junction labelings)*	
4	Unchanged	Unchanged	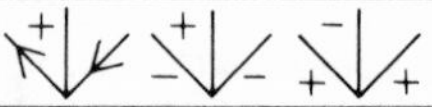 *(junction labelings)*
5	Unchanged	Unchanged	Unchanged
6	Unchanged	Unchanged	*(junction labelings)*
7	Unchanged	*(junction labelings)*	Unchanged
8	 *(junction labelings)*	Unchanged	Unchanged

Figure B5–7.   Label sets assigned to each junction during the steps of the constraint-satisfaction algorithm.

8. Similarly, the current label set of junction C dictates that line AC must be labeled with +. This eliminates one labeling of junction A.

This procedure continues until all junctions have been labeled and the effects of all changes have been allowed to propagate.

This procedure is called a *Waltz filtering algorithm* because it strips out inconsistent labels as it proceeds. If a unique labeling for each junction in the picture has not been generated when the algorithm terminates, a direct tree search can be used to enumerate possible labelings. The three labelings generated in our example are shown in Figure B5–8.

Conclusion

It is interesting to note that even though Waltz allowed many more line labels than previous researchers (enabling him to interpret more realistic scenes), his procedure usually converges on a single interpretation. Our example was simplified for the purpose of explanation and did not illustrate the full power of Waltz filtering; a more compelling example is given by Waltz (1972).

An interesting outcome of Waltz's research is that the inclusion of more detailed information does not complicate interpretation but, rather, it

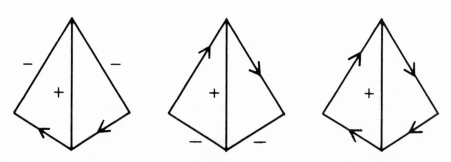

Figure B5–8.   Three labelings of Figure B5–5.

constrains and facilitates interpretation. For example, vision researchers prior to Waltz regarded shadows as an annoying complication, but Waltz was able to show that the constraints contributed by shadows make the algorithm converge more quickly and apply to more pictures.

References

Waltz's research is described in his paper in *The Psychology of Computer Vision* (Winston, 1975).

B6. Obtaining Line Drawings: Y. Shirai

THE PROGRAMS described in the five previous articles all work from a line drawing of a scene; Roberts' program (Article XIII.B1) identifies known objects and finds their positions, sizes, and orientations; Guzman's SEE (Article XIII.B2) infers association of regions into objects from topological, heuristic considerations of line junctions; Falk (Article XIII.B3) attempted to handle noisy input; Huffman and Clowes (Article XIII.B4) developed a systematic method for finding consistent interpretations of line drawings; and Waltz (Article XIII.B5) extended this work to include other features as constraints in an algorithm, based on constraint propagation. Shirai's research (1973) is consistent with these other approaches, but is primarily concerned with the problem of *finding* lines. His program generates lines directly from the intensity array in a photograph; it simultaneously generates and interprets the line drawing, using the partially developed interpretation as top-down information to search for lines in the photograph.

Finding lines in an intensity array of picture points is a very difficult problem. Edges often generate only very small intensity differences, and these may be masked by noise. Noise has two sources: The sensor (e.g., a camera) generates noisy and distorted information, and the scene itself has texture, shadows, multiple reflections, and dirt, all of which result in noisy information. If a line finder is too sensitive, it will interpret noise as lines; if it is not sensitive enough, it will miss legitimate lines.

Prior to Shirai's research, the generation and interpretation of line drawings were treated as separate tasks. The drawing-generation task suffered from the difficulty that a single set of sensitivity parameters for the line finder would generally not be adequate for the entire picture: Some noise-produced lines are stronger than real ones.

Shirai's approach was to introduce knowledge about polyhedral scenes into the line-finding process. For example, by knowing or hypothesizing that a particular object is a block, the strong lines can be used to guide a search for the weaker ones. Thus, by knowing where to expect a line, sensitivity parameters can be locally adjusted to find it if it exists. Heuristics are applied during line finding to suggest places to look for new lines or for the continuations of current lines.

Shirai divides the lines in a picture into three classes:

1. *Contour lines*, or lines formed at the boundary between the objects in a picture and the outer background. In Figure B6–1, lines *AB*, *BC*, ..., *ZV* are contour lines.

2. *Boundary lines*, or lines on the borders of the objects. All contour lines are also boundary lines. In Figure B6–1, the boundary lines are the

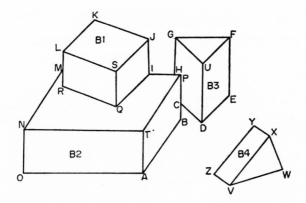

Figure B6–1.   A typical line drawing (from Shirai, 1973).

contour lines plus the lines on the boundaries between objects, that is, *CP, PH, IQ, QR,* and *RM.*

3. *Internal lines,* or lines resulting from the intersection of two surfaces of the same object. In Figure B6–1, lines *JS, LS, . . . , XV* are internal lines.

The overall strategy of Shirai's program is first to extract the contour lines in a picture and then to search within each contour for other boundary lines and internal lines. Boundary lines are sought before internal lines because boundaries often provide good cues for guessing internal lines. It is not difficult to find contour lines, because scenes are always set up with high contrast between white objects and their black background. In Figure B6–1, for example, there are two contours, one for objects B_1, B_2, and B_3 and another for object B_4.

Searches for lines may be over large or small areas of the picture, and Shirai's program gives higher priority to searching smaller areas. For example, in Figure B6–1, we could search over a small area from *C* to *P* to find an extension of line *BC.* In contrast, to find the line *IQ,* we would need to search all possible line directions between *IH* and *IJ.* Thus, the former search has priority over the latter.

Shirai used many heuristics to propose where to search for lines. Some of these are:

1. If two boundary lines meet at a concave point, look for collinear extensions of them. In Figure B6–1, the boundary lines *IH* and *GH* meet at the concave point *H,* and *HP* is searched for as an extension of *IH.*

2. If no extensions of two concave lines are found, look for another line that starts from the concave point. In Figure B6–1, the line *IQ* would be sought starting at the concave point *I.*

3. If the boundary lines of an object are known, select vertices of the boundary that might have internal lines starting from them. At each such vertex, look for an internal line that is nearly parallel to some boundary line. In Figure B6–1, for example, internal line *JS* is parallel to boundary lines *KL* and *IQ*.

4. If two internal lines meet at a vertex, look for another line starting at this vertex. Suppose, in Figure B6–1, that the internal line *JS* is not found at vertex *J* (using rule 3) because of very little difference in brightness between the adjacent faces near this vertex. Suppose, also, that *LS* and *QS* have already been found. This rule will look for a line near vertex *S*, where the contrast may be high enough to find it. Once a line segment is found near *S*, this line may be tracked all the way to *J*.

5. After a line has been tracked as far as possible, if it is still unconnected, an extension or a junction is sought by circularly scanning near the endpoint. If this process does not find a new line near the endpoint, the line is extended by a small length and tested to see if there is now a connection to other lines. If not, the circular scan process is repeated. This process can be continued until it is successful, that is, until the line is connected to other lines or additional line segments are found by circular scanning. For example, in Figure B6–2, line *MN′* has been tracked and left unconnected at point *N′*. A circular scan near *N′* fails to find any new lines. The line is therefore extended to P_1 and the circular scan is again attempted. This process is repeated until a connection to line *KL* is found at point *N*.

These heuristics and others not only find lines, but they also find objects and their relationships. Notice that when a complete set of boundary lines has been found, all the objects can be identified; that is, each enclosing set of boundary lines defines a separate object. In Figure B6–1, for example, four enclosing boundaries are found and four objects are defined. Also, finding

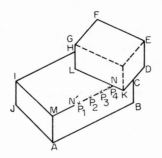

Figure B6–2.   Repetitive line extension (from Shirai, 1973).

boundary lines often gives clues to the relationships between objects. For example, rule 1, which extends concave boundary lines, usually results in a situation like that shown in Figure B6–1, where one object (object B_2) hides another (object B_3). When line IH or line GH is extended, it is easy to see which object the line belongs to and, thus, to determine the "hiding" relationship.

Figure B6–3 is a complete example of Shirai's line finder.

Conclusion

Shirai's program used top-down information (from the partly developed line-drawing) to facilitate line-finding. Shirai introduced a semantic approach

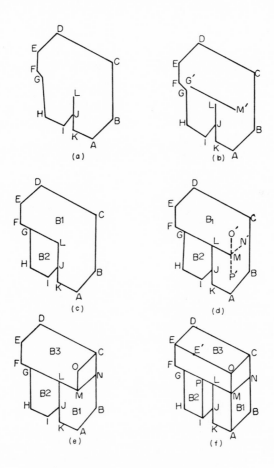

Figure B6–3.   Shirai's line finder.

in which knowledge of the task domain is used to direct low-level vision processes. This topic is discussed further in Article XIII.C4.

References

See Shirai (1973).

B7. Reasoning About Surface Orientations:
A. K. Mackworth

GIVEN a line drawing, the Huffman-Clowes-Waltz labeling scheme (Articles XIII.B4 and XIII.B5) can interpret it as a three-dimensional scene of trihedral objects by assigning line labels to it. Two important points should be noted about labeling. First, line labels characterize the shape only qualitatively. For example, the convex label "+" signifies that two plane surfaces meet and make a convexity along an edge, but it does not specify anything about the angle at which the planes meet. Thus, the labeling of Figure B7-1 says only that it has a convex corner; it does not yet represent a cube corner and, in fact, the Figure B7-1 need not be a cube.

The second point about the Huffman-Clowes-Waltz labeling scheme is that legal labelings obtained by the method are sometimes not realizable as polyhedra. Figure B7-2 is an example of a legal labeling that cannot possibly exist; clearly, regions R_1 and R_2 cannot make convex edges at both AB and CD. Why does the labeling not detect this inconsistency?

The problem of unrealizable labelings is closely related to the question of what information about a scene is represented by labels. For its solution we need to develop an approach that enables us to represent geometrical relationships among plane surfaces in a more quantitative way. Huffman (1971) introduced the idea of the *gradient space* for this purpose, and Mackworth used it extensively in his program POLY (1973, 1974). Before describing POLY, we must define the gradient space.

Gradient Space

Figure B7-3 represents an imaging geometry (see Article XIII.C1): The viewer is at the origin, the z-axis is taken as the optical axis of the viewer,

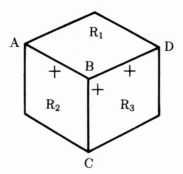

Figure B7-1.   Labeling that represents a convex corner.

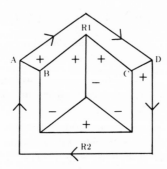

Figure B7–2. Legal labeling for which the corresponding polyhedron cannot exist.

and the picture plane is at $z = 0$ and parallel to the x-y plane. Let us denote
a surface in the space as

$$-z = f(x, y),$$

where $-z$ is the depth of the surface point. An increase in $-z$ represents an
increase in the distance from the viewer.

An ordered pair of values (p, q), where

$$p = \partial f / \partial x = -\partial z / \partial x$$
$$q = \partial f / \partial y = -\partial z / \partial y$$

is called the gradient. A gradient is no more than the first derivative of the
function f, which is the depth of a surface at a point (x, y). In other words,
the gradient (p, q) measures the instantaneous change in the depth of a surface
at point (x, y), or it measures the *tilt* of the surface at that point with respect
to the z-axis. The *gradient space* is simply the set of all possible gradients
(p, q).

In general, p and q change with x and y. A plane is a special case in which
p and q remain constant for all values of x and y, just as a straight line is a
special case in which the slope remains constant for all values of x. And

$$-z = px + qy + c$$

denotes planes with a gradient (p, q). The gradient of a plane is a single point
in gradient space; a curved surface is represented by a set of points in gradient
space.

To illustrate the concept of gradients, imagine viewing Figure B7–4 so
that plane P_0 is flat (parallel to the image plane). Since depth $(-z)$ does
not change on P_0, its gradient is $G_0 = (0, 0)$. Plane P_1 in Figure B7–4 tilts
"away" from the viewer from left to right at a 45-degree angle. It has a

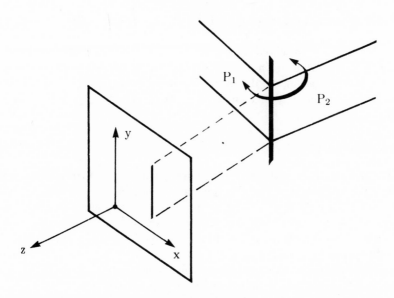

Figure B7–3. Two planes P_1 and P_2 intersect at an edge, which is projected onto the image plane and imaged as a line.

gradient $G_1 = (1,0)$. Since the depth increases as x increases, and since the tilt of the plane is 45 degrees, $p = \partial f/\partial x = 1/1 = 1$; and since the depth does *not* change with respect to y, $q = \partial f/\partial y = 0$. Similar reasoning applies to the other planes in Figure B7–4; assuming they all tilt at 45 degrees with respect to the x or y axis, their gradients are $G_2 = (-1,0)$, $G_3 = (0,1)$, and $G_4 = (0,-1)$.

A surface, of course, may be tilted with respect to both the x and y axes (neither p nor q equals 0), and the angle of tilt need not be 45 degrees

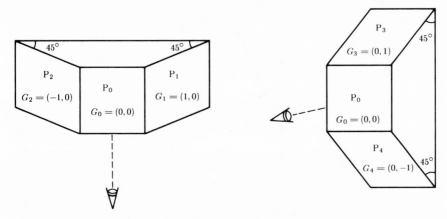

Figure B7–4. Examples of surface orientations and their gradients.

(p and q are something other than 1 or -1). Figure B7–5 shows the gradient space. Note that the axes of this space are p and q, not x and y. The gradient of the surface is represented by a point (p, q). In general, the *direction* of the vector from the origin to (p, q), that is, $\tan^{-1}(q/p)$, describes the direction of the steepest change in the depth on the surface; the *distance* to the origin, $(p^2 + q^2)^{1/2}$, is the rate of change of depth along the direction of steepest change.

Line Labels and Gradients

For the remainder of this discussion we assume an orthographic projection in the imaging process rather than perspective projection (see Article XIII.C1). That is, in Figure B7–3, a point (x, y, z) in three-dimensional space is projected to a point (x, y) in the image plane rather than being foreshortened.

There is an important relationship between line labels and the gradient space: If two surfaces meet along a concave or convex edge, their gradients lie along a line in gradient space that is *perpendicular* to that edge in the image. For example, if two planes intersect at an edge that is imaged as vertical in the image plane, then the gradients of the two planes must lie on a horizontal line in gradient space.

Let us see why this is the case. Figure B7–3 shows a vertical line parallel to the y-axis in the image. The corresponding edge is the intersection of two planes, P_1 and P_2. Let us denote their gradients as $G_1 = (p_1, q_1)$ and $G_2 = (p_2, q_2)$.

Note that $q_1 = q_2$. To see why this is so, recall that we measure $q = \partial(-z)/\partial y$ by moving along a line parallel to the y-axis and measuring

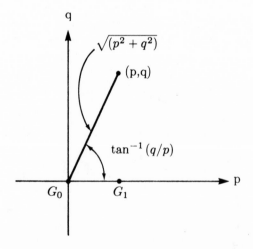

Figure B7–5.   The gradient space.

the change in $-z$. We can do that for the line corresponding to the edge of the intersection between P_1 and P_2 since it is parallel to the y-axis. Since the edge includes both planes, the value of q obtained for this line holds for both planes, that is, $q_1 = q_2$.

Since $q_1 = q_2$, the gradients G_1 and G_2 must therefore lie along a horizontal line in gradient space and, thus, perpendicular to the edge in the image.

We can generalize this result—that the gradients of two surfaces lie along a line in gradient space that is perpendicular to the line of intersection of the surfaces in the image—to the case where the image line is at any angle. We simply imagine rotating the x-y axes (i.e., rotating the camera) until the edge is vertical; then the observation of perpendicularity can be made.

Once the gradient-space line on which G_1 and G_2 lie is fixed, the relationship of G_1 and G_2 within it determines the property of the edge. The situation is most easily understood by imagining a hinge made by the two planes. Suppose we fix G_1 (i.e., the orientation of plane P_1 on the left side of the edge) and rotate only plane P_2 around the hinge axis as shown in Figure B7–3. The corresponding movement of G_2 in the gradient space is shown in Figure B7–6. If plane P_2 is facing to the very far right (i.e., G_2 is far to the right of G_1), the edge is a very sharp convex edge. As it rotates back toward the left, G_2 moves on the gradient-space line toward the left and closer to G_1: the convexity decreases. When the plane P_2 comes to have the same orientation as plane P_1 ($G_1 = G_2$), then we do not see the edge. When plane P_2 rotates further and faces more left than plane P_1, the edge becomes concave. From these observations, we have the following rule: If an edge is convex $(+)$, the

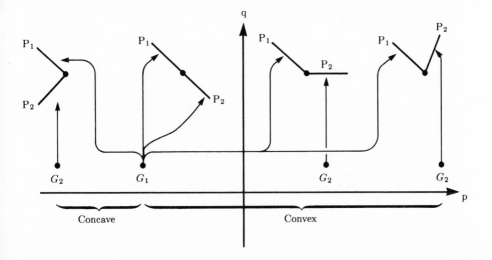

Figure B7–6.   Relationships of gradients with convex and concave edges.

gradients of its planes are ordered in the same order as are the corresponding regions in the picture. If the edge is concave, their order is reversed.

In this way, the line labels $(+, -)$ can be related with properties of the gradients. For instance, Figure B7–7a shows what the labeling of Figure B7–1 means in terms of gradients. Suppose the gradient of R_1 is at G_1. Since R_1 and R_2 are connected by a convex line AB, the gradient of R_2 must be on a line that passes through G_1 and is perpendicular to AB. Suppose it is at G_2. Region R_3 is connected to both R_1 and R_2 by convex lines, BD and BC. Therefore, its gradient G_3 is determined at the intersection of lines extending from G_1 and G_2 in the direction perpendicular to BD and BC, respectively. Thus, G_1, G_2, and G_3 form a triangle of a particular shape. From the way we choose G_1 and G_2, we see that the location and the scale of the triangle are arbitrary, but the shape and orientation are strictly determined by the picture. These are exactly the constraints that the labeling of Figure B7–1 represents.

For Figure B7–2, we can now easily show that this labeling is not realizable. When the gradient of R_1 is fixed, the gradient of R_2 cannot satisfy both constraints imposed by the convex edges AB and CD. This is illustrated in Figure B7–7b.

POLY

Mackworth's POLY is a program to interpret line drawings as three-dimensional scenes. Unlike the labeling schemes of Huffman, Clowes, and Waltz, it does this by reasoning about surface orientations based on the properties of the gradient space.

Given a line drawing, POLY first finds a coherent interpretation in which the gradients of planes can have consistent relationships and as many edges as possible are *connect edges* (either convex or concave). These connect edges are important because they represent a physical connection between surfaces, which corresponds to the gradient-space constraint described above. POLY searches for such an interpretation in a binary-tree-search manner: First, it examines the interpretation in which all edges are connect edges; then, if it is incoherent, interpretations with all edges but one as connect edges; and so on. Next, POLY determines convexity or concavity of the connect edges. Finally, it interprets occluding edges (nonconnect edges) and determines which surface of the line is in front of the other.

Consider how POLY works for the example of Figure B7–8. It first picks up the background surface A and arbitrarily assigns a gradient of $(0,0)$ (origin of the gradient space) to it. Next, it takes region B. Surfaces A and B are bounded by lines 1 and 2. Assume that line 1 is a connect edge. The gradient of B must be on a gradient-space line (perpendicular to line 1) that passes through the gradient of A. Let us choose G_B at a unit distance from G_A, as shown in Figure B7–9a. Notice that the origin and the scale of this figure are arbitrary.

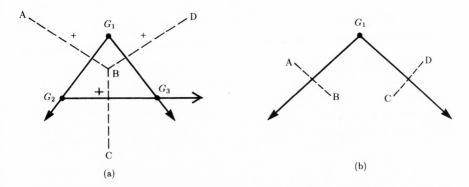

Figure B7–7.   (a) Gradients for the labeling of Figure B7–1; (b) proof that
the labeling of Figure B7–2 is not realizable.

POLY now proceeds to line 2. It cannot be a connect edge, because if it were, G_B in Figure B7–9a would have to lie on a line perpendicular to line 2 through G_A; thus, line 2 is occluding.

Proceed to line 3, which bounds between regions B and C. If line 3 is a connect edge, G_C must be on a line perpendicular to line 3 through G_B. Region C shares lines 4 and 5 with the interpreted region A. Obviously, they both cannot be connect edges. The interpretation in which lines 1, 3, and 5 are connect edges and lines 2 and 4 are occluding edges is rejected by the single rule that three noncollinear points in space (the corners a, b, and c) cannot simultaneously lie on two planes (A and B). So a legal interpretation is that lines 1, 3, and 4 are connect edges, while lines 2 and 5 are not. At this point, the situation in the gradient space is found to be either one of the two cases in Figure B7–9b.

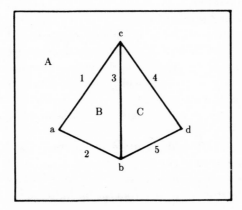

Figure B7–8.   A simple line drawing.

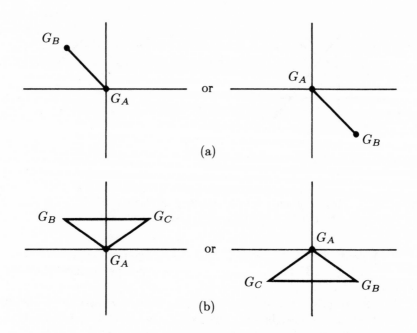

Figure B7–9.   (a) Gradients G_A and G_B for line 1 to be a connected
               edge; (b) gradients G_A, G_B, and G_C for the case in which
               lines 1, 3, and 4 are connected edges.

Next, POLY decides convexity or concavity of connect edges. This is done
by referring to the gradient-space constraints the program has established so
far. For the case on the left of Figure B7–9b, we can easily see that lines 1
and 4 are concave and line 3 is convex. For the case on the right, lines 1 and
4 are convex and line 3 is concave.

Finally, the program looks at the nonconnect edges (lines 2 and 5). It
uses the fact that if two surfaces intersect in a connect edge that is known to
be, say, convex, then at any position in the picture it will be apparent which
surface is in front. For the case in which connect edges 1 and 4 are concave
and 3 is convex, on the right side of line 1, B is always in front of A. In
this way, we know that occluding edges 2 and 5 belong to surfaces B and C,
respectively.

Continued search will yield one more interpretation with three connected
edges: Lines 2, 3, and 5 are connect edges and 1 and 4 are occluding. The
program continues to generate interpretations with fewer connect edges; for
example, the tetrahedron separated from the background has only one connect
edge, namely, line 3.

Huffman's $\phi(\phi')$-point Test

We should note that the coherency in the gradient space is still only a necessary condition for the shape to be realizable by planar surfaces. One of the most illustrative examples is a *truncated pyramid;* Figure B7–10a is the side view and Figure B7–10b is the top view. Surfaces *A*, *B*, and *C* connect each other at convex edges 1, 2, and 3. This drawing may seem perfect to most people, but it is actually unrealizable.

For this configuration to be realizable, lines 1, 2, and 3 must meet at a point: Three planes meet only at a point. In the gradient space, however, the constraints on their gradients are coherent and cannot detect the inconsistency in the relationships of the three planes. The reason is obvious from the equation $-z = px + qy + c$: The gradient takes into account only the orientation (p, q) but not the location (c) of the plane.

Huffman (1977) presents a $\phi(\phi')$-point test as the necessary and sufficient condition for a *cut set* of lines (equivalently, a set of regions separated by those lines) to be realizable by plane surfaces. Consider again the example shown in Figure B7–10b, and take the set of lines 1, 2, and 3 cut by the dotted loop. First, the $\phi(\phi')$-point test gives each line belonging to the cut set of lines an orientation shown as a big arrow according to its label, either coming into the loop if the label is "+" or going out from it if the label is "−" (see Fig. B7–10c). Then the $\phi(\phi')$-point is a point that is to the right (left) of some line of the cut set and that is not to the left (right) of any other lines. The $\phi(\phi')$-point test simply checks whether either a ϕ-point or a ϕ'-point exists, and if either one exists, then the cut set is unrealizable. In fact, unless 1, 2, and 3 meet at a single point, ϕ or ϕ' points exist, and therefore the configuration of Figure B7–10 is unrealizable. Unfortunately, it

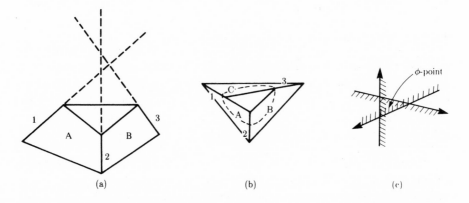

Figure B7–10.   Impossible truncated pyramid: (a) side view; (b) top view; (c) Huffman's $\phi(\phi')$-point test.

can *not* be said that if all the cut sets in the interpretation pass the $\phi(\phi')$-point test, the whole interpretation is realizable by only plane surfaces. That is, the $\phi(\phi')$-point test is the necessary and sufficient condition for the realizability of a cut set of lines, but not of the whole interpretation.

Conclusion

Mackworth used the gradients of planes to constrain interpretations of lines in an image. In so doing, he moved a step away from qualitative labeling schemes to a quantitative scheme. This approach was continued by Kanade, whose research is discussed in Article XIII.B8.

References

See Mackworth (1973) for the explanation of POLY. More results and details can be found in his thesis (Mackworth, 1974). Mackworth (1977) presents an interesting overview of scene analysis.

B8. The Origami World and Shape Recovery:
T. Kanade

FOR MOST line drawings, the Huffman-Clowes-Waltz labeling method gives a unique interpretation that looks very natural to human viewers. However, the method exploits no constraints other than those implicit in the assumption of a trihedral world and, therefore, there is no reason to expect it to give a natural interpretation. Furthermore, as was pointed out in Article XIII.B7, labeling does not quantitatively specify the shape of an object; as a matter of fact, one cannot generate a rotated view of the object from the labeling. The work of Kanade (1979, 1980b) sheds light on the issue of multiple interpretations and quantitative shape recovery of "natural" interpretations. Kanade introduced the *Origami world*.

Origami World Labeling

The Origami world is composed of planar surfaces, rather than solids. In this world, line drawings can be labeled by a technique much like the Huffman-Clowes-Waltz method, but the Origami world allows more objects than are allowed by trihedral worlds. For example, although the *box* line drawing in Figure B8–1 looks simple and perfect, the trihedral-world labeling scheme cannot generate its interpretation, because the trihedral world assumes solid objects, whereas corners like *a* in the figure are made of only two surfaces (if the object is a box).

In the Origami world, it is assumed that no more than three surfaces meet at a vertex (in the trihedral world exactly three surfaces are assumed). Specifically, the 12 quadrant planes obtained by intersecting three full planes are considered as primitives, as shown in Figure B8–2. The vertices that can be generated by those primitives are called *up-to-three-surface* vertices.

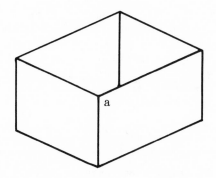

Figure B8–1.   A line drawing of a "box."

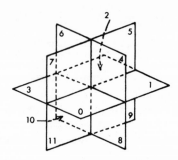

Figure B8–2.   Twelve quadrant planes to generate
up-to-three-surface vertices.

All legal junction labels (i.e., the possible appearances of all up-to-three-surface vertices) can be enumerated by fixing the eye position in one of the eight octants bounded by the quadrant planes and generating all possible $(2^{12} = 4,096)$ combinations of occupied and vacant quadrants. This method is analogous to the one that generates trihedral junction labels; in the trihedral world, the primitives were the eight octant subspaces rather than the 12 quadrants. Table B8–1 shows the number of legal junctions in the Origami world, as compared with the trihedral junction world.

Given the junction dictionary, Waltz filtering might be used to assign labels to line drawings. However, labeling in the Origami world cannot rely only on the filtering of junction labels, because the weaker restrictions at the vertices result in a large number of interpretations that are consistent with the junction dictionary but do not correspond to any physically realizable configurations. More thorough and global constraints concerning surface orientations are needed to eliminate this problem.

TABLE B8–1

Comparison of the Junction Dictionaries
for L, ARROW, FORK, and T Junction Types

Junction type	Huffman-Clowes dictionary	Origami-world dictionary[*]
L	6	8
ARROW	3	15
FORK	3	9
T	4	16

[*]The Origami-world dictionary includes other junction types, such as K, X, and PSI.

The junction dictionary for the Origami world is augmented by constraints in the gradient space that must be satisfied by the surfaces incident at the junction. As shown in Figure B8–3, the constraints are represented by links that connect a pair of related regions and that include information about the constraints on their gradients. The relationships between gradients and line labels are used in generating these constraints.

In junction labelings such as those shown in Figure B8–3b, the line of intersection of two surfaces is hidden from the viewer (occluded) by one of the surfaces. This junction label is typically the result of folding a sheet of paper along BC: Region R_1, which is folded toward the viewer, occludes a part of R_2. However, this junction label may represent a more general case: Regions R_1 and R_2 might be separate sheets of paper, whose intersection line lies anywhere in R_1 (as in the middle of Fig. B8–3b). That is, if we remove the right-hand part of R_1 that is occluding R_2, the rest of R_1 and R_2 will form a convex intersection line, and it can be anywhere in the angle ABC.

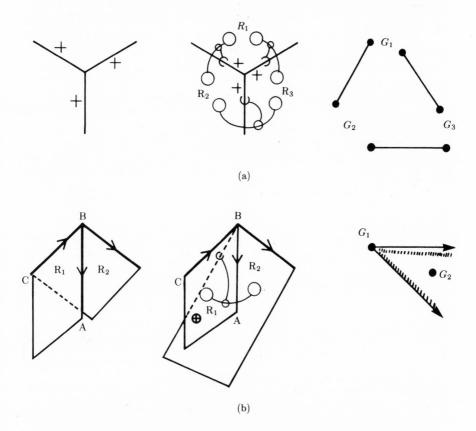

(a)

(b)

Figure B8–3.   Augmented junction dictionary in the Origami world.

The constraint to be satisfied is, therefore, that the gradient G_2 should be inside of the fan-shaped area whose origin is at G_1 and is bounded by lines perpendicular to AB and BC. This constraint will be represented by a *link* attached to the junction dictionary entry for this junction labeling. The line of intersection can be called an *occluded intersection line* and denoted by the label " $\oplus$."

Labeling Procedure

The labeling procedure of the Origami world uses the augmented dictionary described above. First, Waltz filtering on the junction labels is performed. Next, the procedure begins to assign a junction label to each junction, one by one. When a junction label is assigned to a junction, the gradient-space constraints represented by the associated links are instantiated by using the directions of the lines at that particular junction.

The labeling procedure of the Origami world tests the consistency of surface orientations by using these instantiated gradient-space constraints. The test can be performed systematically with another iterative operation that filters out possible relative positions for the gradient of each surface. Details are presented in Kanade (1980b).

Interestingly, the labeling of the Origami world usually results in multiple labelings for a single line-drawing. A *cube* scene has three interpretations, as shown in Figure B8–4: a convex corner, a concave corner, and a peculiar shape made as shown in Figure B8–4d. Similarly, the *box* line drawing of Figure B8–1 has eight labelings, two of which are shown in Figure B8–5: The labeling in Figure B8–5a corresponds to an "ordinary" box—the two front faces form a convex intersection and partially occlude the rear two faces, which form a concave intersection. The labeling in Figure B8–5b corresponds to a "squashed box"—the front two faces, as well as the rear two, form a concave intersection.

When we, as humans, interpret these line drawings, we do not usually think of such peculiar shapes as Figure B8–4d and Figure B8–5b even as *possible* interpretations. They look very unnatural. But it is important to note that all labelings are equally natural in terms of geometrical realizability.

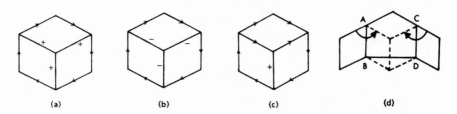

Figure B8–4.   Interpretation of the "cube" line drawing.

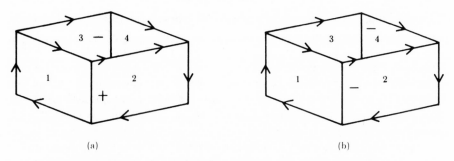

(a)   (b)

Figure B8–5.   Two interpretations of a "box" line drawing.

Quantitative Shape Recovery and "Natural" Interpretations

Labeling a line drawing only qualitatively characterizes shape; it does not give a specific shape. In fact, the two figures in Figure B8–6 have the same labelings (the same constraints in terms of realizability), even though they seem to depict different shapes. This suggests that we interpret line drawings using other constraints than those that concern realizability. Kanade developed a method for mapping image properties into shape constraints for recovering three-dimensional quantitative shapes. He introduced the idea of regularity heuristics, specifically, a *parallel-line heuristic* and a *skewed-symmetry heuristic*.

Parallel-line heuristic. The parallel-line heuristic is:

> If two lines are parallel in the picture,
> they depict parallel lines in the scene.

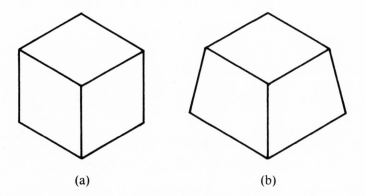

(a)   (b)

Figure B8–6.   These have the same set of labelings, even though usually (a) is perceived as a "cube" and (b) as a "trapezoidal block."

Under orthographic projection, this is not always the case. The converse, however, is always true: Parallel lines in the scene will be depicted as parallel lines in the image. (Under perspective projection, substitute "converging lines" for "parallel lines"; see Kender, 1979.)

Consider the constraint that this heuristic puts on the gradients of two planes if a pair of their boundary lines is parallel in the picture, as shown in Figure B8–7: Their gradients should be on a gradient-space line that is perpendicular to the parallel boundary lines in the image. In fact, if a pair of boundary lines is really parallel in the three-dimensional space, we can translate one of the planes toward the other, without changing its orientation, and make the two planes intersect along those boundary lines. Therefore, the gradients of the two planes should have the same relationship that holds for surfaces connected by a convex or concave line. (See Article XIII.B7 for the properties of the gradient space.)

Skewed-symmetry heuristic. Symmetry in a two-dimensional picture has an axis for which the opposite sides are reflective: The symmetrical property is found along the transverse lines perpendicular to the symmetry axis. The concept of *skewed symmetry* relaxes this condition a little, referring to the class of two-dimensional shapes in which symmetry is found along lines not necessarily perpendicular to the axis, but at a fixed angle to it. Figure B8–8 shows a few examples. Formally, these shapes are defined as two-dimensional, linear (affine) transformations of real symmetries. A skewed symmetry defines two directions, called the *skewed-symmetry axis* and the *skewed-transverse axis*, as shown in Figure B8–8.

The skewed-symmetry heuristic is:

> A skewed symmetry in the image depicts a real symmetry
> in the scene viewed from some (unknown) viewing angle.

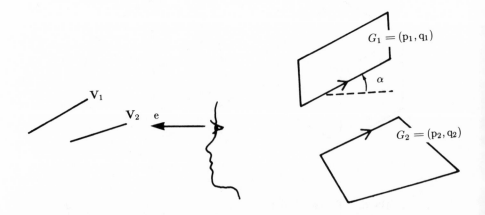

Figure B8–7.   Parallel-line heuristics.

We can transform this heuristic into constraints in the gradient space. Let α and β denote the directional angles of the skewed-symmetry axis and the skewed-transverse axis, respectively, as shown in Figure B8–8d. Let $G = (p, q)$ be the gradient of the plane that includes the skewed symmetry. The heuristic demands that the two three-dimensional space vectors corresponding to the skewed-symmetry axis and the skewed-transverse axis be perpendicular.

It can be shown that the gradient $G = (p, q)$ is on the hyperbola shown in Figure B8–9. That is, the skewed symmetry defined by α and β in the picture can be the projection of a real symmetry if and only if the gradient is on this hyperbola. It might appear that if we assume the skewed symmetry in the picture to be a projection of a real symmetry, the surface orientation is uniquely determined; actually, we have still an infinite number of possible orientations represented by the points on the hyperbola in gradient space.

The vertices G_T and G'_T of the hyperbola represent special orientations with interesting properties. Since they are closest to the origin of the gradient space, and since the distance from the origin to a gradient represents the magnitude of the surface slant, G_T and G'_T correspond to the least slanted orientations that can produce the skewed symmetry in the picture from a real symmetry in the scene.

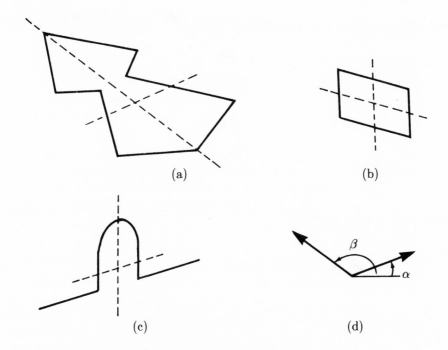

(a)

(b)

(c)

(d)

Figure B8–8.   Skewed symmetry.

Unique Determination of Gradients

A "cube" scene has three labelings, as shown in Figure B8–4; the first is reproduced in Figure B8–10a. The labeling indicates that there are three totally visible surfaces, S_1 ($=$ $V_3 V_4 V_7 V_2$), S_2 ($=$ $V_5 V_6 V_7 V_4$), and S_3 ($=$ $V_1 V_2 V_7 V_6$), and that their gradients G_1, G_2, and G_3 should form a triangle as shown in Figure B8–10b. On the other hand, S_1, S_2, and S_3 have skewed symmetries: Their skewed-symmetry axes and skewed-transverse axes are shown in Figure B8–10a as dotted lines. If we assume these skewed symmetries to be projections of real symmetries, we can draw the hyperbola for each surface as shown in Figure B8–10c.

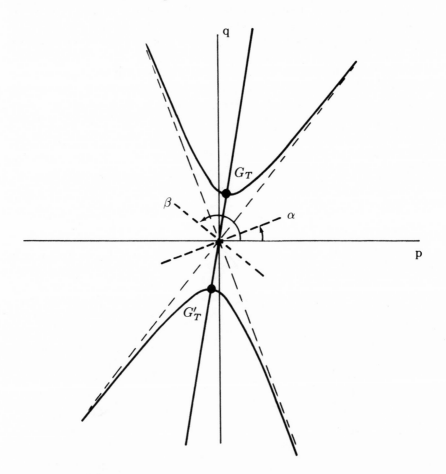

Figure B8–9.   A hyperbola corresponding to the skewed symmetry defined
by angles α and β.

Now, our problem is thus reduced to placing the triangle of Figure B8–10b in Figure B8–10c by shrinking, expanding, and translating it so that each vertex of the triangle is on the corresponding hyperbola. Kanade proved that the location shown in Figure B8–10c is the only possibility and that the corresponding three-dimensional shape is a cube.

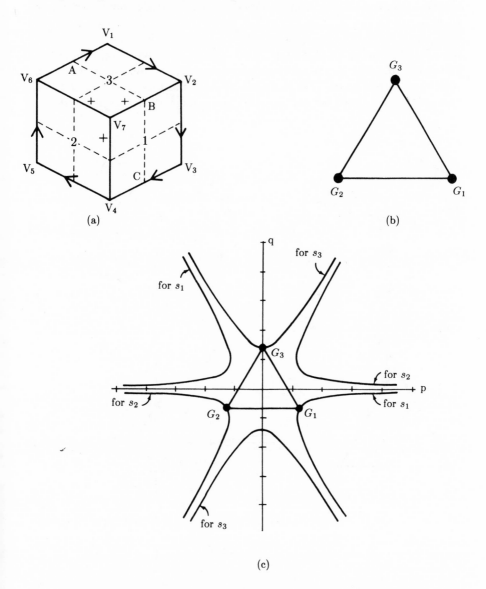

Figure B8–10.   Quantitative shape recovery of a "cube" scene.

Now consider the line drawing of the trapezoidal-block scene in Figure B8–11. As we have noted, this line drawing has the same qualitative interpretations (line labelings) as a cube scene but it seems to depict a quantitatively different shape. What makes the difference? The same interpretation process that applied to the cube applies to the trapezoidal block, but with a different shape. The labeling imposes the same constraints on the gradients of the surfaces S_1, S_2, and S_3 as the convex-corner interpretation for the cube scene, and they also have skewed symmetries. However, the axes for the skewed symmetries of S_1 and S_2 are slightly different from the case of Figure B8–10, so the shape and location of the corresponding hyperbolas also change. As a result, the gradient-space triangle must be placed as shown in Figure B8–11d. When we compare this assignment with Figure B8–10, the

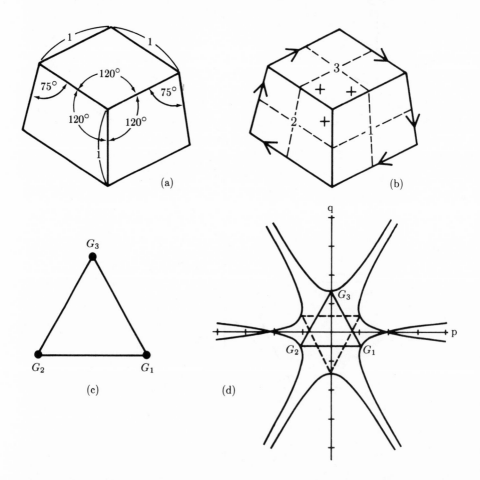

Figure B8–11.   Quantitative shape recovery of a trapezoidal-block scene.

location of G_3 is the same, but G_1 and G_2 are closer to G_3. In this assignment of gradients, the angle made by S_1 and S_3 is equal to that made by S_2 and S_3 and is larger than 90 degrees.

Kanade also showed that the "usual" box shape can be recovered from the labeled line drawing of Figure B8–5a by similar means.

The Violation of Regularity Heuristics by "Strange" Shapes

The labelings treated so far all correspond to the most "natural" interpretations of the pictures. Recall that the theory of the Origami world yields other labelings. Kanade showed that those shapes implied by the labelings are possible but violate some of the regularity heuristics.

The labeling of Figure B8–5b represents a "squashed" box with the front two faces going in. Figure B8–12 illustrates the constraints on the gradient space imposed by the labeling: G_1 lies right of G_2, and G_3 and G_4 should be within the right and left hatched areas, respectively. Lines V_1V_7 and V_2V_3 are parallel. For the parallel-line heuristic to hold, G_1 and G_4 (the gradients of surfaces that include those lines) must be on a line perpendicular to V_1V_7 (or V_2V_3). However, the diagram indicates that this is not possible.

Of course, it is possible to assign the gradients if we violate the heuristics. For example, Figure B8–13a is a possible selection of gradients for a "phony" box that corresponds to the interpretation of Figure B8–5b. This curious shape, illustrated in Figure B8–13b, appears as an ordinary box only when seen from a particular position. Notice that the image regularity (parallelism) we observed in the original view has disappeared. In contrast, the "ordinary" box shape conserves these regularities, no matter from what direction it is seen.

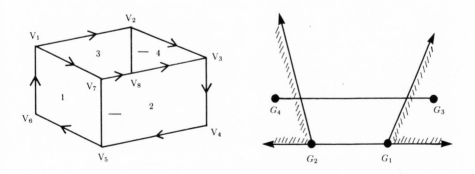

Figure B8–12.   Constraints imposed by the labeling of Figure B8–5b. The parallel-line heuristic cannot be satisfied in this case.

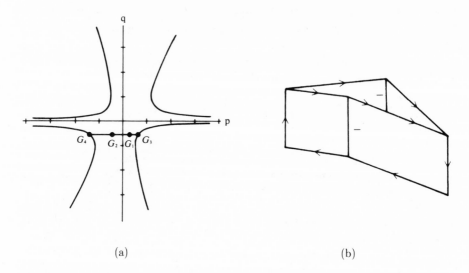

(a)   (b)

Figure B8–13.   A "phony-box" interpretation: (a) selection of gradients; (b) its view from the other direction.

Conclusion

Kanade introduced a representation, called the Origami world, that admits more objects than the trihedral world does. Because line labels were not enough to recover the shape, Kanade's junction dictionary was augmented with constraints on gradients. He also tackled the question of what makes one interpretation of a scene more "natural" than another; by introducing two heuristics that filtered out unnatural interpretations he showed explicitly how much geometrical assumption was necessary to resolve multiple interpretations.

References

See Kanade (1979, 1980b) for details. Kanade and Kender (1980) extend the idea of heuristics on shape constraints into a more general form.

C. EARLY PROCESSING OF VISUAL DATA

C1. Visual Input

COMPUTER VISION SYSTEMS must be able to sense their environment. This sensing is not limited to intensity (i.e., brightness), but includes depth, color, and texture information as well. This article, however, is mainly concerned with the physical means of intensity imaging—with the geometry of picture-taking, image-input devices, and the digitization of video signals. Depth sensing is discussed in Articles XIII.D3 and XIII.D4, and color in Article XIII.C2.

The discussion here will be technical and a little removed from what we normally consider Artificial Intelligence. Vision systems are very different from other AI systems in that some of the information they process is taken from a real, noisy, variable, physical environment. Thus, this article is concerned with the "eyes" of a vision system and with the issues involved in designing and representing these sensors so that they provide high-quality information for the rest of the system.

The Camera Model

The relationship between a camera and a scene defines the *geometry* of the picture-taking process. We begin with the simple *pinhole-lens* model of a camera and derive the direct perspective transform that tells how points on an object are projected onto points in an image. We then represent the perspective transform and its inverse as linear transformations by expressing them with *homogeneous coordinates*. A more thorough introduction to the camera model and the use of homogeneous coordinates is found in Duda and Hart (1973).

The pinhole camera and central projection. The simplest model of the picture-taking process is the pinhole-camera model in which the lens is replaced by a pinhole and the image plane lies at a distance, f, behind the pinhole. Because this configuration gives a mapping from the scene to the image plane in which the images are flipped left to right and upside down, it is more convenient to express this model as a *central projection*. In the central-projection model, the image plane is located *in front* of the pinhole by a distance f, as shown in Figure C1–1. For simplicity we define the center of the image plane as the origin, and the z-axis as the line that intersects the pinhole and the origin. Thus, the pinhole is at $(0, 0, f)$ and points on the image plane are at $(x_p, y_p, 0)$. We shall denote points on the image plane with the subscript p.

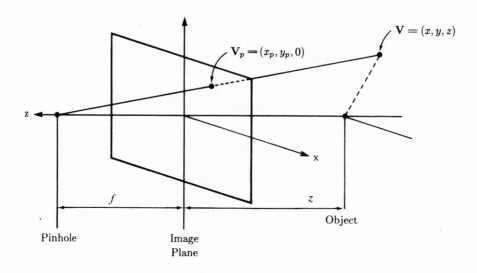

Figure C1–1.   Visual input.

Expressing the camera model as a central projection enables us to deter-mine the projection of a point on an object $\mathbf{V} = (x, y, z)^T$ onto a point in the image plane $\mathbf{V}_p = (x_p, y_p, 0)^T$:

$$\frac{x_p}{f} = \frac{x}{f - z}, \qquad \frac{y_p}{f} = \frac{y}{f - z}$$

or   (1)

$$x_p = \frac{fx}{f - z}, \qquad y_p = \frac{fy}{f - z}.$$

Equivalently, we can determine the *back projection* from each point in the image plane onto a line in three-dimensional space:

$$x = \frac{x_p(f - z)}{f}, \qquad y = \frac{y_p(f - z)}{f}. \tag{2}$$

These equations represent the line passing from the pinhole through the image point $\mathbf{V}_p$, where z (depth) is a free parameter. In other words, all points $(x, y, z)^T$ on this line are projected to an image point $\mathbf{V}_p = (x_p, y_p, 0)^T$. We can write the equations with an auxiliary variable, $\lambda = (f - z)/f$, to obtain

$$\begin{aligned} x &= x_p \lambda \\ y &= y_p \lambda \\ z &= f(1 - \lambda). \end{aligned} \tag{3}$$

Equations (1) and (2) are nonlinear. It is often useful to express this projection as a linear transformation, at the expense of adding an extra dimension to our system. This representation is called *homogeneous coordinates*. The vector $\mathbf{V} = (x, y, z)^T$ is expressed as

$$\tilde{\mathbf{V}} = (wx, wy, wz, w)^T, \tag{4}$$

where w is an arbitrary constant. The original vector, $\mathbf{V}$, can be recovered from the first three components by dividing by the fourth. Thus, $(x, y, z, 1)$ and (wx, wy, wz, w) denote the same three-dimensional points. We will use the " $\tilde{\ }$ " notation to denote homogeneous coordinates.

With homogeneous coordinates we can now express the perspective transform as a linear matrix operation. An object point $\mathbf{V}$ is mapped onto an image point $\mathbf{V}_p$ by

$$\tilde{\mathbf{V}}_p = \mathbf{P}\tilde{\mathbf{V}}, \tag{5}$$

where $\mathbf{P}$ is the matrix

$$\mathbf{P} = \begin{pmatrix} 1 & 0 & 0 & 0 \\ 0 & 1 & 0 & 0 \\ 0 & 0 & 1 & 0 \\ 0 & 0 & \frac{-1}{f} & 1 \end{pmatrix}. \tag{6}$$

In fact, we can see that by substituting $\tilde{\mathbf{V}} = (x, y, z, 1)^T$,

$$\tilde{\mathbf{V}}_p = \begin{pmatrix} x \\ y \\ z \\ \frac{f-z}{f} \end{pmatrix} = \begin{pmatrix} x \\ y \\ z \\ \lambda \end{pmatrix}. \tag{7}$$

By dividing the first three components by the fourth, we obtain the vector $(x/\lambda, y/\lambda, z/\lambda, 1)^T = (x_p, y_p, z/\lambda, 1)^T$. The first and second components are the coordinates of the points $\mathbf{V}_p$ in the image. The third component determines the position of the point on the line that projects from the pinhole through the image point $\mathbf{V}_p$.

Having found $\mathbf{P}$, we are ready to determine the inverse of the linear transformation $\mathbf{P}$,

$$\tilde{\mathbf{V}} = \mathbf{P}^{-1}\tilde{\mathbf{V}}_p. \tag{8}$$

$\mathbf{P}^{-1}$ is found to be

$$\mathbf{P}^{-1} = \begin{pmatrix} 1 & 0 & 0 & 0 \\ 0 & 1 & 0 & 0 \\ 0 & 0 & 1 & 0 \\ 0 & 0 & \frac{1}{f} & 1 \end{pmatrix}. \tag{9}$$

However, if we simply plug an image point $\mathbf{V}_p = (x_p, y_p, 0, 1)^T$ into equation (8) and then convert to Cartesian coordinates, we get a point $\mathbf{V} = (x_p, y_p, 0)^T$ when what we desire is a line.

The way out of this difficulty is to allow the z coordinate of $\mathbf{V}_p$ to be nonzero, say, β. Upon evaluating equation (8) and then converting to Cartesian coordinates, we get:

$$
\mathbf{V} = \begin{pmatrix} \frac{fx_p}{f+\beta} \\ \frac{fy_p}{f+\beta} \\ \frac{f\beta}{f+\beta} \end{pmatrix}.
\tag{10}
$$

By denoting $\lambda = f/(f + \beta)$ we have the same equation as equation (3).

It is often desirable to denote object points with respect to a "world coordinate," which may not be the same as the coordinate system that is fixed to the camera. Consider the process of taking a picture. The camera is first located at a standard position, whose location and orientation are known in the world-coordinate system. Then we move the camera to a desired position and point it in the desired direction by *panning*, rotation in the horizontal plane; *tilting*, rotation in the vertical plane; and *rolling*, rotation around the optical axis. Thus, transformation from the world coordinate to the image coordinate can be accomplished by expressing the position and orientation of the camera as a series of linear transforms in homogeneous coordinates.

Let us use the following symbols to denote transformations involved in mapping world coordinates into image coordinates:

T: Translation of the camera center from the origin of the world-coordinate system;

R: Rotation (pan, tilt, and roll) about the camera center;

G: Translation of the lens position from the camera center.

Then the projection of a point $\tilde{\mathbf{V}}^*$ in three-dimensional space that is expressed in world coordinates to an image point $\tilde{\mathbf{V}}_p$ that is expressed in image coordinates is accomplished by

$$
\tilde{\mathbf{V}}_p = \mathbf{P} \ \mathbf{G} \ \mathbf{R} \ \mathbf{T} \ \tilde{\mathbf{V}}^* .
\tag{11}
$$

Inversely,

$$
\tilde{\mathbf{V}}^* = \mathbf{T}^{-1}\mathbf{R}^{-1}\mathbf{G}^{-1}\mathbf{P}^{-1}\tilde{\mathbf{V}}_p .
\tag{12}
$$

Since we do not use this formula in the present discussion, the matrices **G**, **R**, and **T** are not given here; see Duda and Hart (1973) for more detail. Determining the transformation $\mathbf{K} = \mathbf{P} \ \mathbf{G} \ \mathbf{R} \ \mathbf{T}$ is called *camera calibration*, or calculating the *camera model*. It is an important step in the interpretation of aerial photographs, for example, in stereo vision (see Article XIII.D3).

Imaging Devices

There are two types of components in a visual sensing system: illuminators and light sensors. Illumination may be totally uncontrolled, as in an outdoor scene. Or illumination may be controlled and focused, as a moving spot, as a stripe, as shape of light, or as single-source illumination from a known reference point (see Article XIII.D4 for more detail). Similarly, light sensing may be general, as in a simple photomultiplier or photodiode, or focused, as in a TV camera. In a useful vision system, either the illuminator or the light sensor must be an *imaging* device; that is, it must have the ability to access distinct elements of the scene separately.

One issue in choosing between *raster-scanning* devices like a TV camera and *random-access* devices is the time-space trade-off. If computer-memory usage must be minimized, random-access devices are advantageous, since complete images need not be stored. However, the cost of memory is being continually reduced, and a random-access frame buffer—into which an imaging device writes image data continuously and from which the computer reads image data randomly—is available, so that most vision systems today use this kind of hardware.

Slow random-access devices or image-storage devices with long exposure times are not useful in a scene that contains dynamically changing picture elements. In a dynamic world, quick snapshots must be taken with the faster devices. Moving objects are usually tracked by taking repeated snapshots and applying software techniques (see Article XIII.D2).

Noise and unpredictable signal fluctuation are inevitable in any system that measures light-intensity levels, because of the quantum nature of light. The severity of noise depends on several factors, including the light level, the exposure time, the dynamic range, the architecture of the sensor, and the amplification system. The signal-to-noise (S/N) ratio in a system is the ratio between the level of signal (or meaningful information) and the level of noise. The *dynamic range* is the ratio between the brightest and dimmest light levels. The *gray scale* of a sensor is the number of discrete levels of light that it can represent. If a large gray scale is required, a high S/N ratio must be guaranteed to maintain a given confidence level. In general, longer *exposure times* are needed for higher S/N ratios. The relation between gray-scale values and actual light levels is an important factor in sensing systems. Most typically, the relation is adjusted to be either linear or logarithmic. The *resolution* of a sensor is the number of discriminable points in its field of view.

Most imaging sensors exhibit interactions between the light levels measured for adjacent picture elements. This tends to cause a slight blurring in the picture. In the worst case, called *blooming*, very bright picture-elements cause nearby sensor elements to give excessive light-level readings.

Vidicon and CCD Cameras

The standard technology for electronic imaging is the vidicon camera. Most vidicon cameras include built-in electronics to produce a TV image in the standard, composite video format. They can be made to accept external horizontal and vertical synchronization. Video sensitivity is typically that of a black-body radiator at 2,854K. Spectral sensitivity ranges from 350 to 700 nanometers. Light is focused onto a photosensitive target, on which an image pattern is generated as a charge. The target is scanned by an electron beam to produce the video signal. The electron beam is generated in an evacuated glass bottle. This tends to make vidicon cameras bulky and fragile. In addition, the deflection of the electron beam tends to drift with time. Thus, a vidicon-based imaging system must be calibrated frequently. Vidicons also require a high voltage source (approximately 900 V) and have a typical mean time between failure of 1,000 hours. For these reasons, solid-state cameras (most representatively, Charge Couple Devices, or CCDs) are becoming preferable for most vision applications.

CCD cameras can be purchased as linear (one-dimensional) arrays (also known as Linear Imaging Devices, or LIDs) or as two-dimensional arrays (also known as Area Imaging Devices, or AIDs). A CCD array is composed of discrete light-sensitive elements. The light energy falling on each element builds up a charge proportional to the integrated light intensity, and then these charges are collected in capacitors beneath each element. A two-phase clock transfers these charge packets off the array and into an amplifier. The image then appears as a series of voltages at the output of the amplifier.

CCD linear arrays typically come in sizes of 256, 512, 1,024, 1,728, and 2,048 elements. CCD two-dimensional cameras typically come in sizes of 244 by 190 cells and 488 by 380 cells. These cameras are small, lightweight, and highly shock resistant. Because they are solid state, they are very reliable. Unlike vidicons, CCD cameras do not require high-voltage power and can operate on less than 50 milliwatts. They produce an output signal of approximately 1 V and have none of the lag or drift associated with vidicons. The spectral sensitivity of a CCD camera ranges from 420 to 1,100 nanometers. Most manufacturers of CCD cameras also make available the electronics for converting the image signal to the standard TV format.

One of the problems with CCDs is that sensitivity may change from cell to cell by up to 10%. However, since this deviation is stable over time, a camera can be calibrated (see Article XIII.C3). Caution is also necessary in that in most two-dimensional CCD arrays, except those for industrial applications, the cells are not square but rectangular to match the TV standards.

TV Signals

The Electronics Industries Association (EIA) has defined a standard format for TV signals. This standard, which is used in the United States, is designated RS–170. The image is divided into two fields, each consisting of 240 lines, scanned top to bottom. The fields are "interlaced" to define an image consisting of 480 lines. That is, one field contains all of the odd-numbered lines; the other, the even-numbered lines.

Between each interlace field, the scan has $22\frac{1}{2}$ line-periods to return to the top of the screen. Thus the total number of horizontal scan-line periods per image is 525. Scanning one field takes 1/60 of a second, so a complete image is produced every 1/30 of a second.

The EIA RS–170 composite video signal consists of luminance information, a horizontal synchronization period, and a vertical synchronization period. Figure C1–2 shows a typical signal for a scan line. The luminance information is contained in a signal that ranges from .7 V (black) to 1.5 V (white). Each scan line ends with an approximately 11-μsec. period for horizontal synchronization. During this time the signal is held at 0 V for approximately 4.7 μsec. (the horizontal synchronization signal). After 240 scan lines, the signal is held at 0 V for approximately 68.25 μsec. (21 scan lines) to mark the end of an interlace field. This is the vertical synchronization pulse.

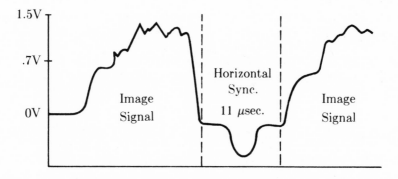

Figure C1–2. A horizontal line-period of a video signal with horizontal synchronization.

Digitization

Computer vision systems do not work with continuous signals direct from a TV camera but, rather, with digitized signals. The continuous-intensity signal is sampled at each pixel position and digitized by an analog-to-digital (A–D) converter. The number of bits required to encode the analog intensity depends on the dynamic range and the S/N ratio of the input device, but 6 to 8 bits is a typical range for most applications. For standard TV signals, 200 to 500 samples—pixels—are taken from a scan line in approximately 60 μsec. This means that sampling and A–D conversion happens every .12 to .3 μsec., and data throughput is between 3 Mbyte/sec. and 7.5 Mbyte/sec. When fast-access computer memory was expensive, many methods were devised to reduce this throughput. Today, however, the cost of memory is so low that it is common to have a buffer memory for one or more frames, and the video signal is digitized in real time. In fact, a combination buffer memory and digitizer is commercially available.

Conclusion

In this article we have introduced the front end of vision systems: imaging geometry and input devices and their characteristics. There is no Artificial Intelligence discussed here, but it is important to realize that, unlike most AI programs, vision systems interpret a real, noisy, physical world. The "eyes" of a vision system—discussed here—affect what it sees and what its "intelligence" has to work with.

References

See Duda and Hart (1973) for further discussion of the camera model.

C2. Color

MOST image-understanding research to date has dealt with black-and-white pictures only. However, there is an increasing amount of work being done with color pictures, because the additional information provided by color can be exploited in a number of ways (see, e.g., the discussion of Ohlander's algorithm in Article XIII.C5).

Color Features

A color image is produced by digitizing a scene or picture viewed through color filters. Although there is no rigid standardization of color filters for image understanding, the most common filters are Wratten filters 25, 47B, and 58, which resemble the National Television Standards Committee's (NTSC's) standard filters for color television. Because these three filters transmit primarily red, green, and blue wavelengths, respectively, color pictures digitized with these filters are sometimes called "red-green-blue" (RGB) images.

Each pixel in a color picture digitized through color filters will have several values, in this case, a red value, R, a green value, G, and a blue value, B. Typically, the R, G, and B images can be used as inputs to the color "guns" of a color-TV monitor to produce a fair reproduction of the original scene. Commercial cameras and displays are available that allow convenient input and output of RGB images; this is the primary reason for the popularity of RGB color images.

Once a picture is digitized and its pixel values are inside a computer, it is possible to transform the RGB values into some other set of color features. This can be viewed as the selection of an alternative coordinate system and set of axes for the same three-dimensional color space. Several alternatives have been popular in processing color images.

Hue, saturation, and density (or intensity). Psychologists usually measure human color perception in these terms. *Hue* (H) refers to the color name (e.g., blue, red, orange). *Saturation* (S) indicates the purity or grayness of a color (red is highly saturated; pink has the same hue but a lower saturation). *Density* (D) measures the overall brightness or darkness of the color. *HSD* coordinates form a cylindrical coordinate system in color space, where density runs along the axis of the cylinder, saturation is the radial distance from the axis, and hue is the angular displacement from some standard (such as pure red). The D-axis is sometimes called the *intensity axis*. In computer vision, *HSD* coordinates are computed by formulas (see Kender, 1977) that are intended to model roughly the psychological meanings of the terms hue, saturation, and intensity.

Normalized colors. These are computed by dividing each *RGB* coordinate by the total density (usually $R + G + B$): $r = R/(R + G + B)$, $g = G/(R + G + B)$, $b = B/(R + G + B)$. The resulting coordinates describe the density-independent (i.e., chromatic) aspect of a color. It is common to specify only density plus two normalized coordinates, such as r and g, since the other color value is easily derived. Such a system might be called *Drg*.

YIQ: Color-TV features. When a commercial color-TV signal is encoded for transmission, the *RGB* values received from the camera are transformed by a linear transformation into three features called *Y*, *I*, and *Q*. The feature *Y* is very much like density and is the only signal seen on a black-and-white TV set. The other features, *I* and *Q*, are chromaticity measures. Because the *I*- and *Q*-axes point in different directions in color space, the *YIQ* system is sometimes purported to be a model of the *opponent-color theory* of human vision. However, this resemblance is a superficial one. The *Y*, *I*, and *Q* features were strategically selected by the NTSC to model some overall effects. of the color-perception performance of humans.

XYZ: Colorimetric features. These are another linear transform of *RGB* and are standard features used in *colorimetry* (the measurement of surface colors). They do not seem to have the qualities considered desirable for computer vision, such as orthogonality or correlation with important features of typical images.

UVW (etc.): Uniform color spaces. A Euclidean distance metric in *RGB*, *YIQ*, *HSD*, or *XYZ* space does not correspond well to the subjective perceptions of color difference in humans. Psychologists have adopted some sets of nonlinear transformations into other spaces, such as *UVW*, in which Euclidean distance does match human perceptions fairly well. Unfortunately, these coordinate systems do not appear to be useful unless the vision input conforms to the tightly controlled viewing situations in which psychological color measurements are made.

Kender (1977) notes some problems that arise when performing any of these transformations on digitized images, due to the small number of bits per feature value at each pixel (typically, 6 or 8). Nonlinear transformations, which usually include a division operation, do not produce uniform distributions of transformed values, given a uniform distribution of *RGB* values. Linear transformations do not suffer from such severe problems. (See Article XIII.C5 for a discussion of linear, but highly discriminating, transforms of color features for use in region analysis.)

In addition to *RGB* input from a camera, *infrared* input has sometimes been used. This is most frequent in analysis of ground coverage from aerial or satellite images; for example, vegetation reflects green and infrared radiation and is thus relatively easy to detect.

Conclusion

Color-image-understanding programs have used different color distance metrics as well as different spaces. While the Euclidean metric is the most common, others, such as the maximum difference in any feature and the sum of differences in all features, have been successfully applied.

References

An excellent description of color science and color spaces can be found in Judd and Wyszecki (1975).

C3.   Preprocessing

PREPROCESSING is the first step of visual data processing. Its objectives are (a) *reconstruction* of the ideal, high-fidelity image from the low-quality, distorted input image and (b) *improvement* or *enhancement* of the quality of the input image by suppressing noise and emphasizing selected features to facilitate later stages of image processing.

All preprocessing techniques involve modifying an image to make it more like an *ideal* image. In this article we examine three kinds of modifications:

1. Geometrical correction,

2. Gray-scale modification,

3. Sharpening and smoothing.

Sharpening and smoothing are especially pertinent to edge detection (see Article XIII.C4). Most of the preprocessing associated with these techniques can be done in either the *spatial* domain or the *frequency* domain. The spatial domain is the distribution of intensities on the image plane that varies as a function of x and y. The frequency (Fourier) domain refers to the spatial frequencies in the image. Edges constitute high frequency; homogeneous or blurred regions, low frequency.

Geometrical Correction

An important image-enhancement technique is the correction of geometrical distortion. The most common distortion is the perspective projection that depends on the position and orientation of the imaging device relative to the object. Another distortion is the aberration in an optical sensor or an electronic scanning device.

Geometrical distortion is defined by a set of transforming equations from ideal coordinates (x, y) to distorted coordinates (x', y'):

$$x' = h_1(x, y)$$
$$y' = h_2(x, y) \, .$$

Then the ideal image $f(x, y)$ becomes the distorted image $g(x', y')$. As shown in Figure C3–1, we have sampled the distorted image at a coordinate (x', y'), but what we want are the values at the coordinate (x, y) in the ideal image. The geometrical correction to recover $f(x, y)$ from $g(x', y')$ is accomplished by first constructing the *distortion model* (h_1, h_2) and then placing the pixel value $g(x', y')$ in the correct position (x, y) to give the ideal image $f(x, y)$. The latter process is called *resampling*. There are cases in which resampling is not

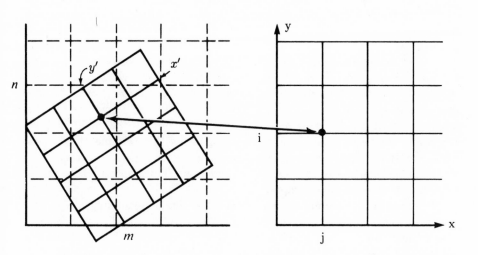

Figure C3–1. Coordinates (x, y) of the ideal image and (x', y') of the distorted image.

necessary; it is sometimes possible to do image processing with the original image and the distortion model, avoiding the expense of resampling.

Construction of the distortion model. If there are a satisfactory number of *control points*, or *landmarks*, in an image, the distortion model can be constructed from them. A control point is a point that can be found in the distorted image and whose location in the ideal image is already known precisely. This method of constructing the distortion model is called *direct modeling*.

The simplest form of the distortion equation is the linear or affine model:

$$x' = a_1 x + b_1 y + c_1$$
$$y' = a_2 x + b_2 y + c_2 \, .$$

A bilinear distortion equation is also used frequently:

$$x' = a_1 x + b_1 y + c_1 xy + d_1$$
$$y' = a_2 x + b_2 y + c_2 xy + d_2 \, .$$

Most local distortions in an image are accurately modeled by linear or bilinear equations, since more complex distortions can be approximated by linear distortions within a small area. However, for large areas and more severe distortions, higher order polynomials are necessary. Alternately, a large image may be divided into a number of smaller patches to which a linear or bilinear equation is applied.

For all these models, the coefficients are estimated by a least-squares error method. It is important to use reliable control points to attain high accuracy of modeling.

Direct modeling requires prior knowledge about the position of points in the ideal image. An alternative is *indirect modeling*, in which a structural model of distortion is derived from knowledge of the imaging process. For example, it is possible to infer a distortion model from knowledge of the angle of regard and other parameters. The parameters in the model may be determined by logging data from the imaging device, for example, the camera parameter (focal length) and the vehicle parameters (x, y, and z coordinates in three-dimensional space, and roll, pitch, and yaw). This approach is common in interpreting aerial photographs.

Resampling. Resampling involves constructing an ideal image by determining for each pixel (x, y) the corresponding pixel in the distorted image. The intensity value of the pixel in the distorted image is then copied into its undistorted position in the ideal image. Unfortunately, a pixel position (i, j) in an ideal image will usually not map to an *integer* coordinate (m, n)—the exact pixel position whose value is sampled in the distorted image—but to a point (x', y') between pixel locations (see Fig. C3–1). How, then, is the value at (x', y')—the value to be copied into pixel (i, j)—to be determined? There are two common solutions to this problem. One is to copy the value of the *nearest neighbor* to (x', y') into the ideal image. The other is to *interpolate* a value based on the values of pixels in a window around (x', y').

Gray-scale Modification

There are two kinds of *gray-scale modification* with different purposes. One is *gray-level correction*, and the other is *gray-scale transformation*.

Gray-level correction. Gray-level correction compensates for the non-uniformity of sensitivity of sensors in the sensor plane. The gray level sensed by each pixel is corrected according to the sensitivity at its location. The sensitivity of pixels can be calibrated by illuminating the sensor plane with a source of uniform brightness.

Gray-scale transformation. Gray-scale transformation is typically done to modify the gray level (or intensity) of pixels in an image in order to stretch its contrast, that is, the range between the darkest and lightest points in the image. It is common to emphasize an interesting region of gray level, as shown in Figure C3–2. A relatively small interval (a) of input intensities is stretched to emphasize it.

A third transformation related to the gray scale involves modifying the histogram of the intensity of pixels over the image. The histogram is a plot of the relative frequency of each level of intensity (Fig. C3–3a); a peak in the histogram implies a relatively large number of pixels with that intensity level.

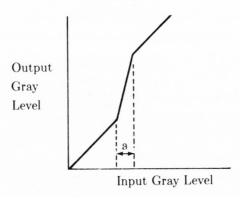

Figure C3–2.   Contrast stretching.

There are several ways to modify the histogram, depending on one's purposes, but most representative is histogram flattening.

Histogram flattening. The principle of histogram flattening is to reduce the frequency of very numerous intensity values and increase the frequency of relatively rare values. This can be done by dividing the *cumulative frequency distribution* (CFD)—the sum of the histogram values up to each intensity level—into a large number of increments for relatively frequent values and a smaller number of increments for rarer values. The first step of histogram flattening is to chop the vertical axis of the CFD into equal intervals, as shown by the horizontal lines in Figure C3–3b. Each line is drawn up to the CFD and then runs vertically down between two original intensity values. Thus, the original set of 32 intensity values (in Fig. C3–3a) is broken into sets of varying intervals, but with an approximately equal total number of pixels in each. Next, each interval is given a new intensity value, as shown below the original intensity axis in Figure C3–3b. The histogram of the new intensity values should be flatter (Fig. C3–3c).

Histogram flattening involves some loss of information when it is done digitally, since the number of intensity values is reduced (in the case of Fig. C3–3, from 32 to 9). It has the effect of sharpening images, because relatively rare intensity values, such as those at edges, are emphasized at the expense of common intensity values, such as those in regions. It is also a useful adjustment before comparing two images of similar scenes taken under different lighting conditions (i.e., with different original intensity scales).

Sharpening

Sharpening, or deblurring, improves the quality of blurred images. The simplest methods include *spatial differentiation* and *high-emphasis frequency filtering*. However, special treatment is necessary when an image is noisy.

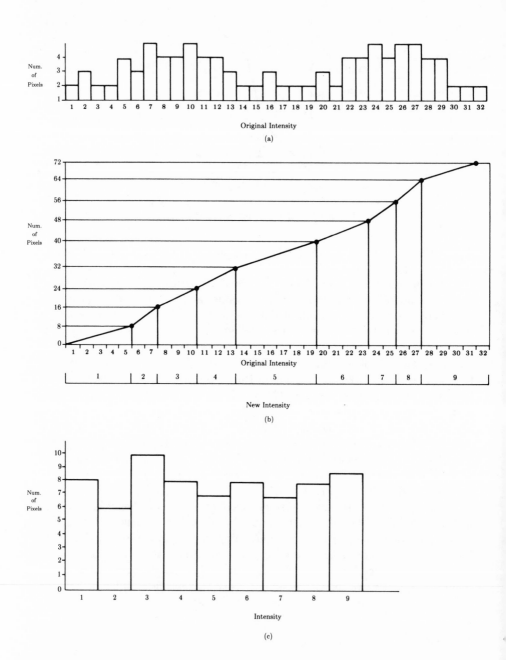

Figure C3–3. Histogram flattening: (a) Original histogram; (b) cumulative frequency distribution; (c) new histogram.

Differentiation and high-emphasis filtering tend to emphasize noise in addition to intensifying edges. One approach to this problem is to apply these operators only to the frequency region in which the signal is stronger than the noise. Another approach is first to remove the noise by *smoothing* and then to sharpen the image.

Spatial differentiation. The principle of this method is illustrated in Figure C3–4. Intensifying edges can be accomplished by subtracting the second derivative of a function from the function itself. Figure C3–4 shows this for a one-dimensional curve; for a two-dimensional image, sharpening involves subtracting the sum of the second-order derivatives (Laplacian) of a picture function from the function itself.

Since an image is represented by discrete pixels, the derivative of the picture function at a pixel is approximated by the difference between the intensities of adjacent pixels. Thus, the first differences in the x and y directions are as follows:

$$f_x(i,j) = f(i,j) - f(i-1,j)$$
$$f_y(i,j) = f(i,j) - f(i,j-1),$$

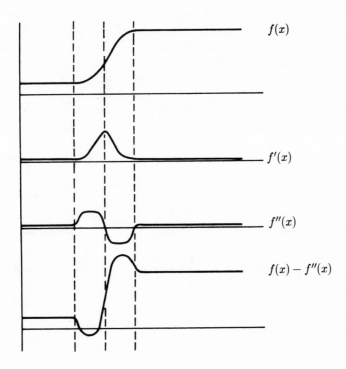

Figure C3–4. Sharpening by spatial differentiation.

where f is the image intensity and i and j are row and column coordinates, respectively.

The higher order differences can be derived by repeating the first-order differences. In particular, the second-order differences are:

$$f_{xx}(i,j) = f_x(i+1,j) - f_x(i,j)$$
$$= f(i+1,j) + f(i-1,j) - 2f(i,j)$$
$$f_{yy}(i,j) = f(i,j+1) + f(i,j-1) - 2f(i,j) \,.$$

The discrete version of the Laplacian operator is, thus, given as follows:

$$\nabla^2 f(i,j) = f_{xx}f(i,j) + f_{yy}(i,j)$$
$$= [f(i+1,j) + f(i-1,j) + f(i,j+1) + f(i,j-1)] - 4f(i,j) \,.$$

Notice that the second differences, f_{xx} and f_{yy}, can be represented by the one-dimensional windows shown in Figure C3–5a, and the Laplacian operator ∇^2 can be represented by the window in Figure C3–5b. Each window has as many cells as there are terms in its corresponding equation, and each cell contains the coefficient of one of the terms. To derive a *Laplacian image*—an image of the second derivative of the original image—the window is centered over a pixel, and the values in the pixels corresponding to the window positions are multiplied by the coefficients in the window (see Fig. C3–6). The sum of these multiplications is the output of the operator at the picture pixel corresponding to the center cell of the window. The window is moved over the entire image to derive an array of these values—a Laplacian image. The original image can be sharpened by subtracting the Laplacian image from it.

High-emphasis filtering. The differentiation of an image is grossly interpreted in the frequency domain as filtering that emphasizes higher frequency components. Actually, any linear operator in the spatial domain (such as the discrete version of the Laplacian) can be converted into an equivalent

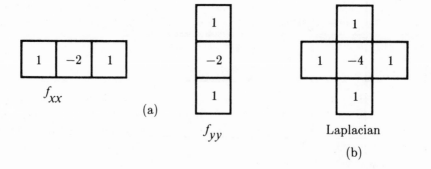

Figure C3–5.   Operators for the second derivatives (a) and Laplacian (b).

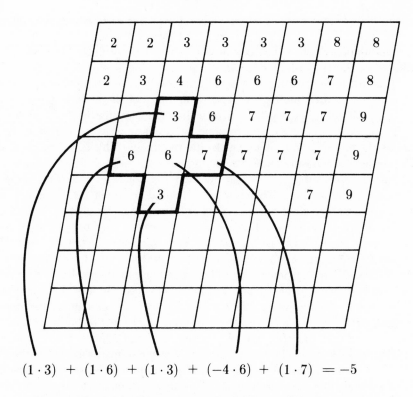

$$(1 \cdot 3) + (1 \cdot 6) + (1 \cdot 3) + (-4 \cdot 6) + (1 \cdot 7) = -5$$

Figure C3–6.   Applying the Laplacian operator to an image.

transfer function in the frequency domain. Just as a linear operator can be designed to emphasize abrupt changes in intensity, so a transfer function can be designed to emphasize areas of high frequency (i.e., areas with abrupt changes in intensity). These are two approaches with the same result: Edges and other high-frequency components of an image are sharpened.

Now, we can also design transfer functions and linear operators that *de*-emphasize areas with abrupt changes in intensity; this technique is called *smoothing*.

Smoothing

The image taken by an imaging device is often contaminated by noise, the simplest kind of which is *additive noise*. The aim of *smoothing* is to remove the noise from an image. Since smoothing techniques tend to blur the image, the main problem for smoothing methods is to remove noise without introducing undesirable blurring of details such as edges.

If the pixels contaminated with noise can be distinguished from the other pixels, the noise can be removed without adverse effects on the image. Once a noise pixel is detected, its intensity is replaced by some reasonable value—usually given by interpolating from neighboring pixels. This technique is effectively applied when the noise appears as stripes with equal intervals or as *salt and pepper* (i.e., isolated dots).

Ensemble averaging. A very effective way to reduce noise without loss of detail is to obtain multiple independent copies of the desired image. Then the image detail in each will be identical, while the superimposed noise will vary randomly. Averaging corresponding pixels across the multiple copies cancels the noise without affecting the desired image. This corresponds to the effect of longer exposure time.

Local averaging. A simple method for optically removing noise in an image is defocusing. This can be simulated by replacing the gray-scale intensity of every point by an average of the image intensity within some window around the point. In general, the average may be weighted, with lower weights assigned to points farther from the center of the window. This processing can be accomplished by a linear operator in much the same way as was illustrated for sharpening. It will remove noise at the expense of blurring the image. Reducing the size of the window will result in less blurring, but it is less effective for removing noise. An alternative is to change a pixel only if its value differs from the average by more than a given threshold. This is less likely to blur desired detail but still removes salt-and-pepper noise effectively.

We can also avoid blurring edges with a *median* operator, rather than an averaging operator. Since the median of a distribution is the value between the lower half and the upper half of the distribution, it tends to preserve edges. For example, if a 3×3 window covered an area with these intensities

$$
\begin{array}{ccc}
8 & 8 & 2 \\
8 & 2 & 2 \\
2 & 2 & 2,
\end{array}
$$

an averaging operator would return a value of 4 for the middle cell, but a median operator would return a value of 2, preserving the edge.

Local averaging is especially efficient for binary images, since a binary pixel has only two values (light and dark), and a pixel's value can be made consistent with that of the immediate neighborhood simply by complementing it or by leaving it unchanged. Binary input and output values permit *logical averaging*, in which the averaging function is defined as a logical function of the binary pixels in the neighborhood.

Low-emphasis filtering. It is common to use filters for noise removal. A simple low-pass filter will remove high-frequency noise, that is, will smooth the image, but it will also blur high-frequency components of the image signal (such as those corresponding to edges and junctions). In some systems this will be acceptable, especially if much of the noise energy is above the highest desired frequency. If not, it may still be possible to improve the image by filtering a selected band of frequencies, allowing the high-frequency edge detail to remain. Bandpass filtering is especially useful if the noise energy is concentrated at a particular frequency (e.g., if it is periodic). Restoration techniques can be used to obtain the optimal filter when the characteristics of the frequency domain, such as the spectrum of the noise, are known.

Conclusion

We have presented an introduction to techniques for preprocessing and image-enhancement. We discussed three kinds of modifications: geometrical modifications, gray-scale modifications, and sharpening and smoothing.

References

The primary introductory textbooks on preprocessing are Rosenfeld and Kak (1976) and Duda and Hart (1973).

C4. Edge Detection and Line Finding

EDGE DETECTION is an important step in segmenting an image. Its purpose is to locate boundaries of meaningful regions that may be defined by a relatively uniform color, gray level, or texture. Thus, edges are detected by finding abrupt discontinuities of such image features. The forms of the change in intensity across an edge are called edge profiles, of which the *step edge* is an ideal one (Fig. C4–1a). In actuality, the edge profile tends to be a slope (Fig. C4–1b) because of noise and blur.

Edge detection is basically a two-step process. First, candidate edge elements are found by a local operator and, second, smooth lines or curves are extracted and specified either as line formulas or as contiguous elements. The remainder of this article discusses techniques for these two steps.

Spatial Differentiation

Since we are interested in places where the picture function changes, it is reasonable to consider using a derivative of the picture function $f(x, y)$ to indicate edge elements. The spatial first derivative of f is called the *gradient* and it is made of a pair of partial first derivatives $\partial f / \partial x$ and $\partial f / \partial y$.

The gradient is a vector, and its magnitude G and orientation θ can be expressed as:

$$G(x, y) = \{(\partial f / \partial x)^2 + (\partial f / \partial y)^2\}^{1/2}$$
$$\theta(x, y) = \tan^{-1}\{(\partial f / \partial y)/(\partial f / \partial x)\}.$$

Many operators have been devised to approximate this gradient in digital images. One of the earliest was the so-called Roberts Cross Operator, $R(i, j)$ (Roberts, 1965). It computes the sum of squares of the differences between diagonal pixels in a 2×2 window:

$$R(i, j) = \{(f(i, j) - f(i + 1, j + 1))^2 + (f(i + 1, j) - f(i, j + 1))^2\}^{1/2}.$$

(a)   (b)

Figure C4–1.   (a) An ideal step-edge profile; (b) a real edge profile.

Of course, we can use operators to approximate $\partial f/\partial x$ and $\partial f/\partial y$. The simplest one is derived from the differences of intensity values of horizontal and vertical neighbors:

$$f_x(i,j) = f(i+1,j) - f(i,j)$$
$$f_y(i,j) = f(i,j+1) - f(i,j).$$

These operations are conveniently expressed in the form of local operators with a window of weights (see Fig. C3–5, in Article XIII.C3). The 3×3 operators shown in Figure C4–2 also compute first derivatives, and they are often referred to as the *Sobel operators*. In these windows, larger weights are given to the pixels close to the central point (i,j). This makes Sobel operators less sensitive to noise.

One problem with many edge detectors is that they rely on computations based on fixed-sized neighborhoods. Figure C4–3 shows that the window size is crucial in detecting slope edges: In general, the window size should be as big as the extent of the slope of the edges to be detected. Notice that there is a trade-off between large windows that are immune to noise and small windows that have higher resolving power. Rosenfeld and Thurston (1971) have suggested one operator that uses windows of variable size. The calculation begins by taking the difference of the average gray levels of a pair of the smallest neighborhoods on opposite sides of a point. Then the size of the neighborhoods is increased by powers of 2 until the difference drops significantly; the largest opposite neighborhoods before the decrease are used.

Edge elements are selected by thresholding the output of the edge detector, resulting in a binary image. If the output of an edge detector at a pixel exceeds a certain threshold, that pixel is determined to be an edge-element candidate and given a value of 1; otherwise, it is given a value of 0. However, as shown in Figure C4–3, the output of the first derivatives across the slope edge tends to be bell-shaped or flat over the extent of the slope. As a result, the located edges may be several pixels wide. One method to overcome this is to follow the local maxima of the detector output. Alternately, the second derivatives can be used. As shown earlier in Figure C3–4, the second

-1	0	1
-2	0	2
-1	0	1

for $f_x(i,j)$

1	2	1
0	0	0
-1	-2	-1

for $f_y(i,j)$

Figure C4–2. Sobel operators.

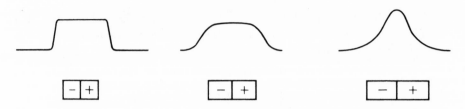

Figure C4–3.   Output of first-derivative operators with different
window sizes applied to a slope edge.

derivative changes its sign at the position of the steepest slope in the edge.
Therefore, the point at which the second derivative crosses the x-axis, called
the *zero-crossing*, unambiguously indicates the position of the edge. Since the
picture function is two-dimensional, we actually use the zero-crossing of the
Laplacian image (i.e., the sum of $\partial^2 f/\partial x^2$ and $\partial^2 f/\partial y^2$). The Laplacian has
long been useful in computer vision, but recently Marr and Hildreth (1980)
proposed, as a model of psychophysical aspects of edge detection in human
vision, zero-crossing in the image obtained by applying a circularly symmetric
Laplacian with Gaussian low-pass filtering.

Pattern Matching

Pattern matching for edge detection assumes a model of an edge, and
its location in the image is determined to be where its intensity profile best
matches the model. A theoretical system that has been adapted and applied
in real vision systems is the *Hueckel operator* (Hueckel, 1971, 1973). Given
a circular region D about the origin of an x-y coordinate system, Hueckel's
ideal edge (Fig. C4–4) is the step function:

$$f(x, y, c, s, p, b, d) = \begin{cases} b & \text{if } cx + sy \le p; \\ b + d & \text{otherwise.} \end{cases}$$

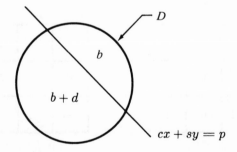

Figure C4–4.   Hueckel's ideal edge.

The ideal edge is a function of the background intensity b, the intensity difference d across the edge, and the parameters for the edge orientation and location c, s, and p.

If $f(x, y)$ is the picture function, we would like to "fit" an ideal edge to $f(x, y)$ by minimizing

$$E(c, s, p, b, d) = \int_D (f(x, y) - F(x, y, c, s, p, b, d))^2 dx\, dy \ . \tag{1}$$

This is accomplished with polar-coordinate Fourier analysis. Let $H(i)$ be a basis function (separable into angular and radial components) and define

$$a(i) = \int_D H(i)(x, y) f(x, y)\, dx\, dy$$

$$s(i) = \int_D H(i)(x, y) F(x, y, c, s, p, b, d)\, dx\, dy \ .$$

Now $a(i)$ is constant and $s(i)$ is variable, and the problem is reduced to minimizing the error E:

$$E(c, s, p, b, d) = \sum_{i=0}^{\infty} (a(i) - s(i))^2 \ .$$

Because of real limitations from resolution and noise, this sum need only be carried out for the first eight terms. For each neighborhood, Hueckel's system returns the optimal edge and an indication of goodness of fit (i.e., the value of E). The value of the intensity difference d can be used to determine whether it corresponds to a real edge element.

Color Edge Detection

Whereas each pixel of a gray-scale image has a scalar value of intensity, a pixel from a color image has a three-dimensional vector value (*Red, Green, Blue*) corresponding to the three principal components of color. More generally, a multispectral image can have an arbitrary number of components (see Article XIII.C2). Edge detection in color images is very like its counterpart in intensity images.

Let d be a differential operator and H a threshold operator, and assume that R, G, and B are the component intensities of a color image. Then the operator $H(dR + dG + dB)$ thresholds the sum of the differences of each feature and produces a binary image indicating whether the total color difference was above the threshold (Yachida and Tsuji, 1971). Alternately, the operator $HdR + HdG + HdB$ computes the sum of binary images given from differentiation and thresholding of each color. It gives a result whose value can be 0,

1, 2, or 3 and indicates the number of color features that show a significant difference. The likelihood of an edge at a pixel is indicated by this number.

Nevatia (1976) extended the Hueckel operator to the detection of color edges. He assumed that the ideal edge in each color feature must have the same orientation $((c, s, p)$ in terms of the previous model) at a given pixel. First, the ideal edge model $F(x, y, c, s, p, b, d)$ is matched separately for each color feature. The orientations (c, s, p) are then averaged to compute (c_0, s_0, p_0), which is taken as the orientation of the color edge. Then the remaining parameters in the tuple are determined separately for each feature to minimize the total error,

$$E = E_R^2 + E_G^2 + E_B^2 \, ,$$

where the components E_R, E_G, and E_B are defined as in equation (1).

Extraction of Line Descriptions

The edge detector produces as output a set of edge elements—for example, the set of points where the gradient of the picture function exceeds a certain threshold. The next problem is how to group edge elements that form a continuous contour and segment them into lines and curves.

Tracking. Tracking links edge elements into a longer contour by visiting the neighboring elements one after another. A typical method is to scan the edge-element image left to right and top to bottom and, when an edge element is found, check whether any of its eight neighbors are edge elements. If one is, mark it and move to it, and repeat the process. The edge elements that have been visited must be marked as such, so that no duplicate tracking occurs. If two or more neighbors are edge elements, remember their positions in a stack as branch points. If there is no neighboring edge element, the present position is the terminal of a contour, and processing continues from the last branch point. If there are no more branch points, the image is scanned for another starting point. This process will eventually visit all edge elements.

This fundamental algorithm has many difficulties. First, it implicitly assumes that an edge contour is just one pixel wide. A *thinning* operation is usually carried out to thin the width of the line before tracking. Second, because of noise, false edge elements are found, as are gaps in a continuous line. The tracking algorithm is fooled, and it detours from the true straight lines or smooth curves or is stranded in the middle of them. One remedy is to give the tracking algorithm inertia so that it continues its current direction of search. Tracking thus searches for a continuation of the last few edge elements; when it encounters a gap, it continues tracking if it finds a line of the same orientation beyond the gap.

A third problem is that tracking is inevitably local, even with tricks to bridge gaps and avoid false edges. To do a really good job of line finding, certain global knowledge, often domain knowledge, is introduced. For example,

Shirai's semantic line finder (see Article XIII.B6) incorporates blocks-world knowledge. Another method is to use a figure of merit to constrain the shape of contours to be traced. For example, suppose we are interested in extracting a curve that is as smooth as possible and across which the intensity difference is as large as possible. Then we can define

$$C = \sum_{(i,j) \text{ on a curve}} [c_1 r(i,j)^2 + c_2 d(i,j)^2]$$

as a figure-of-merit function of a curve, where $r(i,j)$ is the curvature radius, $d(i,j)$ is the intensity difference, and c_1 and c_2 are positive constants. Then the tracking problem becomes an optimization problem of searching for a path in the image that maximizes C. It can be solved with dynamic programming (Montanari, 1971), depth-first search (Chien and Fu, 1974), or heuristic search (Martelli, 1976).

Segmenting a contour into lines and curves. Once a contour is identified, it is sometimes necessary to segment it into a sequence of straight line segments and primitive curves. There is a very simple algorithm for generating a multiple-line description from a given set of points, called an *iterative endpoint fit* (see Fig. C4–5). It begins by choosing from the set two extreme points, A and B, and approximates the entire set by the line joining these two endpoints. If the fit is good, the procedure stops; otherwise, it chooses the point farthest from the fitted line, C, and replaces the one-line description AB by a two-line description, AC, CB. The process is repeated on each of these segments, and so on, until sufficiently good matches are achieved for all segments. Unfortunately, this simple algorithm can be strongly influenced by a single noise point. It is essential that it operate in a virtually noise-free environment, perhaps provided by an earlier smoothing process.

Another important idea is to represent the contour as a function of its length s from its starting point—specifically, to represent the slope of the

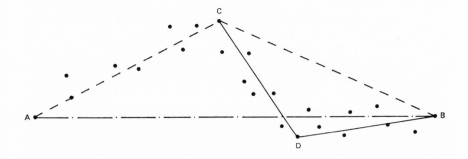

Figure C4–5. An iterative endpoint fit method (from Duda and Hart, 1973).

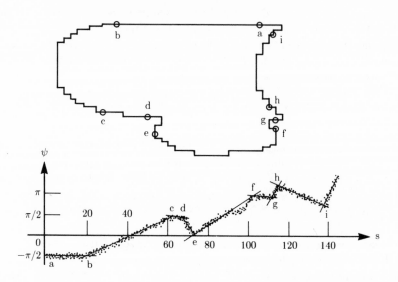

Figure C4–6.   A ψ-s transform (from Turner, 1974).

tangential line, ψ, or curvature, δ, as a function of s. For example, as shown in Figure C4–6, ψ and s can be used to segment a contour into lines and arcs. When we plot ψ against s, the linear portion of the contour becomes a horizontal line in the ψ-s graph, and the arc portion becomes a line with a slope. Then we can divide the ψ-s graph into piecewise linear segments, and use the position of break points to segment the original contour into line segments and arc segments depending on the slope of the corresponding ψ-s segments.

The Hough transform. It is possible to detect multiple straight lines from a set of edge points with a clustering method. To do so, we represent a line in the x-y picture plane by

$$x \cos \theta + y \sin \theta = \rho \ .$$

A graphical interpretation of this equation is shown in Figure C4–7a. Let us imagine a parameter space made of (ρ, θ). The previous equation is then a transformation from (x, y) to (ρ, θ) with the following properties:

1. A line in the x-y space is transformed to a point (ρ, θ) in the ρ-θ space, and vice versa.

2. A point (x, y) is transformed to a sinusoidal curve in the ρ-θ space, and vice versa. Notice that the (ρ, θ) on this sinusoidal curve mean all the lines that pass the point (x, y).

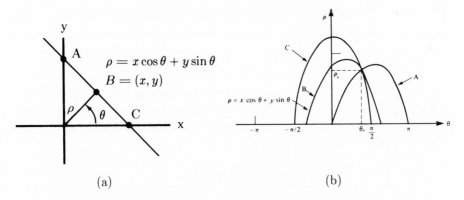

Figure C4–7.   Hough transform.

Suppose we have a set of edge-element points (x_i, y_i), $i = 1 \sim N$, and transform them into N sinusoidal curves in the ρ-θ space. If the original points are on a line, say, $x \cos \theta_0 + y \sin \theta_0 = \rho_0$, then the sinusoidal curves should intersect at (ρ_0, θ_0), as shown in Figure C4–7b. Therefore, we can find a group of points in the x-y space that form a line by detecting a point in the ρ-θ space at which many curves intersect. Actually, we represent the ρ-θ space as an array of accumulators, (ρ_m, θ_m), each of which is responsible for a short interval of ρ and θ. For an edge element at (x_i, y_i), we compute the corresponding sinusoidal curve and add 1 to the content of the accumulators on which the curve passes. After all points are transformed, the accumulators that contain a large number suggest lines whose formulas are given by the associated (ρ_m, θ_m).

Since this method generates $N^2/2$ intersections for N original points, detecting significant clusters is not trivial. An alternative is to compute the orientation θ_i at an edge element (x_i, y_i) by means of the gradient operators for edge detection discussed in this article. Rather than transforming an edge element to a sinusoidal curve in the ρ-θ space, we transform it into a point (ρ_i, θ_i), where $\rho_i = x_i \cos \theta_i + y_i \sin \theta_i$, and augment the single corresponding accumulator. This class of methods, transforming into a parameter space, has the advantage that the set of points that constitute a line can be detected despite gaps or noise points.

Conclusion

Numerous operators and techniques for edge detection have been developed, and we have covered only a fraction of them in this article. Some techniques are relatively general, while others are tuned for particular applications. Most vision systems need some kind of edge detection to get line descriptions of images. This requires a sequence of operations, from edge-element detection to line description.

References

For a standard book of edge-detection techniques, see Rosenfeld and Kak (1976); for a survey, see Davis (1975). One example of a complete line finder that starts with an image and generates line descriptions is Nevatia and Babu's system (1979).

C5. Region Analysis

AN IMAGE is represented as a two-dimensional array of pixels conveying image-feature values. The task of region analysis is to group together the pixels in an image that share some values of a feature. For example, an image can be segmented into regions of similar color, under the assumption that these regions correspond to surfaces in the scene that produced the image.

The regions produced by region segmentation typically have several properties. Such regions are mutually exclusive—that is, no pixel belongs to more than one region—and they are usually exhaustive—that is, each pixel belongs to some region. Each region consists of a single cluster of contiguous pixels; it is *simply connected*. Each region satisfies some predicate, which usually indicates uniformity in the desired features, and no two adjacent regions satisfy the same set of predicates—that is, no two adjacent regions look the same.

Region-segmentation techniques are attractive for a number of reasons. For one, there are usually far fewer regions than pixels, so region segmentation is a form of data compression. Moreover, regions are groups of pixels with (presumably) the same semantic interpretation, so they are convenient units for later stages of image understanding (such as naming objects). The boundaries of regions form outlines of important areas of the image, and since these outlines are guaranteed to be connected and unique, region segmentation avoids some of the problems inherent in edge-based techniques (see Article XIII.C4).

One weakness of region segmentation is that it makes assumptions about the uniformity of image features, for instance, that all pixels with the same color correspond to the same surface. Violations of these assumptions will produce erroneous results. For example, highlights will violate the assumption above, causing a single surface to be split into several regions or producing tiny *noise regions*.

There are two primary approaches to region segmentation:

1. *Region growing.* Starting with many tiny, trivial regions, such as individual pixels, merge similar regions until the only regions that remain are uniform and no further merging is possible.

2. *Region splitting.* Starting with a single large region, such as the entire image, split it into several pieces. Continue splitting pieces until only uniform regions remain.

Region Growing

Region growing begins with many tiny *atomic regions*, often individual pixels or collections of adjacent pixels that have an identical gray level, color, or the like. Adjacent similar regions are merged until no two adjacent regions are sufficiently similar to be merged. Regions are similar if their pixel values do not vary significantly, for example, if the means of their gray levels are approximately the same. Variance is measured by standard deviation, range, or a similar statistic.

There are two common organizations for the region-growing algorithm. In the first, processing begins in any atomic region, say, the upper left-hand corner, and then an adjacent atomic region is examined. If it can be merged with the first, this is done. The next atomic region that is adjacent to any part of the current region is then tested, and so on. When no more adjacent atomic regions can be merged with the current region, another atomic region is selected and a new region is created. Processing continues in this sequential manner until all atomic regions belong to some region.

Another organization is to compute initially, for each pair of adjacent regions, the worth of merging them. Next, the pair that is judged most worthy of merging is merged, and the worth of merging this new region with its neighbors is recomputed. Processing continues in this parallel manner until no pair of regions is judged worthy of merging.

There have been several variations on the basic region-growing idea. For example, the criteria for merging regions might be based on properties of the region shapes as well as on their pixel values. Along these lines, Brice and Fennema (1970) developed two heuristics for deciding whether to merge adjacent regions with a weak boundary. (A boundary is weak if the gray-level difference across it fails to exceed some threshold.) The first heuristic, called the *phagocyte heuristic*, merges two regions if the weak part of their common boundary exceeds some fraction of the perimeter of one region or the other. This has the effect of merging only if one region is contained (or almost contained) within the other. The second heuristic, called the *weakness heuristic*, merges two regions if the length of the weak part of their common boundary exceeds some fraction of the total common boundary.

Yakimovsky and Feldman (1973) use semantic interpretations of regions to guide region growing. They would merge regions only if the interpretation to be assigned to the resulting region was compatible with the interpretations of other adjacent regions. Harlow (1973) allowed the threshold for merging to vary, depending upon the interpretation of the region being generated.

Region Splitting

Region splitting is a recursive procedure in which a single region is examined and possibly split into pieces that, as regions themselves, are then examined and split in exactly the same way. Initially, the entire image is considered to be a single region.

The usual technique for deciding when to split a region is to form a *histogram* of the pixel values within the region—a graph that indicates, for each pixel value, how many pixels have that value. Under the assumption that each surface or object will contain many pixels of similar value, peaks in the histogram will indicate surfaces. If a region consists of a single surface or object, its histogram will therefore consist of a single peak; if the histogram contains several peaks, the region may contain several surfaces and is a candidate for splitting.

It is possible to judge the uniformity of a region of pixel values statistically, with a measure of variance such as the standard deviation of pixel values, and to use this measure—rather than a histogram—to decide whether to split a region. Robertson, Swain, and Fu (1973) proposed dividing a region vertically or horizontally into two regions of equal size if the variance of pixel values was large.

If a histogram is made, it can be used to decide how to split a region. A valley in the histogram between two peaks corresponds to a pixel value that does not occur, or occurs only infrequently. The pixel value at the valley can be used as a threshold, and the region can be split into two collections of pixels: those whose value is above the threshold and those whose value is below the threshold. Groups of contiguous pixels from either collection become new regions. Each is examined by the same technique to see if it should be split further.

This technique, developed by Prewitt (1970) and often referred to as the *mode method,* is suitable for pictures with a single feature, such as black-and-white images. Tsuji and Tomita (1973) and Ohlander (1975; Ohlander, Price, and Reddy, 1978) extended the idea to include multiple histograms. The resulting technique is perhaps the most common region-splitting method used today. Each region is histogrammed separately for each of the color bands (or other features). Then each histogram is examined separately, and potential thresholds are determined for each feature. The histograms and potential thresholds are then compared to determine which feature appears most promising. Usually, the feature that shows the best separation of peaks is chosen. Finally, thresholding of the image using the selected feature proceeds as described above. With this technique, the feature with the most discriminative power is the basis for segmentation.

Other Approaches to Region Splitting

Another approach to region splitting involves examining a distribution of the image features in a multidimensional feature space. Like peaks in one-dimensional histograms, clusters of feature points in a multidimensional space are assumed to correspond to meaningful regions in the image. *Clustering,* the name given to techniques for developing the distribution of feature-values in a multidimensional space, is a common practice in the fields of statistical data analysis and statistical pattern recognition.

MILLS COLLEGE
LIBRARY

Coleman and Andrews (1979) describe a region-segmentation method, based on multidimensional space clustering, that uses both color and texture features. The idea is to form a histogram over the feature space and then to break the space into parts wherever a cluster—a local maximum over some sizable neighborhood—appears in the histogram. Since we do not usually know the number of meaningful regions in the image, we need some criterion for selecting clusters. Coleman and Andrews used the product of between-cluster and within-cluster scatter averages, and selected the number of clusters for which this product is a maximum. Once the clusters are identified, each pixel is labeled with the name of the cluster it belongs to, and the image is partitioned by merging adjacent pixels with identical cluster labels into a single region.

The selection of color features for Ohlander's algorithm has been examined in detail by Ohta (see Ohta, Kanade, and Sakai, 1980). He used a Karhunen-Loeve (K–L) expansion to measure the axis of primary variation of pixel values for each region undergoing segmentation. A statistical analysis showed that certain axes were much more likely than all the rest to represent optimally the variation of pixel values. The most common was the intensity axis, $I_1 = R+G+B$ (see Article XIII.C2). The second and third most commonly used axes were approximately $I_2 = R - B$ and $I_3 = 2G - R - B$, respectively.

It should be noted that these features are simple linear transformations of RGB data and, thus, are immune to the nonuniformity of feature-value distributions that are introduced by nonlinear transformations as an artifact (see Article XIII.C2; Kender, 1977). Ohta compared segmentation using I_1, I_2, and I_3 to segmentation using RGB, XYZ, YIQ, HSD, UVW, and other similar features. He concluded that his features performed for a wide variety of images at least as well as any of these other feature sets. Statistically, it is optimal to compute the K–L transform for each region to be split; using Ohta's features allows a sort of precomputation of the K–L transform (under the assumption that one's images are likely to be statistically similar to Ohta's).

Postprocessing for Region Extraction

Region splitting with histograms exploits global information about features of the image, but it fails to exploit the local spatial information that region-growing methods can use. Because of this, when an image is divided into collections of pixels by thresholding, there are typically some pixels (with values close to the threshold) that seem to have the wrong label. These *noise regions* must be eliminated. Ohlander (1975) used binary smoothing operators (see Article XIII.C3) to eliminate thin regions or holes. Shafer (1980) eliminated any region whose area was less than some constant.

There are a number of ways to do postprocessing on a histogram-based segmentation. One is a kind of smoothing (Article XIII.C3): If most of the neighbors of pixel P are labeled C, then P is relabeled with C. This type of postprocessing has been used in remote-sensing applications where regions are expected to be uniform—where a "wheat" pixel is not expected to appear in the middle of the "corn" field. A slightly modified method is the *conservative threshold* (e.g., Nagin, Hanson, and Riseman, 1977). This involves delaying classification of pixels with feature values near the threshold (or near the boundary of the discriminant surface). These pixels are classified in a second pass, according to the labels of their neighbors.

Another postprocessing technique is *relaxation* (Rosenfeld, 1978). Instead of assigning a single label to each pixel, the probability p_i that P belongs to class C_i is estimated based on the distribution of image-feature values. Then these probabilities are adjusted by some relaxation formula so that p_i is revised iteratively using the previous values of its own and neighboring pixels. (See Article XIII.E4 for a discussion of probabilistic relaxation algorithms.) Rosenfeld reports that, in his experiments, error removal by this method is five times better than simple postprocessing.

Supplementary information can facilitate postprocessing in region analysis. For example, Milgram and Kahl (1979) compared the boundaries of proposed regions with the edges found by an edge-detecting operator; regions were discarded if their boundaries did not correspond sufficiently well with the supplementary edges.

The problem of threshold detection from a histogram has received considerable attention. A survey of this area is presented in Weszka (1978).

Conclusion

A region has been defined intuitively as a group of pixels with certain consistent characteristics; region-segmentation methods rely mostly on spectral and spatial distributions of the image-feature values. However, the problem of region segmentation requires more than simply analyzing image-feature values, because the ultimate goal of region segmentation is to find a segmentation that separates out *meaningful* objects or parts of objects, such as "nucleus of cell," "sky," and "tree." It is recognized in vision research that region-segmentation programs must have knowledge about the world from which the images are taken.

References

For a survey of region-analysis techniques and issues, see Zucker (1976a), Riseman and Arbib (1977), and Kanade (1980a); the last reference also discusses the issue of incorporating knowledge into region-segmentation programs.

C6. Texture

IMAGES of textiles, terrains, and tree barks all include textures—fine-grained patterns of small elements, arranged with a certain structure. Regions of texture appear homogeneous. Texture thus provides important cues for distinguishing objects and natural scenes. Gradual change in texture is a cue to depth and orientation; texture gradients were proposed by Gibson (1950) as part of his model of human perception. In computer vision, texture analysis is an important segmentation technique. It is also used to recognize types of surfaces and their quality and to recover three-dimensional information from images. This article will discuss the description and extraction of two-dimensional patterns of textural features; the problem of relating texture with three-dimensional shapes is discussed in Article XIII.D5.

Extraction of Textural Features

There are many applications of vision research that depend on discriminating textures. For example, quality control and aerial survey can both be done by examining the textural properties—or features—of images. In quality control, different mixtures of materials show up as different textures in microscopic images of samples. In aerial survey, different terrains such as grassland and forest appear as different textures. To exploit these textural differences, it is necessary to define and extract features that discriminate between textures. Various textural features have been proposed; some are motivated by specific applications and others by a desire to explain human texture discrimination.

Statistical features. The simplest textural features are first-order statistics that describe the distribution of individual pixel features such as intensity. Histograms of intensity and other features can be compared directly with the Kolmogorov-Smirnov test; alternately, the distribution can be summarized by the mean, variance, skewness, and kurtosis (the first, second, third, and fourth moments of the distribution, respectively), and these can be used as texture features.

Second-order, or *dipole*, statistics summarize the probability of the intensity values of a pair of pixels. These statistics are computed for pairs of pixels in different positional relations and are summarized in a *co-occurrence matrix*. Let $\delta = (r, \theta)$ denote a vector in the image that represents a displacement by r in the orientation of θ. $P_\delta(I_1, I_2)$ denotes a probability that a pair of pixels displaced by δ has intensities I_1 and I_2: The first pixel has intensity I_1 and the second, displaced by δ from the first, has intensity I_2. If intensity takes one of n possible values, a co-occurrence matrix is an $n \times n$ matrix and records all the $P_\delta(I_1, I_2)$, $1 \leq I_1, I_2 \leq n$, for one δ.

Finding co-occurrence matrices for all δ involves a prohibitive amount of computation. Haralick, Shanmugam, and Dinstein (1973), who first used co-occurrence matrices to classify terrains in aerial photographs, computed just four co-occurrence matrices for $r = 1$ and $\theta = 0°$, $45°$, $90°$, and $135°$—that is, the second-order statistics for pairs of pixels that are one pixel distant in each of four orientations. From each matrix, they defined 14 feature values for discriminating between textures.

Statistics on differences of intensities (rather than combinations of intensities) can be also used as textural features. Let $P_\delta(k)$ be the probability that a pair of pixels separated by δ has a difference of intensity k. P_δ can be derived from a co-occurrence matrix $P_\delta(I_1, I_2)$, because

$$P_\delta(k) = \sum_{|I_1 - I_2| = k} P_\delta(I_1, I_2).$$

$P_\delta(k)$ provides a simpler set of statistics than $P_\delta(I_1, I_2)$; they have been tested for terrain classification and material inspection (Weszka, Dyer, and Rosenfeld, 1976).

Various other statistical texture features have been proposed, including the power spectrum of an image (Bajcsy, 1973), coefficients in an autoregression or a linear-prediction model, and autocorrelations of an image. The co-occurrence matrix and these features are interrelated: One feature can be mathematically derived from another. Higher order statistics might also be used; however, they involve more computation and do not necessarily give better results. In fact, Julesz (1975) conjectured that two textures are not discriminable if their second-order statistics are identical. Recently, some counterexamples to this conjecture have been found; nonetheless, it is possible that second-order statistics are the most that need be computed for texture discrimination.

Local Features

The statistics we have discussed are based on pixel-level intensity values. An alternative is to extract local features and take statistics on them. The most representative of this method are edge statistics. Edge strength and orientation are computed by edge operators (see Article XIII.C4) and are summarized by various statistics. For example, Tamura, Mori, and Yamawaki (1978) computed a directional co-occurrence matrix that summarized statistics on the combinations of edge orientations for pairs of edge elements with certain geometrical relationships.

Marr's *primal sketch* is consistent with this approach. In his original proposal (Marr, 1976), an image is processed with edge and bar masks of various sizes to detect primitives like edges, lines, and blobs. Each primitive has attributes such as orientation, size, and contrast. The primal sketch was proposed as an explicit, symbolic representation of this information. It also makes explicit the two-dimensional relations between primitives, including parallelism between nearby edges and relative positions and orientation of significant places in the image. These places are marked by *place-tokens*, and the geometrical relations between them are represented by inserting *virtual lines* between nearby tokens. Figure C6–1 is an example of the primal sketch. Statistics derived from histograms of intensity, contrast, line-fragment length, line-fragment orientation, and so on are used for texture discrimination. Marr argues that this model explains experimental evidence on texture discrimination by humans. In the line-and-point textures that Schatz (1977) examined,

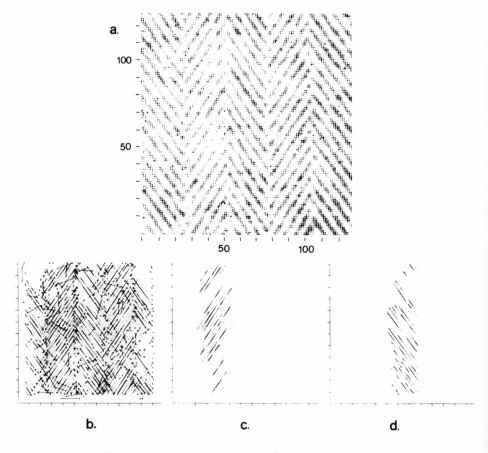

Figure C6–1. Primal sketch (from Marr, 1976).

length and orientation of actual lines and of local virtual lines between terminators were sufficient for texture discrimination.

Segmentation of Texture Regions

Texture features can be used to segment images into regions, if the appropriate features are known a priori. However, since textural features are derived from statistics taken over a region, it is difficult to get meaningful statistics unless the region is delimited a priori.

One solution to this problem is to detect *texture edges* (and, thus, regions) by measuring a change in texture over a small window. This is most useful for those textures that can be discriminated on the basis of intensity distributions, such as random-dot textures. However, if the window is too small, the edge detector's output fluctuates due to local intensity variation, and if it is too large, the boundary is blurred. Rosenfeld and Thurston (1971) used a variable-sized edge detector: Several window sizes were tried at each pixel position to compute the local derivative, and the one that satisfied a certain criterion was used as the strength of the texture edge.

A second approach is to smooth an image (Article XIII.C3) so that pixels in a single texture region will have similar values in the smoothed image. This image can then be segmented as an ordinary intensity image. However, the neighborhood over which the smoothing is performed has to be carefully selected in order not to blur the boundaries. Tomita and Tsuji (1977) considered the five neighborhoods for each pixel position shown in Figure C6-2 to be used for smoothing. The value for the pixel is taken to be the value of the average over the most uniform of the five neighborhoods. This method

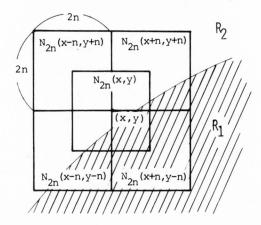

Figure C6-2. Five neighborhoods of point (x, y)
(from Tomita and Tsuji, 1977).

allows only one texture region to be included for averaging even when the pixel is on a boundary—in the case of Figure C6–2, the neighborhood in the upper left. Thus, texture edges are preserved in the smoothed image. Figures C6–3a and C6–3b show an example of segmentation by this method. For comparison, Figure C6–3c shows the result of smoothing with a fixed neighborhood: We can observe in this case blurring near the boundaries of texture regions.

Another approach is to use multiple histograms of the properties of textural elements (e.g., histograms derived from the primal sketch) to find appropriate thresholds to split images. This is the same approach as in region splitting (see Article XIII.C5). In fact, one of the first applications of multiple histograms to recursive region splitting employed texture features. Tomita, Yachida, and Tsuji (1973) segmented the image in Figure C6–4 with histograms of the area, perimeter, and moments of its primitive elements. The histograms for Figure C6–4 are shown in Figure C6–5a. The perimeter, whose histogram shows the most conspicuous bimodality, was first used for segmentation, resulting in the regions shown in Figures C6–5b and C6–5c. Figure C6–5b is further divided with a moment (Fig. C6–5d).

Conclusion

Texture provides important cues in analyzing natural scenes. Recently, it has attracted increasing attention in computer-vision research. It is also being studied in perceptual psychology, and this research has had an influence on computer vision. Models for *generating* textures have also been studied; among them, Markov models, a statistical model—a noise function plus a transfer function (Pratt, Faugeras, and Gagalowicz, 1978), a random mosaic model (Schachter, Rosenfeld, and Davis, 1978), and a syntactic model (Rosenfeld and Lipkin, 1970; Zucker, 1976b).

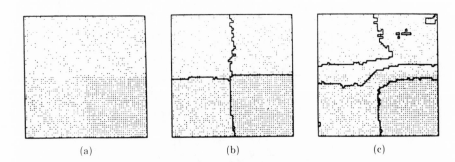

(a)   (b)   (c)

Figure C6–3.   Segmentation by local averaging: (a) input image, (b) variable neighborhood, and (c) fixed neighborhood (from Tomita and Tsuji, 1977).

Figure C6–4.   An image with textural primitive elements obtained from
a real image (from Tomita, Yachida, and Tsuji, 1973).

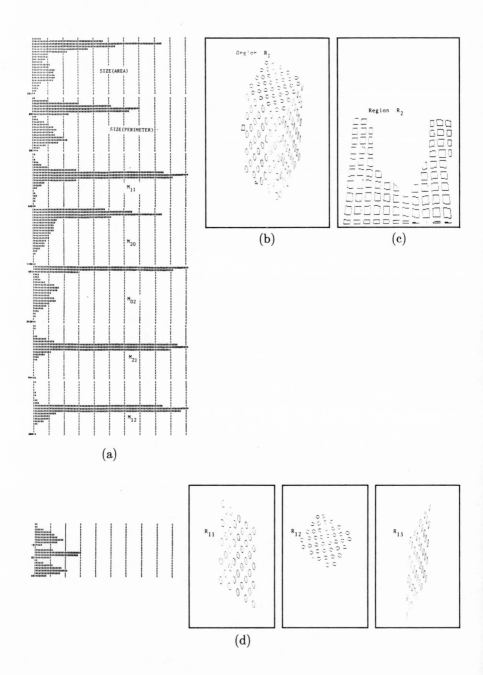

Figure C6–5.   Segmentation of texture regions by use of multiple histograms
              (from Tomita, Yachida, and Tsuji, 1973).

References

Brodatz (1966) contains many pictures of textures. Rosenfeld and Kak (1976) include basic techniques for texture segmentation. Haralick (1978) surveys research on a statistical and structural approach to texture.

D.   REPRESENTATION OF SCENE CHARACTERISTICS

D1.   Intrinsic Images

IMAGE UNDERSTANDING typically involves analysis of an image to determine some features and matching those features with entries in a database of objects to determine which objects are present. Segmentation techniques attempt to determine features in the *image,* such as regions of uniform color or intensity; in general, these can be matched to database entries only if the objects are presented in specific orientations (i.e., with known outlines in the image). A more powerful approach is to determine features of the *scene,* such as the orientation of each surface and its distance from the camera. These features can then be interpreted in terms of object shapes in the scene, which can probably be matched with the database under a wider variety of conditions. The distinction is between determining two-dimensional *image* features and determining three-dimensional *scene* features from the image.

The most basic features of a scene include *orientation* (which way a surface is tipped), *distance* from the camera, *reflectance* (how light or dark it is), and the amount of *incident illumination.* These are called the *intrinsic characteristics* of the scene.

We can represent intrinsic characteristics iconically, that is, as images. The various intrinsic values are computed for each individual pixel, representing the intrinsic characteristics of the surface that is imaged in that pixel. In this representation, there is an image for reflectance values, one for orientations, one for distance, and one for incident illumination (see Fig. D1-1). These are all in registration with the original image. The idea of computing images of scene characteristics emerged from Horn's work (1977) with *albedo maps;* the idea was furthered and aptly named *intrinsic images* by Barrow and Tenenbaum (1978; Tenenbaum, Fischler, and Barrow, 1980).

In addition to the iconic representation, each intrinsic image contains an explicit list of points at which there is a discontinuity in the value (e.g., intensity) and another list of points at which the gradient (two-dimensional derivative) of the value is discontinuous. These correspond to the solid and dashed lines in Figure D1-1. This information is extremely important, since discontinuities in intrinsic values usually correspond to surface and shadow boundaries in the scene, and these lists allow programs to find these features quickly.

The $2\frac{1}{2}$-*D sketch* of Marr (1978) is also a set of intrinsic images. Marr, like Barrow and Tenenbaum, presumes that the iconic data will be supplemented by explicit lists of discontinuities in the values of the intrinsic characteristics.

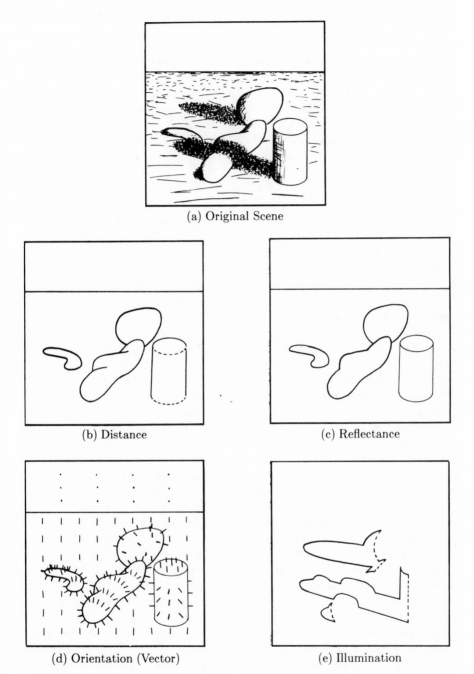

Figure D1–1.   Intrinsic images (from Barrow and Tenenbaum, 1978).

Intrinsic images are most useful because they indicate important physical features of the scene. With intrinsic images, it is possible to perform segmentation, for example, to produce a line drawing in which each surface is outlined. In contrast, reliable segmention from raw intensity data cannot usually be achieved because the intensity of each pixel in the original image is determined by a combination of several physical parameters.

Intrinsic images are also believed to be good models for some aspects of human perception. Psychological phenomena such as *size constancy, shape constancy, brightness constancy,* and *color constancy* may suggest that humans compute these intrinsic parameters at an early stage in the visual process.

Calculating Intrinsic Images

Barrow and Tenenbaum (1979) have performed experiments with synthetic images of scenes from a limited domain to demonstrate that intrinsic images can be calculated from intensity data. Surfaces in this simplified domain are *continuous*—there are no sharp edges—and they have *uniform diffuse reflectance*—there are no markings or colored patches on a surface. Illumination is assumed to come from a *distant point source* with additional *diffuse background* light. This simulates sun and sky. Other assumptions are that there is no *secondary reflection* (i.e., surfaces do not illuminate each other), the view is *monocular* but free of spurious coincidences of edges, and the camera has been *gamma-corrected* to respond linearly with respect to light energy and is noise-free. This domain is described as similar to a picture of "Play-Doh" objects with smooth surfaces, viewed outdoors by a perfect TV camera.

In this domain, the intrinsic parameters are fairly well-behaved. Surface orientation varies continuously across a surface; it is only discontinuous at edges. At the edge of a surface, the orientation must be orthogonal to the line of sight (i.e., the surface has curved away from the camera). Surface reflectance is constant across a surface and discontinuous at surface boundaries. The distance of a point from the camera varies smoothly across a surface and is discontinuous at surface boundaries. Note that the distance is the integral of the surface orientation gradient. The amount of incident illumination varies with surface orientation (i.e., smoothly across a surface), with discontinuities at surface and shadow boundaries. Within a shadow, the incident illumination is constant.

Also, in this domain, there are only three types of edges. *Occlusion edges* are found at the boundary of an object where it occludes part of the background or other objects. *Shadow edges* are found where a shadow from one object falls across another object. Lastly, *self-shading edges* happen when an object curves away from the light source and the incident illumination drops smoothly until the surface normal is orthogonal to the incident light; then, the illumination will be constant in the shadowed area on the far side of this point. Note that all discontinuities in intensity can be accounted for by these edges, because of the assumptions made in this limited domain.

The above simplifications strongly suggest a computational approach. First, the intensity image is examined for discontinuities. These are tentatively called *edges*. The result of this step is a line drawing, which probably contains imperfections. Next, the behavior of intensity is examined in the vicinity of each edge. If the intensity of a region is constant near the edge, it must be a shadow region. If it varies, the region must be illuminated. If it varies with a certain photometrically derived property, the edge must be tangent to the camera, that is, a surface boundary. A small *edge table* is consulted to determine the properties of the intrinsic images (distance, orientation, reflectance, and illumination) along each edge, depending on the region types. The result of this step will be that each intrinsic image contains values for those pixels that correspond to intensity edges. The intrinsic image values at other pixels are initialized to some arbitrary constant, indicating that no information is yet available about these pixels.

The crucial step in the process is a relaxation step, in which two types of consistency are enforced:

1. Each pixel value in each intrinsic image must be compatible (i.e., smooth) with the values of neighboring pixels in the same image, except at the edges. While continuity is easily specified for reflectance, distance, and illumination, there are several kinds of continuity for surface orientation. Barrow and Tenenbaum (1979) have developed a method for performing relaxation on surface orientation values.

2. Each pixel value must be compatible with the pixel values of other intrinsic images at this same position. There are photometric conditions, explained in Horn (1977) and Barrow and Tenenbaum (1978), that relate the various intrinsic image parameters to image intensity by the formula $L = (I_b + [I_s \cos i])R$, where L is image intensity, I_b is the background illumination, I_s is the illumination from the point source, i is the angle of incidence (i.e., the angle between the incident light and the surface normal, which depends on the surface orientation), and R is the reflectance of the surface. For a shadowed point, I_s is zero. This equation must be satisfied at each pixel; thus, when the relaxation suggests that the value of some intrinsic parameter be changed at a pixel, the other intrinsic parameters must change simultaneously to satisfy the equation.

The entire relaxation process is carried out in such a manner that the intrinsic values for edge pixels are not changed, since these were established by physical concerns during the initialization and their values are thus assumed to be correct. Relaxation fills in values for the points within each region.

During the course of relaxation, it is sometimes necessary to postulate additional edges that were not determined in the original segmentation. Note the crucial difference between adding these edges during the computation of intrinsic images and adding them during edge-based segmentation. In the former case, edges are suggested by the laws of physics and geometry to which the scene is subject; in the latter case, edges are suggested only by heuristics based on image-intensity variations, which may result from any of a variety of physical phenomena. Thus, adding edges during the computation of intrinsic images is a much sounder practice than adding edges during traditional segmentation.

Finally, when the intrinsic images have been computed, they may be analyzed to determine the extent of each surface. Traditional segmentation techniques applied to intrinsic data perform much more reliably than when applied to intensity data; for example, regions of uniform reflectance and continuous orientation are almost guaranteed to correspond to surfaces in the scene.

The simplicity of Barrow and Tenenbaum's domain gives rise to some skepticism about the generality of their approach, particularly when extended to intrinsic images of natural scenes. Barrow and Tenenbaum (1978) explain how the technique might be extended to deal with creases (i.e., polyhedral objects), moderate sensor noise, colored areas of the surfaces, unknown illumination, and nonpoint (extended) light sources.

Other Intrinsic Images

Other intrinsic characteristics can be computed, including *specularity,* the amount of specular reflection, such as highlights; *luminosity,* or light sources within the image; *transmittance,* the amount of light that passes through a surface; and three-dimensional texture. Barrow and Tenenbaum note that, as the scene becomes more complex, there is more to be computed but, at the same time, there are more constraints by which to compute the additional information.

Several other researchers have also computed intrinsic characteristics of a scene. Texture descriptions have been produced by Kender (1980). Marr and Poggio (1976) have worked with stereo images, describing disparity by an intrinsic image. From disparity, distance can be calculated. Horn and Schunck (1980) have analyzed optical flow, producing intrinsic images that describe velocity. This can be analyzed to determine object location and relative motion with respect to the camera.

Conclusion

The twin ideas of calculating intrinsic scene characteristics and representing them with intrinsic images have recently become important areas of research. The rich descriptions and convenient representation of a scene that intrinsic characteristics provide make them important for all aspects of image understanding.

References

Intrinsic images are fully described in Barrow and Tenenbaum (1978) and the similar $2\frac{1}{2}$-D sketch is described in Marr (1978). The photometric basis for much of this work is provided by Horn (1977).

D2. Motion

VISION RESEARCHERS use the term *motion* to denote the study of multiple images over time. One of the advantages of multiple views of objects is that they may make it possible to complete three-dimensional structural object descriptions. Objects or parts of objects that are hidden in some frames are frequently revealed in subsequent frames, resolving structural ambiguities. Three-dimensional structure can also be derived from movement. While in theory there is no unique structure consistent with a given motion in two-dimensional space, in most cases humans correctly perceive three-dimensional structures from a two-dimensional movie, for example. This ability, known as the *kinetic depth effect* (Wallach and O'Connell, 1953), is not yet completely understood.

Another advantage of studying time-varying information is the redundancy it provides, especially when frame-to-frame changes are small. This redundancy helps to eliminate noise interference.

Motion cues can also be used for segmentation of objects. Objects that exhibit complex gray-scale patterns or those that are partially occluded can be perceived correctly if the parts exhibit consistent motion. The human visual system uses motion to segment objects from background information. This is especially important for object tracking and collision avoidance.

Several problems are encountered in studying time-varying imagery. First, adding another dimension (time) in image analysis means dealing with massive amounts of information, maybe more than can be handled efficiently by conventional computers. Second, the relation between changes in a sequence of two-dimensional images and movements in the three-dimensional world is not simple. Changes in brightness in images may not be directly related to movements of objects. Apparent changes in images may represent object motion, but they can also represent changes in illumination or movement of the observer. On the other hand, object motion does not always cause brightness changes. For example, a flat surface that is moving in its plane shows no brightness changes as long as the boundaries are not seen. Again, a uniform sphere that is rotated exhibits a constant brightness pattern, since the shading does not move with the surface. Thus, tracking objects involves distinguishing among various sources of change, such as lighting, occlusion, and actual motions, and dealing with inconsistencies between actual and perceived motion.

There are three basic problems in analyzing motion:

1. *The correspondence problem.* To track objects in a sequence of images, one must establish which points on an object in one frame correspond to points in a succeeding frame. Determining the correspondence of points from one frame to the next is called the correspondence problem. (It also arises when points in stereo images are matched for stereo depth analysis;

see Article XIII.D3.) This problem may seem trivial if the objects have already been identified in each frame; however, in most cases, one analyzes motion prior to object identification.

2. *Analyzing motion in three dimensions.* Inferring depth information is a problem inherent in analyzing planar imagery. However, motion information gives its own cues to three-dimensional structure. This is evidenced by the ability of humans to perceive three-dimensional structure and motion from sequences of two-dimensional images. Ullman (1979) and others have tried to understand this human capability and duplicate it in a machine.

3. *Interpreting image-derived information.* The final step in all image analysis is relating all of the image measurements to the real world.

The Correspondence Problem

Before attempting to solve the correspondence problem with a machine, it is helpful to realize that the human visual system does solve it. Humans probably perform the correspondence task at a low level. They are able to react very quickly to motion in order to control eye movements or avoid collisions. It seems likely that identification of objects is not required when humans respond in this way, nor is there time for identification.

The correspondence problem can be studied at three levels:

1. *Pixel level.* Motion can be thought of as the apparent changes in gray scale from one image to the next. At this level, the velocity distribution over the image is referred to as optical flow. Without prior knowledge about the structure of various scene components, measurement must rely on local information about the intensity distribution and the temporal and spatial gradients.

2. *Region or feature level.* Most methods of determining velocities from a sequence of images are based on matching features. A particular pattern, such as a vertex, is identified in one image frame and is searched for in succeeding frames.

3. *Object level.* Objects are first identified in each frame and then the changes that take place between frames are analyzed. Most object-based systems are domain dependent, so that they generally handle known objects and expected changes.

Pixel level. At the pixel level, there is only one constraint on the velocity vector at a given point: the change in gray scale from one frame to the next. We need to impose additional constraints to establish correspondence of points in successive frames so that the velocity vector can be determined. Horn defines optical flow as the distribution of apparent velocities of moving brightness patterns in an image (see Horn and Schunck, 1980). He uses local gray-scale information and additional assumptions to measure the optical flow. He assumes that the basic intensity pattern does not change over time and that velocity varies smoothly in space. These constraints are imposed by simultaneously minimizing the change in intensity of corresponding points and the velocity change from one point to the next. In places where there is no local information, such as flat surfaces where the intensity gradient is zero, the velocity estimate is derived from the surrounding border points. The assumption of velocity smoothness does not hold at object boundaries and, as expected, Horn's simulation results tend to show larger errors at the boundaries.

Region or feature level. At this level, the objective is to match corresponding regions or features in successive frames and thereby determine their velocities. A common approach has been to identify a localized region in one image and use a cross-correlation measure to find the same region in the next image. This method has been applied to the motions of clouds seen in satellite images (Leese, Novak, and Clark, 1971). If the clouds are not changing greatly and form only one layer, this sort of technique works quite well. However, overlapping cloud layers are difficult to distinguish, except on the basis of consistent motion: Tracking objects in a highly occluded domain is very difficult.

Aggarwal and Duda (1975) looked at a simplified version of the problem of tracking overlapping clouds. They represented clouds as polygons moving in planes perpendicular to the viewer and then attempted to track the polygons. They matched clouds in successive frames on the basis of two types of vertices: "true" vertices that corresponded to vertices of the original polygons and "false" vertices that resulted when two polygons overlapped. It is easy to distinguish the two, since the angles at the true vertices stay constant as the polygons move, while the angles and edges at the false vertices tend to change. Only the true vertices are matched. Once a polygon has been successfully tracked in two images, a velocity estimate and a prediction can be made to locate the polygon in the next image. Aggarwal and Duda based matches between true vertices on a criterion function that is determined by the distance of the vertex from the predicted position and the error in the angle of the vertex. They were able to track objects that moved in various directions and occluded each other in fairly complex ways. The work has been extended to curved planar objects by Chow and Aggarwal (1977).

Object level. Once three-dimensional objects have been identified in each frame, finding correspondences is usually not as difficult as it is with pixel or feature information. One of the interesting problems to be solved at this level is the derivation of a semantic description of motions (see Badler, 1975).

Motion in Three Dimensions

Humans are readily able to perceive three-dimensional structure on the basis of motion information alone. For example, when presented with a sequence of binary images of points on a moving object, humans can usually perceive the structure of the the object, even if it is unfamiliar and the individual images are totally unrecognizable. Ullman (1979) has tried to duplicate this capability in a machine. Under the assumptions that the correspondence problem has been solved and that the objects are rigid bodies, Ullman has derived what he calls the *structure-from-motion theorem*. The theorem states that three separate views of four noncoplanar points on a rigid object uniquely define the three-dimensional structure and motion of the object.

Ullman's implementation of the structure-from-motion theorem involves the following steps. The image is divided into sets of four points and each set of points is tested to see whether it has a consistent rigid-body interpretation in the three views. In many cases, after this first pass there will be at least one consistent set for each object in the image. Each remaining point can then be tested to see if it belongs to one of the rigid-body sets. In this way, the objects are segmented and their three-dimensional structure and motion are determined at the same time.

Interpretation

The interpretation of actual scenes in terms of motions of objects is a very difficult problem. Most applications have dealt with a fairly restricted domain, such as cloud motion or motion of the internal boundary of the heart. Jain and Nagel (1979) have attempted to interpret actual TV sequences in two dimensions using as little domain-dependent information as possible. The objects they study are usually cars or people moving along streets. They track regions not by directly matching features but by looking at what information can be derived from changes between the first frame and subsequent frames. They generate a *first-order-difference picture* (FODP) based on whether a sample area in a particular frame is incompatible with the first frame. Incompatibility is tested with the mean gray value and its variance from the current and reference frame.

A first-order-difference picture is accumulated by counting the number of times sample areas from the second and subsequent frames are incompatible with the first frame. After the first few frames, an object moving along in a particular direction should produce two regions of incompatibility in the FODP—one in which the background is being uncovered and another in which it is being covered over. Once the object has moved the length of its diameter, the two regions should merge. Jain and Nagel also compute a second-order-difference picture that indicates the areas in which two successive FODPs differ. When an object has moved a distance greater than its boundary, the second-order-difference picture will show two regions, one indicating where the object was originally and the other where the object is in the current frame.

When there are two such regions in the second-order-difference picture that correspond to one incompatibility region in the FODP, an object is identified. Each of the two regions found in the second-order-difference picture should outline the contour of the moving object.

The primary constraint on this method is that in order to identify or track an object, one must observe a displacement by more than the object diameter along the direction of displacement. This means that movement must be primarily in one direction and primarily in the plane of the image.

Conclusion

To date, much of the attention in motion studies has been directed to applications, for example, tracking cloud motions and detecting geological changes from satellite images, as well as to analyzing the dynamic shape of the heart and tracking circulatory flow from x-ray data. However, the study of time-varying imagery is becoming more theoretical, and there are three primary research problems. The first involves solving the correspondence problem, the second concerns deriving three-dimensional structural information from motion cues, and the third is to apply this research to real problems and relate image-derived motion measurements to the movements of real objects.

References

See Huang (1981) and Aggarwal and Badler (1980), which include recent work on motion and image-sequence analysis.

D3. Stereo Vision

THE CENTRAL PROBLEM of general image-understanding is to recover the three-dimensional form of an object that produced a two-dimensional image. One approach is to measure quantitatively the distance from a camera to each point of interest in a scene. If views of the same object from two different positions are available, we can measure the distance from camera to object by triangulation. This technique is known as *stereo* or *binocular vision;* it is a primary source of information for humans about three-dimensional objects in their environment.

A schematic of a binocular pair of cameras viewing the same scene is shown in Figure D3–1. The image of an object in a camera view is formed by a ray of light originating at the object and passing through the center of the lens. Inversely, the center of the lens and a point in the image uniquely determine a line along which the object must fall. The question is where in space along this line the object is located—how far away it is. This is easily determined with a second image from another camera. If we can find a point in the second image that corresponds to a point in the first, then that point and the center of its lens determine a second ray of light. If the two points are indeed produced by the same object, if our knowledge of the relative camera positions is correct, and if the cameras are linear, then the object must be located at the point at which the two rays are calculated to intersect.

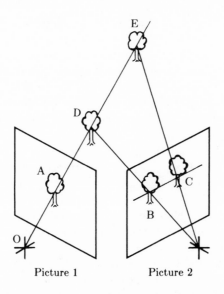

Figure D3–1. Binocular views of a scene.

This model is very general in that it describes both conventional stereo and *motion parallax*. In conventional stereo, as in human vision, two images are taken by laterally displaced sensing devices—eyes or cameras. In motion parallax, a single camera may take images from arbitrary positions and orientations, for example, as an aerial camera takes images from two points in a flight.

The problem of extracting depth information from a stereo pair of images has, in principle, four components: finding features of an image that are easily recognized in both images, matching these features in the two images, determining the relative camera positions, and inferring the distances from the camera to the objects that cast the features in the images.

Given accurate knowledge of the camera model, the search for the match for a given feature in one image is restricted to a line in the other, rather than to the whole image. Figure D3–1 shows that the object responsible for the feature A in the left image must lie along a ray starting at the origin of the left coordinate system, O, and proceeding through the feature A. The image of the object in the right picture must lie somewhere along the projection of the ray OA onto the right image plane, which is the line BC. This line is called an *epipolar line*. Note that every point on a given epipolar line in the right image must match some point along the corresponding epipolar line in the left image, and vice versa. Even if we do not know the exact camera parameters, the search for a match is still restricted to a narrow region along the epipolar line.

Finding Features

The objective of feature finding is to find features in one image that are likely to have an unambiguous match in the other image. For example, an individual pixel has little information content: The fact that two pixels in two images have the same gray level is little evidence that they were produced by the same object in the scene. Unambiguous matches are more likely to be found in regions of the pictures that have high information content, or high variance. Moravec's *interest operator* (1980) is a technique for finding such regions. It first computes the sum of the squares of the differences between each pixel in a window and the pixel's neighbors in each of four directions (horizontal, vertical, and two diagonals). This results in four sums, and the interest measure for each pixel is the minimum of the sums. Interesting points are those for which the interest measure attains a local maximum. Thus, interesting points have a high variance in all directions and so are likely to find an unambiguous match in the other image. For example, the interest operator tends to select corners.

Another good source of points for unambiguous matches are edges of objects, because they tend to correspond to sharp changes in intensity. For stereo, edges may be extracted by the usual edge-detection methods (see

Article XIII.C4). A computational model of human stereo vision (Marr and Poggio, 1977; Grimson, 1980) uses zero-crossings in the *Laplacian* image after Gaussian low-pass filtering (smoothing). Zero-crossings are the points at which the second derivatives of an image change their sign (see Article XIII.C4). Two considerations with regard to edges should be noted. First, only linear features oriented across the epipolar lines provide an accurate match. Second, since edges usually represent discontinuities in depth, it is likely that what appears behind an edge will be different in the two views. Therefore, edge-based stereo uses the information about location and orientation of edges but makes little use of intensity across the edges.

Matching

Matching is a search process. As such, it has two components: a difference measure and a search strategy.

Difference measures. Two kinds of difference measures are used to evaluate matches between corresponding features of two images. One kind is appropriate when the features are *areal*, that is, constitute regions, and another kind is used for *lineal* features such as edges.

A typical measure of the difference between two areal features is the sum over the region of the squares of the differences between corresponding pixels, called the L_2 *norm*, $\sum(E_1 - E_2)^2$, where E_1 and E_2 are the pixel values of the two images, and the summation extends over the region of interest. This measure requires a multiplication for each pixel in the regions and, although an algorithm can replace the multiplication by a table lookup (Moravec, 1980), this may still be computationally expensive. The L_1 *norm*, $\sum |(E_1 - E_2)|$, requires only absolute values.

Both measures are sensitive to changes in contrast (gain) and brightness (bias) between the images. These differences occur when two views of the same object are processed differently, when images are taken separately under different lighting conditions, and because the apparent brightness of a surface changes with the angle from which it is viewed (e.g., specular reflection). A measure of the similarity between two images that is insensitive to contrast and brightness changes is the *normalized correlation:*

$$\frac{\sum E_1 E_2}{\sqrt{\sum E_1^2 \sum E_2^2}}.$$

Lineal features are similar if they have the same orientation and if the intensity gradient across them is the same. As we mentioned earlier, matched edges may be adjacent to regions of dissimilar appearance. Thus, one may wish to ignore the appearance of the image near an edge and record only the fact that there is an edge. Alternately, to consider two edges to be a match, one might require only that the intensity gradients across the edges have the same sign (e.g., Marr and Poggio, 1977).

Search strategies. Finding matching points in two images is the most difficult problem of stereo image interpretation. The best feature-finding systems will still select features that match in appearance more than one feature in the other image. In fact, if the scene has a repeating pattern, like windows of a building, matching is inevitably ambiguous. Moreover, because of occlusion, there will be features in one image that are not visible in the other; it is impossible to find a match for these features.

Matching is also complicated by expensive searches of large areas. Imagine that we find N areal features in one image, each with an average area of W^2 pixels. In the worst case, in which we have no idea of the camera positions, it can be very expensive to find the pixel positions in the other image that correspond to the center pixels in the areal features. It involves a search of W^2 pixels from each pixel position in the other image, for each of the N features. This requires NW^2L^2 comparisons, where L^2 is the area of the other image.

There are two properties of matter—*cohesiveness* and *opacity*—that can help to decide between ambiguous matches. Because of the cohesiveness of matter, the distance from the camera to objects that appear near each other in the image tends to be approximately the same. Because of opacity of matter (in general), each point in each image will have a unique depth associated with it and, thus, each point in each image will have at most one match in the other image. Marr and Poggio (1976) suggest a *cooperative* or *relaxation algorithm* that implements both of these constraints. The partially determined disparity for a given pixel adjusts the disparity for nearby pixels in an iterative updating procedure, so that neighboring pixels have similar disparities. This implements the constraint of cohesiveness. Opacity is implemented by a technique of inhibition between different disparity detectors for a given pixel.

Mori, Kidode, and Asada (1973) and Marr and Poggio (1976) used a *coarse-fine* approach to finding matches. A low-resolution depth map of low-resolution versions of the images provides initial disparity estimates for higher resolution matches. This allows larger disparities to be tolerated without ambiguity of match, since in frequency-limited images a disparity of up to about one-half the wavelength of the highest frequency in the image can be tolerated before the match becomes ambiguous.

There are several search strategies for finding a matching point. For areal features, the *sequential similarity-detection algorithm* (SSDA; Barnea and Silverman, 1972) is a kind of best-first search. This technique requires a cumulative measure of difference, such as L_1 or L_2. For a given feature, a running count is kept of the best match thus far, and each subsequent search in another area of the image is abandoned if it does not produce a match that is at least as good as the current best. Guidance for the next position to search can be provided by the spatial intensity gradient of the image, resulting in an iterative hill-climbing method for stereo (Lucas and Kanade, 1981).

If the camera parameters are known, matching can be facilitated by taking advantage of the fact that the matching occurs only along the epipolar lines. This is especially important in computational models of human stereo vision in which the search is limited along horizontal scan lines of the same vertical position in both images.

For edge-based stereo, the problem is to pair features along an epipolar line in one image with features along the corresponding epipolar line in the other. Some features may not have matches because of occlusion. Useful constraints are that nearby features in one image make pairs with nearby features in the other and that the order of matched features be preserved along the epipolar lines. We can define a measure of the degree of satisfaction of these constraints combined with goodness of the local match of individual features. Then, conventional search techniques, such as dynamic programming and branch and bound, can be used (Baker, 1980; Henderson, Miller, and Grosch, 1979) to find the best pairings.

Solving for the Camera Model

The information about the relative position of the two cameras is called the *camera model*. A priori knowledge or kinds of log data (e.g., a flight record) often provide this information, but it also can be derived from a given stereo pair when we know a set of more than five matching points in it. Gennery (1979) discusses an iterative method to find camera models. If the camera parameters are known exactly, then the point that corresponds to a given point in the left image must lie somewhere along the corresponding epipolar line in the right image. The location of the epipolar line depends on the camera parameters, and if they are not exact, the matching point will lie somewhere off the epipolar line. The distance between the matching point and the epipolar line is thus a measure of the error of the current camera parameters. Gennery's method finds camera parameters that minimize the sum of the errors over the known matching points. It will converge to the correct camera model, if the initial estimate of the camera parameters is fairly accurate.

Conclusion

Stereo has been used as a primary source of three-dimensional information for navigation (Hannah, 1980), a robot rover (Moravec, 1979; Arnold, 1978), and cartographic applications (Mori, Kidode, and Asada, 1973).

References

For a basic discussion of the geometry of stereo vision, see Duda and Hart (1973). Barnard and Fischler (1981) present a survey and discussion of stereo.

D4. Range Finders

VISION SYSTEMS that work from intensity images must infer three-dimensional structure from two-dimensional data; an alternative is to measure depth directly. There are several techniques for measuring depth. In this article we discuss *time-of-flight* and *triangulation* methods. Time of flight measures the distance from a source of light (or sound) to an object in terms of the time required for the light or sound to travel to the object and back. Triangulation in *stereo vision* is discussed in Article XIII.D3; it finds corresponding points in two images and infers lines extending from these points, through the centers of their respective lenses, and out into space to where the lines intersect. The intersecting lines and the baseline between the two lenses constitute a triangle. We discuss here the technique of replacing one of the cameras in stereo vision by an active projection of a *light spot* or a *light stripe*. This method is called *active illumination* and has an advantage over stereo vision in that it avoids the difficult problem of finding corresponding points in two images.

Time of Flight

Time-of-flight systems measure the time required for a waveform to propagate to an object and reflect back. The waveform may be either sound or laser light. Given that the propagation speed of the wave form is V, the distance to the object, d, is given by the time measured between transmission of the pulse and its return to the receiver, T:

$$d = \frac{VT}{2} \; .$$

Two important parameters that determine the accuracy of a time-of-flight system are the beam width, W, and the smallest measurable unit of time, δt. The size of resolution elements in the dimension perpendicular to the sensor in a *depth map* depends on W, the beam width. The size of the resolution element in the depth dimension is determined by δt and V.

Sound has the desirable property of a relatively slow propagation velocity, permitting fairly accurate depth resolution. However, it is difficult to form a narrow beam with sound, and so sound systems are not useful for producing a precise depth map. For robotic applications, detection systems based on sound have been designed to warn if an object is within a specified distance (e.g., with the commercially available Polaroid ultrasonic transceiver set).

Laser light, on the other hand, is ideal for generating a narrow beam, but since the propagation speed of light is very high relative to the precision of instruments that measure time, some laser range-finders have poor depth resolution—on the order of meters. They are used for large outdoor scenes (e.g., for the Mars Explorer robot; see Johnston, 1973).

One solution to the depth-resolution problem is to modulate the amplitude of the laser beam and measure the phase shift of the reflected beam. Such a system was constructed at SRI International (Nitzan, Brain, and Duda, 1977) to sense a 128×128 depth map with a range of 1 to 5 meters and a depth resolution of 1 centimeter. It used a 9 MHz oscillator ($\lambda = 33.3$ m), which meant that a phase shift of $.0006\lambda$ corresponded to a depth change of 1 centimeter. In addition to the depth map, the intensity of the reflected beam was used to form a television-quality intensity image, from which an *intrinsic* image of the reflectance of the object points (see Article XIII.D1) was generated.

Photon noise dominates such a system. In general, for a given signal-to-noise (S/N) ratio there is a trade-off between scanning time and laser signal power. The SRI system uses a 15 mW laser for safety reasons. To achieve a high S/N ratio, each sample is integrated for 500 msec. Thus, a 128×128 image requires over two hours to generate. A more practical system could employ some combination of a greater transmit power, a larger receiver area, and a shorter modulator wavelength to reduce this time.

Triangulation-based Depth Sensors with Active Illumination

There are several different triangulation methods for measuring depth. One approach, stereo vision, is discussed in Article XIII.D3. In the following, we describe system configurations with one passive element, namely, a one- or two-dimensional camera, and one active element, namely, a spot or stripe projector.

A simple, two-dimensional, triangulation-based depth sensor. Let us introduce the mechanics of triangulation-based depth sensing with a simple two-dimensional system. After discussing the parameters of this system, we extend this system to the third dimension.

A two-dimensional system is illustrated in Figure D4–1, in which the passive component is a linear CCD photodetector array (see Article XIII.C1) with its associated optics. (For simplicity, the CCD array in Fig. D4–1 has only five elements, although a practical system would typically have 256 to 2,048 elements.) Here, the x-z coordinates are situated so that the x-axis is the baseline connecting the lens center and the light projector and the origin is at its middle point. The lens center is located at $(-a/2, 0)$. Each photodetector array element has a field of view that diverges at an angle of γ, and the center of the field of view is oriented at an angle ϕ from the x-axis. The active component of the illustrated system is a beam projector, located at position $(a/2, 0)$, which projects a beam with a divergence of δ and angle of ψ.

The intersection of the beam with the camera's field of view defines a set of quadrilateral resolution cells. Two such cells are labeled C_1 and C_2

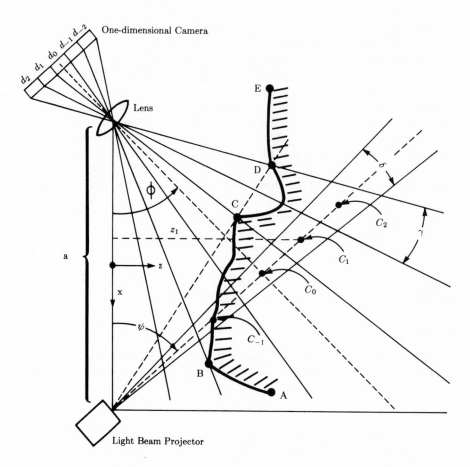

Figure D4–1.   A triangulation-based depth-measurement system with active illumination.

in Figure D4–1. The presence of a surface in a cell, C_i, will cause light from the beam to be reflected and imaged onto the corresponding detector, d_i, in the linear photodetector array. In the case of Figure D4–1, C_{-1} interrupts the light beam, which is detected by d_{-1}. If we define the *depth* z_i to the surface as depth to the center of the cell, we can see from the figure that

$$z_i = \frac{a}{\cot \psi + \cot (\phi + \gamma i)} \tag{1}$$

for $-2 \le i \le 2$.

There are two limitations to this depth-finding apparatus. First, with a single beam angle ψ, we can measure depth only to surface points that are on the beam. To obtain a depth map—in this case, a one-dimensional array of the depth of all points between A and E—we would have to *scan* over areas by changing the angle of the beam, ψ. Even then, we are unable to find the depth of some areas of the scene: The area between C and D cannot be illuminated by the beam, and the area between A and B is the "far side" of the camera and is invisible to it.

Second, because of the divergence of the light beam and the camera's field of view, the size and shape of the quadrilateral resolution cells C_i vary. They also depend on the beam angle ψ. This means that the precision of depth measurement varies from place to place. In general, it is desirable to keep the beam as narrow as possible (small δ) and to use a camera with as many elements as possible (small γ). As equation (1) suggests, a larger baseline (parameter a, the distance between the camera and projector) helps increase the precision, but it also results in larger unmeasurable areas.

Spot sensing. The simple system described above produces only a one-dimensional array of depth measurements. To obtain a two-dimensional array of depth measurements, the scene must be scanned in both directions x (within the page) and y (perpendicular to the page). The simplest way to scan is to reflect a spot beam with two rotating mirrors whose axes of rotation are orthogonal: The first mirror rotates about the y-axis to orient the beam within x-z plane (the page), and the second one orients the beam perpendicular to the x-z plane.

A simple sensing device for this scheme is a camera with a two-dimensional field of view (usually a two-dimensional TV camera—vidicon or CCD array; see Article XIII.C1) for detecting the spot position. This involves scanning the field of view and finding the brightest spot in it. With conventional TV cameras, a spot detection requires one *frame*—typically 1/60 sec.—per measurement.

Once the projected spot is detected, its three-dimensional location can be calculated to be the intersection of two lines—the light beam and the line of sight—in three-dimensional space.

This scheme can be improved in several ways. First, the direction of the light beam can be controlled to trace only interesting portions of the scene. Such a device is called a *tracker*. Second, faster (random-access) sensors such as image disectors can decrease the spot-detection time. Recently, a PIN diode position-sensitive chip was used (Kanade and Asada, 1981) because it directly outputs the x-y position of the spots without scanning the field of view. Typical spot-based ranging devices operate at a speed of 300 to 2,000 points per second.

We should mention that we do not need to know two lines in three-dimensional space to determine a three-dimensional point: It suffices to know one three-dimensional line and one plane. This suggests that the camera can actually be one-dimensional. We can place a cylindrical lens vertically before the camera, and only the horizontal position of the spot is sensed by the one-dimensional camera (Roeker and Kiessling, 1975). This will determine the vertical plane that includes the projected spot and, therefore, together with the known light beam (three-dimensional space line), we can compute the three-dimensional position of the surface point.

Light-stripe sensing. Another practical method for measuring depth is to use a *stripe* of light (instead of a spot beam) and a two-dimensional television camera. This is a simple extension of the principle illustrated in Figure D4–1. We can imagine that Figure D4–1 shows a single *cross-section* of a light-stripe sensing apparatus: The receptor cells are a single scan line of a two-dimensional sensor, and the light beam is a result of slicing a stripe perpendicular to the page. We can imagine that a light-stripe sensor has as many of these cross-sections as it has scan lines. Light-stripe sensing was pioneered by Shirai and Suwa (1971) and Agin and Binford (1973).

With this method, one depth measurement for each scan line of the camera can be obtained within one frame. With a camera with 256 scan lines, we can measure the depth of up to 256×60 points per second. To get a complete depth map, the light stripe has to be moved or rotated to scan the scene, but it need be moved only in the direction orthogonal to the camera scan lines, that is, about one axis instead of the two required for spot sensing.

Since light-stripe sensing is simple and fast, it is widely used today for robotic applications; for example, the camera-projector pair can be mounted at the end of a robot arm to guide the arm toward the object to be grasped (Vanderbrug, Albus, and Borkmeyer, 1979).

Multiple-stripe and grid-coding methods. Instead of a single stripe, it is possible to use a grid of horizontal and vertical stripes. From the position of the camera, the square grid pattern is seen as distorted by the surface orientation and curvature. By identifying the nature of these distortions, we can infer the surface orientations and curvatures. (Notice the relationship of this idea to shape from texture; Article XIII.D5.) However, the benefit of obtaining an entire scene in one shot is often offset by a complicated image-processing task.

We can also employ an encoding scheme. Each stripe can be encoded by color, intensity, width, or position. When the positional encoding is used, a set of stripes can be turned on and off in a binary pattern in a sequence of images. Then, 2^N stripe positions can be identified from a set of N images, rather than 2^N images. Each stripe is assigned a unique N-bit number from 0 to $2^N - 1$. Then, when taking the Kth image ($1 \leq K \leq N$), each stripe is turned on or off depending on whether the Kth bit of its assigned number is 1 or 0. Some redundancy can be added to this encoding to increase reliability. This type of encoding scheme requires far fewer images than the single-stripe method (Altschuler, Altschuler, and Taboada, 1981).

A related method is to project onto the scene multiple stripes that are out of alignment with the TV scan lines. This produces a moiré pattern in which each contour is a locus of the same depth. Thus, the moiré method is very useful for detecting fluctuations in surface depths. However, the moiré pattern alone does not provide information about the *absolute* depth of a contour.

Conclusion

We have discussed a number of methods for measuring depth. First, we considered time-of-flight systems that measure the time required for sound or light to propagate to an object and reflect back. There is a trade-off in these systems between light, which can be precisely focused but which travels too fast to be useful in measuring small distances, and sound, which cannot be accurately focused but which travels slowly enough for good depth resolution.

We also discussed triangulation-based systems that use an active light projector and a passive sensor. Several variations were considered, including spot sensing and stripe sensing.

The related technique of stereo analysis is discussed in Article XIII.D3, and Article XIII.D6 explains some of the ways that range data are used in scene analysis.

References

Nitzan, Brain, and Duda (1977) give a basic discussion of depth measurement by time of flight. Bolles, Kremers, and Cain (1981) treat the light-striping method concisely and clearly.

D5. Shape-from Methods

IN the first article in this section (Article XIII.D1), the importance of recovering intrinsic scene characteristics was emphasized. Shading, textures, edges, contours, and highlights play important roles in determining shape from a monocular image. However, two-dimensional images provide only ambiguous shape information; to recover shape, assumptions that relate image characteristics to scene characteristics are needed. For example, in Article XIII.B8, we described quantitative shape recovery from line drawings (i.e., contours and edges) of the Origami world. We used the assumptions concerning image properties—such as parallelism and skewed symmetry. Recently, a class of methods has been developed for recovering shape from shading, textures, and contours in monocular images under reasonable assumptions. They make it possible for us to represent the constraints that images provide and to aggregate them to recover a shape. They are called *shape-from* methods, after the pioneering work in shape-from-shading by Horn (1975, 1977). In this article, we discuss shape-from-shading and shape-from-texture methods.

Shape from Shading

A model of image formation and the reflectance map. To use shading to recover shape, we need to know how the image intensity at a pixel is determined: We need a model of image formation. The model includes both the geometry of image projection and the radiometry of intensity formation. We will follow the discussion given by Woodham (1978). Figure D5–1 shows a basic model. It includes a light (illumination) source, a surface, and a picture plane. As in Article XIII.B7, we place a coordinate system so that the viewer's central line of sight (optical axis) is the z-axis, and the picture plane is the x-y plane. Imagine a small surface patch at (x, y, z). It is illuminated by the light source and part of the reflected light is recorded at a corresponding pixel position in the image.

In general, the intensity recorded at a pixel depends on the illumination position, surface material, surface position, surface orientation, and viewer position. However, for simplicity, we assume that the incident illumination is parallel and constant at each surface position and that the image projection is orthographic. This corresponds well to the case in which the illumination source and viewer are both far from the object.

The reflectance characteristics of an object surface can now be represented as a function $\phi(i, e, g)$ of the three angles defined in Figure D5–1: The incident angle i is the angle between the incident light and the surface normal, the

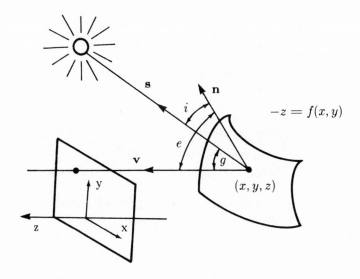

Figure D5–1.   A model of image formation.

view angle e is the angle between the emergent light (which is also the line of sight) and the surface normal, and the phase angle g is the angle between the incident and emergent light.

Orientation in three-dimensional space can be represented by means of gradient space (see Article XIII.B7). Assuming that $-z = f(x, y)$ denotes the surface, the gradient (p, q) is defined as

$$p = \partial f/\partial x = \partial(-z)/\partial x, \quad q = \partial f/\partial y = \partial(-z)/\partial y \,,$$

where $-z$ is the depth. Then, the surface normal $\mathbf{n}$ at (x, y, z), which points to the viewer, is given by

$$\mathbf{n} = (p, q, 1) \,.$$

Thus, we can regard a gradient as representing a three-dimensional space vector whose x and y components are p and q and whose z component is 1, and vice versa. Similarly, we can represent other orientations with gradients. A three-dimensional vector $\mathbf{s} = (p_s, q_s, 1)$ points in the direction of illumination; that is, the gradient (p_s, q_s) represents the orientation of illumination. Similarly, the viewer's line of sight can be represented as $(0, 0)$ in the gradient space, because under orthographic projection it is parallel to the z-axis; this vector is $\mathbf{v} = (0, 0, 1)$.

One of the simplest surface-reflectance models is a perfectly diffuse (lambertian) surface, in which the reflection is uniform for all the view angles, and the amount of reflection varies as the cosine of the incident angle; that is,

$$\phi(i, e, g) = \rho \cos i,$$

where ρ is called the reflectivity constant.

Because of the property of inner products, we can write this equation in terms of gradients:

$$\begin{aligned}
\phi(i, e, g) &= \rho \cos i = \rho(\mathbf{s} \cdot \mathbf{n})/|\mathbf{s}||\mathbf{n}| \\
&= \rho(pp_s + qq_s + 1)/\sqrt{(p_s^2 + q_s^2 + 1)(p^2 + q^2 + 1)} \\
&= R(p, q).
\end{aligned} \tag{1}$$

This means that, given a surface patch at (x, y, z) with orientation (p, q), we can determine the image intensity $I(x, y)$ observed at the corresponding pixel (x, y) to be

$$I(x, y) = R(p, q).$$

The function $R(p, q)$ is called a reflectance map. This is, in fact, generally the case under our assumptions: Since we assume a constant illumination, the surface-reflectance characteristics $\phi(i, e, g)$ solely determine the image intensity, and since we assume orthographic projection, a pixel at (x, y) images the surface patch at (x, y, z) and therefore its pixel value is equal to $\phi(i, e, g)$. The angles i, e, and g can be represented in terms of the vectors $\mathbf{n}$, $\mathbf{s}$, and $\mathbf{v}$, which are represented by the gradients.

Figure D5–2 shows the reflectance map of equation (1), drawn as a series of *iso-intensity contours* for the case $p_s = .7$, $q_s = .3$, and $\rho = 1$. The surface orientations on a single contour generate the same image intensity. Those to the left of the straight lines $p_s p + q_s q + 1 = 0$ correspond to the orientations that face away from the illumination and, thus, do not give rise to any brightness.

Reflectance maps have been calculated for various cases (Horn, 1979) and used for automatic generation of hill-shading of terrains. The synthesized images can be matched with real images to normalize them.

Shape-recovery process. The reflectance map of Figure D5–2 shows that under the assumptions about the imaging geometry and surface reflectivity, the observed intensity at a pixel *does* constrain the surface orientations on the corresponding iso-intensity contour of gradients, and yet this constraint is not strong enough to determine surface orientations uniquely. Additional constraints are needed.

The utility of the reflectance map is illustrated for the case of the block scene in Figure D5–3a. Suppose this is a convex corner. Then the gradients of the three faces should form the triangle shown in Figure D5–3b, whose shape is determined by the orientations of lines in Figure D5–3a, but whose location and size are ambiguous. Suppose also that the imaging condition is the same

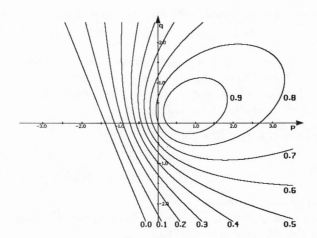

Figure D5–2.   The reflectance map for a lambertian surface with $p_s = .7$, $q_s = .3$, and $\rho = 1$ in
equation (1) (from Woodham, 1978).

as discussed above: Image intensities should be constant over each planar face
because it has a constant gradient. The observed intensities constrain surface
orientations on the iso-intensity contours. If we put together the two types
of constraints—the triangle and the iso-intensity contours—we may be able
to determine the surface orientations. We can translate, shrink, and expand
the gradient-space triangle until each corner lies on the iso-intensity contour
that corresponds to the observed intensity (see Fig. D5–3c). In this way, we
can determine the surface orientations of the three faces.

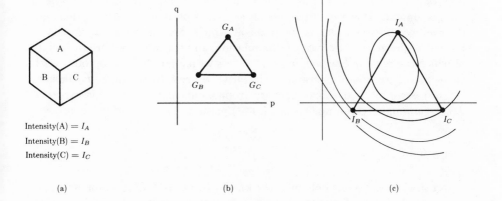

Figure D5–3.   A simple example of using the reflectance map.

More generally, for curved objects, we must find surface orientations (gradients) for each point, rather than for a whole surface. To do this, we can exploit two general constraints: Each image point is assigned to at most one surface orientation, and orientations vary smoothly almost everywhere except at boundaries. These constraints are called *uniqueness* and *continuity*, respectively. Suppose we assign $(p_{i,j}, q_{i,j})$ to pixel position (i, j). Then we can define a measure of error of that assignment as

$$
\begin{aligned}
E_{i,j} = {} & (I(i, j) - R(p_{i,j}, q_{i,j}))^2 \\
& + \lambda\{(p_{i+1,j} + p_{i,j+1} + p_{i-1,j} + p_{i,j-1} - 4p_{i,j})^2 \\
& + (q_{i+1,j} + q_{i,j+1} + q_{i-1,j} + q_{i,j-1} - 4q_{i,j})^2\},
\end{aligned}
$$

where λ is a positive constant.

The first term of this equation is the difference of the observed intensity $I(i, j)$ from the expected intensity $R(p_{i,j}, q_{i,j})$, and the second term is the sum of the squared Laplacians to measure the smoothness (see Article XIII.C3). Then we define the total error E as the summation of $E_{i,j}$ over the image:

$$
E = \sum_i \sum_j E_{i,j}\,.
$$

We minimize this error to obtain a shape that globally satisfies the constraints. Iterative or cooperative relaxation algorithms (see Article XIII.E4) can be used for minimization. Boundary information gives explicit orientations at certain points and provides anchor points for an algorithm. Ikeuchi (1980a) used occluding contours and self-shadow boundaries to obtain anchor points. At an occluding contour, the line of sight is tangent to the object surface, and its surface normal is uniquely determined as perpendicular to both the contour line and the line of sight. A self-shadow boundary is the place at which the illumination ray is tangent to the surface. It corresponds to the line $p_s p + q_s q + 1 = 0$ in Figure D5–2, but unfortunately the surface normals are not unique. However, there are three points on it whose orientations are determined uniquely: One is the point at which the self-shadow boundary is perpendicular to the direction of illumination, and the other two are the points at which the self-shadow boundary intersects with an occluding contour. With these boundary conditions and an iterative process to minimize E, Ikeuchi (1980b) accomplished shape recovery from monocular images, for example, from scanning-electron-microscope (SEM) pictures.

Shape from Texture

Historically, textural change was known to be useful for shape and pattern discrimination; for example, the term *texture gradient* has been used to suggest the change of density due to distance and orientations. However, it is only recently that texture has been studied mathematically, so that computer vision systems can directly relate texture with shape. Notable work here includes Kender (1979, 1980), Stevens (1980), Witkin (1980), Kender and Kanade (1980), and Ikeuchi (1980b). This article will present a simple example of shape from texture.

Parallels between shading and texture. Close parallels can be drawn between shape from shading and shape from texture. We can imagine a small texture element—called a *texel*—that corresponds to a pixel. Just as the intensity at a pixel changes with surface orientation, so does the appearance of a texel in the image; its appearance includes its shape and its local density. Just as shape from shading needed certain assumptions, so does shape from texture. One such assumption is homogeneity of surface texture; that is, the original "print" on the surface is homogeneous and any variation observed in the image is due to the change in shape and view angle. Under this assumption, observed textural properties such as shape distortion and density change constrain the orientations of the surface patches, but they are not enough to determine uniquely the orientations. Assumptions of surface uniqueness and continuity are required—as they were for shape from shading—to propagate the constraints and to facilitate the search for a globally correct solution.

In most vision research, perspective projection is a source of difficulty because its nonlinearity makes theories less tractable. We have seen that orthographic projection is often preferred as an approximation because of its simplicity. Interestingly, the perspective projection is one of the main sources of constraints in the shape-from-texture method.

The case of parallel lines. Converging lines in a perspective image suggest parallel lines in the corresponding scene. More than one set of converging lines can specify the orientation of a surface on which they lie. Typical examples are lines formed by tiles or windows on the wall of a building. A human can perceive the orientation of the wall from such an image. An elegant solution to this problem was presented by Kender (1979).

Suppose we have a set of converging lines in an image (Fig. D5–4a). Then we can transform each line as follows:

1. Represent a line in the x-y picture plane as $\rho = x \cos\theta + y \sin\theta$;

2. Transform the line into a point T in u-v space where $T = (u, v) = ((K/\rho)\cos\theta, (K/\rho)\sin\theta)$ and K is a positive constant.

When we transform a set of lines that converge to a point C in the image, the transformed points lie on a single line in the u-v space. The reason for this is illustrated in Figure D5–4b. First, think of a point $T' = (\rho\cos\theta, \rho\sin\theta)$. T' is just the leg of a perpendicular line from the origin O to the picture line, such as T'_1 for line l_1. All T' for the converging lines should be on a circle whose diameter coincides with OC, because the angle $OT'C$ is always a right angle. Now, notice that T is the point located on the line OT', so that

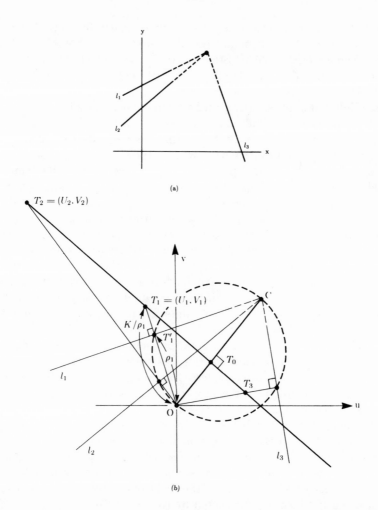

Figure D5–4.   Obtaining surface orientation from converging lines.

$OT = K/OT' = K/\rho$. Let us define T_0 on OC so that $OT_0 = K/OC$.
Since O and C are fixed points, T_0 is also a fixed point. Then it is easy to
show that point T (the transformed point of a convergent line) is always on
the line that passes T_0 and is perpendicular to OC. For example, assume
T_1. Triangles OT_0T_1 and OT'_1C are similar, and thus angle OT_0T_1 is equal
to angle OT'_1C, which is equal to a right angle. Kender showed that under
perspective projection, if we choose K equal to the focal length, then the u-v
plane coincides with the gradient-space p-q plane. After all, if we assume that
the convergent lines are originally parallel lines on a single plane surface, the
surface orientation should be such that its gradient is on this line. If the

surface includes more than one set of parallel lines, like the boundary lines of repetitive windows on a wall of a building, we have two such gradient-space lines, and thus the surface orientation can be determined as an intersection of the two gradient-space lines. To do this involves several steps:

1. Detect short edge elements and their direction θ;
2. Transform them into the p-q place as defined above (with K = focal length);
3. Detect straight lines in the p-q plane;
4. Obtain their intersection point as the gradient of the original surface.

Conclusion

Not only are individual shape-from methods useful, but the approach that is common to them is a powerful paradigm in vision research. Indeed, this approach is the theme of Section XIII.D, namely, to understand the geometrical and physical basis of the imaging process and to derive constraints by making assumptions (such as uniformity and continuity) explicit. Recent formulations of other shape-from methods—shape from contours, from motion, from stereo, and so forth—have been strongly influenced by the approach described here.

References

Horn (1975) did the first work on shape from shading. Kender (1980) presents basic tools for shape-from methods as well as his results on shape from texture.

D6. Three-dimensional Shape Description and Recognition

ONE OF THE REASONS that image understanding is so difficult is that the gray value of a point in a scene is the product of many factors. It depends on an object's reflectance function, the illumination, the orientation of the surface with respect to the light and to the viewer, mutual illumination, and shadowing. Furthermore, spatial information is lost by projection in forming the image (see Article XIII.D4).

This problem can be overcome if range data, derived from an active range finder (Article XIII.D4) or by stereo (Article XIII.D3), are used to compute the three-dimensional position of each observable point in a scene. This is usually the most useful measure of a scene, because the size, shape, and orientation of objects can be derived from it. For robotic vision, range information is essential.

Range information does have its limitations. One is that painted surface markings cannot be read from positional data alone (although some laser range-finders can also measure per-point reflectance; see Duda, Nitzan, and Barrett, 1979; Kanade and Asada, 1981). A second limitation is that triangulation-based range finders can measure only the points visible to both ends of the "eye" baseline. (The physical construction of range finders is described in Article XIII.D4.) Third, range finders are usually accurate only over a small volume.

Despite these limitations, range data are very important for scene analysis. The first part of this article discusses how objects in scenes are represented in terms of range information; the second part of the article presents several vision systems that make use of range data.

Shape Description

Recognition of objects in a scene involves constructing a shape description of objects from sensed data and then matching the description with stored object *models*. Shape descriptions of models and objects must be represented by similar terms and, for range-data analysis, these terms must describe the relative positions of elements of a scene.

A few types of primitives are used for shape descriptions:

1. *Vertex and edge.* Describing the data in terms of vertices and edges is appropriate when the world model contains only polyhedra. Roberts and Falk (Articles XIII.B1 and XIII.B3) represented objects in terms of vertices.

2. *Surface.* An object can be represented by a collection of surfaces, of which planes are the simplest. Quadratic (second-order) surfaces are also popular (see the discussion of Oshima and Shirai's work later in this article).

3. *Volume.* A volume description defines the space taken up by an object. A range finder sees only surfaces, so a volume description must be developed by fitting its surface to the sensed data.

Generalized cylinders. The most popular type of volume description is the *generalized cylinder* (Agin and Binford, 1973). As the name suggests, generalized cylinders are a class of objects obtained by extending the definition of a cylinder. An ordinary cylinder (Fig. D6–1a) is the volume swept out by a circular disc moving along a straight line segment through its center. The disc is kept normal (perpendicular) to the line segment that is the axis, or the *spine*, of the cylinder.

The cylinder can be generalized by one or more extensions: The spine may be curved (Fig. D6–1b). The radius of the disc may vary as a function of its position along the spine (Fig. D6–1c); this function is known as the *sweeping rule*. The cross-section may be some planar figure other than a circular disc (Fig. D6–1d). The cross-section may be held at some nonperpendicular angle to the spine (Fig. D6–1e).

Many complex objects can be modeled as clusters of generalized cylinders; for example, Figure D6–2 shows a model of a Lockheed TriStar (from Brooks, Greiner, and Binford, 1978). It is composed of generalized cylinders with straight spines, circular or rectangular cross-sections, and constant or linear sweeping rules. The airfoils and nose and tail cones are generated by cross-sections held at nonperpendicular angles to their spines.

Models composed of generalized cylinders can be expressed at various levels of detail. For example, Figure D6–3 shows levels of detail for a model of a human (from Marr and Nishihara, 1978). At the least detailed level, a single, vertically oriented cylinder suffices. Next, one cylinder is used for the trunk and one each for the head, arms, and legs. An arm can be further refined into a forearm and an upper arm, and so on. With a hierarchy of detail, image interpretation can begin with gross features, and then finer details can be filled in under the guidance of the grosser match. This coarse-to-fine strategy reduces the combinatorics of matching. It might also be recognized as the strategy that reduces search in *hierarchical planning* (see Article XV.C).

The generalized-cylinder representation works best with objects composed of elongated parts, since these are often recognizable as stick figures: the "sticks" are the spines of the generalized cylinders. Non-elongated shapes may be represented as generalized cylinders, but the choice of spine is less obvious. A cube has three equally good choices for a spine; a short, squat, circular cylinder has its spine parallel to its shortest dimension.

Issues in Shape Description

In addition to the primitive units for describing surfaces and volumes, a representation scheme must specify a means of composing them into object

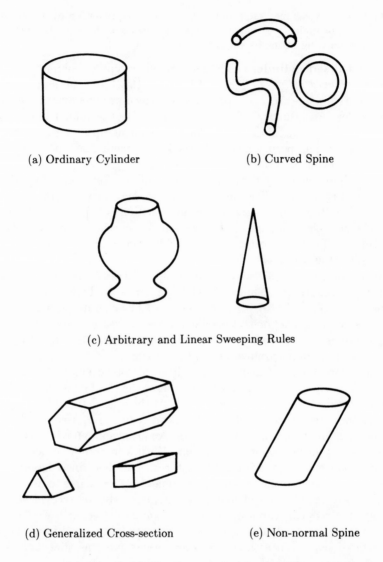

(a) Ordinary Cylinder   (b) Curved Spine

(c) Arbitrary and Linear Sweeping Rules

(d) Generalized Cross-section   (e) Non-normal Spine

Figure D6–1. Generalized cylinders.

models. For example, a description of a hammer contains not just descriptions of the handle and the head, but also the fact that the end of the handle is joined with the bottom of the head. (See Article XIII.E3 for a discussion of syntactic rules for composing objects.)

Uniqueness and *continuity* are two important qualities of a representation scheme, especially a scheme for object recognition. It is often desirable to have a single, unique representation for each shape in the world; otherwise, a

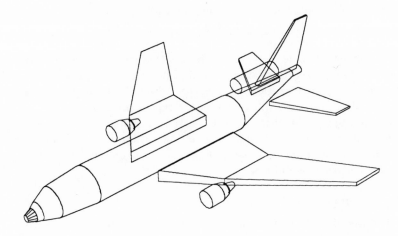

Figure D6–2.   A Lockheed TriStar by a generalized-cylinder
representation (from Brooks, Greiner, and Binford, 1978).

program may be faced with the task of choosing from a large set of substantially different representations, and matching becomes difficult. The criterion of continuity is that similar shapes should have similar representations and that very different shapes should have very different representations. A representation should not change drastically with a small change in shape.

A problem for range-data analysis is picking an appropriate level of detail for models: A very detailed description of a particular object, say, a chair, in a particular orientation is relatively useless in that it will fail to recognize the chair in a slightly different orientation, just as it will fail to recognize similar chairs. Therefore, a model of a chair must express the essential features of the shape of a chair. Such a model has its own reference frame, independent of

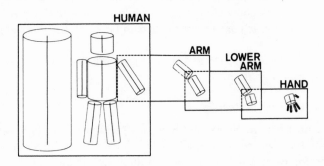

Figure D6–3.   Detail hierarchy of a three-dimensional model of
a human (from Marr and Nishihara, 1978).

its position or orientation in the scene. Thus, it is said to be *object-centered,* as opposed to *camera-centered.* (See Articles XIII.E2 and XIII.E3 for other discussions of the problem of choosing primitives for scene analysis.)

An important issue of representation is that, while there are advantages to object-centered representations, the first description of an object extracted from sensed data is necessarily camera-centered. Consequently, object recognition involves these two different types of representations.

Lastly, object recognition involves partial matching, because a range finder can see only one side of an object. The description derived from the sensed data cannot match hidden parts of a stored model, unless it contains a hypothesis of what is hidden.

Shape Recognition

The raw data from most range-finding sensors are not in the form of a depth map (see Article XIII.D4); however, it is often used for scene analysis in raw (or nearly raw) form because it is a fairly faithful representation of the physical structures of objects in a scene. For example, a light-stripe range finder produces many frames of TV images of light stripes; other researchers reduce their data to an array of displacement values: D_{ij} represents a horizontal displacement of the jth light stripe on TV frame-row i. Although the conversion from these input forms to three-dimensional surface points is straightforward, many researchers examine features in this representation directly, before (or without) converting to three-dimensional coordinates.

Scene analysis on the raw range-sensor data prior to, or in place of, converting to three-dimensional coordinates is done most often with triangulation range-finders that produce light stripes. An occluding edge is manifest as a discontinuity of stripe displacement, either within a stripe or between adjacent stripes. Intersection of two planar surfaces may be detected by a discontinuity in the direction (bend) of a light stripe when tracing along its length, or by a change in interstripe pitch. If we assume vertical stripes with the camera to the right of the illuminator, a horizontal concave edge will produce a bend in the stripe that is convex rightward, while a horizontal convex edge will produce a bend that is convex leftward. Similar relationships hold for other orientations.

The remainder of this article discusses individual scene-analysis programs that work from range data.

Range-data Analysis Systems

Shirai and Suwa. Shirai and Suwa (1971) first used a light-stripe range finder to analyze and recognize polyhedra. Their range finder produced one TV picture for each position of the illuminating stripe. They thresholded and smoothed each image and tracked the stripes, which were segmented into nearly linear portions and replaced with straight line segments. Neighboring lines were grouped into planes, according to their orientation and their intervals. (When light planes at equal intervals intersect a planar surface, the TV camera sees a set of stripes with common orientation, located at equal intervals.) Once a planar patch was found, its lines were projected back into three dimensions, and the equation of the plane was found by least squares. After all the planes were found, they were grouped into polyhedra.

Agin, Binford, and Nevatia. At Stanford University, the generalized cylinder representation has been used extensively for analyzing range data from light stripes. Agin fit generalized cylinders to range data (Agin and Binford, 1973). He worked directly from the raw data, delaying conversion to three-dimensional coordinates. He started with two sets of light stripes, obtained by illuminating the subject with two sets of light sheets, one perpendicular to the other. Parallel elliptical arcs suggest a generalized cylinder and its radius and axis, as shown in Figure D6–4a. Each detected stripe was thinned and linked into a chain. Then adjacent chains representing consecutive laser scans were grouped together if they were roughly parallel in the TV image. Each such group was then modeled as a generalized cylinder. As an initial guess for the cylinder's axis, the midpoints of a group of chains were converted into three-dimensional coordinates. The diameter of the cylinder was gauged from the length of the chains and their orientation with respect to the axis. The cylinder description was iteratively refined by marching along the cylinder's spine, passing a plane orthogonal to the spine, and fitting a circle to the surface points near the cylinder in that plane. This refined the notion of the diameter at that point, as well as of the location of the spine.

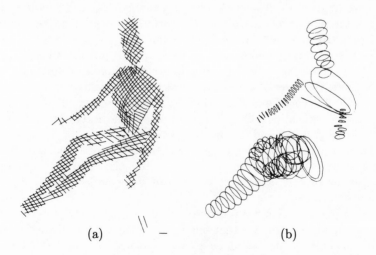

(a)   (b)

Figure D6–4.   (a) Light-stripe image of a Barbie doll and
(b) generalized cylinders obtained from (a)
(from Agin and Binford, 1973).

Thus, the shape of a Barbie doll is represented by generalized cylinders (see Fig. D6–4b).

Nevatia and Binford (1973) extended Agin and Binford's work. The construction of the generalized cylinders was much the same, but it omitted conversion to three-dimensional coordinates and generalized the cylinders further by removing the assumption of a circular cross-section. Also, boundary information was derived by linking the discontinuities in the range data. They segmented a single object into simpler parts (such as leg and torso), each of which was extracted as a smooth generalized cylinder (see Fig. D6–5). The segmented parts were connected at joints, and their connectivity relations were represented as a graph with joints as nodes and parts as arcs. The part descriptions included their size and shape (length of axis, average cross-section width, etc.); the joint descriptions included the parts connected at the joints and their relations. The graph descriptions that are constructed from one view were stored as models, and a new scene was recognized by matching the graph description with stored model descriptions.

Popplestone, Brown, Ambler, and Crawford. Popplestone and his associates (1975) used a light-stripe range finder to provide data for interpreting scenes composed of planar surfaces and walls of cylinders with circular cross-sections. Because of this restriction on the scene objects, sections of light stripes observed in the TV frames were known to be either straight line segments or parts of ellipses. The stripes were segmented and fit with straight line segments or were assumed to be curved. Their three-dimensional coordinates were calculated. Groups of parallel lines arising from sequential laser scans were fit to planes by means of least squares. A poor fit indicated that the lines were not on planes, but on the surface of a cylinder, parallel to the axis. Groups of curves also indicated a cylinder wall.

The first step in pursuing a cylinder hypothesis was to estimate the axis orientation. This was trivial for a cylinder that was manifest as a set of straight lines. For a set of curves, the direction was estimated by finding the direction (in TV coordinates) in which successive stripes may be shifted to coincide with each other. Once this shift was found in two dimensions, the third coordinate was found for the axis vector.

The data points were then projected onto a plane orthogonal to the axis. This caused the elliptical stripes to project onto a circle. By fitting a circle to the projection by least squares, the radius of the cylinder and a point on its axis were determined.

Once a plane or cylinder was determined, the list of stripes was scanned to find unexplained segments that might lie on the surface. If such segments were found, they would be added to the evidence for the surface and the surface would be refit to the data.

Sugihara. Sugihara (1979) exploited the constraints of a junction dictionary like those of Huffman, Clowes, and Waltz. Whereas the earlier work used the dictionary to deduce line labels, Sugihara derived those labels directly

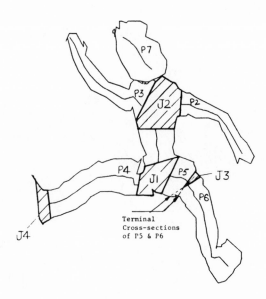

Figure D6–5.   Segmentation of range data into parts and
joints (from Nevatia and Binford, 1973).

from analysis of the range image. The dictionary was used to suggest edges
that had originally escaped detection. It contained not only physically possible
junctions, but also impossible junctions that would become possible if one
or more additional incident edges were discovered. These junctions were
linked together in a directed acyclic graph, in which an arc from junction
A to junction B denoted an edge that, if found, would convert junction A to
junction B.

Scene analysis was done on stripe data in the image domain, taking
advantage of features that reflected those of the scene. For example, occluding
edges are manifest as range jumps, which are detected as sudden changes in
the x-coordinate within a stripe or between adjacent stripes. A set of operators
detected each type (convex or concave) of edge in the light-stripe image. After
initial edge detection and linking, the resulting junctions were examined. As
we just mentioned, impossible junctions may really be possible junctions for
which an edge has not yet been detected. Thus, impossible junctions were
located in the dictionary and an additional edge proposed. Figure D6–6 shows
an example of Sugihara's program at intermediate stages of analysis.

With minimal modification to the junction dictionary, Sugihara applied
his techniques to a world with curved objects. The dictionary was applied
by considering the tangents to curves coming into a junction. There was no
attempt to model the shapes of surfaces or the enclosed volumes, but heuristic
rules were used to partition groups of edges into bodies.

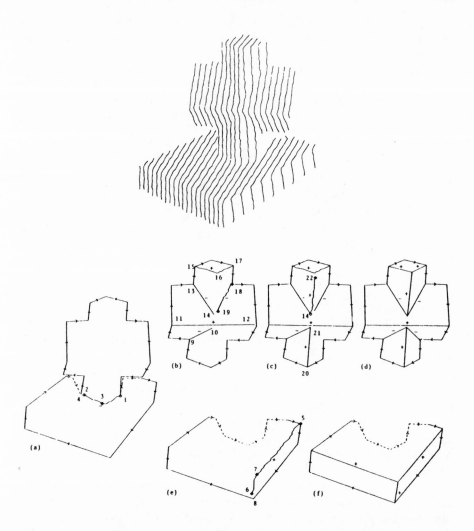

Figure D6–6.   Analysis of range data by means of a junction dictionary (from Sugihara, 1979).

Oshima and Shirai.   Oshima and Shirai (1979) developed an area-based system that did all of its work in three dimensions. It assumed a world consisting of planar and quadratic (second-degree) surfaces. Processing started with partitioning the range image into small, overlapping patches and determining the orientation of each patch by fitting a plane by least squares. Next, contiguous patches were merged into larger, approximately planar regions. Regions were classified as planar, curved, and ambiguous, depending upon the variation in orientation of the region: If the variation is small, the patch is planar; if it is large, the patch is curved; otherwise, it is ambiguous. Curved regions were grown outward by devouring neighboring curved or ambiguous regions; larger regions were favored as kernels for region growing. Next, leftover ambiguous regions were merged into neighboring regions. When all regions were merged, quadratic surfaces were fit to the curved regions. Edges between adjoining surfaces were found by intersecting the equations of the two surfaces. The edges were classified as convex or concave.

An advantage of this approach is that, for ambiguous portions of the image, action is deferred until more context is available from the more reliable parts. Edge finding in this manner is more reliable than with an edge detector, because it takes into consideration all the points in the surfaces. It is not influenced as much by noise right at the edges.

Duda, Nitzan, and Barrett. Duda and his associates found planar surfaces by using registered range and reflectance images (Duda, Nitzan, and Barrett, 1979). Horizontal planes were found first. This was done by plotting, in a histogram, the relative frequency of the heights of all points. A peak in the histogram indicates a horizontal plane, since it suggests a relatively large number of points of the same height.

To pursue a plane hypothesis, the points that lay near the plane were aggregated into regions. Small regions were discarded. A plane was fit to each region and its orientation was compared with the hypothesized orientation. This weeded out groups of points that were on surfaces that passed through the hypothesized plane but were not in it. If a region was accepted, it would be refined by repeating this process but using its measured orientation for the plane hypothesis. Finally, the points of the accepted region would be removed from the data. This would allow a new plane to become dominant. (This technique is similar to histogram-based region-segmentation methods; see Article XIII.C5.)

Next, vertical surfaces were located. The data points were projected onto a horizontal plane, forming a two-dimensional histogram. Vertical surfaces show up as straight lines in this histogram. These lines were found by using the *Hough transform* (see Article XIII.C4). The equation of the line, coupled with the knowledge that the surface is vertical, yields a surface hypothesis to be tested.

Finding slanted planes is more complicated. The Hough transform is computationally unattractive, because, for a plane, it produces a histogram in a three-dimensional parameter space. To solve the problem, Duda and his associates used the reflectance image that the range finder had produced in registration with the range image. They assumed that points on a planar surface have the same reflectance. All points that lay on surfaces already extracted were deleted from the reflectance image. The remaining contiguous areas were processed by the histogram method; that is, the relative frequencies of reflectances were plotted on a histogram so that peaks in the histogram corresponded to areas in which many points have the same reflectance. The highest peak was used to locate a contiguous area of pixels with constant reflectance. By fitting a plane to these pixels (using the range data), a plane hypothesis was obtained.

Conclusion

Range (depth) information is one of the most important *intrinsic characteristics* of a scene (Article XIII.D1), and the approach discussed here is to represent and recognize three-dimensional shapes from range data. The most popular representation of objects that is based on depth information is the *generalized cylinder*. The raw data to which cylinders can be fit are usually obtained with a light-stripe range finder (Article XIII.D4). Several systems were discussed.

References

Badler and Bajcsy (1978) present a survey and discussion of 3-D representation.

E.   ALGORITHMS FOR VISION

E1.   Pyramids and Quad Trees

VISION ALGORITHMS sometimes use hierarchically organized images with multiple levels of resolution. For example, Kelly (1971) introduced the idea of *planning* in edge detection with two levels of resolution. He first detected edges in a low-resolution image and used them to plan a detailed search for the edges in the higher resolution image. Since the gross location of the edges was known, the tracing program could cope with local gaps and noise in the detailed image. Similarly, multiple resolution images are useful in region segmentation (see Article XIII.C5) and stereo vision (Article XIII.D3). (Hierarchical representations are popular in AI; for example, see Articles XV.D1 and XV.D2 on hierarchical planning.)

Pyramids and quad trees are hierarchical image representations that facilitate the efficient implementation of vision algorithms (Tanimoto and Pavlidis, 1975). They were motivated partly by two aspects of human visual perception. First, the eye itself has multiple levels of resolution; photoreceptors are densely packed in the fovea and more sparsely distributed elsewhere. Second, humans naturally attend to areas of high information and ignore less interesting areas. This is called *selective attention*.

Pyramids

A pyramid may be visualized as a sequence of two-dimensional arrays—like those in Figure E1–1—representing the same visual scene in more and more detail. Usually the dimensions of the arrays double at each step in the sequence. For example,

$$P = \langle A^{1 \times 1}, A^{2 \times 2}, A^{4 \times 4}, \ldots, A^{512 \times 512} \rangle$$

is a pyramid of 10 levels. The arrays consist of pixels that may contain binary, gray-scale, multispectral, or local feature information. Alternately, a pyramid may be described as the set P of cells (based on the combined sets of pixel indices of all the arrays) together with a function *Val* that assigns a value to each cell:

$$P = \{(k, i, j) \mid 0 \leq k \leq L;\ 0 \leq i, j \leq 2^k - 1;\ Val : P \to R\}.$$

279

Usually R is a real, positive value and we insist that an *averaging rule* hold:

If $0 \leq k \leq L, \quad 0 \leq i,j \leq 2^k - 1$,

$$Val(k,i,j) = \sum_{p=0}^{1} \sum_{q=0}^{1} \frac{Val(k+1, 2i+p, 2j+q)}{4} \ .$$

That is, $Val(k,i,j)$ is the average for four cells $(k+1, 2i, 2j)$, $(k+1, 2i, 2j+1)$, $(k+1, 2i+1, 2j)$, $(k+1, 2i+1, 2j+1)$, as is illustrated in Figure E1–1. The pyramid in the figure is constructed from a picture (e.g., 512×512 pixels) by forming successive reductions ($256 \times 256, 128 \times 128, \ldots$) by averaging 2×2 blocks of cells, until the 1×1 or root level is reached.

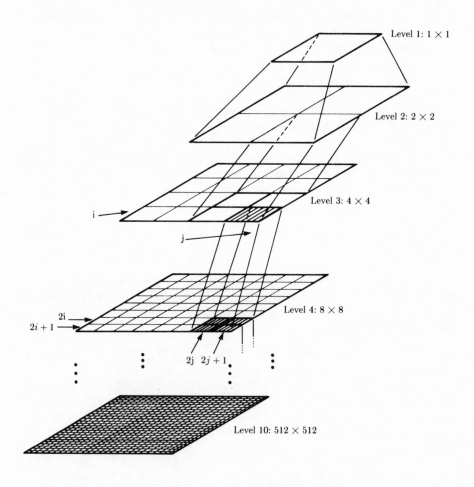

Figure E1–1.   The pyramid structure.

A typical use of the pyramid is seen in the following edge-detection algorithm. A level s will be examined for edges: All edges found in the input pyramid INP at level s will be indicated in the output pyramid OUTP at level s. The algorithm proceeds by computing edges at each input pixel according to some function BNDRY, which may be any edge-detection operator, such as Roberts' cross operator (see Article XIII.C4). In the algorithm, GET and STORE access pyramid values.

If the edge strength (the output of BNDRY) at a pixel is greater than THRESHOLD, the edge will be REFINEd recursively. The four corresponding pixels will be examined at the next higher level of resolution—level $s+1$. If any have a strength greater than THRESHOLD, then level $s+2$ will be examined, and so on, up to the maximum resolution level L of the pyramids.

This algorithm illustrates both varying resolution and selective attention. Varying resolution pinpoints edges precisely and ignores large areas of relatively uniform intensity, since recursion to a more detailed level occurs only for edge pixels. Selective attention is a consequence of limiting the algorithm to examining those parts of the image with interesting information, that is, edges.

```
PROCEDURE alledges (inp,outp: pyramid; s: integer);
VAR i,j: integer
BEGIN
    FOR i:=0 to 2**s-1 DO BEGIN
        FOR j:=0 to 2**s-1 DO BEGIN
        store (outp,s,i,j,bndry(inp,s,i,j));
        IF get(outp,s,i,j) > threshold THEN
            refine(inp,outp,s,i,j);
        END;
    END;
END;

PROCEDURE refine (inp,outp: pyramid; k,i,j: integer);
VAR di,dj: integer; temp: real;
BEGIN
    IF k < L THEN BEGIN
        FOR di:=0 to 1 DO BEGIN
            FOR dj:=0 to 1 DO BEGIN
            temp:=bndry(inp,k+1,2*i+di,2*j+dj);
            store(outp,k+1,2*i+di,2*j+dj,temp)
            IF temp > threshold THEN
            refine (inp,outp,k+1,2*i+di,2*j+dj)
            END;
        END;
    END;
END;
```

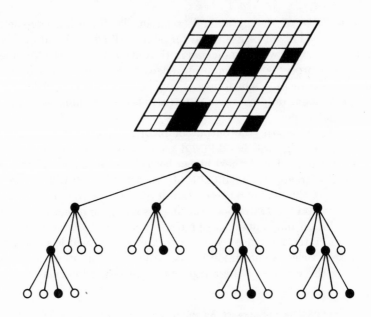

Figure E1–2.   A quad tree.

This algorithm is reasonably insensitive to noise, ignoring those edges in level L that are not supported in levels s through $L - 1$. The computation time it requires is proportional to the edge complexity of the pyramid and to the chosen threshold; a pyramid with no edges will be processed very quickly.

Quad Trees

Quad trees are data structures that are similar to pyramids. They have nodes that correspond to the cells of a pyramid, and each nonterminal node has four children nodes in the level below. Unlike a pyramid, a quad tree may be pruned so as to be unbalanced. For example, when all nodes in a subtree have the same gray value, the subtree may be represented by its root without loss of information (see Fig. E1–2). Properly implemented, a quad tree may allow significant storage savings in representing many kinds of images. More significantly, quad trees allow some operations to be performed efficiently by recursive procedures. For example, image superposition and bitmap union and intersection are easily formulated and executed.

References

See Tanimoto and Klinger (1980).

E2.   Template Matching

ONE WAY to determine which patterns exist in a scene is to compare them with stored patterns that are already named. This approach is called *template matching*. Classically, template matching has been applied to digitized images directly, using a pixel-by-pixel comparison. More recently, however, higher level templates have also been used.

Pixel-level Templates

Low-level, pixel templates come in four varieties: (a) *total templates*, which are fixed against a background; (b) *partial templates*, which are free of the background; (c) *piece templates*, which match one feature of a figure; and (d) *flexible templates*, which are modified to match possible distortions in the scene. Each of these categories provides more flexibility than the previous one, but at the expense of time and complexity during the matching process.

Total templates. These require an exact match between a scene and a template. Each template must contain as many picture elements (pixels) as the input scene contains. Because the matching requirements are so stringent, any displacement or orientation error of the "correct" pattern will be rejected.

Partial templates. Partial matching frees the desired pattern from the background. This allows for multiple successful matches against a single scene. Storage requirements are limited to the representation of the desired pattern. While partial matching solves the displacement problems of total templates, incorrect matches can occur if the pattern is embedded in a larger object; for example, the "F" template matches against an "E" scene. Furthermore, if a black template is not to be a trivial match with an all-black region, a white border must be included. The technique for matching the template to the scene is known as cross-correlation; it moves the template across the figure looking for one or more points of maximum coincidence.

Piece templates. These templates break up a pattern into its component segments; for example, the pattern "A" could be recognized with a combination of "/", "\", and "–" piece templates. The order in which the templates are compared to the scene is important: The largest piece templates must be tried first, since these contain the most information and may also subsume smaller templates. For example, if the "scene" were running text, the template "there" should be tried before "the" against the target "therefore." An advantage in using piece templates is that storage requirements are kept to a minimum. Furthermore, because of the primitive nature of piece templates, they can sometimes be described by mathematical functions instead of a point-by-point picture.

To use piece templates, they must be partially ordered according to any properties that dominate other templates. When the templates are checked against the scene, an ordered list of matches is generated. To decide which combination of located piece templates is the most appropriate, the component templates are weighted by size and scored against a prototype list of expected features. This template-matching scheme is less sensitive to distortions in the original scene but may lose information about the spatial arrangement of the pieces. For example, "\", "/", and "–" will match the "∀" symbol as well as "A," which may or may not be the intended result. If we add a piece template that provides corner orientation, a more specific decision could be made. To help solve this problem, piece templates may also include positioning information relative to the background.

Positional information is important in the navigation system for an underwater robot developed by Thorpe (1981), who used a variation of a technique developed by Davis (1976). The navigation system, which works with sonar images and which uses descriptions rather than raw images to match, is an interesting variant of template matching, since the sonar images are themselves the "pieces" that are matched to a much larger template map. Normally, images are larger than templates, but in this case the opposite is true. The navigation system decides its exact location by matching sonar images to a stored map of the area. Since individual rocks on a smooth sea floor do not produce sufficiently consistent echoes to be reliably recognized, the distances and angles between rocks are the components of the sonar images.

Each object in the sonar image that produces an echo is abstracted to a point, with only x and y coordinates and approximate echo strength recorded. The stored map consists of a list of such points with known positions. The general problem is to get the sonar image of the area surrounding the vehicle, produce a description of the objects in that image, and then use that description as a template to see what part of the map that area most accurately matches. From there, basic geometry gives the vehicle's location and heading.

Flexible templates. Also called rubber masks, these templates are designed to handle the problems of stretching, misorientation, and other deviations from the prototype. The flexible template starts with a good prototype of a known object. After each comparison with the unknown object, the rubber mask is parametrically modified to obtain a better fit. This relaxation procedure is continued until no more improvement is obtained. The object can now be encoded as the template plus a series of modifications, which can be compared against the results with other starting templates to determine the best match. A good example of this technique is sorting chromosome images to get a karyotype. A standard H-shaped chromosome is picked as the initial template and modified in length, width, bend, and curvature of the H until the natural chromosome is matched. The same technique has been used to locate peaks in a chromatographic image; the rubber mask is the sum of several adjustable Gaussian peaks with parameters of x position, amplitude, and narrowness.

Some problems remain with pixel-level templates. Working with typical two-dimensional inputs such as handwritten characters or TV pictures proves difficult for any simple template scheme. TV pictures may be blurred, stretched, and peppered with noise. Additional problems arise from rotations, shape variations, offsets, and gaps. Handwritten characters are subject to differences among authors and inconsistencies in any individual's script. These problems can be partially solved by carefully choosing piece templates, made more forgiving by allowing for "don't care" slots in noncrucial locations in the template or by using the flexible templates. Also, learning is difficult within the template paradigm. If a new template is added for each variation in the handwriting example, the set of templates becomes too large. Deciding when a match has been found between a template and a pattern presents another problem. Solutions usually involve a threshold or difference criterion to determine that one match is significantly better than the rest.

High-level Templates

Thus far, template matching has been discussed mostly at the level of the digitized image. It is certainly possible, however, to do template matching at a higher level, in which images and templates are described symbolically and description is matched to description rather than pixel to pixel. Parts of an image can be described in terms such as "Area = 28 pixels" or "Average intensity = 40." Relations between parts of the image can also be represented, such as "A is above B" or "X is larger than Y."

The high-level approach was taken by Barrow and Popplestone (1971) in one of the earliest uses of this kind of template matching. They broke an image into regions of approximately uniform brightness. For each region they recorded shape information, and between pairs of regions they defined relations such as "bigger than," "adjacent to," "above," and "distance between." All further processing was done on the basis of these descriptions, without ever referring back to the original image. In *training mode*, several views of each known object were shown to the system, and these descriptions and their identifications were stored. Next, during *processing mode*, an image of an unknown object was divided into regions and described in the same way and then compared with the stored descriptions. The object with the best match was, in almost every case, the correct identification.

Testing every possible combination of matches would obviously have been computationally expensive, so Barrow and Popplestone (1971) incorporated a *best-first search* heuristic (see Article II.C3a, in Vol. I). Partial matches were built up region by region, and only the best were candidates for combination with matches from other regions.

Winston's (1975) work on learning blocks-world structures (see Article XIII.C3c) uses an expanded piece-template approach for description matching. Each component piece, such as a block or a pyramid, is recognized, and the relations between objects, for example, "supported-by," are used to match a prototype template built up over several training sessions. The matching process is governed by weights associated with the links in the prototype.

Conclusion

Template matching involves matching an image to a stored representation and evaluating the fit with some function. Template matching is a simple and relatively old technique that has been applied in many areas of vision research.

References

For basic techniques of template matching, see Duda and Hart (1973).

E3. Linguistic Methods for Computer Vision

STATISTICAL METHODS for classifying patterns are well established in the field of pattern recognition (see Article XIV.D2). Patterns in pictures are recognized by determining whether the features of the picture match a stored set of features sufficiently well. This approach to computer vision was criticized in AI for its lack of *descriptive power*. Pattern-recognition programs only classify patterns; they do not describe them. Syntactic methods emerged as attempts to generate picture descriptions from sets of picture primitives and formal picture grammars.

Syntactic methods of scene analysis constitute a *language theory* of vision. Patterns are regarded as sentences in a language defined by a formal grammar. Just as a natural-language sentence might consist of a noun phrase followed by a verb phrase, a pattern might consist of a vertical stroke followed by a horizontal one. Thus, the process of recognizing the structure of a pattern or scene is analogous to the process of parsing an English sentence. The syntactic approach assumes a *picture grammar* and a *parser*, for building a formal representation of the objects and interrelationships in a scene, and a set of *semantic primitives*, such as edges or primitive bodies. These are the meaningful units from which interpretations of a scene are constructed. (See the articles in Secs. IV.C and IV.D, in Vol. I, for a discussion of grammars and parsing.)

Picture Grammars in Syntactic Analysis

A *grammar* is a set of *rewrite rules*, or *productions*, of the form:

```
<left-hand side> ::= <right-hand side>.
```

Depending on the grammar, there are different restrictions on what can appear on either side of the rule. These regulate what atomic elements can appear in the rules, as well as how the elements are to be combined. For example, a *web grammar* is one whose atomic elements are restricted to pieces of a labeled directed graph. Similarly, *array grammars* and *tree grammars* limit the atomic elements to arrays and trees, respectively.

Both the left-hand side and the right-hand side of the rules are made up of symbols and connectives, or *operators*. Concatenation is usually a sufficient connective for one-dimensional input; for example, `Sentence ::= Noun Phrase + Verb Phrase` means that a verb phrase follows a noun phrase in the time dimension. However, a problem in extending a one-dimensional grammar to analysis of patterns in two dimensions is that the two-dimensional plane has no natural ordering. For two-dimensional pictures, the relevant connectives seem to be relational, for example, "on top of," "below," "to the left of," and "to the right of."

The problem of defining appropriate connectives between primitives has been approached in several ways. One is to analyze a figure in terms of its boundaries. For example, a *quadrilateral* might be defined as

```
quadrilateral ::= line + line + line + line
```

where "+" means concatenation and it is understood that concatenation must close on itself.

Another approach is to give every primitive two distinguished points, a *head* and a *tail*. Concatenation of two primitives is then taken to mean head-to-tail concatenation of the two primitives. (This idea can be extended to a nonprimitive if its tail is the tail of the first primitive in its definition and its head is the head of the last primitive.) For example, the line drawing in Figure E3–1 might be analyzed in terms of the primitives shown in Figure E3–2.

If "+" denotes the head-to-tail concatenation operation and "∼" means "reverse the head and tail of the primitive," we could define a cylinder as

```
cylinder ::= ∼v + b + v + ∼t + b.
```

We might also define an operator "*" to mean "head of p touching head of q and tail of p touching tail of q"; then a cylinder would be described by the following grammar:

```
(1) cylinder ::= side * top
(2) side ::= ∼v + b + v
(3) top ::= t * b.
```

Parsing Strategies

A parser takes some input and a grammar and produces a representation of the input in terms of the grammar.

Parsing typically follows a *top-down*, a *bottom-up*, or a *hybrid* strategy. A top-down approach is *goal-directed*: It expects to find certain elements in

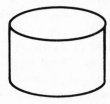

Figure E3–1.   Line drawing of a cylinder.

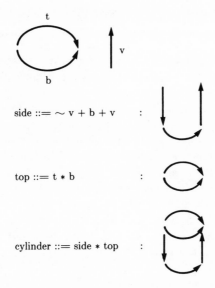

side ::= ~ v + b + v   :

top ::= t * b   :

cylinder ::= side * top :

Figure E3–2.   A set of pictorial primitives for a cylinder drawing.

the input. Consequently, a top-down parser can erroneously interpret noisy data as one of the patterns it is looking for. Bottom-up parsing, on the other hand, is data-driven. A bottom-up parser identifies each element in the input as an instance of one of the primitives in the grammar and then tries to combine the elements according to the rules of the grammar to produce a sentence or a picture. A disadvantage of bottom-up processing is that one must identify all of the primitives in the input before parsing. A pure bottom-up approach can be inefficient if the primitives cannot be identified without the aid of top-down expectations (e.g., recall that Shirai used partly developed line-drawings to guide the search for low-contrast lines; see Article XIII.B6). Similarly, a purely top-down strategy is too "hallucinatory," too susceptible to finding what it is looking for in noisy input. Consequently, a hybrid of these strategies is often most efficient. (For a detailed discussion of this issue, see Articles V.B and IV.D1, in Vol. I.)

    Consider a top-down parsing of the object in Figure E3–1 with the "cylinder grammar" that we just discussed. The question for a top-down parser is, "Does the input match my expectations of it?" or, in this case, "Is there a cylinder in the input?" Productions 1 and 2 in the cylinder grammar specify that a cylinder must have a side and that a side must have a downward-pointing vertical line, a bottom, and an upward-pointing vertical line. Therefore, the parser looks for a downward-pointing vertical line. Having found one, the parser directs its attention to the head of the line to find a bottom primitive. If one is found, parsing continues; otherwise, the parser backtracks and looks for a different vertical line.

An important aspect of the top-down approach is that it directs the attention of the parser. This is not so much an issue when parsing sentences, because the next component of the sentence is always contiguous, but it is a great advantage in parsing a picture. It guarantees that only certain local areas of the picture must be scanned and, thus, reduces the time required for scene analysis.

A bottom-up parse of the drawing in Figure E3–1 starts with identification of all the primitives in the picture. Subsequently, the parser looks for combinations of primitives in the picture that match the right-hand sides of rules in the cylinder grammar. For example, after identifying the lower half of the figure as two vertical lines and a bottom, it matches them to the left-hand side of production 2 to identify the combination as a side. If it can then find a top, it will have satisfied the left-hand side of production 1 and will conclude that the input contains a cylinder. Bottom-up processing lacks direction: It does not know where in the picture to look for primitives, and, when it finally finds some, it does not use the rules of the grammar to direct search for others. Since knowing where to look for information is a considerable advantage in image understanding, undirected bottom-up processing tends to be inefficient.

Semantic Primitives in Syntactic Analysis

A problem for syntactic analysis is to define the appropriate semantic primitives; an associated problem is to design processes or mechanisms capable of detecting these primitives. Unlike linguistic grammars, for which natural primitives are word stems and endings, we do not know what the primitives are in patterns. It seems that the choice of primitives depends, to some extent, on the application of a vision system and on the availability of mechanisms to recognize the primitives. For example, when these methods are applied to low-level vision, the primitives are usually edge elements. The edge elements of a picture can be encoded as a sentence, according to a regular or context-free grammar. In the case of 3-D shape recognition, the semantic primitives could be *generalized cylinders* (see Article XIII.D6). Of course, the procedures for detecting these primitives are more complicated than those used in edge detection.

The choice of primitives is very important. A related problem concerns the epistemological adequacy of semantic primitives; that is, is there a set of primitives that are adequate for representing any scene, or that are at least very general? This is not so much a question of application as a general question for a theory of representation. Many primitives have been suggested for different problems: generalized cones (Marr and Nishihara, 1978) and spheres (Badler, O'Rourke, and Tolzis, 1979) for three-dimensional shape descriptions; ribbons (Brooks, Greiner, and Binford, 1978) for relating image features to generalized cylinders; camera parameters *pan, tilt, focus,* and *aperture,* and the X and Y dimensions of a picture for camera control and recognition (Bourne, 1981).

Generating Pictures

If pictures can be parsed, they can also be generated by reversing the parsing process; for example, the cylinder grammar above can be seen as a procedure for generating cylinders. Syntactic models are used to generate texture patterns (see Article XIII.C6). Gips (1974) proposed a theory of aesthetics based on the restrictions he imposed on his pattern-generating grammars.

Templates can be generated by grammars, so that matching between actual and expected images can be done in the image domain, rather than by comparing parse trees. O'Rourke (1980) took this approach in his analysis of human motion.

Conclusion

Syntactic methods in the narrowest definition (picture primitives plus formal grammars) suffer from a lack of descriptive power. They are usually applicable only when the picture is built up from a small set of well-defined, easily recognized primitives and when the relationships between primitives are simple. Much effort has been devoted to designing more sophisticated grammars, for example, stochastic, fuzzy, and error-correcting grammars. However, descriptive power and flexible control seem to result from adding more programmable mechanisms, as was the case with ATNs in natural-language processing (see Article IV.D3, in Vol. I). For example, Turner (1974) used procedures in POPLER to represent the hierarchical structure of objects. The goal statements of these procedures, which try to prove the existence of objects, provide top-down control, and the assertion statements, which add objects to a database as they are discovered, provide bottom-up control.

References

Rosenfeld (1979) discusses a wide variety of picture languages and their formal properties. Fu (1974) and Pavlidis (1977) include syntactic methods in pattern analysis.

E4. Relaxation Algorithms

MANY TASKS in vision can be viewed as constraint-satisfaction problems, for which *relaxation algorithms* are efficient problem-solving methods. A relaxation algorithm iteratively assigns values to mutually constrained objects in such a way as to ensure a consistent set of values, that is, a set for which no constraint is violated. Consider, for example, the task of labeling a blocks-world picture (see Sec. XIII.B). This involves finding a unique label for each line, such that each junction has line labels allowed by the junction dictionary and each line has a single label along its entire length. These two conditions constitute constraints on the final solution of the line-labeling problem. There are several search methods for solving this type of problem, including generate and test, backtracking, and relaxation. The approach used by Waltz (called *Waltz filtering;* see Article XIII.B5) is a relaxation method.

The values assigned to the objects in relaxation can be discrete or probabilistic. In the case of blocks-world line labeling, either a discrete label satisfies the constraints or it does not. In other applications, relaxation does not eliminate inconsistent interpretations but, rather, updates their probabilities. Probabilistic relaxation methods exploit constraints to render an interpretation more or less likely.

A Simple Blocks-world Problem

Consider the problem of labeling a picture of a box with a rectangular hole (shown in Fig. E4–1). Assume that the lines can be labeled only as $+$, $-$, $\leftarrow$, and $\rightarrow$, and that the allowable junction labelings for junctions 1, 2, and 3 are known to be in the small set in Figure E4–2.

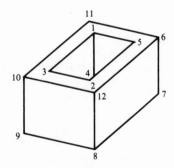

Figure E4–1.   A box with a rectangular hole
(from Duda and Hart, 1973).

292

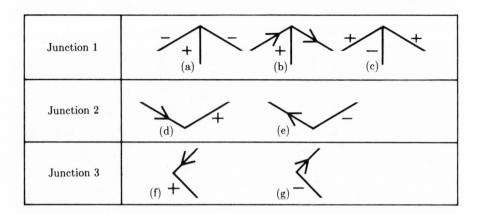

Figure E4–2. Possible labelings for junctions 1, 2, and 3 in Figure E4–1.

The relaxation method for solving this problem (Waltz filtering) was presented in Article XIII.B5. For comparison, let us try to label the drawing by the method of search with backtracking.

Search with backtracking for a complete labeling of Figure E4–1 begins by sequentially assigning a single junction label to each junction in the picture. When an adjacent pair of junctions has been labeled, the line that connects the junctions is checked to make certain that it has a single label along its entire length. If it does, labeling continues. Otherwise, the process backtracks to the most recently labeled junction that still has untried labelings in the dictionary. A new label is assigned to this junction, and the process continues.

To illustrate the procedure, consider the initial portion of the search tree for this example, shown in Figure E4–3. We have arbitrarily decided to examine junctions in the order that they are numbered in Figure E4–1. Each node in the search tree is shown with the partial solution developed to that node. Backtracking happens whenever a partial solution fails to satisfy the constraint that each line has a single label along its length.

The order in which nodes are searched is indicated by numbers above each node. In node 2, junction 1 is arbitrarily assigned the label of Figure E4–2a; then, at node 3, junction 2 is assigned the label of Figure E4–2d. But when, at node 4, junction 3 is assigned the label of Figure E4–2f, lines 1-3 and 2-3 violate the constraint of a single label for a line, and the process backtracks to junction 3—the most recently processed junction. At node 5 a new label, that of Figure E4–2g, is assigned to junction 3. But again, this results in two labels for one line. Since there are no remaining untried labelings for junction 3, the process backs up to junction 2. It still has untried labelings, so at node 6 it is assigned the label of Figure E4–2e. The process continues as, once again, junction 3 is assigned the label of Figure E4–2f, and, once again, it fails.

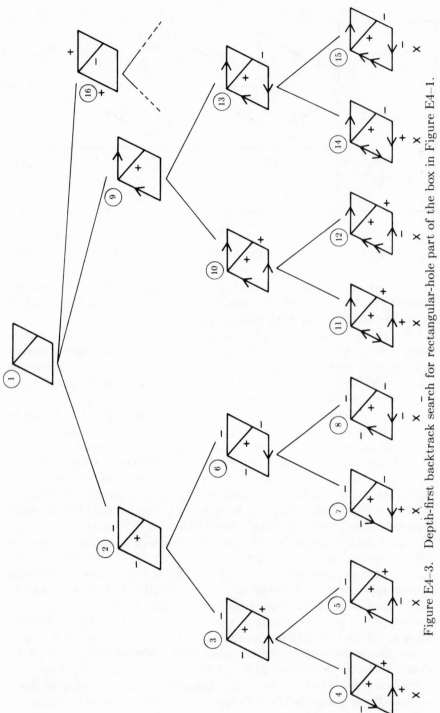

Figure E4-3.   Depth-first backtrack search for rectangular-hole part of the box in Figure E4-1.

One reason that backtracking is inefficient is that it rediscovers the same mistakes. For example, if junction 2 is assigned the labeling of Figure E4–2d, there is no possible labeling for junction 3 such that line 3-2 has a single label along its length. In the search tree, this causes failure at nodes 4, 5, 11, and 12. The same is true if junction 2 is given the labeling of Figure E4–2e; it causes failure at nodes 7, 8, 14, and 15. Yet, in backtracking search, these failures are discovered again and again.

A more efficient approach to this problem would apply the following rule: Given two adjacent junctions i and j, if junction i can be labeled with x but there is no labeling for junction j such that the connecting line has a consistent single label along its length, then x can be eliminated from the set of possible labelings for junction i. In this manner, once a failure between adjacent junction labelings is discovered, it is eliminated as a possibility and need not be rediscovered. This rule would eliminate the labelings of Figures E4–2d and E4–2e for junction 2, and since only these labelings are possible (in this example), the rule swiftly demonstrates the impossibility of a consistent labeling of the object in Figure E4–1 (assuming, of course, the limited set of labels in Fig. E4–2; the object can be labeled with the full Huffman-Clowes set of labels). Exhaustive search with backtracking, on the other hand, must try all combinations of labelings before it can claim that a consistent labeling is impossible.

The rule stated above may be generalized by substituting any objects in the problem domain for junctions and substituting any constraint for the one involving unique line labels. This process is called *Waltz filtering* after Waltz and because labels of objects are filtered by constraints. Notice that the rule takes explicit advantage of local constraints. This property is the conceptual basis of relaxation algorithms.

Region Interpretation

Tenenbaum and Barrow (1976b) used a relaxation algorithm to interpret a picture that was correctly partitioned into regions. Figure E4–4a shows a picture of an empty room partitioned into six regions corresponding to the *floor, wall, door, baseboard, picture,* and *doorknob.* The problem is to interpret the picture by assigning the correct label to each region. Some knowledge about pictures of rooms is assumed; for example, the *doorknob* is surrounded by the *door,* which is above the *floor,* and so on. This knowledge is expressed in the form of constraints, as indicated in Figure E4–4b. In terms of a relaxation rule, these are the constraints used in the filtering process, while the picture regions are the objects to be uniquely labeled.

Initially, each region is assigned all six possible labels because, prior to considering the knowledge in Figure E4–4b, there is no reason to favor one label over another. However, in considering the constraints, we immediately notice that constraint 4 requires pictures and doorknobs to be small. Since

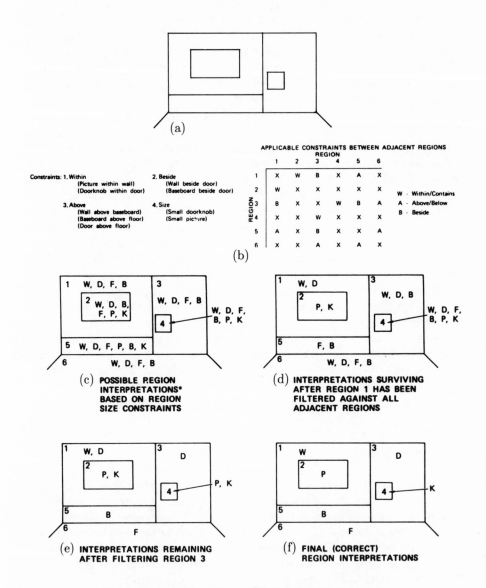

Figure E4–4. Application of relaxation to region interpretation (from Tenenbaum and Barrow, 1976b).

regions 1, 3, and 6 are large regions, the labels *picture* and *knob* are dropped from them. This stage of the labeling is shown in Figure E4–4c.

The constraints are now applied to each pair of adjacent regions in order of region number. Since region 2 is within region 1, constraint 1 applies, and it can be satisfied if region 2 is a *picture* and region 1 is a *wall*, or if region 2 is a *doorknob* and region 1 is a *door*. Therefore, all labelings other than *wall* and *door* are deleted from the set of possible labels of region 1, and all labelings other than *picture* and *doorknob* are deleted from the set of possible labels of region 2. Next, regions 1 and 3 are filtered by constraint 2. The labels for region 1 are reduced to *wall* and *door;* the labels for region 3 are reduced to *wall, door,* and *baseboard.* Finally, regions 1 and 5 are filtered by constraint 3. According to this constraint, region 5 may be labeled only *floor* or *baseboard.* The stage of labeling at this point is shown in Figure E4–4d. Note that region 1 has not been filtered with regions 4 and 6, since they are not adjacent.

Region 2 is now due for filtering with its neighbor, region 1. However, because no labels have been eliminated from either region since the last time the pair was filtered, further application of constraints will result in no additional eliminations.

We therefore proceed to region 3 and its neighbors. Regions 3 and 1 are not filtered for the same reason that regions 1 and 2 are not filtered. Regions 3 and 4 are filtered by constraint 1, which constrains region 3 to be either a *wall* or *door* and region 4 to be either a *picture* or *doorknob*. Regions 3 and 5 are filtered next by constraint 2, which limits the labeling of region 5 to *wall, door,* and *baseboard.* The previous set of labels for region 5 contained only *floor* and *baseboard,* and since the current constraint does not permit *floor* as a label, the only possible labeling for region 5 is *baseboard.* Since constraint 2 allows only a *door* beside a *baseboard,* region 3 is uniquely labeled *door.*

Regions 3 and 6 are filtered next by constraint 3. Since region 3 is a *door,* region 6 must be a *floor.* This stage of labeling is shown in Figure E4–4e.

Region 4 is filtered next with its single neighbor, region 3, by constraint 1. Since region 3 is a *door,* region 4 must be a *doorknob.* Region 5 is then filtered with region 1 by constraint 3; region 1 is labeled as a *wall.*

At this point, all pairs of adjacent regions have been filtered once. All pairs of regions whose labels have changed since the last time they were filtered are now reconsidered. In particular, constraint 1 is reapplied to regions 1 and 2. Region 1 currently has the unique label *wall,* so region 2 must be a *picture.* The final interpretation of the picture is shown in Figure E4–4f.

Probabilistic Relaxation

There are two significant characteristics of the relaxation algorithms described above. First, discrete labels are assigned to the objects. This notion can be generalized by attaching a level of certainty to each label. For example, a region may be a *wall* with a certainty of .3 and a *door* with a certainty of .7. A second characteristic of the previous relaxation algorithms is that they are sequential. Each object is filtered in sequence, using the label sets resulting from previous filterings. An alternative approach is to filter the objects in parallel, filtering each object with its neighbors without reference to results of filtering other objects. For results to propagate, however, this procedure is performed iteratively. During each iteration, the objects are filtered in parallel with their neighbors, using the label sets resulting from the previous iteration. The filtering of each object during an iteration is independent of other filterings during that iteration.

Relaxation algorithms that attach certainties to the labels and that are applied in a parallel-iterative manner are called *probabilistic,* as opposed to the *discrete* relaxation algorithms considered previously. Probabilistic relaxation is useful in many low-level vision tasks in which the problem is to convert the intensity array into a vocabulary of low-level symbols, such as those representing lines or edges. Typically a local-feature detector (e.g., line detector, edge detector) is applied to the intensity array. Such detectors, however, respond to noise as well as to the presence of the feature. Probabilistic relaxation can be used to draw out features and eliminate noise on the basis of consistency in neighboring feature detector responses. For example, if relaxation is used in line detection, the probability that a pixel point P is a line point can depend on whether or not P extends a line that has already been detected with high probability. This example will be discussed next.

Line and Curve Enhancement

The research of Zucker, Hummel, and Rosenfeld (1977) is an application of probabilistic relaxation to the enhancement of lines and curves. Many approaches to locating lines or curves in pictures begin by applying local line detectors that find small line segments throughout the picture. Another process joins these into more global lines or curves. However, noise in the picture and gaps in the curves often cause local detectors to return strong responses when no line segment is present, or weak responses when segments are present. Relaxation offers a way to enhance the local detector outputs, making it easier for a subsequent process to follow the lines and curves.

The goal of the relaxation process is therefore to extract consistently oriented line segments from the intensity array. In the formulation of Zucker et al. (1977), each picture point has a set of nine labels. Eight of these correspond to unit line segments at eight orientations between $\pi/2$ and $-\pi/2$, and the ninth corresponds to the case in which no line is present.

The initial probability for each label is obtained by evaluating a local line detector at every picture point in the eight orientations. If the detector's response is strong for only one orientation, the initial probability is set to be high on that label and the probabilities on the other labels at that point are set to be low. If there is no strong response for any orientation at some point, the "no-line" probability is set high.

The relaxation process that applies here does not discard labels, as in discrete relaxation. Instead, the probabilities of the labels are updated. This is accomplished by *compatibility functions,* which are the continuous counterparts to the constraint relations of discrete relaxation. For each pair of neighboring points a_i, a_j and each pair of labels λ, λ', the compatibility function $r_{ij}(\lambda, \lambda')$ is a measure of the compatibility between point a_i with label λ and point a_j with label λ'. For example, let a_i, a_j be vertically adjacent points, let λ represent a vertical line, and let λ' represent a horizontal line. Then the compatibility of both a_i and a_j having label λ is very high, but the compatibility of a_i having label λ and a_j having label λ' (or vice versa) is very low.

Let us assume that the compatibility function r has values $-1 \leq r \leq 1$, where -1 is complete incompatibility, $+1$ is complete compatibility, and 0 is irrelevancy (a "don't care" condition). For the line-enhancement problem, the compatibilities between lines of different orientations are shown in Figure E4–5. Line segments oriented in the same direction support each other, while perpendicular line segments contradict each other. Note, however, that the negative compatibility for perpendicular line segments is set to $-.25$ rather than -1.0, since it is possible for curves to make right-angle turns. The "no-line" label is supported by neighboring "no-line" labels and by line segments not directed toward or away from it; it is contradicted by line segments directed toward it.

The updating process consists of adjusting the probabilities at each point on the basis of the neighboring probabilities and their associated compatibility functions. Let $p_i(\lambda)$ be the probability of label λ for picture point a_i. Then the updating process should satisfy the following properties:

1. If $p_j(\lambda')$ is high and $r_{ij}(\lambda, \lambda')$ is close to $+1$, then $p_i(\lambda)$ should be increased.

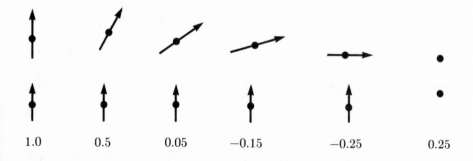

| 1.0 | 0.5 | 0.05 | −0.15 | −0.25 | 0.25 |

Figure E4–5.   Compatibility weights between line labels (from Zucker, Hummel, and Rosenfeld, 1977).

2. If $p_j(\lambda')$ is high and $r_{ij}(\lambda, \lambda')$ is close to -1, then $p_i(\lambda)$ should be decreased.

3. If $p_j(\lambda')$ is low, or $r_{ij}(\lambda, \lambda')$ is close to 0, then $p_i(\lambda)$ should not change significantly.

A simple expression that satisfies these properties is $p_j(\lambda') \cdot r_{ij}(\lambda, \lambda')$. This product may be used, for all neighboring points a_j and labels λ', to increment the probability $p_i(\lambda)$ of point a_i having label λ. An updating rule that uses these products is

$$p_i^{k+1}(\lambda) = \frac{p_i^k(\lambda)[1 + q_i^k(\lambda)]}{\sum_\lambda p_i^k(\lambda)[1 + q_i^k(\lambda)]} \tag{1}$$

where

$$q_i^k(\lambda) = \sum_j c_{ij} \sum_{\lambda'} r_{ij}(\lambda, \lambda') p_j^k(\lambda').$$

Briefly, the rule states that the probability of label λ on point a_i at the $(k + 1)$st iteration is a function of both the previous estimate for that probability, $p_i^k(\lambda)$, and the contribution from the neighboring points, $q_i^k(\lambda)$, which represents the increment due to the sum of products $p_j(\lambda') r_{ij}(\lambda, \lambda')$ over the neighbors and their possible labels. The denominator in equation (1) normalizes the net increment to $p_i(\lambda)$ to ensure that the updating rule results in probabilities.

The rule of equation (1) has been successful in the line-enhancement problem, suppressing noisy line responses and enhancing long, smooth lines, after only 5 to 10 iterations. This technique has also been applied to other low-level vision tasks such as histogram modification, noise cleaning, edge detection, angle detection, curve thinning, and template matching.

Conclusion

Relaxation methods provide efficient solutions for many vision tasks by exploiting local constraints in the problem domain. Although discrete methods preceded continuous ones, it quickly became apparent that the multitude of uncertainties in low-level vision tasks required a probabilistic approach, thus, *probabilistic relaxation*.

The main shortcoming of relaxation is that it is not usually effective in building global interpretations; its main utility lies in reducing local ambiguities. However, as a preprocessor for exhaustive search, relaxation greatly improves efficiency.

References

Waltz (1972) introduced relaxation in vision. One of the first applications of probabilistic relaxation for low-level vision is found in Zucker, Hummel, and Rosenfeld (1977). Mackworth (1977a) presents a good discussion on the problem of consistency in networks of constraints.

F. VISION SYSTEMS

F1. Robotic Vision

THE GOAL of robot-vision research is to develop a visual-sensing technology for industrial robots and anthropomorphic manipulators that allows them to operate in an unpredictable physical environment. Robotic vision is especially useful in industrial applications, exploration of hazardous environments, and medical applications. Currently, most of the work in robotic vision has been in industrial applications. This article examines the general factors that influence the design of such systems and describes two systems in detail—one for transistor wire bonding (Kashioka, Ejiri, and Sakamoto, 1976) and another for material handling (Holland, Rossol, and Ward, 1979).

Industrial Applications

There are three objectives in using robots in industrial applications: (a) to increase productivity, (b) to improve quality, and (c) to eliminate repetitive jobs. However, one of the biggest barriers to successful robot applications has been the lack of visual sensing.

In manufacturing, visual sensing is needed for the assembly, handling, and inspection of materials and goods. Assembly and material-handling operations require that parts be identified and that their precise position and orientation be known. Without visual sensing, a robot must find a part blindly; touch can be used if the parts are in approximately the right position and orientation, but vision is needed if the parts are placed randomly. Vision also offers the advantages of speed and accuracy over touch. Furthermore, vision can automate tedious and costly inspection tasks that are not accomplished accurately by humans. Image-processing and pattern-recognition techniques can improve the quality and lower the costs of inspection.

Parameters of Robotic Vision Systems

The most important factors in designing a robotic vision system are cost, real-time operation, reliability, and flexibility. Since most robotic vision systems are used in industry, they must be cost-effective; in particular, they must cost less than human labor for comparable work. Real-time operation is obviously required to compete with human workers, and this usually requires the image-processing system to process an image in one second or less. For this reason, the trade-off between performance and the amount of information processed is often resolved by processing the smallest practical amount of information. This influences the design of image-input devices, the choice between gray-scale and binary representations, the choice of resolution and the size of the image, and the choice between software and hardware implementation of algorithms. Using binary images (just black or white) and finding an optimum image size are two especially important techniques. The optimum image size is one that achieves a balance between the required resolution and the real-time operation. For instance, an automatic system for transistor wire bonding uses binary images of 160×120 pixels (Kashioka et al., 1976); on the other hand, an inspection system for integrated-circuit (IC) chips requires only 50×50 pixels, but it has four-bit gray-level images (Baird, 1978). Some design decisions will change with time because prices of memory, solid-state array sensors, custom-designed IC chips, and microprocessors are decreasing.

Reliability is another important factor in practical robotic-vision systems. To achieve reliable performance, careful attention must be paid to the imaging device, illumination settings, threshold techniques, selection of reliably extractable features, and the recognition algorithm. In addition, designers and users must understand the limitations of the system and the situations in which it fails. Noise and worst-case studies are important because the images vary according to the surrounding conditions. These considerations are illustrated in the next section.

Finally, vision systems must be flexible, especially in the case of medium- and low-volume production runs. The system must be easily adapted to different tasks; otherwise, it is uneconomical. However, a flexible system often costs more than a special-purpose one, so if production runs are very large, a manufacturer will opt for special-purpose devices.

To date, the successful vision systems in production are those that were designed specifically for a particular environment. The key factors in their success seem to have been a careful analysis of the task and the fact that the burden on the vision system is minimized.

Case Studies

A transistor wire-bonding system. A fully automatic system for transistor wire bonding, developed by Kashioka, Ejiri, and Sakamoto (1976) at Hitachi, was one of the first production robotic-vision systems to use image-processing functions extensively. The system visually locates a transistor chip and automatically bonds gold wires between the electrodes on the chip and the outer leads. It assembles 2,000 chips per hour (1.8 sec./chip)—twice the speed of traditional semiautomatic wire-bonding machines—with an accuracy of more than 99%. One of the features of this system is that up to five groups of 10 bonding machines share a central minicomputer, and the bonding machines in a group share an image hardware processor.

The task of the vision system is to extract the precise x-y coordinates of the base electrode B and the emitter electrode E on the chip and to send the information to the x-y servomechanism of a bonder. To do this, an area of $1,100 \times 800$ micrometers is first scanned by a TV camera through a microscope and the image is then binarized into 160×120 pixels. To locate the chip position and orientation, two or three local standard patterns are searched in the input image, where each standard pattern consists of 12×12 pixels. The search for matching patterns is done by special hardware that receives a frame of input image from the TV camera and a standard pattern from the minicomputer. The matching is accomplished within a one-frame scanning time, 16.7 ms, and the evaluation of the position is done by the central minicomputer during the one-frame blanking time.

Identifying local patterns P_1 and P_2 is enough to identify the coordinates of the chip; however, the following additional processing increases precision and reliability. If the distance and direction angle between the located P_1 and P_2 are not what was expected, a third local pattern P_3 is found and the distances and direction angles between P_1 and P_3 and between P_2 and P_3 are evaluated. Because the matching rate decreases rapidly when the inclination of chips exceeds ± 7 degrees, the system uses two other sets of standard patterns that are rotations of P_1, P_2, and P_3, by 10 degrees right and left, respectively. Finally, to achieve high precision, four repeated measurements are made for each chip. Incompatible measurements are thrown out, and the others are averaged to yield the final x-y coordinates. Averaging produces a resolution of one-half of a pixel, or 3.5 micrometers. In a trial, the average recognition accuracy was ± 9.3 micrometers and the average recognition time was .15 seconds per chip.

The system has the flexibility to handle various types of transistors. The standard patterns for these transistors are generated interactively. Special-purpose hardware displays an image of a transistor chip with a 12×12 pixel overlay to a human operator, who indicates one set of standard patterns. These are then stored in binary form in the computer.

At the time that Kashioka and his associates (1976) published their report, a 20-machine system was assembling 10 million transistors per month. The success of this system has led to similar systems for integrated circuits (see, e.g., Mese et al., 1977; Naruse et al., 1979).

Transferring parts from belt conveyors. CONSIGHT–I, developed by Holland, Rossol, and Ward (1979) at General Motors Research Laboratories, is a vision-based robot system that picks up parts that have been randomly placed on a moving conveyor belt. Its vision system, operating in a visually noisy environment, determines the position and the orientation of parts on the belt. After each piece is located, the belt is stopped and the robot transfers the parts to a predetermined location.

An important feature of the system is that it can obtain a reliable binary image of objects that do not always have a high contrast with the background of a conveyor belt. For example, foundry castings blend with the background when placed on a belt. To overcome this difficulty, the system projects a narrow and intense line of light to the conveyor belt surface by using two sets of long light tubes and cylindrical lenses. The projected line is sensed by a linear-array camera with 256 photocells. When an object comes to the lighted position, it intercepts the light before it reaches the surface, with the result that the belt surface appears bright and the object dark. Two light sources are used to avoid a shadowing effect. Though some internal features, like holes, are still subject to distortion or occlusion due to shadowing, the system gives a sharp-edged silhouette for a wide range of objects.

The camera scans the belt at a constant rate, independent of the belt speed. One scan line is sampled for each equal increment of belt travel by measuring the position and the speed of the belt. This continuous sampling of scan lines produces a two-dimensional image. In fact, the system does not store the entire image but processes it line by line. As objects pass through the slit of view, statistics on each component (dark area) are continuously updated. When two components in a previous scan line are connected to one component in a new line, the system updates its statistics on the object. These include position, color (black or white), count of pixels, sums of x coordinates and y coordinates, and sums of products of x and y coordinates. When a component has passed completely through the slit of view, these statistics are used to calculate numerical shape descriptors. The system then identifies the object and computes its position and orientation.

The system uses run-length coding to perform the connectivity analysis effectively. This minimizes the amount of memory and processing required. For a line image of n pixels, a straightforward binary connectivity analysis requires on the order of n^2 operations, while the algorithm using run-length coding requires on the order of n operations. In general, run-length coding is an effective technique for reducing the amount of information processing and storage.

SRI International has developed a leading machine-vision system called the SRI Vision Module (Gleason and Agin, 1979). The techniques developed at SRI include connectivity analysis with run-length coding, numerical shape descriptors, and recognition (identification) of parts with a nearest-neighbor method. The principal components of the vision module are a solid-state TV camera with 128×128 resolution, an interface unit for digitizing the video signal, and an LSI–11/2 microcomputer. The system is a package of useful programs with all necessary hardware for many visual sensing and inspection tasks.

Conclusion

The application of robotic-vision technologies in industry has important implications, not only for industrial manufacturing processes, but also for vision technology. Powerful industrial-vision systems have been developed by careful attention to the trade-offs between cost, flexibility, speed, and reliability.

References

Operating industrial vision systems are discussed in Ejiri et al. (1973); Kashioka, Ejiri, and Sakamoto (1976); Uno, Ejiri, and Tokunaga (1976); Mese et al. (1977); Baird (1978); Holland, Rossol, and Ward (1979); and Uno et al. (1979). Thompson (1980) includes several survey papers on industrial applications of vision.

F2. Organization and Control of Vision Systems

THIS CHAPTER has thus far described the theory and methods of various aspects of vision, but there has been little discussion of integrated vision systems. In the previous article (XIII.F1) we described some industrial robotic-vision systems. This article and the next survey four vision systems that were developed as AI projects and that have organization and control schemes representative of vision systems. We discuss three of these systems here: a multiband aerial-photo interpretation system from Kyoto University, the VISIONS system from the University of Massachusetts, and a query-oriented system from the University of Rochester. The ACRONYM system, developed at Stanford University, is presented in Article XIII.F3.

A key attribute of an image-understanding system is the interaction between high-level knowledge—object models—and low-level knowledge—image or scene features. While the general flow of information is *bottom-up*, from pixels to image features, to scene features, to object labeling, many systems also have some *top-down* information flow from object models to image features. Kelly (1970), for example, wrote a program to recognize human faces in which a model of the arrangement and intensity characteristics of typical faces guided all of the low-level processing. After finding the outline of the head, the program would estimate the probable position of the eyes, and look for the dark spots that characterize the pupils in and around the predicted locations. This *model-driven* processing can be both efficient and effective. However, programs that depend very much on high-level control of low-level processing tend to be too domain-dependent and respond poorly when viewing conditions change even slightly. The following descriptions of vision systems focus on mechanisms for achieving cooperation and flow of control between low-level and high-level processing stages. In fact, we emphasize flow of control at the expense of detailed descriptions of vision processes in this article.

Interpreting Multiband Aerial Photographs

Nagao, Matsuyama, and Ikeda (1978, 1979) developed a system that interpreted a class of multiband aerial photos acceptably well. Their image-interpretation system employs multiple, independent knowledge sources that operate on a common, multilevel database. This database, or *blackboard*, is represented as shown in Figure F2–1. The abstraction levels of image information are *elementary region, cue region, object*, and *object category*. Models are described in terms of two-dimensional features that can be observed in images. In general, it is not possible to do scene interpretation with two-dimensional models, but it is an acceptable technique for aerial photography because the

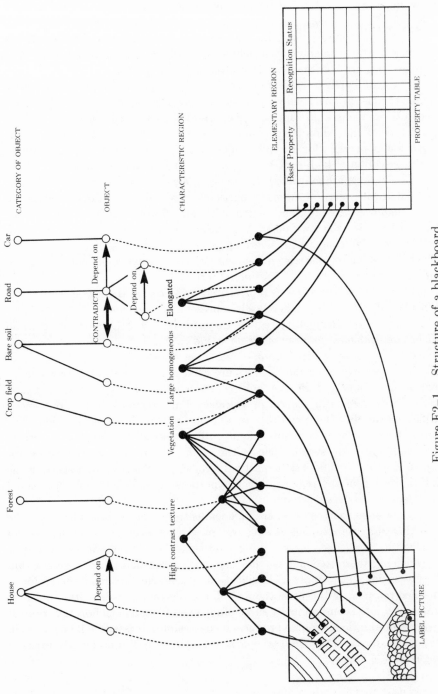

Figure F2–1. Structure of a blackboard.

view angle is so constrained that object shapes change little and occlusion is not much of a problem.

The first step of processing is to smooth the image (see Article XIII.C3). A nonsemantic segmenter then defines a set of elementary regions—a set of patches that are homogeneous in multispectral properties.

The next step is to extract cue regions. The types of cue regions are large homogeneous regions, shadow and shadow-causing regions, elongated regions, vegetation regions, high-contrast regions, and high-contrast vegetation regions. Each type of cue region triggers one or more object recognizers. Different cue regions may overlap; for example, high-contrast vegetation regions are simply the intersection of high-contrast regions and vegetation regions.

Cue regions are extracted by screening elementary regions; for example, any patch with very low intensity, particularly in red and infrared, is classified as a shadow. An adjacent region with an appropriate boundary on the sunward side is a shadow-maker. Vegetation regions have a high ratio of infrared to red; high-contrast areas are aggregations of small elementary regions. Shadow-making regions trigger the house detector, while high-contrast vegetation regions are likely to be considered forest.

Each elementary region is represented by a node in the lowest level of the blackboard. Nodes at higher levels represent cue regions and objects; they are linked to the elementary regions they subsume. Furthermore, a node can have a dependency link to another node, indicating that its interpretation was aided by the prior interpretation of the other node.

The property table shown in Figure F2–1 stores the coordinate range, or *bounding rectangle,* of a region and records whether the region is *unanalyzed, recognized, irregularly shaped,* or *rejected.* Each region has only one entry, which means that there can be only one object hypothesis for a region. The first interpretation of a region is kept until a contradiction arises. To resolve contradictions, the system deletes the conflicting region interpretation for which it is least confident. It marks the region as unanalyzed, restarting the interpretation of the region; object hypotheses that depend on the deleted node are themselves deleted.

Knowledge sources (KSs) are independent, but they communicate via the blackboard and a message-passing system. A central executive cycles control among the knowledge sources. When a KS is invoked, it looks at the cue region in which it is interested and, if it finds an unclassified elementary region within its cue region, it attempts a classification. If classification fails, the region is marked *rejected.* In this case, the KS will not reattempt classification unless it gains additional constraints by successfully classifying a neighboring region. If a different knowledge source produces a constraint, a message will be placed in the message box. This could trigger a reexamination of a previously rejected region.

VISIONS

The University of Massachusetts' VISIONS system (Hanson and Riseman, 1978b) is patterned after the HEARSAY–II speech-understanding system (Erman et al., 1980; see also Article V.C1, in Vol. I). In VISIONS, hypotheses are posted and accessed on a *blackboard* by independent procedural *knowledge sources:* KS activation and scheduling are under the control of a central executive. The system has been tested with outdoor scenes. Figure F2–2 outlines the structure of VISIONS.

The blackboard in this system represents a layered description of the contents of an image. The lowest levels represent *regions, segments,* and *vertices;* they form a structure called an *RSV graph.*

Preprocessing stages are shown in the left half of Figure F2–2. There are three stages of information representation. The first is the image itself, represented by a resolution pyramid (see Article XIII.E1). The second stage comprises separate edge and region analysis. The third stage is a merged representation of the results of a correlation between the edge analysis and region analysis. The representations at these low levels are of image characteristics, rather than of scene characteristics.

The next two levels in the blackboard work with surfaces and volumes. At these levels, the system attempts to reconstruct the three-dimensional configuration of the scene. The top two levels work with representations of

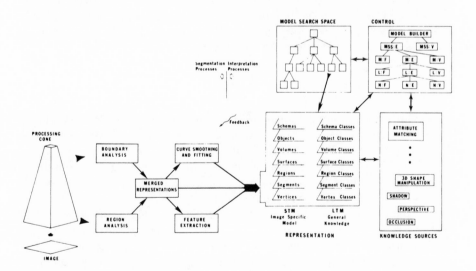

Figure F2–2.   Overview of the VISIONS system.

objects and schemas. At the object level, hypotheses are formed about what the objects in the scene must have been to result in the observed image. The schema level imposes constraints on the selection of object models. There may be office schemas, airport schemas, and so on. Schemas serve the same purpose as Minsky's frames (1973; see also Article III.C7, in Vol. I).

The blackboard model in Figure F2–2 illustrates the distinction made in VISIONS between a priori models and image-specific models, though both may be represented in the same manner. The a priori models are stored in *long-term memory* (LTM), while the image-specific models are stored in *short-term memory* (STM). Recognizing that they did not have adequate KSs to make surface and volume hypotheses reliably, the designers of VISIONS compensated by relying heavily on top-down hypotheses represented by models in LTM. By projecting these models into two dimensions, they construct RSV-level models of objects, and these are matched to the actual image.

VISIONS chooses a KS by traversing a decision tree. Its *model builder* decides to expand or to develop a new hypothesis for a model. To expand a model, the *level focuser* first decides which level of the blackboard to work on. Then, that level is expanded under the control of the *node focuser,* the *node expander,* and the *node verifier.* The focuser selects a node from the blackboard to process further, the expander calls a KS to create new hypotheses, and the verifier checks the results for satisfaction of constraints.

VISIONS incorporates a checker to follow along after each KS activation to test each new hypothesis. The system's confidence in a hypothesis is affected by a number of factors, including its confidence in other competing or supporting hypotheses and whether a hypothesis supports a higher level hypothesis in which the system has confidence.

A Query-oriented Vision System

Ballard, Brown, and Feldman (1978) at the University of Rochester have developed a query-oriented vision system. It abandons the approach of exhaustive processing at the low levels. Instead, it processes just enough information to answer a query. A description of the content of the image is maintained and expanded with each query. All processing is done in the two-dimensional image domain; no three-dimensional models are used.

Information is represented in three *layers:* an *image data structure,* a *model layer,* and a *sketchmap.* This is shown in Figure F2–3. The image data structure contains the spectral bands of the raw image at various resolutions, along with derived information about edges, texture, and regions. The model is a semantic network, representing the appearances of and relationships

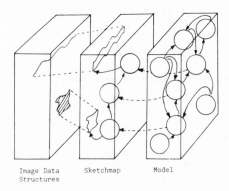

Figure F2–3.   Basic layer structure.

between objects as projected into two dimensions. An object node in the model layer is linked by constraint relations to other object nodes. A node in the sketchmap represents a correspondence between a feature of the image and an object node in the semantic network. These associations are built up during image interpretation and constitute the answers to queries.

Types of queries are precoded as *executive procedures* that roughly outline how to answer queries. An executive procedure imposes a search strategy, based on information contained in *mapping procedures* that are associated with objects in the model plane. Mapping procedures encode how to find instances of the models in the image data structure. Each is specialized to one particular object, but an object node in the model layer may be associated with any number of mapping procedures. A mapping procedure has a precondition, a postcondition, an a priori reliability, and an expected cost (in CPU time). An executive procedure can examine these characteristics to select the mapping procedure that best fulfills its needs.

Figure F2–4 shows a sample executive procedure, written in a stylized version of SAIL. It looks for ribs in chest radiographs. The *Node* variable in Figure F2–4 refers to a node in the sketchmap.

The executive can use (or cause to be used) the information built up in answering previous queries in order to construct new sketchmap nodes to be verified.

Conclusion

We have discussed three integrated vision systems, concentrating on the flow of control within each. Two of these systems use flexible and powerful

```
PROCEDURE MatchRib(Node)
  BEGIN
  if there is an INSTANCE of Node then
    BEGIN
    print("rib", Node, "already matched.");
    return
    END
  else BEGIN
    Find x such that
      x is a RIB-PROCEDURE of Node,
      and RELIABILITY of x is acceptable,
      and COST of x is no greater than that of any other reliable
        RIB-PROCEDURE of Node;
    ApplyProc (x, Node);
    For each v such that
      v is a RIB,
      and v is a NEIGHBOR of Node
      do MatchRib(v)
    END
  END
```

Figure F2–4.   A simplified executive procedure for ribs, from the system
of Ballard, Brown, and Feldman (1978).

blackboard control structures, which are well-suited to processing large amounts
of information and developing partial hypotheses incrementally from noisy
data.

Other well-developed computer vision systems that interpret natural scenes
include Shirai (1978), Rubin (1978), and Ohta (1980).

References

Kanade (1977) discusses the issues of model representation and control
structure in vision systems.

F3.   ACRONYM

ACRONYM (Brooks, 1981a) is intended as a domain-independent, model-driven interpretation system: A user describes the objects expected in an application domain, along with their possible relationships, and the system tries to interpret images as specializations of the domain. ACRONYM attempts to identify and classify instances of modeled objects and, at the same time, extract three-dimensional information from a monocular image concerning the shape, structure, and three-dimensional location and orientation of the objects. The major modules (boxes) and data structures (ellipses) of ACRONYM are shown in Figure F3–1.

The principal domains in which the system has been tested are aerial-photograph interpretation, specifically of airport scenes, and low-angle views of automated assembly work-stations with a wide range of industrial parts.

The ACRONYM project divides model-based vision into four parts: *modeling, prediction, description,* and *interpretation.* The user models both specific objects and generic classes of objects in terms that are independent of images. The program automatically predicts which image features to expect, how to look for them, how to coarsely filter candidate features, and how to use image

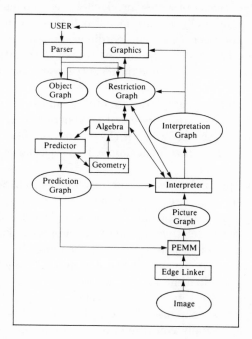

Figure F3–1.   The ACRONYM system.

313

measurements to deduce three-dimensional information about tentative object interpretations. Description is the process of bottom-up reduction of the gray-level image to a higher level, model-independent description of it. Interpretation relates the description of the image to the prediction, applying the instructions included in the prediction to produce a three-dimensional understanding of the scene. These four phases of image understanding are discussed in detail in the remainder of the article.

The ACRONYM system uses two symbolic reasoning systems in all phases of its operation other than description. A *geometric* system reasons about complex products of coordinate transforms—typically 10 to 20 transforms with 10 or more free parameters. An *algebraic* reasoning system takes sets of nonlinear algebraic symbolic inequalities and bounds trigonometric and other expressions of the satisfying sets of those inequalities. This system is based on a method for reasoning about linear inequalities over integers introduced by Bledsoe (1975) for proving properties of programs.

Modeling

The user gives ACRONYM models of objects and their spatial relationships, as well as classes of models and their subclass relationships. The first provides a geometric component of the representation scheme, stored as the *object graph*. The second provides an algebraic component and is stored as the *restriction graph*. Objects are modeled by the volumes they occupy and by transforms between the local coordinate systems of these volumes. Classes (and thus subclasses) are defined by sets of inequalities (constraints) on algebraic expressions (perhaps nonlinear) over parameters of the geometric model.

The nodes of the object graph denote objects and subobjects; they refer to volume primitives that are represented as generalized cones (see Article XIII.D6). For example, the body of an electric motor (like those shown in Fig. F3–2) might be represented by a simple, right circular cylinder—a circle swept along a straight axis.

There are two types of directed arcs in the object graph. *Subpart* arcs represent the coarse-to-fine subpart hierarchy of complex objects. Electric motors have subparts such as a base, attachment flanges, and a drive shaft. *Affixment* arcs describe the spatial relationships between subparts. For instance, the drive shaft has its axis collinear to the axis of the motor body.

Many parameters must be specified to describe fully a generalized cone, a subpart arc, or an affixment arc. The user may give specific numeric values for these parameters and thus completely specify particular objects; alternatively, he (or she) may also choose to leave some parameters as free variables and perhaps supply constraints on the values allowed for them as arbitrary nonlinear algebraic inequalities.

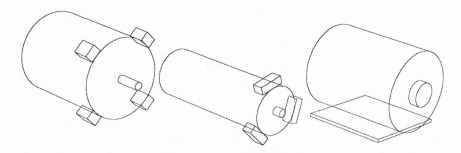

Figure F3–2.   Three specializations of the generic class of small electric
motors.

A user may want to describe a class of small electric motors that vary in
shape and structure but have similar masses. Further, the motors may have
volumes roughly proportional to their masses but constrained to lie in some
range. Finally, the motors may have different lengths and diameters. Thus,
the user might leave the body length as a parameter MOTOR–LENGTH and
body radius as a parameter MOTOR–RADIUS and specify that

$$70.0 \leq \text{MOTOR–LENGTH} \times \text{MOTOR–RADIUS} \times \text{MOTOR–RADIUS} \leq 160.0$$

with additional constraints that

$$6.0 \leq \text{MOTOR–LENGTH} \leq 9.0 \,,$$
$$2.0 \leq \text{MOTOR–RADIUS} \leq 3.0 \,.$$

This is how variations in size and shape are represented by constraints on
parameters of the nodes of the object graph.

Similarly, constraints on parameters of subpart arcs can be used to represent variations in object structure, and variations in spatial relationships
can be represented by constraints on parameters of the affixment arcs. For
instance, a parameter for the number of attachment-flange subparts might be
allowed either to be 0 or to lie in the range from 3 to 6. This constrains the
allowable structures of electric motors. Parameters in the affixment arcs relating attachment flanges to the motor body may constrain them to lie equally
spaced about one end of the body.

Sets of constraints on model parameters form the nodes of the restriction
graph. They are organized in a lattice defined by directed specialization arcs.
Thus, there might be a node giving all the constraints for some generic class of
small electric motors. It may have two specializations—each a more restrictive
set of constraints. One might be the subclass of motors with flanges and no
base, and the other the subclass of motors with a base and no flanges. Each of
these may have further specializations. Figure F3–2 presented three instances
of such a parameterized model, obtained in each case by specializing all the
parameters down to specific numeric values.

During modeling, the user can explictly define parts of the restriction graph. Later, during interpretation, ACRONYM adds more nodes, corresponding to hypothesized instances of objects. Starting with a hypothesized instance that matches the geometric description of an object, ACRONYM tries to find the most specialized restriction node that is consistent with algebraic constraints implied by the image. Thus, it carries out subclass identification of objects.

The ACRONYM modeling system is also used for tasks other than vision. Soroka (1980) has made it the basis of a real-time simulation system for off-line programming of robots. Brooks (1981a) has used it to explore techniques of planning automated assemblies.

Prediction

Given a set of models and their relationships, geometric reasoning techniques are used to predict features that will be invariantly observable, that is, features that will be observable over the modeled range of variations in size, structure, and spatial relations. Image relations between those features are also predicted. This requires analysis of the ranges of those variations in the object-model classes. ACRONYM does not predict the complete appearance of objects from all possible viewpoints but, rather, it predicts features that allow it to identify instances of objects, and also their orientation and position.

The major result of prediction is the *prediction graph*. The nodes of the graph are predictions of image features, and the arcs specify relations expected to hold between the features. Predictions have two functions. First, they provide a coarse filter for hypothesizing object-to-image feature matches. Second, they contain instructions on how to use noisy measurements of an image feature to deduce three-dimensional information about the object to which it has been hypothetically matched.

The predictor module of ACRONYM is implemented as a set of about 280 production rules. These are executed according to a backward-chaining control strategy, augmented by the possibility of setting up subgoals on an agenda. Meta-rules examine the agenda for goal conflicts, eliminate them, and then invoke the rule mechanism on each subgoal in the agenda. Rule selection is through a unification pattern match of rule advertisements to subgoal specifications.

Shape prediction. The image features predicted by ACRONYM are shapes, represented as ribbons (the two-dimensional analogue of generalized cylinders) and ellipses. Ribbons are a good representation of the images generated by a generalized cone. Consider a ribbon that corresponds to the image of the swept surface of a generalized cone. For straight spines, the projection of the cone spine into the image would closely correspond to the spine of the ribbon. Thus, a good approximation to the observed angle between the spines of two generalized cones is the angle between the spines of the two ribbons in the image corresponding to their swept surfaces. Ellipses are a good way of describing the shapes generated by the ends of generalized cones, since the perspective projections of ends of cones with circular cross-sections are ellipses.

Shape prediction involves deciding what shapes will be visible, predicting ranges for shape parameters—to be used as a coarse filter during interpretation and also to guide the low-level descriptive processes—and deriving instructions about how to invert locally the perspective transform and hence use image measurements to generate constraints on the original three-dimensional models.

The perspective transform and the process of inverting it are illustrated in Figure F3–3, which shows a simple camera geometry. An object of length l is at distance d from the camera focus, and parallel to the image plane of the camera. The camera has focal ratio r. The image of the object will measure rl/d; thus, this expression can be used to make predictions about the appearance of the object in the image. Since the object and its relation to the camera may be specified in terms of many free parameters, any or all of r, l, and d may be symbolic algebraic expressions rather than specific numbers. The algebraic reasoning system is able to find upper and lower bounds on rl/d that give a range approximation for possible image sizes of the object. Let that predicted range be $P = [p_l, p_h]$. Suppose that, later, some image feature is hypothesized to match the object and that its measured length, with error estimates, is the range $M = [m_l, m_h]$. Then if $P \cap M$ is empty, the hypothesis should be rejected, as the observed feature cannot possibly fall in the predicted range. Otherwise, however, the hypothesis can be tentatively accepted. Further, if the hypothesis is correct, it must be the case that

$$m_l \leq rl/d \leq m_h .$$

Thus, the hypothesis produces algebraic constraints, called *back constraints*, on the underconstrained parameters of the original model. When combined with other constraints from such local inversions, and from the user-supplied model constraints, the unknown parameters of the model's size, structure, position, and orientation in the world are gradually refined.

Predicting relations. In addition to shapes, relations between shapes are also predicted. Observable relationships predicted between shapes include *exclusivity, collinearity, connectivity, relative spine angle,* and *distance* within the image. Many relations (e.g., angle and distance) include back constraints, analogous to those provided with shapes, which permit three-dimensional information to be extracted from image measurements.

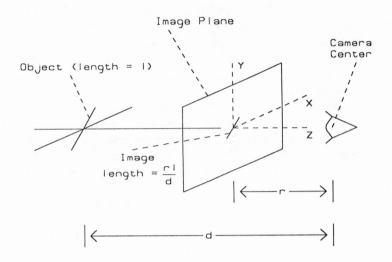

Figure F3–3.   The coordinate system used for ACRONYM camera
models.

Description

The descriptive modules of ACRONYM try to describe images as a *picture
graph* in the same terms as the *prediction graph*, that is, as ribbons and ellipses.

A *line-finder*, first developed by Nevatia and Babu (1981), summarizes
a gray-level image as a collection of linked and straightened line segments.
Typically, about 1,000 lines are produced. The line-finder works in a purely
bottom-up fashion. Figure F3–4a shows the lines found by the line-finder for
an aerial image of an airplane.

The *prediction graph* provides general guidelines for the shapes and sizes
that can be expected, and the *edge mapper* looks for these shapes, but with
no particular concern for which shape corresponds to which prediction. The
result is the *picture graph*, consisting of shape descriptions and their relative
locations and orientations in the two-dimensional image. The picture graph
contains no explicit three-dimensional information. Figure F3–4b shows the
ribbons contained in a picture graph produced from the edges in Figure F3–4a,
when the system was looking for wide-bodied jet aircraft, but had no idea of
the scale to expect.

Interpretation

ACRONYM interprets images by trying to find subgraph isomorphisms
between the picture-graph description of the image and the prediction-graph

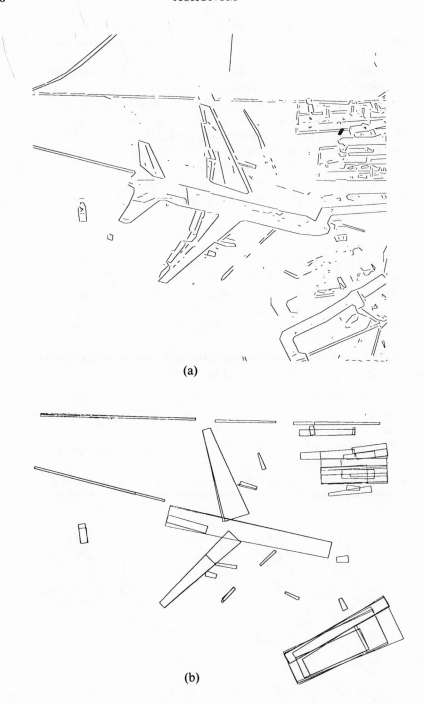

(a)

(b)

Figure F3–4.   (a) Line segments for the image; (b) ribbon description.

expectations. Not only must image features coarsely match predictions, and support observed relations that match those predicted, but all the locally generated back constraints must be consistent. Since ACRONYM does subgraph matching, partial obscurations or failures in the descriptive processes do not necessarily preclude reliable interpretations.

Figure F3–5 shows two specializations of a modeled generic class of wide-bodied passenger jet aircraft used to interpret the image of Figure F3–4a. The subclasses specified by the user included Boeing–747s and Lockheed L–1011s. Figure F3–5 shows specializations of each of these two classes. The full geometric model has approximately 30 parameters related by inequalities, which, for example, express the fact that the wing span of wide-bodied jets is roughly proportional to fuselage length. More specific inequalities are provided to specify the subclasses.

Given that the camera was somewhere in the range of 1,000 to 12,000 meters above ground, with a focal ratio of 20, and some small pitch and roll, ACRONYM produced the interpretation of Figure F3–4b shown in Figure F3–6. In addition, it deduced a large number of inequalities on the model parameters. These were consistent with the constraints for the generic model and for L–1011s, but not for Boeing–747s; therefore, ACRONYM deduced that the aircraft was an L–1011. Note that this deduction was not based on the size of the image, but on relationships between the subparts of the aircraft, such as the ratio between the wing span and the fuselage length and the angle between the wing and the fuselage.

Conclusion

ACRONYM combines geometric matching and algebraic consistency-checking to obtain reliable and accurate three-dimensional interpretations of images. Details of other image interpretations can be found in Brooks (1981a).

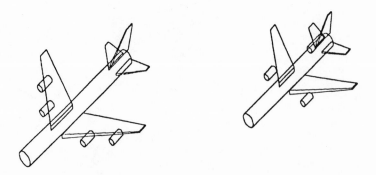

Figure F3–5. Models of the Boeing–747 and the Lockheed L–1011.

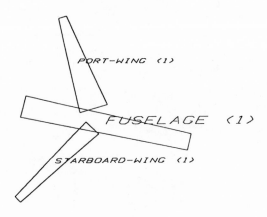

Figure F3–6.   Interpretation of Figure F3–4a.

References

The ACRONYM system is discussed in Brooks' doctoral dissertation (1981a) and in his *AI Journal* paper in the special issue devoted to vision (1981b).

Chapter XIV

Learning and Inductive Inference

CHAPTER XIV: LEARNING AND
INDUCTIVE INFERENCE

A. OVERVIEW

LEARNING is a very general term denoting the way in which people (and computers) increase their knowledge and improve their skills. From the very beginnings of AI, researchers have sought to understand the process of learning and to create computer programs that can learn.

There are two fundamental reasons for studying learning. One is to understand the process itself. By developing computer models of learning, psychologists have attempted to gain an understanding of the way humans learn. Philosophers since Plato have also been interested in learning research, because it may help them understand what knowledge is and how it grows.

The second reason for conducting learning research is to provide computers with the ability to learn. It has long been a goal of AI to develop computer systems that could be taught rather than programmed. Many other applications of computers, such as intelligent programs for assisting scientists, involve the acquisition of new knowledge. Thus, learning research has potential for extending the range of problems to which computers can be applied.

In this overview article, we first present a short history of AI research on learning. This is followed by a review of AI perspectives on learning, from which a simple model of learning is developed. This model allows us to discuss some of the major factors affecting the design of learning systems.

A Brief History of AI Research on Learning

AI research on learning has evolved through three stages. The first, and most optimistic, stage of work centered on self-organizing systems that modified themselves to adapt to their environments (see Yovits, Jacobi, and Goldstein, 1962). The hope was that if a system were given a set of stimuli, a source of feedback, and enough degrees of freedom to modify its own organization, it would adapt itself toward an optimum organization. Attempts were made, for example, to simulate evolution in the hope that intelligent programs would result from the processes of random mutation and natural selection (Friedberg, 1958; Friedberg, Dunham, and North, 1959; Fogel, Owens, and Walsh, 1966). Various computational analogues of neurons were developed and tested; foremost of these was the perceptron (Rosenblatt, 1957). Unfortunately, most of these attempts failed to produce systems of any complexity or intelligence (see Article XIV.D2 on adaptive learning).

Theoretical limitations were discovered that dampened the optimism of these early AI researchers (see Minsky and Papert, 1969). In the 1960s, attention moved away from learning toward knowledge-based problem solving and natural-language understanding (Minsky, 1968). Those people who continued to work with adaptive systems ceased to consider themselves AI researchers; their research branched off to become a subarea of linear systems theory. Adaptive-systems techniques are presently applied to problems in pattern recognition and control theory.

The beginning of the 1970s saw a renewal of interest in learning with the publication of Winston's (1970) influential thesis. In this second stage of learning research, workers adopted the view that learning is a complex and difficult process and that, consequently, a learning system cannot be expected to learn high-level concepts by starting without any knowledge at all. This view has led researchers, on the one hand, to study simple learning problems in depth (such as learning single concepts) and, on the other, to incorporate large amounts of domain knowledge into learning systems (such as the Meta-DENDRAL and AM programs discussed in Articles XIV.D4b and XIV.D4c) so that they could discover high-level concepts.

A third stage of learning research, motivated by the need to acquire knowledge for expert systems, is now under way. Unlike the first two phases of learning research, which focused on rote learning and learning from examples, the current work looks at all forms of learning, including advice-taking and learning from analogies.

Four Perspectives on Learning

Herbert Simon (in press) defines learning as *any process by which a system improves its performance.* His definition assumes that the system has a task that it is attempting to perform. It may improve its performance by applying new methods and knowledge or by improving existing methods and knowledge to make them faster, more accurate, or more robust.

A more constrained view of learning, adopted by many people who work on expert systems, is that learning is *the acquisition of explicit knowledge.* Many expert systems represent their expertise as large collections of rules that need to be acquired, organized, and extended. This view emphasizes the importance of making the acquired knowledge explicit, so that it can be easily verified, modified, and explained. Researchers are presently working on knowledge-acquisition systems that discover new rules from examples or accept new rules from experts and integrate them into the knowledge base of the system.

A third view is that learning is *skill acquisition.* Psychologists have pointed out that long after people are told *how* to do a task, such as touch typing or computer programming, their performance on that task continues to improve through practice (Norman, 1980). It appears that although people can easily understand verbal instructions on how to perform a task, much work remains to be done to turn that verbal knowledge into efficient mental or muscular operations. Researchers in AI and cognitive psychology have sought to understand the kinds of knowledge that are needed to perform skillfully. The processes by which people acquire this knowledge through practice are little understood.

The collective enterprise of science is usually considered to be one of the most effective ways that our culture learns about the world. Thus, a fourth view of learning is that it is *theory formation, hypothesis formation, and inductive inference.* Work on theory formation has centered on understanding how scientists build theories to describe and explain complex phenomena. A necessary part of theory formation is hypothesis formation—the activity of finding one or more plausible hypotheses to explain a particular set of data in the context of a more general theory. Another aspect of theory formation is inductive inference—the process of inferring general laws from particular examples.

A Simple Model of Learning and Its Implications for the Design of Learning Systems

Of these four views of learning, Simon's (in press) is perhaps the most encompassing. Taking his definition as a starting point, we have developed the simple model of learning systems shown in Figure A–1. Throughout this chapter, we use this simple model to organize our discussion of learning systems.

In the model, the circles denote declarative bodies of information (e.g., facts represented in predicate calculus or statements made by an expert), while the boxes denote procedures. The arrows show the predominant direction of data flow through the learning system. The environment supplies some information to the learning element, the learning element uses this information to make improvements in an explicit knowledge base, and the performance element uses the knowledge base to perform its task. Finally, information gained during attempts to perform the task can serve as feedback to the learning element. This model is primitive and omits many important functions. It is useful, however, in that it allows us to classify learning systems according to how they "fill" these four functional units. In any particular application, the environment, the knowledge base, and the performance task determine the nature of the particular learning problem and, hence, the particular functions that the learning element must fulfill. In the following three sections, we

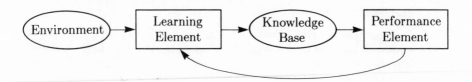

Figure A–1.   A simple model of learning systems.

examine the role of each of these three functional units that surround the learning element.

The Environment

The most important factor affecting the design of learning systems is the kind of information supplied to the system by the environment—particularly the *level* and *quality* of this information.

The *level* of information refers to the degree of generality (or domain of applicability) of the information relative to the needs of the performance element. High-level information is abstract information that is relevant to a broad class of problems. Low-level information is detailed information that is relevant to a single problem. The task of the learning element can be viewed as the task of bridging the gap between the level at which the information is provided by the environment and the level at which the performance element can use the information to carry out its function. Thus, if the learning system is given very abstract (high-level) advice about its performance task, it must fill in the missing details, so that the performance element can interpret the information in particular situations. Correspondingly, if the system is given very specific (low-level) information about how to perform in particular situations, the learning element must generalize this information—by ignoring unimportant details—into a rule that can be used to guide the performance element in a broader class of situations.

Since its knowledge is imperfect, the learning element does not know in advance exactly how to fill in missing details or ignore unimportant details. Consequently, it must guess—that is, *form hypotheses*—about how the gap between the levels should be bridged. After guessing, the system must receive some feedback that allows it to evaluate its hypotheses and revise them if necessary. It is in this way that a learning system learns: by trial and error.

The level of the information provided by the environment determines the kinds of hypotheses that the system must generate. Four basic learning situations can be discerned:

1. *Rote learning*, in which the environment provides information exactly at the level of the performance task and, thus, no hypotheses are needed.

2. *Learning by being told*, in which the information provided by the environment is too abstract or general and, thus, the learning element must hypothesize the missing details.

3. *Learning from examples*, in which the information provided by the environment is too specific and detailed and, thus, the learning element must hypothesize more general rules.

4. *Learning by analogy*, in which the information provided by the environment is relevant only to an analogous performance task and, thus, the

learning system must discover the analogy and hypothesize analogous rules for its present performance task.

Each of these learning situations is discussed in more detail below.

The *quality* of information can have a significant effect on the difficulty of the learning task. Induction is easiest, for example, when the training instances are selected by a cooperative teacher who chooses "clean" examples, classifies them, and presents them in good pedagogical order. Learning by induction is particularly difficult when the training instances are made up of noise-ridden, unclassified data that are "presented" by nature in an uncontrollable fashion. Similarly, in advice-taking systems, information is of little use if it is provided by an unreliable and inarticulate expert; rote learning cannot succeed with poor-quality, possibly contradictory data; and analogies are useless if they are cluttered with errors.

The Knowledge Base

The second factor affecting the design of learning systems is the knowledge base, its *form* and *content*. We discuss first the *form*, or representational system, in which the knowledge base is expressed; it is a particularly important design consideration (see Chap. III, in Vol. I, on representation of knowledge). Most work in learning has used one of two basic representational forms— feature vectors and predicate calculus—although other forms, such as production rules, grammars, LISP functions, numerical polynomials, semantic nets, and frames, have also been used. These representational forms vary along four important dimensions: expressiveness, ease of inference, modifiability, and extendability.

Expressiveness of the representation. In any AI system it is important to have a representation in which the relevant knowledge can be easily expressed. Feature vectors, for example, are useful for describing objects that lack internal structure. They describe objects in terms of a fixed set of features (such as color, shape, and size) that take on a finite set of values (such as red or green, circle or square, and small or large). Predicate calculus, on the other hand, is useful for describing structured objects and situations. A situation in which a red object is on top of a green one, for example, can be expressed as $\exists x, y : \text{RED}(x) \wedge \text{GREEN}(y) \wedge \text{ONTOP}(x, y)$.

Ease of inference within the representation. The computational cost of performing inference is another important property of a representational system. One type of inference frequently required in learning systems is the comparison of two descriptions to determine whether they are equivalent. It is very easy to test two feature-vectors for equivalence. The comparison of two predicate-calculus expressions is more costly. Since many learning systems must search large spaces of possible descriptions, the cost of comparisons can severely limit the extent of these searches.

Modifiability of the knowledge base. A learning system must, by its very nature, modify some part of the knowledge base to store the knowledge it is gaining. Consequently, most learning systems have employed explicit, stylized representations (such as feature vectors, predicate calculus, and production rules) in which it is easy to add knowledge to the knowledge base. Very little attention has been given to the problem of adding to knowledge bases in which substantial revision and integration must be performed. These problems arise, for example, in systems that refer to time or state information (e.g., procedural representations) and in systems that make default assumptions that may later need to be retracted.

Extendability of the representation. For a learning program to manipulate explicitly its acquired knowledge, there must be a meta-level description within the program that tells how the representation is structured. This meta-level knowledge has usually been embodied in procedures that manipulate the data structures of the representation. Of recent interest in learning research, however, are representational systems in which this meta-knowledge is also made an explicit part of the knowledge base (see Davis, 1976). The purpose is to allow the program to examine and alter its own representation by adding vocabulary terms and representational structures. This ability in turn provides the possibility of developing learning systems that are open-ended—that is, that can learn successively more complex units of knowledge without limit. The outstanding example of an extendable representation is Lenat's (1976) AM program (see Article XIV.D4c), which allows new concepts to be defined in terms of old ones. Recent work on RLL (Greiner and Lenat, 1980; Greiner, 1980) has pushed this idea much further toward allowing a program to define new representations dynamically.

Now that we have examined issues relating to the *form* of the knowledge base, we turn our attention to its *content*. A learning system does not gain knowledge by starting "from scratch," that is, without any knowledge at all. Some knowledge must be employed by every learning system to understand the information provided by the environment, to form hypotheses, and to test and refine those hypotheses. Thus, it is more appropriate to view a learning system as extending and improving an existing body of knowledge. Unfortunately, in most learning systems, the knowledge employed is not explicit; it is built into the program by the designer. Throughout this chapter, we try to point out the ways in which domain-specific knowledge has entered into existing learning systems.

The Performance Element

The performance element is the focus of the whole learning system, since it is the actions of the performance element that the learning element is trying to improve. There are three important issues related to the performance element: complexity, feedback, and transparency.

First, the *complexity* of the task is important. Complex tasks require more knowledge than simple tasks. For instance, a simple task like binary classification, in which objects are classified into one of two groups, requires only a single classification rule. On the other hand, a program that can play a reasonable poker game (Waterman, 1970) needs about 20 rules, and a medical-diagnosis system like MYCIN (Shortliffe, 1976) employs several hundred rules.

In learning from examples, three classes of performance tasks can be distinguished according to their complexity. The simplest performance task is *classification* or *prediction* based on a *single concept* or *rule*. Indeed, the problem of learning single concepts from examples has received more study than any other problem in AI learning research. Slightly more complex are tasks involving multiple concepts. An example is the problem of predicting which bonds of an organic molecule will be broken in the mass spectrometer; the DENDRAL prediction program employs a set of cleavage rules to perform this task. The most complex tasks for which learning systems have been developed are small planning tasks in which a set of rules must be applied *in sequence*. Symbolic integration, for example, is a task that requires chaining together several integration rules to obtain a solution. The articles on learning from examples consider these three classes of performance tasks and their corresponding learning methods.

As the performance task becomes more complex and the knowledge base grows in size, the problems of *integrating new rules* and *diagnosing incorrect rules* become more complicated. The *integration problem*—that is, the problem of integrating a new rule into an existing set of rules—is difficult, because the learning system must consider possible interactions between the new rule and the previous rules. During the construction of the MYCIN system, for example, there were several cases in which a new rule caused existing rules to be applied incorrectly or to cease being applied altogether (see Article VIII.B1).

The problem of diagnosing incorrect rules—also known as the *credit-assignment problem* (Minsky, 1963)—can be very difficult in systems that perform a sequence of actions before receiving any feedback. Consider, for example, the problem of learning to play chess by first playing a complete game, then determining who won and lost, and finally updating the knowledge base accordingly. The credit-assignment problem is the problem of assigning credit or blame to the individual decisions that led to some overall result—in this case, the individual chess moves that contributed most to the win or loss.

The second important issue related to the performance task is the role of the performance element in providing *feedback* to the learning element. All learning systems must have some way of evaluating the hypotheses that have been proposed by the learning element. Some programs have a separate body of knowledge for such evaluation. The AM program, for example, has many heuristic rules that assess the interestingness of the new concepts developed by the learning element. A more frequently used technique, however, is to have the environment, often a teacher, provide an external *performance standard*.

Then, by observing how well the performance element is doing relative to this standard, the system can evaluate its current store of hypotheses.

In systems that learn a single concept from training instances, the performance standard is the correct classification of each training instance (as to whether it is, or is not, an instance of the concept to be learned). In most systems, the training instances are preclassified by a reliable teacher. In the Meta-DENDRAL system (see Article XIV.D4b), the performance standard is the actual mass spectrum produced when a molecule of known structure is placed in the mass spectrometer.

The third issue regarding the performance task is the *transparency* of the performance element. For the learning element to assign credit or blame to individual rules in the knowledge base, it is useful for the learning element to have access to the internal actions of the performance element. Consider again the problem of learning how to play chess. If the learning element is given a trace of all the moves that were *considered* by the performance element (rather than only those moves that were actually chosen), the credit-assignment problem is easier to solve.

Overview of the Chapter

In the previous section, we discussed the interaction between the information provided by the environment and the problems that are presented to the learning element. From this analysis, four learning situations could be discerned. In this section, we discuss these four situations in detail and give an example of a learning problem in each situation. The remainder of this chapter is organized around these four situations, with a separate set of articles devoted to each.

Rote learning. The simplest learning situation is one in which the environment supplies knowledge in a form that can be used directly by the performance element. The learning system does not need to do any processing to understand or interpret the information supplied by the environment. All it must do is memorize the incoming information for later use. This is a form of rote learning—if it is considered learning at all. Virtually every computer system can be said to do rote learning insofar as it stores instructions for performing a task.

An important AI study of rote learning was undertaken by Samuel (1959, 1967). He developed a checkers-playing program that was able to improve its performance by memorizing every board position that it evaluated. The program used a standard minimax look-ahead search (see Chap. II, in Vol. I) that evaluated potential future board positions. A simple polynomial evaluation function measured board properties such as center control, fork threats, and possible exchanges. In terms of our primitive learning-system model, the look-ahead search portion of Samuel's program served as the "environment." It supplied the learning element with board positions and their backed-up minimax values. The learning element simply stored these board positions and indexed them for rapid retrieval. Interestingly, the look-ahead search portion of Samuel's program also served as part of the performance element that played a game of checkers against an opponent. It used the previously memorized board positions to improve the speed and depth of its look-ahead search during subsequent games.

Learning by being told—Advice-taking. When a system is given vague, general-purpose knowledge or advice, it must transform this high-level knowledge into a form that can be used readily by the performance element. This transformation is called *operationalization*. The system must understand and interpret the high-level knowledge and relate it to what it already knows. Operationalization is an active process that can involve such activities as deducing the consequences of what it has been told, making assumptions and "filling in the details," and deciding when to ask for more advice. McCarthy's (1958) proposal for an "advice taker" was the first description of a system that could learn by being told. More recent work in the area of learning by being told includes the TEIRESIAS program (Davis, 1976) and Mostow's program FOO (Mostow and Hayes-Roth, 1979; Mostow, 1981).

FOO, for example, is told the rules of the game of Hearts and is given vague strategic advice such as "Avoid taking points." It operationalizes this advice into specific strategies such as "Play lower than the highest card so far in the suit led." This kind of operationalization is similar to the kind of processing performed by ordinary language compilers that convert unexecutable high-level languages into directly interpretable machine code. In the same trivial sense that every computer system can be said to do rote learning, every system can also be said to learn by being told: Advice in the form of a high-level language program is compiled and assembled into an executable object program.

Learning from examples—Induction. One way to teach a system how to perform a task is to present it with examples of how it should behave. The system must then generalize these examples to find higher level rules that can be applied to guide the performance element. Examples can be viewed as being pieces of very specific knowledge that cannot be used efficiently by the performance element. These are transformed into more general, higher level pieces of knowledge that can be used effectively.

For example, consider the problem of teaching a program to recognize poker hands that contain a *pair*. The program would be presented with sample hands that, it is told, contain pairs. Here is such a training instance:

4 of clubs, 4 of spades, 5 of diamonds, 6 of hearts, jack of diamonds.

This training example is a very specific piece of knowledge. If the program merely memorized it (by rote learning), it would now *know* that the hand

4 of clubs, 4 of spades, 5 of diamonds, 6 of hearts, jack of diamonds

contains a pair. It would *not* know that the hand

   4 of clubs, 4 of spades, 5 of diamonds, 6 of hearts, 8 of diamonds

also contains a pair, since the program has not *generalized* its knowledge. To recognize all possible pair hands, the program needs to discover that the hand must contain two cards of the same rank and that the remaining cards are irrelevant. The generalization of knowledge to make it apply to a broader class of situations is the key inference process in learning from examples.

Learning by analogy. If a system has available to it a knowledge base for a related performance task, it may be able to improve its own performance by recognizing analogies and transferring the relevant knowledge from the other knowledge base. Thus far, however, very little work has been done in this area. Some of the open research questions are: What exactly is an analogy? How are analogies recognized? How is the relevant knowledge transferred from the analogous knowledge base and applied to accomplish the desired tasks?

Suppose, for example, that a program has available to it a knowledge base describing how to diagnose diseases in human beings and someone wants to use the same program to diagnose computer-system failures. By finding the proper analogies, the program can develop classes of computer failures ("diseases") and possible solutions ("therapies"). Diagnostic procedures can be transferred as the analogy is developed (e.g., x-rays can be analogized to core dumps).

We do not include in this chapter any articles discussing learning by analogy, since this area has not received much attention.

Conclusion

This introduction has surveyed AI research on learning and presented a simple model of AI learning systems. The model has been used to discuss the factors that bear upon the design of the learning element. These include the level and quality of the information provided by the environment, the form and content of the knowledge base, and the complexity and transparency of the performance element. Of these factors, the most important is the level of the information provided by the environment. This has been used to develop the simple taxonomy of four learning situations that provides an organization for the remainder of this chapter.

References

Buchanan et al. (1977) survey several systems and present a general model of learning systems. See also Lenat, Hayes-Roth, and Klahr (1979) and Dietterich and Michalski (1979).

B. ROTE LEARNING

B1. Issues

ROTE LEARNING is memorization; it is saving new knowledge so that when it is needed again, the only problem will be *retrieval*, rather than a repeated computation, inference, or query. Two extreme perspectives on rote learning are possible. One view says that memorization is such a basic necessity for any intelligent program that it cannot be considered a separate learning process at all. An alternate view regards memorization as a complex subject that is vital to any effective cognitive system and well worth study and modeling on its own. This article takes a less extreme perspective, partly because the former viewpoint leaves nothing to say about rote learning and the latter would require more than is appropriate here. (See Chap. XI for a discussion of AI investigations into human memory processes.)

Rote memorization can be seen as an elementary learning process, not powerful enough to accomplish intelligent learning on its own (because not everything that needs to be known in any nontrivial domain can be memorized), but an inherent and important part of any learning system. All learning systems must remember the knowledge that they have acquired so that it can be applied in the future. In a rote-learning system, the knowledge has already been gained by some method and is in a directly usable form. Other, more sophisticated learning systems first acquire the knowledge from examples or from advice and then memorize it. Thus, all learning systems are built on a rote-learning process that stores, maintains, and retrieves knowledge in a knowledge base.

Rote learning works by taking problems that the performance element has solved and memorizing the problem and its solution. Viewed abstractly, the performance element can be thought of as some function, f, that takes an *input pattern* $(X_1, \ldots, X_n)$ and computes an *output value* $(Y_1, \ldots, Y_p)$. A rote memory for f simply stores the *associated pair* $[(X_1, \ldots, X_n), (Y_1, \ldots, Y_p)]$ in memory. During subsequent computations of $f(X_1, \ldots, X_n)$, the performance element can simply retrieve $(Y_1, \ldots, Y_p)$ from memory rather than recomputing it. This simple model of rote learning is depicted in Figure B1–1.

Consider, for example, an automobile insurance program that determines the cost of repairs for damaged automobiles. The input pattern is a description of the damaged automobile, including make and year, and a list of the damaged portions of the car. The output value is the estimated cost of the repairs. The system has only a rote memory. To estimate the cost of repairs, it looks in its memory for a previous automobile of the same make, model,

$$(X_1, \ldots, X_n) \quad \xrightarrow{f} \quad (Y_1, \ldots, Y_p) \quad \xrightarrow{\text{store}} \quad [(X_1, \ldots, X_n), (Y_1, \ldots, Y_p)]$$

Input	Performance	Output value	Associated
pattern	function	of computation	pair

Figure B1–1.   Simple model of rote learning.

and damage description and retrieves the corresponding cost. If it cannot find such an automobile, it uses a set of rules (published by a consortium of insurance companies) to guess the cost of the repairs and then saves its estimate for future use. This computed estimate, along with the description of the damaged automobile, forms the associated pair that is memorized.

Lenat, Hayes-Roth, and Klahr (1979) provide an interesting perspective on rote learning. They point out that rote learning (or "caching") can be viewed as the lowest level of a hierarchy of *data reductions*. The reductions are analogous to *computer language compilation:* The purpose is to refine the original information down to the essentials for performance. In rote learning, we generally attempt to save the input/output details of some calculation and so bypass a future need for the intermediate computation process. Thus, a *calculation* task, if valuable and stable enough to be remembered, is reduced to an *access* task (see Fig. B1–2, below).

Just as calculations can be reduced to retrievals by caching, so can other inferential processes be reduced to simpler tasks. For instance, *deductions* can be reduced to *calculations*. The first time we are asked to solve a quadratic equation, for example, we must follow lengthy deductive chains to find the quadratic formula. Subsequently, we can simply compute the roots of a quadratic equation directly from the formula. We have distilled the results of a deductive search and summarized them as an efficient algorithm. Going one step further, the process of induction can convert a huge body of training instances into a single heuristic rule. Once again, the primary gain is in efficiency: It is no longer necessary to consult a huge body of examples to find out how to behave in a new situation.

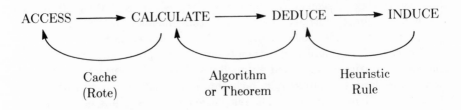

Figure B1–2.   Spectrum of data reductions (from Lenat et al., 1979).

Issues in the Design of Rote-learning Systems

There are three important issues relevant to rote-learning systems: memory organization, stability, and the store-versus-compute trade-off.

Memory organization. Rote learning is useful only if it takes less time to retrieve the desired item than it does to recompute it. Retrieval can be made very rapid by properly organizing memory. Consequently, indexing, sorting, and hashing techniques have been thoroughly studied in the computer science subfields of data structures (Aho, Hopcroft, and Ullman, 1974) and database systems (Wiederhold, 1977; Date, 1977; Ullman, 1980).

Stability of the environment and the frame problem. Rote learning is not very helpful or effective in a rapidly changing environment. One important assumption underlying rote learning is that information stored at one time will still be valid later. If, however, the information changes frequently, this assumption can be violated. Consider, for example, information gathered about automobile repair costs during the early 1950s. Such information would be of little value for estimating automobile repair costs in the 1980s because the world has changed in critical ways: The makes and models of cars presently manufactured did not exist in the 1950s; furthermore, inflation has made the direct comparison of dollar costs impossible. A rote-learning system must be able to detect when the world has changed in such a way as to make stored information invalid. This is an instance of the *frame problem* (see Chap. III, in Vol. I).

Some solutions to this problem have been developed. One approach is to monitor every change to the world and keep the stored information always up to date. Thus, when an old model of automobile is discontinued, all information about that model could be removed from the knowledge base. This approach requires that the relevant aspects of the world be continually monitored.

A second approach to solving the frame problem is to check, when the information is retrieved for use, that it is still valid. Typically, this requires storing, along with the information itself, some additional data about the state of the world at the time the information was memorized. When the information is retrieved, the stored state can be compared to the current state, and the system can determine whether or not the information is still valid. This approach requires that the relevant aspects of the world (such as the current value of the dollar) be anticipated and stored with the data.

Many other approaches are possible. If the system can determine *how* the world has changed (e.g., by knowing the inflation rate), it may be able to make appropriate modifications to restore the validity of the memorized information (e.g., by converting the 1950 prices into 1980 equivalents).

Store-versus-compute trade-off. Since the primary goal of rote learning is to improve the overall performance of the system, it is important that the rote-learning process itself does not decrease the efficiency of the system.

It is conceivable, for instance, that the cost of storing and retrieving the memorized information is greater than the cost of recomputing it. This is certainly the case with the multiplication of two numbers; virtually all computers recompute the product of two numbers rather than store a large multiplication table.

There are two basic approaches to resolving the store-versus-compute trade-off. One is to decide at the time the information is first available whether or not it should be stored for later use. A cost-benefit analysis can be performed that weighs the amount of storage space consumed by the information and the cost of recomputing it against the likelihood that the information will be needed in the future. A second approach is to go ahead and store the information and later decide whether or not to forget it. This procedure, called *selective forgetting*, allows the system to determine empirically which items of information are most frequently reused.

One of the most common selective-forgetting techniques is called the *least recently used* (LRU) replacement algorithm. Each item stored in memory is tagged with the time when it was last retrieved. Every time an item is retrieved, its "time of last use" is updated. When a new item is to be memorized, the least recently used item is forgotten and replaced by the new one. Variations on this scheme take into consideration the amount of storage required for the item, the cost of recomputing the item, and so on.

References

Lenat, Hayes-Roth, and Klahr (1979) provide an excellent discussion of various learning methods, including rote learning. Samuel (1959) remains the best example of research into rote processes.

B2. Rote Learning in Samuel's Checkers Player

SAMUEL conducted a series of studies (1959, 1967) on how to get a computer to learn to play checkers. Among the earliest investigations of machine learning, they remain some of the most successful both in terms of improved performance (i.e., demonstrated improvements in the performance element) and in terms of lessons for AI. His experiments with three different learning methods—rote learning, polynomial evaluation functions, and signature tables—showed that significant improvement in playing checkers could be obtained. This article focuses on his thorough analysis of the question of how much rote learning alone can contribute to expertise and improved performance. Other aspects of Samuel's work are discussed later in Article XIV.D4a.

The Game of Checkers as a Performance Task

Checkers is a difficult game to play well. It is estimated that a full exploration of all possible moves in checkers would require roughly 10^{40} moves. Samuel's program was provided with procedures for playing the game *correctly;* that is, the rules of checkers were incorporated into the program. He sought to have the program learn to play *well* by having it memorize and recall board positions that it had encountered in previous games.

At each turn, Samuel's program chose its move by conducting a *minimax game-tree search* (see Articles II.B3 and II.C5, in Vol. I). In principle, of course, a program could try all possible moves and all possible consequences of each move and thereby search the entire checkers game-tree. Such a calculation—which is equivalent to playing every possible game of checkers—is not feasible because the search space is too large. Every potential move by one player generally leads to many possible countermoves, each of which has still more possible responses. The resulting combinatorial explosion (see Article II.A, in Vol. I) prevents any program from searching the whole tree.

Consequently, the standard approach to conducting a game-tree search is to search only a few moves (and countermoves) into the future and then apply a *static evaluation function* to estimate which side is winning. The program then chooses the move that leads to the best estimated position.

Suppose, for example, that at some board position, A, it is the program's turn to move (see Fig. B2–1). The program searches ahead three moves by considering first all possible moves that it could make, then all possible countermoves available to its opponent, and finally all possible replies to those countermoves. At this point, the program applies a static evaluation function to estimate its net advantage at each of the board positions shown on the right in the figure. These values are then "backed up" by assuming that

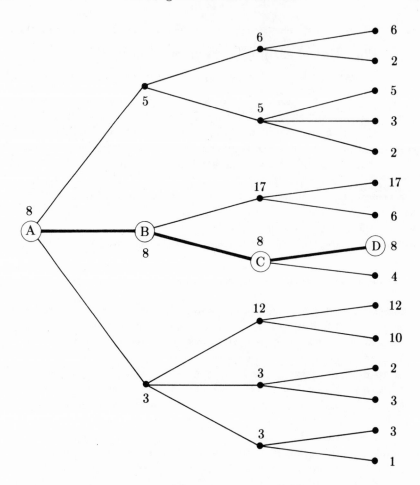

Figure B2–1.   An example of a minimax game-tree search.

the opponent will always take the move that is worst for the computer (and vice versa). Thus, the best move for the program is the one that leads to position *B*. The program expects that the opponent will countermove to *C*, to which the program can reply with *D*. The static evaluation function has estimated the value of *D* to be 8, so this is the backed-up value of position *A*.

Improving the Performance of the Checkers Player

There are two basic ways to improve the performance of a game-tree search. One method is to search farther into the future and thus better approximate a full search of the tree. This is known as improving the *look-ahead power* of the program. The other method is to improve the static evaluation function, so that the estimated value of each board position is more accurate. Samuel's rote-learning studies aimed at improving the look-ahead power by memorizing the backed-up values of board positions. The techniques discussed in Article XIV.D5a address the problem of improving the evaluation function.

The rote-learning approach employed by Samuel saved every board position encountered during play, along with its backed-up value. In the situation shown in Figure B2–1, for instance, Samuel's program would memorize the description of board position A and its backed-up value of 8 as an associated pair, $[A, 8]$. When position A is encountered in subsequent games, its evaluation score is retrieved from memory rather than recomputed. This makes the program more efficient, because it does not have to compute the value for A with the static evaluation function.

There is a more important benefit of retrieving the backed-up value of A from memory, however. The memorized value of A is more accurate than the static value of A, because it is based on a look-ahead search. Thus, the look-ahead power of the program is improved. Figure B2–2 shows an example of this improvement. The program is considering which move to make at position E. It searches ahead three moves and then applies the static evaluation function. For position A, however, the program is able to retrieve the memorized value based on the previous search to position D.

This approach improves the effective search depth for E. As more and more positions are memorized, the effective search depth improves from its

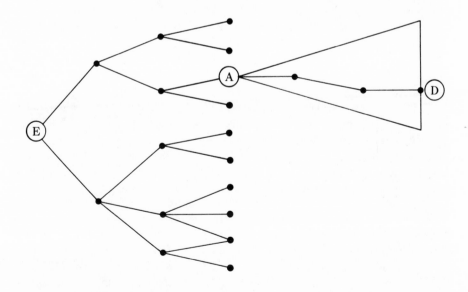

Figure B2–2.   Improving look-ahead power by rote learning.

original value of 3 moves, up to 6, then to 9, and so on. Rote learning is thus used in Samuel's program to save the results of previous partial game-tree searches, so that they can gradually be extended and deepened. Rote learning converts a computation (tree search) into a retrieval from memory.

Memory Organization

Samuel employed several clever techniques to store the evaluated board positions, so that they took up little space and could be retrieved rapidly. To store the positions compactly, Samuel took advantage of several symmetries (e.g., positions in which it was Red's turn to move were converted into the corresponding Black-to-move positions; king positions are symmetric in two ways). Efficient retrieval was accomplished by indexing the boards according to many different characteristics (including the number of pieces on the board, presence or absence of kings, and piece advantage) and writing them onto a tape in the order they would most likely be needed during a game. The use of magnetic tape was necessary because the program was running on a relatively small IBM-704 computer, and only a few board positions could be kept in the computer's core memory. During rote learning, the program would accumulate a number of board positions before reading, sorting, and rewriting them onto the memory tape.

Samuel resolved the store-versus-compute trade-off with a variation of *least recently used* (LRU) replacement. Each board position was given an age. Whenever a position was retrieved from memory, its age was divided by 2. When the memory tape was rewritten, the ages of all stored positions were increased by 1, and very old positions were forgotten—that is, not written back onto tape.

Results

The program was trained in several ways: by playing against itself, by playing against people (including some checkers masters), and by following published games between master players (so-called book games). After training, the memory tape contained roughly 53,000 positions. As the program learned more, it improved slowly but steadily, becoming, in Samuel's words, a "rather better-than-average novice, but definitely not ... an expert" (Samuel, 1959, p. 218). Success in learning varied markedly depending on the phase of the game. The program became capable of playing a very good opening game, since the number of board variations is relatively small near the start of the game. Performance during the midgame, with its far greater range of possible configurations, did not greatly improve with rote learning. During the end game, the program became able to recognize winning and losing positions well in advance, but it needed some improvement before it was able to force the game to a successful conclusion (see below).

On the whole, Samuel's experiments demonstrated that significant and measurable learning can result from rote processes alone, but that on its own, rote learning is limited in several ways. The first and most obvious limitation is in storage space and retrieval. One question that interested Samuel is the following: If rote learning produces steady improvement of performance as it gathers new positions (up to a limit determined by available space and the efficiency of indexing algorithms), could it ever reach a performance level considered expert before exceeding the storage and indexing limits? If so, how much data would it need to remember, and how long would it take to gather the data?

Samuel estimated that his program would need to memorize about one million positions to approximate a master level of checkers play. Unfortunately, even a system with sufficient storage capacity and rapid retrieval methods would require an impractical amount of machine playing in order to gather a million useful positions. However, Samuel suggests that even this long acquisition period would be shorter than the time taken by humans to improve from complete beginners to masters.

The inability of the program actually to effect a win once it had a winning position was a curious problem. It was caused by the *mesa effect* (Minsky, 1963)—that is, once the program has found a winning position, all moves look equally good, and the program tends to wander aimlessly. Samuel solved the problem by storing, along with each board position and value, the length of the search path that was used to compute the board value. The move-selection procedure was modified to select the best move that also had the shortest associated search distance. This change gave the program a sense of direction, so that it was able to press forward to win the game (or stall as much as possible to avoid losing a game).

Another interesting problem arose when Samuel attempted to combine rote learning with learning techniques that modified the static evaluation function. Unfortunately, changes to the evaluation function tended to invalidate previously memorized positions (see Article XIV.B1, on the frame problem). Samuel's solution was to avoid this problem by postponing rote learning until the evaluation function had been effectively learned.

Conclusion

Besides showing that real improvement of performance could be gained by the conceptually simplest form of learning—rote memorization—Samuel identified and elaborated several issues that need to be handled if rote is to offer significant gains. In general, the value of rote learning is to gain problem-solving power in the form of speed. By retrieving the stored results of extensive computations, the program can proceed deeper in its reasoning. The price is storage space, access time, and effort in organizing the stored knowledge.

Samuel found that for rote learning to be effective, knowledge had to be carefully organized for efficient retrieval, stabilized to avoid using values whose meanings had changed, augmented with search-depth information, and selectively forgotten so that only the most useful information would tend to be saved. In the case of Samuel's checkers player, rote learning may have had enough power on its own to lead eventually to expert performance, but the time and space required for that much improvement were beyond the available resources.

References

Samuel (1959) describes the rote-learning research in detail.

C. LEARNING BY TAKING ADVICE

C1. Issues

IN ONE of the earliest AI papers on learning, McCarthy (1958) proposed the creation of an advice-taking system that could accept advice and make use of it to plan and execute actions in the world. Until the late 1970s, however, there were very few attempts to write programs that could *learn by taking advice*. The recent emphasis in AI on expert systems has focused new attention on the problem of converting expert advice into expert performance (see Barr, Bennett, and Clancey, 1979).

Research on advice-taking systems has followed two major paths. One approach has been to develop systems that accept abstract, high-level advice and convert it into rules that can effectively guide the performance element. This research seeks to automate all phases of the advice-taking process. The other approach has been to develop sophisticated tools—such as knowledge-base editing and debugging aids—that make it easier for the expert to transform his own abstract expertise into detailed rules. In this second approach, the expert is an integral part of the learning system, detecting and diagnosing bugs and repairing and refining the knowledge base. The former approach shows promise of eventually developing completely instructable systems, while the latter approach has proved invaluable for creating knowledge-based expert systems. This article describes both of these research paths. We will discuss the more highly automated approach first and return later to the research on knowledge-base editing and debugging aids.

Steps for Automatic Advice-taking

Hayes-Roth, Klahr, and Mostow (1980, 1981) provide an outline of the processes required to convert expert advice into program performance. This outline can be summarized as follows:

1. *Request*—request advice from expert,
2. *Interpret*—assimilate into internal representation,
3. *Operationalize*—convert into usable form,
4. *Integrate*—integrate into knowledge base,
5. *Evaluate*—evaluate resulting actions of performance element.

Request. The first step is for the program to request advice from the expert. The request can be simple—just asking the expert to give some general advice—or it can be sophisticated—identifying a shortcoming in the knowledge base and asking the expert how to repair it. Some systems are completely passive and simply wait for the expert to interrupt them and provide advice, while others are very careful to focus the attention of the expert on a particular problem.

Interpret. The next step in advice-taking is to accept the advice and represent it internally. McCarthy (1958) points out that in order for a program to accept advice, the program must have an *epistemologically adequate* representation for the advice (see Article III.C1, in Vol. I), that is, a representation that is capable of expressing the advice without losing any information. This interpretation step can be very difficult if the advice is given in a natural language. The program must understand the natural language sufficiently well to convert it into an unambiguous internal representation. See Chapter IV, in Volume I, for a detailed survey of AI research into natural-language understanding.

Operationalize. Once the advice has been accepted and interpreted into an unambiguous representation, it still may not be directly executable by the performance element. The third step—*operationalization*—seeks to bridge the gap between the level at which the advice is provided and the level at which the performance element can apply it.

Mostow's (1981) program FOO, for example, accepts advice about how to play the card game of Hearts. English-language advice, such as "Avoid taking points," is interpreted by FOO's human user and given to the program as the lambda-calculus statement (AVOID (TAKE–POINTS ME) (CURRENT TRICK)). However, even though this advice has been interpreted into an unambiguous internal representation, it is still not *operational* since FOO has no procedures or methods to avoid taking points. FOO *does* have methods for selecting and playing cards, however. Thus, the advice must be converted into a form, such as [ACHIEVE (LOW (CARD–OF ME))] (i.e., "Play a low card"), that requires only these operations.

FOO accomplishes this task by applying many different operationalization methods (see Article XIV.C2). It tries to re-express the advice, using known relationships, until it can recognize that one of its operationalization methods is applicable. These methods then allow it to develop a procedure for carrying out all or part of the advice. The steps of reformulating the advice and applying operationalization methods are repeated until the advice is completely executable.

This process is similar to the approach taken by automatic-programming systems that convert high-level program specifications into efficient implementations (see Chap. X, in Vol. I). However, unlike those systems, which seek to create provably correct programs, FOO is not foolproof. The gap between the advice and the performance element is usually too wide, and the operationalization methods are usually too weak, to permit error-free operationalization.

For example, it is often necessary for FOO to make assumptions and approximations in order to transform the advice. FOO cannot always successfully "avoid taking points" in Hearts, since it is impossible for the program to know the contents of its opponents' hands. Instead, FOO applies heuristic methods to reduce the likelihood that points will be taken. Its strategy of playing low cards is, consequently, a tentative *hypothesis* about how to avoid taking points. The tentative hypotheses developed by operationalization must be tested and debugged before they can be accepted.

Integrate. When knowledge is added to the knowledge base, care must be taken to see that it is properly integrated (see Article XIV.A). New advice can result in new mistakes if it takes precedence over previous knowledge in situations in which the old knowledge is still correct. Yet the new advice must take precedence in the intended situations. The learning program must know enough about how the performance element applies the knowledge to be able to anticipate and avoid any bad side-effects that could result from adding the knowledge to the knowledge base.

Two common problems of integration are (a) overlapping applicability and (b) contradictory recommendations. Consider an expert system, such as MYCIN, whose knowledge base is represented as a set of production rules. When a new rule is added, its left-hand side (or condition part) may be overly general, causing it to trigger in situations in which some other rule is properly applicable. One solution to this problem is to specialize the rules, so that this overlap of applicability no longer occurs. Another approach—the *meta-rule approach*—is to add ordering rules (*meta-rules*) that explicitly indicate which regular rules should be applied before others.

When the right-hand sides (or action parts) of two production rules recommend inconsistent actions in the same situation, the problem of contradictory recommendations arises. Again, either the right-hand sides can be modified to remove the contradiction or a meta-rule can be added to indicate which action should take precedence. There are many other integration problems aside from these two typical ones.

Evaluate. Since the new knowledge received from the expert is only tentative—that is, it is the result of interpretation, operationalization, and integration—it must be evaluated somehow. The learning system may be able to recognize some errors and inconsistencies in the advice when it integrates the advice into the knowledge base. More frequently, however, it is necessary to test the advice empirically by actually employing it to perform some task and then assessing whether the system is working properly.

Evaluation requires some performance standard against which the actual behavior of the system can be compared. In some domains, the performance standard can be built into the program. Game-playing programs, for example, can tell if the system is doing well by whether or not the system wins the game. In other domains, however, the system needs to set up detailed expectations about how the new knowledge will affect the performance of the system. These expectations allow the program to detect and locate bugs in the knowledge base.

Evaluation can naturally feed back into the *request* step (the first of these five steps). When the program detects that the performance element is not functioning properly, it can announce this to the expert and request additional advice. A more sophisticated approach is for the program to do *credit assignment*—that is, to determine which parts of the knowledge base are incorrect. Once the bug has been located, the advice-taking system can ask the expert to tell it how to repair the particular piece of knowledge that is incorrect.

Now that we have discussed the five basic steps in an advice-taking system, we describe some systems that have been developed as aids for creating, modifying, and debugging large knowledge bases.

Aids for Knowledge-base Maintenance

Instead of fully automating these five steps, many researchers working on expert systems have built tools for assisting in the development and maintenance of expert knowledge bases. EMYCIN (van Melle, 1980; Davis, 1976), AGE (Nii and Aiello, 1979), and KAS (Reboh, 1981), for example, all provide certain functions to assist a domain expert or knowledge engineer in carrying out these five steps. Particular assistance has been provided for integrating new knowledge into the knowledge base (intelligent editors, flexible representation languages) and for evaluating and debugging the knowledge base (explanation and tracing facilities). This semiautomated approach to advice-taking places the knowledge engineer in the role of requesting, interpreting, and operationalizing the expert's advice.

To assist the knowledge engineer, these systems must be able to communicate effectively. It is particularly important for the engineer to get good feedback from the system during testing and debugging. Thus, a great deal of effort has been expended on the development of tracing and explanation facilities for expert systems (see Article VII.B, in Vol. II; Davis, 1976).

Conclusion

Research on advice-taking systems is still in its infancy, although important ideas and methods are available from the related areas of natural-language understanding and automatic programming. Present research is advancing along two paths: the theoretical path of automatic operationalization of expert advice and the practical path of providing aids to help knowledge engineers build and debug expert systems. The development of fully automatic systems remains an active research area.

A few AI systems have been developed that perform some kind of advice-taking. Mostow's FOO system is described in Article XIV.C2. The reader is also directed to the articles on TEIRESIAS (Article VII.B, in Vol. II) and on Waterman's poker player (Article XIV.D5b) for other examples of advice-taking systems.

References

Davis's work (1976, 1978) describes pioneering efforts in interactive advice-taking. Hayes-Roth, Klahr, and Mostow (1981) and Mostow and Hayes-Roth (1979) present the most comprehensive analyses of advice-taking as a whole.

C2. Mostow's Operationalizer

A GROUP of researchers at the Rand Corporation, Carnegie-Mellon University, and Stanford University has recently been developing the *machine-aided heuristic programming* methodology in which a computer would be instructed to perform a new task in much the same way that a person is taught (see Hayes-Roth, Klahr, Burge, and Mostow, 1978; Hayes-Roth, Klahr, and Mostow, 1981). A central effort in this project is understanding the problem of *operationalization* (see Article XIV.C1). Mostow's program FOO (First Operational Operationalizer) is one of the first results of this work. It investigates principles, problems, and methods involved in converting high-level advice into effective, executable procedures.

Accepting Advice About the Game of Hearts

Mostow, in his research with FOO, has dealt primarily with operationalization problems taken from the card game of Hearts. The game is played as a sequence of tricks. In each trick, one player—who is said to *have the lead*—starts the trick by playing a card and each of the other players continues the trick by playing a card during his (or her) turn. If he can, each player must follow suit, that is, play a card of the same suit as the suit led. The player who played the highest valued card in the suit led takes the trick and any point cards contained in it. Every heart counts as one point, and the queen of spades is worth 13 points. The goal of the game is to avoid taking points. Hayes-Roth et al. (1978) provide a more complete explanation of the game.

Hearts is a game of partial information, with no known algorithm for winning. Although the possible situations in the game are extremely numerous, beginning players often hear general advice such as "Avoid taking points," "Don't lead a high card in a suit in which an opponent is void," and "If an opponent has the queen of spades, try to flush it." The task of the FOO program is to take such general advice and render it directly applicable by a performance program. This task can be viewed as a kind of *planning* task. A piece of advice, such as "Avoid taking points," can be viewed as a goal. The operationalization program must develop an executable plan for achieving that goal. What makes this advice difficult to operationalize, however, is that the goal can be ill-defined and unattainable. It is impossible, for example, always to avoid taking points. Instead, the program must develop approximate strategies. The advice-giver intends the goal to *suggest*, but not *specify*, the desired behavior.

FOO is not able to accomplish this advice-taking task unaided. First, it does not perform the interpretation step at all but, instead, relies on the user to translate the English form of the advice into an unambiguous lambda-calculus representation. Second, FOO cannot perform the operationalization step without human assistance. Although FOO has a large knowledge base of transformation rules and an interpreter for applying those rules, it must be told by the user which rules to apply. The user must operate FOO by repeatedly selecting an appropriate rule and indicating which expression or subexpression should be transformed. Finally, FOO does not integrate the operational knowledge it develops into a knowledge base that could drive a Hearts-playing program. No performance element has been developed that could provide an empirical test of the operationalized knowledge. Despite these shortcomings, Mostow's work on FOO provides an in-depth analysis of the techniques required to perform operationalization.

The primary way in which advice is operationalized in FOO is by applying *operationalization methods*, such as heuristic search, the pigeonhole principle, and finding necessary or sufficient conditions. Mostow claims that this is precisely what knowledge engineers and AI researchers do when they are faced with a new problem to solve: They look in their bag of tricks for a method, such as worst-case analysis, that allows them to construct an effective, but inefficient, program. This program can then be further refined by applying other knowledge and advice. Mostow's work can thus be viewed as formalizing the knowledge and techniques used by AI researchers to do heuristic programming.

The most sophisticated of FOO's operationalization methods is the *heuristic-search method*. When FOO needs to evaluate a predicate, such as (TAKE–POINTS ME), over a sequence, such as the sequence of cards in a trick, it is able to reformulate this problem as a heuristic search of the space of all possible tricks. FOO starts with a basic generate-and-test algorithm (discussed in Article II.A, in Vol. I) and refines it into a heuristic search by improving the ways the algorithm (a) selects the next node to expand, (b) selects possible expansions of the node to apply, (c) prunes nodes from the search tree, and (d) prunes possible expansions prior to applying them. The overall effect of these refinements is to move constraints from the *test* portion of the algorithm, that is, the step that checks to see whether the goal has been achieved, into the *generate* portion of the algorithm, that is, the step that chooses which nodes to expand and how they should be expanded. Some refinements actually move constraints out of the search altogether by precompiling them into tables or by modifying the algorithm to search a smaller space.

In the "Avoid taking points" problem, for example, FOO starts with a simple generate-and-test algorithm that generates all possible tricks and tests to see if ME (FOO's performance persona) takes any points. This is gradually converted into a heuristic search in which the only tricks considered are those in which ME plays a card higher than any card played so far in the suit led. Additional heuristics, such as generating tricks that contain points first and pruning tricks in which the opponents play cards higher than ME, are extracted from the test and applied earlier in the search to order and prune the search tree.

Underlying all of FOO's operationalization methods is its basic ability to reformulate an expression in many different ways. For example, in order to evaluate (VOID P1 S1) (i.e., player P_1 is void in suit S_1), FOO must reformulate VOID in terms of observable variables such as the number of cards already played in the suit S_1. In order for FOO to *recognize* that an operationalization method is applicable, it must often do some reformulations. Then, in order actually to *apply* the method, FOO may need to do some further reformulations. The heuristic search method, for instance, is applicable only to a problem that is expressed as a search through some space. Consequently, in order to use heuristic search to operationalize the "Avoid taking points" advice, FOO must first reformulate the advice as a predicate over the search space of all possible tricks. The heuristic search can then search this space for those tricks that do not contain points.

The reformulation and operationalization process is accomplished by approximately 200 transformation rules (Mostow, in press). These rules employ analysis techniques and domain knowledge to successively reformulate the advice into an operational form. In this article, we trace a portion of FOO's operationalization of the "Avoid taking points" advice to show how these reformulation techniques are applied. Before doing this, however, we describe the knowledge that FOO has initially and how it is represented.

FOO's Initial Knowledge Base

FOO's performance knowledge is made up of *domain concepts*, plus *rules* and *heuristics* that are composed in terms of these concepts. The advice offered to the program likewise consists of domain concepts, plus *compositions* of concepts. So as long as these compositions of basic concepts can be described in general ways, both the performance knowledge and the advice for building and improving it can be used and manipulated by domain-independent methods (see Hayes-Roth et al., 1981, for further discussion).

For example, in the domain of the card game Hearts, *basic concepts* include:

> deck, hand, card, suit, spades, deal, round, trick, avoid, point, player, play, take, lead, win, follow suit.

Examples of advice in the form of behavioral *constraints* include:

> The lead of the first trick is by the player with the 2C.
> Each player must follow suit if possible.
> The player of the highest card in the suit led wins the trick.
> The winner of a trick leads the next trick.

Advice in the form of *heuristics* includes:

> If the queen of spades has not been played, then flush it out.
> Take all the points in a round.
> If you can't take all the points in a round, then take as few
>   as possible.
> If necessary, take a point to prevent someone else from taking
>   them all.

A constraint such as "The lead of the first trick is by the player with the 2C" is represented as a composition, using domain-independent concepts like *first* and *with* and domain-dependent concepts like *lead, trick, player,* and *2C.*

An Example: Operationalizing "Avoid Taking Points"

After advice has been *interpreted* into an internal representation that is precise and unambiguous, it might be in an operational form, for example, "Play a low card." On the other hand, it may be far more general: "Avoid taking points." Experienced Hearts players will recognize that the first, specific piece of advice is a possible strategy for carrying out the latter, general advice. But it is a rather simplistic strategy, more appropriate for the later stages of a game than for the beginning. Furthermore, repeated attempts to play low cards will sometimes conflict with other advice. For purposes of illustration, however, operationalizing even a quite simple goal can require a wide range of knowledge and methods (see Mostow, 1981; Hayes-Roth et al., 1981). For the remainder of this article, several of the methods and problems of operationalization will be illustrated by showing how advice such as this can be converted into directly executable procedures.

First, consider how a person might handle advice such as "Avoid taking points." He might apply it to a specific situation by reasoning as follows:

1. To avoid taking points in general, I should avoid taking any points in the current *trick* (a single round in which one card is played by each player).

2. Thus, if the trick contains *points* (either a heart or the queen of spades), I should try not to win it.

3. I can do this by trying not to play the winning card.

4. That can be done by my playing a card lower than some other card played in the suit led.

Each step above is an attempt to implement the previous statement as closely as possible by restatement in successively more specific, operational terms. Some restatements may fully preserve the truth or accuracy of the previous one, while others may be very suppositional (i.e., valid given certain assumptions) or more restrictive (i.e., valid only in certain situations). The final statement above is not a very sophisticated plan, but it is at least a reasonable operationalization of the initial advice, and it represents a kind of process that seems very common in human learning. A *problem-reduction* strategy is employed until the advice can be applied directly in the given situation.

Now that we have a sense of how a person might operationalize "Avoid taking points," we trace the methods applied by FOO to accomplish this task. The following example is based on Derivation 6 in Mostow (1981) in which he guided FOO to reformulate "Avoid taking points" as "Play a low card." This particular trace shows the use of several simple operationalization and reformulation methods but does not show the application of the heuristic-search method discussed above.

To begin with, the advice must be *interpreted* into a tractable representational form, such as:

(avoid (take-points me) (trick))

That is, "Avoid the event in which ME takes points during the current trick." In FOO, this is done manually by the advice-giver.

A useful beginning in operationalization is to *elaborate* the original advice by expanding definitions (first of "avoid" and then of "trick"). The point is to unfold high-level terms so that the expression can be more easily manipulated. The results are

```
[achieve (not (during (trick) (take-points me)))]
```
and
```
(achieve (not (during [scenario
                        (each p (players)(play-card p))
                        (take-trick (trick-winner))]
                        (take-points me)))).
```

The advice in this form is still not operational, since it depends on the outcome of the trick, which is not generally knowable at the time ME needs to choose an action in accordance with the advice. Therefore, a *case analysis* is done on the subexpression (during...). The idea is to reformulate a single concept as several disjoint expressions that can be evaluated separately. To this end, the single (during...) expression is split into two expressions that depend on alternative assumptions. Here, taking points during the two-part "scenario" above can be considered as either of two possible cases: that taking points occurs during (a) the playing of cards or (b) the taking of the trick. The transformation results in:

```
(achieve (not (or [during (each p (players) (play-card p))
                          (take-points me)]
                   [during (take-trick (trick-winner))
                          (take-points me)]))).
```

The next transformation eliminates impossible cases. When expressions cannot be achieved because of impossible conditions, the learner should recognize this and drop them from consideration. Here, the first case can be ignored because there is no way to take points during the play of the cards (it is possible only after all players have played, when the trick is taken). FOO recognizes this by an *intersection search*. It searches through the knowledge base of defined concepts for a common subevent of the two events (each p (players) (play-card p)) and (take-points me). Since no common subevent is found for these two, FOO concludes that the situation is an impossible one and eliminates it. (For the second case, take-trick and take-points have a common sub-event, take.) The advice now is:

```
(achieve (not [during (take-trick (trick-winner))
                       (take-points me)])).
```

The advice is still far from operational. One difficulty is that neither take-trick nor trick-winner is immediately evaluable at the time a card must be chosen for play. At this point, the problem can be reduced by reexpressing different concepts in *common terms*. This is possible here by again elaborating definitions and restructuring the subexpressions. Since take-points occurs during take-trick, the expression can be reformulated as:

```
(achieve (not [exists c1 (cards-played)
                      (exists c2 (point-cards)
                              (during (take (trick-winner) c1)
                                      (take me c2)))])).
```

This says, "Make sure the situation does not happen where ME takes a point card (c2) during the time that the winner of the trick takes the cards played."

A process of *partial matching* recognizes that the two events in the during subexpression are closely related and thus are candidates for simplification, depending on the constraints of the during predicate. Using domain knowledge of relationships among the concepts, the terms can be combined and the subexpression made less complex. Instead of the complicated relation during, the events become joined by the far simpler predicates = and and. We now have:

```
(achieve (not (exists c1 (cards-played)
                      (exists c2 (point-cards)
                              [and (= (trick-winner) me)(= c1 c2)])))).
```

Further analysis at this point shows that *simplification* of some forms is possible. The central purpose of searching for simplifications is to *restructure* expressions to make them more amenable to further analysis. Examples of simplifying methods are deleting null clauses from a disjunction, transforming an expression into a constant (by evaluation), applying logical transformations (such as De Morgan's laws), or removing quantifiers when possible. The last of these methods is appropriate here, since c1 and c2 denote the same object: a point card. Thus with some reformulation employing domain knowledge, one variable can be replaced by the other, and the condition that they be equal can be dropped. The expression is transformed into:

```
(achieve (not [and (= (trick-winner) me)
                   (exists c1 (cards-played)
                           (in c1 (point-cards)))])).
```

Another kind of pattern-matching can accomplish another kind of simplification: By looking for canonical constructions, the operationalizer can *recognize known concepts.* If the form of a lower level expression fits the definition of a higher level concept, the former can be replaced by its simpler equivalent. (Note that this is the inverse of the first transformation mentioned above: expanding definitions.) In this case, the last two lines of the above expression match the definition of `trick-has-points`. This is analogous to the psychological process of *chunking.* In addition to all the analytical advantages gained by simplification, the recognition of known concepts can also enable the application of previously learned knowledge about them (e.g., ways to predict the likelihood that a trick will have points in it). Our expression is now reduced to not winning a trick that has points:

```
(achieve (not (and (= (trick-winner) me) [trick-has-points]))).
```

The expression is still not operational, since `trick-winner` is not generally knowable at the time of choosing which card to play. The concept of `trick-winner` is further analyzed, and, in fact, it takes about 20 further transformations to reformulate the above expression, "Try not to win a trick that has points," into "If you're following suit in a trick with points, try to play lower than some other card played in the suit led." Symbolically, this looks like:

```
(achieve (⇒ [and (in-suit-led (card-of me))
                  (trick-has-points)]
            [lower (card-of me)
                   (find-element (cards-played-in-suit-led))])).
```

But this still is not operational, since in general the set `cards-played-in-suit-led` is not fully known at the time that ME must choose a card. Since Hearts is a game of imperfect information, this set cannot generally be known, but the data available (cards already played) can be used to *approximate* the result. Here, the binary relation `lower` is approximated by the unary predicate `low`. In other words, in the absence of complete information for evaluating a comparative predicate (`lower x1 x2`), use instead an estimating function (`low x1`) that may not be exact but can produce a result from the available data. The approximation is:

```
(achieve (⇒ (and (in-suit-led (card-of me))
                 (trick-has-points))
            [low (card-of me)])).
```

This is now very close to being operational. `Low` is an imprecise term but can be treated as a *fuzzy* predicate (see Zadeh, 1979)—that is, it could be used to order potential candidates for the choice variable, `card-of me`.

The only remaining barrier to full operationality is the predicate (`trick-has-points`). This also is not always knowable at the time of choosing a card to play. However, further analysis leads to application of a rule that formulates an assertion as `possible` (effectively assuming it to be true) in the absence of any knowledge to the contrary. Even when a predicate p is not evaluable, (possible p) will be.

Thus, the fully operational (though approximate) reformulation of the original "Avoid taking points" is "If following suit in a trick that may have points, play a low card." Again, the result may not always be the most effective action and may be in conflict with other advice. These are issues to be decided by the evaluating module of the learning element and by the performance element of the program. The symbolic form of the operationalized advice is:

```
(achieve (⇒ [and (in-suit-led (card-of me))
                 [possible (trick-has-points)]]
            [low (card-of me)])).
```

Conclusion

The example given above is a useful one because of the diversity of its reformulations, not because of any completeness. Among the most useful contributions of this research has been an introduction to the considerable complexity of operationalizing advice. Of the 13 examples of operationalized advice given in Mostow's thesis (1981), a couple required only a handful of transformations (a minimum of 8), but several required over 100. About 10 domain-independent transformational rules were mentioned in the example above, but over 200 such rules have been formulated and included in the system. Mostow (1981) gives a taxonomy of operationalization methods according to their *purpose*, *scope*, and *accuracy*. This taxonomy is outlined in Figure C2–1; each category is illustrated by one or more methods.

The greatest shortcoming of the work on FOO is the lack of a control structure that could apply these operationalization methods automatically. The development of such a control regime may be quite difficult. Mostow suggests using means-ends analysis (see Article II.D2, in Vol. I) and describes how his execution of rules often conformed to the following pattern:

1. *Reformulate* an expression until it is possible to
2. *recognize* that the method is applicable and decide to apply it, so
3. *reformulate* the expression to match the method problem statement and
4. *fill in* additional information required by the method; then
5. *refine* the instantiated method by applying additional domain knowledge.

A second shortcoming of FOO is that its methods are quite specific to the game of Hearts and similar tasks. The development of a general-purpose operationalization program will require the explication of many more operationalization methods. Still, these first steps in operationalization should prove valuable either for the overall project of *machine-aided heuristic programming* (see the beginning of this article) or for future efforts at implementing advice-taking systems.

1. **Methods for evaluating an expression**

   a. Procedures that always produce a result (assuming their inputs
      are available)
      "Pigeonhole principle"
      "Historical reasoning"
      "Heuristic search"

   b. Procedures that sometimes produce a result
      "Check a necessary or sufficient condition"
      "Make a simplifying assumption that restricts the scope
      of applicability"

   c. Procedures that produce an approximate result
      "Apply formula for probability that randomly chosen
      subsets overlap"
      "Characterize a quantity as an increasing or decreasing
      function of some variable"
      "Use an untested simplifying assumption"
      "Predict others' choices pessimistically"

2. **Methods for achieving a goal**

   a. Sound methods (introduce no errors)—execution of plan (when
      feasible) will achieve goal
      "To empty a set, remove one element at a time"
      "Find a sufficient condition and achieve it"
      "Restrict a choice to satisfy the goal"
      "Modify a plan for one goal to achieve an additional goal"
      "To achieve a goal with a future deadline, satisfy it now
      and then avoid violating it"

   b. Heuristic methods—execution of plan may not always
      achieve goal
      "Simplify the goal by arbitrarily choosing a value for
      one of its variables"
      "Find a necessary condition and achieve it"
      "Order choice set with respect to goal"

Figure C2–1.   Taxonomy of operationalization methods.

References

Mostow (1981) is the most comprehensive description of FOO. The articles by Hayes-Roth, Klahr, and Mostow (1980, 1981) and by Hayes-Roth, Klahr, Burge, and Mostow (1978) provide a good overview of the idea of machine-aided heuristic programming. Mostow (in press) describes the work on heuristic search.

D. LEARNING FROM EXAMPLES

D1. Issues

THE PROSPECT of creating a program that can learn from examples has attracted the attention of AI researchers since the 1950s. McCarthy (1958, p. 78) said, "Our ultimate objective is to make programs that learn from their experience as effectively as humans do." Of course, the attainment of this goal still lies in the distant future. The area of learning from examples is, however, the best understood aspect of learning.

A program that learns from examples must reason from specific instances to general rules that can be used to guide the actions of the performance element. The learning element is presented with very low level information, in the form of a specific situation and the appropriate behavior for the performance element in that situation, and it is expected to *generalize* this information to obtain general rules of behavior.

Consider, for example, a program that is learning to play checkers. One way to train the program is to present it with particular checkers-board situations and tell it what the best moves are. The program must generalize from these particular moves to discover strategies for good play. Similarly, if we are teaching a program the concept of a *dog*, for example, we might present the program with various animals (and other things) and tell it whether or not they are dogs. The program must develop general rules for recognizing dogs and distinguishing them from everything else in the world.

Simon and Lea (1974), in an important early paper on induction, describe the problem of learning from examples as the problem of using training instances, selected from some space of possible instances, to guide a search for general rules. They call the space of possible training instances the *instance space* and the space of possible general rules the *rule space*. Furthermore, Simon and Lea point out that an intelligent program might select its own training instances by actively searching the instance space in order to resolve some ambiguity about the rules in the rule space. Thus, if the program were unsure whether all dogs have four legs, it might search the instance space for animals with different numbers of legs to see which ones are dogs. Simon and Lea view a learning system as moving back and forth between an instance space and a rule space until it has converged on the desired rule.

This *two-space view* of learning from examples as a simultaneous, cooperative search of the instance space and the rule space is a good perspective for organizing this article. We will use the terms *instance space* and *rule space* even in situations where the rule space does not contain rules but, instead,

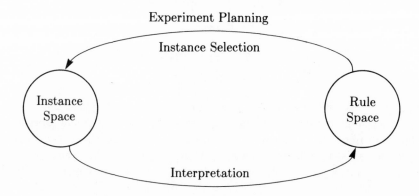

Figure D1–1.   The two-space model of learning from examples.

contains some other high-level descriptions of the knowledge needed by the performance element.

   Figure D1–1 shows a schematic diagram of the two-space model of learning from examples. In addition to the instance space and the rule space, the processes of *interpretation* and *experiment planning* are depicted. In some learning situations, the training instances are provided in a form far removed from the form of the rules in the rule space. As a result, when the program moves from the instance space to the rule space, special processes are needed to interpret the raw training instances so that they can guide the search of the rule space. Similarly, when the program needs to gather some new training instances, special experiment-planning routines are needed so that the current high-level hypotheses can guide the search of the instance space.

   As an example of the two-space model, consider the problem of teaching a computer program the concept of a *flush* in poker (i.e., a hand in which all five cards have the same suit). The instance space in this learning problem is the space of all possible poker hands. We can represent an individual point in this space as a set of five ordered pairs, for example,

$$\{(2, clubs), (3, clubs), (5, clubs), (jack, clubs), (king, clubs)\}.$$

Each ordered pair specifies the rank and suit of one of the cards in the hand. The entire instance space is the space of all such five-card sets.

   The rule space in this problem could be the space of all predicate calculus expressions composed of the predicates SUIT and RANK; the variables c_1, c_2, c_3, c_4, c_5 for the cards; any necessary free variables; the constant values of *clubs, diamonds, hearts, spades, ace, 2, 3, 4, 5, 6, 7, 8, 9, 10, jack, queen,* and *king;* the conjunction operator $(\wedge)$; and the existential quantifier $(\exists)$. This rule space includes concepts such as *contains at least three cards of the same rank:*

$$\exists \; c_1, c_2, c_3 : \text{RANK}(c_1, x) \wedge \text{RANK}(c_2, x) \wedge \text{RANK}(c_3, x) \,,$$

and also the desired concept of a *flush:*

$$\exists \; c_1, c_2, c_3, c_4, c_5 : \text{SUIT}(c_1, x) \wedge \text{SUIT}(c_2, x) \wedge \text{SUIT}(c_3, x) \wedge$$
$$\text{SUIT}(c_4, x) \wedge \text{SUIT}(c_5, x) \,.$$

Note that this rule space does *not* contain the concept of a *straight.*

A learning program for searching these two spaces might operate as follows. First, the program selects a training instance from the instance space and asks the teacher whether it is an instance of the desired concept. This information (the instance and its classification) is converted by the interpretation procedures into a form that can help guide the search of the rule space. When some plausible candidate concepts are found in the rule space, experiment-planning routines decide which training instances should be examined next. If the learning program works properly, it will eventually choose, as its best candidate concept, the flush concept shown above.

Learning systems that employ the two-space approach are making use of the *closed-world assumption,* that is, the assumption that the rule space contains the desired concept. The closed-world assumption allows programs to locate the desired concept by progressively excluding candidate concepts that are known to be incorrect.

This two-space view of learning from examples helps to elucidate many of the design issues for learning systems. In this article, we follow this two-space model full circle. We examine, in turn, the issues concerning the instance space, the interpretation process, the rule space, and the experiment-planning process.

Instance Space

The first issue involving the instance space is the *quality* of the training instances. High-quality training instances are unambiguous and thus provide reliable guidance to the search of the rule space. Low-quality training instances invite multiple, conflicting interpretations and, consequently, provide only tentative guidance to the rule-space search.

Consider again the problem of teaching a program the concept of a *flush.* There are several sources of ambiguity that could make it difficult for the program to discover the concept from training instances.

First, the instances may contain errors. If the descriptions of the instances are incorrect, for example, if a 2 of clubs is incorrectly observed to be a 2 of spades, the error is a *measurement error.* If, on the other hand, the classification of the hand (as being a flush or not being a flush) is incorrect, the error is a *classification error.* Two kinds of classification errors can occur. The program can be told that a sample hand is a flush when in fact it is not—a *false positive* instance—or that it is not a flush when in fact it is—a *false negative* instance.

A second source of ambiguity arises if the program must learn from *unclassified training instances*. In these so-called *unsupervised learning situations*, the program is given heuristic information that it must use to classify the training instances itself. If this heuristic knowledge is weak and imperfect, the rule-space search must treat the resulting classifications as being potentially incorrect.

A third factor relating to the quality of the training instances is the *order in which they are presented*. A good training sequence systematically varies the relevant features to determine which features are important. When a program is selecting training instances, it attempts to construct a good training sequence for itself. The task of learning is made much easier if there is a teacher who can be counted on to perform this function. In such cases, a program can reason about a puzzling instance by trying to infer "what the teacher was getting at" in presenting the example.

The main point, then, is that high-quality training instances are unambiguous. Under such favorable conditions, the program can be designed to embody a whole set of constraining assumptions about the examples that permit it to locate rapidly the appropriate high-level rules in the rule space. Low-quality instances, again, are ambiguous, because the program must consider a much larger space of hypotheses. Thus, if it is possible that the training instances contain errors, the program must consider the hypothesis that any given instance is incorrect due to either measurement error or classification error. In general, the more constraints a program can assume about the data, the more easily it can learn from them.

The second design issue concerning the instance space is the question of how it should be searched. This issue has not received much attention in AI research, since most work has assumed either that the instances are presented all at once or else that the program has no control over their selection. (See, however, Rissland and Soloway, 1980, for recent work on instance selection.) Programs that can update their hypotheses as additional training instances are selected (or are made available by the environment) are said to perform *incremental learning*. Programs that explicitly search the instance space are said to perform *active instance selection*.

Most methods of searching the instance space make use of a set, *H*, of hypotheses in the rule space that are currently believed by the program to be most plausible. One approach is to try to *discriminate* as much as possible among the alternatives within *H*. A training instance can be chosen that "splits *H* in half," so that half of the hypotheses can be ruled out when the new instance is obtained. Another approach is to choose the most likely hypothesis in *H* and try to *confirm* it by checking additional training instances (particularly instances with extreme characteristics). Using a confirmatory strategy, the learning system can determine the limits of applicability of the hypothesis under consideration. A third approach, called *expectation-based filtering*, selects training instances that *contradict* the hypotheses in *H* (see Lenat, Hayes-Roth, and Klahr, 1979). The hypotheses in *H* are used to filter out those instances that are expected to be true (i.e., those that are consistent with *H*), so that the learning program can focus its attention on those instances in which its current hypotheses break down. Finally, an important consideration may be the size of *H*, or other computational costs associated with the learning process. In such cases, new instances may be selected to *minimize* these computational costs. For example, the program might try to rule out only one factor at a time in order to reduce the cost of comparing a drastically different training instance with each hypothesis in *H*.

Interpretation Processes

Once the training instances have been selected, they may need to be transformed before they can be used to guide the search of the rule space. This transformation process can be quite difficult, especially in perceptual learning tasks. Suppose, for example, that we wish to train a computer to recognize the concept of an arch constructed from toy blocks. The program will be presented with a line drawing of a scene involving a structure of blocks and told whether or not the scene contains an arch. Winston's (1970) program that solves this learning task (see Article XIV.D3a) makes extensive use of "blocks-world knowledge" to interpret the line drawing and extract a relational graph structure that indicates which blocks are resting on top of which other blocks, which blocks are touching, and so forth. These are the relations needed to express the concept of an arch.

Another learning program that performs extensive interpretation of the training instances is Soloway's (1978) BASEBALL system. The raw training instances are roughly 2,000 noise-free "snapshots" of a baseball game. The snapshots give the locations of the nine players on the two teams (e.g., (AT P1 FIRST-BASE)), the location of the ball, and the state of the scoreboard. The program is composed of a sequence of nine steps that employ various kinds of knowledge to interpret and generalize the training instances. The first three steps apply general knowledge about games to filter out periods of inactivity and focus on cycles of high activity. The next three steps apply knowledge about physics and about competition and cooperation to interpret these cycles of activity as competitive or cooperative episodes. To identify these episodes, the program must assign goals to the different players (e.g., (WANT-TO-EXECUTE (AT P1 FIRST-BASE))). It also guesses that the overall goal of an episode is that of the last action taken by a player. The final three steps search the rule space to discover generalized episodes and episode goals such as *hit* and *out*. These concepts are far removed from the original training instances, but because the previous steps have properly interpreted the data in terms of goals and actions, this rule-space search is easily accomplished.

The basic purpose of interpreting the training instances is to extract information that is useful for guiding the search of the rule space. This usually involves converting the raw training instances into a representational form that allows syntactic generalization to be easily accomplished (see below).

Rule Space

Two main issues are related to the rule space of high-level knowledge: What is the space, and how can it be searched? The rule space is usually defined by specifying the kinds of operators and terms that can be used to represent a rule. The designer of a learning system seeks to choose a rule space that is easy to search and that contains the desired rule or rules. In the sections that follow, we first discuss two factors that influence the choice of a representation language for the rule space: the kinds of inference supported by the representation and the single-representation trick. Then we survey the four methods for searching the rule space. We conclude the discussion of rule-space issues by examining problems that arise when the representation is found to be inadequate for expressing the desired rule or rules.

Syntactic rules of inference. Both the expressiveness of a representation and the ease of searching the rule space depend on the kind and complexity of the inferences supported by the representation. The most common inference process needed for learning from examples is *generalization*. We say that one description, *A*, is *more general than* another description, *B*, if *A* applies in all of the situations in which *B* applies and then some more. Thus, the set of situations in which *A* is relevant is a superset of the set of situations in which *B* is relevant. For example, the rule that *All ravens are black* is more general than the rule that *All one-eyed ravens are black*, since the set of all ravens strictly includes the set of one-eyed ravens. Often, a description *A* is more general than a description *B* because *A* places fewer constraints on any relevant situations. The *all ravens* rule omits the *one-eyed* constraint and, hence, is more general.

It is important to choose a representation for the rule space in which generalization can be accomplished by inexpensive syntactic operations. Predicate calculus, for example, is quite amenable to certain kinds of syntactic generalization. Below are some examples of syntactic rules of inference that accomplish generalization in predicate calculus. Some recent work in learning (Larson, 1977; Larson and Michalski, 1977; Michalski, 1980) has sought to identify rules of inference that are particularly useful in learning systems. It is important to note that these rules of inference do not preserve truth—the rules are inductive.

1. **Turning constants to variables.** Suppose we want a program to discover the concept of a flush in poker. We might give some training instances of the form:

Instance 1. SUIT(c_1, *clubs*) $\wedge$ SUIT(c_2, *clubs*) $\wedge$
SUIT(c_3, *clubs*) $\wedge$ SUIT(c_4, *clubs*) $\wedge$
SUIT(c_5, *clubs*) $\Rightarrow$ FLUSH(c_1, c_2, c_3, c_4, c_5).

Instance 2. SUIT(c_1, *spades*) $\wedge$ SUIT(c_2, *spades*) $\wedge$
SUIT(c_3, *spades*) $\wedge$ SUIT(c_4, *spades*) $\wedge$
SUIT(c_5, *spades*) $\Rightarrow$ FLUSH(c_1, c_2, c_3, c_4, c_5).

From these, the program could hypothesize the rule

Rule 1. SUIT(c_1, x) $\wedge$ SUIT(c_2, x) $\wedge$ SUIT(c_3, x) $\wedge$ SUIT(c_4, x) $\wedge$
SUIT(c_5, x) $\Rightarrow$ FLUSH(c_1, c_2, c_3, c_4, c_5).

by replacing the atomic constants of clubs and spades by the variable x (where x stands for any suit).

2. **Dropping conditions.** Suppose again that we are teaching a program the concept of a flush, but now we present instances of the form:

Instance 1. SUIT(c_1, *clubs*) $\wedge$ RANK($c_1, 3$) $\wedge$
SUIT(c_2, *clubs*) $\wedge$ RANK($c_2, 5$) $\wedge$
SUIT(c_3, *clubs*) $\wedge$ RANK($c_3, 7$) $\wedge$
SUIT(c_4, *clubs*) $\wedge$ RANK($c_4, 10$) $\wedge$
SUIT(c_5, *clubs*) $\wedge$ RANK(c_5, *king*)
$\Rightarrow$ FLUSH(c_1, c_2, c_3, c_4, c_5).

In order to discover rule 1, the program must not only turn constants into variables, but it must also "forget" all of the RANK predicates, since rank is irrelevant. This can be accomplished by *dropping conditions*. Any conjunction can be generalized by dropping one of its conditions. We can view a conjunctive condition as a constraint on the set of possible instances that could satisfy the description. By dropping a condition, we are removing a constraint and generalizing the rule.

3. **Adding options.** A further way to generalize a rule is to add another option to the rule so that more instances may conceivably satisfy it. Suppose we are trying to teach a program the concept of a *face card* (i.e., jack, queen, or king). We might give examples of the form:

Instance 1. RANK(c_1, *jack*) $\Rightarrow$ FACE(c_1).
Instance 2. RANK(c_1, *queen*) $\Rightarrow$ FACE(c_1).
Instance 3. RANK(c_1, *king*) $\Rightarrow$ FACE(c_1).

The program can discover the rule by forming the disjunction of the possibilities:

Rule 2. RANK(c_1, *jack*) $\vee$ RANK(c_1, *queen*) $\vee$ RANK(c_1, *king*)
$\Rightarrow$ FACE(c_1).

Notice that this decision to add options is a less drastic generalization than that of turning the jack, queen, and king constants into a single variable to get

Rule 3 (wrong). RANK(c_1, y) $\Rightarrow$ FACE(c_1).

An alternative to ordinary disjunction is what Michalski (1980) terms an *internal disjunction*. If we allow sets and set membership in our representation, we can express our instances as

Instance 1'. $\text{RANK}(c_1) \in \{jack\}$ $\Rightarrow$ $\text{FACE}(c_1)$.
Instance 2'. $\text{RANK}(c_1) \in \{queen\}$ $\Rightarrow$ $\text{FACE}(c_1)$.
Instance 3'. $\text{RANK}(c_1) \in \{king\}$ $\Rightarrow$ $\text{FACE}(c_1)$.

The generalization can then be expressed as

Rule 2'. $\text{RANK}(c_1) \in \{jack,\ queen,\ king\}$ $\Rightarrow$ $\text{FACE}(c_1)$.

This latter representation is more compact.

Similar rules of generalization can be defined for numerical representations that use a linear combination of features, as follows:

4. **Curve fitting.** Suppose a program is attempting to discover how the output, z, of a system is related to two inputs, x and y. The program is provided with training instances in the form of (x, y, z) triples that show the output of the system for particular values of the inputs:

Instance 1. $(0, 2, 7)$.
Instance 2. $(6, -1, 10)$.
Instance 3. $(-1, -5, -16)$.

By a curve-fitting technique, such as least-squares regression, the program fits the line

Rule 1. $z = 2x + 3y + 1$,

or, alternately, the ordered triple $(x, y, 2x + 3y + 1)$, to these data. This generalizes the relationship, so that it holds for many more (x, y, z) triples than just the three training instances. The program can now predict the z output for any values of the x and y inputs. This process is analogous to the turning-constants-into-variables generalization rule.

5. **Zeroing a coefficient.** The program can further generalize this relationship by zeroing the y coefficient and fitting a plane to the three training instances. In this case, it obtains

Rule 2. $z = 2.59x - 3.99$.

Alternately, the ordered triple is $(x, y, 2.59x - 3.99)$. (The y coordinate can be anything.) By giving y the coefficient of zero, the program has dropped it as a condition and reduced the dimensionality of the function $z = F(x, y)$ to make it $z = G(x)$. The program has decided that y is irrelevant to the value of z. The relationship now holds for an even larger set of (x, y, z) triples. This rule is analogous to the dropping-condition rule of generalization.

Notice that these rules of inference correspond to particular features of the representation language. For example, the method of turning constants into variables makes use of free variables, the method of adding options uses the disjunction operator, and the coefficient-zeroing technique makes use of the multiplication operator. To the extent that the representation language has fewer of these features, fewer inference rules will be applicable and, consequently, the search of the rule space will be easier to accomplish. But since each of these language features contributes to the expressiveness of the representation, the designer of a learning system faces a trade-off between the increased expressiveness of the representation and the increased difficulty of searching the rule space.

The single-representation trick. Another factor relating to the difficulty of searching the rule space (and the instance space) is the difference between the representation used for rules and the representation used for the training instances. If the representations for the rule space and the instance space are far removed from each other, then the searches of the two spaces must be coordinated by complex interpretation and experiment-planning procedures. One trick commonly used to avoid this problem is to choose the same representation for both spaces. Training instances are viewed literally as highly specific pieces of acquired knowledge. Suppose, for example, that we are trying to teach a program the concept of a *pair* in poker. We want the program to learn the rule

Rule 4. $\exists$ $card_1, card_2$: RANK($card_1, x$) $\wedge$ RANK($card_2, x$) $\Rightarrow$ PAIR.

(This is only an approximate definition of PAIR. An exact definition would require a more complex representation involving equality.)

As was shown above, specific hands could be represented "naturally" as sets of five ordered pairs—the rank and suit of each of the cards. With such a representation for the hand made up of the 2 of clubs, 3 of diamonds, 2 of hearts, 6 of spades, and king of hearts, we would obtain

Instance 1. $\{(2, clubs), (3, diamonds), (2, hearts), (6, spades), (king, hearts)\}$
     $\Rightarrow$ PAIR.

But this representation makes it difficult to discover the concept of a pair in poker with the syntactic rules of inference described above. A less natural, but more useful, representation would describe the hand in predicate calculus— the same representation that we will eventually need for the acquired concept (rule 4). Thus, we would say of our hand

Instance 1′. $\exists$ c_1, c_2, c_3, c_4, c_5 : RANK($c_1, 2$) $\wedge$ SUIT($c_1, clubs$) $\wedge$
                        RANK($c_2, 3$) $\wedge$ SUIT($c_2, diamonds$) $\wedge$
                        RANK($c_3, 2$) $\wedge$ SUIT($c_3, hearts$) $\wedge$
                        RANK($c_4, 6$) $\wedge$ SUIT($c_4, spades$) $\wedge$
                        RANK(c_5, K) $\wedge$ SUIT($c_5, hearts$) $\Rightarrow$ PAIR.

Now the process of generalization merely involves dropping the SUIT conditions and replacing the constant 2 by a variable x. Of course, there are many other possible generalizations of instance 1′, and the search of the rule space would still be nontrivial. The advantage of using the single-representation trick is that we have chosen a representation that allows this search to be accomplished by simple syntactic processes.

The problems of interpretation and experiment planning are eased when the single-representation trick is used. Many learning programs sidestep these problems completely by assuming that the training instances are provided by the environment in the same representation as used for the rule space. In more practical situations, the interpretation and experiment-planning routines serve to translate between the *raw* instances (as they are received from the environment) and the *derived* instances (after they have been interpreted as specific points in the rule space).

Methods of searching the rule space. Now that we have discussed the issue of how to represent the rule space, we can turn our attention to the four main methods that have been used to search the rule space. All of these methods maintain a set, H, of the *currently most plausible rules*. They differ primarily in how they refine the set H so that it eventually includes the desired points in the rule space. A useful classification of search methods distinguishes methods in which the presentation of the training instances drives the search (so-called *data-driven methods*) from those methods in which an a priori model guides the search (so-called *model-driven methods*).

The first data-driven method is the *version-space method* (and several related techniques). This approach uses the single-representation trick to represent training instances as very specific points in the rule space. The set H is initialized to contain all hypotheses consistent with the first positive training instance. New training instances are examined one at a time and pattern-matched against H to determine whether the hypotheses in H should be generalized or specialized.

The second method, also a data-driven method, does not use the single-representation trick. Instead, special procedures (or production rules) examine the set of training instances and decide how to refine the current set, H, of hypotheses. The program can be viewed as having a set of *hypothesis-refinement operators*. In each cycle, it uses the data to choose one of these operators and then applies it. Lenat's (1976) AM system is an example of this approach.

The third approach is *model-driven generate and test*. This method repeatedly generates and tests hypotheses from the rule space against the training instances. Model-based knowledge is used to constrain the hypothesis generator to generate only plausible hypotheses. The Meta-DENDRAL program is the best example of this approach (see Buchanan and Mitchell, 1978).

Finally, the fourth approach is *model-driven schema instantiation*. It uses a set of *rule schemas* to provide general constraints on the form of plausible rules. The method attempts to instantiate these schemas from the current set of training instances. The instantiated schema that best fits the training instances is considered the most plausible rule. Dietterich's SPARC program

(Dieterich, 1979; Dieterich and Michalski, in press), which discovers secret rules in the card game Eleusis, applies the schema-instantiation method.

Data-driven techniques generally have the advantage of supporting incremental learning. A feature of the version space method, in particular, is that the H set can easily be modified to account for new training instances without any backtracking by the learning program. In contrast, model-driven methods, which test and reject hypotheses based on an examination of the whole body of data, are difficult to use in incremental learning situations. When new training instances become available, model-driven methods must either backtrack or search the rule space again, because the criteria by which hypotheses were originally tested (or schemas instantiated) have changed.

A strength of model-driven methods, on the other hand, is that they tend to have good noise immunity. When a set of hypotheses, H, is tested against noisy training instances, the model-driven methods need not reject a hypothesis on the basis of one or two counterexamples. Since the whole set of training instances is available, the program can use statistical measures of how well a proposed hypothesis accounts for the data. In data-driven methods, H is revised each time on the basis of the current training instance. Consequently, a single erroneous instance can cause a large perturbation in H (from which it may never recover). One approach that allows data-driven methods to handle noise is to make very slight, conservative changes in H in response to each training instance. This minimizes the effect of any erroneous training instances, but it causes the learning system to learn much more slowly.

The problem of new terms. In some learning problems, the program can assume that the desired rule or rules exist somewhere in the rule space. Consequently, the search has a well-defined goal. In many situations, however, there is no such guarantee, and the learning program must confront the possibility that its representation of the rule space is inadequate and should be expanded. This is called the problem of *new terms*.

One approach to expanding the rule space is to add new terms to the representation. Consider again the problem of teaching a program the concept of a *pair* in poker. In the section above, the program was able to represent the *pair* concept by using a predicate-calculus representation with the suit and rank terms. Such a representation would not permit the program to discover the concept of a *straight*, however. One way to represent the *straight* concept would be to create a new term called $\text{SUCC}(x, y)$, which is true if and only if $x = y + 1$. Now the *straight* concept can be represented as:

$$\text{RANK}(c_1, r_1) \wedge \text{RANK}(c_2, r_2) \wedge \text{RANK}(c_3, r_3) \wedge \text{RANK}(c_4, r_4) \wedge \text{RANK}(c_5, r_5) \wedge$$
$$\text{SUCC}(r_1, r_2) \wedge \text{SUCC}(r_2, r_3) \wedge \text{SUCC}(r_3, r_4) \wedge \text{SUCC}(r_4, r_5).$$

The problem of defining new terms is quite difficult to solve. An advantage of the hypothesis-refinement operator approach to searching the rule space is that it is fairly easy to incorporate operators that create new terms. The

BACON (Langley, 1980) and AM programs both have operators that create new terms by combining and refining existing terms.

Experiment Planning

Once the learning element has searched the rule space and developed a set, H, of plausible hypotheses, the program may need to gather more training instances to test and refine them. When the instance space and the rule space are represented in very different ways, the process of determining which training instances are needed and how they can be obtained can be quite involved. Suppose, for example, that a genetics learning program is attempting to discover which portions of DNA are important. To test a high-level hypothesis (or several hypotheses), it may be necessary to plan a very involved experiment to synthesize a particular strand of DNA and insert it into the appropriate bacterial cells to observe the resulting behavior of the cells.

The AM program is an example of an AI learning program that performs some experiment planning. After one of AM's refinement operators creates a new concept, AM must gather examples of that concept to evaluate and refine it. Several techniques are used to generate good training instances, for example, by symbolically instantiating the concept definition or by inheriting examples from more general or more specific concepts. AM has a special body of heuristics for locating positive and negative boundary examples (i.e., examples that barely succeed, or barely fail, to be instances of the concept).

Taxonomy of Work in Learning from Examples

Now that we have described the two-space model, we present a rough taxonomy of work in the area of learning from examples. Several subareas of research have developed within this area, ranging from philosophically oriented inductive learning to highly engineering-oriented pattern-classification work. These different areas can be characterized by two components of the simple learning model presented in Article XIV.A: the representation used in the knowledge base and the task that the performance element carries out. In the remainder of this chapter, a separate article is devoted to each of these subareas.

Systems that use numerical representations. Researchers in electrical engineering and systems theory have developed learning methods that represent acquired knowledge in the form of polynomials and matrices. The performance elements of these learning systems, which are usually called *adaptive systems*, typically perform tasks such as pattern classification, adaptive control, and adaptive filtering. The strengths of these adaptive methods are that they can be used in noisy environments, in environments whose properties are changing rapidly, and in situations where analytic solutions based on classical systems theory are unavailable. We include an article on this subject because of its historical relationship to AI and because of the possibility that useful hybrid systems may be constructed in the future.

Systems that use symbolic representations. Most AI work on learning has used symbolic representations such as feature vectors, first-order predicate calculus, and production rules to represent the knowledge acquired by the learning element. It is useful to classify this work according to the complexity of the task being performed by the learning system:

1. *Learning single concepts.* The simplest performance task is to classify new instances according to whether they are instances of a single concept. The problem of learning single concepts has received a lot of attention and is probably the best understood learning task in AI.

2. *Learning multiple concepts.* Many performance tasks involve the use of a *set* of concepts that operate independently. Disease diagnosis, for example, is a task in which the program seeks to assign one or more disease classes to a patient. The problem of learning a set of concepts has received some attention in AI. The Meta-DENDRAL and AM systems, for example, discover many concepts in order to describe their training instances and guide the performance element.

3. *Learning to perform multiple-step tasks.* The most complex performance tasks for which learning techniques have been developed are relatively simple planning tasks that require the performance element to apply a *sequence* of operators to perform the task. Unlike the multiple, but independent, concepts used in Meta-DENDRAL and AM, the rules in these systems must be chained together into a sequence. Consequently, many difficult problems of integration and credit-assignment arise.

References

Simon and Lea (1974) describe the two-space model of rule induction. Dieterich and Michalski (1981) provide some perspectives on systems that learn from examples. See also Buchanan, Mitchell, Smith, and Johnson (1977).

D2. Learning in Control and Pattern Recognition Systems

THERE ARE many applications in engineering and science for which learning systems have been developed. These systems, usually called *adaptive systems*, are useful when classical systems techniques cannot be applied because of insufficient knowledge about the underlying system. Such situations often arise in extremely noisy and rapidly changing environments.

Classical systems theory addresses itself to problems in the design and analysis of *systems*, where a system is viewed abstractly as an operator that maps a vector of inputs, $\mathbf{x}$, to a vector of outputs, $\mathbf{y}$. Two important engineering problems for which learning systems have been developed are *control* and *pattern recognition*.

Consider the control problem shown in Figure D2–1. The system is an automobile engine. The inputs—in this case, control inputs—are the amount of gasoline and the setting of the spark-plug advance. The single output is the speed of the engine. The control problem is to determine the settings of the inputs over time, so that the output follows a particular curve. We want the speed of the engine to track the desired speed as commanded by the driver of the automobile. If we have a mathematical model of the engine—say, as a set of differential equations relating x_1 and x_2 to y—we can often solve this control problem. To obtain the model, we can usually inspect the system directly and apply the laws of physics. But in complex, time-varying systems, such an approach may be impossible. Instead, it may be necessary to *identify* the system—that is, construct a model by observing the system in operation and finding an empirical relationship between the inputs and the outputs.

Pattern recognition—the other task for which adaptive learning is useful—also can be viewed as a system-identification problem. The pattern-classification system shown in Figure D2–2 takes an input object—represented as a vector, $\mathbf{x}$, of features—and maps it into one of m pattern classes. The

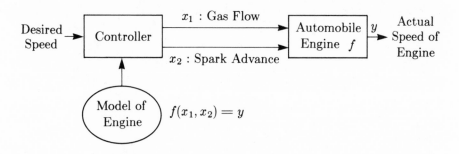

Figure D2–1.   A simple control problem.

373

Input **x** → | Character Recognizer | *y* → Character Class
Image | (person) | $\{A, B, \ldots, Z, 1, 2, \ldots, 9, \ldots\}$

Figure D2-2. A simple pattern-classification problem.

archetypal pattern-classification problem is optical character recognition, in which the inputs are images of handwritten or printed characters and the output is a classification of each image as one of the letters, numerals, or punctuation symbols. Suppose we want to build a computer system that can recognize characters. We have available an unknown system—in this case, a person—that can perform the task reliably. If we can identify the system, we will then have a computer model that can recognize handwritten characters.

Figure D2-3 illustrates the general setup for adaptive system identification. The unknown system and the model are configured in parallel. Their outputs—the true output, **y**, and the estimated output, **ỹ**—are compared, and the error, *e*, is fed back to the learning element, which then modifies the model appropriately. In the terminology of our simple learning-system model, the unknown system is the environment. It provides training instances, in the form of $(\mathbf{x}, \mathbf{y})$ pairs, to the learning element. The learning element modifies certain parts of the model (i.e., the knowledge base), so that the model system (i.e., the performance element) more accurately models the unknown system.

Conceptually, therefore, adaptive system identification, adaptive control, and pattern recognition are all problems of learning from examples. The

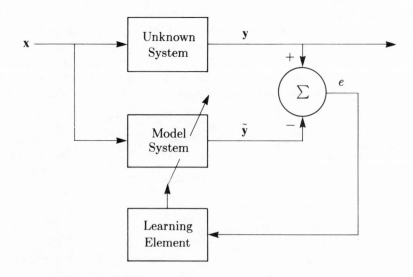

Figure D2-3. Adaptive system identification.

unknown system provides the training instances and the performance standard (i.e., the true **y** values).

In this article, we discuss the methods that have been used to accomplish this learning. We have divided the methods into four groups according to the representations that are used to model the unknown system:

1. *Statistical algorithms,* which employ probability density functions to create a Bayesian decision procedure;

2. *Parameter learning,* which uses a vector of parameters and a linear model;

3. *Automata learning,* which uses stochastic and fuzzy automata (discussed below) to model the unknown system; and

4. *Structural learning,* which uses pattern grammars and graphs to represent classes of objects for pattern classification.

Statistical Learning Algorithms

In pattern recognition (and sometimes in control), it is possible to view the unknown system as making a decision to assign the input, **x**, to one class, y, out of m classes. By defining a loss function that penalizes incorrect decisions (i.e., decisions in which $\tilde{y}$ differs from y), a minimum-average-loss Bayes classifier can be used to model the unknown system. The problem of identifying the unknown system then reduces to the problem of estimating a set of parameters for certain probability density functions. These parameters, such as the mean vector and the variance-covariance matrix, can be estimated from the training instances in a fairly straightforward fashion (see Duda and Hart, 1973).

In the terminology of Simon and Lea (1974), the set of all possible **x** vectors forms the instance space, and the set of possible values for the parameters of the probability distributions forms the rule space. The rule space is searched by direct calculation from the training instances. The instance space is not actively searched.

Unfortunately, these methods rely on assuming a particular form (e.g., multivariate normal) for the probability distributions in the model. These assumptions frequently do not hold in real-world problems. Furthermore, the computational costs of the estimation may be very high when there are many features.

Parameter Learning

In parameter learning, a fixed functional form is assumed for the unknown system. This functional form has a vector of parameters, **w**, that must be determined from the training instances. Unlike the statistical methods, there is little or no probabilistic interpretation for the unknown parameters and, consequently, probability theory provides no guidance for estimating them from the data. Instead, some sort of criterion, usually the squared error $(y - \tilde{y})^2$ averaged over all training instances, is minimized. The rule space is thus a space of possible parameter vectors, and it is searched by hill-climbing (also called *gradient descent*) to find the point that minimizes the error between the model and the unknown system.

The most popular form assumed for the unknown system is a linear functional:

$$y = \mathbf{wx} = \sum_i w_i x_i \ .$$

The output is assumed to be a linear combination of the input feature vector, $\mathbf{x}$, with a weight vector, $\mathbf{w}$. The elements of the weight vector are the unknown parameters. The rule space is thus the space of all possible weight vectors, known as the *weight space*.

An important special case arises when the unknown system is a *binary* pattern classification system similar to the system shown earlier in Figure D2–2. In binary pattern classification, the classifier must indicate in which of the two pattern classes the input pattern, $\mathbf{x}$, belongs. This is typically accomplished by taking the output, y, of a linear functional and comparing it to a threshold, b:

If $y > b$, then $\mathbf{x}$ is in class 1.
If $y < b$, then $\mathbf{x}$ is in class 2.

Usually, the instance space is normalized, so that the threshold b is zero. This *linear-discriminant function* can be thought of as a hyperplane that splits the instance space into two regions (class 1 and class 2). For example, if $\mathbf{x} = (x_1, x_2)$ is a two-dimensional feature vector and $\mathbf{w} = (-1, 2)$, the instance space is split as shown in Figure D2–4.

The learning problem of finding $\mathbf{w}$ can thus be viewed as the problem of finding a hyperplane that separates training instances of class 1 from training instances in class 2. When it is possible to find such a hyperplane, the training instances are said to be *linearly separable*. Often, however, the training instances are not linearly separable. In such cases, we must either use a more complex functional form, such as a quadratic function, or else settle for the hyperplane that makes the fewest errors on the average.

How can the desired hyperplane, or, equivalently, the desired weight vector, be found? We describe three basic algorithms for computing the weight vector. The first two algorithms are hill-climbing methods that process the training instances one at a time. After each training instance, $\mathbf{x}_k$, the weight vector, $\mathbf{w}_k$, is updated to give $\mathbf{w}_{k+1}$.

The first algorithm, called the *fixed-increment perceptron algorithm*, seeks to minimize the classification errors made by the model. If $\mathbf{x}_k$ is an instance of class 1 and $\tilde{y} = \mathbf{w}_k \mathbf{x}_k$ is less than 0, instead of greater than 0, an error

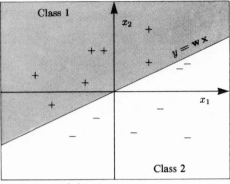

+ : Instance of class 1
− : Instance of class 2

Figure D2–4.   An example of a linear-discriminant function.

has been made. The magnitude of this error is $e = 0 - \mathbf{w}_k\mathbf{x}_k$, that is, the difference between the desired value for the output of the system ($y = 0$) and the value computed by the model ($\tilde{y} = \mathbf{w}_k\mathbf{x}_k$). This is usually written as the perceptron criterion,

$$\mathbf{J}_p = -\mathbf{w}_k\mathbf{x}_k \,,$$

and the goal of learning is to minimize $\mathbf{J}_p$. The fixed-increment algorithm updates $\mathbf{w}_k$ whenever $\mathbf{J}_p > 0$ according to

$$\mathbf{w}_{k+1} = \mathbf{w}_k + \mathbf{x}_k \,. \tag{1}$$

We can think of $\mathbf{J}_p$ as a surface over the *weight space*, the space of possible values for the weight vector $\mathbf{w}$ (see Fig. D2–5). Mathematical analysis shows that $\mathbf{x}$ can be viewed as a vector in this weight space (as well as in instance space) pointing in the direction of steepest descent for $\mathbf{J}_p$. Thus, this algorithm takes a fixed-size step in the direction of steepest descent.

Similarly, if $\mathbf{x}_k$ is in class 2 and $\mathbf{w}_k\mathbf{x}_k > 0$, an error has been made. The solution is to adjust $\mathbf{w}$ as

$$\mathbf{w}_{k+1} = \mathbf{w}_k - \mathbf{x}_k \,.$$

Equivalently, all training instances in class 2 can be replaced by their negatives, and all instances can be processed as though they were in class 1. Equation (1) can then be used to perform the entire learning process.

The fixed-increment algorithm converges in a finite number of steps if the training instances are linearly separable. It has been shown for the two-class case that the number of training instances should be at least twice the number of features in the instance space (see Nilsson, 1965).

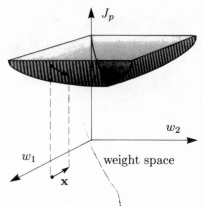

Figure D2–5.   A schematic diagram of the perceptron algorithm.

Historically, the fixed-increment algorithm is associated with Rosenblatt's (1957, 1962) perceptron, which was developed within the study of bionics and neural mechanisms. The simplest perceptron, shown in Figure D2–6, is a device that assigns patterns to one of two classes. It consists of an array of sensory units connected in a random way to an array of unmodifiable threshold units, each of which computes some desired feature of the sensory array and produces a +1 or −1 output, depending on whether the feature is present or absent. The outputs of these feature-extraction units are then connected to a modifiable unit that weights each input and sums the result (i.e., computes **wx**). The resulting value is compared with a threshold, and the perceptron produces an output of +1 if **wx** is greater than the threshold and −1 otherwise. Thus, the simplest perceptron implements a linear-discriminant function. The original publication of the perceptron model sparked a large

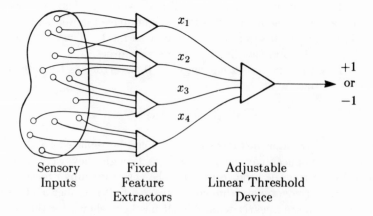

Figure D2–6.   The simplest form of perceptron.

amount of research, and a fair amount of speculation, concerning the potential for building intelligent machines from perceptrons. Minsky and Papert (1969) attempted to quiet this speculation by proving several theorems about the limits of perceptron-based learning. The introduction to their book provides several criticisms of AI learning research that remain valid today.

The fixed-increment perceptron algorithm can be improved in several ways by choosing how far in the direction of the gradient to go at each step. The LMS (least-mean-square) algorithm (Widrow and Hoff, 1960), for example, updates $\mathbf{w}$ according to

$$\mathbf{w}_{k+1} = \mathbf{w}_k + \rho e_k \mathbf{x}_k \,,$$

where ρ is a positive value and e_k is the magnitude of the error, that is, $-\mathbf{w}_k \mathbf{x}_k$. This algorithm tends to minimize the mean-squared error

$$\mathbf{J}_s = \sum_k \left(\mathbf{w}_k \mathbf{x}_k \right)^2$$

even when the classes are not linearly separable. The algorithm is also very easy to implement.

More robust, but harder to compute, algorithms are based on traditional linear-regression and linear-programming techniques (see Duda and Hart, 1973). Given a set of training instances, linear regression can be used to minimize $\mathbf{J}_s$. The weight vector is computed from the data as

$$\mathbf{w} = (\mathbf{X}^T \mathbf{X})^{-1} \mathbf{X}^T \mathbf{y} \,,$$

where $\mathbf{y}$ is the true output of the unknown system and $\mathbf{X}$ is a matrix of training instances, one instance in each row. Unfortunately, this method requires computing the pseudo-inverse $(\mathbf{X}^T \mathbf{X})^{-1} \mathbf{X}^T$ of $\mathbf{X}$, which is an expensive step. Less costly recursive algorithms have been developed that can compute $\mathbf{w}$ incrementally as the training instances become available, rather than collecting all of the instances and computing $\mathbf{w}$ once and for all (Goodwin and Payne, 1977).

Linear-programming techniques can be used to minimize the perceptron criterion, $\mathbf{J}_p$. These methods also conduct a hill-climbing search of the weight space. Further details are available in Duda and Hart (1973).

Some of these linear-discriminant algorithms can be modified slightly to put them on sound statistical foundations. The regression techniques, for example, can be adjusted to converge in the limit to an optimum Bayes classifier. Their rate of convergence is slower than the unmodified algorithms. Consequently, the simpler, faster algorithms shown above are often chosen in favor of the statistically more rigorous methods.

All of these methods for finding discriminant functions can be generalized to handle classification problems for more than two classes. Typically, a separate discrimination function is learned for each of m classes, and $\mathbf{x}$ is classified to that class i for which the value of the discriminant function $f_i(\mathbf{x})$ is largest. Another approach to multiple-class problems is to perform a multistage classification in which $\mathbf{x}$ is first classified into one of a few classes and then each of these is in turn split into subclasses until $\mathbf{x}$ is properly classified. By decomposing the classification problem into subproblems, other a priori knowledge about different classes—and the features relevant to those classes— can be incorporated into the system. Most large, multicategory problems do not lend themselves to straightforward general solutions. Instead, the structure and organization of the classification strategy are usually highly dependent on the particular problem and domain-specific knowledge. Consequently, many of these classification problems overlap problems in AI.

Learning Automata

An alternate representation for an unknown system is as a finite-state automaton (Fu, 1970b). The goal is to find a finite-state automaton whose behavior imitates that of the unknown system. Two quite similar approaches have been pursued. One models the unknown system as a deterministic finite-state machine with randomly perturbed inputs. The learning program is given an initial state transition probability matrix, $\mathbf{M}$, which tells overall for each state, q_i, what the probability is that the next state will be q_j. From $\mathbf{M}$, an equivalent deterministic machine can be derived, and the probability distribution of the input symbols can be determined. This approach requires that the internal states of the unknown system can be precisely observed and measured.

A second approach models the unknown system as a stochastic machine with a random transition matrix for each possible input symbol. Reinforcement techniques are applied to adjust the transition probabilities. Unfortunately, this requires a large amount of training information in order to exercise all possible transitions. As with the first approach, assumptions about the observability of all internal states must be made.

Fuzzy automata based on Zadeh's *fuzzy set* concept provide an alternate, but similar, approach to that used with stochastic automata (Wee and Fu, 1969). Set-membership criteria are applied, rather than probabilistic constraints, in the selection of transitions and outputs. Fuzzy automata are also able to make higher order transitions than stochastic automata and, consequently, they can usually learn faster.

The basic ideas of automata learning have been extended to take into account the interactions of a number of automata operating in the same environment. Such automata may interact in either cooperative or competitive modes. This has led to the formulation and study of automata games (Fu, 1970b).

Automata methods have the advantage over parameter-learning methods in that they do not require that there be a performance criterion with a unique minimum point. Furthermore, automata provide a more expressive representation for describing the unknown system. The principal disadvantage of automata learning methods is that they are relatively slow compared to parameter learning techniques. In addition, they are usually suitable only for application in stationary (i.e., non-time-varying) environments. Consequently, automata methods have not yet seen much practical application.

Structural Learning

Structural learning techniques have been used primarily in situations in which the objects to be classified have important substructure (Fu, 1974). The parametric linear-discriminant approaches described above can represent only the global features of objects. By employing pattern graphs and grammars, important substructures, such as the pen strokes that make up a character and the phonemes that make up a spoken word, can be represented along with their interrelationships. A first step in setting up a structural learning scheme involves identifying a set of primitive structural elements associated with the problem. These primitives may be thought of as the alphabet for describing all possible patterns associated with the application. They need to be higher level objects than simple scalar measurements (e.g., characters, shapes, and phonemes instead of height, width, and curvature). Legal and recognizable patterns are formed from combinations of the primitives according to certain syntactic rules.

Formal language theory provides a theoretical framework that accommodates the structural or descriptive formulation of pattern recognition. Here, the alphabet corresponds to the set of structural primitives. A number of formalisms have been used to express structural descriptions. In linguistic terms, a pattern may be thought of as a string or sentence, and a grammar may be associated with each pattern class. The grammar controls the structure of the language in such a way that the sentences (patterns) produced belong exclusively to a particular pattern class; a grammar is therefore needed for each pattern class. Parsing techniques can help determine whether a sentence (pattern) is grammatically correct for a given language. Both deterministic and stochastic grammars have been employed in pattern classification. (See Article XIII.E3 for a discussion of grammatical approaches to image understanding.)

Stochastic grammars (see Article XIV.D5e) have been used in an attempt to accommodate the possibilities of ambiguity and error in pattern description. These grammars make it possible for probabilistic assignments to be made. Before such a grammar can be used for classification, the production probabilities must be determined, for example, by "learning" them from a set of training examples.

There are still several difficulties associated with the structural approach to pattern classification. In contrast to the statistical and parameter learning methods, very few practical structural training algorithms have presently been proposed. The problem of learning a grammar from training instances is called *grammatical inference*. Article XIV.D5e describes the current state of work in that area. In addition to the problem of learning the grammar, the steps of segmentation into primitives and formation of structural descriptions are only partly solved.

Relevance for Artificial Intelligence

This survey of learning systems in engineering shows that many of the problems addressed are analogous to those encountered in the design of AI learning systems. Engineering systems are particularly adept at handling noisy training instances—a problem that few AI systems have addressed. It has also been possible to develop detailed analyses of these learning algorithms, including convergence proofs and investigations of their statistical foundations.

The primary drawback of these methods is their reliance on simple feature-vector representations. Although there are many practical applications for which these representations suffice, most problems of interest to AI researchers require more expressive representations. The more recent attempts to use automata and pattern-grammar representations are much more relevant to AI research.

Some aspects of the work in engineering may be important for AI researchers. In addition to work on the problem of noise, some progress has been made on solving the problem of choosing a good set of features with which to perform the learning process. One approach is to estimate the discriminatory ability of each feature given choices of the other features. Dynamic-programming techniques can help determine a good ordering of the features (from most relevant to least relevant). A second interesting approach—called *dimensionality reduction*—is to take a large set of features and compute a new, smaller set by forming linear combinations of the old features. The Karhunen-Loève expansion can be used to create such derived features (see Fu, 1970a, and Article XIII.C5).

References

A very readable introduction to linear-discriminant functions can be found in Nilsson (1965). Duda and Hart (1973) provide an excellent survey of pattern recognition techniques. Tsypkin (1973) develops a formal, unified treatment of learning methods in engineering.

D3.   Learning Single Concepts

MANY PROGRAMS have been developed that are able to learn a single concept from training instances.   This article describes the single-concept learning problem and discusses a few, selected learning programs that give a sense of the techniques that have been applied to this problem.

What does it mean to learn a concept from training instances? The term *concept* is used quite loosely in the AI literature.   In this article, we take a concept to be a predicate, expressed in some description language, that is TRUE when applied to a positive instance and FALSE when applied to a negative instance of the concept. A concept is thus a predicate that partitions the instance space into positive and negative subsets. For example, the concept of *straight* can be thought of as a predicate that indicates, for any poker hand, whether or not that hand is a straight.

The single-concept learning problem is the problem of discovering such a concept predicate from training instances—that is, from a sample of positive and negative instances in the instance space. The standard solution to this problem is to provide the learning program with a space of possible concept descriptions that the learning program searches to find the desired concept description (see Article XIV.D1).

Formally, the single-concept learning problem can be stated as follows:

Given: (1) A representation language for concepts.   This implicitly defines the rule space: the space of all concepts representable in the language.

(2) A set of positive (and usually negative) training instances. In most work to date, these training instances are noise free and classified in advance by the teacher.

Find: The unique concept in the rule space that best covers all of the positive and none of the negative instances. Most work to date assumes that if enough instances are presented, exactly one concept exists that is consistent with the training instances.

To gain insight into the origin of the single-concept learning problem, it is useful to examine the performance tasks that make use of the concept once it is learned. The standard performance task is *classification;* the system is presented with new unknowns and is asked to classify them as positive or negative instances of a concept. Another common task is *prediction;* if the training instances are successive elements of a sequence, the system is asked to predict future elements in the sequence. A third task is *data compression;* the system is given all possible instances (the full instance space) and is asked to find a concept that compactly describes them. The concept-classification and sequence-prediction tasks both arose as laboratory paradigms within cognitive psychology (see Hunt, Marin, and Stone, 1966). Sequence extrapolation is also a paradigm example of induction as discussed by philosophers (Carnap, 1950). Data compression is of practical value for storage and classification.

The two key assumptions made in all of this work are (a) that the training instances are all examples (or counterexamples) of a single concept and (b) that that concept can be represented by a point in the given rule space. When the first assumption is violated, it is necessary to find a *set* of concepts that account for the training instances. The systems described in the article on multiple concepts (Article XIV.D4) address this problem. When the second assumption is violated, it is necessary to alter the rule space so that it *does* contain the desired concept. Very little attention has been given to this problem in single-concept learning. The BACON program employs some simple methods to alter the rule space by adding new terms to the representation language (see Article XIV.D3b).

Approaches to Solving the Single-concept Learning Problem

In Article XIV.D1, we described four basic techniques—version spaces, refinement operators, generate and test, and schema instantiation—that are used to search the rule space. Each of these search methods has been applied to the single-concept learning problem. The remainder of this article is divided into four subarticles—one devoted to each method. The first two subarticles describe data-driven methods. Mitchell's version-space method is discussed first. It provides a useful framework for describing several related systems developed by Hayes-Roth, Vere, and Winston. Then two refinement-operator systems, BACON and CLS/ID3, are presented. The second pair of subarticles describes model-driven methods: a generate-and-test method developed by Dietterich and Michalski (1981) and a schema-instantiation method, SPARC, that plays the card game Eleusis.

References

See Mitchell (1978, 1979).

D3a. Version Space

RECENT WORK by Mitchell (1977, 1979) provides a unified framework for describing systems that use a data-driven, single-representation approach to concept learning. Mitchell has noted that, in all representation languages, the sentences can be placed in a partial order according to the *generality* of each sentence. Figure D3a–1 illustrates this general-to-specific ordering with a few sentences in predicate calculus containing the predicates RED and BLACK. The concept $\exists\, c_1 : \mathrm{RED}(c_1)$, for example, describes the set S of all poker hands that contain at least one red card. This concept is more general than the concept $\exists\, c_1\, c_2 : \mathrm{RED}(c_1) \wedge \mathrm{RED}(c_2)$ that describes the set T of all poker hands containing at least two red cards, since the set S strictly contains the set T. The set of cards described by $\exists\, c_1\, c_2\, c_3 : \mathrm{RED}(c_1) \wedge \mathrm{RED}(c_2) \wedge \mathrm{BLACK}(c_3)$ is smaller still and, thus, is even more specific than the $\exists\, c_1\, c_2 : \mathrm{RED}(c_1) \wedge \mathrm{RED}(c_2)$ concept.

It should be evident that the syntactic rules of generalization described in Article XIV.D1 can be used to generate this partial ordering. In this example, the *dropping-conditions* rule of generalization was applied to the three most specific concepts to generate the others. In general, any rule space can be partially ordered according to the general-to-specific ordering.

The most general point in the rule space is usually the null description (in which *all* conditions have been dropped), which places no constraints on the training instances and thus describes anything. The most specific points in the rule space correspond to the training instances themselves— represented in the same representation language as that used for the rule space (see Fig. D3a–2).

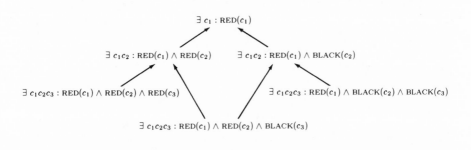

Figure D3a–1.   A small rule space and its general-to-specific ordering.

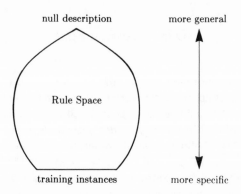

Figure D3a–2.   A schematic diagram of the rule space.

Mitchell has pointed out that programs can take advantage of this partial ordering to represent the set H of plausible hypotheses very compactly. A set of points in a partially ordered set can be represented by its *most general* and *most specific* elements. Thus, as shown in Figure D3a–3, the set H of plausible hypotheses can be represented by two subsets: the set of most general elements in H (called the G set) and the set of most specific elements in H (called the S set). Once H has been represented in this manner, the rules of generalization must be used to fill in the subspace between the G set and the S set whenever the full H set is needed.

The Candidate-elimination Learning Algorithm

Mitchell's learning algorithm, called the *candidate-elimination algorithm*, takes advantage of the boundary-set representation for the set H of plausible

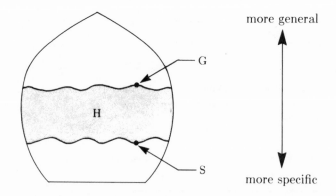

Figure D3a–3.   Using the boundary sets to represent a subspace of the rule space.

hypotheses. Mitchell defines a plausible hypothesis as *any* hypothesis that has not yet been ruled out by the data. The set H of all plausible hypotheses is called the *version space*. Thus, the version space, H, is the set of all concept descriptions that are consistent with all of the training instances seen so far.

Initially, the version space is the complete rule space of possible concepts. Then, as training instances are presented to the program, candidate concepts are eliminated from the version space. When it contains only one candidate concept, the desired concept has been found. The candidate-elimination algorithm is a *least-commitment* algorithm, since it does not modify the set H until it is *forced to do so* by the training information. Positive instances force the program to generalize—thus, very specific concept descriptions are removed from the H set. Conversely, negative instances force the program to specialize, so very general concept descriptions are removed from the H set. The version space gradually shrinks in this manner until only the desired concept description remains.

To see how training instances force the version space to shrink, consider once again the problem of teaching a program the *flush* concept in poker. Suppose the program has already seen the positive training instance

$$\{(2, \mathit{clubs}), (5, \mathit{clubs}), (7, \mathit{clubs}), (\mathit{jack}, \mathit{clubs}), (\mathit{queen}, \mathit{clubs})\} \quad \Rightarrow \quad \text{FLUSH}.$$

Since the candidate-elimination algorithm is a least-commitment algorithm, it makes the most specific possible assumption about the *flush* concept. Namely, it sets up the S set to contain

$$
\begin{aligned}
S = \{ &\text{SUIT}(c_1, \mathit{clubs}) \wedge \text{RANK}(c_1, 2) \wedge \\
&\text{SUIT}(c_2, \mathit{clubs}) \wedge \text{RANK}(c_2, 5) \wedge \\
&\text{SUIT}(c_3, \mathit{clubs}) \wedge \text{RANK}(c_3, 7) \wedge \\
&\text{SUIT}(c_4, \mathit{clubs}) \wedge \text{RANK}(c_4, \mathit{jack}) \wedge \\
&\text{SUIT}(c_5, \mathit{clubs}) \wedge \text{RANK}(c_5, \mathit{queen}) \}.
\end{aligned}
$$

This hypothesis is very specific indeed. It says that there is only one hand that could possibly be a flush. At the same time, however, the candidate-elimination algorithm makes the most general possible assumption, namely, that *every* possible hand is a *flush*. The G set contains the null description. This means that the version space—the H set—of all plausible hypotheses contains S, G, and every hypothesis in between.

Now, suppose the positive training instance

$$\{(3, \mathit{clubs}), (8, \mathit{clubs}), (10, \mathit{clubs}), (\mathit{king}, \mathit{clubs}), (\mathit{ace}, \mathit{clubs})\} \quad \Rightarrow \quad \text{FLUSH}$$

is presented. The candidate-elimination algorithm realizes that its initial assumption for the S set was too specific—there *are* other hands that can be flushes. Thus, it is forced to generalize S to contain, among other hypotheses, the rule

$$S = \{\text{SUIT}(c_1, clubs) \wedge \text{SUIT}(c_2, clubs) \wedge \text{SUIT}(c_3, clubs) \wedge$$
$$\text{SUIT}(c_4, clubs) \wedge \text{SUIT}(c_5, clubs)\}.$$

The G set does not change. Suppose, however, that a negative training instance

$$\{(3, spades), (8, clubs), (10, clubs), (king, clubs), (ace, clubs)\} \implies \neg \text{FLUSH}$$

is presented. This forces the candidate-elimination algorithm to realize that its assumption for the G set, that *any* hand could be a flush, was wrong. It must specialize the G set in some way, so that it does not wrongly classify this hand as a *flush*.

In full detail, the candidate-elimination algorithm proceeds as follows:

Step 1. Initialize H to be the whole space. Thus, the G set contains only the null description, and the S set contains all of the most specific concepts in the space. (In practice, this is not actually done due to the huge size of S. Instead, the S set is initialized to contain only the first positive example. Conceptually, however, H starts out as the whole space.)

Step 2. Accept a new training instance. If the instance is a positive example, first remove from G all concepts that do not cover the new example. Then update S to contain all of the maximally specific common generalizations of the new instance and the previous elements in S. In other words, generalize the elements in S *as little as possible*, so that they will cover this new positive example. This is called the Update-S routine.

If the instance is a negative example, first remove from S all concepts that cover this counterexample. Then update the G set to contain all of the maximally general, common specializations of the new instance and the previous elements in G. In other words, specialize the elements in G *as little as possible* so that they will *not* cover this new negative example. This is called the Update-G routine.

Step 3. Repeat step 2 until $G = S$ and this is a singleton set. When this occurs, H has collapsed to include only a single concept.

Step 4. Output H (i.e., either G or S).

Here is an example of a complete run of the candidate-elimination algorithm. Suppose we have the following feature-vector representation language: The instance space is a set of objects, each object having two features—*size* and *shape*. The size of an object can be *small* or *large*, and the shape of an

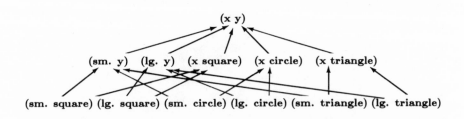

Figure D3a–4. The initial version space and the general-to-specific
              partial order.

object can be *circle, square,* or *triangle.* Figure D3a–4 shows the entire rule
space for this representation language.

Each point in the rule space specifies either a variable or a value for both
of the features. If a feature is specified by a variable, then *any* value of that
feature can be applied.

Suppose we want to teach the program the concept of a *circle.* This is
represented as (x circle) where x represents any size. First we initialize the
H set to be the entire rule space. This means that the G set is

$$G = \{(\text{x y})\},$$

representing the most general possible concept, and the S set is

$$S = \{(\text{small square}) \ (\text{large square}) \ (\text{small circle}) \ (\text{large circle})$$
$$(\text{small triangle}) \ (\text{large triangle})\}.$$

Now we present the first training instance: a positive example of the
concept, a small circle. The Update-S algorithm is applied in step 2 to yield:

$$G = \{(\text{x y})\}$$
$$S = \{(\text{small circle})\}.$$

Figure D3a–5 shows the resulting version space. Solid lines connect concepts that are still *in* the version space. In practical implementations of the
candidate-elimination algorithm, the version space is usually initialized at this
point rather than explicitly listing the entire instance space as in the step
above.

The second training instance is (large triangle)—a negative example of
the concept. This forces the G set to be specialized. Update-G is applied to
produce

$$G = \{(\text{x circle}) \ (\text{small y})\}$$
$$S = \{(\text{small circle})\}.$$

Figure D3a–6 shows the resulting version space.

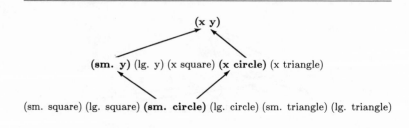

Figure D3a–5.   The version space after the first training instance.

Notice how the (x y) description was specialized in two distinct ways, so that it no longer covered the negative example (large triangle). A third possible specialization (x square) is not considered, since it was removed from the version space during the previous training instance. Of course, further specializations such as (small circle) are not considered because the Update-G algorithm specializes as little as possible.

In this case, the G set grew larger as a result of the specialization. The Update-G and Update-S algorithms often expand the size of the G and S sets. It is the size of these sets that limits the practical application of this algorithm.

Finally, we present the algorithm with another positive example: (large circle). Update-S first prunes G to eliminate (small y), since it does not cover (large circle). Then S is generalized as necessary:

$$G = \{(x \; circle)\}$$
$$S = \{(x \; circle)\}.$$

Since $G = S$, the algorithm halts and prints (x circle) as the concept.

It is possible to give intuitive interpretations of the G and S sets. The set S is the set of sufficient conditions for a new example to be an instance

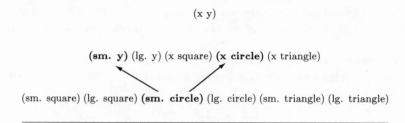

Figure D3a–6.   The version space after two training instances.

of the concept. Thus, after the second training instance, we know that if the new example is a (small circle), it is an instance of the concept; (small circle) is a sufficient condition for positive classification. The set G is the set of necessary conditions. After the second training instance, we know that an object either must be a circle or must be small in order to be an instance of the concept. Neither of these conditions is sufficient. The algorithm terminates when the necessary conditions are equal to the sufficient conditions—that is, the algorithm has found a necessary and sufficient condition.

It is important to note that the candidate-elimination algorithm conducts an exhaustive, breadth-first search of the given rule space, guided only by the training instances. This makes the algorithm infeasibly slow for large rule spaces. The efficiency of the algorithm can be improved (at the cost of possibly failing to find the desired concept) by employing heuristics to prune the S and G sets. We postpone further discussion of the strengths and weaknesses of the candidate-elimination algorithm until after we have discussed the related methods developed by Hayes-Roth, Vere, and Winston.

Methods Related to the Version-space Approach

Two learning methods similar to the Update-S procedure of the version-space algorithm were developed prior to it. One method, termed *interference matching*, was developed by Hayes-Roth and McDermott (1977, 1978). The other method, the *maximal unifying generalization* method, was developed by Vere (1975, 1978). These methods can both be viewed as implementations of the Update-S procedure with respect to slightly different representation languages in that they learn from positive training instances only.

Interference matching was developed to discover concepts expressed in Hayes-Roth's Parameterized Structural Representation (PSR), which is roughly equivalent to an existentially quantified conjunctive statement in predicate calculus. Recall that Update-S seeks to generalize the descriptions in S as little as possible in order to cover each new positive training instance. When the descriptions are represented as predicate calculus expressions, this is equivalent to finding the largest common subexpressions, because the largest common subexpression is that subexpression for which the *fewest* conjunctive conditions need to be dropped. As an example, suppose that the set S contains the description

$$S = \{\text{BLOCK}(x) \wedge \text{BLOCK}(y) \wedge \text{RECTANGLE}(x) \wedge \text{ONTOP}(x,y) \wedge \text{SQUARE}(y)\}$$

and the next positive training instance (I_1) is

$$I_1 = \text{BLOCK}(w) \wedge \text{BLOCK}(v) \wedge \text{SQUARE}(w) \wedge \text{ONTOP}(w,v) \wedge \text{RECTANGLE}(v).$$

Update-S will produce the following common subexpressions:

$$S' = \{s_1, s_2\},$$

where $s_1 = \text{BLOCK}(a) \wedge \text{BLOCK}(b) \wedge \text{SQUARE}(a) \wedge \text{RECTANGLE}(b)$, and $s_2 = \text{BLOCK}(c) \wedge \text{BLOCK}(d) \wedge \text{ONTOP}(c, d)$.

The s_1 description corresponds to the hypothesis that the ONTOP relation is irrelevant to the concept. The s_2 description, on the other hand, corresponds to the hypothesis that the shapes of the objects involved are irrelevant. Notice that there is no consistent way to match I_1 to S that preserves a one-to-one correspondence of the variables x and y with w and v; either the rectangle and square predicates conflict (e.g., when x is matched with w) or else the order of the arguments to ONTOP conflict (e.g., when x is matched to v).

The interference-matching algorithm starts out as a breadth-first search of all possible matchings of one PSR with another. The search proceeds by "growing" common subexpressions until a space limit is reached. Unpromising matches are then pruned with a heuristic utility function, and the growing process continues in a more depth-first fashion. The utility of a partial match is equal to the number of predicates matched less the number of variables matched. If the space limit is approximately the same as the largest common subexpression, the algorithm becomes truly depth-first, since only one subexpression "fits" within the space limit. Thus, the interference-matching algorithm tends to find one good common subexpression rather than finding all maximal common subexpressions (as in the Update-S algorithm).

Vere's algorithm for finding the maximal unifying generalization of two first-order predicate-calculus descriptions is very similar to the interference-matching algorithm. The representation language used by Vere, however, permits a many-to-one binding of parameters during the matching process (Vere, 1975). Vere's method also conducts a breadth-first search of possible matchings but does not do any pruning of this search.

Winston's Work on Learning Structural Descriptions from Examples

Winston's (1970) influential work on structural learning served as a precursor to the other learning methods described above. The method has the same basic data-driven approach as in the version-space and related algorithms: Training instances are accepted one at a time and matched against the concept descriptions in the set H. Unlike those breadth-first algorithms (e.g., Update-S and Update-G), however, Winston's system conducts a *depth-first* search of the concept space. Instead of maintaining a *set* of plausible hypotheses, Winston's program uses the training instances to update a *single* current concept description. This description contains all of the program's knowledge about the concept being learned.

The task of the program is to learn concept descriptions that characterize simple toy-block constructions. The toy-block assemblies are initially presented to the computer as line drawings. A knowledge-based interpretation program converts these line drawings into a semantic-network description.

Winston also uses this semantic-network representation to describe the current concept and some background knowledge about toy blocks.

Figure D3a–7 shows a line drawing of an arch and the corresponding semantic network. The network is roughly equivalent to the predicate-calculus expression

ONE–PART–IS($arch, a$) $\wedge$ ONE–PART–IS($arch, b$) $\wedge$

ONE–PART–IS($arch, c$) $\wedge$ HAS–PROPERTY–OF($a, lying$) $\wedge$

A–KIND–OF($a, object$) $\wedge$ MUST–BE–SUPPORTED–BY(a, b) $\wedge$

MUST–BE–SUPPORTED–BY(a, c) $\wedge$ MUST–NOT–ABUT(b, c) $\wedge$

MUST–NOT–ABUT(c, b) $\wedge$ LEFT–OF(b, c) $\wedge$ RIGHT–OF(c, b) $\wedge$

HAS–PROPERTY–OF($b, standing$) $\wedge$ HAS–PROPERTY–OF($c, standing$) $\wedge$

A–KIND–OF($b, brick$) $\wedge$ A–KIND–OF($c, brick$) ,

along with statements of blocks-world knowledge such as

A–KIND–OF($brick, object$)

A–KIND–OF($standing, property$)

and statements relating different predicates in the representation language, such as

OPPOSITES(MUST–ABUT, MUST–NOT–ABUT)

MUST–FORM–OF(IS–SUPPORTED–BY, MUST–BE–SUPPORTED–BY) .

A distinctive aspect of Winston's concept representation is that it allows *necessary conditions* to be represented explicitly. For example, the condition that in an arch the posts *must not touch* can be directly represented by a MUST–NOT–ABUT link. This allows Winston's program to express necessary and sufficient conditions in one combined network structure.

Winston's learning algorithm works as follows:

Step 1. Initialize the current concept description, H, to be the network corresponding to the first positive training instance.

Step 2. Accept a new line drawing and convert it into a semantic-network representation.

Step 3. Match the training instance with H (using a graph-matching algorithm) to obtain the common skeleton. The skeleton is a maximal common subgraph of the two graphs. Annotate the skeleton by attaching comments indicating those nodes and links that did *not* match.

Step 4. Use the annotated skeleton to decide how to modify the current concept description H.

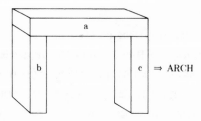

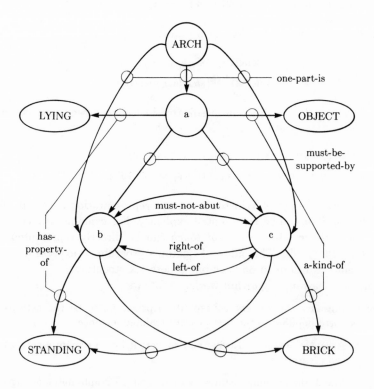

Figure D3a–7.   A training instance and its internal representation.

If the new instance is a positive example of the concept, then generalize *H* as necessary. The algorithm generalizes either by dropping nodes and links or by replacing one node (e.g., **cube**) by a more general node (e.g., **brick**). In some cases, the algorithm must choose between these two generalization techniques. The program chooses the less drastic method (node replacement) and places the other choice on a backtrack list.

If the new instance is a negative example of the concept, a necessary condition (represented by a **must**-link) is added to *H*. If there are several differences between the negative training instance and *H*, the algorithm applies some ad hoc rules to choose one difference to "blame" for causing the instance to be a negative instance. This difference is converted into a necessary condition. The other differences are ignored.

Repeat steps 2, 3, and 4 until the teacher halts the program.

Since the algorithm searches in depth-first fashion, it is possible for contradictions to arise in step 4. For example, after seeing a negative training instance such as shown in Figure D3a–8, the algorithm might assume in step 4 that the reason this is not an arch is the triangular lintel rather than the fact that the posts are touching. Subsequently, when the program sees the positive instance shown in Figure D3a–9, a contradiction arises. When this happens, the system backtracks to the last point at which a choice was made, and the algorithm makes a new choice.

This learning algorithm is somewhat weak and ad hoc, since it does not concern itself either with the possibility that the training instance matches *H* in multiple ways or with the problem that there are multiple ways of generalizing or specializing *H*. Winston makes two important assumptions that allow this algorithm to ignore these problems. First, it is assumed that the training instances are presented in good pedagogical order, so that contradictions and choice-points are unlikely to arise; the teacher is assumed to have chosen the examples so as to vary only one aspect of the concept in each example. The second assumption is that the negative training instances

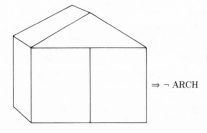

Figure D3a–8.   A near-miss negative example of an ARCH.

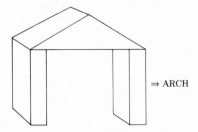

Figure D3a–9.   A positive example of an ARCH.

are all *near misses*, that is, instances that just barely fail to be examples of the concept in question. These two assumptions permit the learning system to perform fairly well in the domain of toy-block concepts.

Weaknesses of the Version-space Approach (and Related Approaches)

There are several weaknesses in these methods that limit their practical application. This section discusses these problems and examines some proposed solutions.

Noisy training instances. As with all data-driven algorithms, these methods have difficulty with noisy training instances. Since these algorithms seek to find a concept description that is consistent with *all* of the training instances, any single bad instance (i.e., a false positive or false negative instance) can have a big effect. When the candidate-elimination algorithm is given a false positive instance, for example, the S set becomes overly generalized. Similarly, a false negative instance causes the G set to become overly specialized. Eventually, noisy training instances can lead to a situation in which there are no concept descriptions that are consistent with all of the training instances. In such cases, the G set "passes" the S set, and the version space of consistent concept descriptions becomes empty. The methods of Hayes-Roth, Vere, and Winston also overgeneralize in the presence of false positive training instances.

In order to learn in the presence of noise, it is necessary to relax the condition that the concept descriptions be consistent with *all* of the training instances. One solution, proposed by Mitchell (1978), is to maintain several S and G sets of varying consistency. The set S_0, for example, is consistent with *all* of the positive examples, and the set S_1 is consistent with *all but one* of the positive examples. In general, each description in the set S_i is consistent with all but i of the positive training instances. Similarly, each description in the set G_i is consistent with all but i of the negative training instances. Figure D3a–10 gives a schematic diagram of these sets. Mitchell provides a fairly efficient algorithm for updating these multiple boundary sets.

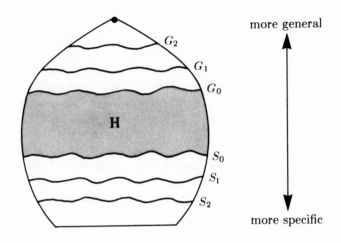

Figure D3a–10.   The multiple-boundary set technique.

When G_0 crosses S_0, the algorithm can conclude that no concept in the rule space is consistent with *all* of the training instances. The algorithm can recover and try to find a concept that is consistent with *all but one* of the training instances. If that fails, it can look for a concept consistent with all but two instances, and so forth. This approach to error recovery works for learning problems containing a few erroneous training instances, but it requires a large amount of memory to store all of the S and G boundary sets.

Disjunctive concepts. A second, important weakness of these data-driven algorithms is their inability to discover disjunctive concepts. Many concepts have a disjunctive form. For instance, an *uncle* is either the brother of a parent or the spouse of a sister of a parent:

$$\text{UNCLE}(x) = \text{BROTHER}(\text{PARENT}(x)) \vee$$
$$\text{UNCLE}(x) = \text{SPOUSE}(\text{SISTER}(\text{PARENT}(x))).$$

Parent itself might be expressed disjunctively as $\text{PARENT}(x) = \text{FATHER}(x) \vee \text{PARENT}(x) = \text{MOTHER}(x)$. However, if disjunctions of arbitrary length are permitted in the representation language, the data-driven algorithms described above never generalize. In the candidate-elimination algorithm, for example, the S set will always contain a single disjunction of all of the positive training instances seen so far. This is because the least generalization of a new training instance and the current S set is simply the disjunction of the new instance with the S set. Similarly, the G set will contain the disjunction of the negation of each of the negative training instances. Unlimited disjunction allows the partially ordered rule space to become infinitely "branchy."

The basic difficulty is that all of these algorithms are least-commitment algorithms that generalize only when they are forced to. Disjunction provides a way of avoiding any generalization at all—so the algorithms are never forced to generalize. In order to develop a useful technique for learning disjunctive concepts, some method must be found for controlling the introduction of disjunctions. The learning algorithms must be guided toward generalizing in certain ways to exclude the *trivial disjunction*.

One solution (proposed in different forms by Michalski, 1969, and by Mitchell, 1978) is to employ a representation language that does not contain a disjunction operator and to perform repeated candidate-elimination runs to find several conjunctive descriptions that together cover all of the training instances. We repeatedly find a conjunctive concept description that is consistent with *some* of the positive training instances and *all* of the negative training instances. The positive instances that have been accounted for are removed from further consideration, and the process is repeated until all positive instances have been covered:

Step 1. Initialize the S set to contain one positive training instance. G is initialized to the null description—the most general concept.

Step 2. For each negative training instance, apply the Update-G algorithm to G.

Step 3. Choose a description g from G as one conjunction for the solution set. Since Update-G has been applied using *all* of the negative instances, g covers *no* negative instances. However, g may cover several of the positive instances. Remove from further consideration all positive training instances that are more specific than g.

Step 4. Repeat steps 1 through 3 until all positive training instances are covered.

This process builds a disjunction of descriptions that covers all of the data. It tends to find a disjunction containing only a few conjunctive terms. Figure D3a–11 is a schematic diagram of how this process works.

The point s_1 is the first positive training instance selected in step 1. After all of the negative instances have been processed with Update-G, g_1 is selected from the G set in step 3. Notice that g_1 covers several positive instances in addition to s_1, but that not all positive instances are yet covered. The point s_2 is then chosen and g_2 is developed. Similarly, s_3 is chosen and g_3 is developed. As the figure shows, the conjunctive concepts, g_i, need not be disjoint. Also, the set of concepts g_i that is obtained by this procedure varies depending on the order in which the positive training instances are selected in step 1.

An algorithm very similar to this, called the A^q algorithm, was developed by Michalski (1969, 1975) for use with an extended propositional calculus representation. The A^q algorithm makes use of an additional heuristic in

Instance Space

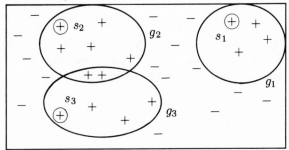

+ : Positive Instance   − : Negative Instance

Figure D3a–11. Schematic diagram of an iterative version-space algorithm for finding disjunctive concepts.

step 1. It selects as a "seed" positive training instance one that has not been covered by *any* description in *any* previous *G* set. This has the effect of choosing training instances that are "far apart" in the instance space. Larson (1977) elaborated A^q to apply it to an extended predicate-calculus representation.

The effect of this iterative version-space approach is to find a description with virtually the fewest number of disjunctive terms. Finding such a description is not always desirable. Programs searching for symmetrical descriptions, for example, may hypothesize a disjunctive term for which there is, as yet, no evidence. Consider how a program would learn the direction of wind rotation about a weather system. After seeing the following two training instances

Instance 1. HEMISPHERE = *north* ∧ PRESSURE = *high*
      ⇒ ROTATION = *clockwise*

Instance 2. HEMISPHERE = *south* ∧ PRESSURE = *high*
      ⇒ ROTATION = *counterclockwise* ,

the program might hypothesize that

HEMISPHERE = *north* ∧ PRESSURE = *high* ∨

HEMISPHERE = *south* ∧ PRESSURE = *low*

⇒ ROTATION = *clockwise* ,

even though the *simplest* hypothesis would be

HEMISPHERE = *north* ⇒ ROTATION = *clockwise* .

The problem of learning disjunctive concepts is still largely unexamined by AI researchers.

References

Mitchell (1977, 1979) provides good descriptions of the version-space approach. Hayes-Roth and McDermott (1978), Vere (1975), and Winston (1970) present detailed descriptions of their methods. See Dietterich and Michalski (1981) for a critical comparison of these methods.

D3b. Data-driven Rule-space Operators

THE SECOND FAMILY of data-driven methods does not employ partial matching to search the rule space. Instead, these methods develop a set of hypotheses in a rule space that is separate from the instance space (i.e., the single-representation trick is not used). The hypotheses are modified by *refinement operators*, which are selected by heuristics that inspect the training instances. The following is a general outline of these operator-based algorithms:

Step 1. Gather some training instances.

Step 2. Analyze the instances to decide which rule-space operator to apply.

Step 3. Apply the operator to make some change in the current set, $\overset{\cdot}{H}$, of hypotheses.

Repeat steps 1 through 3 until satisfactory hypotheses are obtained.

In this article, two systems are described that use this technique: BACON and CLS.

BACON

BACON is a set of concept-learning programs developed by Pat Langley (1977, 1980). These programs solve a variety of single-concept learning tasks, including "rediscovering" such classical scientific laws as Ohm's law, Newton's law of universal gravitation, and Kepler's law. The programs are also capable of using the learned concepts to predict future training instances.

The idea underlying BACON is simple: The program repeatedly examines the data and applies its refinement operators to create new terms. This continues until it finds that one of these terms is always constant. A single concept is thus represented in the form *term = constant value*.

BACON uses a feature-vector representation to describe each training instance. A distinguishing aspect is that the features may take on continuous real values as well as discrete symbolic or numeric values. For example, suppose we want BACON to discover Kepler's law: The period of a planet's revolution around the sun, p, is related to its distance from the sun, d, as $d^3/p^2 = k$, for some constant k. First, BACON is supplied with training instances of the form:

	Features		
Instance	*Planet*	*p*	*d*
I_1	Mercury	1	1
I_2	Venus	8	4
I_3	Earth	27	9

BACON is told that p and d are dependent on the value of the planet variable. Once BACON has gathered a few training instances, it examines them to see if any of its rule-space operators are triggered. In this case, since p and d are both increasing and are not linearly related, an operator that creates the new term d/p is triggered. This rule-space operator is executed, and the training instances are reformulated to give:

		Features		
Instance	Planet	p	d	d/p
I_1	Mercury	1	1	1.0
I_2	Venus	8	4	.5
I_3	Earth	27	9	.33

Again, BACON checks to see if any of its rule-space operators are triggered. This time, the product operator is executed to create the term $(d/p)d$, since d and d/p are varying inversely. The data are reformulated to give:

		Features			
Instance	Planet	p	d	d/p	d^2/p
I_1	Mercury	1	1	1.0	1.0
I_2	Venus	8	4	.5	2.0
I_3	Earth	27	9	.33	3.0

On the third iteration, BACON again checks to see if any operators apply. The product operator is again triggered to create the term $(d/p)(d^2/p)$. The data are reformulated to give:

		Features				
Instance	Planet	p	d	d/p	d^2/p	d^3/p^2
I_1	Mercury	1	1	1.0	1.0	1.0
I_2	Venus	8	4	.5	2.0	1.0
I_3	Earth	27	9	.33	3.0	1.0

BACON examines these data, and its constancy operator is triggered to create the hypothesis that the d^3/p^2 term is constant. BACON then gathers more data to test this hypothesis before it halts.

BACON's Rule-space Operators

The various BACON programs have different rule-space operators. Each operator is stored as a production rule, of which the left-hand side performs extensive tests to search for possible patterns in the data and the right-hand side creates the new terms. Here is a brief survey of the operators implemented in the BACON.1 program:

1. *Constancy detection.* This operator is triggered when some dependent variable takes on the same value, v, at least two times. It creates the hypothesis that this variable is always constant with value v.

2. *Specialization.* This operator is triggered when a previously created hypothesis is contradicted by the data. It specializes the hypothesis by adding a conjunctive condition.

3. *Slope and intercept term creation.* This operator detects that two variables are varying together linearly and creates new terms for the slope and intercept of this linear relation.

4. *Product creation.* This operator detects that two variables are varying inversely without a constant slope. It creates a new term that is the product of the two variables.

5. *Quotient creation.* This operator detects that two variables are varying monotonically (increasing or decreasing) without constant slope. It creates a new term that is the quotient of the two variables.

6. *Modulo-n term creation.* This operator notices that one variable, v_1, takes on a constant value whenever an independent variable, v_2, has a certain value modulo n. The new term v_2-*modulo-n* is created. Only small values of n are considered.

Extensions to BACON

BACON.2 is an extended version of BACON.1 that includes two additional operators for detecting recurring sequences and for creating polynomial terms by calculating repeated differences. BACON.2 can solve a larger class of sequence extrapolation tasks as a result.

BACON.3 is another extension of BACON.1 that uses hypotheses proposed by the constancy-detection operators to reformulate the training instances. For BACON.3 to discover the ideal gas law (PV/NT is equal to a constant), for example, it is given the following training instances:

	Features			
Instance	V	P	T	N
I_1	.0083200	300,000	300	1
I_2	.0062400	400,000	300	1
I_3	.0049920	500,000	300	1
I_4	.0085973	300,000	310	1
I_5	.0064480	400,000	310	1
I_6	.0051584	500,000	310	1
I_7	.0088747	300,000	320	1
I_8	.0066560	400,000	320	1
I_9	.0053248	500,000	320	1
$\vdots$	$\vdots$	$\vdots$	$\vdots$	$\vdots$

	Features			
Instance	*V*	*P*	*T*	*N*
$\vdots$	$\vdots$	$\vdots$	$\vdots$	$\vdots$
I_{25}	.0266240	300,000	320	3
I_{26}	.0199680	400,000	320	3
I_{27}	.0159740	500,000	320	3

By applying the product-creation operator followed by the constancy-detection operator, BACON develops the hypothesis that PV is constant for particular values of N and T. This hypothesis, which BACON must rediscover for each particular value of N and T, is used to recast the data to give the following derived training instances:

	Features		
Instance	*PV*	*T*	*N*
I'_1	2,496	300	1
I'_2	2,579.1999	310	1
I'_3	2,662.3999	320	1
I'_4	4,991.9999	300	2
I'_5	5,158.3999	310	2
I'_6	5,324.7999	320	2
I'_7	7,488	300	3
I'_8	7,737.5999	310	3
I'_9	7,987.2	320	3

Each of these derived instances results from collapsing three of the original training instances. Thus, I'_1 is derived by noticing that PV takes on the constant value 2,496 in I_1, I_2, and I_3. By applying the slope-intercept operator to these derived instances, BACON develops the hypothesis that PV/T is constant for particular values of N. It uses this hypothesis to recast the training instances into the following form:

	Features	
Instance	*PV/T*	*N*
I''_1	8.32	1
I''_2	16.64	2
I''_3	24.95	3

By applying the slope-intercept operator to these doubly derived instances, BACON develops the hypothesis that PV/NT is constant and, thus, posits the ideal gas law.

BACON's Rule Space

What is the rule space that BACON is searching? BACON expresses hypotheses as feature vectors, some of whose values are omitted (i.e., turned to variables). For example, Kepler's law is expressed as

Features:	*Planet*	p	d	d/p	d^2/p	d^3/p^2
Values:		–	–	–	–	1.0

Thus, the rule space is the space of such feature vectors whose features are any terms that BACON can create with its operators.

BACON conducts a sort of depth-first search through this space. The conditions under which the operators are triggered are quite specialized. The constancy-detection operator, for example, only checks the values of the most recently created dependent variable against the most recently varied independent variable. Most of the other operators are invoked under similarly constrained conditions.

Strengths and Weaknesses of BACON

BACON's primary strength is its ability to discover simple laws relating real-valued variables. Also of interest is BACON's use of rule-space operators to create new terms as combinations of existing terms. Further, the BACON.3 strategy of reformulating the training instances when partial regularities are discovered may be important for future learning programs. Simon (1979) has discussed BACON as a model of data-driven theory formation in science.

There are some difficulties with the present BACON programs, however. First, the fact that the operators are evoked only under highly specialized conditions causes the program to be sensitive to the order of the variables and to the particular values chosen for the training instances. For some sets of training instances, for example, BACON is unable to discover Ohm's law (see Langley, 1980, p. 104). It is necessary to adjust the order of the variables and the particular training instances to get BACON to discover concepts efficiently. For example, when BACON is discovering the pendulum law, 40% more time is required if the variables are poorly ordered. Similarly, it cannot handle irrelevant variables well.

Second, BACON is unable to handle noisy training instances. The triggering of the constancy detectors, for example, is based on the near equality of the values seen in as few as *two* training instances. Such calculations are highly sensitive to noise. The slope detectors are similarly sensitive.

Third, BACON can handle only relatively simple concept-formation tasks involving nonnumeric variables. The program cannot, for example, discover concepts that involve internal disjunction (such as the concept of a *red or green cube*). It is also unable to discover the simple concept underlying the

letter sequence ABTCDSEFR ... and similar sequences appearing in Kotovsky
and Simon (1973).

In summary, BACON is interesting primarily for its use of rule-space
operators to create product, quotient, slope, and intercept terms and for its
ability to recast the training instances on the basis of developed hypotheses.

CLS/ID3

CLS (Concept Learning System) is a learning algorithm devised by Earl
Hunt (see Hunt, Marin, and Stone, 1966). It is intended to solve single-
concept learning tasks and uses the learned concepts to classify new instances.
A more recent version of the CLS algorithm, ID3, was developed by Ross
Quinlan (1979, in press). In this article, we discuss the ID3 algorithm and its
application to data compression and concept formation.

Like BACON, ID3 uses a feature-vector representation to describe the
training instances. The features must each have only a small number of possible discrete values. Concepts are represented as decision trees. For example,
if the features of size (small, large), shape (circle, square, and triangle), and
color (red, blue) are used to represent the training instances, the concept of a
red circle (of any size) could be represented as the tree shown in Figure D3b–1.

An instance is classified by starting at the root of the tree and making
tests and following branches until a node is arrived at that indicates the class
as YES or NO (see Article XI.D). For example, the instance (*large, circle, blue*)
is classified as follows. Starting with the root node (shape), we follow the
circle branch to the color node. From the color node we take the blue branch
to a NO node indicating that this instance is not an instance of the concept
of a red circle.

Decision trees are inherently disjunctive, since each branch leaving a decision node corresponds to a separate disjunctive case. The tree in Figure D3b–1,

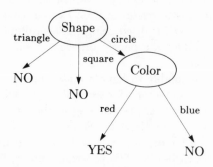

Figure D3b–1.   Decision tree for the concept of a *red circle*.

for example, is equivalent to the predicate calculus expression:

$$\neg\text{SHAPE}(x, \textit{triangle}) \lor \neg\text{SHAPE}(x, \textit{square}) \lor$$
$$\text{SHAPE}(x, \textit{circle}) \land [\text{COLOR}(x, \textit{red}) \lor \neg\text{COLOR}(x, \textit{blue})]\,.$$

Consequently, decision trees can be used to represent disjunctive concepts such as *large circle or small square* (see Fig. D3b–2).

A drawback of decision trees is that there are many possible trees corresponding to any single concept. This lack of a unique concept representation makes it difficult to check that two decision trees are equivalent.

The CLS Learning Algorithm (as Used in ID3)

The CLS algorithm starts with an empty decision tree and gradually refines it, by adding decision nodes, until the tree correctly classifies all of the training instances. The algorithm operates over a set of training instances, C, as follows:

Step 1. If all instances in C are positive, then create a YES node and halt.
If all instances in C are negative, create a NO node and halt.
Otherwise, select (using some heuristic criterion) a feature, F, with values $v_1, \ldots, v_n$ and create the decision node:

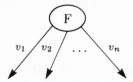

Step 2. Partition the training instances in C into subsets $C_1, C_2, \ldots, C_n$ according to the values of V.

Step 3. Apply the algorithm recursively to each of the sets C_i.

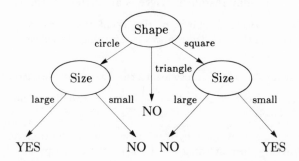

Figure D3b–2.   Decision tree for a disjunctive concept.

The criterion used in step 1 by ID3 is to choose the feature that best discriminates between positive and negative instances. Hunt et al. (1966) describe several methods for estimating which feature is the most discriminatory. Quinlan chooses the feature that leads to the greatest reduction in the estimated entropy of information of the training instances in C. The exact criterion is to choose the feature F (with values $v_1, v_2, \ldots, v_n$) that minimizes

$$\sum_i \left[-V_i^+ \log_2 \left(\frac{V_i^+}{V_i^+ + V_i^-} \right) - V_i^- \log_2 \left(\frac{V_i^-}{V_i^+ + V_i^-} \right) \right],$$

where V_i^+ is the number of positive instances in C with $F = v_i$, and V_i^- is the number of negative instances in C with $F = v_i$.

This CLS algorithm can be viewed as a refinement-operator algorithm with only one operator:

> Specialize the current hypothesis by adding a new condition (a new decision node).

The CLS algorithm repeatedly examines the data during step 1 to decide which new condition should be added. The final decision tree developed by CLS is a generalization of the training instances, because in most cases not all features present in the training instances need to be tested in the tree. Thus, CLS begins with a very general hypothesis and gradually specializes it, by adding conditions, until a consistent tree is found.

The ID3 Learning Algorithm

The CLS algorithm requires that all of the training instances be available on a random-access basis during step 1. This places a practical limit on the size of the learning problems that it can solve. The ID3 algorithm (Quinlan, 1979, in press) is an extension to CLS designed to solve extremely large concept-learning problems. It uses an active experiment-planning approach to select a good *subset* of the training instances and requires only sequential access to the whole set of training instances. Here is an outline of the ID3 algorithm:

Step 1. Select a random subset of size W of the whole set of training instances (W is called the *window size*, and the subset is called the *window*).

Step 2. Use the CLS algorithm to form a rule to explain the current window.

Step 3. Scan through *all* of the training instances serially to find exceptions to the current rule.

Step 4. Form a new window by combining some of the training instances from the current window with some of the exceptions obtained in step 3.

Repeat steps 2 through 4 until there are no exceptions to the rule.

Quinlan has experimented with two different strategies for building the new window in step 4. One strategy is to retain all of the instances from the old window and add a user-specified number of the exceptions obtained from step 3. This gradually expands the window. The second strategy is to retain one training instance corresponding to each leaf node in the current decision tree. The remaining training instances are discarded from the window and replaced by exceptions. Both methods work quite well, although the second method may not converge if the concept is so complex that it cannot be discovered with *any* window of fixed size *W*.

Application of the ID3 Algorithm

The ID3 algorithm has been applied to the problem of learning classification rules for part of a chess end-game in which the only pieces remaining are a white king and rook and a black king and knight. ID3 has discovered rules to describe the concept of "knight's side lost (in at most) *n* moves" for $n = 2$ and $n = 3$. Table D3b–1 shows the results of these processes.

The features describing the board positions have been chosen to capture patterns believed to be relevant to the concept of *lost in n moves*. The actual raw data for the *lost in 2 moves* concept comprise 1.8 million distinct board positions. By choosing appropriate features, Quinlan was able to compress these into 428 distinct feature vectors. This is an excellent example of the importance to concept learning of good representation and of knowledge-based interpretation of the raw data. Quinlan (in press) points out that an important task for future learning research is to develop a program that can discover a good set of features.

Strengths and Weaknesses of CLS and ID3

The ID3 and CLS programs with their very simple representations and straightforward learning algorithms perform impressively on the single-concept

TABLE D3b–1

The Application of ID3 to a Chess End-game

Concept	Number of training instances	Number of features	Size of decision tree	Solution time
Lost in 2 moves	30,000	25	334 nodes	144 seconds[a]
Lost in 2 moves	428	23	83 nodes	3 seconds[a]
Lost in 3 moves	715	39	177 nodes	34 seconds[b]

[a]Using PASCAL implementation on a DEC KL–10.

[b]Using PASCAL implementation on a CDC CYBER 72.

learning problem. Much of the power of the ID3 algorithm derives from its sophisticated selection of training instances. This form of instance selection has been termed *expectation-based filtering* by Lenat, Hayes-Roth, and Klahr (1979). The basic value of expectation-based filtering is that it focuses the attention of the program on those training instances that violate its expectations. These are precisely the training instances needed to improve the program's representation of the concept being learned. Even this simple form of experiment planning allows ID3 to solve large learning problems efficiently.

One of the chief difficulties of the CLS/ID3 method is that the representation for learned concepts is a decision tree, and decision trees are difficult to check for equivalence. What is more important, it is difficult for people to understand the learned concept when it is expressed as a large decision tree.

References

The best discussion of BACON is Langley (1980). The ID3 algorithm is well described in Quinlan (in press).

D3c. Concept Learning by Generating and Testing Plausible Hypotheses

THE two model-driven approaches discussed in Article XIV.D1 on issues—generate-and-test and schema instantiation—have received little attention from people doing learning research. This article describes one method, developed by Dietterich and Michalski, that discovers a single concept from examples by model-driven generate and test. In spite of using only a very simple model, this method exhibits the strengths and weaknesses that are typical of model-driven methods: It is quite immune to noise but cannot incrementally modify its concept description as new training instances become available.

The INDUCE 1.2 Algorithm

Dietterich and Michalski (1981) address the problem of learning a single concept from positive training instances only. Their program, INDUCE 1.2, is intended to be applied in *structural-learning* situations, that is, situations in which each training instance has some internal structure. Winston's toy-block constructions, for example, are structural training instances; a toy-block construction is represented as a set of nodes connected by structural relations like ONTOP, TOUCH, and SUPPORTS (see Article XIV.D3a). Dietterich and Michalski's model, which guides the search for generalizations, expects the learned concept to be a conjunction involving both structural relations and ordinary features.

INDUCE 1.2 seeks to find a few concepts in the rule space, each of which covers all of the training instances while remaining as specific as possible. This learning problem is similar to the problem of finding the S set in the candidate-elimination algorithm. INDUCE 1.2, however, applies some model-based heuristics to drastically prune the S set so that only a few generalizations are discovered.

The program assumes that the training instances have been transformed so that they can be viewed as very specific points in the rule space (i.e., it uses the single-representation trick). A random sample of the training instances is chosen. These points in rule space serve as the starting points for a beam search upward through the rule space, that is, from the very specific training instances toward more general concepts. The concept descriptions are generalized by dropping conjunctive conditions and adding internal disjunctive options until they cover all of the training instances. By starting at the most specific points in the rule space and stopping as soon as it finds concepts that cover all of the training instances, INDUCE 1.2 is guaranteed to find the most specific concepts that cover the data.

The beam-search process has the following steps:

Step 1. *Initialize.* Set H to contain a randomly chosen subset of size W of the training instances (W is a constant called the *beam width*).

Step 2. *Generate.* Generalize each concept in H by dropping single conditions in all possible ways. This produces all the concept descriptions that are minimally more general than those in H. These form the new H.

Step 3. *Prune implausible hypotheses.* Remove all but W of the concept descriptions from H. The pruning is based on syntactic characteristics of the concept description, such as the number of terms and the user-defined cost of the terms. Another criterion is to maximize the number of training instances covered by each element of H.

Step 4. *Test.* Check each concept description in H to see if it covers all of the training instances. (This information was obtained previously in step 3.) If any concept does, remove it from H and place it in a set C of output concepts.

Repeat steps 2, 3, and 4 until C reaches a prespecified size limit or H becomes empty.

A schematic diagram of the beam-search process is shown in Figure D3c–1.

Extensions to the Basic Algorithm

Structural learning problems of the kind INDUCE 1.2 was designed to attack require binary (and higher order) predicates to represent the desired

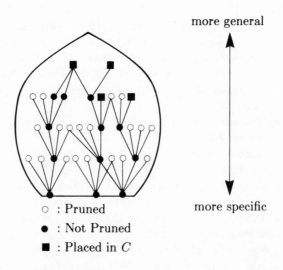

Figure D3c–1.   A schematic diagram of INDUCE 1.2's beam search.

concepts. The binary predicates are needed to express relationships among the parts (e.g., toy blocks) that make up each training instance. In Winston's arch training instances, for example, binary predicates could be used to represent the fact that two blocks are touching—TOUCH(a, b)—or that one block is supporting another—SUPPORTS(a, b). Unary predicates and functions are, of course, still needed as well. Typically, they represent the attributes of the parts of an instance. In Winston's arches, for example, unary predicates could represent the size and shape of each block. The syntactic distinction between unary and binary predicates thus corresponds to a semantic distinction between feature values and binary relationships.

Although it is *possible* to represent structural relationships using only unary predicates or functions, such a representation is cumbersome and unnatural. Consequently, this distinction—by which binary and higher order predicates correspond to structural relationships and unary predicates and functions correspond to feature values—holds in most structural learning situations.

Dietterich and Michalski take advantage of this dichotomy to improve the efficiency of INDUCE 1.2's rule-space search. Two separate rule spaces are used. The first rule space, called the structure-only space, is the space of all concepts expressible using only the binary (and higher order) terms in the representation language. The training instances are abstracted into this space (by dropping all unary predicates and functions), and then the generate-and-test beam search is applied to this abstract rule space.

Once the set, C, of candidate structure-only concepts is obtained, each concept, c_i, in C is used to define a new rule space, consisting of all concepts expressible in terms of the attributes of the subobjects (e.g., blocks) referred to in c_i. This space can be represented with a simple feature-vector representation. The training instances are transformed into very specific points in this space, and another beam search is conducted to find a set, C', of plausible concept descriptions. The descriptions in C' specify the attributes for the subobjects referred to in c_i. Taken together, one concept in C' combined with c_i provides a complete concept description.

As an example of this two-space approach, consider the two positive training instances depicted below:

Instance 1.   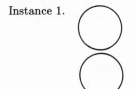 $\exists\, u, v : \text{LARGE}(u) \wedge \text{CIRCLE}(u) \wedge$
$\text{LARGE}(v) \wedge \text{CIRCLE}(v) \wedge \text{ONTOP}(u, v)$.

Instance 2. 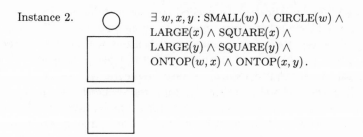 $\exists\ w, x, y : \text{SMALL}(w) \wedge \text{CIRCLE}(w) \wedge$
$\text{LARGE}(x) \wedge \text{SQUARE}(x) \wedge$
$\text{LARGE}(y) \wedge \text{SQUARE}(y) \wedge$
$\text{ONTOP}(w, x) \wedge \text{ONTOP}(x, y)\,.$

When these two training instances are translated into the structure-only rule space, the following abstract training instances are obtained:

Instance 1′. $\exists\ u, v : \text{ONTOP}(u, v)\,.$

Instance 2′. $\exists\ w, x, y : \text{ONTOP}(w, x) \wedge \text{ONTOP}(x, y)\,.$

The INDUCE 1.2 beam search discovers that $C = \{\text{ONTOP}(u, v)\}$ is the only, least general, structure-only concept consistent with the training instances. Now a new attribute-vector rule space is developed with the features of u and v:

$$\langle \text{SIZE}(u), \text{SHAPE}(u), \text{SIZE}(v), \text{SHAPE}(v) \rangle\,.$$

The training instances are translated to obtain:

Instance 1″.   ⟨large, circle, large, circle⟩.

Instance 2.1″.   ⟨small, circle, large, square⟩.

Instance 2.2″.   ⟨large, square, large, square⟩.

Notice that two alternative training instances are obtained from instance 2′, since $\text{ONTOP}(u, v)$ can match instance 2 in two possible ways (u bound to w, v bound to x; or u bound to x, v bound to y). During the beam search, only one of these two instances, 2.1″ and 2.2″, need be covered by a concept description for that description to be consistent.

The second beam search is conducted in this feature-vector space, and the concepts ⟨large, *, large, *⟩ and ⟨*, circle, large, *⟩ are found to be the least general concepts that cover all of the training instances ("*" indicates that the corresponding feature is irrelevant). By combining each of these feature-only concepts with the structure-only concept $\text{ONTOP}(u, v)$, two overall consistent concept descriptions are obtained:

$$C_1: \exists\ u, v : \text{ONTOP}(u, v) \wedge \text{LARGE}(u) \wedge \text{LARGE}(v)\,,$$
$$C_2: \exists\ u, v : \text{ONTOP}(u, v) \wedge \text{CIRCLE}(u) \wedge \text{LARGE}(v)\,.$$

These correspond to the observations that in both instance 1 and instance 2 there are (C_1) "always a large object on top of another large object" and (C_2) "always a circle on top of a large object."

Strengths and Weaknesses of the INDUCE 1.2 Approach

The basic algorithm suffers from the absence of a strong model to guide the pruning of descriptions in step 3 and the termination of the search in step 4. The present syntactic criteria, of minimizing the number of terms in a proposed concept, minimizing the user-defined cost of the terms, and maximizing the number of training instances covered, are very weak. Dietterich and Michalski claim that domain-specific information could easily be applied at this point to improve the model-based pruning.

A second weakness is that step 2 involves exhaustive enumeration of all possible single-step generalizations of the hypotheses in H. This can be very costly in a large rule space. The method of plausible generate and test works best if the generator can be constrained to generate only plausible hypotheses. The generator in INDUCE 1.2 relies on a subsequent pruning step, which is quite costly.

A third weakness of the method is that, because it prunes its search, it is incomplete (see Dietterich and Michalski, 1981). It does not find all minimally general concepts in the rule space that cover all of the training instances.

As with all model-driven methods, this approach does not work well in incremental learning situations. All of the training instances must be available to the learning algorithm simultaneously.

The advantages of the algorithm are that it is faster and uses less memory than the full version-space approach. As with all model-based methods, INDUCE 1.2 has good noise immunity. In particular, if INDUCE 1.2 is to be given noisy training instances, then step 4 can be modified to include in C the concepts that cover *most,* rather than all, of the training instances.

References

Dietterich and Michalski (1981) describe INDUCE 1.2.

D3d. Schema Instantiation

SCHEMA–INSTANTIATION techniques have been used in many AI systems that perform comprehension tasks such as image interpretation, natural-language understanding, and speech understanding. Few learning systems have employed schema-instantiation methods, however. These methods are useful when a system has a substantial number of constraints that can be grouped together to form a schema, an abstract skeletal rule. The search of the rule space can then be guided to only those portions of the space that *fit* one of the available schemas. In this section, we describe one learning system, SPARC, that uses schema instantiation to discover single concepts.

Discovering Rules in Eleusis with SPARC

Dietterich's (1979) SPARC system attempts to solve a learning problem that arises in the card game Eleusis. Eleusis (developed by Robert Abbott, 1977; see also Gardner, 1977) is a card game in which players attempt to discover a secret rule invented by the dealer. The secret rule describes a linear sequence of cards. In their turns, the players attempt to extend this sequence by playing additional cards from their hands. The dealer gives no information aside from indicating whether or not each play is consistent with the secret rule. Players are penalized for incorrect plays by having cards added to their hands. The game ends when a player empties his hand.

A record of the play is maintained as a layout (see Fig. D3d–1) in which the top row, or *main line,* contains all of the correctly played cards in sequence. Incorrect cards are placed in *side lines* below the main-line card that they follow. In the layout shown in Figure D3d–1, the first card correctly played was the 3 of hearts (3H). This was followed by another correct play, the 9 of spades (9S). Following the 9, two incorrect plays were made (JD and 5D) before the next correct card (4C) was played successfully.

Main line:	3H	9S	4C	9D	2C	10D	8H	7H	2C	5H
Side lines:		JD		AH	AS			10H		
		5D		8H	10S					
				QD						

If the last card is odd, play black; if the last card is even, play red.

Figure D3d–1. An Eleusis layout and the corresponding secret rule.

The scoring in Eleusis encourages the dealer to choose rules of intermediate difficulty. The dealer's score is determined by the difference between the highest and lowest scores of the players. Thus, a good rule is one that is easy for some players and hard for others.

Schemas in Eleusis

In ordinary play of Eleusis, certain classes of rules have been observed. Dietterich has identified three rule classes and developed a parameterized schema for each:

1. **Periodic rules.** A periodic rule describes the layout as a sequence of repeating features. For example, the rule *Play alternating red and black cards* is a periodic rule. Dietterich's rule schema for this class can be described as an N-tuple of conjunctive descriptions:

$$\langle C_1, C_2, \ldots, C_N \rangle.$$

The parameter N is the length of the period (the number of cards before the period starts to repeat). The above-mentioned periodic rule would be represented as a 2-tuple:

$$\langle \text{RED}(card_i), \text{BLACK}(card_i) \rangle.$$

More complex periodic rules may refer to the previous periods. Thus, the rule

$$\langle \text{RANK}(card_i) \geq \text{RANK}(card_{i-1}), \text{RANK}(card_i) \leq \text{RANK}(card_{i-1}) \rangle$$

describes a layout composed of alternating ascending and descending sequences of cards.

2. **Decomposition rules.** A decomposition rule describes the layout by a set of *if-then* rules. For example, the rule *If the last card is odd, play black; if the last card is even, play red* is a decomposition rule. The rule schema for this class requires that the set of *if-then* rules have single conjunctions for the *if* and *then* parts of each rule. The *if* parts must be mutually exclusive, and they must span all possibilities. The above-mentioned rule can be written as:

$$\text{ODD}(card_{i-1}) \Rightarrow \text{BLACK}(card_i) \vee$$
$$\text{EVEN}(card_{i-1}) \Rightarrow \text{RED}(card_i).$$

3. **Disjunctive rules.** The third class of rules includes any rules that can be represented by a single disjunction of conjunctions (i.e., an expression in disjunctive normal form, or DNF). For example, the rule *Play a card of the same rank or the same suit as the preceding card* is a DNF rule. This is represented as:

$$\text{RANK}(card_i) = \text{RANK}(card_{i-1}) \vee \text{SUIT}(card_i) = \text{SUIT}(card_{i-1}).$$

Each schema has a few parameters that control its application. The N (length of period) parameter of the period schema has already been described. Each schema also has a parameter L, called the lookback parameter, that indicates how many cards back into the past the rule may consider. Thus, when $L = 0$, no preceding cards are examined. When $L = 1$, the features of the current card are compared with the previous card, and expressions such as $\text{RANK}(card_i) \geq \text{RANK}(card_{i-1})$ are permitted. Larger values of L provide for even further lookback.

Searching the Rule Space Using Schemas

Each schema can be viewed as having its own rule space—the set of all rules that can be obtained by instantiating that schema. SPARC uses the single-representation trick to reformulate the layout as a set of very specific rules for each of the schema-specific rule spaces. The overall algorithm works as follows:

Step 1. *Parameterize a schema.* SPARC chooses a schema and selects particular values for the parameters of that schema.

Step 2. *Interpret the training instances.* Transform the training instances (i.e., the cards in the layout) into very specific rules that fit the chosen schema.

Step 3. *Instantiate the schema.* Generalize the transformed training instances to fit the schema. SPARC uses a schema-specific algorithm to accomplish this step.

Step 4. *Evaluate the instantiated schema.* Determine how well the schema fits the data. Poorly fitting rules are discarded.

SPARC conducts a depth-first search of the space of all parameterizations of all schemas up to a user-specified limit on the magnitudes of the parameters. Notice that a separate interpretation step is required for each parameterized schema.

When these steps are applied to the game shown in Figure D3d–1, for example, step 1 eventually chooses the decomposition schema with $L = 1$. Step 2 then converts the training instances into very specific rules in the corresponding rule space. In this case, the first five cards produce the training instances shown below. The instances are represented by the feature vector $\langle \text{RANK, SUIT, COLOR, PARITY} \rangle$ to describe each card. (SPARC actually generates 24 features to describe each training instance.)

Instance 1 (positive). $\langle 3,\ hearts,\ red,\ odd \rangle \quad \Rightarrow \quad \langle 9,\ spades,\ black,\ odd \rangle$.
Instance 2 (negative). $\langle 9,\ spades,\ black,\ odd \rangle \quad \Rightarrow \quad \langle jack,\ diamonds,\ red,\ odd \rangle$.
Instance 3 (negative). $\langle 9,\ spades,\ black,\ odd \rangle \quad \Rightarrow \quad \langle 5,\ diamonds,\ red,\ odd \rangle$.
Instance 4 (positive). $\langle 9,\ spades,\ black,\ odd \rangle \quad \Rightarrow \quad \langle 4,\ clubs,\ black,\ even \rangle$.

Step 3 produces the following instantiated schema (with irrelevant features indicated by $*$):

$$\langle *, *, *, odd \rangle \;\; \Rightarrow \;\; \langle *, *, black, * \rangle \vee \langle *, *, *, even \rangle \;\; \Rightarrow \;\; \langle *, *, red, * \rangle.$$

Step 4 determines that this rule is entirely consistent with the training instances and is syntactically simple. Consequently, the rule is accepted as a hypothesis for the dealer's secret rule.

The schema-instantiation method works well when step 3, the schema-instantiation step, is easy to accomplish. A good schema provides many constraints that limit the size of its rule space. In SPARC, for example, the periodic and decomposition schemas require that their rules be made up of single conjuncts only. This is a strong constraint that can be incorporated into the model-fitting algorithm. On the other hand, the DNF schema provides few constraints and, consequently, an efficient instantiation algorithm could not be written. The general-purpose A^q algorithm (see Article XIV.D3a) was used instead.

Strengths and Weaknesses of SPARC

The schema-instantiation method used in SPARC was able to find plausible Eleusis rules very quickly. This is the primary advantage of the schema-instantiation approach—large rule spaces can be searched quickly. A second advantage of this approach is that it has good noise immunity. The schema-instantiation process has access to the full set of training instances, and, thus, it can use statistical measures to guide the search of rule space.

There are three important disadvantages of the schema-instantiation method as used in SPARC. First, it is difficult to isolate a group of constraints and combine them to form a schema. The three schemas in SPARC, although they cover most "secret rules" pretty well, are known to miss some important rules. The task of coming up with new schemas, however, is particularly difficult. A second problem with the schema-instantiation approach is that special schema-instantiation algorithms must be developed for each schema. This makes it difficult to apply the approach in new domains. The third disadvantage is that separate interpretation methods need to be developed for each schema. This was less of a problem in the Eleusis domain, because the interpretation processes for the different schemas were very similar.

References

Dietterich (1979) is the original description of the SPARC program. Dietterich (1980) is a more accessible source. See also Dietterich and Michalski (in press).

D4.   Learning Multiple Concepts

A FEW AI learning systems have been developed that discover a *set* of concepts from training instances. These systems perform tasks, such as disease diagnosis and mass-spectrometer simulation, for which a single concept or classification rule is not sufficient.

To understand the problems of learning multiple concepts, it is helpful to review single-concept learning. In single-concept learning (see Sec. XIV.D3), the learning element is presented with positive and negative instances of some concept, and it must find a concept description that effectively partitions the space of all instances into two regions: positive and negative. All instances in the positive region are believed by the learning system to be examples of the single concept (see Fig. D4–1).

In multiple-concept learning, the situation is slightly more complicated. The learning element is presented with training instances that are instances of several concepts, and it must find several concept descriptions. For each concept description, there is a corresponding region in the instance space (see Fig. D4–2). An important multiple-concept learning problem is the problem of discovering disease-diagnosis rules from training instances. The learning element is presented with training instances that each contain a description of a patient's symptoms and the proper diagnosis as determined by a doctor. The program must discover a set of rules of the form:

⟨description of symptoms for disease A⟩ ⇒ Disease is A,

⟨description of symptoms for disease B⟩ ⇒ Disease is B,

$$\vdots$$

⟨description of symptoms for disease N⟩ ⇒ Disease is N.

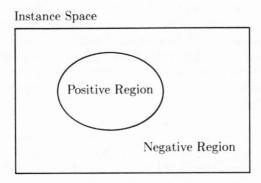

Figure D4–1.   A single concept viewed as a region
of the instance space.

Instance Space

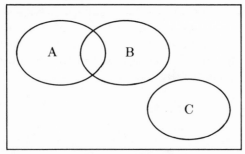

Figure D4–2.   Regions of the instance space corresponding to different rules.

The left-hand side of each rule is a concept description that corresponds to
a region in the instance space of all possible symptoms (see Fig. D4–2). Any
patient whose symptoms fall in region A, for example, will be diagnosed as
having disease A.

An important issue arising in multiple-concept learning is the problem
of overlapping concept descriptions—that is, overlapping left-hand sides of
diagnosis rules. In Figure D4–2, for example, when a patient's symptoms fall
in the area where regions A and B overlap, the system will diagnose the patient
as having both diseases A and B. This overlap may be correct, since there
are often cases in which a patient has more than one disease simultaneously.
On the other hand, it is often the case in multiple-concept problems that
the various classes are intended to be mutually exclusive. For example, if,
instead of diagnosing diseases, the performance task is to classify images of
handwritten characters, it is important that the system arrive at a unique
classification for each character.

The problem of overlap among multiple concepts can lead to *integration*
problems, as described in Article XIV.A. When a new rule or concept is added
to the knowledge base in a multiple-concept system, it may be necessary to
modify the left-hand sides of existing rules, particularly if the concept classes
are intended to be mutually exclusive.

The systems described in this section differ from those described in the
Section XIV.D5 on multiple-step tasks in that the performance tasks discussed here can all be accomplished in a single step. The various disease-
classification rules, for example, can be applied simultaneously to classify a
patient's symptoms. Tasks for which this is not the case—like playing checkers or solving symbolic integration problems—are discussed in Section XIV.D5.

We first discuss the work of Michalski and his colleagues on the AQ11
program, which learns a set of classification rules for the diagnosis of soybean

diseases. Second, we describe the Meta-DENDRAL system, which learns a set of cleavage rules that describe the operation of a chemical instrument called the mass spectrometer. Finally, the AM system, which discovers new concepts in mathematics, is discussed in some detail. Since these systems do not all address the same learning problem, we begin each article with a description of the particular learning problem being attacked and then discuss the methods employed to accomplish the learning.

D4a.   AQ11

MICHALSKI and his colleagues (Michalski and Larson, 1978; Michalski and Chilausky, 1980) have developed several techniques for learning a set of classification rules. The performance element that applies these rules is a pattern classifier that takes an unknown pattern and classifies it into one of n classes (see Fig. D4a–1). Many performance tasks, such as optical character recognition and disease diagnosis, have this form.

The classification rules are learned from training instances consisting of sample patterns and their correct classifications. For the classifier to be as efficient as possible, the classification rules should test as few features of the input pattern as necessary to classify it reliably. This is particularly relevant in areas like medicine, where the measurement of each additional feature of the input pattern may be very costly and dangerous. Consequently, Michalski's learning program AQ11 (Michalski and Larson, 1978) seeks to find the *most general rule* in the rule space that discriminates training instances in class c_i from all training instances in all other classes c_j $(i \neq j)$. Dieterich and Michalski (1981) call these *discriminant descriptions* or *discrimination rules*, since their purpose is to discriminate one class from a predetermined set of other classes.

Using the A^q Algorithm to Find Discrimination Rules

The representation language used by Michalski to represent discrimination rules is VL_1, an extension of the propositional calculus. VL_1 is a fairly rich

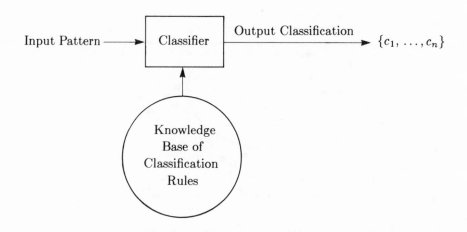

Figure D4a–1.   The n-category classification task.

language that includes conjunction, disjunction, and set-membership operators. Consequently, the rule space of all possible VL_1 discrimination rules is quite large. To search this rule space, AQ11 uses the A^q algorithm, which is nearly equivalent to the repeated application of the candidate-elimination algorithm (see Article XIV.D3a). AQ11 converts the problem of learning discrimination rules into a series of single-concept learning problems. To find a rule for class c_i, it considers all of the known instances in class c_i as positive instances and all other training instances in all of the remaining classes as negative instances. The A^q algorithm is then applied to find a description that covers all of the positive instances without covering any of the negative instances. AQ11 seeks the most general such description, which corresponds to a necessary condition for class membership. Figure D4a–2 shows schematically how this works. The dots represent known training instances, and the circle represents the set of possible training instances that are covered by the description of class c_1.

For each class c_i, such a "concept" is discovered. The result is shown schematically in Figure D4a–3.

Note that the discrimination rules may overlap in regions of the instance space that have not yet been observed. This overlap is useful because it allows the performance element to be somewhat conservative. In the areas in which the discrimination rules are ambiguous (i.e., overlap), the performance element can report this to the user rather than assign the unknown instance to one arbitrarily chosen class.

AQ11 also has a method for finding a nonoverlapping set of classification rules. Since the A^q algorithm uses the single-representation trick, it can accept not only single points in the instance space (as represented by very specific points in the rule space) but also generalized "instances" that are conjuncts

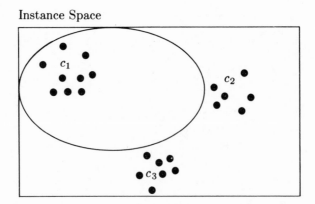

Figure D4a–2. Learning c_1 by treating all other classes
as negative instances.

Instance Space

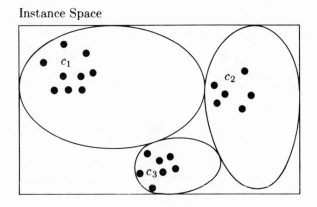

Figure D4a–3.   Finding single concepts for each class.

in the rule space corresponding to *sets* of training instances. This allows AQ11 to treat the *concept descriptions* themselves as negative examples when it is learning the concept description for a subsequent class. Thus, in order to obtain a nonoverlapping set of discrimination rules, AQ11 takes as its positive instances all known instances in c_i and as its negative instances all known instances in c_j $(j \neq i)$ *plus* all conjuncts that make up the discrimination rules for previously processed classes c_k $(k < i)$. The resulting disjoint rules are shown schematically in Figure D4a–4 (assuming the classes were processed in the order c_1, c_2, c_3).

The rules that are developed split up the unobserved part of the instance space in such a way that c_1 gets the largest share, c_2 covers any space not covered by c_1, c_3 covers any space not covered by c_1 or c_2, and so on. The way in which the space is divided up depends on the order in which the classes are

Instance Space

Figure D4a–4.   Finding nonoverlapping classification rules.

processed. A performance element that uses such a disjoint set of concepts will be reckless in the sense that it will assign an unknown instance to an arbitrary class. The classifier arbitrarily prefers c_1 to c_2, c_2 to c_3, and so on.

The discrimination rules developed by AQ11 correspond (roughly) to the set of most general descriptions consistent with the training instances—the G set in the candidate-elimination algorithm (see Sec. XIV.D3). In many situations, it is also good to develop, for each class c_i, the most specific (S-set) description of that class. This permits very explicit handling of the unobserved portions of the space. Figure D4a–5 shows such a set of descriptions.

When S and G sets are both available, the performance element can choose among definite classification (the instance is covered by the S set), probable classification (the instance is covered by only one G set), and multiple classification (the instance is covered by several G sets). AQ11 has the ability to calculate an approximate S set for each class. When the description of the class is disjunctive, the S set is also disjunctive.

Applications of AQ11

The AQ11 program has been applied to the problem of discovering disease-diagnosis rules for 15 soybean diseases (Michalski and Chilausky, 1980). Here is an example of a classification rule for the disease Rhizoctonia root rot obtained by the overlapping-concept approach discussed above:

leaves ∈ {normal} ∧ stem ∈ {abnormal} ∧
stem cankers ∈ {below soil line} ∧ canker lesion color ∈ {brown} ∨

leaf malformation ∈ {absent} ∧ stem ∈ {abnormal} ∧
stem cankers ∈ {below soil line} ∧ canker lesion color ∈ {brown}
⇒ Rhizoctonia root rot .

Instance Space

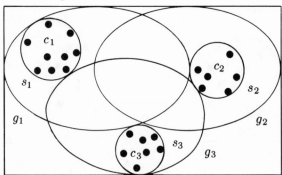

Figure D4a–5.   Learning both the G and S set descriptions
for each class.

An interesting experiment was conducted as part of the soybean disease project. The goal was to compare the quality of rules obtained through consultation with expert plant pathologists with rules developed by learning from examples. Descriptions of 630 diseased soybean plants were entered into the computer (as feature vectors involving 35 features) along with an expert's diagnosis of each plant. A special instance-selection program, ESEL, was used to select 290 of the sample plants as training instances. ESEL attempts to select training instances that are quite different from one another—instances that are "far apart" in the instance space. The remaining 340 instances were set aside to serve as a testing set for comparing the performance of the machine-derived rules with the performance of the expert-derived rules.

AQ11 was then run on the 290 training instances to develop overlapping rules such as the rule above. Simultaneously, the researchers consulted with the plant pathologist to obtain a set of rules. They adopted the standard knowledge-engineering approach of interviewing the expert and translating his expertise into diagnosis rules. The expert insisted on using a description language that was somewhat more expressive than the language used by AQ11. The expert's rules, for example, listed some features as necessary and other features as confirmatory; AQ11 was unable to make such a distinction.

As a consequence of the differing description languages, slightly differing performance elements had to be developed to apply the two sets of rules, and each performance element was adjusted to get the best performance from its classification rules. Surprisingly, the computer-generated rules outperformed the expert-derived rules. Despite the fact that the expert-derived rules were expressed in a more powerful language, the machine-generated rules gave the correct disease top ranking 97.6% of the time, compared to only 71.8% for the expert-derived rules. Overall, the machine-generated rules listed the correct disease among the possible diagnoses 100% of the time, in contrast to 96.9% for the expert's rules. Furthermore, the computer-derived rules tended to list fewer alternative diagnoses. The conclusion of the experiment was that automatic rule induction can, in some situations, lead to more reliable and more precise diagnosis rules than those obtained by consultation with the expert.

References

Michalski and Larson (1978) describe the AQ11 and ESEL programs in detail. The soybean work is described in Michalski and Chilausky (1980).

D4b. Meta–DENDRAL

META-DENDRAL (Buchanan and Mitchell, 1978) is a program that discovers rules describing the operation of a chemical instrument called a *mass spectrometer*. The mass spectrometer is a device that bombards small chemical samples with accelerated electrons, causing the molecules of the sample to break apart into many charged fragments. The masses of these fragments can then be measured to produce a *mass spectrum*—a histogram of the number of fragments (also called the *intensity*) plotted against their mass-to-charge ratio (see Fig. D4b–1).

An analytic chemist can infer the molecular structure of the sample chemical through careful inspection of the mass spectrum. The Heuristic DENDRAL program (see Sec. VII.C2, in Vol. II) is able to perform this task automatically. It is supplied with the chemical formula (but not the *structure*) of the sample and its mass spectrum. Heuristic DENDRAL first examines the spectrum to obtain a set of constraints. These constraints are then supplied to CONGEN, a program that can generate all possible chemical structures satisfying the constraints. Finally, each of these generated structures is tested by running it through a mass-spectrometer simulator. The simulator applies a set of *cleavage rules* to predict which bonds in the proposed structure will be broken. The result is a simulated mass spectrum for each candidate structure. The simulated spectra are compared with the actual spectrum, and the structure whose simulated spectrum best matches the actual spectrum is ranked as the most likely structure for the unknown sample.

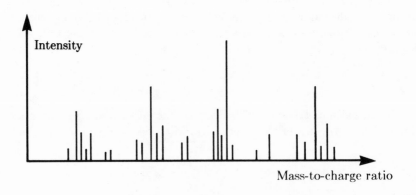

Figure D4b–1. A mass spectrum.

The Learning Problem

Meta-DENDRAL was designed to serve as the learning element for Heuristic DENDRAL. (For an alternate view of Meta-DENDRAL as an expert system, see Article VII.C2c, in Vol. II.) Its purpose is to discover new cleavage rules for DENDRAL's mass-spectrometer simulator. These rules are grouped according to *structural families*. Chemists have noted that molecules that share the same structural skeleton behave in similar ways inside the mass spectrometer. Conversely, molecules with vastly different structures behave in vastly different ways. Thus, no single set of cleavage rules can accurately describe the behavior of all molecules in the mass spectrometer.

Figure D4b–2 shows an example of a structural skeleton for the family of monoketoandrostanes. Particular molecules in this family are constructed by attaching keto groups (OH) to any of the available carbon atoms in the skeleton.

The learning problem addressed by Meta-DENDRAL is to discover the cleavage rules for a particular structural family. The problem can be stated as follows:

Given: (a) A representation language for describing molecular structures and substructures; and

(b) A training set of known molecules, chosen from a single structural family, along with their structures and their mass spectra;

Find: A set of cleavage rules that characterize the behavior of this structural family in the mass spectrometer.

This learning problem is difficult because it contains two sources of ambiguity. First, the mass spectra of the training molecules are noise-ridden. There may be falsely observed fragments (false positives) and important fragments that may not have been observed (false negatives). Second, the cleavage rules need

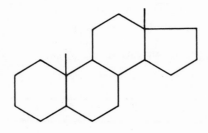

Figure D4b–2.   The structural skeleton for the monoketo-
androstane family.

not be entirely consistent with the training instances. A rule that correctly predicts a cleavage in more than half of the molecules can be considered to be acceptable; the rules need not be cautious. It is safer—from the point of view of DENDRAL's simulation task—to predict cleavages that do not occur than it is to fail to predict cleavages that do occur.

Meta-DENDRAL's representation language corresponds to the ball-and-stick models used by chemists. The molecule is represented as an undirected graph in which nodes denote atoms and edges denote chemical bonds. Hydrogen atoms are not included in the graph. Each atom can have four features: (a) the atom type (e.g., carbon, nitrogen), (b) the number of nonhydrogen neighbors, (c) the number of hydrogen atoms that are bonded to the atom, and (d) the number of double bonds in which the atom participates. A cleavage rule is expressed in terms of a *bond environment*—a portion of the molecular structure surrounding a particular bond. The bond environment makes up the condition part of a cleavage rule. The action part of the rule specifies that the designated bond will cleave in the mass spectrometer. Figure D4b–3 shows a typical cleavage rule.

The performance element (the simulator) applies the production rule by matching the left-hand-side bond environment to the molecular structure that is undergoing simulated bombardment. Whenever the left-hand-side pattern is matched, the right-hand-side predicts that the bond designated by $*$ will break.

The Interpretation Problem and the Subprogram INTSUM

Meta-DENDRAL employs the method of model-driven generate-and-test to search the rule space of possible cleavage rules. Before it can carry out this search, however, it must first interpret the training instances and convert them into very specific points in the rule space (i.e., into very specific cleavage rules).

$$x—y—z—w \;\Rightarrow\; x—y \;*\; z—w$$

Node	Atom type	Neighbors	H-neighbors	Double bonds
x	carbon	3	1	0
y	carbon	2	2	0
z	nitrogen	2	1	0
w	carbon	2	2	0

Figure D4b–3.   A typical cleavage rule.

The interpretation process is accomplished by the subprogram INTSUM (INTerpretation and SUMmary). Recall that the training instances have the form:

⟨whole molecular structure⟩ ⇒ ⟨mass spectrum⟩.

INTSUM seeks to develop a *set* of very specific cleavage rules of the form:

⟨whole molecular structure⟩ ⇒ ⟨one designated broken bond⟩.

To make this conversion, INTSUM must hypothesize which bonds were broken to produce which peaks in the spectrum. It accomplishes this by means of a "dumb" version of the DENDRAL mass-spectrometer simulator. Since Meta-DENDRAL is attempting to discover cleavage rules for this particular structural class, it cannot use those same cleavage rules to drive the simulation. Instead, a simple *half-order theory* of mass spectrometry is adopted.

The half-order theory describes the action of the mass spectrometer as a sequence of complete fragmentations of the molecule. One fragmentation slices the molecule into two pieces. A subsequent fragmentation may further split one of those two pieces to create two smaller pieces, and so on. After each fragmentation, some atoms from one piece of the molecule may migrate to the other piece (or be lost altogether). The half-order theory places certain constraints on this *split-and-migrate* process. It says that all bonds will break in the molecule *except* the following:

1. Double and triple bonds do not break;
2. Bonds in aromatic rings do not break;
3. Two bonds involving the same atom do not break simultaneously;
4. No more than three bonds break simultaneously;
5. At most, only two fragmentations occur (one after the other);
6. No more than two rings can be split as the result of both of the fragmentations.

Constraints are also placed on the kinds of migrations that can occur:

1. No more than two hydrogen atoms migrate after a fragmentation;
2. At most, one H_2O is lost;
3. At most, one CO is lost.

The parameters of the theory are flexible and can be adjusted by the user of Meta-DENDRAL.

Based on this theory, INTSUM simulates the bombarding and cleaving of the molecular structures provided in the training instances. The result is a simulated spectrum in which each simulated peak has an associated record of the bond cleavages that caused that peak to appear. Each simulated peak is compared with the actual observed peaks. If their masses match, then INTSUM infers that the "cause" of the simulated peak is a plausible explanation of the observed peak. If a simulated peak finds no matching observed peak, it is ignored. If an observed peak remains unexplained, it is also ignored. However, unexplained peaks are reported to the chemist. A large proportion of unexplained peaks would indicate that the half-order theory was inadequate to explain the operation of the mass spectrometer in this training instance.

The half-order theory contributes another source of ambiguity to the learning problem. The interpreted set of training instances can easily contain erroneous instances. INTSUM's half-order theory tends to predict cleavages that did not, in fact, occur. It is also not unusual for the half-order theory to fail to predict cleavages that did occur. Thus, the training instances that guide the rule space search are very noisy indeed.

The Search of the Rule Space

Meta-DENDRAL searches the rule space in two phases. First, a model-driven generate-and-test search is conducted by the RULEGEN subprogram. This is a fairly coarse search from which redundant and approximate rules may result. The second phase of the search is conducted by the RULEMOD subprogram, which cleans up the rules developed by RULEGEN to make them more precise and less redundant.

RULEGEN. This subprogram searches the rule space of bond environments in order from most general to most specific. The algorithm repeatedly generates a new set of hypotheses, H, and tests it against the (positive) training instances developed by INTSUM, as follows:

Step 1. *Initialize H to contain the most general bond environment.*

$x * y$

Node	Atom type	Neighbors	H-neighbors	Double bonds
x	any	any	any	any
y	any	any	any	any

This bond environment matches every bond in the molecule and thus predicts that every bond will break. Since the most useful (i.e., most accurate) bond environment lies somewhere between this overly general environment $(x * y)$ and the overly specific, complete molecular structure (with specified bonds breaking), the program generates refined environments by successively specializing the H set.

Step 2. *Generate a new set of hypotheses.* Specialize the set H by making a change to all atoms at a specified distance (radius) from the $*$ bond—the bond designated to break. The change can involve either adding new neighbor atoms or specifying an atom feature. All possible specializations are made for which there is supporting evidence. The technique of modifying *all* atoms at a particular radius causes the RULEGEN search to be coarse.

Step 3. *Test the hypotheses against the training instances.* The bond environments in H are examined to determine how much evidence there is for each environment. An *improvement criterion* is computed for each environment that states whether the environment is more plausible than the parent environment from which it was obtained by specialization. Environments that are determined to be more plausible than their parents are retained. The others are pruned from the H set. If all specializations of a parent environment are determined to be less plausible than their parent, the parent is output as a new cleavage rule and is removed from H.

Repeat steps 2 and 3 until H is empty.

Figure D4b–4 shows a portion of the RULEGEN search tree. Horizontal levels in the tree correspond to the contents of the H set after each iteration. Starting with the root pattern, S_0, the *number-of-neighbors* attribute is specialized (i.e., the pattern graph is expanded) for each atom at distance zero from (adjacent to) the break to give pattern S_1. The *atom type* is then specified for atoms adjacent to the break in S_2 and for atoms one bond removed from the break in S_3. At each step, there are many other possible successors corresponding to assignments of other values to these same attributes or to other attributes.

The improvement criterion used in step 3 states that a daughter environment graph is more plausible than its parent graph if:

1. It predicts fewer fragmentations per molecule (i.e., it is more specific);

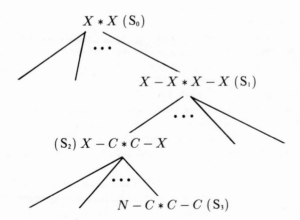

Figure D4b–4.   A portion of the RULEGEN search tree.

2. It still predicts fragmentations for at least half of all of the molecules (i.e., it is sufficiently general);

3. It predicts fragmentations for as many molecules as its parent—unless the parent graph was "too general" in the sense that the parent predicts more than 2 fragmentations in some single molecule or on the average it predicts more than 1.5 fragmentations per molecule.

This algorithm assumes that the improvement criterion increases monotonically to a single maximum value (i.e., it is unimodal). This is usually true for the mass-spectrometry learning task. RULEGEN can thus be viewed as following monotonically increasing paths down through the partial order of the rule space until the criterion attains a local maximum value.

RULEMOD. The rules produced by RULEGEN are very approximate and have not been tested against negative evidence. RULEMOD improves these rules by conducting fine hill-climbing searches in the portions of the rule space near the rules located by RULEGEN. The subprogram RULEMOD proceeds in four steps:

Step 1. *Select a subset of important rules.* RULEGEN can produce rules that are different from one another but that explain many of the same data points. RULEMOD attempts to find a small set of rules that account for all of the data. Negative evidence is gathered for each rule by re-invoking the mass-spectrometer simulator. Each candidate rule is tested to see how many incorrect predictions are made as well as how many correct predictions. The rules are ranked according to a scoring function $(I \times (P + U - 2N)$, where I is the average intensity of the positively predicted peaks, P is the number of correctly predicted peaks, U is the number of correct peaks predicted uniquely by this rule and no other, and N is the number of incorrectly predicted peaks). The top-ranked rule is selected. All evidence peaks explained by that rule are removed, and the ranking and selection process is repeated until all positive evidence is explained or until the scores fall below a specified threshold.

Step 2. *Specialize rules to exclude negative evidence.* RULEMOD attempts to specialize the rules in order to exclude some negative evidence while retaining the positive evidence. For each candidate rule, RULEMOD attempts to fill in additional values for features that were left unspecified by RULEGEN. RULEMOD first examines all of the positive instances predicted by the candidate rule and obtains a list of all possible feature values that are common to all of the positive instances. Each of these feature values could individually be added to the rule without excluding any positive instances. RULEMOD attempts to select a mutually compatible set of values that will exclude a large amount of negative evidence.

The selection process uses a hill-climbing search. The feature value that excludes the largest number of negative instances is chosen and added to the candidate rule. Incompatible feature values are pruned from the list of possible refinements, and the process is repeated until further refinement is not possible or all negative evidence has been excluded.

Step 3. *Generalize rules to include positive evidence.* RULEMOD attempts to generalize the rules in order to include some positive evidence without including any new negative evidence. This is accomplished by relaxing the legal values for atom features that were specified by RULEGEN. RULEMOD examines each atom in the bond environment of the rule, starting with the atoms most distant from the * bond. It first checks to see if the whole atom can be removed from the graph without introducing any negative evidence. If it cannot, then a hill-climbing search is performed that iteratively removes the one atom feature that allows the rule to include the largest amount of new positive evidence without introducing any negative evidence. When the outermost atoms have been generalized as much as possible, RULEGEN examines the set of atoms that are one bond closer to the fragmentation site. This search continues until all possible changes have been made.

Step 4. *Select the final subset of rules.* The procedure used in step 1 is re-applied to select the final set of rules.

The key assumption made by RULEMOD is that RULEGEN has located rules that are approximately correct. RULEGEN points out the regions of the rule space in which detailed searches are needed.

Notice that RULEMOD must frequently invoke the mass-spectrometer simulator to assess the negative (incorrect) predictions of a proposed rule. INTSUM provides only positive training instances to RULEGEN. Negative instances are not provided to RULEGEN directly because there are many more negative instances than there are positive instances. This is a problem that frequently arises in systems that are attempting to explain why some particular set of events took place. Negative information must indicate everything that did *not* occur.

All three of Meta-DENDRAL's subprograms make use of some form of the mass-spectrometer simulator. These versions of the simulator are flexible and transparent. They allow the learning element to interpret the training instances and to reason about the performance of a hypothetical modification to the cleavage rules. Similar transparent performance elements are used in systems that learn to perform multiple-step tasks (see Sec. XIV.D5).

Experiment planning and the search of the instance space. Meta-DENDRAL does not conduct a search of the instance space. Such a search would require that Meta-DENDRAL select a molecular structure and ask the chemists to synthesize it and obtain its mass spectrum. To choose an appropriate molecule, Meta-DENDRAL would need to invert the INTSUM process. Given a set of possible bond cleavages that it wanted to verify, Meta-DENDRAL would need to determine a molecule in which those bonds would cleave. Once the molecule was chosen, existing organic-synthesis programs could be used to plan the synthesis process (see Article VII.C4, in Vol. II). The chosen molecule might be difficult or impossible to synthesize. Instance-space searching was not incorporated into Meta-DENDRAL because of the complex and time-consuming nature of these procedures.

Another View of the Meta-DENDRAL Learning Algorithm

In the previous section, we discussed the RULEGEN/RULEMOD pair of subprograms as a coarse search followed by a fine search. Another view of this process is that RULEGEN converts a multiple-concept learning problem into a set of single-concept learning problems. This view regards the output of RULEGEN *not* as a set of rules but as a clustering of the training instances. Once RULEGEN has completed its search, the program knows approximately which training instances belong together as instances of a single cleavage rule. At this point, a single-concept learning algorithm could be applied to discover this rule directly from the RULEGEN-supplied cluster of training instances rather than by incremental modifications of the RULEGEN-supplied rule.

As part of his thesis work, Mitchell (1978) applied the candidate-elimination algorithm to this learning problem. Each approximate rule developed by RULEGEN was used to build a set of positive and negative training instances that were then processed by the version-space approach. This technique resulted in a better set of cleavage rules than those developed with RULEMOD. The version-space approach has the advantage of supporting incremental learning, so Mitchell's system can incorporate new training instances as they become available.

Strengths and Weaknesses of the Meta-DENDRAL System

Meta-DENDRAL is an effective learning system applied to a real-world domain. Meta-DENDRAL has discovered cleavage rules for five structural families of molecules. The system provides solutions to the problem of interpreting training instances and to the problem of learning in the presence of certain kinds of noise. These solutions are based on the incorporation into the program of a large amount of domain-specific knowledge. This knowledge enters the system in the form of the half-order theory of mass spectrometry (to guide interpretation) and in the use of a model-directed search of rule space.

The two-phase search of the rule space provides an efficient method for searching a large space and also suggests how a multiple-concept learning problem can be converted into a set of single-concept learning problems.

Among the weaknesses of the system are its domain-specific representation and the fact that much of the domain knowledge is buried in the code rather than represented as an explicit knowledge base.

References

Lindsay, Buchanan, Feigenbaum, and Lederberg (1980) present a comprehensive survey of the many programs developed during the DENDRAL project. Buchanan and Mitchell (1978) describe Meta-DENDRAL as an AI learning system. Mitchell (1978) discusses the application of the candidate-elimination algorithm to Meta-DENDRAL.

D4c. AM

AM is a computer program written by Douglas Lenat (1976) that discovers concepts in elementary mathematics and set theory. Unlike most of the learning systems described in this chapter, AM does not learn concepts for use in some performance task. Instead, it seeks simply to define and evaluate interesting concepts on the basis of a knowledge of mathematical aesthetics. It employs a refinement-operator approach (see Article XIV.D1) to conduct a heuristic search of a space of mathematical concepts.

AM starts with a substantial knowledge base of 115 concepts selected from finite set theory. As AM runs, it collects examples of these concepts, creates new concepts, and hypothesizes conjectures relating the concepts to each other. During one typical run of a few CPU hours' duration, AM defined about 200 new concepts, half of which were quite well known in mathematics. One of the synthesized concepts was equivalent to the concept of natural numbers. AM's knowledge of mathematical aesthetics led it to pursue this concept in depth, and it spent much time developing elementary number theory, including conjecturing the fundamental theorem of arithmetic (i.e., every number has a unique prime factorization). This impressive performance can be traced to AM's large body of knowledge about mathematics and its ability to apply this knowledge to discover new concepts and conjectures.

In this article, we first describe AM's architecture in terms of its representation for concepts and its control structure for deciding what tasks to perform. Then we change our perspective and show how AM can be viewed as searching an instance space and a concept space by the refinement-operator method. Third, we examine the initial contents of AM's knowledge base and review briefly the concepts that it discovered. Finally, we attempt to summarize the strengths and weaknesses of AM's approach to concept discovery.

AM's Architecture

AM is a blend of three powerful methods: *frame representation, production systems,* and heuristically guided *best-first search.* We discuss each of these in turn.

Frame representation. The concepts that AM discovers and manipulates are represented as frames (see Article III.C7, in Vol. I), each containing the same fixed set of slots. Each concept has slots for its *definition,* for known positive and negative *examples,* for links to other concepts that are *specializations* and *generalizations* of the concept, for telling the *worth* of the concept, and for several other things. Figure D4c–1 shows the frame representation of the PRIMES concept after it has been discovered and filled in by AM.

NAME: Prime Numbers

DEFINITIONS:

    ORIGIN: Number-of-divisors-of(x) = 2

    PREDICATE-CALCULUS: $\text{Prime}(x) \equiv (\forall z)(z \mid x \Rightarrow z = 1 \oplus z = x)$

    ITERATIVE: (for x > 1): For i from 2 to sqrt(x), $\neg(i \mid x)$

EXAMPLES: 2, 3, 5, 7, 11, 13, 17

    BOUNDARY: 2, 3

    BOUNDARY-FAILURES: 0, 1

    FAILURES: 12

GENERALIZATIONS: Nos., Nos. with an even no. of divisors,
    Nos. with a prime no. of divisors

SPECIALIZATIONS: Odd Primes, Prime Pairs, Prime Uniquely-addables

CONJECTURES: Unique factorization, Goldbach's conjecture,
    Extremes of Number-of-divisors-of

ANALOGIES:
    Maximally divisible numbers are converse extremes of
    Number-of-divisors-of,
    Factor a nonsimple group into simple groups

INTEREST: Conjectures associating Primes with TIMES
    and with Divisors-of

WORTH: 800

Figure D4c–1.   AM's frame representation of the PRIMES concept.

The DEFINITIONS slot is the most important. It provides one or more LISP predicates that can be applied to determine whether something is an example of the concept. AM knows a concept when it has a definition for it. However, the frame representation allows AM to represent more knowledge about a concept than just its definition. The CONJECTURES, SPECIALIZATIONS, and GENERALIZATIONS slots, for example, all describe different ways in which concepts are related to each other. Furthermore, attached to each slot in a concept are *heuristic rules* (not shown in the figure) that can be executed to *fill in* the contents of a slot or to *check* the contents to see if they are correct. These heuristic rules form a production system that carries out the actual discovery process.

Production systems. AM operates as a *modified production system.* Each of the 242 heuristic rules attached to the concept slots of AM's knowledge base is written, as in all production systems, as a condition part and an action part. The condition part tells under what conditions the rule should be executed, and the action part carries out some task such as creating a new concept or finding examples of an existing concept. For instance, the following heuristic rule is attached to the EXAMPLES slot of the ANY–CONCEPT frame:

> If: The current task is "Fill in examples of X"
> and X is a specialization of some concept Y,
>
> Then: Apply the definition of X to each of the examples of Y
> and retain those that satisfy the definition.

The main difference between AM's production-system architecture and the standard recognize-act cycle is the way rules are selected for execution. Recall that in an ordinary production system, the condition part of each rule is compared to the contents of a working memory, and all rules that match are executed. In contrast, AM is much more selective about which rules it executes. It operates from an *agenda of tasks* of the form "Fill in (or check) slot S of concept C." Each task has a numeric "interestingness" rating. AM repeatedly selects the most interesting task from the agenda, gathers all heuristic rules relevant to performing that task, and executes those rules that are actually applicable.

To locate those heuristics that are relevant to the task "Fill in (or check) slot S of concept C," AM looks at slot S of concept C to see if it has any attached heuristics. If it does, those heuristics are executed. If not, AM examines relatives of concept C to see if any of them have heuristics that can be *inherited* by C and applied. For example, when AM is looking for rules relevant to the task "Fill in examples of sets," it finds no heuristics attached to the EXAMPLES slot of SETS. Consequently, it looks at concepts such as ANYCONCEPT, which are more general than SETS. The EXAMPLES slot of ANYCONCEPT has an attached heuristic that says:

> If: The current task is "Fill in examples of X"
> and X has a recursive definition,
>
> Then: Instantiate the base step of the recursion to get
> a boundary example.

When AM applies this heuristic rule, it creates the *null set* as a boundary EXAMPLE of SETS. Heuristics that are closely related to C are executed before heuristics of distant relatives.

A heuristic rule can do one or more of the following:

1. *Fill in slot S of some concept C.* This covers many activities, including finding new examples for a concept, proposing conjectures, and providing guidance for the search by modifying the WORTH slot of a concept.

2. *Check slot S of concept C.* The process of checking a slot involves verifying that the contents of the slot are correct and noticing interesting facts about a slot. Often, a rule will check a slot and notice that some new task should be performed as a result. For example, one rule notices that all of the examples of one concept, X, are also examples of a more specific concept, Y. It conjectures that X and Y are equivalent and proposes the task "Check examples of Y" to see if Y is actually equivalent to an even more specific concept, Z.

3. *Create new concepts.* New concepts are created by adding a new frame to the knowledge base and filling in the DEFINITIONS slot of the frame. Usually the WORTH slot is filled in as well.

4. *Add new tasks to the agenda.* Often, a rule will propose that a new task be added to the agenda. For example, a rule that creates a new concept, X, will propose the new task "Fill in examples of X." Most rules that generate examples of X will propose the task "Check examples of X."

5. *Modify the interestingness of a task on the agenda.* The numerical interestingness of a task is computed from a list of "reasons" for performing the task. Thus, a rule can add a new reason to an existing task. This is another way of providing guidance in the search for concepts and conjectures.

Best-first search. The procedure of always choosing the most interesting task from the agenda gives AM the flavor of best-first search. This search is well guided by heuristics that modify the INTERESTINGNESS and WORTH slots of concepts and that propose and justify agenda tasks. AM has 59 heuristics for assessing the interestingness of concepts and tasks. One rule, for example, says that a concept is interesting if each of its examples accidentally satisfies an otherwise rarely satisfied predicate P. (The satisfaction is accidental if the concept was not deliberately defined as the set of things satisfying P.)

Without heuristic guidance and the agenda mechanism, AM would be swamped by a combinatorial explosion of new concepts. However, the fact that it creates only 200 new concepts and that half of them are acceptable to a mathematician shows that its search is quite restrained. AM is an excellent example of the power of well-informed best-first search.

AM and the Two-space View of Learning

Thus far, we have discussed the architecture of AM. We now turn our attention to how this architecture is used to accomplish learning. Although its 242 heuristic rules are extremely varied and can perform many diverse functions, AM tends to behave as if it were executing the following loop:

Repeat:

Step 1. Select a concept to evaluate and generate examples of it.

Step 2. Check these examples looking for regularities. Based on the regularities,

(a) update the assessment of the interestingness of the concept,

(b) create new concepts, and

(c) create new conjectures.

Step 3. Propagate the knowledge gained (especially from new conjectures) to other concepts in the system.

In terms of the two-space view of learning, step 1 searches a space of instances, step 2 examines these instances and searches the space of concepts (the rule space) and conjectures, and step 3 performs bookkeeping to maintain the consistency and integration of the knowledge base. We examine each of these steps in more detail.

Searching the instance space. When a concept is created, AM knows very little about that concept aside from its LISP definition. In fact, when AM is first started up, none of its 115 initial concept frames has any examples filled in. Thus, one of the first tasks it must perform—in order to assess the value of the concepts and develop conjectures—is to gather examples (and negative examples) of its concepts. AM has more than 30 heuristic rules to guide this example-generating process. Here are some of the techniques they use:

1. *Symbolic instantiation of definitions.* Symbolic instantiation converts the definition of a concept into an example. Typically, each concept has, as one of its definitions, a recursive LISP predicate. The base step of this recursion can be instantiated to give an instance that satisfies the definition. For example, one of the definitions of the SET concept is:

   ```
   (lambda (s)
       (or (= s {})
           (set.definition (remove (any-member s) s)))) .
   ```

   Since the first thing this definition checks is to see if *s* is the null set, we can conclude that the null set is an example of a set. Similarly, AM knows that *removing* is the opposite of *inserting*, so it can deduce that {{}} is also a set by inserting {} into itself.

2. *Generate and test.* Another approach used by the program is to generate examples and test them against the concept definition. In order to generate examples of some concept *C*, the program looks at "nearby" concepts in the knowledge base. For example, AM may look at generalizations of *C* (concepts more general than *C*), operations that have *C* in their range, cousins of *C* (concepts that share a common generalization or specialization with *C*), and even random LISP atoms from various internal lists inside AM (such as the list of users of the system).

3. *Inheritance of examples.* If concept *C* has other concepts that are more specialized than it, any example satisfying these more specialized concept definitions will satisfy *C*. Examples can thus be inherited "up" the

generalization hierarchy. Similarly, negative examples can be inherited "down" the generalization hierarchy.

4. *Applying the algorithm of the concept.* So-called active concepts (i.e., operators such as SET–UNION) have algorithms that compute an element in the range of the concept when given valid arguments from the domain. Thus, by randomly selecting domain items and applying these algorithms, AM can produce new examples. For instance, if $\{A\}$ and $\{B\}$ are sets, then SET–UNION.ALGORITHMS produces $\{A, B\}$, and the list $\langle\{A\}, \{B\}, \{A, B\}\rangle$ forms a positive example of SET–UNION.

5. *Reasoning by views or by analogy.* The VIEWS slot of a concept provides an algorithm for converting instances of one concept into instances of another. The ANALOGY slot gives less precise information about how instances of one concept are related to instances of another concept. AM can use these two slots to map existing examples into examples of the concept under construction.

When AM needs to fill in examples of a concept, it attempts to apply these methods until it has developed 26 examples of the concept (or until it has exhausted its time or space quota for the current task).

A particularly interesting feature of AM is its ability to locate the *boundary* of a concept. Examples of a concept are classified according to whether they are:

1. Normal positive examples,

2. Boundary positive examples,

3. Boundary negative examples (i.e., what Winston, 1970, calls *near misses*),

4. Normal negative examples, or

5. Just plain weird (i.e., have the wrong data structure).

Most examples produced by the above-mentioned techniques will turn out to be normal positive examples (or normal negative examples, if they do not satisfy the concept definition). Some of the example-generation techniques, however, are faulty. They can accidentally generate negative examples. A particular case is the VIEW slot of SETS that tells AM that it can view a bag as a set by changing the [ ] brackets (that represent a bag) to { } braces. This does not always work (e.g., when the bag $[a, b, a]$ is viewed as that set $\{a, b, a\}$ which contains an impermissible duplicate element). When AM checks these examples against the definition of a set, it discovers that they fail. Such negative examples are classified as boundary negative examples.

Boundary positive examples can be found by such techniques as instantiating the base case of a recursion (which almost always produces a boundary case) or by taking boundary non-examples of more specialized concepts and determining that they satisfy the concept definition. Another technique is to take a normal positive example and progressively modify it until it fails to satisfy the definition. This isolates the boundary of the concept quite well.

By applying all of these techniques, AM is able to gather a good set of examples that can be used for analysis and generalization. AM can also assess how much effort was expended to obtain these examples. Thus, it can conclude that a predicate is "rarely satisfied" or "easily satisfied." All of these empirical data are used to drive the search of the rule space and the search for interesting conjectures.

Searching the rule space. The rule space for AM is the space of all possible instantiations of its concept frame. This is indeed an immense space. To search it, AM applies a refinement-operator method similar to the techniques employed by BACON and ID3 (see Article XIV.D3b). The current set of concept frames can be thought of as AM's current set of hypotheses. These hypotheses are repeatedly refined and extended by applying operators (i.e., heuristics) that create new concepts and conjectures.

AM has roughly 40 heuristics that create new concepts. These can be broken into two sets. One set of heuristics is general and can be applied to virtually any concept in AM. The second set is applicable only to functions and relations—active concepts that can be viewed as mapping elements from some domain set into some range set. The general methods are:

1. *Generalization.* AM implements, in some form, virtually all rules of generalization that have appeared in other AI programs. The dropping-condition, adding-option, and turning-constants-to-variables rules are all used. Also implemented is the technique of specializing a negative conjunct (e.g., $A \wedge \neg B$ is generalized to $A \wedge \neg B'$, where B' is more specific than B). AM can generalize expressions involving quantification, for example, converting $\exists x \in S : P(x)$ to $\exists x \in S' : P(x)$, where S' is a larger set than S. Since the definitions of concepts are typically recursive LISP functions, AM contains many rules of generalization that are applicable to recursion. For instance, a definition can be generalized by eliminating one of a conjoined pair of recursive calls or by disjoining a new recursive call. In particular, AM knows that if one recursive call involves CAR (or CDR), the other recursive call should use CDR (or CAR, respectively).

2. *Specialization.* AM also implements a wide variety of rules of specialization. These are the reversals of the rules of generalization mentioned above.

3. *Handling exceptions.* When a concept has a lot of exceptions (negative boundary examples), a new concept can be created whose instances are these negative examples. Also, AM can create the concept whose instances are those positive examples, but not boundary examples, of the original concept. This allows AM to represent the conjecture that all prime numbers are odd—except the number 2.

4. *Reasoning by analogy.* If J is a conjecture and J' is an analogous conjecture, then AM can create the concept $\{b' \mid J'(b')\}$ and also the concept

$\{b' \mid \neg J'(b')\}$, that is, the set of objects for which J' is true and the set of objects for which J' is false.

AM's concept-creation methods that apply to active concepts (mappings) usually produce new active concepts. New concepts can be created by the following:

1. *Generalization.* The domain and range of an existing concept can be expanded.

2. *Specialization.* The domain and range of an existing concept can be contracted (restricted).

3. *Inversion.* The inverse of an existing relation can be created. AM can also create interesting concepts such as the inverse image of an interesting subset of the range and the inverse image of an interesting value in the range.

4. *Composition.* Two functions $F(x)$ and $G(y)$ can be composed to obtain the new functions $F(G(y))$ and $G(F(x))$.

5. *Projection.* An existing multiple-argument function F can be projected onto a subset of its arguments. For example, $\text{Proj2}(F(x,y))$ is just y.

6. *Coalesce.* The arguments of $F(x,y)$ can be coalesced to produce a new function, $G(x) = F(x,x)$.

7. *Canonization.* This method takes two predicates, P_1 and P_2, and defines a function, F, and a set, the range of F, such that $P_1(x,y) = P_2(F(x), F(y))$. If x and y are instances of concept C, then F maps C to the set of canonical C. Thus, P_2 applied to canonical C is the same as P_1 applied to C. AM uses this operation to invent NUMBERS by taking SAME–SIZE(x,y) as P_1, and EQUAL(x,y) as P_2, and applying them to bags to create the canonizing function SIZE–OF(x) and the concept of CANONICAL–BAGS (i.e., bags that contain only T). CANONICAL–BAGS can be interpreted as numbers.

8. *Parallel-replace and parallel-join.* These concept-creation operators come in many varieties and are used to create new concepts by repeated application of old concepts. Multiplication, for example, can be created by repeated addition (with the parallel-replace method).

9. *Permutation.* The arguments of a function or relation can be permuted to give a new function or relation.

10. *Cartesian product.* A new concept can be obtained by taking the Cartesian product of existing concepts.

Many of the refinement operators in this group (e.g., COALESCE, COMPOSITION) are also *concepts* defined in AM. It is perhaps only in mathematics that the means of study are also the objects of study.

Representing and proposing conjectures. Roughly 30 of AM's rules also propose conjectures based upon examination of the empirical data. Conjectures take one of the following forms:

1. C_1 is an example of C_2;
2. C_1 is a specialization (generalization) of C_2;
3. C_1 is equivalent to C_2;
4. C_1 is related by X to C_2 (where X is some predicate);
5. Operation C_1 has domain D or range R.

Most of these conjectures are discovered by performing rough statistical comparisons of examples. If all of the examples of C_1 are also examples of C_2, then AM conjectures that C_1 is a specialization of C_2. If AM is unable to find negative examples of C_1, it conjectures that C_1 is trivially true. If all examples of elements in the range of C_1 seem to be numbers, then AM conjectures that C_1 has numbers as its range. If all of the range elements of C_1 are equal to corresponding domain elements, then perhaps C_1 is the same as the identity function.

Conjectures, once proposed, are believed completely by AM. The relevant slots are changed, and the changes are propagated throughout the knowledge base. If two concepts are conjectured to be equivalent, they are merged and the space occupied by one is released. AM can also modify the LISP definitions to take advantage of new conjectures.

Propagating acquired knowledge. Several heuristics (including those that locate and generate examples) serve to propagate new information throughout the network of frames that constitutes AM's knowledge base. These are fairly straightforward and make heavy use of the three sets of inheritance links (IS–AN–EXAMPLE–OF/EXAMPLES, SPECIALIZATIONS/GENERALIZATIONS, DOMAIN/RANGE).

To complete our review of AM from the perspective of the two-space view of learning, we note that, although the example-generation techniques discussed above perform sophisticated instance selection, there is no corresponding need for complex interpretation routines like those found in Meta-DENDRAL. On the contrary, since mathematical objects are easily represented and manipulated in LISP, there is no need to convert them to some alternate representation. More sophisticated instance selection and interpretation routines would probably be needed for nonmathematical domains.

AM's Initial Knowledge Base

We now turn our attention to AM's actual performance. First we describe the knowledge that it started with, and then we give a summary of the concepts and conjectures it found.

AM's initial knowledge base contains the basic concept hierarchy shown in Figure D4c–2. In addition, beneath the concept of STRUCTURE are many important data structures: SETS, ORDERED SETS, BAGS, LISTS (i.e., ordered BAGS), and ORDERED PAIRS. Under the ACTIVITY concept are many operations such as SET–INTERSECT, SET–UNION, SET–DIFFERENCE, and SET–DELETION (and analogous operations for BAGS, ORDERED SETS, and LISTS). Also, several of the concept-creation operators such as PARALLEL–JOIN, RESTRICT, PROJECTION, and so forth, are included here. Under PREDICATES are the constant predicates TRUE and FALSE, as well as the concept of EQUALITY. Finally, the most important part of the initial knowledge base is the body of 242 heuristic rules attached to various concepts in this tree. Most of these were summarized above.

Results: AM as a Mathematician

Now we review the mathematics that AM explored. Throughout, AM acted alone, with a human user watching it and occasionally renaming some concepts for his (or her) own benefit. Like a contemporary historian summarizing the work of the Babylonian mathematicians, we will use present-day terms to describe AM's concepts, and we will criticize its behavior in light of our current knowledge of mathematics.

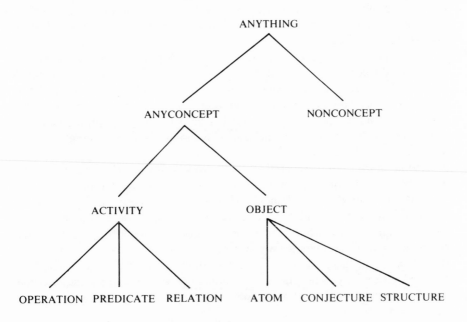

Figure D4c–2. AM's initial concept tree (partially shown).

AM began its investigations with scanty knowledge of a few set-theoretic concepts. Most of the obvious set-theoretical relations (e.g., de Morgan's laws) were eventually uncovered; since AM never fully understood abstract algebra, the statement and verification of each of these was quite obscure. AM never derived a formal notion of infinity, but it naively established conjectures like "A set can never be a member of itself" and procedures for making chains of new sets ("Insert a set into itself"). No sophisticated set theory (e.g., diagonalization) was ever done.

After this initial period of exploration, AM decided that "equality" was worth generalizing and thereby discovered the relation "same size as." Natural numbers were based on this discovery, and, soon after, most simple arithmetic operations were defined.

Since addition arose as an analogue to union, and multiplication as a repeated substitution, it came as quite a surprise when AM noticed that they were related (namely, $N + N = 2 \times N$). AM later rediscovered multiplication in three other ways: as repeated addition, as the numeric analogue of the Cartesian product of sets, and using the cardinality of the power set of the union of two sets.

Raising to fourth-powers and taking fourth-roots were discovered at this time. Perfect squares and perfect fourth-powers were isolated. Many other numeric operations and kinds of numbers were found to be of interest: odds, evens, doubling, halving, integer square root, and so on. Although it isolated the set of numbers that had no square roots, AM was never close to discovering rationals, let alone irrationals. No notion of "closure" was provided to—or discovered by—AM.

The associativity and commutativity of multiplication indicated to AM that it could accept a bag of numbers as its argument. When AM defined the inverse operation corresponding to "times," this property allowed the definition to be: "any bag of numbers greater than 1 whose product is x." This was just the notion of factoring a number x. Minimally factorable numbers turned out to be what we call primes. (Maximally factorable numbers were also thought to be interesting.)

Prime pairs were discovered in a bizarre way: by restricting the domain and range of addition to primes (i.e., solutions of $p + q = r$ in primes).

AM conjectured the fundamental theorem of arithmetic (unique factorization into primes) and Goldbach's conjecture (every even number greater than 2 is the sum of two primes) in a surprisingly symmetric way. The unary representation of numbers gave way to a representation as a bag of primes (based on unique factorization), but AM never came up with exponential notation. Since the key concepts of remainder, greater than, greatest common denominator, and exponentiation were never mastered, progress in number theory was arrested.

When a new base of *geometric* concepts was added, AM began finding some more general associations. In place of the strict definitions for the equality of lines, angles, and triangles came new definitions of concepts comparable to parallel, equal measure, similar, congruent, translation, and rotation, together with many that have no common name (e.g., the relationship of two triangles sharing a common angle). A clever geometric interpretation of Goldbach's conjecture was found: Given all angles of a prime number of degrees $(0°, 1°, 2°, 3°, 5°, 7°, 11°, \ldots, 179°)$, any angle between 0 and 180 degrees can be approximated (to within $1°$) as the sum of two of those angles. Lacking a geometry "model" (an analogical representation like the one Gelernter, 1963, employed; see Article II.D3, in Vol. I), AM was doomed to propose many implausible geometric conjectures (see Article III.C5, in Vol. I).

Perhaps a full appreciation for the depth of AM's search of the concept space can be gained by examining Figure D4c-3, which shows the derivation path for prime numbers. It is eight levels deep and requires 14 concept-creation operations. This derivation is quite impressive, both because of its depth, and because the final concept is so far removed semantically from the initial concepts. Note, in particular, the fascinating way in which a new concept, SELF-COMPOSE, is used as a new operator to derive TIMES21 and TIMES22. AM is able to search in a highly directed, rational fashion.

Evaluating AM

It is important to ask how general the AM program is: Is the knowledge base "just right" (i.e., finely tuned to elicit this one chain of behaviors)? The answer is no: The whole point of this project was to show that a relatively small set of general heuristics can guide a nontrivial discovery process. Keeping the program general and not finely tuned was a key objective. Each activity or task was proposed by some heuristic rule (like "Look for extreme cases of X") that was used time and time again, in many situations. It was not considered fair to insert heuristics that provide guidance in only a single situation. For example, the same heuristics that lead AM to decompose numbers (using TIMES-inverse) and thereby discover unique factorization, also lead to decomposing numbers (using ADD-inverse) and the discovery of Goldbach's conjecture.

AM does, however, have some weaknesses. Although AM was able to discover and refine many interesting new concepts, it had no way of improving its stock of heuristic rules. Consequently, as AM ran longer and longer, the concepts it defined were further and further from the primitives it began with, and the efficacy of its fixed set of heuristics gradually declined. Lenat (1980) has proposed a solution to this problem. He advocates turning each heuristic rule into a concept and developing additional operators for creating new heuristics. The EURISKO project is presently pursuing this research.

A deeper problem has to do with some of the characteristics of the domain of mathematics that may not hold in other domains. One important fact about elementary mathematics is that the density of interesting concepts

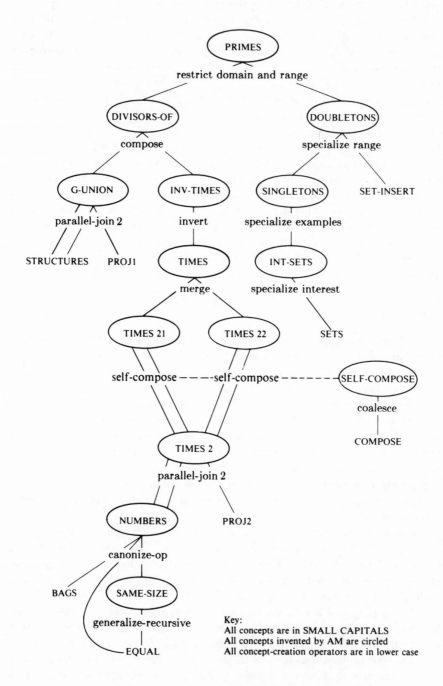

Figure D4c–3.   The derivation tree for PRIMES.

is quite high. AM relies on the ability to build up complex concepts from more primitive concepts in a step-by-step fashion. At each step, the partial concepts must appear to AM to be interesting. In many domains, however, it is not possible to assess the interestingness of partial solutions. Consider, for example, the problem of credit assignment in a game such as chess. For a novice chess player, it is necessary to play an entire game before receiving any feedback on the quality of individual moves. Even as a player becomes expert, it is still necessary to search several moves in advance in order to evaluate a particular choice. Future efforts to develop AM-style discovery systems in other domains may face difficulties in evaluating the worth of concepts. More sophisticated interestingness heuristics may need to be developed. Work on the EURISKO project may provide some answers to these questions.

Conclusion

AM is a powerful discovery system that investigates and refines concepts in elementary set and number theory. It begins with a large body of knowledge about what kinds of concepts are mathematically interesting and how they can be synthesized from existing concepts. This knowledge can then carry AM far beyond its initial store of concepts to discover prime numbers and the fundamental theorem of arithmetic.

References

Lenat (1976) provides complete details on AM; see also Lenat (1977). Lenat (1980) describes the EURISKO project.

D5.   Learning to Perform Multiple-step Tasks

MOST of the learning programs discussed so far in this chapter were designed
to learn how to perform *single-step tasks*—that is, tasks in which one rule, or a
set of independent rules, can be applied in one step to accomplish the performance task. In pattern classification (Article XIV.D2) and single-concept learning (Sec. XIV.D3), the performance element takes an unknown object or pattern
and assigns it to one of two classes (e.g., an arch or a "nonarch"). These systems apply a single classification rule, or concept, to perform the classification.
Even the sequence-extrapolation problems addressed by BACON (Article
XIV.D3b) and SPARC (Article XIV.D3d) involve applying a single rule to predict
the next item in the sequence from the previous items. Similarly, in the
multiple-rule tasks of soybean-disease diagnosis (Article XIV.D4a) and mass-
spectrometry simulation (Article XIV.D4b), several rules are applied in parallel
to determine the unknown disease or to predict how the unknown molecule
will break apart.

Multiple-step Tasks

In contrast, this section surveys a few learning systems that learn how
to perform *multiple-step tasks*—that is, tasks in which several rules must be
chained together into a sequence. Examples of multiple-step tasks include
the game of checkers, in which rules for making individual moves must be
chained together to play a whole game, and symbolic integration, in which
several rules of integration must be applied sequentially to solve each integral.
The goal of the learning system is to acquire a good set of rules for performing
these tasks.

Multiple-step tasks are essentially *planning tasks* in which the performance element must find a sequence of operators to get from some starting
state (e.g., the opening position in checkers) to some goal state (e.g., a won
game). The chapters on search (Chap. II, in Vol. I) and planning (Chap. XV)
describe various methods that have been used to accomplish this *state-space
search* (see Article II.C3, in Vol. I). So far, AI learning systems have been developed only for simple, forward-chaining planning programs. No attempts have
been made to learn how to perform hierarchical or constraint-based planning.

Viewing the Performance Element as a Production System

The first four systems described in this section—Samuel's (1959) checkers
player, Waterman's (1970) poker player, Sussman's (1975) HACKER planning
system, and Mitchell's LEX system for symbolic integration (Mitchell, Utgoff,

and Banerji, in press)—are all simple, forward-chaining problem solvers and, thus, can be viewed as simple production systems. The grammatical-inference systems discussed in the fifth article (Article XIV.D5e) employ context-free grammars, which can also be considered production systems. The knowledge base for each of these systems contains a set of production rules of the form:

$$\langle \text{situation}_1 \rangle \;\; \Rightarrow \;\; \langle \text{action}_1 \rangle$$
$$\langle \text{situation}_2 \rangle \;\; \Rightarrow \;\; \langle \text{action}_2 \rangle$$
$$\vdots$$
$$\langle \text{situation}_n \rangle \;\; \Rightarrow \;\; \langle \text{action}_n \rangle .$$

The performance element repeatedly selects a rule whose situation part (left-hand side) matches the current state and applies the rule by performing the action indicated (right-hand side). The action usually has the effect of moving the performance element to a new state, closer to the goal.

For most of the programs discussed in this section, the possible actions are provided in advance. The problem addressed by the learning element is to determine under what situations the actions should be applied. This learning problem is similar in many ways to the problems addressed in Section XIV.D4 on learning multiple concepts.

However, two factors make this learning problem more difficult. First, because the rules must be chained together, the learning element has to consider possible interactions among the rules when it modifies the knowledge base. In LEX, for example, the learning element might decide that in any integral of the form

$$\int c f(x)\, dx ,$$

the constant c should always be factored out. This is expressed in LEX as the production rule

If the integral has the form $\int c f(x)\, dx$, then apply OP03 ,

where OP03 converts $\int c f(x)\, dx$ to $c \int f(x)\, dx$. Unfortunately, if the constant c is 0 or 1, this is not an advisable step. Instead, OP08 (convert $1 \cdot f(x)$ to $f(x)$) or OP15 (convert $0 \cdot f(x)$ to 0) should be applied. When LEX is learning the production rule for OP03, it must take into account these possible interactions with OP08 and OP15. In fact, LEX's goal is to discover the best operator to apply in every situation. Thus, any time more than one operator is applicable because of overlapping left-hand sides, LEX must eliminate the overlap. In this case, the appropriate rule for OP03 is:

If the integral has the form $\int c f(x)\, dx \wedge c \neq 0 \wedge c \neq 1$, then apply OP03 .

This is a particular instance of the general problem of incorporating new knowledge into the knowledge base (see Article XIV.A).

The second difficult aspect of multiple-step tasks is the problem of credit assignment. In single-step tasks, the system has available a *performance standard* that can be employed immediately after a rule is applied to determine whether or not the rule is correct. In disease diagnosis, for example, the learning element receives the correct disease classification along with each training instance. The performance element can apply its diagnosis rules and receive immediate feedback on the correctness of those rules. The performance standard can even be incorporated directly into the learning process as in the version-space method, in which the correct classification determines how the version space is updated.

In multiple-step tasks, however, feedback from the performance standard is not usually available until the game is completed or the problem is solved. The program can determine only whether the entire sequence of rules was good or bad. The credit-assignment problem is the problem of converting this overall performance standard into a performance standard for each rule. The overall credit or blame must be parceled out somehow among the individual rules that were applied.

The Importance of a Transparent Performance Element

To solve these problems of integration and credit assignment, it is critically important for the performance element to be transparent. A transparent performance element can provide the learning element with a trace of all actions that it *considered*, as well as those it actually performed. This allows the learning element to determine all of the rules that might have been applicable at each step of the problem-solving process. Such information makes it easier to solve the problem of integrating new rules into the knowledge base.

A complete performance trace also aids the credit-assignment task. During credit assignment, it is very useful to know why the performance element chose the rules that it did and what it expected those rules to do. By comparing the goals and expectations of the performance element with what really transpired, credit and blame can be assigned to individual decisions.

Extracting Local Training Instances from the Performance Trace

When the learning system for a multiple-step task is presented with a training instance—such as a board position in checkers and knowledge of which side can win from that position—it cannot immediately learn from the training instance. Instead, it must actually perform the task—that is, play out the checkers game—and compare the result with the information supplied by the performance standard—that is, which side should have won. During credit assignment, it can actually decide which individual decisions were good and which bad, and these evaluated decisions can serve as training instances for learning the left-hand sides of the production rules in the knowledge base.

By performing the task and assigning credit and blame, the "global" training instances can be converted into "local" training instances.

For example, in LEX, a global training instance consists of an integral such as

$$\int 2x^2 \, dx$$

along with knowledge of whether or not the integral can be solved. The solution trace (see Fig. D5–1) shows that OP12 should not have been applied, since it leads to a complicated expression that requires several more steps to solve, but that OP03 and OP02 were used correctly.

Thus, three local training instances can be extracted:

$$\int 2x^2 \, dx \;\Rightarrow\; \text{OP12 (negative)}.$$

$$\int 2x^2 \, dx \;\Rightarrow\; \text{OP03 (positive)}.$$

$$2\int x^2 \, dx \;\Rightarrow\; \text{OP02 (positive)}.$$

Once local training instances have been extracted, the techniques for doing concept learning discussed in Sections XIV.D3 and XIV.D4 can be applied to learn the left-hand sides of the production rules in the knowledge base. Figure D5–2 shows a slight perturbation of the simple learning-system model presented in Article XIV.A. The model now contains a loop in which the performance trace is analyzed by the learning element to extract local training instances. Global training instances are still supplied by the environment.

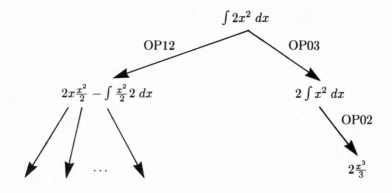

Figure D5–1. A sample performance trace.

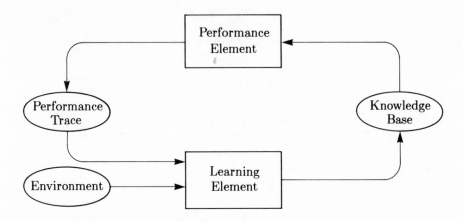

Figure D5–2.   A modified model of learning systems.

Outline of This Section

The five systems presented in this section all perform multiple-step tasks and, consequently, must address problems of integrating new rules and assigning credit and blame. Waterman, and to some extent Samuel, simplifies the credit-assignment problem by obtaining a move-by-move performance standard from the environment. Furthermore, all of the systems, except Waterman's poker system, ignore the problem of integrating new rules into the knowledge base. Work in this area is still in its infancy, and more sophisticated learning systems for multiple-step tasks can be expected in the future.

References

Buchanan, Mitchell, Smith, and Johnson (1977) provide another perspective on the use of feedback in learning systems.

D5a. Samuel's Checkers Player

FROM 1947 to 1967, Arthur Samuel conducted a continuing research project aimed at developing a checkers-playing program that was able to learn from experience. Samuel investigated three different representations for checkers knowledge—memorized moves, polynomial evaluation functions, and signature tables—and two different training methods—self-play and book-move learning. The work on rote learning of checkers moves is discussed in Article XIV.B2. The present article discusses two specific learning situations: (a) self-play as it was used to learn a polynomial evaluation function and (b) book-move training as it was used to learn a set of signature tables. Samuel experimented with several other combinations of training methods and representations (for more details, see Samuel, 1959, 1967).

The performance element in all of Samuel's systems employs a look-ahead, game-tree search to determine which moves to make (see Articles II.B3 and II.C5, in Vol. I). The performance element uses a *static evaluation function* (Article II.C5) to evaluate possible future positions in the game and applies alpha-beta minimaxing to determine the best move to make. The goal of the learning process is to establish and improve this static evaluation function through experience.

Learning a Polynomial Evaluation Function Through Self-play

The first static evaluation function investigated by Samuel was a polynomial of the form

$$\text{value} = \sum_i w_i f_i \, ,$$

where f_i are board features and w_i are real-valued weights (coefficients). For most of Samuel's experiments, a polynomial with 16 features was employed. Each board feature provides a numerical measure of some aspect of the board position under evaluation. For example, the EXCH feature measures the *relative exchange advantage* of the player whose turn it is to move. EXCH is computed by taking $T_{current}$, the total number of squares into which the player to move may advance a piece, and in so doing force an exchange, and subtracting $T_{previous}$, the corresponding quantity for the previous move by the opposing player.

Samuel's program faced two tasks in attempting to learn such a polynomial evaluation function: (a) discovering which features to use in the function and (b) developing appropriate weights for combining the various features to obtain a value for the board position. We describe the weight-learning task first and later return to the problem of discovering which features to use.

457

In the self-play mode of training, the checkers program learns by playing a copy of itself. The version of the program that is doing the learning is referred to as Alpha, while the copy that serves as an opponent is called Beta. The learning procedure employed by Alpha is to compare at each turn its estimate of the value for the current board position with a performance standard that provides a more accurate estimate of that value. The difference between these two estimates controls the adjustment of the weights in the evaluation function. Alpha's estimate is developed by conducting a shallow minimax search applying the evaluation polynomial to tip board positions and backing up these values (see Article II.C5a, in Vol. I). The performance standard is obtained by conducting a deeper minimax search into future board positions using the same evaluation function as in the shallow search. Samuel takes advantage of the fact that a deep search is usually more accurate than a shallow one.

How does Alpha use this move-by-move performance standard to guide its search for proper weighting coefficients? First, the difference, Δ, between the performance standard and Alpha's estimate is computed. If Δ is negative, Alpha's polynomial is overestimating the value of the position. If Δ is positive, Alpha is underestimating it. For each board feature, a count is kept of the times that the sign of that feature agrees or disagrees with the sign of Δ. From these tallies, a correlation coefficient is developed that indicates the degree to which that feature predicts Δ. The goal of the learning procedure is to minimize Δ (so that Alpha is duplicating the evaluations of the performance standard). The weights of the polynomial are determined by scaling the correlation coefficients onto the range -2^{18} to 2^{18}. Large positive coefficients are given to features that strongly predict positive values of Δ and vice versa, so that the polynomial will tend to "follow" Δ and thus reduce it.

The overall effect of this scheme is to independently assign blame for Alpha's estimation errors to the individual features. This is sensible, since the features are combined independently (i.e., by addition, without any interaction terms) to form the polynomial.

Alpha can be viewed as conducting a hill-climbing search through the "rule space"—the space of possible weights. Each move in the checkers game serves as a training instance to guide this search. The correlation coefficients summarize the entire body of training instances and indicate in which direction the search must move in order to minimize Δ.

Hill-climbing is known to have many drawbacks, including convergence to local maxima. Samuel addresses this problem as follows. When Alpha and Beta commence play, they are identical. However, while Alpha proceeds to search the rule space, Beta does not change. As Alpha improves, it begins to defeat Beta regularly. When Alpha has won a majority of the games played, Beta adopts Alpha's improved evaluation function, and the count of games won and lost is started again from zero. Beta is thus used to "remember" a good point in the rule space. If Alpha is at a local maximum, however, its performance will tend to worsen whenever it makes a minor modification to its polynomial. To prevent a local maximum from halting Alpha's improvement, an arbitrary change is made to Alpha's scoring polynomial whenever Alpha loses three games to Beta. The largest weight in Alpha's polynomial is set at zero to jump Alpha to some new point in the rule space.

Now that we have seen how Samuel's program determines the weights for the evaluation polynomial, we turn our attention to the first learning problem—determining what features should be used to evaluate a board position. This is a variant of the *problem of new terms* (see Article XIV.D1): How can a learning program discover the appropriate terms for representing its acquired knowledge? Samuel offers a partial solution to this problem, namely, *term selection*. The learning program is provided with a list of 38 possible terms. Its learning task is to select a subset of 16 of these terms to include in the evaluation polynomial.

The selection process is quite straightforward. The program starts with a random sample of 16 features. For each feature in the polynomial, a count is kept of how many times that feature has had the lowest weight (i.e., the weight nearest zero). This count is incremented after each move by Alpha. When the count for some feature exceeds 32, that feature is removed from the polynomial and replaced by a new term. At all times, 16 features are included in the polynomial, and the remaining 22 features form a reserve queue. New features are selected from the top of the queue, while features removed from the polynomial are placed at the end of the queue. Viewed in the context of credit assignment, Samuel's program assigns blame to features whose weights have values near zero, since those features are making no contribution to the evaluation function.

Samuel (1959) was dissatisfied with this term-selection approach to the new-term problem. He writes:

> It might be argued that this procedure of having the program select new terms for the evaluation polynomial from a supplied list is much too simple and that the program should generate terms for itself. Unfortunately, no satisfactory scheme for doing this has yet been devised. (p. 220)

The feature-selection and weight-adjustment learning processes take place concurrently. In Samuel's experiment with these learning methods, the set of selected features and their weights started to stabilize after roughly 32 games of self-play. The resulting program was able to play a "better-than-average" game of checkers (Samuel, 1959, p. 222).

Learning a Signature Table by Book Training

The second kind of static evaluation function investigated by Samuel was a system of *signature tables*. A signature table is an n-dimensional array. Each dimension of the array corresponds to one of the measured board features.

To obtain the estimated value of a board position, we measure each of the board features and index these values into the signature-table array. The contents of each cell in the table is a number that gives the value of the corresponding board position. In a sense, the signature table maps all possible board positions into a small n-dimensional feature space. Every point in that feature space is represented as a cell in the signature table that gives the value of all board positions mapped to that point.

Suppose, for example, that we had only three features: KCENT (king center control), MOB (total mobility), and GUARD (back-row control). The cube shown in Figure D5a–1 is a schematic diagram of the resulting signature table. Notice that KCENT and GUARD take on only the values -1, 0, and 1, while MOB is allowed to take on values from -2 to $+2$. If we have a board position for which KCENT $= 1$, GUARD $= 0$, and MOB $= 2$, then we look into the signature table at the cell addressed by $(1, 0, 2)$ to obtain the value: .8.

It is possible to view this signature table as a set of $3 \times 3 \times 5 = 45$ production rules. There is one rule for every possible combination of features—every cell—in the table. The rule for the situation illustrated in Figure D5a–1 could be stated as

If: KCENT $= 1 \wedge$ GUARD $= 0 \wedge$ MOB $= 2$,
Then: Value of position $= .8$.

Signature tables are more expressive than linear polynomials because they can capture interactions among all of the features. Their main drawbacks, however, are their large size and related problems with learnability. A full signature table for the entire set of 24 terms used by Samuel would contain roughly 6×10^{12} cells—far too large to be stored or effectively learned. Two techniques were applied to overcome these problems. First, the number of possible values for each feature was substantially reduced. Most features were restricted to three values: $+1$ (if the position is good for the program), 0 (if the position is even), and -1 (if the position is bad for the program). Second,

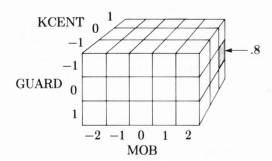

Figure D5a–1. A three-dimensional signature table.

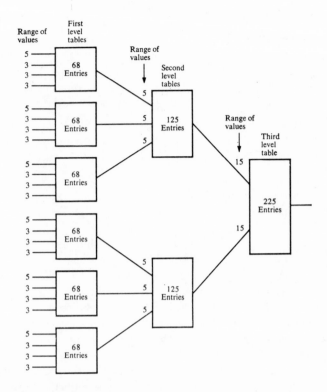

Figure D5a–2. Three-level hierarchy of signature tables
(from Samuel, 1967).

instead of one giant signature table, Samuel adopted the three-level hierarchy
shown in Figure D5a–2.

The 24 board features are partitioned into six important subgroups, and
a separate signature table is developed for each group. The outputs of the
six first-level signature tables are values between −2 and +2 that are used as
indexes to two second-level signature tables. The second-level tables produce
values between −7 and +7 that are used as indexes to the final signature
table to obtain the estimated value of the board position. This hierarchical
system was found to be expressive enough to support excellent checkers play
and small enough to be learnable.

The program learns the values for the cells in these tables by following
"book games" played between two master checkers-players. Approximately
250,000 board situations of master play were presented to the program. Most
of these moves were selected from games ending in a draw. The program
operates as follows. Each cell in the signature table is associated with two
counts, called A (agree) and D (differ). Initially, A and D are zero for each
cell. At each move, the program is faced with a set of alternative moves, one

of which is the book-designated move. Each of these possible moves can be mapped into one cell in *each* signature table. The program adds a one to the D count of each cell whose corresponding move was *not* the book-preferred move. A total of n (where n is the number of nonbook moves) is added to the A count of each cell corresponding to the book-preferred move. Periodically, the contents of the signature-table cells themselves are updated to reflect the A and D counts. Each cell is given the value

$$C = \frac{(A - D)}{(A + D)},$$

which is a rough correlation coefficient indicating the extent to which the board positions mapped to that cell are the book-preferred moves. The correlation coefficients are then scaled into the -2 to $+2$ (or -7 to $+7$) range.

This learning process can be viewed as a technique of learning from examples. Each move provides a training instance that is used to update several signature-table entries. Credit assignment is easy, because the book provides a fairly reliable performance standard on a move-by-move basis. Credit is assigned to the signature-table cell corresponding to the book move, and blame is allotted to all cells corresponding to rejected alternative moves. It is the learning-by-doing approach that allows the program to determine which moves are the alternative moves.

The second- and third-level tables are trained at the same time, and by the same techniques, as the first-level tables. The current contents of the signature tables are used to determine which second- and third-level cells correspond to the alternative moves under consideration, and their A and D totals are updated during each move. The learning process is quite erratic at the start, since most of the first-level signature-table cells contain zeros initially. Thus, incorrect second- and third-level cells are selected during the early stages of learning. As learning progresses, these errors are overcome.

To make the tables more reliable during the early stages of training, some smoothing is done to fill in cells for which the A and D counts are still near zero. Smoothing is a form of generalization involving interpolating and extrapolating from surrounding cells in the table. The smoothing has no effect on the A and D counts—these are used later to replace the interpolated values with more accurate, induced values.

One other refinement of the signature-table system is to break the game of checkers into seven chronological *phases* and to use a different signature table for each phase. Samuel reasoned that the board features relevant to determining good moves during the opening of the game are unlikely to be the same as those used during the ends of games. The seven-phase approach leads to an increase in the number of cells, thus making the tables more difficult to learn. However, Samuel was able to fill in empty cells by smoothing from the tables of adjacent phases.

Results

Samuel's signature-table system was much more effective as a checkers player than any of the other configurations he tested. To assess the goodness of play, Samuel tested the program on 895 book moves that were not used during the training. A count was made of the number of times that the program rated 0, 1, 2, etc., moves as equal to or better than the book-recommended move. After training on 173,989 book moves, the test gave the results shown in Table D5a–1. By summing the first two columns, we see that the program chooses the best move or the second-best move, as defined by the book, 64% of the time. These ratings are made without employing any forward search. Minimax look-ahead search improves the performance of the program substantially.

Despite this impressive level of performance, champion checkers players are still able to beat the program. In 1965, the world champion, W. F. Hellman won all four correspondence games played against the program. He drew with the program during one "hurriedly played cross-board game" (Samuel, 1967, p. 601, n. 2).

Comparison of the Signature-table and Polynomial Methods

The signature-table method substantially outperformed the polynomial-evaluation-function approach. Even when both methods were trained by following book moves, the moves chosen by the polynomial evaluation function correlated with the book-indicated moves only half as well as the moves chosen by the signature tables. This difference is due to the improved representational power of the signature tables. The signature table can represent nonlinear relationships among the various terms, since there is a different table cell for each possible combination of terms. In the polynomial representation, only linear relationships are possible. Such a representation assumes that each term contributes independently to the value of a board position. This assumption is evidently incorrect for checkers.

Conclusion

Samuel developed and tested several different representations and training techniques for teaching a program to play checkers. Among the contributions

TABLE D5a–1
Evaluation of Signature-table Performance

Number of moves rated as better than or equal to book move	0	1	2	3	4	5	6
Relative proportion	38%	26%	16%	10%	6%	3%	1%

of this work are (a) the demonstration that machine-learning techniques can be highly successful, (b) the technique of using a deeper search and book-supplied moves to solve the credit-assignment problem, (c) the term-selection methods for determining which features to include in the polynomial evaluation function, and (d) the demonstration that signature tables provide a much more effective representation for checkers knowledge than either the linear-polynomial or the rote-learning techniques.

References

All of this work is discussed in Samuel (1959, 1967). See Buchanan, Mitchell, Smith, and Johnson (1977) for a discussion of Samuel's term-selection technique as an instance of a *layered* learning system.

D5b. Waterman's Poker Player

As PART of his thesis project, Donald Waterman (1968) developed a computer program that learns to play draw poker. Draw poker is a game of imperfect information in which psychological factors, such as how easily one's opponent is bluffed, become important. Minimax look-ahead search is not possible because the overall state of the game (i.e., the contents of all the hands) is not completely known. Instead, approximate heuristic methods must be used. Waterman developed a production system (see Article III.C4, in Vol. I) to encode a set of heuristics for poker, and he sought to have his program discover these production rules through experience. In this article, we first describe Waterman's production-rule knowledge representation and its application in the poker-playing performance element; we then discuss in detail the methods used in the learning element to acquire and refine these production rules.

Waterman's Performance Element for Draw Poker

Each game of draw poker is divided into five stages. First, each player is dealt five cards. This is followed by a betting stage in which the players alternately choose to place a bet larger than the opponent's bet (RAISE), place a bet equal to the opponent's bet (CALL), or give up (DROP) the hand; a CALL or DROP action ends this stage. In the third stage, each player has the option of replacing up to three of his (or her) cards with new cards drawn from the deck. This is followed by another betting stage like the first. Finally, the hands are compared (except in a DROP), and the player with the best hand wins the game.

Waterman's performance element has built-in routines for carrying out the deal, the draw, and the final comparison of hands. The two betting stages, however, are performed by a modifiable production system. It is the production rules making up this production system that the program attempts to learn and improve.

The production system developed by Waterman contains two basic kinds of rules: *interpretation rules* that compute important features of the game situation and *action rules* that decide which action (CALL, DROP, or RAISE) to take.

The action rules make their decisions based on the values of seven key variables that make up the so-called *dynamic state vector:*

(VDHAND, POT, LASTBET, BLUFFO, POTBET, ORP, OSTYLE) .

VDHAND, for example, is a measure of the value of the program's hand, POT is the current amount of money in the pot, and BLUFFO is an estimate of the opponent's "bluffability."

The interpretation rules compute the values of these seven variables from directly observable quantities. To compute the value of BLUFFO, for example, features such as OBLUFFS (the number of times the opponent has been caught bluffing) and OCORREL (the correlation between the opponent's hands and his bets) are examined. Once numeric values for the seven variables have been computed, they are converted into symbolic values that describe important subranges of values. For example, the rule

If POT > 50, then POT = BIGPOT.

gives POT the symbolic value BIGPOT whenever POT is larger than 50.

The action rules are stated solely in terms of these symbolic values. A typical action rule is

(SUREWIN, BIGPOT, POSITIVEBET, *, *, *, *)
⇒ (*, POT + (2 × LASTBET), 0, *, *, *, *) CALL,

which can be paraphrased as

If:	VDHAND =	SUREWIN
and	POT =	BIGPOT
and	LASTBET =	POSITIVEBET,
Then:	POT :=	POT + (2 × LASTBET)
	LASTBET :=	0
	CALL .	

The condition and action parts of the rule have the same form as the state vector. The left-hand side of the rule is a pattern that is matched against the state vector to determine whether the rule should be executed. The right-hand side of the rule indicates which action to take and provides instructions for modifying the value of the state vector.

These production rules are applied by the performance element as follows. First, all of the interpretation rules are used to analyze the current game situation in order to develop the dynamic state vector. Next, the action rules are examined one by one in a *fixed order* until a rule is found whose condition pattern matches the state vector. That rule is executed to make the program's move. This fixed ordering for the production rules serves as a conflict-resolution technique (see Article III.C4, in Vol. I). If more than one rule is applicable in a given situation, only the first rule in the list is executed. Hence, when new rules are acquired or old rules are modified, the order of the rules must be carefully considered.

There are two basic ways to generalize the left-hand side of an action rule. One method is to drop a condition by replacing one of the symbolic values on the left-hand side (e.g., BIGPOT) by *, which matches *any* value. The other method is to modify the interpretation rule that defines a symbolic value so that it includes a larger set of underlying numeric values (e.g., changing BIGPOT to be any POT > 40). This is the same as Michalski's method of generalizing by internal disjunction (see Article XIV.D1). We will see below how Waterman makes use of these two generalization methods.

Learning to Play Poker

Waterman sought to have the program learn the interpretation rules, the action rules, and the ordering of the action rules by playing poker games against an expert opponent. As the poker games proceed, the learning element analyzes each of the decisions of the performance element and extracts training instances. Each training instance is in the form of a *training rule,* that is, a specific production rule that would have made the correct decision had it been chosen and executed. The training rules guide the learning element as it determines which production rules to generalize and specialize.

The task of extracting a training rule is quite difficult, because the environment provides very little information that could serve as a performance standard. Unlike deterministic games such as checkers or chess that have no chance element, poker is probabilistic. Even an expert player will lose from time to time. Thus, the program must play several hands before it can assess the quality of the production rules in its knowledge base. As discussed in the introduction to this section (Article XIV.D5), however, even when a reliable performance standard is available on a full-game basis, the problem of assigning credit or blame to individual moves in that game is still very difficult. Consequently, Waterman sought to provide the program with some form of move-by-move performance standard. Three different techniques were developed: advice-taking, automatic training, and analytic training.

In advice-taking, the program plays a series of poker games against a human expert. After each turn by the performance element, the learning element asks the expert whether the performance-element action is correct. The expert responds either with (OK) or with some advice such as (CALL BECAUSE YOUR HAND IS FAIR, THE POT IS LARGE, AND THE LASTBET IS LARGE). This advice provides the training rule directly.

In the automatic-training approach, an expert program serves as the opponent and advice-giver. The expert program uses a knowledge base of production rules developed by Waterman himself to determine, at each move, what action to take. During play against the learning program, the expert program compares each move made by the learning program with the move it would have made and provides advice exactly as a human expert would.

Finally, the most interesting method of instruction, the analytic method, involves no advice-taking whatsoever. After each full round of play (i.e., each single hand), the learning element analyzes the moves made by the performance element and attempts to deduce which moves were incorrect. In place of an externally supplied performance standard, the learning element is provided with a predicate-calculus axiomatization of the rules of poker. From these axioms, the program is able to deduce, after the hand is over, what the correct decisions would have been, thus providing the learning element with a performance standard.

Once the learning element has a move-by-move performance standard, it can extract a training rule and modify the production system. The modification process works by first locating the production rule that made the incorrect decision and then examining the list of production rules for a rule before or after the error-causing rule that could have made the correct decision. If such a rule is found, generalization and specialization techniques are applied to modify the production rules so that the proper rule would have been executed. If no such rule is found, the training rule itself is inserted into the production-rule list immediately in front of the error-causing rule.

In the remainder of this article, we discuss how each of these three training techniques allows the learning element to develop a training rule. For the advice-taking and automatic-training methods, this is straightforward. In the analytic approach, however, a series of credit-assignment problems must be solved. We describe Waterman's solutions in detail. Finally, we describe how the training rule acquired by any one of these methods is used to modify the current set of production rules in the knowledge base.

Advice-taking and Automatic Training

In the advice-taking and automatic-training methods, the program is supplied after each move with advice such as:

> (CALL BECAUSE YOUR HAND IS FAIR, THE POT IS LARGE,
> AND THE LASTBET IS LARGE) .

This advice provides the training rule directly. The proper action (i.e., the right-hand side of the training rule), CALL, is indicated along with the relevant variables and their values. This advice is equivalent to the production rule:

> (FAIR, LARGE, LARGE, *, *, *, *)
> $\Rightarrow$ (*, POT + (2 $\times$ LASTBET), 0, *, *, *, *) CALL .

The details of the right-hand side of the rule can be filled in automatically for each action from knowledge of the rules of the game. In this case, for example, CALL requires the program to match its opponent's bet, and thus the POT must increase by twice LASTBET, once for the opponent's bet and again for the program's reply. The other possibilities, DROP and RAISE, are handled similarly.

It is interesting to note that Waterman's program accepts fairly low-level advice. The expert's advice can easily be interpreted in terms of the present game situation, so there is no need to interpret or operationalize the advice (see Article XIV.C1). Waterman's advice-taking research concentrates, instead, on the problem of integrating this advice into the current knowledge base. We describe how this happens after we discuss the methods employed during analytic training to obtain the training rule.

Learning by the Analytic Technique

The main difficulty facing Waterman's program during analytic training is credit assignment. The learning element has to deal with a pair of credit-assignment problems. The first problem is *determining the quality of a round of play*. As we mentioned above, the probabilistic nature of draw poker makes this difficult, since the loss of a single hand does not necessarily indicate that the program is playing poorly. Furthermore, the fact that poker is a game of imperfect information leads to difficulties. If, for example, the program "drops" its bid (i.e., folds its hand and gives in to the other player), the contents of the opponent's hand are never known. The program solves this first credit-assignment problem by always "calling" the bid (i.e., meeting the opponent's bet and requesting to see his hand), instead of dropping, and by applying its knowledge of the rules of poker to deduce whether the program could have improved its play within the round.

If the program could have done better, it turns its attention to the second credit-assignment problem—*determining which individual moves were poor*. During the round of play, a complete trace of the actions of the performance element is kept. To solve the second credit-assignment problem, the learning element applies its axiomatization of the rules of poker to evaluate each move in detail. The rules of poker are axiomatized in predicate calculus as a set of implications such as:

ACTION(CALL) ∧ HIGHER(YOURHAND, OPPHAND)
⊃ ADD(LASTBET, POT) ∧ ADD(POT, YOURSCORE) .

These statements define the effects of each of four possible actions: BET HIGH, BET LOW, CALL, and DROP. To evaluate a particular move in the game, the learning element takes the value of the dynamic state vector at that point and uses it to determine the truth value of certain predicates in this axiom system (e.g., GOOD(OPPHAND), HIGHER(OPPHAND, YOURHAND)). Then it tries to prove the statement

MAXIMIZE(YOURSCORE)

by backward-chaining through the axiom system (see Article III.C4, in Vol. I). The resulting proof indicates the action that should have been performed and provides the move-by-move performance standard. When the performance standard differs from the move made by the program, blame is assigned to that move, and the learning element builds a training rule.

The correct decision, obtained from the performance standard, forms the right-hand side (action part) of the training rule. Waterman axiomatized the

RAISE action as two possible subactions, BET HIGH and BET LOW, so that the program would not have to learn how big a bet to make. For BET HIGH, the performance element chooses a random bet between 10 and 20. Similarly, a BET LOW action leads to a random bet between 1 and 9. Thus, the performance standard provides the complete right-hand side of the training rule.

The left-hand side of the training rule is obtained by examining a table called the *decision matrix*. The decision matrix contains four abstract rules, one for each possible action. These rules tell which values of the seven state variables are relevant for the indicated action. The exact values of the variables are not given—only a general indication of whether the values should be large or small. For instance, the abstract rule for the DROP action is

(CURRENT, LARGE, LARGE, SMALL, SMALL, CURRENT, LARGE) ⟹ DROP,

or more clearly,

If:	VDHAND = ⟨current symbolic value of VDHAND⟩
and	POT = LARGE
and	LASTBET = LARGE
and	BLUFFO = SMALL
and	POTBET = SMALL
and	ORP = ⟨current symbolic value of ORP⟩
and	OSTYLE = LARGE,
Then:	DROP.

Once the learning element has deduced from the axioms that the proper action would have been DROP, it takes the corresponding rule from the decision matrix and uses it as the training rule. Notice that the level of abstraction of the rules in the decision matrix is the same as the level of abstraction of the advice supplied by the human expert or expert program.

It could be argued that the use of the decision matrix is improper, since it provides the learning element with essential information that a person who was learning to play poker would have to discover himself. Waterman (1968) suggests some methods by which the decision matrix could be learned from experience, but none of these was implemented.

Using the Training Rule to Modify the Knowledge Base

Once the training rule is obtained, whether by advice from a person, by advice from the expert program, or by analysis, it must be used to modify the production rules in the knowledge base. The training rule is first used to modify the interpretation rules. The left-hand side of the training rule is compared with the state vector computed by the interpretation rules. LARGE matches symbolic values that correspond to large values of the underlying variable. Similarly, SMALL matches small values. If a symbol does not match, the interpretation rules that computed that symbol are assigned blame. They are then either modified or augmented to include a new interpretation rule.

Suppose, for example, that the state vector listed POT as having the value P3, where P3 is derived by the interpretation rule:

```
If POT > 20, then POT = P3.
```

Furthermore, suppose that the value of POT in the game situation being analyzed is 45. By comparing P3 with LARGE, the learning element determines that this interpretation rule is incorrect (since P3 can refer to very small values of POT). The learning element can either modify the rule (by substituting 44 for 20) or create a new rule. A user-supplied parameter, KK, specifies the largest allowable change that can be made to a numeric value in an interpretation rule. In this case, we will assume that the learning element creates the new rule

```
If POT > 44, then POT = P4.
```

and modifies the state vector so that POT has the value P4.

Once the interpretation rules have been checked and modified, the updated state vector is matched against the action rules to find the rule that made the incorrect decision. This rule is called the *error-causing rule*. The training rule is then used to locate a production rule that could have made the correct decision had it been executed. This is accomplished by comparing the right-hand side of the training rule with each production rule in the rule base.

Waterman's program classifies action rules as either *recently hypothesized* or *accepted*. A recently hypothesized rule is one that was recently added to the knowledge base, whereas an accepted rule is one that the program believes to be nearly correct. The learning element follows a strategy of first attempting to make minor changes in accepted rules and then, if minor changes do not suffice, attempting to make major changes in recently hypothesized rules. Finally, if a suitable recently hypothesized rule cannot be found, the training rule is added to the rule base and is labeled as recently hypothesized.

The learning element searches upward ahead of the error-causing rule for an accepted rule that would have made the correct decision. If such a rule is found, it is checked to see if the pattern of its left-hand side can be generalized to match the current state vector. Only minor generalizations— that is, changes to the interpretation rules—are considered. No conditions are dropped (i.e., replaced by *).

If no accepted rule can be found, the learning element again searches upward before the error-causing rule, this time looking for a recently hypothesized rule that would have made the correct decision. If such a rule is found, major changes—including both dropping conditions and modifying interpretation rules—are made in the left-hand-side pattern so that it matches the state vector.

If no suitable rules can be found before the error-causing rule, the learning element searches for an accepted rule *after* the error-causing rule. If an appropriate rule is found there, the error-causing rule and all intervening rules must be specialized so that they will *not* match the state vector, and the target rule must be generalized—by changing the interpretation rules—so that it *will* match the state vector.

Finally, if no rules can be found that could be generalized to make the correct decision, the training rule is inserted into the ordered list of production rules immediately in front of the error-causing rule. The training rule is marked as being recently hypothesized. Figure D5b–1 depicts this four-step process of modifying the rule base.

This four-step process combines the task of integrating new knowledge into the knowledge base with the task of generalizing the training rule. Notice that the integration process must have knowledge about how the performance element chooses which rule to execute, so that it can decide how to update the rule base. The generalization process is fairly ad hoc. For example, recently hypothesized rules become accepted when enough conditions are dropped from the left-hand side so that only N conditions remain (N is a parameter given to the program). This is a very weak technique for preventing rules from becoming overgeneralized.

Results

Waterman's poker program learned to play a fairly good game of poker. Separate tests were conducted with each of the three training techniques. In each case, the program started with only one rule: "In all situations, make a random decision." For advice-taking from a human expert and for learning

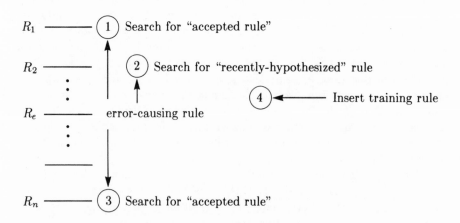

Figure D5b–1. The four steps to modifying the production-rule base.

from the expert program, training was continued until the program played one complete game of five hands without once making an incorrect decision (as judged by the expert). For the analytic method, the program continued to play games until the original "random decision" production rule was executed only 5% of the time. The results are shown in Table D5b–1.

The rightmost column shows the results of a proficiency test in which the program and a human expert played two sets of 25 hands. During the first set of 25 hands, the cards were drawn at random from a shuffled deck as in ordinary play. However, during the second set of 25 hands, the same hands were used as in the first set, except that the program received the hands originally dealt to the person and vice versa. At the end, the cumulative winnings of the program and person were compared.

The results show that in all three training methods, performance improved markedly. The automatic training provided the best performance improvement, perhaps because the automated expert played more consistently than the human expert. Although the analytic method performed the poorest, the results are not strictly comparable, since the axiom set provided it with only four possible actions, whereas the advice-based methods were given eight possible actions. Consequently, the analytic method may not actually be inferior to the two advice-taking methods.

Conclusion

Waterman's poker-playing program faces a very difficult learning problem. Poker is a multiple-step task that provides very little feedback to the learning program. For the two advice-taking methods, this problem is sidestepped by allowing the program to accept a training rule directly from an expert. However, for the analytic method, two credit-assignment problems must be solved: evaluating a round of play and evaluating a particular move. To solve these problems, the program modifies its betting strategy (to call instead

TABLE D5b–1

Comparison of Three Training Methods (from Waterman, 1970)

Training method	Number of training trials	Final number of rules	Percent difference in winnings[a]
Before training	0	1	−71.0
Advice-taking	38	26	−6.8
Automatic training	29	19	−1.9
Analytic method	57	14	−13.0

[a]These percentages are computed by subtracting the amount of money won by the opponent from the amount of money won by the program and dividing by the amount of money won by the opponent. In all cases, the program won less than the opponent and, hence, the percentages are all negative.

of dropping) and applies knowledge available from the axiom set and from the decision matrix. This permits the credit-assignment process to extract a training rule from the trace of decisions taken by the performance element. Once the training rule is acquired by any of these three methods, it is used to guide the generalization and specialization of the production rules in the knowledge base. Since only positive training instances are available, the program must make use of arbitrary constraints to prevent overgeneralization.

References

Waterman (1970) describes this work in detail.

D5c. HACKER

HACKER is a learning system developed by Gerald Sussman (1975) to model the process of acquiring programming skills. HACKER's performance task is to plan the actions of a hypothetical one-armed robot that manipulates stacks of toy blocks. This planning task is described in detail in Article XV.C.

HACKER learns by doing. It develops plans and simulates their execution. The plan and the trace of the execution are examined by HACKER to acquire two kinds of knowledge: *generalized subroutines* and *generalized bugs*. A generalized subroutine is similar to a STRIPS macro operator (see Article II.D5, in Vol. I), in that it provides a sequence of actions for achieving a general goal. A generalized bug is a *demon* that inspects new plans to see if they contain an instance of the bug and provides an appropriate bug fix.

An example of a generalized subroutine is the following procedure for stacking one block on top of another:

```
(TO (MAKE (ON a b))
    (HPROG
        (UNTIL (y) (CANNOT (ASSIGN (y) (ON y a)))
                   (MAKE (NOT (ON y a)))
        (PUTON a b))).
```

The goal of this procedure is (MAKE (ON a b)): The procedure changes the world so that (ON a b) is true. This subroutine is general and works for any two blocks a and b (a and b are variables that are bound to particular blocks—denoted by capital letters—when the subroutine is invoked). The procedure removes everything that is on a and then picks up a and puts it on b.

Viewed as a production rule, this procedure could be written as:

```
(MAKE (ON a b))  ⇒  (HPROG
                        (UNTIL (y) (CANNOT (ASSIGN (y) (ON y a)))
                                   (MAKE (NOT (ON y a)))
                        (PUTON a b)).
```

From this perspective, we see that when HACKER learns a generalized subroutine, it is learning both a generalized left-hand side, the goal, and a generalized right-hand side, the plan. As we will see below, the left-hand sides of the production rules are generalized by turning constants into variables, while the right-hand sides are developed by concatenating subplans and ordering them properly to form macro operators.

An example of the other kind of knowledge gained by HACKER—a generalized bug—is the demon:

```
(WATCH-FOR  (ORDER (PURPOSE 1line (ACHIEVE (ON a b)))
                   (PURPOSE 2line (ACHIEVE (ON b c))))
            (PREREQUISITE-CLOBBERS-BROTHER-GOAL
                              current-prog 1line 2line
                              (CLEARTOP b))).
```

It tells HACKER to watch for plans in which one step, 1line, has the goal of achieving (ON a b) and a subsequent step, 2line, has the goal of achieving (ON b c). In such cases, the prerequisite of the second step—that b have a clear top—requires undoing the goal of the first step. When this demon detects such bugs, it invokes the PREREQUISITE-CLOBBERS-BROTHER-GOAL repair procedure to fix them.

Generalized bugs can also be viewed as production rules. This particular bug demon could be written as:

```
(ORDER   (PURPOSE 1line (ACHIEVE (ON a b)))
                     (PURPOSE 2line (ACHIEVE (ON b c))))  ⇒
(PREREQUISITE-CLOBBERS-BROTHER-GOAL
                 current-prog 1line 2line
                 (CLEARTOP b)) .
```

HACKER learns both the left- and the right-hand sides of these bug demons.

HACKER's Architecture

HACKER is a complex program that contains several interleaved components (see Fig. D5c–1). These include:

1. The *planner,* which develops plans by pattern-directed expansion of planning operators;

2. The *critics' gallery,* which inspects the plans for known generalized bugs;

3. The *simulator,* which simulates the execution of the plans and checks for errors;

4. The *debugger and generalizer,* which locate and repair bugs in the plans for later use by the critics' gallery; and

5. The *generalizer and subroutinizer,* which generalize plans and install them in HACKER's knowledge base.

The first two components comprise the performance element, which develops block-stacking plans. The simulator creates a performance trace of the simulated execution of the plan. The last two components perform the actual process of learning generalized subroutines and generalized bugs.

These components interact continually. As the planner is developing the plan, for example, the critics' gallery is interrupting to repair known bugs and the simulator is symbolically executing the evolving plan. The debugger may step in to fix a new bug and then resume the planning process. In this article, however, we describe each of these components separately and pretend that the plan is first developed in its entirety and then successively criticized, simulated, debugged, and generalized. This false architecture corresponds fairly closely to our simple model of learning multiple-step tasks. There are two learning elements, however: one for developing generalized subroutines and one for developing generalized bugs. Figure D5c–1 summarizes this false architecture. We will explain the operation of HACKER by following the flow through this model.

HACKER's Performance Element:
The Planner and the Critics' Gallery

HACKER employs a simple problem-reduction planner (Chap. XV; see also Article II.B2, in Vol. I), which is presented with an initial situation and a goal block-structure to create. Figure D5c–2 shows a sample situation and goal.

The goal is matched against HACKER's knowledge base of known plans, subroutines, and refinement rules. If a known plan or subroutine is found that

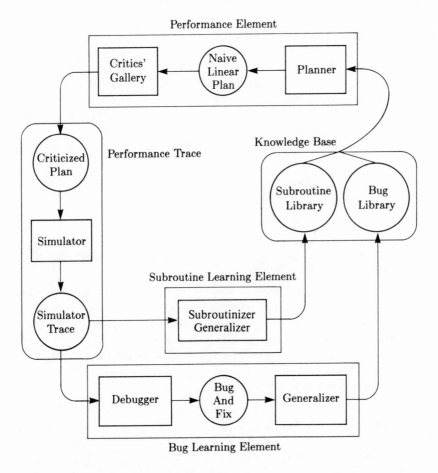

Figure D5c–1.   A simplified architecture for HACKER.

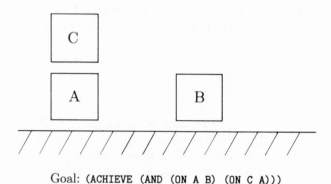

Goal: (ACHIEVE (AND (ON A B) (ON C A)))

Figure D5c–2.   A sample situation and goal.

can accomplish the goal, it is used. Otherwise, a refinement rule is applied to reformulate the goal as a set of subgoals. These subgoals, in turn, are matched against the knowledge base to locate known methods for achieving them. The expansion into subgoals proceeds until HACKER finds existing plans or primitive operators that can achieve each of the subgoals.

HACKER is noted for its *linearity assumption*. Whenever the planner is faced with the problem of achieving a pair of conjunctive subgoals, it assumes that they can be achieved *independently*. This assumption is represented in the AND rule for refining a conjunctive goal:

```
(TO  (ACHIEVE (AND a b))
     (AND  (ACHIEVE a)
           (ACHIEVE b))).
```

This says "To achieve goals *a* and *b*, first achieve *a* and then achieve *b*." As a result of this linearity assumption, the plan developed by the planner is a naive plan that may not work (see Article XV.C).

The naive plan is criticized by the critics in the critics' gallery, which attempt to find instances of the generalized bugs kept in the bug library. When a bug is found, the associated bug fix is applied to improve the plan— usually by rearranging plan steps. The result of this criticism is a plan that reflects all of HACKER's past experience but still may not be correct.

HACKER's Performance Trace:
Plans and Simulation

HACKER's plans contain a large amount of information about the planning process itself. Each step of a plan is justified by giving the *purpose* of the step—the subgoal it is intended to achieve. There are two fundamental kinds of steps: main steps and prerequisite steps. Main steps are directed at goals relating to the goals of the overall plan. Prerequisite steps are computations

needed to establish preconditions for the main steps. For example, the plan
for the problem of Figure D5c–2 contains three steps:

Step 1. (PUTON C TABLE) [purpose: (CLEARTOP A) span: step 2] .

Step 2. (PUTON A B) [purpose: (ON A B) span: full plan] .

Step 3. (PUTON C A) [purpose: (ON C A) span: full plan] .

Steps 2 and 3 are main steps, while step 1 is a prerequisite step needed to
clear off the top of A so that the robot can move A. As HACKER simulates the
execution of the plan, it verifies that the goal of each step has been attained.

Each step in the plan also includes an indication of the *time span* of the
goal it is attaining. The purpose of a step may be to accomplish something
that will remain true for only a short time. In this example, (CLEARTOP A) will
be true only until step 3. For HACKER to know that this is *not* a bug, step 1
includes a time-span indication that its goal is intended to be true only until
the end of step 2.

The criticized plan is simulated to verify that it works properly. The
simulator detects bugs in three forms: illegal operations, failed steps, and
unaesthetic actions. An illegal operation is one that is considered impossible
in the hypothetical blocks world. For instance, it is illegal to pick up a
block unless it has a clear top. A failed step is one that does not achieve its
goal for the designated time span. The simulator uses the goal information
attached to each plan step to verify that at all times the goals intended by the
planner have actually been met. Lastly, an unaesthetic action is a situation
in which the robot moves the same block two times in succession without
any intervening actions. These three methods for detecting bugs provide a
performance standard for HACKER, which states that a plan must execute
legally, achieve all intended goals and subgoals, and also be aesthetically
correct. The simulation halts whenever one of these problems is identified,
and a trace of the simulation is provided to the bug learning element.

HACKER's Learning Elements:
The Subroutine Learning Element and the Bug Learning Element

As mentioned above, there are two learning elements in HACKER. One,
the subroutine learning element, inspects the criticized plan and simulation
trace to identify possible subroutines. The other, the bug learning element,
examines the performance trace to diagnose and correct bugs uncovered by
the simulation.

The subroutine learning element attempts to detect when two subgoals
in the plan are sufficiently similar to allow a single subroutine to accomplish
both. The trace of the planning and simulation processes indicates which
constants in a goal or subgoal—for example, the constants A and B in the
goal (ON A B)—can be generalized. A constant cannot be generalized if the

plan somehow refers to that constant explicitly (e.g., the constant TABLE has special status). HACKER generalizes each subgoal in the plan by turning all generalizable constants into variables. The generalized subgoal is then compared with all other goals in the program. Any two subgoals found to have an allowable common generalization are replaced by calls to a parameterized procedure. This generalization process is similar to the technique used in STRIPS to generalize macro operators.

As an example, consider the block-stacking task of Figure D5c-2. The initial plan involves separate steps for achieving (ON A B) and (ON C A). However, traces of the planning and simulation processes indicate that the code for (ON A B) will work for any variables u and v. The generalized goal (ON u v) is checked against other goals in the plan and found to match the subgoal (ON C A). As a result, HACKER formulates a generalized subroutine, (MAKE-ON u v), and replaces the subplans for steps 2 and 3 with calls to MAKE-ON. The MAKE-ON subroutine is placed in the knowledge base for use in future plans as well.

The subroutine learning element can be regarded as learning from examples. The goals and subgoals in a particular plan form the training instances, which are generalized by turning constants into variables. The distinctive aspect of the HACKER approach is that the search of the rule space is accomplished very directly. HACKER (and its predecessor, STRIPS) is able to reason about how the different steps in the plan depend on particular values for the arguments of the goal statement. From this dependency analysis, the correct generalization can be deduced directly. HACKER thus differs from most of the other learning methods described in this chapter in that it is able to use the meanings of its operators to guide the generalization process.

The bug learning element faces a much more difficult learning task. It must determine why the plan failed and repair the plan. Then it must attempt to generalize the discovered bug and create a bug critic that will prevent the bug from reappearing in future plans. The first task—determining why the plan failed—is the problem of credit assignment. The traditional credit-assignment problem is to determine which rule, used in the performance element, led to the mistake. In HACKER's case, there is one fundamental source of error: the linearity assumption as implemented by the AND rule. HACKER's credit assignment, instead, involves determining how the current planning task violates this linearity assumption—that is, how do the subplans in this problem interact?

HACKER's solution to the credit-assignment problem is to compare the intentions and expectations of the performance element with what actually happened. This approach again relies on knowledge of the semantics of the operators to assign blame to individual steps. This is more direct than the weaker, more empirical approach of comparing many possible plans obtained through a more widespread search, as in Samuel's checkers program and the LEX system.

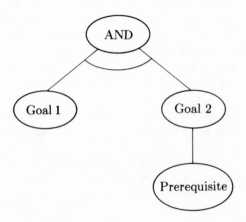

Figure D5c–3.   The PREREQUISITE-CLOBBERS-BROTHER-GOAL
bug schema.

HACKER has a small library of schemas that describe possible subgoal
interactions. Credit assignment is accomplished by matching these schemas
to the goal structure of the current plan and performance trace. For example,
one class of interactions, the PREREQUISITE-CLOBBERS-BROTHER-GOAL, involves
the goal structure depicted in Figure D5c–3.

The prerequisite step of goal 2 somehow makes goal 1 no longer true. For
example, if the overall goal is (ACHIEVE (AND (ON A B) (ON B C))), we have
the subgoal structure shown in Figure D5c–4.

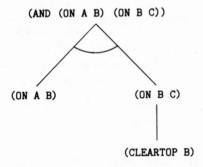

Figure D5c–4.   A subgoal structure that matches the bug schema
of Figure D5c–3.

HACKER simulates this plan by first placing block A on block B, then clearing off B so that it can place B on C. The clearing-off process makes (ON A B) false—the prerequisite of goal 2 has clobbered goal 1. (This is detected by the simulator when it checks the time span of each subgoal.)

Each of HACKER's bug schemas describes some general goal structure that can be matched to the goal structure of the current plan. The matching process is implemented in an ad hoc fashion as a series of six questions that the debugger asks of the performance trace. As a result of the matching process, the bug is ignored as innocuous, is properly classified, or is found to be too difficult to repair.

The process of repairing the plan is straightforward. Each bug schema contains instructions on how to repair the bug. These can involve reordering plan steps, creating new subplans that establish prerequisite conditions, and even removing unnecessary plan steps. The resulting repaired plan is simulated again to detect further bugs.

The process of generalizing the bug is also easily accomplished. Each bug schema contains instructions regarding which components of the goal structure can be generalized by turning constants into variables. For instance, the bug schema for PREREQUISITE-CLOBBERS-BROTHER-GOAL contains the instructions

```
(CSETQ  goal1 (VARIABLIZE (GOAL line1))
        goal2 (VARIABLIZE (GOAL line2))
        prereq (VARIABLIZE pre)) ,
```

where line1 refers to the first goal (whose prerequisite was clobbered), line2 refers to the search goal, and prereq refers to the prerequisite that did the clobbering. These instuctions tell HACKER to analyze the dependencies in the performance trace and generalize all three of these goal expressions. The resulting generalized goal structure shown in Figure D5c–5 is compiled into a demon and added to the bug library for use in subsequent criticism of naive plans.

The bug learning element can be regarded as learning by schema instantiation. Over time, HACKER discovers new situations in which particular kinds of subgoal interactions occur, generalizes these situations, and watches for them in future plans. It does not tackle the problem of discovering these classes of bugs in the first place, nor does it address the problem of discovering techniques for fixing bugs.

Conclusion

HACKER is a system that learns to develop plans for manipulating toy blocks. It acquires two kinds of knowledge—generalized subroutines and generalized bugs. Both of HACKER's learning elements make extensive use of the performance trace, which consists of the plan (annotated with goal information) and a trace of the simulated execution of the plan. The subroutine

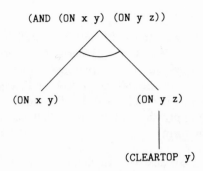

Figure D5c–5.   A generalized goal structure.

learning element generalizes by analyzing the goal structure in the performance trace to determine which constants can be turned into variables. The bug learning element accomplishes credit assignment by instantiating schemas that describe bug-inducing goal structures. The schemas provide guidance for bug repair and generalization. Much of HACKER's impressive behavior derives from its ability to reason about the semantics of its task. The value of a transparent performance element for credit assignment and generalization is very evident in HACKER.

References

HACKER is described in Sussman's (1973) thesis. Doyle (1980) describes a formalization of the concepts of *goal* and *intention* as used by HACKER. An alternative to the linearity assumption is described in Article XV.D1.

D5d. LEX

LEX, a system designed by Thomas Mitchell (see Mitchell, Utgoff, and Banerji, in press; Mitchell, Utgoff, Nudel, and Banerji, 1981), learns to solve simple symbolic integration problems from experience. LEX is provided with an initial knowledge base of roughly 50 integration and simplification operators, some of which are shown in Table D5d–1. The goal of LEX is to discover *heuristics* for *when* to apply these operators. That is, LEX seeks to develop production rules of the form

$$\langle \text{situation} \rangle \quad \Rightarrow \quad \text{Apply operator OP}i,$$

where ⟨situation⟩ is a pattern that is matched against the current integration problem. The situations are expressed in a *generalization language* of possible patterns. For instance, a heuristic rule for operator OP12 might be:

$$\int f(x)\,\text{transc}\,(x)\,dx \quad \Rightarrow \quad \text{Apply OP12 with } u = f(x) \text{ and } dv = \text{transc}\,(x)\,dx.$$

This tells the LEX performance element that if it sees any problem whose integrand is the product of any function, $f(x)$, with a transcendental function, $\text{transc}\,(x)$, then it should apply OP12 with u bound to $f(x)$ and dv bound to $\text{transc}\,(x)\,dx$. The concepts of $f(x)$ and $\text{transc}\,(x)$ are part of the generalization language (illustrated later in Fig. D5d–4).

Mitchell calls these production rules *heuristics* because they provide heuristic guidance to LEX's performance element, which is a simple, forward-chaining production system (see Sec. II.B, in Vol. I). Without any heuristic rules, the performance element conducts a blind uniform-cost search (see Article II.C1, in Vol. I) of the space of all legal sequences of operator applications. Consider the problem of integrating $\int 3x \cos x\,dx$. Without any heuristics, LEX produces the rather large search tree shown in Figure D5d–1. It is no surprise that

TABLE D5d–1

Selected Integration Operators in LEX

OP02	convert	$\int x^r\,dx$	to	$x^{r+1}/(r+1)$ (power rule)
OP03	convert	$\int r f(x)\,dx$	to	$r \int f(x)$ (factor out a real constant)
OP06	convert	$\int \sin x\,dx$	to	$-\cos x$
OP08	convert	$1 \cdot f(x)$	to	$f(x)$
OP10	convert	$\int \cos x\,dx$	to	$\sin x$
OP12	convert	$\int u\,dv$	to	$uv - \int v\,du$ (integration by parts)
OP15	convert	$0 \cdot f(x)$	to	0

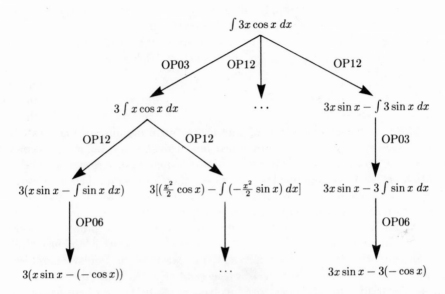

Figure D5d–1.   Partial search tree for $\int 3x \cos x \, dx$ without heuristics.

when LEX has no heuristics, it often cannot solve integration problems before exhausting the time and space available to it.

The task of learning the left-hand sides of heuristic rules can be thought of as a set of concept-learning tasks. LEX tries to discover, for each operator OPi, the definition of the concept *situations in which* OPi *should be used*. It accomplishes this by gathering positive and negative training instances of the use of the operator. By analyzing a trace of the actions taken by the performance element, LEX is able to find cases of appropriate and inappropriate application of the operators. These training instances guide the search of a rule space of possible left-hand-side patterns. The candidate-elimination algorithm (see Article XIV.D3a) is employed to search the rule space, and partially learned heuristics, for which the candidate-elimination algorithm has not found a unique left-hand-side pattern, are stored as version spaces of possible patterns. Thus, the general form of a heuristic rule in LEX is:

⟨version space represented as S and G sets⟩   ⟹   Apply OPi.

For example, after a few training instances, LEX might have the following partially learned heuristic for the integration-by-parts heuristic, OP12:

Version space for OP12:

$G = \int f(x)g(x) \, dx \;\Rightarrow\; \text{OP12, with } u = f(x) \text{ and } dv = g(x) \, dx\,;$

$S = \int 3x \cos x \, dx \;\Rightarrow\; \text{OP12, with } u = 3x \text{ and } dv = \cos x \, dx\,.$

This heuristic tells LEX to apply OP12 in any situation in which the integral has the form $\int f(x)g(x)\,dx$. It also indicates that the correct left-hand-side pattern lies somewhere between the overly specific S pattern, $\int 3x \cos x\,dx$, and the overly general G pattern, $\int f(x)g(x)\,dx$. Below, we show how this partially learned heuristic was discovered by LEX.

LEX's Architecture

LEX is organized as a system of four interacting programs (see Fig. D5d–2) that correspond closely to our modified model of learning for multiple-step tasks. The *problem solver* is the performance element. It solves symbolic integration problems by applying the current set of operators and their heuristics. When the problem solver succeeds in solving an integral, a detailed trace of its performance is provided to the *critic*, which examines the trace to assign credit and blame to the individual decisions made by the problem solver. Once credit assignment is completed, the critic extracts positive (and negative) instances of the proper (and improper) application of particular operators. These training instances are used by the *generalizer* to guide the search for proper heuristics for the operators involved. Finally, the *problem generator* inspects the current contents of the knowledge base (i.e., the operators and their heuristics) and chooses a new problem to present to the problem solver.

LEX thus incorporates all four components of our simple model: the knowledge base (of operators and heuristics), the performance element, the performance trace, and the learning element (composed of the critic and the generalizer). Furthermore, LEX is one of the few AI learning systems to include an experiment planner—the problem generator.

In this article, we first present an example of how LEX solves problems and refines the version spaces of its heuristics. Then we describe each of LEX's components in detail and discuss some open research problems.

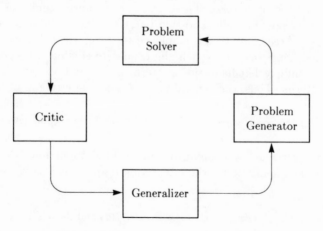

Figure D5d–2.   LEX's architecture.

An Example

To show how LEX works, suppose that the problem generator has chosen the problem $\int 3x \cos x \, dx$ and the problem solver has produced the trace shown earlier in Figure D5d–1. The critic analyzes the trace and extracts several training instances, including:

$$\int 3x \cos x \, dx \;\Rightarrow\; \text{OP12, with } u = 3x \text{ and } dv = \cos x \, dx \text{ (positive)}.$$

$$\int 3 \sin x \, dx \;\Rightarrow\; \text{OP03, with } r = 3 \text{ and } f(x) = \sin x \quad \text{(positive)}.$$

$$\int \sin x \, dx \;\Rightarrow\; \text{OP06} \qquad\qquad\qquad\qquad\qquad \text{(positive)}.$$

We will watch how the generalizer handles the training instance for OP12. Let us assume that this is the first training instance that has been found for this operator, so the knowledge base does not yet contain any heuristics for when to use it. Consequently, the generalizer will create and initialize a new OP12 heuristic. The left-hand side of the heuristic is a version space of the form:

Version space for OP12:

$$G = \int f(x)g(x) \, dx \;\Rightarrow\; \text{OP12, with } u = f(x) \text{ and } dv = g(x) \, dx \,;$$
$$S = \int 3x \cos x \, dx \;\Rightarrow\; \text{OP12, with } u = 3x \text{ and } dv = \cos x \, dx \,.$$

Notice that S is a copy of the training instance and G is the most general pattern for which OP12 is *legal*. This heuristic will recommend that OP12 be applied in any problem whose integrand is less general than $\int f(x)g(x) \, dx$. This is not a highly refined heuristic.

To see how LEX refines this heuristic, let us assume that the other training instances shown above have been processed. At this point, the problem generator chooses the problem $\int 5x \sin x \, dx$ to solve. The problem solver will apply OP12, since the G set of the heuristic matches the integrand. Figure D5d–3 shows a portion of the solution tree.

Some of the training instances extracted by the critic are:

$$\int 5x \sin x \, dx \;\Rightarrow\; \text{OP12, with } u = 5x \text{ and } dv = \sin x \, dx \text{ (positive)}.$$

$$\int 5 \cos x \, dx \;\Rightarrow\; \text{OP03, with } r = 5 \text{ and } f(x) = \cos x \quad \text{(positive)}.$$

$$\int \cos x \, dx \;\Rightarrow\; \text{OP10} \qquad\qquad\qquad\qquad\qquad \text{(positive)}.$$

$$\int 5x \sin x \, dx \;\Rightarrow\; \text{OP12, with } u = \sin x \text{ and } dv = 5x \, dx \text{ (negative)}.$$

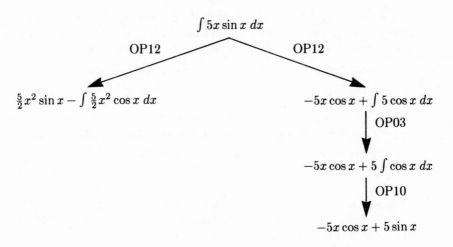

Figure D5d–3.   The solution tree for $\int 5x \sin x \, dx$.

The generalizer updates the version space for OP12 to contain:

$$G = \{g_1, g_2\}, \text{ where}$$
$$g_1: \int \text{polynom}\,(x)g(x)\,dx \;\; \Rightarrow \;\; \text{OP12}\,,$$
$$\text{with } u = \text{polynom}\,(x) \text{ and } dv = g(x)\,dx\,;$$
$$g_2: \int f(x)\,\text{transc}\,(x)\,dx \;\; \Rightarrow \;\; \text{OP12}\,,$$
$$\text{with } u = f(x) \text{ and } dv = \text{transc}(x)\,dx\,;$$

$$S = \{s_1\}, \text{ where}$$
$$s_1: \int kx\,\text{trig}\,(x)\,dx \;\; \Rightarrow \;\; \text{OP12}\,,$$
$$\text{with } u = kx \text{ and } dv = \text{trig}\,(x)\,dx\,.$$

The positive training instance forces the constants 3 and 5 to be general-ized to k, which represents any integer constant, and "sin" and "cos" to be generalized to "trig," which represents any trigonometric function, as shown in s_1. Similarly, the negative training instance leads to two alternative specializa-tions. In g_1, f was specialized to "polynom" to avoid $u = \sin x$, and in g_2, g was specialized to "transc" to avoid $dv = 5x\,dx$. These two specializations no longer cover the negative training instance. With a few more training instances, the heuristic for OP12 converges to the form shown at the start of this article, that is, $\int f(x)\,\text{transc}\,(x)\,dx$. The concepts "$k$," "trig," "polynom," and so on, are all part of the generalization language known to LEX from the start (see Fig. D5d–4, shown later).

Now that we have seen an example of LEX in action, we describe each of the four components of LEX in turn.

The Problem Solver

As discussed above, the problem solver conducts a forward search of possible operator applications in an attempt to solve the given integration problem. Initially, this search is blind. However, as the heuristics for the operators are refined, the search becomes more focused.

The problem solver conducts a *uniform-cost search*. At each step, it chooses the one expansion of the search tree that has the smallest estimated cost. The search tree is maintained as a list of *open* nodes—that is, nodes to which not all legal integration operators have been applied. The cost of an open node is measured by summing the cost of each search step (for both time and space) back to the root of the search tree. In addition, the cost of a proposed expansion is weighted to reflect the strength of the heuristic advice available. In detail, the problem solver chooses an expansion as follows:

Step 1. For each open node and each legal operator, compute the "degree of match" according to the formula:

0   if no heuristic recommends this operator for this node;

m/n if there is a heuristic, and m out of the n patterns in the boundary sets of the version space (i.e., the S and G sets) match the current situation.

Step 2. Choose the expansion that has the lowest weighted cost, computed as:

$$(1.5 - \text{degree of match}) \times (\text{cost so far} + \text{estimated expansion cost}).$$

The effect of the $(1.5 - \text{degree of match})$ weight on the cost is to emphasize the cost of the path when little heuristic guidance is available but to ignore cost considerations as the heuristic recommendation becomes stronger.

The problem solver continues to select nodes and apply operators until the integral is solved. Notice that, in LEX, a simple performance standard is available: solution of the integral. This is a substantially simpler situation than that faced by Waterman's poker player, which needs to play several hands to evaluate how well it is doing. LEX knows when it is doing well. LEX also knows when it is doing poorly. For each integration problem, the problem solver is given a time and space limit. If it runs out of time or space before solving the problem, it gives up and the problem generator selects a new problem to solve.

The Critic

The problem solver provides the critic with a detailed trace of each successfully solved problem. The critic's task is to extract positive and negative training instances from this trace by assigning credit and blame to individual decisions made by the problem solver. The critic solves the credit-assignment problem as follows:

1. Every search step along the minimum-cost solution path found by the problem solver is a positive instance;

2. Every step that (a) leads from a node on the minimum-cost path to a node not on this path and (b) leads to a solution path whose length is greater than or equal to 1.15 times the length of the minimum-cost path is a negative instance.

These criteria are intended to produce applicability heuristics that guide the performance element to *minimum-cost solutions*. To evaluate these criteria (especially 2b), the critic must re-invoke the problem solver to follow out paths that appear to be bad. This deeper search is in some ways analogous to the deep search Samuel used in his checkers-playing program for solving the credit-assignment problem. The criterion of minimum-cost solution is convenient because it can be measured by the computer itself—by its own experience in attempting to solve the problem.

The critic is fairly conservative. It provides the generalizer only with the training instances that can be most reliably credited or blamed. However, the critic is not infallible. It can produce false positive and false negative training instances when the knowledge base contains incorrect heuristics. Since the problem solver follows the guidance provided by the heuristics in the knowledge base, it may believe it has found the lowest cost solution when in fact, the heuristics have led it astray. Since LEX does not conduct an exhaustive search of the space, it will not always detect this fact. As a result, the critic may create false positive and false negative instances. Its reliability can be improved by increasing the safety factor (normally 1.15) when the problem solver is re-invoked by the critic. This causes the problem solver to search more deeply along alternative paths and improves the chances of finding the true minimum-cost path.

The Generalizer

The generalizer simply applies the candidate-elimination algorithm to process each of the training instances provided by the critic and to refine the version spaces of each of the operators. The multiple-boundary-set form of the algorithm (see Article XIV.D3a) was adopted to handle erroneous training instances.

The generalizer is able to learn disjunctions in certain cases. During generalization based on a positive training instance, for example, if the version space would normally be forced to collapse because no consistent rule exists, a second version space is created instead. This second version space contains the patterns that are consistent with all of the negative instances and the single new positive instance. As additional positive instances are received, they are processed against any version space whose G set covers them. When more than one heuristic rule is created for a single operator, the effect is the same as if a single disjunctive heuristic had been developed.

The generalization language (and, thus, the rule space) in LEX is based on the tree of functions shown in Figure D5d–4. The most general pattern is $f(x)$, that is, any real function. The most specific functions are integer and real constants, sine, cosine, tangent, and so on. This language is known to have shortcomings (e.g., it cannot describe the class of twice continuously differentiable functions), but it is adequate for expressing some of the heuristics useful in the domain of symbolic integration.

LEX relies entirely on syntactic generalization methods. It cannot, for example, analyze the solution of $\int 3x \cos x \, dx$ and realize that, since OP03 requires only a real constant r, the particular constant 3 can be generalized to any real constant. This kind of analysis, based on the semantics of the operators, is done in STRIPS and HACKER. The advantage of LEX's syntactic approach is that it is general—it can be applied to any generalization language.

The Problem Generator

The purpose of the problem generator is to select a set of integration problems that form a good teaching sequence (see Article XIV.A). This portion of LEX is still under development, so only some strategies that have been proposed for the design of the problem generator are discussed here.

One strategy for selecting a new problem is to find an operator whose version space is still unrefined and select a problem that "splits" the version space—that is, an integral that matches only half of the patterns in the S and G sets. If the problem solver can solve such a problem, LEX will be able to refine the version space for that operator.

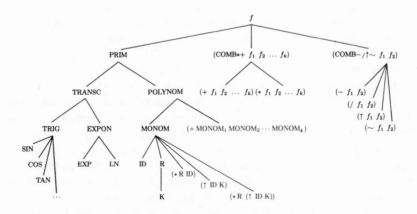

Figure D5d–4.   Function hierarchy used in LEX's generalization language.

A second, related strategy is to take a problem that LEX has already solved and modify it in some way. For instance, having solved the integral $\int 3x \sin x \, dx$, LEX could consider attempting the integral $\int 5x \sin x \, dx$. This would force it to generalize its version space to indicate that any constant could appear (not just 5 or 3). The generalization hierarchy in Figure D5d–4 can be used to create such training problems.

A third strategy is to look for overlaps in the knowledge base. If there are two operators whose version spaces overlap, the problem generator can choose a problem for which both operators are believed to be applicable. The resulting attempt to solve the problem may show that only one of the operators should be used in such situations.

Finally, when LEX is just beginning to learn, it may be necessary to apply the inverses of the integration operators to create problems of known difficulty for the problem solver to solve. This is analogous to the technique of providing students in chemistry courses with an "unknown" that is, in fact, deliberately synthesized by the professor. LEX must learn how to control its search so that it can solve the training problem without being overwhelmed by combinatorial explosion.

The problem generator, more than any other component of the LEX system, must have meta-knowledge of what LEX already knows and where its weaknesses are. It must keep a history of previous problem-solving attempts, so that it does not repeatedly propose unsolvable or uninformative problems. The design of the problem generator is, in fact, the most difficult part of the LEX project.

Conclusion

LEX learns *when* to apply the standard operators of symbolic integration. For each integration operator, the system learns a heuristic pattern. The problem solver matches these patterns against the expression being integrated to determine which operators should be applied. LEX obtains training instances by observing its own attempts to solve integration problems. Similarly, LEX obtains its performance standard by computing the cost of the shortest solution path that it found when it tried to solve the problem. The credit-assignment problem is solved by conducting a deeper search and crediting those decisions that led to the minimum-cost solution. Decisions that caused the problem solver to depart from the minimum-cost path are blamed. Positive and negative training instances are thus extracted and processed by the generalizer to update the version spaces of the integration operators.

Experiment planning is implemented in LEX by the problem generator, which employs a variety of strategies to select problems that will help the other components of the system refine the knowledge base.

The primary weakness of LEX, and a source of its generality, is that it employs only syntactic methods of generalization. It is unable to reason about the meanings of its operators, and thus it cannot use knowledge about dependencies among operators to determine how the heuristics should be generalized.

LEX does not attack the problems of learning new operators (i.e., right-hand sides of heuristic rules) or learning operator sequences (i.e., macros). To learn a new integration operator, LEX would need much more knowledge about mathematics and the goals of integration. This is a very difficult learning problem. The problem of learning macro operators (i.e., useful sequences of operators) and their applicability conditions has been addressed in HACKER and STRIPS. Further work on LEX may include the learning of such operators.

References

Mitchell, Utgoff, and Banerji (in press) and Mitchell, Utgoff, Nudel, and Banerji (1981) provide descriptions of LEX.

D5e.   Grammatical Inference

MOST AI RESEARCHERS employ numerical or logical representations in their learning systems. In work on adaptive systems, for example, the concept to be learned is often represented as a vector of numerical weights. Most of the other systems described in this chapter represent their knowledge in logic-based description languages (e.g., predicate calculus, semantic nets, feature vectors). A number of researchers, however, have developed systems that employ formal grammars to represent the learned concepts. This article discusses the body of work, known as *grammatical inference*, that seeks to learn a grammar from a set of training instances.

The primary interest in grammar learning can be traced to the use of formal grammars for modeling the structure of natural language (see Chomsky, 1957, 1965). The question of how people learn to speak and understand language led to studies of language acquisition; interest in modeling the languages of other cultures encouraged the development of computer programs to help field researchers construct grammars for unfamiliar languages (Klein and Kuppin, 1970); and recent attempts by pattern recognition researchers to use grammars to describe handwritten characters, visual scenes, and cloud-chamber tracks have created a need for grammatical-inference techniques. Thus, all of these researchers are interested in methods for learning a grammar from a set of training instances.

A grammar is a system of rules describing a *language* and telling which sentences are allowed in the language (see Article IV.C1, in Vol. I). Grammars can describe natural languages—that is, languages spoken by people—and formal languages—that is, simple languages amenable to mathematical analysis. In natural languages, grammar rules indicate the generally accepted ways of constructing sentences. In formal languages, however, grammars are applied much more strictly. A formal grammar for a language, *L*, can be viewed as a predicate that tells, for any sentence, whether it is *grammatical*, that is, "in" the language *L*, or *ungrammatical*, that is, not a legal sentence in *L*. From this formal perspective, a language is simply a potentially infinite set of all legal sentences, and a grammar is simply a description of that set.

One might expect the task of learning a grammar to be the same as the task of learning a single concept (see Sec. XIV.D3), since a single concept can also be viewed as a predicate describing some set of objects. Usually, however, this is not the case. Most formal languages are too complex to be described by a single concept or rule. Instead, a grammar is usually written as a set of rules that describe the *phrase structure* of the language. For example, we might have one rule that says: *A sentence is an article followed by a noun phrase followed by a verb phrase*. This could be written as the grammar rule:

494

$$\langle \text{sentence} \rangle \rightarrow \langle \text{article} \rangle \langle \text{noun phrase} \rangle \langle \text{verb phase} \rangle .$$

This rule describes the overall structure of a sentence. Of course, there are many different kinds of noun and verb phrases. These can also be described by phrase-structure rules. We might, for example, write another rule

$$\langle \text{verb phrase} \rangle \rightarrow \langle \text{verb} \rangle$$

for the simplest case in which the verb phrase is just a single word, as in *The boy cried.* A more complex verb phrase could be written as

$$\langle \text{verb phrase} \rangle \rightarrow \langle \text{verb} \rangle \langle \text{article} \rangle \langle \text{noun phrase} \rangle$$

for sentences like *The program learned the grammar.*

A grammar can thus be built out of a set of phrase-structure rules (also called *productions*). These rules break the problem of determining whether a sentence is *grammatical* into the subproblems of determining whether it is composed, for example, of a grammatical article followed by a grammatical noun phrase followed by a grammatical verb phrase. In this way, the single concept *grammatical sentence* is broken into the subconcepts of *noun phrase* and *verb phrase*. Moreover, such subconcepts are not independent but interact according to the grammar rules. Thus, determining whether a sentence is grammatical is a *multiple-step* task involving the sequential application of phrase-structure rules. It is for this reason that we include grammatical inference in our survey of systems that learn to perform multiple-step tasks.

In this article, we first introduce formal grammars and their uses and then discuss the theoretical limits of grammatical inference. The problem of learning a grammar from training instances has received a fair amount of mathematical analysis. We describe the principal results of this work along with their relevance for practical learning systems. Finally, we present the four major methods that have been developed for learning grammars.

Grammars and Their Uses

In the theory of formal languages, a language is defined as a set of strings, where each string is a finite sequence of symbols chosen from some finite vocabulary. In natural languages, the strings are sentences, and the sentences are sequences of words chosen from some vocabulary of possible words. To describe languages, Chomsky (1957, 1965) introduced a hierarchy of classes of languages based on the complexity of their underlying grammars. We will focus primarily on the *context-free languages* (and grammars).

A context-free language is defined by the following:

1. A *terminal vocabulary* of symbols—the words of the language;
2. A *nonterminal vocabulary* of symbols—the syntactic categories (e.g., "noun," "verb") of the language;

3. A set of *productions*—the phrase-structure rules of the language; and

4. The *start symbol.*

The best way to understand these definitions is by considering an example. Examine the following context-free grammar, G, with

(a) the terminal vocabulary {a, the, boy, girl, petted, held, puppy, kitten, wall, hill, by, on, with};

(b) the nonterminal vocabulary $\{Z, S, V, A, P, W, O, X\}$;

(c) the productions

$Z \to ASV$,
$V \to X$, $V \to XAO$, $V \to VP$,
$P \to WAS$, $P \to WAO$,
$A \to$ a, $A \to$ the,
$S \to$ boy, $S \to$ girl,
$W \to$ by, $W \to$ on, $W \to$ with,
$O \to$ puppy, $O \to$ kitten, $O \to$ hill, $O \to$ wall,
$X \to$ petted, $X \to$ held; and

(d) the start symbol, Z.

This grammar, G, describes a language of simple sentences such as *The boy held the puppy* and *The girl on the hill held a kitten*. It describes a sentence by *deriving* it from the start symbol. We start with the symbol Z and choose a production that has Z as the left-hand side. There is only one such rule in G: $Z \to ASV$. We apply this rule by *rewriting* Z as the string ASV. Now we choose one of the nonterminals, A, S, or V, and find a rule that can be used to rewrite it. If we choose the rule $V \to XAO$, our current sentence becomes $ASXAO$. We continue rewriting nonterminals (according to the production rules) until the sentence contains only *terminal* symbols. A complete derivation for the sentence *The boy held the puppy* is as follows:

Current sentence	Chosen production rule
Z	
	$(Z \to ASV)$
ASV	
	$(V \to XAO)$
$ASXAO$	
	$(A \to$ the$)$
the $SXAO$	
	$(S \to$ boy$)$
the boy XAO	
	$(X \to$ held$)$
the boy held AO	
	$(A \to$ the$)$
the boy held the O	
	$(O \to$ puppy$)$
The boy held the puppy	

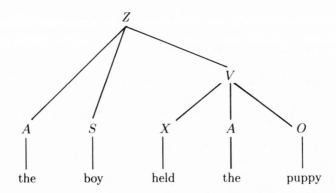

Figure D5e-1.   Derivation tree for the sentence *The boy held the puppy*.

This is usually depicted as a derivation tree (see Fig. D5e-1).

Depending on which rules we choose during the rewriting process, we get different sentences. If we choose "$O \to$ kitten" instead of "$O \to$ puppy," we get the sentence *The boy held the kitten*. The context-free language described by G is the set of *all possible* sentences that can be derived from Z by the rewrite rules in G. Notice that we can also start our derivation with some symbol other than Z. If we start with the nonterminal V, for example, we generate the *sublanguage* of all verb phrases in G. Each nonterminal has a sublanguage. Thus, each nonterminal represents a subconcept, such as *noun phrase* (S) or *verb phrase* (V), of the overall concept of *grammatical sentence* (Z).

In pattern recognition and language understanding, the performance task facing a computer program is not the generation of grammatical sentences but their recognition. Given a sentence, the problem of determining whether it is grammatical—that is, of finding a derivation for the sentence—is called *parsing*. Many efficient algorithms have been developed for parsing sentences in context-free languages (see Article IV.D, in Vol. I; Hopcroft and Ullman, 1969).

Extensions to Context-free Grammars

Context-free grammars are able to capture much of the structure of natural and artificial languages, especially computer programming languages. However, many problems require extensions to the basic context-free grammar framework.

Transformational grammars.   Some characteristics of natural language cannot be modeled with context-free grammars. One example that is frequently cited is the "respectively" construction in sentences such as *The* *boy and the girl held the puppy and the kitten, respectively.* Other examples include the conversion of sentences from active to passive voice and discontinuous constituents like *throw out* in the sentence *He threw the junk out.* In response to these shortcomings of context-free grammars, Chomsky (1965) developed the theory of *transformational grammar* (see Article IV.C2, in Vol. I), in which a sentence is first derived as a so-called *deep structure*, then manipulated by *transformation rules*, and finally converted into *surface form* by phonological rules. The deep structure, which corresponds to the basic declarative meaning of the sentence, is derived by a context-free grammar. The transformation rules can modify the structure—but not the meaning—by altering the derivation tree. For example, a transformation rule can convert a declarative sentence into a question by flipping branches of the tree to change the word order. Under such a transformation, the sentence *The boy is holding the dog* becomes the question *Is the boy holding the dog?* Some methods have been developed for learning transformation rules, as well as context-free grammars, from examples. Particular attention has been given to learning these rules under conditions believed to be similar to those under which a child learns a language.

Stochastic grammars. Although context-free grammars (and transformational grammars) can represent the phrase structure of a language, they tell nothing about the relative frequency or likelihood of appearance of a given sentence. It is common, for instance, in context-free grammars to use *recursive productions* to represent repetition. In our sample grammar above, the production $V \rightarrow VP$ is recursive. If we apply it over and over again, we can generate sentences like *The boy held the puppy on the wall by the hill with the kitten...* Although the sentence is technically grammatical, it would be nice to represent the degree of acceptability of such a sentence.

Stochastic grammars provide one approach to this problem. Each production in a stochastic grammar is assigned a probability of selection—that is, a number between zero and one. During the derivation process, productions are selected for rewriting according to their assigned probabilities. Consequently, each string in the language has a probability of occurrence computed as the product of the probabilities of the rules in its derivation. If we took our sample grammar, for instance, and assigned probabilities of .5 to all of the rules except $X \rightarrow ASV$ (probability 1.0) and $V \rightarrow XAO$ (probability .33), the string "The boy held the puppy" has probability $1(.33)(.5)(.5)(.5)(.5)(.5) = .01$, while the string "The boy held the puppy on the wall by the hill with the kitten" has probability 1.58944×10^{-7}. This expresses the intuition that the second sentence is very unlikely to be considered acceptable.

Stochastic grammars have been employed by pattern recognition researchers in noisy and uncertain environments where it is better to have an indication of the degree of grammaticality of a sentence than a single yes-no decision. Stochastic grammars also allow grammatical-inference programs to represent uncertainty about the true language when noisy and unreliable training instances are presented.

Graph grammars. In syntactic pattern-recognition problems, it is often important to represent the two- or three-dimensional structure of "sentences" in the language. Traditional context-free grammars, however, generate only one-dimensional strings. Context-free *graph grammars* have been developed that construct a *graph of terminal nodes* instead of a string of terminal symbols (see Article XIII.E3). Rewrite rules in the grammar describe how a nonterminal node can be replaced by a subgraph. Evans (1971) employs a set of graph grammars to describe visual scenes. Other researchers have applied graph grammars to the pattern recognition of handwritten characters and cloud-chamber tracks. This latter use of grammars is especially appropriate in that the rewrite rules in the grammar directly correspond to properties of the pattern. For example, subatomic particles decay into other particles only in certain ways, and these decay events can be modeled naturally with productions whose left-hand sides have the decaying particles and whose right-hand sides state the corresponding particles into which they decay.

Theoretical Limitations of Grammatical Inference

Now that we have reviewed some of the important kinds of formal languages and grammars, we turn our attention to the problem of learning these formal languages from examples. As with other forms of learning from examples, it is profitable to view grammatical inference as a search through a rule space of all possible context-free grammars for a grammar that is consistent with the training instances chosen from an instance space. In language learning, the training instances are usually sample sentences that have been classified by a teacher to indicate whether or not they are grammatical. The goal of the grammatical-inference program is to find a grammar for the "true" language that underlies the training instances.

Under what conditions is it possible to learn the correct context-free language from a set of training instances? This question has received a fair amount of study, and several results have been obtained. The most important result is that it is impossible to learn the correct language (or the correct single concept) from positive examples alone. Gold (1967) proved that if a program is given an infinite sequence of positive examples—that is, sentences known to be "in" the language—the program cannot determine a grammar for the correct context-free language in any finite time. To see why this is so, consider that at some point the program has received k strings $\{s_1, s_2, \ldots, s_k\}$. There are many possible languages that are consistent with these examples. The most general, *universal language*, which contains all possible strings of the terminal symbols, certainly contains all of the strings in the sample. Similarly, the trivial language $L = \{s_1, s_2, \ldots, s_k\}$ is the most specific language that contains all of the strings in the sample. There are many possible languages between these two extremes. No finite sample will allow the learning program to choose the correct language from these various possibilities.

Fortunately, in most learning situations, additional information is available that can help constrain the choices of the learning program so that a reasonable language, and its grammar, can be found. Let us examine possible sources of this additional information.

Negative examples. Negative training instances allow the program to eliminate grammars that are too general (see Article XIV.D3a, on the candidate-elimination algorithm). Gold (1967) showed that if the learning program could pose questions to an *informant*, that is, ask a person whether or not a given string was grammatical, the true language could be learned. The informant could be used to obtain complete positive and negative examples and thus determine exactly the true language. Gold called this learning situation *informant presentation*.

Stochastic presentation. When a program is trying to learn a *stochastic* context-free grammar, learning is also possible if the training instances are presented to the program repeatedly, with a frequency proportional to their probability of being in the language. In this *stochastic-presentation* method, the program can estimate the probability of a given string by measuring its frequency of occurrence in the finite sample. In the limit, stochastic presentation gives as much information as informant presentation of positive and negative examples: Ungrammatical strings have zero probability, and grammatical strings have positive probability.

Prior distributions. As we have seen above, even after a set of positive instances has been processed, there are still many possible languages, and hence many possible grammars, for the learning program to choose from. Furthermore, even when a unique language has been determined, as with informant presentation, there may be several different grammars that all generate the same language. One way to tell a program how to choose the right grammar is to define a prior probability (or desirability) distribution over all possible grammars. The program can then choose the most probable grammar that is consistent with the training instances. Horning (1969) employs a prior distribution that makes simple grammars more likely than complex ones, where simple grammars are those that have fewer nonterminals, fewer productions, shorter right-hand sides, and so on.

Semantics. According to cognitive psychologists, children receive little negative feedback when they are learning a language. Consequently, we are faced with the puzzle of how people are able to learn natural language almost entirely from positive training instances. One important source of information for children may be the meaning of the sentences they hear. A few psychological theories, and some computer programs (see below), have been developed that incorporate semantic constraints as a source of information. These theories basically claim that the grammatical structure of a language parallels the semantic structure of the internal representation that people employ.

Structural presentation. One technique employed by pattern recognition researchers to aid grammatical inference is *structural presentation*, in which the program is given some information about the derivation tree of the sample sentences. This is similar to the use of book training in Samuel's checkers program. The derivation tree provides a move-by-move (or, in this case, a rule-by-rule) performance standard along with each training instance.

Grammar restriction. One final way to get around Gold's results is to learn only special subclasses of the context-free languages. In particular, grammatical inference is much easier for *regular* and *delimited* languages, which, though not as powerful as the context-free languages, have important practical applications.

In summary, then, although Gold's theorems show that the formal problem of learning a context-free grammar from positive instances alone is impossible, there are many alternative sources of information that allow programs, and presumably people, to learn language.

Methods of Grammatical Inference

In this section, we survey four basic techniques that have been used to learn context-free grammars from training instances. The various methods, some of which parallel the basic learning methods discussed in Article XIV.D1, differ primarily in the way that they search the rule space and the kinds of information that they use to guide that search.

The first approach we discuss is *enumeration*. Enumerative, or generate-and-test, methods propose possible grammars and then test them against the data. The second basic grammatical-inference technique is *construction*. Constructive methods usually learn from positive examples only. They collect information about the structure of the sample strings and use it to build a grammar reflecting that structure. *Refinement* methods form a third important class of grammatical-inference techniques. They start with a hypothesis grammar and gradually improve it by means of various heuristics based on additional training instances. Finally, *semantics-based* methods employ knowledge of the meanings of the sample sentences to decide how to search the rule space. Most semantics-based methods have been developed to model how children learn natural languages.

Rules of generalization and specialization for grammars. Before describing these learning methods in more detail, we first discuss three methods for the syntactic generalization and specialization of grammars:

1. *Merging.* A context-free grammar can be generalized by an operation called *merging.* Suppose the grammar G contains two nonterminals, A

and B. We can modify G to obtain a more general grammar by merging A and B—that is, by creating a new nonterminal, Q, and replacing all occurrences of A and B by Q. This has the effect of pooling the sublanguages of A and B to create a new sublanguage, Q, whose strings may appear anywhere that either the strings of A or the strings of B could have appeared. Suppose, for example, that in our sample grammar discussed above, we merged S (subjects) and O (objects) to obtain Q. The productions of the grammar G become:

$Z \to AQV$
$V \to X, \quad V \to XAQ, \quad V \to VP,$
$P \to WAQ,$
$A \to a, \quad A \to$ the,
$W \to$ by, $\quad W \to$ on, $\quad W \to$ with,
$Q \to$ puppy, $\quad Q \to$ kitten, $\quad Q \to$ hill, $\quad Q \to$ wall,
$\quad\quad Q \to$ boy, $\quad Q \to$ girl,
$X \to$ petted, $\quad X \to$ held .

Previously ungrammatical sentences like *The puppy petted the boy* are now allowed. The language is thus larger and, consequently, more general.

2. *Splitting.* The inverse of merging is a specialization process called *splitting.* We can specialize a grammar by splitting the sublanguage of one nonterminal, N, into two smaller sublanguages, N_1 and N_2. This is accomplished by replacing some occurrences of N in the grammar by N_1 and others by N_2. In the grammar above, for instance, we could split the A (article) nonterminal into A_1 and A_2 to obtain the grammar:

$Z \to A_1 QV,$
$V \to X, \quad V \to XA_2 Q, \quad V \to VP,$
$P \to WA_2 Q,$
$A_1 \to a, \quad A_2 \to$ the,
$W \to$ by, $\quad W \to$ on, $\quad W \to$ with,
$Q \to$ puppy, $\quad Q \to$ kitten, $\quad Q \to$ hill, $\quad Q \to$ wall,
$\quad\quad Q \to$ boy, $\quad Q \to$ girl,
$X \to$ petted, $\quad X \to$ held .

Now all sentences must begin with "a," and all prepositional phrases and object phrases must use "the." The previously grammatical sentence *The boy petted the puppy* is now illegal. This language is therefore more specialized.

3. *Disjunction.* One operation that is similar to merging is called disjunction. In disjunction, we choose two *strings*, s_1 and s_2, and create a new nonterminal, D, whereby the rules $D \to s_1$ and $D \to s_2$ are added to the grammar. Every occurrence of the strings s_1 and s_2 in existing productions is replaced by D. For example, we could disjoin AO and AS in our sample grammar to create the new nonterminal, N (noun phrase). The grammar then becomes:

$Z \rightarrow NV,$
$V \rightarrow X, \quad V \rightarrow XN, \quad V \rightarrow VP,$
$P \rightarrow WN,$
$N \rightarrow AS, \quad N \rightarrow AO,$
$A \rightarrow$ a, $\quad A \rightarrow$ the,
$S \rightarrow$ boy, $\quad S \rightarrow$ girl,
$W \rightarrow$ by, $\quad W \rightarrow$ on, $\quad W \rightarrow$ with,
$O \rightarrow$ puppy, $\quad O \rightarrow$ kitten, $\quad O \rightarrow$ hill, $\quad O \rightarrow$ wall,
$X \rightarrow$ petted, $\quad X \rightarrow$ held .

This operation is similar to merging, except that it can be applied to *strings* of terminals and nonterminals. If both of s_1 and s_2 are simple nonterminal symbols, disjunction has the same effect as merging. If only one of s_1 or s_2 is a nonterminal, the operation is called *substitution*.

These rules of generalization can be applied to move from one point in the rule space (i.e., one grammar) to another. We now turn our attention to the four basic methods of grammatical inference and show how they apply these operations to search the space of possible context-free grammars.

Enumerative Methods

Enumerative methods generate grammars one by one and test each to determine how well it accounts for the training instances. The first enumerative method we consider is that of Horning (1969), who developed a procedure for finding the most plausible stochastic grammar consistent with a set of stochastically presented training instances. The general idea behind Horning's method is to enumerate all possible grammars in order of simplicity and choose the first grammar that is consistent with the training data. The actual algorithm is somewhat more complicated, however, since Horning seeks the *most likely* stochastic grammar, that is, the grammar G that is most likely to have generated the observed set S of sample strings. This is expressed formally as the grammar G that maximizes $P(G \mid S)$, that is, the probability of G given S. Unfortunately, it is difficult to compute $P(G \mid S)$ directly from the training instances. Bayes' theorem, however, provides a way of computing $P(G \mid S)$ from three other quantities, $P(G)$, $P(S \mid G)$, and $P(S)$:

$$P(G \mid S) = \frac{P(G) \times P(S \mid G)}{P(S)},$$

where $P(G)$ is the a priori probability that G is the "true" grammar, $P(S)$ is the a priori probability of observing the particular sample S, and $P(S \mid G)$ is the probability of observing S given the grammar G. Since $P(S)$ is independent of G, we can maximize $P(G \mid S)$ by just maximizing the numerator $P'(G \mid S) = P(G) \times P(S \mid G)$. The probabilities $P(G)$ and $P(S \mid G)$ can be computed for any particular grammar G.

The probability $P(S \mid G)$ that the training instances S will be generated by the stochastic grammar G can be computed directly from G by parsing each sentence in S. The problem of computing $P(G)$ is more difficult, however. Horning sought to have the a priori probability of G reflect the complexity of the grammar G. Simple grammars should be highly probable; complex grammars should be improbable. Consequently, he developed the idea of a grammar-grammar, that is, a stochastic grammar that generates a *stochastic grammar* as its terminal string. Such a grammar-grammar can be constructed from a terminal vocabulary of symbols such as A, B, C, Z, $\rightarrow$, etc. Since, as we have seen above, a stochastic grammar generates short strings with a much higher probability than it does long strings, the grammar-grammar generates simple grammars with a much higher probability than it does complex ones. In particular, the probability $P(G)$ is the probability that the grammar-grammar would generate G.

Since we can compute $P(G)$ and $P(S \mid G)$, we can use Bayes' theorem to compute $P'(G \mid S)$. Therefore, if we compute $P'(G \mid S)$ for all possible grammars, G, we can find the grammar that most likely generated S. Such a procedure is impossibly inefficient, however. Instead, Horning used the following technique. First, he developed a procedure that could enumerate all possible stochastic grammars starting with the most likely grammar, G_1, and continuing on in order of decreasing probability $P(G_i)$. Next, he noticed that $P'(G_i \mid S)$ did not have to be computed for all grammars but only for those grammars whose probability $P(G_i)$ was greater than $P'(G_1 \mid S)$. This is because once $P(G_i)$ falls below $P'(G_1 \mid S)$, there is no way that multiplying by $P(S \mid G_i)$ will ever exceed $P'(G_1 \mid S)$, since $P(S \mid G_i)$ is always less than or equal to 1.

Consequently, Horning's method enumerates all grammars G_i starting with G_1 and continuing until $P(G_i) < P'(G_1 \mid S)$. The probability $P'(G_i \mid S)$ is computed for each grammar G_i, and the grammar that maximizes $P'(G_i \mid S)$ is output as the grammar most likely to have produced the set of examples, S.

The algorithm is theoretically correct—it always finds the best grammar—but it is still too inefficient for all but the smallest grammars. Therefore, Horning modified the grammar generator to generate only grammars that were *deductively acceptable* (DA). A grammar is deductively acceptable if it generates every string in the sample, S, and if every production in G is used to derive at least one of the training instances. In other words, a DA grammar must be consistent with the training instances and must not be overly specific or cluttered by useless productions. It can be shown that all DA grammars with $k + 1$ nonterminals can be obtained by splitting DA grammars with k nonterminals. Furthermore, once a grammar ceases to be deductively acceptable, no further splits will make it deductively acceptable, since it is already overly specific.

These facts were used by Horning to organize the rule-space search. Starting with the most general (and most likely) DA grammars, repeated splits are made until either the grammars cease to be deductively acceptable or their a priori probability $P(G_i)$ falls below the bound $P'(G_1 \mid S)$. The probability $P'(G_i \mid S)$ is computed for all of the generated grammars, and the grammar that maximizes $P'(G_i \mid S)$ is selected. This procedure, although more efficient than the first one, is still of theoretical interest only.

A second enumerative method makes use of training instances to guide the enumeration of plausible grammars. Pao (1969) describes an approach to grammatical inference that resembles the plan-generate-test paradigm of the DENDRAL program (see Sec. VII.C2, in Vol. II). In the initial planning phase, Pao's algorithm analyzes the (positive) training instances and constructs a trivial grammar—that is, a very specific grammar that generates only the training examples. A partially ordered set (actually, a lattice) of plausible grammars can be generated by merging nonterminals from this trivial grammar. During the generate-and-test phase, Pao's algorithm enumerates all of these grammars in order, from most specific to most general, and tests them by consulting an informant.

Pao's algorithm generates two grammars at a time, G and H, and uses an informant to eliminate one of the two. The informant is presented with a new sentence, s, that is generated by G but not by H. If the informant says s is in the "true" language, then H and all grammars more specific than H are removed from further consideration. Also, the set of grammars more general than H (but not more general than G) is searched in order from general to specific, and grammars that do not generate s are discarded. If, on the other hand, the informant says that s is not in the "true" language, then G and all grammars more general than G are removed from further consideration. The generating and testing of possible grammars continues until only one possible grammar remains. This search through the partially ordered set of all possible grammars is similar to Mitchell's (1978) candidate-elimination algorithm (see Article XIV.D3a). In Pao's program, though, an active experimentation approach is employed to search the space rather than waiting for new training instances to drive the search.

Unfortunately, this method does not work for general context-free grammars. The basic algorithm works only for regular grammars—that is, grammars whose productions all have the form $N \rightarrow tM$ or $N \rightarrow t$ for t, a single terminal symbol, and M, a single nonterminal symbol. In regular languages, there is no difficulty finding a test sentence s to distinguish between two grammars G and H. Unfortunately, this cannot be done for general context-free languages. Pao has extended the method to handle delimited grammars— a somewhat larger class of grammars than the regular grammars.

Constructive Methods

Constructive methods attempt to build a plausible grammar using only the information from a positive sample with no informant. From Gold's theorems, it is clear that this problem is ill-formed, since no unique language is determined by a set of positive instances. However, various heuristics have been developed for constructing simple, fairly general grammars from positive instances only.

One important set of heuristics is based on the idea of the *distribution* of substrings in the language. In context-free languages, certain classes of strings, such as noun phrases and prepositional phrases, tend to appear in the same contexts in different sentences. This suggests that we might be able to discover interesting classes of strings by looking at their surroundings in the set of sample sentences. For instance, the words *a* and *the* both tend to occur at the beginnings of sentences, so perhaps they should be grouped together to form the class of *articles*. This is done by creating a nonterminal A and inventing the production rules "$A \to$ a" and "$A \to$ the." Distributional analysis has been employed by Harris (1964), Fu (1975), Kelley (1967), and Klein and Kuppin (1970).

For regular grammars, Fu (1975) has applied a particular kind of distributional analysis based on the idea of the *formal derivative* of a string. The formal derivative of a string s is the set of strings

$$D_s L = \{t \mid \text{the string } st \text{ is in the language } L\},$$

that is, all of the strings t that follow s in the given language L in sentences where s is at the beginning of the sentence.

Formal derivatives can be employed to construct regular grammars in a straightforward way. Imagine that we have a grammar G, and we are in the process of generating a sentence. Suppose that, so far, we have generated the string sU, where U is a nonterminal and s is a terminal string. If we take formal derivatives for every string sa that appears in the sample (where a is a single terminal symbol), we can create new nonterminals for each distinct formal derivative. We can add the productions

$$U \to a V_1$$
$$U \to b V_2$$
$$\vdots$$
$$U \to m V_k$$

to the grammar, G, where $V_1, V_2, \ldots, V_k$ correspond to the formal derivatives of $sa, sb, \ldots, sm$. The effect of this construction is to group together all of the strings in the formal derivative of sa, for example, and place them in the sublanguage for V_1. We can construct the entire grammar G by initially taking s to be the null string and U to be the start symbol.

The chief difficulty of distributional methods is that some definition of *similar contexts* is needed so that strings that appear in similar contexts can be grouped into the sublanguage for a new nonterminal symbol. Problems can also arise when one string is in two different sublanguages and therefore appears in different contexts. The word *program*, for example, can be both a noun and a verb.

Another approach to constructive inference of grammars is to look for repetition in the sample and model it as a recursive production. This method is rarely sufficient in itself to construct the whole grammar, but it can be used in combination with other methods. Consider, for example, the set of training instances $\{a, aaa, aaaa\}$. A reasonable grammar to infer has the productions $S \rightarrow a$ and $S \rightarrow Sa$ and generates all possible strings of repeated as.

To employ this repetition heuristic, it is helpful to know the properties of repetition for different kinds of grammars. For regular grammars, iteration always takes the form of repeated choice of a string without reference to any other strings. However, for context-free languages, repetition can be more complicated. One important theorem about context-free languages (called the *uvxyz* theorem) states that if a sufficiently long string $uvxyz$ is in the language, then so is the string uv^kxy^kz as well; that is, v and y are repeated an equal number of times. This can be represented by a *self-embedding* production of the form $X \rightarrow VXY$. Solomonoff (1964) and Maryanski (1974) describe inference methods based on searching for double cycles of the uv^kxy^kz variety. Once a possible cycle is found, it can be tested by consulting an informant.

Refinement Methods

Refinement methods formulate a hypothesis grammar and then refine it by applying simplification heuristics or by gathering new training instances. Knobe and Knobe (1977), for example, present an algorithm that creates an initial hypothesis grammar, G, and then enters a refinement cycle in which it repeatedly accepts a new grammatical string, refines G to include the string, and generalizes and simplifies G. The initial grammar includes a distinct nonterminal for each of the terminal symbols. In the course of the algorithm, these nonterminals are generalized by merging. The basic learning cycle proceeds as follows:

Step 1. Accept a grammatical string (i.e., a positive training instance) and attempt to parse the string with the current grammar, G. If the parse succeeds, repeat step 1; otherwise, go to step 2.

Step 2. Compute a list of partial parses and sort it according to generality. (A *partial parse* is a string of terminals and nonterminals in which parts of the original training string have been partly parsed into nonterminals; the more general partial parses are shorter, since most of the sentence has been successfully parsed.) Hypothesize the production $S \rightarrow P$, where S is the start symbol and P is the most general partial parse. (This allows the training instance to be parsed successfully.) Use the modified grammar to generate a test sentence, and ask the informant if the test sentence is grammatical. If it is, go to step 3; otherwise, try the next most general partial parse, and repeat until a sufficiently specific production has been found.

Step 3. Generalize and simplify the grammar by applying some of the merging and substitution heuristics described below.

The third step of generalization and simplification is important, because it is in this step that the new production $S \rightarrow P$ is integrated into the grammar and connected to existing production rules. Many different simplification and generalization techniques have been developed by various researchers. We survey a number of these here.

Generalization by disjunction. One important simplification technique is to apply disjunction (see above) to replace two similar strings s and t, which appear on the right-hand sides of productions, by a single nonterminal. There are two basic heuristics for deciding whether s and t are similar: *internal similarity* and *external similarity*. The internal-similarity heuristic compares the sublanguages generated by s and t. If the sublanguages are similar, the heuristic proposes that s and t are similar and should be disjoined. The external-similarity heuristic, on the other hand, compares the contexts in which s and t appear. As in the constructive technique of distributional analysis, if s and t appear in similar contexts, the heuristic recommends that they be disjoined. There are many important special cases of these heuristics:

1. *Heuristics based on internal similarity.* The first internal-similarity heuristic is *subsumption*. If the language generated by s is a superset of the language generated by t, then s and t should be disjoined. This often occurs when s is a single nonterminal, X, and the rule $X \rightarrow t$ is among the productions for X in the grammar.

   If s and t are both single nonterminals, X and Y, a second internal heuristic can be applied. This heuristic compares the right-hand sides, u and v, of production rules of the form $X \rightarrow u$ and $Y \rightarrow v$, to see if they are similar. If they are, X and Y can be merged.

   A third internal-similarity heuristic is *k-tail equivalence*. Two strings s and t are *k-tail equivalent*, for some nonnegative integer k, if the sets of strings of length k or less that they generate are the same. Thus, s and t are judged similar if the short strings that they generate are the same. This heuristic can be applied by choosing a value for k and merging groups of nonterminals that are k-tail equivalent. As k gets small, this heuristic causes more generalization.

2. *Heuristics based on external similarity.* The one heuristic for external similarity is to look at productions in which s and t appear on the right-hand side of productions. If s and t appear in similar contexts within the productions, they can be disjoined. Various special cases of this heuristic have been used, including the case in which s and t are both single nonterminals.

Hypothesizing iteration. As with constructive methods, if productions such as $X \to a$ and $X \to aa$ are present, a recursive production $X \to Xa$ can be introduced.

Shorthand substitution. When a string s appears many times on the right-hand side of productions, it is often good to create a new nonterminal, A, replace all occurrences of s by A, and add the production $A \to s$ to the grammar. This simplifies the grammar without modifying the language that it generates. The advantage of the simplification is that it is easier to apply the various merging heuristics to a simplified grammar.

The k-tail heuristic was employed by Biermann and Feldman (1970) in the inference of regular grammars. Various of the other heuristics are employed by Klein and Kuppin (1970), Evans (1971), Knobe and Knobe (1977), and Cook and Rosenfeld (1976). Cook and Rosenfeld are concerned with stochastic grammars and use their heuristics to simplify grammars with a hill-climbing procedure based on a numerical-complexity measure.

Semantics-based Methods

The fourth basic approach to grammatical inference employs semantic constraints to guide the search for plausible grammars. Most of this work has centered on language acquisition by children. The child is given positive examples of sentences and is assumed to know the meanings of individual words in isolation. Furthermore, the situation in which the sentence was uttered, and, thus, some idea about its overall meaning, is assumed to be known by the child. In most work, no negative examples are provided, nor is an informant available. This is because most research in psychology (e.g., Brown and Hanlon, 1970) has found that children receive little or no feedback concerning the grammaticality of the sentences they utter. Pinker (1979) discusses the work of several researchers who have studied grammatical inference under these assumptions, including Anderson (1977) and Hamburger and Wexler (1975).

Anderson's Language Acquisition System (LAS) attempts to learn a context-free grammar for English from training instances that include a representation of the meaning of each sentence. The Human Associative Memory (HAM; Article XI.E2) network notation is used to represent these sentence meanings. Learning proceeds in a cycle similar to that of Knobe and Knobe (1977): A sentence and its meaning are input, and LAS attempts to parse the sentence. If the parse fails, the grammar is extended according to some refinement heuristics so that the training sentence can be parsed and assigned the correct meaning. One such heuristic adds a word to a sublanguage—for example, it adds *chair* to the sublanguage for ⟨noun⟩—when the word is located at a place in the HAM net similar to the place of other words in the sublanguage. This is a special case of the general heuristic that the structure of the semantic representation is reflected in the structure of the syntax of the language. A more sophisticated version of this heuristic is the *graph deformation condition*, which states that branches in the HAM representation of the sample sentence are not allowed to cross. This heuristic rules out certain parses that would result in an ill-formed HAM structure. Anderson also employs one syntactic heuristic: Two nonterminals are merged if they have similar sublanguages.

The work of Hamburger and Wexler (1975) is more theoretical in nature and is concerned with showing that transformational grammars (see Chomsky, 1965) are learnable. In their model, the learner is repeatedly given a sentence and its meaning, where the meaning is represented as a deep-structure parse tree (based on a deep-structure context-free grammar). The learner must find a set of transformation rules that succeed, for each sample sentence, in converting the deep structure into the given sentence. Hamburger and Wexler are proponents of Chomsky's nativist theory of language acquisition, which asserts that people have built-in limits and biases that provide essential constraints for the language-learning process. Consequently, their model of language learning includes several factors that limit the complexity of possible transformations.

Given these limits, Hamburger and Wexler show that the desired set of transformations can be learned by a program as follows. As each training instance (a sentence and its deep structure) is received, the learner tries to transform the deep structure into the surface sentence by applying its current set of transformations. If this succeeds, the learner goes on to the next input example. If not, the learner randomly adds, deletes, or alters a transformation and goes on. This method will work as long as the learner does not repeat transformation rules known to be incorrect. Plainly, this learning procedure is not practical, but it does demonstrate that learning transformation rules under these assumptions is possible.

Conclusion

The expressiveness of grammars for use in AI knowledge representation is somewhat limited, so interest in the difficult problem of grammatical inference is also correspondingly limited in the AI community. This is especially so because of the impractical nature of many of the grammatical-inference systems developed thus far. However, future work on the problem may yield more powerful inference systems, and an understanding of past work may well be helpful in research on related learning problems.

References

We have surveyed here the motivations, limitations, and methods of grammatical inference. More detailed surveys of grammatical inference in the context of cognitive psychology are given in Pinker (1979) and Reeker (1976).

Surveys of grammatical inference for use in syntactic pattern recognition are given in Fu (1974, 1975), Biermann and Feldman (1972), and Gonzalez and Thompson (1978).

Chapter XV

Planning and Problem Solving

CHAPTER XV: PLANNING AND PROBLEM SOLVING

A. OVERVIEW

PROBLEM SOLVING is the process of developing a sequence of actions to achieve a goal. This broad definition admits all goal-directed AI programs to the ranks of problem solvers; for example, MYCIN (see Article VIII.B1, in Vol. II) solves the problem of determining a bacteremia infection, HARPY (Article V.C2, in Vol. I) solves the problem of understanding speech signals, and AM (Article XIV.D4c) solves the problem of filling in slots in its representations of concepts. It follows that this chapter is not about problem solvers—the entire *Handbook* is about problem solvers. This chapter, like the chapter on search (Chap. II, in Vol. I), is about problem-solving techniques. In particular, it is about *planning*.

In everyday terms, planning means deciding on a course of action before acting. This definition accurately describes the planning systems of this chapter, so we will adopt it. A plan is, thus, a representation of a course of action. It can be an unordered list of goals, such as a grocery list, but usually a plan has an implicit ordering of its goals; for example, most people plan to get dressed to go to the theater, not the other way around. Many plans include steps that are vague and require further specification. These serve as placeholders in a plan; for example, a daily plan includes the goal *eat-lunch*, although the details—where to eat, what to eat, when to leave—are not specified. The detailed plan associated with eating lunch is a *subplan* of the overall daily plan. Most plans have a rich subplan structure; each goal in a plan can be replaced by a more detailed subplan to achieve it. Although a finished plan is a *linear* or *partial* ordering of problem-solving operators, the goals achieved by the operators often have a hierarchical structure (see Fig. A–1). This aspect of plans prompted one of the earliest definitions:

> A Plan is any hierarchical process in the organism that can control the order in which a sequence of operations is to be performed. (Miller, Galanter, and Pribram, 1960, p. 16)

Planning and Problem Solving

Failure to plan can result in less than optimal problem solving; one may go to the library twice, for example, having failed to plan to borrow a book and return another at the same time. Moreover, in cases where goals are not independent, failing to plan before acting may actually preclude a solution to the problem. For example, the goal of building a house includes the subgoals of installing a dry wall and installing electrical wiring, but these goals are not independent. The wiring must be installed first; otherwise, the dry wall will be in the way.

Plans can be used to monitor progress during problem solving and to catch errors before they do too much harm. This is especially important if the problem solver is not the only actor in the problem solver's environment and if the environment can change in unpredictable ways. Consider the example of a roving vehicle on a distant planet: It must be able to plan a route and then replan if it finds that the state of the world is not as it expected. *Feedback* about the state of the world is compared with what is predicted by the plan, which can then be modified in the event of discrepancies. This topic is discussed more fully in Sacerdoti (1975). The benefits of planning can be summarized as reducing search, resolving goal conflicts, and providing a basis for error recovery. These will be discussed in detail in the remainder of this chapter.

Approaches to Planning

Four distinct approaches to planning are discussed in this volume. They are nonhierarchical planning, hierarchical planning, script-based planning, and opportunistic planning. Here we must resolve a confusing ambiguity in the word *hierarchical*. The vast majority of plans have nested subgoal structures—*hierarchical structures*—as shown in Figure A–1. However, the word has another interpretation, one that provides the basis for distinguishing hierarchical from nonhierarchical planning. The distinction is that hierarchical planners generate a hierarchy of *representations* of a plan in which the highest is a simplification, or *abstraction*, of the plan and the lowest

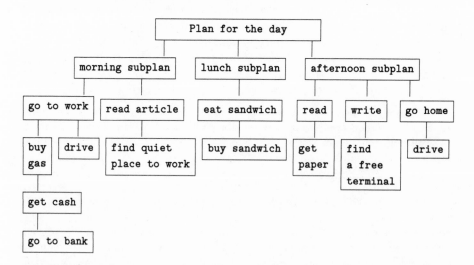

Figure A–1.   Plan for a day, illustrating the hierarchical structure of sub-plans.

is a detailed plan, sufficient to solve the problem. In contrast, nonhierarchical planners have only one representation of a plan. Both kinds of planners generate plans with hierarchical subgoal structures, but only hierarchical planners utilize a hierarchy of representations of the plan. This distinction is discussed further in Article XV.B, in which STRIPS (a nonhierarchical planner) and ABSTRIPS (the hierarchical extension of STRIPS) are compared.

Nonhierarchical planning corresponds roughly to the colloquial meaning of planning; that is, a nonhierarchical planner develops a sequence of problem-solving actions to achieve each of its goals. It may *reduce* goals to simpler ones, or it may use *means-ends analysis* to reduce the *differences* between the current state of the world and that would hold after the problem has been solved. Examples of nonhierarchical planners are STRIPS (Article XV.B), HACKER (Article XV.C), and INTERPLAN (also in Article XV.C).

The major disadvantage of nonhierarchical planning is that it does not distinguish between problem-solving actions that are critical to the success of a plan and those that are simply details. As a result, plans developed by nonhierarchical planners get bogged down in unimportant details. In any plan there are levels of detail that are too picky or too vague and a level of detail that is appropriate for the problem; for example, a too-detailed plan for dinner starts with *Go to the table, sit down, unfold the napkin, pour a glass of water, find matches, light the candles...* A too-vague plan is *Sit down somewhere, have food.* Planning with too many details is a waste of effort, but plans that are too vague do not specify which problem-solving operators should be used; a balance between these extremes is necessary for efficient planning.

To this end, the method of *hierarchical planning* has been implemented in a number of planning systems. The method is first to sketch a plan that is complete but too vague and then to *refine* the vague parts of the plan into more detailed subplans until finally the plan has been refined to a complete sequence of detailed problem-solving operators. The advantage of this approach is that the plan is first developed at a level at which the details are not computationally overwhelming.

Hierarchical planning also takes several forms in these systems. One approach, typified by the ABSTRIPS program (Article II.D6, in Vol. I), is to determine which subgoals are critical to the success of the plan and to ignore, at least initially, all others. (In ABSTRIPS, a *detail* is a subgoal for which a subplan can be found if plans have been found to accomplish goals that are not details.) For example, the problem of buying a piano cannot be solved unless two subgoals are accomplished, namely, *Locate piano* and *Get money.* Thus, an initial plan for buying a piano might simply be *Locate piano, get money, buy piano.* Subsequently, this plan can be *refined* with inessential details, such as *Drive to the store* and *Select piano.* ABSTRIPS plans in a *hierarchy of abstraction spaces*, the highest of which contains a plan devoid of all unimportant details and the lowest of which contains a complete and detailed sequence of problem-solving operators. The advantage of considering the critical subgoals before the details is that it reduces search: By ignoring details, one effectively reduces the number of subgoals to be accomplished in any given abstraction space.

Hierarchical planning was implemented in its earliest form by Newell and Simon (1972, pp. 429–435) in their GPS model of theorem proving in logic. The GPS approach was slightly different from that of ABSTRIPS. In ABSTRIPS, a hierarchy of abstraction spaces is defined by treating some goals as more important than others, while in GPS there was a single abstraction space defined by treating one representation of the problem as more general than others. GPS planned in an abstraction space defined by replacing all logical connectives by a single abstract symbol. The original *problem space* defined four logical connectives, but many problem-solving operators were applicable to any connective. Thus, it could be treated as a detail and abstracted out of the formulation of the problem. A problem could be solved in the abstraction space, the space with only one connective, and the solution could be mapped back into the original four-connective space.

Subsequent implementations of the hierarchical planning approach such as NOAH (Article XV.D1) and MOLGEN (Article XV.D2) are, again, slightly different from either ABSTRIPS or GPS. ABSTRIPS abstracted critical goals, and GPS abstracted a more general representation of an aspect of its problem space. NOAH abstracts problem-solving operators; it plans initially with generalized operators that it later refines to problem-solving operators given in its problem space. MOLGEN goes one step further, abstracting both the operators and the objects in its problem space. In all cases, however, hierarchical planning involves defining and planning in one or more abstraction spaces. A plan is first generated in the highest, most abstract space. This constitutes the skeleton onto which details are fleshed out in lower abstraction spaces. Hierarchical planning provides a means of ignoring the details that obscure or complicate a solution to a problem.

A third approach to planning also makes use of skeleton plans but, unlike hierarchical planning, these skeletons are recalled from a store of plans instead of generated. This approach was adopted in one of the MOLGEN systems (Article XV.E). The stored plans contain the outlines for solving many different kinds of problems. They range in detail from extremely specific plans for common problems to very general plans for broad classes of problems. The planning process proceeds in two steps: First a skeleton plan is found that is applicable to the given problem and then the abstract steps in the plan are filled in with problem-solving operators from the particular problem context. This instantiation process involves large amounts of domain-specific knowledge, often working through several levels of generality until a problem-solving operator is found to accomplish each skeleton-plan step. If a suitable instantiation is found for each abstracted step, the plan as a whole will be successful.

This approach has much in common with that of Schank and his colleagues (see Article IV.F6, in Vol. I). Their approach to natural-language understanding is to use stored *scripts* (and other, more sophisticated structures) to provide top-down expectations about the course of a story.

A fourth approach to planning has been found by Hayes-Roth and Hayes-Roth in human planning (see Article XI.C). It is described as *opportunistic* and is characterized by a more flexible control strategy than is found in the other approaches. The Hayes-Roths have adopted a *blackboard* control structure to model human planning. The blackboard is a "clearinghouse" for suggestions about plan steps, suggestions that are made by planning *specialists*. Each specialist is designed to make a particular kind of planning decision. Specialists do not operate in any particular order; the asynchrony of planning decisions that are made only when there is reason to do so gives rise to the term *opportunistic*. In the Hayes-Roths' model, and apparently in human planning, the ordering of operators that characterizes a plan is developed piecewise—the plan "grows out" from concrete clusters of problem-solving operators.

Opportunistic planning includes a *bottom-up* component, since it is driven by opportunities to include detailed problem-solving actions in the developing plan. It contrasts with the *top-down* refinement process characteristic of hierarchical planning, in which detailed problem-solving actions are not decided until the last possible moment in developing the plan. Another difference between opportunistic planning and other forms is that it can develop *islands* of planning actions—parts of a plan—independently, while hierarchical planners try to develop an entire plan at each level of abstraction. (See Chap. V, in Vol. I, for a discussion of island driving in speech understanding.)

The Hayes-Roths' model is discussed in Chapter XI, on models of cognition, since it is intended as a model of human planning abilities.

Search and the Problem of Interacting Subproblems

Two major, interrelated issues will keep reappearing in this chapter. They are the problem of limiting search and the problem of interacting subproblems. The problem of search is to find an ordering of problem-solving actions that will achieve a goal when there are a huge number of orderings possible, most of which will not achieve the goal. This problem has been called *combinatorial explosion,* since the number of combinations of problem-solving operators increases exponentially with the number of operators (see Chap. II, in Vol. I). The problem of interacting subproblems arises whenever a problem has a *conjunctive goal,* that is, more than one condition to be satisfied. The order in which conjunctive goals are to be achieved is sometimes not specified in the problem, but it can be critical to finding a solution. Sometimes interactions of this sort prevent any solution; for example, if a conjunctive goal is to paint a ladder and paint a ceiling, the second goal *must* be achieved before the first, because one cannot stand on a freshly painted ladder to paint a ceiling. Unfortunately, this information is sometimes not given in the problem but must be inferred.

The problem of search is related to the problem of interacting subproblems because additional search results from premature commitment to an arbitrary ordering of interacting subgoals. In the ladder example, a planner that arbitrarily decided to paint the ladder first would need to *backtrack* and change its plan when it discovered it could not paint the ceiling. Backtracking involves replanning from the *choice point* that failed, in this case, the choice between painting the ceiling and painting the ladder. Backtracking can be very costly.

Interactions between subgoals have been called *constraints* (Stefik, 1980; see also Article XV.D2). They can be inferred from the *preconditions* of operators if the preconditions are explicit. For example, if the operator *Paint ceiling* has several preconditions such as *Have paint, Have brush,* and *Have ladder*, an intelligent planner will infer from these that painting the ladder cannot precede painting the ceiling. A less intelligent planner may construct a plan to paint the ladder first and then realize that it cannot continue; it may then attempt to reorder its actions.

Some of the earliest planners generated initial plans that violated ordering constraints and then tried to go back and fix the plan. They include HACKER, INTERPLAN, and Waldinger's system, all discussed in Article XV.C. These systems applied a powerful heuristic called the *linear assumption*, namely, that

> subgoals are independent and thus can be sequentially achieved in an arbitrary order. (Sussman, 1973, p. 59)

In a historical perspective, this can be seen to be an important heuristic. The number of orderings of problem-solving operators is the factorial of the number of operators, so it is obvious that a problem solver cannot successfully examine *all* orderings in the hope of finding one that does not fail because of interacting operators. The linear assumption says that in the absence of any knowledge about orderings of operators, assume that one ordering is as good as any other and then fix any interactions that emerge. The three programs mentioned above all fix plans by reordering the component operators.

The linear assumption is used in cases where there is no a priori reason to order one operator ahead of another. An alternative assumption is that it is better *not* to order operators than to order them arbitrarily. This assumption arises in slightly different forms in the NOAH planning system (Article XV.D1) and one of the MOLGEN systems (Article XV.D2). NOAH establishes *partial orders* of problem-solving operators by considering their preconditions. For example, it may know that the goal of buying coffee beans has the subgoals *Go to coffee store* and *Get money*, but initially it does not commit itself to an ordering of these operators. However, when it expands each of these goals, it notices that a precondition of getting money, *Be at bank*, interferes with the goal of being at the coffee store; thus, it decides to get money before it goes to the coffee store. NOAH orders operators only to eliminate problems that might arise from picking an arbitrary ordering. MOLGEN also will not order operators until constraints are available to guide it; furthermore, MOLGEN avoids committing itself to using operators or objects without constraints because premature commitment may conflict with other parts of its plan.

The *least-commitment* approach of NOAH and MOLGEN contrasts with the linear assumption, which says, *Commit yourself to any order of operators and then fix it.* This approach works because NOAH and MOLGEN are able to infer constraints that hold between operators. An important aspect of the approach is that it is *constructive;* since planning decisions are made only when the planner is sure they will not interfere with past or future decisions, the planner need never *backtrack* and undo a bad decision. In fact, both of these planners do make bad decisions and can backtrack, but the major research effort has been to avoid backtracking.

Interestingly, human planners do not always use the least-commitment strategy and, consequently, they must sometimes backtrack. Humans *opportunistically* plan to execute an operator when it is convenient to do so. For example, a human may plan to pick up groceries on the way to a football game because it is convenient to do so. Later he (or she) will realize that the groceries will wilt during the game and he will have to replan to avoid this.

Conclusion

We have discussed the structure of plans, concentrating especially on the hierarchical relation between goals and subgoals. When problem solving is discussed in terms of search, it becomes evident that, although finished plans are usually linear or partial orders of problem-solving operators, the search spaces in which the plans are developed are hierarchical. This is because problem-solving operators have preconditions that are subproblems with preconditions of their own, and so on. The term *hierarchical* was shown to refer to two related concepts: Most plans have a *hierarchical structure*, but only hierarchical planners use a *hierarchy of abstraction spaces* to develop a plan.

We have introduced four approaches to planning: nonhierarchical planning as practiced by STRIPS and HACKER; hierarchical planning of the sort done by ABSTRIPS, NOAH, and MOLGEN; script-based planning; and opportunistic planning. Most will be discussed in subsequent articles, although opportunistic planning is covered in Chapter XI, on models of cognition. Nonhierarchical planners are discussed in Article XV.C after a comparison of hierarchical and nonhierarchical planning illustrated by ABSTRIPS and

STRIPS in Article XV.B; NOAH is discussed in Article XV.D1; and the last two articles are devoted to the MOLGEN systems (Articles XV.D2 and XV.E).

The major issue for any planning system is reducing search; instrumental in this are methods for minimizing the effects of interacting subproblems. In particular, the least-commitment approach that derives from hierarchical planning is *constructive,* that is, it requires little or no backtracking.

References

Sacerdoti (1979) is an interesting overview and attempt to taxonomize planning methods. Stefik's (1980) doctoral thesis discusses and compares many planning systems and methods. The references mentioned in this article are representative of the planning literature and provide a readable historical background; one important reference that was not mentioned earlier is Bobrow and Raphael's (1974) review of AI programming languages. Planning has received some attention in cognitive science, and human planning has been examined in AI. References include Schank and Abelson's (1977) book on scripts and plans, Feitelson and Stefik's (1977) study of human experiment-planning, Friedland's (1979) doctoral dissertation on script-based planning, and the research of Barbara and Frederick Hayes-Roth on opportunistic planning (Hayes-Roth, 1980).

B. STRIPS AND ABSTRIPS

HIERARCHICAL PLANNING in the context of the STRIPS and ABSTRIPS planners is the subject of this article (see also Fikes and Nilsson, 1971; Fikes, Hart, and Nilsson, 1972; Sacerdoti, 1974; Articles II.D5 and II.D6, in Vol. I). The two systems are virtually identical except that STRIPS plans in a single abstraction space while ABSTRIPS plans in a hierarchy of them. We present here a single problem—getting a cup of coffee—and show how each of the systems would solve it.

Let us first characterize a problem solver as a program that explores the states that arise from the application of problem-solving operators in search of one that qualifies as a solution to the problem. (Other characterizations of search in problem solving are possible; see Articles II.B1 and II.B2, in Vol. I, for a discussion of *state-space* and *problem-reduction search*.) The first state examined by a problem solver is the *starting state*, and if the problem solver is successful, the last state examined will be the *goal state*.

Problem solvers have available a set of problem-solving operators and objects. When problem-solving operators are executed, they bring about changes in the state of the world. Consider now the problem of getting a cup of coffee. You go to the kitchen and if coffee is made, you pour some. If not, you make some or go out to buy some. If you decide to make some, but there are no coffee beans or ground coffee, you go to the store to get some. If you have no money, you go to the bank first. The relevant operators and objects are:

Operator	Object
Boil water	boiling water
Pour X	kitchen
Buy X	coffee-bean store
Make coffee	coffee beans
Go to X	brewed-coffee store
Get money	bank
	money

Each operator has *preconditions* that must be true before that operator can be executed—for example, if there is no coffee to pour, you must make some. Making a precondition true is a subproblem. Because problem-solving operators usually have preconditions, a developing plan usually has a hierarchical structure.

The operators for this problem can be represented in such a way that their preconditions and effects are explicit:

Operator	Precondition	Effect
Pour coffee	Have brewed coffee	Problem solved
Make coffee	Have beans Have grinder Have boiling water Be in the kitchen	Have brewed coffee
Buy something	Be at store Have money	Have something
Go someplace	Place exists	Be at place Not at any other place
Get money	Be at bank	Have money
Boil water	Be in the kitchen	Have boiling water

The starting state and goal state of the problem can be expressed in these terms also:

Starting state	Goal state
Not have brewed coffee	Have brewed coffee
In kitchen	In kitchen
Have grinder	Have grinder
Have money	Have money
Have boiling water	Have boiling water

If a problem solver knows how each problem-solving operator changes the state of the world and knows the preconditions for an operator to be executed, it can apply a technique called *means-ends analysis* to solve problems (see Article II.D2, in Vol. I, and Article XI.B). Briefly, this technique involves looking for a *difference* between the current state of the world and a desired state and trying to find a problem-solving operator that will reduce the difference. This continues recursively until the desired state of the world has been achieved. STRIPS and ABSTRIPS, and most other planners, use means-ends analysis.

The next few paragraphs illustrate how STRIPS might solve the problem of getting a cup of coffee. First, it compares the starting state and the goal state and immediately finds a difference: *Have brewed coffee*. So it looks for an operator that has *Have brewed coffee* in its list of effects. It finds two: *Make coffee* and *Buy something*, where *something* is instantiated with *brewed coffee*. STRIPS must choose one of them; choosing the first makes the example more interesting, so we will assume it does that.

To make coffee, the four preconditions of the *Make coffee* operator must be fulfilled. STRIPS compares the current state of the world (the starting state) with the first precondition and immediately finds a difference, *Have beans*. Consequently, it goes back and tries to eliminate this difference by searching for an operator that has as its effect *Has beans*. Only one operator applies, namely, *Buy something*, where *something* is instantiated with *beans*. Once again, STRIPS compares the preconditions of the proposed operator with the current state of the world. It notes that the condition *Be at store* is not satisfied, so it must repeat the search once again and find an operator that will get it to the store. There is such an operator, *Go to someplace*, with the single precondition that the place exist; since the store is one of the objects available to STRIPS, the operator can be executed.

At this point, a plan for solving the problem would have the following hierarchical structure:

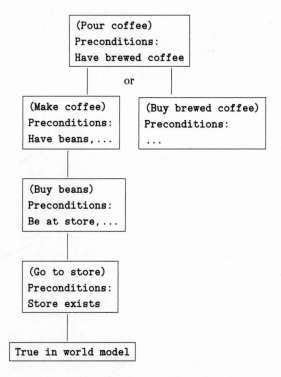

Note that executing the operator *Go to store* changes one aspect of the state of the world. The starting state is *In the kitchen*, but *Go to store* changes this to *At the store*. This change satisfies one of the preconditions of the *Buy beans* operator; STRIPS checks the other precondition, *Have money*. Since this precondition is true in the current state of the world, STRIPS is free to execute the *Buy beans* operator. Its execution fulfills the first precondition of the *Make coffee* operator. Furthermore, STRIPS finds the next two preconditions, *Have grinder* and *Have boiling water*, true in the current state of the world. However, the last precondition, *Be in kitchen*, has been made false by going to the store, so before making coffee, STRIPS must find an operator with the effect of making *Be in kitchen* true again. This is simply *Go to kitchen*, and since it has no preconditions it is immediately applicable. Its execution fulfills all the preconditions of *Make coffee;* consequently, that operator can be executed, fulfilling the single precondition of *Pour coffee* and solving the problem.

The final plan for getting coffee is, thus, *Go to the store, buy beans, go to the kitchen, make coffee, pour coffee.*

Means-ends analysis is a powerful problem-solving method because it reduces the amount of search done by a problem solver. At any point prior to solving a problem, one or more goals must be satisfied. Means-ends analysis recognizes only one type of goal, namely, to reduce a difference between two states. Moreover, an assumption of the method is that problem-solving operators can be classified according to the kinds of differences they reduce. Consequently, only a fraction of the available operators will be applicable to any given goal, and search among the operators for an applicable one will be reduced.

Search and Backtracking

One difficulty with means-ends analysis is that it can still develop large search spaces. Although it restricts the number of operators that apply to a goal, there may still be several applicable operators and no a priori basis for selecting one. Moreover, there is no way of knowing whether the subgoals of an operator can be satisfied or whether their evaluation may eventually lead to a dead end, that is, to a subgoal that cannot be satisfied. For example, if the *Go to someplace* operator had a precondition *Have car* but no car existed, all of the processing that led to that operator would have been in vain and the problem solver would have had to *backtrack* to find an alternate path. In the example above, the only other path involves trying to *Buy brewed coffee,* and it, too, will fail for the same reason. In more complicated problems, one might expect to find several alternative paths that might accomplish a given subgoal, and a substantial amount of backtracking may be needed to solve the problem. Backtracking can be very expensive, so recent planners have been designed to avoid it as much as possible.

Backtracking arises from premature commitment to a problem-solving path. As an illustration, consider again the problem of getting coffee. Assume for a moment that the objects that are available to STRIPS are *kitchen, bank, coffee-bean store, brewed-coffee store.* The *grinder* and the *grinder store* are missing. To solve the problem, STRIPS builds a *search tree,* as shown in Figure B–1.

Briefly, STRIPS would reason that to pour coffee, it must make some or buy some. It opts to make some. To do so, it needs beans, for which it needs money and a bean store. To get money, it must get to a bank, for which a bank must exist. Since a bank does exist, STRIPS plans to go there and get money. It then explores the possibility of going to a bean store; since such

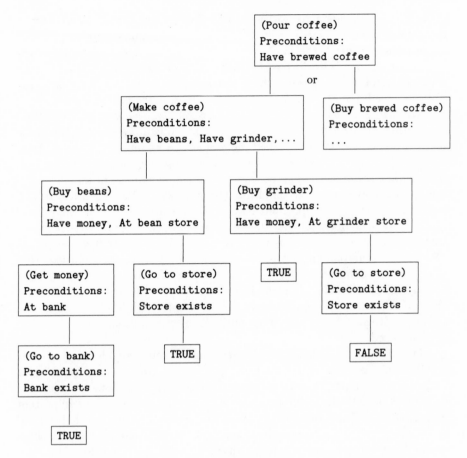

Figure B–1.   A search tree for the problem of pouring coffee.

a store exists, STRIPS can go there. Both preconditions for buying beans are fulfilled, so it plans to buy them and then goes on to consider the next precondition of making coffee, which is having a grinder. Since it does not have one, it decides to buy one, for which the preconditions are having money and being at a grinder store. It has money from its previous visit to the bank, so it plans to go to the grinder store. Unfortunately, no such store exists. All of this processing has been in vain—STRIPS cannot possibly make coffee. Its only option is to backtrack to a *choice point* in the plan and try another path. In this case, it can try to buy some brewed coffee. This part of the plan is not illustrated, but it will succeed since a brewed-coffee store exists.

Part of the expense of backtracking in the previous example derives from planning several operations that are actually unimportant details. Intuitively, one would expect STRIPS to have checked much earlier in the plan to see whether a grinder store existed. Similarly, if STRIPS knew that certain stores existed, it should not have worried about how to get to them until later in the plan; getting to places seems like a detail. One would expect a planner first to plan to do all the important steps in a plan and then to fill in the less important ones after it has sketched out the others. In fact, this method is called *hierarchical planning;* the first planner to use it was an extension of STRIPS called ABSTRIPS. We will now briefly describe how it works.

ABSTRIPS plans in a *hierarchy of abstraction spaces.* An ABSTRIPS abstraction space contains all of the objects and operators given in the initial specification of the problem (called the *ground space*), but some preconditions of some operators are judged to be more important than others. For example, *Have boiling water* seems like an unimportant precondition of making coffee because it is so easy to accomplish. Other preconditions such as *Grinder store exists* seem very important, because if they are not true in the ground space, there is no operator that the problem solver can execute to make them true. Preconditions are assigned importance levels, called *criticalities.* When ABSTRIPS starts planning, it plans to achieve only those preconditions that have the maximum criticality—just those preconditions that are critical to the success of the plan. It plans in the *highest* abstraction space. Next, it plans to achieve the preconditions of the steps in its high-level plan that have the next criticality level, and so on, until all the preconditions in a plan have been achieved.

The first step in this process is assigning criticalities. The method used in ABSTRIPS is for a human to draw up a partial ordering of preconditions by intuitively judging their importance; then ABSTRIPS follows an algorithm to adjust the criticalities further. One might guess that the most important precondition is that a place exist, since if it does not, operators that depend on its existence cannot be used in a plan. One might judge having something as the next most important precondition and being somewhere the least important:

Precondition	Intuitive criticality
Place exists	3
Have something	2
Be somewhere	1

ABSTRIPS adjusts these criticalities as follows: All preconditions whose truth values cannot be changed by any operator are given a maximum criticality. For each of the other preconditions, if a short plan can be found to achieve it—assuming the previous preconditions are true—it is assumed to be a detail and is given a criticality equal to that specified in the partial ordering. If no such plan can be found, it is given a criticality greater than the highest one in the partial order.

The preconditions *Bank exists, Bean store exists,* and *Brewed-coffee store exists* are all assigned a maximum value, say, 5, because their truth cannot be changed by any operator. The four *Have something* preconditions are *Have beans, Have grinder, Have boiling water,* and *Have money;* three of them can be achieved by a short plan, given that the previous preconditions are true. For example, given that the bank exists, a short plan can be found to achieve the precondition *Have money.* These three preconditions are therefore assigned their partial-order rank of 2, and the fourth, *Have grinder,* which cannot be achieved by a simple plan because no grinder store exists, is given the rank of 4, higher than any partial-order rank. Lastly, the *Be somewhere* preconditions are ranked, and since they can all be achieved by simple plans, they are assigned their partial-order rank of 1:

Precondition	Criticality
Bean store exists	5
Brewed-coffee store exists	5
Bank exists	5
Have grinder	4
Have beans, boiling water, money	2
Be at brewed-coffee store, bean store, bank	1

ABSTRIPS now formulates a plan in an abstraction space of criticality 5. This means that at this level, any precondition of an operator that has a smaller criticality value is assumed to be true. At this level, ABSTRIPS finds two plans to get coffee: *Make coffee* and *Buy brewed coffee.* It then expands the *Make coffee* plan in an abstraction space of criticality 4, since the *Have grinder* precondition emerges at this level. ABSTRIPS tries to find a subplan for getting a grinder but cannot. Consequently, it recognizes immediately that its level 5 plan to make coffee will fail. It backs up to level 5 again, picks the alternative plan to buy brewed coffee, and pursues it. Figure B–2 shows a trace of its operation in the five abstraction spaces.

In this trace, ABSTRIPS first plans to make coffee, but this plan fails in the abstraction space of level 4. Thus, it backtracks to level 5 and plans to buy brewed coffee. This plan is not expanded further until level 2, when the precondition of having money becomes apparent. At level 1, a precondition of getting money is found, namely, *Be at bank,* and a precondition of buying coffee is found, namely, *Be at store.* ABSTRIPS plans to go to these places; its final plan is *Go to bank, get money, go to coffee store, buy brewed coffee.*

ABSTRIPS solves problems with much less searching and backtracking than STRIPS because it is a hierarchical planner. It generates a hierarchy of plans in which the highest level plans are very sketchy and the lowest level plans are detailed. Since a complete plan is formulated at each level of abstraction before the next level is considered, ABSTRIPS can find dead ends early, as it did with the problem of finding a coffee grinder. The details of the other parts of the plan to make coffee, for example, boiling water and

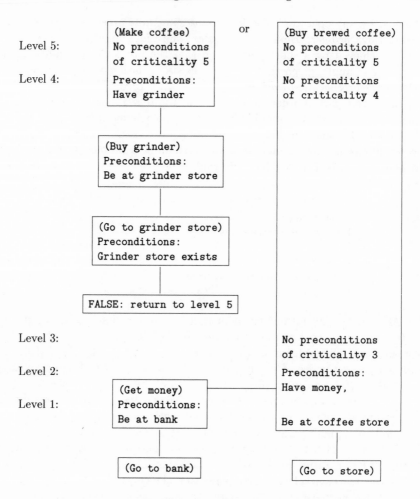

Figure B–2.   A trace of ABSTRIPS in five abstraction spaces.

buying beans, were never considered because ABSTRIPS quickly detected that an important precondition of making coffee could not be satisfied.

References

STRIPS is discussed in Fikes and Nilsson (1971); in Fikes, Hart, and Nilsson (1972); and in Article II.D5 in Volume I of the *Handbook*. ABSTRIPS is discussed in Sacerdoti (1974) and in Article II.D6 (also in Vol. I).

C. NONHIERARCHICAL PLANNING

NONHIERARCHICAL approaches to planning order operations at a single level of abstraction, in contrast to hierarchical planners, which develop entire plans at multiple levels of abstraction. A nonhierarchical planner typically develops a hierarchy of subgoals, but they are all at the same level of abstraction.

The systems discussed in this article are HACKER, INTERPLAN, and the planner developed by Waldinger. They are three attempts to solve the difficult planning task of achieving conjunctive subgoals that are not independent. Many problems are formulated as a conjunction of goals; for example, *spring cleaning* may involve sweeping, washing the floor, washing the windows, beating the rug, and so on. However, these goals are not independent; they cannot be achieved in an arbitrary order. Washing the floor before sweeping is a doomed and grubby operation; a *precondition* of washing the floor is that it be swept clean of loose dirt. Similarly, one should not beat the rug after sweeping, because dragging a dusty rug outside will make the floor dirty and ruin the effect of sweeping. In the terminology of this chapter, beating the rug after sweeping would constitute a *violation of a protected goal,* the goal being a freshly swept house. Similarly, achieving some goals can actually prevent the accomplishment of others, as when washing the floor prevents one from walking across it or using it for any other purpose until it is dry. To any person with minimal housecleaning experience, it will be obvious how and why spring-cleaning tasks must be ordered to avoid their mutual interference, but simple planning programs do not have a priori knowledge about the order in which goals should be accomplished. The problem for these planners is to construct, in the absence of this knowledge, an efficient plan for achieving conjunctive goals that are not independent.

The approach taken by HACKER and INTERPLAN is to formulate plans that are flawed by interferences between subgoals and then to fix them by reordering problem-solving operations in the plan. Waldinger's system is more constructive: Instead of reordering operations in a flawed plan, it develops the plan by inserting operations one by one, checking each for potential interference with established operations.

HACKER and INTERPLAN apply a simplifying heuristic called the *linear assumption* to restrict the number of goal orderings that it considers. It was originally formulated by Sussman (1973) in these terms:

> Subgoals are independent and thus can be sequentially achieved in an arbitrary order. (p. 59)

Of course, this assumption is false for many problems, but it does avoid the problem of searching for an ordering of subgoals in which none interferes. The search space of orderings can be enormous, since it grows with the factorial of the number of subgoals in a plan; for example, there are over 3 million distinct orders in which 10 conjunctive subgoals can be achieved. The linear assumption commits the planner to an arbitrary ordering of subgoals rather than searching for an optimal one and, in the event that the ordering is suboptimal, the planner tries to fix it. (For an alternative, *least-commitment*, approach, see the following two articles.)

HACKER

HACKER was developed as a model of skill acquisition by Gerald Sussman at M.I.T. Sussman defines *skill* as a set of procedures, each of which solves a certain kind of problem from the domain of the skill. If a skill does not include a procedure to solve a problem, a new procedure must be designed. Typically, it implements old procedures as a means of achieving subgoals of the new problem. New procedures can turn out to have "bugs" and not work in all the situations for which they are designed, in which case they can be patched to make them work. Often, bugs can be abstracted; that is, within the domain of a skill there are common bugs that show up in many procedures. One very general bug, the one addressed by all the systems in this article, is found in cases in which *conjunctive subgoals* are to be achieved: Achieving one subgoal may prevent the accomplishment of another. Sussman reasons that this bug (and others) is so common that a model of skill acquisition should know how to *debug* the procedures it designs. HACKER is able to do so in many cases.

Although HACKER was designed as a model of skill acquisition, it is interesting in the context of planning because the procedures it develops for solving problems are plans and because the debugging of plans was considered a useful problem-solving technique. For the purposes of this chapter, we will ignore what HACKER contributes to the subject of learning (for this, see Article XIV.D5c) and concentrate on those aspects of skill acquisition that are relevant to planning.

HACKER was written at a time when *procedural* representations of knowledge were popular (see Chap. III, in Vol. I, on knowledge representation). One result of this is that HACKER's various functions are difficult to separate. Rather than explain their extensive interactions, the functions and the knowledge that supports them are described here in general terms. Those of immediate interest are the *answer library,* which contains problem-solving procedures; the *knowledge library,* which contains facts about the domain; the *programming-techniques library,* which is used to propose problem-solving procedures when appropriate ones are not found in the answer library; and several libraries of bugs and appropriate patches.

Problem solving in HACKER would be much like that in PLANNER (see Article VI.A, in Vol. II) were it not for the need to debug plans. PLANNER had only one mechanism for recovering from a flawed plan, namely, *backtracking*. This was very expensive in terms of search time. In contrast, HACKER proposes a plan and then corrects errors in it with programs that are experts in debugging, rather than by backtracking to the point of failure in a plan and blindly trying another problem-solving operation.

The bug that concerns us here is called *prerequisite-clobbers-brother-goal* by Sussman; it arises from the *linearity assumption*. There are often interactions between goals such that achieving the prerequisites for one goal prevents the accomplishment of another. HACKER can solve some of these interaction problems, but sometimes the solution is not optimal. A popular problem for planners is shown in Figure C–1.

HACKER attempts to solve this problem by finding a procedure in its answer library that matches the pattern of the goal: (MAKE (ON B C)). It finds a procedure that says,

$$\text{(TO (MAKE (ON X Y))}$$
$$\text{(PUTON (X Y))) ;}$$

that is, to get block B on block C, execute the simple procedure PUTON with B and C as arguments. When it simulates the execution of this program, it discovers that it fails, because A is on B. A bug in the proposed plan has been found; HACKER now attempts to patch it up. First, a library of types of bugs is consulted, from which HACKER concludes that the bug is a PREREQUISITE-MISSING type. We will not go into the details of this classification. HACKER knows that a prerequisite to one of its planned actions is missing, but it does not know which prerequisite. In its knowledge library it finds several potentially pertinent facts. One is

$$\text{(FACT (PREREQUISITE (PUTON (X Y) (PLACE-FOR X Y)))) .}$$

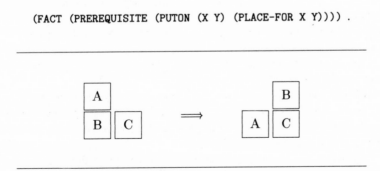

Figure C–1.   A planning problem: Get block B from under A and put it on block C.

That is, to put X on Y there must be a place on Y for X to rest. It checks to see whether there is a place on C for B; since there is, this is not the missing prerequisite. The next fact is more enlightening:

```
(FACT (PREREQUISITE (EXPRESSION (CLEARTOP OBJECT))
                    (HAVE () (MOVES EXPRESSION OBJECT)))) .
```

It says that a prerequisite for moving an object is that the object have a clear top. Since A is stacked on B, this prerequisite is not met for B.

HACKER has discovered the identity of the bug that spoiled its initial plan for getting B on C. It now uses this information to modify the plan, applying general methods for fixing bugs that it has encountered before. One such method says that, to patch a PREREQUISITE–MISSING bug, a procedure for attaining the prerequisite should be inserted into the plan before the prerequisite is needed. The prerequisite to be achieved is (CLEARTOP B). HACKER treats this as a subgoal and returns to the beginning of its problem-solving cycle; it looks in the answer library for a procedure that will achieve the prerequisite. We will assume that this procedure exists; if it did not, HACKER would construct it with the help of its programming-techniques library.

To summarize, HACKER solves problems by searching for a procedure known to be appropriate for such problems. If it finds one but the procedure does not achieve the goal as expected, the reasons for the failure are formalized as bugs. Efforts are then initiated to debug the procedure. At any time during problem solving, HACKER may be required to write procedures to achieve certain goals. These are then tested and debugged exactly like procedures found in the answer library.

There are problems for which HACKER cannot generate an optimal plan. One such problem is shown in Figure C–2 and is discussed in the "Anomalous Situations" chapter of Sussman's thesis (1973).

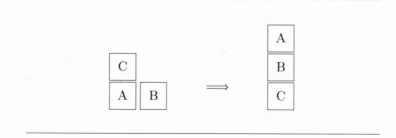

Figure C–2.   A problem for which HACKER cannot provide an optimal solution. The proper goal sequence is (CLEAR A), (ON B C), (ON A B).

HACKER knows from previous experience that it is wise to build from the ground up; therefore, for the problem in Figure C–2, it constructs a plan to

((ACHIEVE (ON B C))
(ACHIEVE (ON A B)))

But when it simulates execution of this plan, it notices that, after putting B on C, it must take it off again, and take C off A, in order to clear A for putting A on B. This constitutes a *protection violation* of the previously achieved goal, namely, (ON B C). HACKER treats protection violations as bugs; unfortunately, this one cannot be fixed simply by reordering its goals. If HACKER tries to solve the problem by achieving (ON A B) and then (ON B C), it finds that, after achieving (ON A B), another protection violation results from trying to (CLEAR B) to put it on C. Regardless of the order in which HACKER attempts to achieve the goals of the problem, a protection violation occurs. The only alternative is suboptimal—to permit the violation and then to achieve the violated goal again at a later time, for example, by putting B on C, then taking it off again, taking C off A, putting B back on C, and finally putting A on top.

When HACKER discovers a protection violation, it tries to reorder the operations in its plan. However, it is limited to reordering operations at one particular level of the plan; in the previous example it tried to reorder the initial goals. To solve the problem, it is necessary to reorder goals at different levels of the plan. HACKER need not reorder the goals (ON B C) and (ON A B), but it must achieve a *subgoal* of (ON A B), namely, (CLEAR A), before it achieves (ON A B). This kind of reordering of levels of goals is too subtle for HACKER. However, another program called INTERPLAN does consider these more complex reorderings.

INTERPLAN

INTERPLAN was developed by Austin Tate at the University of Edinburgh in 1974. It employs a convenient declarative representation called a *tick list* to allow protection violations to be detected easily and to give the system the relevant information for recovery (Tate, 1975a). In the event of a protection violation, INTERPLAN first tries the same reorderings as HACKER; namely, goals are reordered at a single level of the subgoal hierarchy. But if this fails, it considers more general reorderings. In particular, the subgoal at which failure occurred is *promoted*, that is, moved before its superordinate goal, and possibly before other goals as well.

The space of goal orderings considered by INTERPLAN is thus larger than that considered by HACKER, but for this added effort it gains the ability to optimize plans that HACKER could not optimize.

Consider the problem from Figure C–2. INTERPLAN initially proceeds like HACKER:

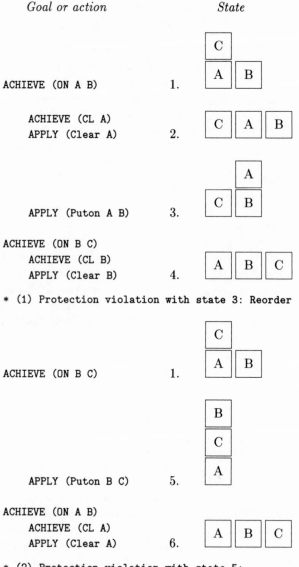

Goal or action   *State*

ACHIEVE (ON A B)   1.

ACHIEVE (CL A)
APPLY (Clear A)   2.

APPLY (Puton A B)   3.

ACHIEVE (ON B C)
  ACHIEVE (CL B)
  APPLY (Clear B)   4.

* (1) Protection violation with state 3: Reorder

ACHIEVE (ON B C)   1.

APPLY (Puton B C)   5.

ACHIEVE (ON A B)
  ACHIEVE (CL A)
  APPLY (Clear A)   6.

* (2) Protection violation with state 5:

At this point in the problem, HACKER resigns itself to a suboptimal plan. It has tried the two possible orderings of the goals (ON A B) and (ON B C), and neither of them produces plans free of protection violations. In order to solve the problem, a *subgoal* of one of the main goals must be achieved before either of the main goals. HACKER is not capable of reordering goals between levels, but INTERPLAN is. It decides to *promote* the subgoal that caused the protection violation; it returns to the starting state of the problem and immediately tries to achieve (CL A):

Goal or action		*State*

PROMOTE (CL A)
ACHIEVE (CL A)   1.

APPLY (Clear A)   7.

ACHIEVE (ON B C)
APPLY (Puton B C)   8.

ACHIEVE (ON A B)
APPLY (Puton A B)   9.

  * (3) Goal achieved

Subgoal promotion is thus a useful method for reordering goals when they interfere with each other. The method and the *tick-list* data-structure that facilitates it are discussed in detail in Tate (1975b).

Goal Regression

HACKER and INTERPLAN *backtrack* when they find a protection violation; they reorder a couple of goals and then start planning to achieve them in the new order. For simple problems like the previous example, this method will suffice, but if there are several conjunctive goals, and many or most goal orderings produce subgoal interactions, the method is very inefficient. Moreover, when these planners reorder their goals, all goals affected by the reordering must be achieved again. This can lead to the same solution being achieved for a subgoal a number of times because superordinate goals interacted with each other.

An alternative approach is to construct a plan by solving one conjunctive subgoal at a time, checking that each solution does not interfere with other goals that have already been achieved and moving the offending goal to a different place in the plan if it does. A planner that works this way was developed by Richard Waldinger (1977). He introduced the concept of *goal regression* to handle interference between goals.

At any point in a plan a goal may have been achieved, but after another step it may have been violated. This was illustrated earlier in the problem in Figure C–2; after (ON B C) had been achieved, it was violated to achieve (CLEAR A). Waldinger noted that for any goal G and operation O, there is no guarantee that G will be true after O, but that a new goal G' can be found such that if G' holds before O, G will hold after O. Finding this new goal G' is *goal regression*, or *passing the goal back over the operator*. Goal regression can be used to guarantee that goals that have been achieved are not violated by subsequent operations. The basic planning algorithm is to achieve the first of the conjunctive subgoals of the problem and then expand the plan by regressing subsequent subgoals from the end of the plan to a point in the plan where their accomplishment will not violate those previously achieved.

Consider again the three-blocks problem. Waldinger's system can solve the problem regardless of the order in which it approaches the subgoals, but we will illustrate it planning to achieve (ON A B) before (ON B C). First, the system removes block C from atop A in order to clear A. The plan looks like this:

Goal or action	*State*

1.

ACHIEVE (ON A B)
    (Clear A)   2.

Now the system puts A on B:

(Put A on B)   3.

The plan consists of two actions, (Clear A), (Put A on B). The system now attempts its second goal, appending it to the end of the plan. However, it finds that achieving one of its preconditions, (Clear B), violates the protected relation A *is on* B. Rather than reordering the conjunctive goals of the plan, as HACKER and INTERPLAN do, the system simply passes the offending goal back over previously achieved subgoals until it finds a place in the plan where the goal will not interfere with any others. In this case, the goal (ON B C) is moved in front of the action (Put A on B). The plan now looks like this:

Goal or action		State

1.

```
 C
 A   B
```

ACHIEVE (ON A B)
(Clear A)   2.

```
 C   A   B
```

ACHIEVE (ON B C)
(Put B on C)   3.

```
 B
 C   A
```

(Put A on B)   4.

```
 A
 B
 C
```

When a proposed operator causes a protection violation, an attempt is made to insert it at earlier points in the plan, checking to see whether the interaction is avoided and to see that no new protection violations occur. However, the choice of where to insert the new operator is not guided by any information. It involves simply searching back in the plan and checking at each position to see if it is suitable. Waldinger's system does not check whether a later step is made redundant by the insertion of the operator, so a less than optimal plan may be produced.

The main advantage of Waldinger's approach is that it is constructive: Plan steps are added one by one, and the only difficulty is finding out where they should go in the plan. This can involve a considerable amount of searching, but it avoids the inefficient repeated achieving of subgoals that HACKER and INTERPLAN must do after reordering.

Conclusion

We have discussed here three nonhierarchical approaches to planning: HACKER, INTERPLAN, and Waldinger's system. Each suffers from interacting subproblems; the first two systems are forced to backtrack and reorder sub-goals, and Waldinger's system, though it avoids backtracking by constructive goal regression, must evaluate the consequences of putting a subgoal at a proposed place in a plan. In the remaining articles of this chapter, we will consider hierarchical and script-based planning as alternatives to nonhierarchical planning.

References

HACKER is discussed in Sussman's doctoral thesis (1973; also Sussman, 1975). INTERPLAN is discussed in Tate's thesis (1975b), although his *IJCAI* article (1975a) is more accessible. See Waldinger (1977) for a presentation of his system.

D. HIERARCHICAL PLANNERS

D1. NOAH

IN NOAH, Earl Sacerdoti made some significant advances in problem solving and planning. NOAH (Nets of Action Hierarchies) was designed as part of the Computer-based Consultant project at SRI International, Inc., around 1975 (see Article VII.D2, in Vol. II). It uses a representation for plans called the *procedural net,* which has a richer structure than previous problem solvers. In contrast to these earlier efforts, the procedural net represents both procedural and declarative knowledge about problem solving. The procedural knowledge (also called *domain knowledge*) includes functions that expand statements of goals into subgoals and that simulate the actions of operators that transform one state into another. Declarative, or *plan,* knowledge represents the effects of executing these functions; for example, if a procedure is executed that puts one block on top of another, NOAH records that the supporting block no longer has a clear top surface. Because the effects of actions are represented explicitly, NOAH can reason about them. In fact, NOAH employs a set of procedures called *critics* that are sensitive to those effects of actions that would jeopardize the success of the plan. Critics are used to detect and correct interactions, eliminate redundant operations, and so forth.

Problem solving in NOAH is accomplished by developing the procedural net. From a single node that represents the goal to be achieved, a hierarchy of nodes is developed that represents levels of subgoals to be achieved before the original goal can be accomplished. The original goal node contains a pointer to a set of functions that expand goals into subgoals. When one or more of these functions are executed, subgoal nodes are added to the procedural net. They are linked to the original goal—their *parent*—and to each other, and, like their parent, they contain pointers to functions that expand goals to subgoals. In addition, the nodes representing the subgoals include a declarative representation of the effects, if any, of executing the functions.

After the original goal node has been expanded, there are two levels of representation of the problem, the first of which is the goal node. The second is a series of subgoals that, when achieved, will have the effect of achieving the original goal. These nodes are themselves expanded as their parent was. NOAH continues to add nodes to the procedural net that are more specific versions of the goals represented by their parents. Eventually, the original goal of the problem is replaced by several levels of more detailed goals and, finally, by a level of goals that can be immediately attained by simple problem-solving operators.

Thus, NOAH plans by developing a hierarchy of subgoals. These will sometimes be called *abstract operators*. A distinction is made here, as elsewhere in this chapter, between the simple *problem-solving operators* specified in the problem space and abstract operators that will eventually be expanded to problem-solving operators. Abstract operators are goals, and their expansions are subgoals, in the sense that such operators specify abstract actions that the planner would like to execute but that it cannot execute until they are expanded to subgoals attainable by problem-solving operators.

In addition to abstract and problem-solving operators, NOAH has *planning actions*. These include the functions that expand goals into subgoals and the actions of various critics. They are not part of the emerging plan but, rather, are the actions by which NOAH develops the plan.

Note that whenever NOAH expands a goal to subgoals, it runs the risk of creating *interacting subproblems* (see Article XV.C). This problem arises when a planner commits itself to an arbitrary order for achieving conjunctive goals. NOAH avoids the problem in two ways: first, by not ordering subgoals until there is some reason to do so and, second, by continually examining the developing plan for potential subgoal interactions and correcting them before they arise. This allows NOAH to solve interaction problems constructively: Operators are not ordered until a potential interaction is detected, and then they are ordered to avoid the interaction. This contrasts with the planners in the previous article; those planners ordered operators arbitrarily, and, if an interaction emerged, they backtracked and replanned to try to avoid the interaction. These planners are said to *overconstrain* a plan by committing themselves to orderings arbitrarily; NOAH is said to *underconstrain* a developing plan by not committing itself to any orderings except to avoid an interaction.

Application

NOAH was applied in the domain of assembly tasks, and it proved useful and powerful. It provided instructions to a human apprentice, who then carried out NOAH's plan. The procedural net was well suited to this task, because it allowed a plan to be specified at any of several levels of detail; for example, NOAH could instruct a trained engineer to *bolt the mounting bracket to the frame*—a high-level instruction—but it could tell a novice how to accomplish this goal in detail if necessary. The procedural net also made it easier to monitor the execution of the plan. If an unexpected situation arose, NOAH could replan by patching the procedural net. The building of the plan was kept distinct from its execution, but control could pass from the planner to the execution monitor at any stage.

The Structure of the Procedural Net

The procedural net contains several levels of representation of a plan, each level more detailed than the previous one. Each consists of a *partially ordered* sequence of nodes that represent goals at some level of abstraction. To avoid overconstraining the order in which goals are achieved, NOAH assumes they can be attained in parallel until it has some reason to put one before or after another.

Each node in the procedural net is attached to its more detailed expansion in the next level; for example, the node representing the abstract goal *Make coffee* may be expanded to a handful of more detailed goals, such as *Grind coffee, Boil water, Put the coffee in a filter, Pour the water through it.* NOAH will not commit itself to any particular ordering of these operators until it has reason to do so.

The statement of the problem goal is the top-level node, representing a plan at a very high level. A simple example of the structure of the net with two levels is given in Figure D1–1. The *S* and *J* nodes represent *split* and *join*, respectively; they are dummy nodes that bound actions that are assumed to be executable in parallel. NOAH uses this formalism to represent operations for which it has not chosen an ordering.

NOAH expands a single goal node in the procedural net into a hierarchy of plans at various levels of abstraction. To do this, it uses procedures that expand abstract operators into more detailed ones. Much *domain* knowledge is implicit in these procedures; for example, one such procedure might be:

> *If the abstract operator is* (MAKE COFFEE),
> *then expand it to the operators* (BOIL WATER), (GRIND COFFEE),
> (PUT COFFEE IN FILTER), (POUR WATER THROUGH).

The problem that NOAH is to solve determines what knowledge will be represented in these procedures; the preceding procedure may be appropriate

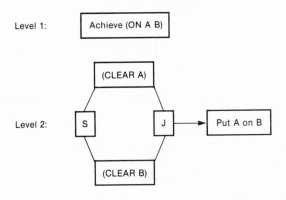

Figure D1–1. An action hierarchy (in a blocks world).

for the *coffee* domain but not for any other. Since these procedures contain so much knowledge about the problem domain, they are called SOUP functions, for Semantics of User Problem. They are written in an extension of QLISP.

Expanding the Procedural Net with SOUP Functions

Consider again the simple blocks-world action hierarchy in Figure D1–1. To achieve it, and to solve simple blocks problems, two SOUP functions are required. One, shown in Figure D1–2, expands any goal of the form (ACHIEVE (ON X Y)), and the other expands any goal of the form (CLEAR X) (these are the only functions required). The main goal of the problem is associated with both functions, since at the outset of the problem it is not known which will apply. However, only (PUTON X Y) matches the *pattern* of the main goal, so only it is applied. (See Article VI.A, in Vol. II, for a discussion of *pattern-directed invocation* of procedures in PLANNER.)

Applying (PUTON X Y) to the main goal of the problem generates three subgoals. The PGOAL forms the basis for constructing subgoals; when a PGOAL is activated, a new node is generated at the next level in the net whose name is the PGOAL's first argument, for example, (CLEAR X). The three PGOALs in PUTON create the nodes (CLEAR A), (CLEAR B), and (Put A on B). The first two are conjunctive, as is specified by the "AND" in the function. NOAH does not choose an order to attain them but assumes they may be attained in parallel and thus surrounds them with *split* and *join* nodes.

The function (PUTON X Y) also specifies the effects of achieving these subgoals. The effects of applying CLEAR to X or Y is to assert CLEARTOP for that

```
(PUTON
 (QLAMBDA (ON +X +Y)
 (PAND
   (PGOAL (Clear X)
          (CLEARTOP X)
          APPLY
          (CLEAR))
   (PGOAL (Clear Y)
          (CLEARTOP Y)
          APPLY
          (CLEAR)))
   (PGOAL (Put X on top of Y)
          (ON X Y)
          APPLY NIL)
   (PDENY (CLEARTOP Y)))))
```

Figure D1–2.   SOUP code for the blocks problem.

block, and the effect of putting X on Y is to DENY the assertion of (CLEARTOP Y). These effects are represented declaratively in the *add list* and *delete list* of a node. The add list is a list of propositions that become true after the goal is achieved, and the delete list represents the propositions that are no longer true after the goal is achieved.

Finally, the SOUP function specifies which other SOUP functions should be applied to expand the subgoals it has just created. It suggests that the appropriate function for the subgoal of clearing A or B is CLEAR. It makes no such suggestion for the third subgoal, Put A on B, because this goal can be accomplished by a single problem-solving operator and need not be further expanded. This mechanism increases the efficiency of problem solving and helps to avoid backtracking. Several SOUP functions might apply to a node in the procedural net, but the parent of the node can specify, at the time the node is created, which function is to be used to expand it. This reduces search. (However, the user may explicitly cause NOAH to consider alternatives by using a POR function inside a SOUP procedure. In this case, alternative expansions are generated in parallel until one is seen to be simpler than the other.)

The Concept of "State" in NOAH

Problem solvers are typically regarded as searching through a space of states for one that qualifies as a solution. One conception of a state in problem solvers like STRIPS and GPS is that a state is a collection of propositions. New states are generated from old ones by the application of operators; that is, operators make some old propositions false and add new true propositions. Eventually, and depending on the power of the problem solver, a state will be generated that includes just the propositions required for the problem to be solved.

NOAH can also be characterized in this way, but the knowledge that makes up a state in NOAH is quite distributed. Some knowledge—that which will never have its truth value changed—is represented in a *world model*. This includes the state of the world that holds when problem solving starts. When some aspect of that state is changed, the proposition describing it is removed from the world model. The changed state of the world is represented by the propositions added to the add list or delete list of the operator that changed the state. Thus, NOAH knows which aspects of its world have not changed— they are represented in the world model—and it distributes its records of changes throughout the procedural net.

Changes are summarized at each level in the net by a *table of multiple effects* (TOME), which contains an entry for every proposition that was asserted or denied by more than one node at that level in the net. TOMEs are used to check for interactions between goals; if a single proposition has its value changed by more than one action in a plan, there is a possibility of interference between the actions.

NOAH uses programs called *critics* to check for interferences. A critic simply checks a TOME for the kinds of conflicts it is designed to correct. When a conflict is found, the critic has a limited number (usually only one) of corrective actions it can take. If all of the critics can successfully eliminate any conflicts found, the next level is expanded. There is presently only a limited ability to backtrack on failure. Three critics are described here.

The RESOLVE–CONFLICTS critic. This examines conjunctive goals that are to be achieved in parallel. If an action taken to achieve one goal removes a precondition of an action in the other, the critic attempts to order the actions so that neither violates a precondition of the other. This critic is similar to the debugging procedure in HACKER for reordering conflicting goals. The important difference is that HACKER backtracks and *reorders* arbitrarily ordered operations, while this critic constructively orders goals that were previously unordered.

The ELIMINATE–REDUNDANT–PRECONDITIONS critic. Sometimes during planning, the same operation gets specified twice when it need be done only once. This critic fixes the problem.

The USE–EXISTING–OBJECTS critic. Formal objects, essentially placeholders, are used whenever there is not a clear choice of what value to give a variable. This critic will substitute a value when a clear choice becomes possible at a lower level of planning.

There are other critics in the system; some have a general purpose like those above, while others are specifically designed for a given domain. More can be added at any time. The critics described here are sufficient for the following example.

Planning in NOAH

The planning algorithm of NOAH operates repeatedly on the current lowest level of the procedural net. Initially, a node is constructed for the goal NOAH is given as its task. All SOUP procedures are available to expand this node; expanded nodes are associated with a much smaller set of SOUP procedures by the procedure that generated them. Once all the nodes in the current level have been expanded to produce a new level, critics check for interactions before another level of expansion is tried.

An Example

This example shows NOAH solving the three-blocks problem that was so difficult for the planners in the previous article.

NOAH's *world model* contains the propositions:

```
(ON C A)
(CLEARTOP B)
(CLEARTOP C)
```

This constitutes the *starting state* of the problem. The goal is also written as a proposition:

(AND (ON A B) (ON B C)).

Graphically, the starting state and the goal look like this:

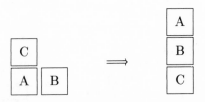

The PUTON and CLEAR functions discussed earlier are used in this problem. The first node in the procedural net is:

Level 1: | Achieve(AND(ON A B)(ON B C)) |

This is expanded to two parallel actions by merit of NOAH's policy about conjunctive goals: They are not ordered until there is some reason to do so.

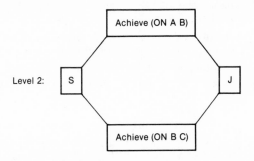

Level 2:

This is a simple expansion; the critics can find nothing to criticize about it. The PUTON function is now used to expand each of the nodes at level 2. (Refer back to Figs. D1–1 and D1–2 for an explanation of how this works.) The result is shown in Figure D1–3.

The RESOLVE–CONFLICTS critic notices that node 3 will delete a precondition of node 6, namely, that *B* is clear (node 4), because node 3 adds a statement to its delete list that DENYs (CLEARTOP B). When a table of multiple effects is compiled for this level, NOAH notices that (CLEARTOP B) is implicated in the effects of both nodes 4 and 6. Since NOAH has not committed itself to achieving any of its goals in a particular order, it need not backtrack to modify its plan in any destructive way. Instead, it uses this conflict as an opportunity to introduce constructively a partial ordering of goals: It decides

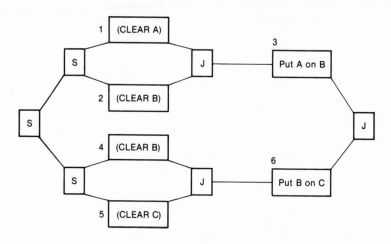

Figure D1–3.   Level 3 before criticism, with nodes numbered for reference.

to accomplish node 3 after it has done everything else. Figure D1–4 shows this reordering.

Next, the REDUNDANT–PRECONDITIONS critic observes that nodes 2 and 4 are redundant and eliminates node 2. This step is shown in Figure D1–5.

NOAH next expands the (CLEAR A) goal at level 3. Actually, that is the only goal that remains to be expanded, since B and C have been clear from the start of the problem, and the (Put X on Y) goals are achieved by simple problem-solving operators. To achieve (CLEAR A), NOAH needs to move C off of it and put C someplace; it does not know where, so it makes up a placeholder. Block C cannot be moved unless it is clear, so the final sequence

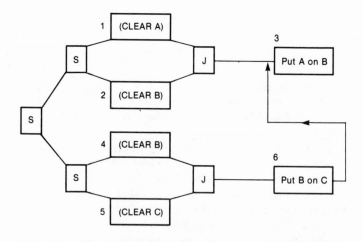

Figure D1–4.   Level 3 after the RESOLVE–CONFLICTS criticism.

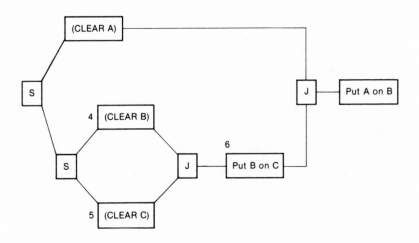

Figure D1–5.   Level 3 after all criticism.

that NOAH plans in order to clear A is (CLEAR C), (Put C on Object1). This is illustrated in Figure D1–6.

NOAH notices that node 6 may interfere with its latest goal, so the RESOLVE–CONFLICTS critic decides to order node 6 after it has achieved (Put C on Object1). See Figure D1–7.

Finally, the ELIMINATE–REDUNDANT–PRECONDITIONS critic notices that (CLEAR C) is mentioned twice in the plan. It eliminates one of the nodes. The final plan is shown in Figure D1–8.

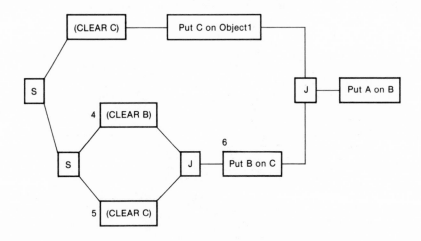

Figure D1–6.   Level 4 before criticism.

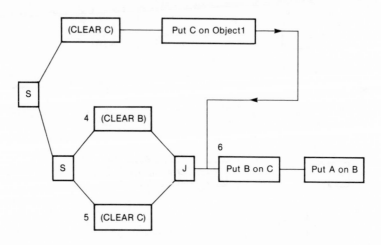

Figure D1–7.   Level 4 after the RESOLVE–CONFLICTS criticism.

Conclusion

NOAH plans with a combination of procedural and declarative knowledge. Initially, all NOAH's knowledge is in procedural form—local domain knowledge in the SOUP code and global knowledge in the critics. At the outset of planning, NOAH is given a world model and a goal that it develops into a hierarchical procedural net. As it plans, it records in a declarative form—in add lists and delete lists—knowledge to help it avoid interaction problems. To reason about interactions and possible orderings of goals, this information is summarized in a table of multiple effects. Critics consult these tables after each level has been expanded; they order and alter the plan constructively.

References

NOAH is discussed in detail in Sacerdoti's doctoral dissertation (printed as an SRI technical note, 1975). NOAH has been extended by Tate (1976), and a distributed implementation is discussed by Corkill (1979).

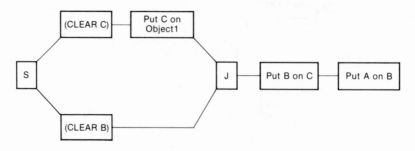

Figure D1–8.   Level 4, final plan.

D2. MOLGEN

THE PREVIOUS articles have demonstrated the utility of *problem-reduction* in planning—dividing a problem into subproblems that are more easily solved. But problem reduction has an associated liability, namely, that subproblems are rarely independent. Solving one may prevent solving another. A number of approaches to this problem have been presented in the previous articles. HACKER and INTERPLAN used destructive reordering of subgoals; Walding-er's system employed a more constructive goal-regression method (see Article XV.C). In NOAH (Article XV.D1), the conceptual leap was to avoid linear orderings of subproblems as long as possible and to plan initially with abstract goals that were refined in such a way as to avoid subproblem interactions.

In this article, we discuss the MOLGEN system—a knowledge-based program that assists molecular geneticists in planning experiments. There are actually two MOLGEN planners, one developed by Friedland (1979; see also Article XV.E) and another, the one this article is about, by Stefik (1980). MOLGEN extends the work on hierarchical planning to include a *layered* control structure for *meta-planning*. Plans are constructed in one layer, decisions about the design of the plan are made in a higher layer, and strategies that dictate the design decisions are made at a still higher level. A key idea in MOLGEN is to represent the interactions between subproblems explicitly and declaratively, so that MOLGEN can reason about them and use them to guide its planning. The structure that represents an interaction is called a *constraint*.

Levels of Planning

Control of planning in MOLGEN switches between three *layers*, or *spaces*. The lowest layer, called the *planning space*, contains a hierarchy of operations and objects typical in a gene-splicing experiment. At the lowest level of this layer are bacteria, drugs, and laboratory operations, which are represented by knowledge structures called *units* (Stefik, 1979); generalizations of these include the general objects *gene, organism,* and *plasmid* and the general laboratory operations *merging, amplifying, reacting,* and *sorting*. Initially, MOLGEN plans experiments with these abstract objects and operators. As it chooses specific operators or objects to replace the abstract ones, it introduces constraints into its plan. For example, it plans at an abstract level to *sort* two kinds of bacteria. At a later time, *sort* is replaced by *screen*, which sorts bacteria by killing one group of them with an antibiotic. This decision results in the constraint that the antibiotic be potent against one kind of bacterium but not the other.

The utility of hierarchical planning is illustrated by the preceding example. It shows that although a planning decision to use a particular operation affects later decisions about the kinds of objects to use, this interaction is absent as long as the plan is formulated at an abstract level. Using hierarchical planning, a complete, abstract plan is constructed without attention to these interactions. Then, as steps in the plan are *refined,* the interactions that arise are explicitly represented as constraints and are resolved. The act of refining plan steps involves replacing an abstract operator with a more specific one or replacing an abstract object with a more specific one. If hierarchical planning were not used, every planning decision would introduce interactions; each decision would affect the decisions following it. Early planners like those discussed in Article XV.C produced initial plans that were crippled by interactions and then attempted to reorder planning steps to alleviate them. These planners were said to *overconstrain* their plans; in contrast, MOLGEN and NOAH (see Article XV.D1) produce *underconstrained* plans and add constraints *constructively.*

The middle layer at which MOLGEN plans is called the *design space.* At this level, MOLGEN makes decisions about how its plan is to develop. The operators of the design space dictate steps taken in the design of a plan, for example, proposing a goal or refining an operator. The objects in this space include *goals* and *constraints.* MOLGEN reasons about plans with the objects and operators in the design space, just as it reasons about molecular genetics with the objects and operators in the planning space.

The top layer of planning for MOLGEN, the *strategy space,* includes four very general operators that dictate planning strategy. These are FOCUS and RESUME, which together propose new planning steps and reactivate old ones that have been "put on hold," and GUESS and UNDO, which make planning decisions heuristically when there is not sufficient information to focus or to resume. UNDO is a backtracking operator that undoes decisions that have overconstrained a plan. Much of the research effort in MOLGEN has gone into avoiding backtracking by developing underconstrained plans, but in the rare cases where a guess must be made about a plan step (e.g., choosing the identity of a bacterium), the unforeseen constraints introduced by the choice may force backtracking and a different choice.

Of the three layers of planning in MOLGEN, only the planning space is unique to a domain, in this case, molecular genetics. The design and strategy spaces contain objects and operators that apply to planning in any domain.

Control of Planning in MOLGEN

The three layers discussed above constitute a hierarchically organized control structure for MOLGEN. At the highest level, the strategy space, decisions are made about the style of planning. Two styles are available, *least commitment* and *heuristic.* During the least-commitment cycle, MOLGEN sends a message to the design operators in the design space asking whether they can suggest any tasks to do. Tasks include proposing a goal (after noticing a difference between the current state and the goal state), refining an object or an operator, and formulating a constraint. MOLGEN may fail to find a task for which it has the constraints to proceed successfully; for example, it may propose to refine an object—a bacterium—to a particular species of bacterium, but it may lack the guarantee that this refinement will not interfere with later steps in the plan. In this case, it will *suspend* this step and look for another. If MOLGEN cannot find any design steps to execute immediately, it checks whether any previously suspended steps can be executed; information may have become available since their suspension that justifies their reactivation. The least-commitment cycle oscillates between finding a planning step to execute and reactivating suspended steps in the light of new information. It is called *least commitment* because it will not commit itself to a plan step that might have to be abandoned at some later point in the development of the plan. If MOLGEN cannot find a plan step that satisfies the requirements of the least-commitment cycle, it switches to the heuristic cycle in which it guesses a plan step.

MOLGEN uses three kinds of operations on constraints. The first, called *constraint formulation*, involves identifying interactions between solutions for goals. Often the goals are to refine abstract objects or operators; for example, the goal of sorting two kinds of bacteria is achieved by *screening* one of them with an antibiotic. When this solution is proposed, a constraint is formulated, saying that the choice of bacterium and antibiotic is now constrained by the requirement that one kind of bacterium should be susceptible to the antibiotic.

The second operation with constraints is called *constraint propagation*. This is the creation of new constraints from old ones, which helps refine abstract parts of a plan. For example, the single constraint described above reduces the number of bacteria or antibiotics that MOLGEN is considering, because not all bacteria are susceptible to all antibiotics. Constraint propagation collects other constraints on the bacterium and antibiotic, formulated perhaps in other parts of the plan. As a result of constraint propagation, abstract plan steps that might have been refined in dozens of ways are constrained to have a relatively small number of potential refinements. Often, individual subproblems are constrained to some extent, but not enough to narrow down the space of solutions significantly. However, when the individual constraints on individual subproblems are propagated, the sum of the constraints often eliminates one or more solutions. For example, during a day, a person may have two goals: to get some exercise and to get to school in a short time for a class. The first problem, to get exercise, is constrained only by the requirement that it is energetic; the second problem, to get to school, is constrained only by the requirement that it take a short time. Propagating these constraints leads to the obvious solution that one should run or ride a bike to school.

Following constraint formulation and propagation, MOLGEN seeks to *satisfy* constraints. In the domain of molecular genetics, this often involves replacing an abstract object with a particular one that satisfies the constraints put on it. For example, it may involve replacing the object *bacterium* with *e. coli* and replacing the object *antibiotic* with *tetracycline*. Whatever the results of constraint satisfaction, it is facilitated by constraint formulation and propagation, which together narrow down the space of refinements that is considered for each subproblem.

The formulation-propagation-satisfaction cycle is a *constructive* process; abstract parts of plans usually are refined only when there are constraints specifying the refinement. The antithesis of this constructive cycle is found in rare cases in which MOLGEN lacks the constraints needed to refine a plan step. It guesses a refinement that may be shown at a later time to interfere with other parts of the plan, in which case the refinement is abandoned for another. This process is destructive, since it may involve throwing away old planning decisions.

An Example

MOLGEN has been used to find plans for the *rat-insulin* experiment (Stefik, 1980). Many organisms produce insulin that is biologically active in humans but can sometimes cause allergic reactions. An alternative to extracting insulin from the pancreas of animals is to design a bacterium that produces insulin. No bacteria are known to produce insulin naturally, so one must be created. To do this, the gene coding for insulin production in rats was spliced into bacteria, altering the genetic makeup of the bacteria and causing them to produce insulin. This experiment was done in 1977; it was selected as a test case for MOLGEN, which successfully designed four different plans for the experiment.

The major steps in the experiment involved finding a medium in which to embed the insulin gene, allowing some bacteria to absorb this medium, killing off the bacteria that did not absorb the medium, and growing the culture of those that did. The plan is simple at this abstract level—that is the advantage of hierarchical planning. The complete plan is actually quite complicated and involves many constraints.

MOLGEN represents the goal of the experiment using the most abstract objects it knows of. The goal is to obtain a culture with

```
ORGANISMS = (A Bacterium with
              EXOSOMES = (A Vector with
                          GENES = (RAT-INSULIN))).
```

Planning in MOLGEN is driven by *means-ends analysis*, which is to say that, at each step of the planning process, MOLGEN seeks operators that will reduce the *differences* between the current state of the plan and its goal. In this case, MOLGEN makes a very abstract plan to build, from available objects, the organism specified in the goal. It plans two *merges* of objects to achieve its goal. The first merge involves the insulin gene and a *vector* (a medium for carrying the gene into the body of a bacterium), and the second merge involves the results of the first merge and the bacterium:

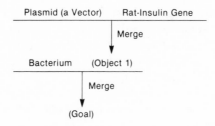

Next, MOLGEN refines the two abstract merges to more specific operations. The second merge, by which a bacterium absorbs a plasmid carrying new genes, corresponds to a laboratory step called a *transformation*. But MOLGEN knows that not all plasmids are absorbed by all bacteria, so it formulates the constraint that they be compatible. MOLGEN also knows that *transformation* operators work by mixing plasmids and bacteria together in a solution and that some bacteria will not absorb the plasmid. This leads to a difference between the goal of the experiment and the state resulting from the plan: The goal is to have a single culture of bacteria carrying a particular gene, but the plan results in a culture of bacteria in which some bacteria do not carry the gene.

Since planning is driven by differences between the current state and the goal, MOLGEN tries to solve the problem of getting rid of the unwanted bacteria. To do this, it proposes to *sort* the culture. *Sort* is an abstract operator that is next refined to *screening* the bacteria with an antibiotic. Note that the antibiotic is not specified because the bacterium is not. However, the refinement of *sort* to *screen* results in two constraints: that the bacteria that absorb the plasmid should resist the antibiotic and that the bacteria that do not absorb the plasmid should perish from the antibiotic.

At this point, MOLGEN *propagates* the constraints about antibiotic resistance. The result of the propagation is that both constraints on the bacteria are replaced by a single constraint on the plasmid itself. The reasoning is that, since the only difference between the two kinds of bacteria is that one carries the plasmid, the plasmid itself must confer immunity to the antibiotic. Notice that this reasoning does not change any of the plan steps that have already taken place, but it does constrain MOLGEN to include a resistance gene for an antibiotic in the plasmid.

So far, MOLGEN has done a little bit of planning at an abstract level and a lot of reasoning about how to refine the abstract plan into a detailed one. It has proposed a *merge* of a gene and a plasmid, a *transformation* of that result into two bacteria, and a *screening* of the bacteria to obtain the desired one. The identities of the bacteria, the screening agent, the resistance gene, and the plasmid that will carry the genes are unknown, but MOLGEN knows some things about these objects in the form of constraints. For example, the resistance gene and the antibiotic must be compatible, and the plasmid must be compatible with the bacterium. As MOLGEN continues to plan, particularly to plan how to insert the desired genes in a plasmid, other constraints will be formulated.

Eventually, MOLGEN will be able to satisfy constraints. By then, it will have refined the plan to a point where the only bacterium that it knows will satisfy all the constraints is *e. coli*. Similarly, it will have found just one method of inserting genes into a plasmid (though this was not done through constraint propagation but because MOLGEN knows of only one such method). It will have found two antibiotics—*tetracycline* and *ampicillin*—and four plasmids that satisfy the constraints. Thus, it finds four solutions to the rat-insulin problem.

MOLGEN's solution to the rat-insulin experiment was more complex than the abbreviated version presented here. In all, a dozen constraints emerged during the planning process. The development of the plan was complex, requiring about 30 pages of printout to document.

Conclusion

We have seen that MOLGEN can develop a complex plan without ever undoing a planning decision. Its *least-commitment* strategy dictates that it defer decisions for which it lacks constraints, and, thus, it rarely commits itself to a decision that it must later undo.

MOLGEN plans at different levels of abstraction, and it also works at three levels of planning actions to accomplish *meta-planning:* At the highest level it makes *strategy* decisions, at the middle level it makes *design* decisions, and at the lowest level it decides how to *instantiate* its design.

References

Stefik's MOLGEN system is discussed in his doctoral dissertation (1980).

E. REFINEMENT OF SKELETAL PLANS

ONE WAY to develop methods for AI systems is to observe the methods that humans use. Such an approach is typically taken by cognitive scientists (see Chap. XI) to develop models of cognition. This article describes a molecular genetics (MOLGEN) planning system developed by Peter Friedland after studying human experiment-planning behavior. The major observation of the study was that scientists rarely invent from scratch the plan for an experiment. Most often, they begin with an abstract, or *skeletal*, plan that contains the basic steps. Then they instantiate each of the plan steps by a method that will work within the environment of the particular problem. Skeletal plans range from general to specific, depending on the experimenter and the problem. This MOLGEN system is one of two such systems developed at Stanford University; the other, by Mark Stefik, is discussed in Article XV.D2.

This article gives an example of skeletal plans in the laboratory and discusses the implementation of the method in the MOLGEN system for the design of experiments in molecular biology.

Two Examples of Analysis Experiments

As an introduction to the skeletal-plan method, two simplified and related examples of analysis experiments in molecular biology are presented, namely, DNA sequencing and restriction-site mapping. Both experiments involve similar sequences of actions; consequently, they are discussed as variants of a single skeletal plan.

DNA sequencing: The problem. DNA is composed of a linear string of molecules called bases. There are four possible bases, adenine, cytosine, guanine, and thymine, usually abbreviated A, C, G, and T. The goal of a sequencing experiment is to determine which of the four bases is present at each position on the molecule. The base sequence is extremely important in determining both the biological function and the physical structure of the entire DNA molecule.

DNA sequencing: The solution. One of the best current experimental plans for DNA sequencing, known as Maxam-Gilbert sequencing (Maxam and Gilbert, 1974), is as follows:

1. Label one end of the molecule with radioactive phosphorus. This gives the experimenter a "handle" for later locating pieces of the molecule attached to the radioactive end. Radioactive-phosphorus labeling is the current method of choice for end-labeling of DNA.

2. Divide the sample into four portions. For each portion, apply a hydrazine-based chemical reaction that cuts the molecule at a particular base. Control the reaction so that, on the average, one base is cut per molecule. Each of the four samples will then contain a population of molecules of lengths determined by the base that was cut in that sample.

3. Determine the lengths of the molecules in each population with a labeled end. This is done by a technique called acrylamide gel electrophoresis, which is currently the most accurate method for the separation of molecules by length.

For example, suppose the starting sequence was AGTTCGA. The sample for which the molecule was cut at the A base would show labeled molecules of lengths 0 and 6, the C sample would show molecules of length 4, the G sample would show molecules of lengths 1 and 5, and the T sample would show molecules of lengths 2 and 3. The sequence can now be "read" directly from these lengths.

Restriction-site mapping: The problem. Restriction enzymes are used to cut DNA molecules at specific locations. The locations are specified by a pattern of four, five, or six bases called a restriction site. The goal of a mapping experiment is to find all of the restriction sites for common enzymes on a molecule. This information tells the molecular geneticist which enzymes to use or not to use in a future experiment that requires restriction cutting.

Restriction-site mapping: The solution. One of the best current methods (Smith and Birnsteil, 1976) is as follows:

1. Label the end with radioactive phosphorus as above.

2. Divide the sample into as many new samples as restriction enzymes for which a map is desired. Then, for each sample, do a "partial digest" with one restriction enzyme. This means to control the laboratory conditions (temperature, pH, time of application) so that only one or two sites are cut on the average molecule. As above, a population of molecules will exist in each sample.

3. Determine the length of the labeled molecules by means of electrophoresis, as above. The length measurements will locate each of the restriction sites for each enzyme tested.

The Skeletal Plan Refinement Method

Clearly, the two experiments described above are closely related. Each had the goal of locating the position of a specific site—either a single base or a string of bases—on the molecule. Each had the same design; they differed only in the middle, cutting step. Both experiments sprang from the same basic idea:

1. Label one end of the molecule;

2. Cut with an agent that makes an average of one cut per molecule at the sites that are being mapped;

3. Determine the length of the labeled fragments.

This is an abstracted or skeletal plan that is useful for locating any type of site for which there is a suitable cutting agent.

The plan is transformed into an actual design for an experiment by refining each step in the plan—by instantiating it with a method that will actually work in the laboratory. The first and third steps of the experiments— phosphorus labeling and gel electrophoresis—were chosen because they were the best methods available. The choice of the second step was directed by the specific choice of site to be mapped.

The idea here, again, is that scientists rarely invent an experimental design from scratch. They find a strategy, a skeletal plan, that was useful for some related experimental goal and then instantiate it with the proper laboratory methods for their specific goal and laboratory conditions. The skeletal plan may be very specific if the goal is similar to one for which a very good experiment has already been designed. It may also be extremely general, as was the plan in the example above.

Implementation in MOLGEN

The skeletal plan method is used successfully in the MOLGEN system. Since the method depends heavily on domain knowledge, a well-organized, expert knowledge base is the central part of the system. The Unit package (Stefik, 1979) is used by domain experts to construct a knowledge base containing both a selection of skeletal plans and the objective and procedural knowledge necessary to instantiate the plans competently. The Unit package permits the domain experts to describe such information in a language natural to them as molecular biologists.

The two major steps in planning by incremental refinement of skeletal plans—plan selection and plan-step refinement—are described separately below.

Choosing a skeletal plan. Skeletal plans are specified at many levels of generality. At the most general level, there are only a few basic plans. These are used as fallbacks when plans that are easier to refine and that are more specific cannot be found. The problem is not just one of finding a plan that might provide a satisfactory solution, but of finding a plan that will require the least refinement work. Skeletal plan finding reduces to a simple lookup when exactly the same problem has been solved before (even if this were done with a completely different set of laboratory and molecular conditions), but it becomes more difficult when only related problems have been solved. Then the task may be to decide whether to choose a detailed plan for a related problem or to choose a more general plan for a class of problems.

The MOLGEN work has only begun to treat these problems of plan selection. Plans are classified according to their perceived utility by molecular geneticists. The specificity of the utilities (any given skeletal plan could have many) is totally up to the experts. The knowledge base contains also a taxonomy of goals in molecular biology. When a problem is described to the planning system, a search is made of the skeletal-plan utilities to see if any exactly match the experimental design goal. If several do, all are tried; if none does, a more general goal is chosen from the taxonomy and the process is repeated.

Refining the skeletal plan. Refinement of the skeletal plan is the process of selecting an appropriate ground-level instantiation for each step in the abstract plan. In the example above, the ground-level instantiation of labeling was radioactive phosphorus. This refinement process is usually hierarchical; a scientist might decide first on the method of cutting, then on a cutting enzyme, and finally on a specific enzyme.

Knowledge about laboratory techniques is organized hierarchically in MOLGEN. There were several broad classes of techniques, with as many subclasses as are deemed natural by the domain experts. In all, about 400 different techniques are described in the knowledge base.

The MOLGEN system proceeds linearly through the steps of a selected skeletal plan. The steps are matched to the techniques in the knowledge base by name, synonym, or function of the step. A specific technique—as specific as can be directly determined from the plan step—is chosen, and then the instantiation process begins.

The knowledge to do the instantiation is stored in the form of an English-like procedural language within the knowledge base. This knowledge represents three major criteria for plan-step instantiation. In order of priority of application they are:

1. Will the technique, if successfully applied, carry out the specific goal of the step; for example, will a separatory method not just do some sort of separation, but also separate all circular DNA from all linear DNA?

2. If the technique satisfies the first criterion, can it be successfully applied to the given molecule under the given laboratory conditions?

3. Is the technique the "best" of those that passed the first two tests? This choice point, while in some sense the least important (since all techniques that make it to this point will work), seems to be the hardest for scientists to define. All the scientists studied gave somewhat different metrics involving reliability, convenience, accuracy, cost, and time to carry out the technique. The heuristic chosen as most representative gave greatest weight to four-point scales of convenience and reliability as an initial filter.

This knowledge is used to proceed down a level in the technique hierarchy; the process is repeated until an actual instance of a technique is chosen. At higher levels of the hierarchy (i.e., with less refined plans), a premium is set on achieving goals; but at lower levels of the hierarchy, a premium is set on making plans efficient and elegant.

This strategy-finding process is common to many disciplines. In his book *How to Solve It*, Polya (1957) describes "mobilizing" problem-solving knowledge:

> Many of these questions and suggestions aim directly at *mobilization* of our formerly acquired knowledge: *Have you seen it before? Or have you seen the same problem in a slightly different form? Do you know a related problem? Do you know a theorem that could be useful?* (p. 159; italics in original)

The idea is to avoid reinventing general strategies and to use plan outlines that have worked in the past on related problems.

Related Work

The concept of a skeletal plan for experimental design has a direct precedent in Schank and Abelson's work in natural-language understanding (see Article IV.F6, in Vol. I). They introduce *scripts*, declarative representations of ordered sequences of events. The detailed knowledge contained in scripts is used to understand, predict, and participate in events one has encountered previously.

Schank and Abelson also introduce generalized scripts, called *plans*, that explain events related to, but not exactly like, those the user has seen before. "Plans are where scripts come from.... The difference is that scripts are specific and plans are general" (Schank and Abelson, 1977, p. 72). In fact, there is a continuum between scripts and plans in Schank and Abelson's work: "There is a fine line between the point where scripts leave off and plans begin.... When a script is available for satisfying a goal, it is chosen. Otherwise a plan is chosen" (p. 77; see also Article IV.F6, in Vol. I).

The idea of abstracted plans is found also in the STRIPS planner (Fikes, Hart, and Nilsson, 1972; see also Article II.D5, in Vol. I). This system parameterized successful plans in order to generalize them. The generalized plans were called MACROPs (for macro-operators).

There are several distinctions between skeletal plan refinement and some of the other methods discussed in this chapter—for example, Stefik's parallel work on planning in molecular biology (see Article XV.D2). Other methods emphasize building the initial abstract plan; this method assumes the initial plan is already known and emphasizes the plan selection and instantiation process. Other methods concentrate on the interaction of plan steps; this method, in large part, considers plan steps to be sufficiently independent that conflicts can be resolved by relatively minor subplans. Finally, other methods place relatively little emphasis on domain-specific expertise, whereas such expertise is the heart of this planning method.

Conclusion

The reader may be surprised by the simplicity of the method of skeletal plan refinement but should remember that it attempts to produce competent—rather than wildly innovative—plans. It is based on the observation that human scientists who know a lot about their domains, and who have flexible cross-associations for choosing steps in an experiment, are usually good at experimental design. There are very few totally new plan outlines discovered, but many new plan instantiations.

References

A source for this article and a good discussion of this implementation of MOLGEN is Friedland's doctoral dissertation (1979).

Bibliography

List of Abbreviations

AAAI	American Association for Artificial Intelligence
ACM	Association for Computing Machinery
AFIPS	American Federation of Information Processing Societies
AMS	American Mathematical Society
CACM	Communications of the Association for Computing Machinery
IEEE	Institute for Electrical and Electronic Engineers
IJCAI	International Joint Conferences on AI
IJCPR	International Joint Conferences on Pattern Recognition
IRE WESCON	Western Conference of the Institute for Radio Engineers
SIGART	ACM Special Interest Group on AI
SIGPLAN	ACM Special Interest Group on Programming Languages
SPIE	Society of Photo-Optical Instrumentation Engineers
TINLAP	Workshops on Theoretical Issues in Natural Language Processing

BIBLIOGRAPHY

Abbott, R. 1977. The new Eleusis. Available from author: Box 1175, General Post Office, New York, NY 10116.

Abelson, R. P. 1973. The structure of belief systems. In R. C. Schank and K. M. Colby (Eds.), *Computer models of thought and language.* San Francisco: Freeman.

Abelson, R. P. 1979. Differences between belief and knowledge systems. *Cognitive Science* 3:355–366.

Abelson, R. P., and Reich, C. M. 1969. Implicational molecules: A method for extracting meaning from input sentences. *IJCAI 1,* 647–748.

Aggarwal, J. K., and Badler, N. 1980. Special issue on motion and time-varying imagery. *IEEE Transactions on Pattern Analysis and Machine Intelligence* PAMI–2:495–588.

Aggarwal, J. K., and Duda, R. O. 1975. Computer analysis of moving polygonal images. *IEEE Transactions on Computers* C–24:966–976.

Agin, G. J., and Binford, T. O. 1973. Computer description of curved objects. *IJCAI 3,* 629–640.

Aho, A. V., Hopcroft, J. E., and Ullman, J. D. 1974. *The design and analysis of computer algorithms.* Reading, Mass.: Addison-Wesley.

Altschuler, M. D., Altschuler, T. B., and Taboada, J. 1981. A laser electro-optic system for rapid 3-D topographic mapping of surface. MIPG51, Computer Science Dept., State University of New York, Buffalo.

Amarel, S. 1968. On representations of problems of reasoning about actions. In D. Michie (Ed.), *Machine intelligence 3.* New York: American Elsevier, 131–171.

Anderson, J. R. 1976. *Language, memory, and thought.* Hillsdale, N.J.: Lawrence Erlbaum.

Anderson, J. R. 1977. Induction of augmented transition networks. *Cognitive Science* 1:125–157.

Anderson, J. R. 1980. On the merits of ACT and information-processing psychology: A response to Wexler's review. *Cognition* 8:73–88.

Anderson, J. R., and Bower, G. H. 1973. *Human associative memory.* Washington, D.C.: Winston.

Arnold, D. 1978. Local context in matching edges for stereo vision. *Proceedings of the Image Understanding Workshop,* 65–72.

Baddeley, A. D. 1976. *The psychology of memory.* New York: Basic Books.

Badler, N. 1975. *Temporal scene analysis: Conceptual descriptions of objects' movements.* Doctoral dissertation, Computer Science Dept., University of Toronto.

Badler, N., and Bajcsy, R. 1978. 3-D representations of computer graphics and computer vision. *Computer Graphics* 12:153–160.

Badler, N., O'Rourke, J., and Tolzis, H. 1979. A spherical representation of a human body for visualizing movement. *Proceedings of the IEEE* 67:1397–1403.

Baird, M. L. 1978. SIGHT–I: A computer vision system for automated chip manufacture. *IEEE Transactions on Systems, Man, and Cybernetics* SMC–8(2):133–139.

Bajcsy, R. 1973. Computer descriptions of textured surfaces. *IJCAI 3*, 572–579.

Baker, H. 1980. Edge-based stereo correlation. *Proceedings of the Image Understanding Workshop*, 168–175.

Ballantyne, A. M., and Bennett, W. 1973. Graphing methods for topological proofs. Memo ATP–7, Mathematics Dept., University of Texas, Austin.

Ballantyne, A. M., and Bledsoe, W. W. 1975. Automatic proofs of theorems in analysis using non-standard techniques. Memo ATP–23, Mathematics Dept., University of Texas, Austin. (Also in *J. ACM*, July, 1977.)

Ballantyne, A. M., and Lankford, D. 1979. New decision algorithms for finitely presented commutative semigroups. Memo MTP–4, Mathematics Dept., Louisiana Tech University.

Ballard, D. H. 1981. Parameter networks: Towards a theory of low-level vision. *IJCAI 7*, 1068–1078.

Ballard, D. H., and Brown, C. M. 1982. *Computer vision*. Englewood Cliffs, N.J.: Prentice-Hall.

Ballard, D. H., Brown, C. M., and Feldman, J. A. 1978. An approach to knowledge-directed image analysis. In A. R. Hanson and E. M. Riseman (Eds.), *Computer vision systems*. New York: Academic Press, 271–281.

Barnard, S. T., and Fischler, M. A. 1981. Computational stereo from an IU perspective. In *Proceedings of the Image Understanding Workshop*, 157–167.

Barnea, D. I., and Silverman, H. F. 1972. A class of algorithms for fast digital image registration. *IEEE Transactions on Computers* C–21(12): 179–186.

Barr, A., Bennett, J., and Clancey, W. 1979. Transfer of expertise: A theme for AI research. Rep. No. HPP–79–11, Heuristic Programming Project, Stanford University.

Barrow, H. G., et al. 1977. Interactive aids for cartography and photo interpretation. *Proceedings of the Image Understanding Workshop*, 111–127.

Barrow, H. G., and Popplestone, P. J. 1971. Relational descriptions in picture processing. In B. Meltzer and D. Michie (Eds.), *Machine intelligence 6*. New York: Elsevier, 377–396.

Barrow, H. G., and Tenenbaum, J. M. 1978. Recovering intrinsic scene characteristics from images. In A. R. Hanson and E. M. Riseman (Eds.), *Computer vision systems*. New York: Academic Press, 3–26.

Barrow, H. G., and Tenenbaum, J. M. 1979. Reconstructing smooth surfaces from partial, noisy information. *Proceedings of the Image Understanding Workshop*, 76–86.

Bibel, W., and Schreiber, J. 1974. Proof search in a Gentzen-like system of first order logic. Bericht Nr. 7412, Technische Universitat, Munich.

Biermann, A., and Feldman, J. 1970. On the synthesis of finite-state acceptors. AI Memo 114, Computer Science Dept., Stanford University.

Biermann, A., and Feldman, J. 1972. A survey of results in grammatical inference. In S. Watanabe (Ed.), *Frontiers of pattern recognition*. New York: Academic Press.

Black, F. 1968. A deductive question-answering system. In M. Minsky (Ed.), *Semantic information processing*. Cambridge, Mass.: MIT Press, 354–402.

Bledsoe, W. W. 1971. Splitting and reduction heuristics in automatic theorem proving. *Artificial Intelligence* 2:55–77.

Bledsoe, W. W. 1974. The sup-inf method in Presburger arithmetic. Memo ATP–18, Mathematics Dept., University of Texas, Austin.

Bledsoe, W. W. 1975. A new method for proving certain Presburger formulas. *IJCAI 4*, 15–21.

Bledsoe, W. W. 1977. Non-resolution theorem proving. *Artificial Intelligence* 9:1–35.

Bledsoe, W. W., and Ballantyne, A. M. 1979. On automatic generation of counterexamples, Memo ATP–44A, Mathematics Dept., University of Texas, Austin.

Bledsoe, W. W., Bruell, P., and Shostak, R. 1979. A prover for general inequalities. Memo TPP–40A, Mathematics Dept., University of Texas, Austin.

Bledsoe, W. W., and Tyson, M. 1975. The UT interactive theorem prover. Memo ATP–17, Mathematics Dept., University of Texas, Austin.

Bobrow, D. G. (Ed.). 1980. Special issue on non-monotonic logic. *Artificial Intelligence* 13(1,2).

Bobrow, D. G., and Collins, A. 1975. *Representation and understanding*. New York: Academic Press.

Bobrow, D. G., and Raphael, B. 1974. New programming languages for artificial intelligence. *Computing Surveys* 6.

Bolles, R. C., et al. 1978. The SRI Road Expert. *Proceedings of the Image Understanding Workshop*, 163–174.

Bolles, R. C., Kremers, J. H., and Cain, R. A. 1981. A simple sensor to gather three-dimensional data. Tech. Note 249, SRI International, Inc., Menlo Park, Calif.

Bourne, D. A. 1981. On automatically generating a program for real time computer vision. *IJCPR* 5:759–764.

Bower, G. H. 1981. Mood and memory. *American Psychologist* 36:129–148.

Boyer, R. S. 1971. *Locking: A restriction of resolution*. Doctoral dissertation, University of Texas, Austin.

Boyer, R. S., and Moore, J. S. 1979. A computational logic. New York: Academic Press.

Brachman, R. J. 1978. On the epistemological status of semantic networks. BBN Rep. No. 3807, Bolt Beranek and Newman, Inc., Cambridge, Mass.

Brice, C. R., and Fennema, C. L. 1970. Scene analysis using regions. *Artificial Intelligence* 1:205–226.

Brodatz, P. 1966. *Textures*. New York: Dover.

Brooks, R. A. 1981a. Model-based three dimensional interpretations of two dimensional images. *IJCAI 7*, 619–624.

Brooks, R. A. 1981b. Symbolic reasoning among 3-d objects and 2-d models. *AI Journal* 16:285–348.

Brooks, R. A., Greiner, R., and Binford, T. 1978. Progress report on a model-based vision system. In L. S. Baumann (Ed.), *Proceedings of the Image Understanding Workshop*, 145–151.

Brown, R., and Hanlon, C. 1970. Derivational complexity and order of acquisition in child speech. In J. Hayes (Ed.), *Cognition and the development of language*. New York: Wiley, 11–53.

Buchanan, B. G., and Mitchell, T. M. 1978. Model-directed learning of production rules. In D. A. Waterman and F. Hayes-Roth (Eds.), *Pattern-directed inference systems*. New York: Academic Press, 297–312.

Buchanan, B. G., Mitchell, T. M., Smith, R. G., and Johnson, C. R., Jr. 1977. Models of learning systems. In J. Belzer, A. G. Holzman, and A. Kent (Eds.), *Encyclopedia of computer science and technology* (Vol. 11). New York: Marcel Dekker, 24–51.

Burstall, R. 1969. Proving properties of programs by structural induction. *Computer Journal* 12(1):41–48.

Carnap, R. 1950. *Logical foundations of probability*. Chicago: University of Chicago Press.

Chang, C., and Lee, R. C. 1973. *Symbolic logic and mechanical theorem proving*. New York: Academic Press.

Cherry, C. 1970. *On human communication*. Cambridge, Mass.: MIT Press.

Chien, Y. P., and Fu, K. S. 1974. A decision function method for boundary detection. *Computer Graphics and Image Processing* 3:125–140.

Chomsky, N. 1957. *Syntactic structures*. The Hague: Mouton.

Chomsky, N. 1965. *Aspects of the theory of syntax*. Cambridge, Mass.: MIT Press.

Chow, W. K., and Aggarwal, J. K. 1977. Computer analysis of planar curvilinear moving images. *IEEE Transactions on Computers* C–26:179–185.

Clowes, M. B. 1971. On seeing things. *Artificial Intelligence* 2:79–116.

Colby, K. M. 1975. *Artificial paranoia*. New York: Pergamon.

Coleman, G. B., and Andrews, H. C. 1979. Image segmentation by clustering. *Proceedings of the IEEE* 67(5):773–785.

Collins, A. M. 1978. Fragments of a theory of human plausible reasoning. *TINLAP–2*, 194–201.

Collins, A. M., and Quillian, M. R. 1969. Retrieval time from semantic memory. *Journal of Verbal Learning and Verbal Behavior* 8:240–247.

Collins, A. M., and Quillian, M. R. 1972. How to make a language user. In E. Tulving and W. Donaldson (Eds.), *Organization and memory*. New York: Academic Press.

Colmerauer, A., Kanoui, H., Pasero, R., and Roussel, P. 1973. Un systeme de communication homme-machine en français. In *Rapport, Groupe d'Intelligence Artificielle, Universite d'Aix-Marseille, Luminy, France*.

Conrad, C. 1972. Cognitive economy in semantic memory. *Journal of Experimental Psychology* 92:149–154.

Cook, C. M., and Rosenfeld, A. 1976. Some experiments in grammatical inference. In J. C. Simon (Ed.), *Proceedings of the NATO Advanced Study Institute on Computer Oriented Learning Processes*. Leyden, The Netherlands: Noordhoff.

Corkill, D. D. 1979. Hierarchical planning in a distributed environment. *IJCAI 6*, 168–175.

Crowder, R. G. 1976. *Principles of learning and memory*. Hillsdale, N.J.: Lawrence Erlbaum.

Dacey, R. 1978. A theory of conclusions. *Philosophy of Science* 45:563–574.

Date, C. J. 1977. *An introduction to database systems* (2nd ed.). Reading, Mass.: Addison-Wesley.

Davis, L. S. 1975. A survey of edge detection techniques. *Computer Graphics and Image Processing* 4:248–270.

Davis, L. S. 1976. Shape matching using relaxation techniques. Tech. Rep. TR–480, Computer Science Center, University of Maryland.

Davis, R. 1976. Applications of meta level knowledge to the construction, maintenance, and use of large knowledge bases. Rep. No. STAN–CS–76–564, Computer Science Dept., Stanford University. (Doctoral dissertation. Reprinted in R. Davis and D. B. Lenat (Eds.). 1980. *Knowledge based systems in artificial intelligence.* New York: McGraw-Hill.)

Davis, R. 1978. Knowledge acquisition in rule-based systems: Knowledge about representations as a basis for system construction and maintenance. In D. A. Waterman and F. Hayes-Roth (Eds.), *Pattern-directed inference systems.* New York: Academic Press, 99–134.

de Kleer, J., et al. 1979. Explicit control of reasoning. In P. H. Winston and R. H. Brown (Eds.), *Artificial intelligence: An MIT perspective* (Vol. 1). Cambridge, Mass.: MIT Press, 93–116.

Dietterich, T. G. 1979. The methodology of knowledge layers for inducing descriptions of sequentially ordered events. Rep. No. UIUC–DCS–80–1024, Computer Science Dept., University of Illinois, Urbana.

Dietterich, T. G. 1980. Applying general induction methods to the card game Eleusis. *AAAI 1,* 218–220.

Dietterich, T. G., and Michalski, R. S. 1979. Learning and generalization of characteristic descriptions: Evaluation criteria and comparative review of selected methods. *IJCAI 6,* 223–231.

Dietterich, T. G., and Michalski, R. S. 1981. Inductive learning of structural descriptions: Evaluation criteria and comparative review of selected methods. *Artificial Intelligence* 16:257–294.

Dietterich, T. G., and Michalski, R. S. In press. Discovering sequence generating rules.

Dodd, G. G., and Rossel, L. (Eds.). 1979. *Computer vision and sensor-based robots.* New York: Plenum.

Doyle, J. 1979. A truth maintenance system. *Artificial Intelligence* 12:231–272.

Doyle, J. 1980. A model for deliberation, action, and introspection. Tech. Rep. AI–TR–581, AI Laboratory, Massachusetts Institute of Technology. (Doctoral dissertation.)

Doyle, J., and London, P. 1980. A selected descriptor-induced bibliography to the literature on belief revision. *SIGART Newsletter* 71:7–23.

Druffel, L. 1981. Summary of DARPA image understanding program. *Proceedings of SPIE—The International Society for Optical Engineering* 281:2–10.

Duda, R. O., and Hart, P. E. 1973. *Pattern classification and scene analysis.* New York: Wiley.

Duda, R. O., Nitzan, D., and Barrett, P. 1979. Use of range and reflectance data to find planar surface regions. *IEEE Transactions on Pattern Analysis and Machine Intelligence* PAMI–1:259–271.

Ejiri, M., Uno, T., Mese, M., and Ikeda, S. 1973. 1973. A process for detecting defects in complicated patterns. *Computer Graphics and Image Processing* 2:326–339.

Erman, L. D., Hayes-Roth, F., Lesser, V. R., and Reddy, D. R. 1980. The HEARSAY–II speech-understanding system: Integrating knowledge to resolve uncertainty. *Computing Surveys* 12:2.

Ernst, G. W. 1971. The utility of independent subgoals in theorem proving. *Information and Control* 18:237–252.

Ernst, G. W. 1973. A definition-driven theorem prover. *IJCAI 3*.

Evans, T. G. 1971. Grammatical inference techniques in pattern analysis. In J. T. Tou (Ed.), *Software engineering* (Vol. 2). New York: Academic Press, 183–202.

Falk, G. 1972. Interpretation of imperfect line data as a three–dimensional scene. *Artificial Intelligence* 3:101–144.

Faught, W. S. 1975. Affect as motivation for cognitive and conative processes. *IJCAI 4*, 893–899.

Faught, W. S., Colby, K. M., and Parkinson, R. 1974. The interaction of inferences, affects, and intentions, in a model of paranoia. Memo AIM 253, AI Laboratory, Stanford University.

Feigenbaum, E. A. 1963. The simulation of verbal learning behaviour. In E. A. Feigenbaum and J. Feldman (Eds.), *Computers and thought*. New York: McGraw-Hill, 297–309.

Feigenbaum, E. A., and Simon H. A. 1962. A theory of the serial position effect. *British Journal of Psychology* 53:307–320.

Feitelson, J., and Stefik, M. 1977. A case study of the reasoning in a genetics experiment. Rep. No. HPP–77–18, Heuristic Programming Project, Computer Science Dept., Stanford University.

Fikes, R. E., Hart, P. E., and Nilsson, N. J. 1972. Learning and executing generalized robot plans. *Artificial Intelligence* 3:251–288.

Fikes, R. E., and Nilsson, N. J. 1971. STRIPS: A new approach to the application of theorem proving to problem solving. *Artificial Intelligence* 2:189–208.

Fogel, L. J., Owens, A. J., and Walsh, M. J. 1966. *Artificial intelligence through simulated evolution*. New York: Wiley.

Friedberg, R. M. 1958. A learning machine: Part I. *IBM J. Research and Development* 2:2–13.

Friedberg, R. M., Dunham, B., and North, J. H. 1959. A learning machine: Part II. *IBM J. Research and Development* 3:282–287.

Friedland, P. E. 1979. Knowledge-based experiment design in molecular genetics. Rep. No. 79–771, Computer Science Dept., Stanford University. (Doctoral dissertation.)

Fu, K. S. 1970a. Statistical pattern recognition. In J. M. Mendel and K. S. Fu (Eds.), *Adaptive, learning, and pattern recognition systems*. New York: Academic Press, 35–80.

Fu, K. S. 1970b. Stochastic automata as models of learning systems. In J. M. Mendel and K. S. Fu (Eds.), *Adaptive, learning, and pattern recognition systems*. New York: Academic Press, 393–432.

Fu, K. S. 1974. *Syntactic methods in pattern recognition*. New York: Academic Press.

Fu, K. S. 1975. Grammatical inference: Introduction and survey. *IEEE Transactions on Systems, Man, and Cybernetics* SMC–5:95–111, 409–423.

Gardner, M. 1977. On playing the new Eleusis, the game that simulates the search for truth. *Scientific American* 237:18–25.

Gelernter, H. 1959. Realization of a geometry theorem-proving machine. *Proceedings of an International Conference on Information Processing.* Paris: UNESCO House, 273–282.

Gelernter, H. 1963. Realization of a geometry theorem proving machine. In E. A. Feigenbaum and J. Feldman (Eds.), *Computers and thought.* New York: McGraw-Hill, 134–152.

Gennery, D. B. 1979. Stereo-camera calibration. In *Proceedings of the Image Understanding Workshop,* 101–107.

Gibson, J. J. 1950. *The perception of the visual world.* Boston: Houghton-Mifflin.

Gips, J. 1974. Shape grammars and their uses. Rep. No. CS–74–413, Computer Science Dept., Stanford University.

Gleason, G. J., and Agin, G. J. 1979. A modular system for sensor-controlled manipulation and inspection. *Proceedings of the Ninth International Symposium of Industrial Robots. Society of Manufacturing Engineers and Robot Institute of America, Washington, D.C.,* 57–70.

Gold, E. 1967. Language identification in the limit. *Information and Control* 16:447–474.

Gonzalez, R. C., and Thompson, M. G. 1978. *Syntactic pattern recognition.* Reading, Mass.: Addison-Wesley.

Goodwin, G. C., and Payne, R. L. 1977. *Dynamic system identification: Experiment design and analysis.* New York: Academic Press.

Green, C. 1969. Theorem-proving by resolution as a basis for question-answering systems. In B. Meltzer and D. Michie (Eds.), *Machine intelligence 4.* New York: American Elsevier, 183–205.

Greiner, R. 1980. RLL–1: A representation language language. Rep. No. HPP–80–9. Heuristic Programming Project, Computer Science Dept., Stanford University.

Greiner, R., and Lenat, D. B. 1980. A representation language language. *AAAI 1,* 165–169.

Grimson, W. E. L. 1980. Aspects of a computational theory of human stereo vision. *Proceedings of the Image Understanding Workshop,* 128–149.

Gumb, R. D. 1978. Summary of research on computational aspects of evolving theories. *SIGART Newsletter* 67:13.

Gumb, R. D. 1979. *Evolving theories.* New York: Haven.

Guzman, A. 1968a. Computer recognition of three-dimensional objects in a visual scene. Tech. Rep. MAC–TR–59, AI Laboratory, Massachusetts Institute of Technology.

Guzman, A. 1968b. Decomposition of a visual scene into three-dimensional bodies. *AFIPS Fall Joint Conferences* 33:291–304.

Hamburger, H., and Wexler, K. 1975. A mathematical theory of learning transformational grammar. *J. Mathematical Psychology* 12:137–177.

Hannah, M. J. 1980. Bootstrap stereo. *Proceedings of the Image Understanding Workshop,* 201–208.

Hanson, A. R., and Riseman, E. M. (Eds.). 1978a. *Computer vision systems.* New York: Academic Press.

Hanson, A. R., and Riseman, E. M. 1978b. Segmentation of natural scenes. In A. R. Hanson and E. M. Riseman (Eds.), *Computer vision systems.* New York: Academic Press, 129–163.

Haralick, R. M. 1978. A statistical and structural approach to texture. *IJCPR* 4:45–49.

Haralick, R. M., Shanmugam, K., and Dinstein, I. 1973. Textual features for image classification. *IEEE Transactions on Systems, Man, and Cybernetics* SMC–3:610–621.

Harlow, C. A. 1973. Image analysis and graphs. *Computer Graphics and Image Processing* 2:60–82.

Harris, Z. 1964. Distributional structure. In J. Fodor and J. Katz (Eds.), *The structure of language.* Englewood Cliffs: Prentice Hall, 33–49.

Hayes, P. J. 1973. Computation and deduction. *Symposium on the Mathematical Foundations of Computer Science, Czechslovakia Academy of Science,* 105–116.

Hayes-Roth, B. 1980. Human planning processes. Rep. No. R–2670–ONR, Rand Corp., Santa Monica, Calif.

Hayes-Roth, B., and Hayes-Roth, F. 1978. Cognitive processes in planning. Rep. No. R–2366–ONR, Rand Corp., Santa Monica, Calif.

Hayes-Roth, F., Klahr, P., Burge, J., and Mostow, D. 1978. Machine methods for acquiring, learning, and applying knowledge. Rand Paper P–6241, Rand Corp., Santa Monica, Calif.

Hayes-Roth, F., Klahr, P., and Mostow, D. 1980. Knowledge acquisition, knowledge programming, and knowledge refinement. Rand Paper R–2540–NSF, Rand Corp., Santa Monica, Calif.

Hayes-Roth, F., Klahr, P., and Mostow, D. 1981. Advice-taking and knowledge refinement: An iterative view of skill acquisition. In J. R. Anderson (Ed.), *Cognitive skills and their acquisition.* Hillsdale, N.J.: Lawrence Erlbaum, 231–253. (Also in Rand Paper P–6517, Rand Corp., Santa Monica, Calif., 1980.)

Hayes-Roth, F., and McDermott, J. 1977. Knowledge acquisition from structural descriptions. *IJCAI 5,* 356–362.

Hayes-Roth, F., and McDermott, J. 1978. An interference matching technique for inducing abstractions. *CACM* 26:401–410.

Henderson, R. L., Miller, W. J., and Grosch, C. B. 1979. Automatic stereo recognition of man-made targets. *Society of Photo-Optical Instrumentation Engineers* 186:240–248.

Hewitt, C. 1971. Description and theoretical analysis (using schemata) of PLANNER: A language for proving theorems and manipulating models in a robot. Rep. No. AI–TR–258, AI Laboratory, Massachusetts Institute of Technology. (Doctoral dissertation.)

Hewitt, C. 1975. How to use what you know. *IJCAI 4,* 189–198.

Hewitt, C., et al. 1973. A universal modular actor formalism for artificial intelligence. *IJCAI 3,* 235–245.

Hintikka, J. 1971. Semantics for propositional attitudes. In L. Linsky (Ed.), *Reference and modality.* London: Oxford University Press, 145–167.

Hintzman, D. L. 1968. Explorations with a discrimination net model for paired-associate learning. *Journal of Mathematical Psychology* 5:123–162.

Holland, S. W., Rossol, L., and Ward, M. R. 1979. CONSIGHT–I: A vision-controlled robot system for transferring parts from belt conveyors. In G. G. Dodd and L. Rossol (Eds.), *Computer vision and sensor based robots.* New York: Plenum, 81–100.

Hopcroft, J. E., and Ullman, J. D. 1969. *Formal languages and their relation to automata.* Reading, Mass.: Addison-Wesley.

Horn, B. K. P. 1975. Obtaining shape from shading information. In P. H. Winston (Ed.), *The psychology of computer vision.* New York: McGraw-Hill.

Horn, B. K. P. 1977. Understanding image intensities. *Artificial Intelligence* 8:201–231.

Horn, B. K. P. 1979. Hill-shading and the reflectance map. *Proceedings of the Image Understanding Workshop,* 79–120.

Horn, B. K. P., and Schunck, B. G. 1980. Determining optical flow. AI Memo 572, AI Laboratory, Massachusetts Institute of Technology.

Horning, J. J. 1969. A study of grammatical inference. Rep. No. CS–139, Computer Science Dept., Stanford University.

Huang, T. S. (Ed.). 1981. *Image sequence analysis.* New York: Springer-Verlag.

Hueckel, A. 1971. An operator which locates edges in digital pictures. *J. ACM* 20:113–125.

Hueckel, A. 1973. A local visual operator which recognizes edges and lines. *J. ACM* 20:634–647.

Huet, G. 1972. Constrained resolution: A complete method for higher order logic. Rep. No. 1117, Jennings Computing Center, Case Western Reserve University. (Doctoral dissertation.)

Huet, G. 1975. A unification algorithm for typed lambda calculus. *Theoretical Computer Science* 1:27–57.

Huffman, D. A. 1971. Impossible objects as nonsense sentences. In R. Meltzer and D. Michie (Eds.), *Machine intelligence 6.* New York: Elsevier, 295–323.

Huffman, D. A. 1977. Realizable configurations of lines in pictures of polyhedra. In E. W. Elcock and D. Michie (Eds.), *Machine intelligence 8.* Edinburgh: Edinburgh University Press, 493–509.

Hunt, E. B., Marin, J., and Stone, P. J. 1966. *Experiments in induction.* New York: Academic Press.

Ikeuchi, K. 1980a. Numerical shape from shading and occluding contours in a single view. AI Memo 566, AI Laboratory, Massachusetts Institute of Technology.

Ikeuchi, K. 1980b. Shape from regular patterns. AI Memo 567, AI Laboratory, Massachusetts Institute of Technology.

Jain, R., and Nagel, H. H. 1979. On the analysis of accumulative difference pictures from image sequences of real world scenes. *IEEE Transactions on Pattern Analysis and Machine Intelligence* PAMI–1:206–213.

Johnston, A. R. 1973. Infrared laser rangefinder. Rep. No. NPO–13460, Jet Propulsion Laboratory, Pasadena, Calif.

Judd, D. B., and Wyszecki, G. 1975. *Color in business, science, and industry* (3rd ed.). New York: Wiley.

Julesz, B. 1975. Experiments in the visual perception of texture. *Scientific American* 232:24–43.

Kanade, T. 1977. Model representations and control structures in image understanding. *IJCAI 5*, 1074–1082.

Kanade, T. 1979. Recovery of the three-dimensional shape of an object from a single view. Rep. No. CMU–CS–79–153, Computer Science Dept., Carnegie-Mellon University. (Also in *Artificial Intelligence* 17:409–460, 1981.)

Kanade, T. 1980a. Region segmentation: Signal vs. semantics. *Computer Graphics and Image Processing* 13:279–297.

Kanade, T. 1980b. A theory of Origami world. *Artificial Intelligence* 13:279–311.

Kanade, T., and Asada, H. 1981. Noncontact visual 3-D sensing devices. *SPIE Technical Symposium, East '81, 3-D, on Machine Perception,* 283.

Kanade, T., and Kender, J. 1980. Skewed symmetry: Mapping image regularities into shape. CMU–CS–80–133, Computer Science Dept., Carnegie-Mellon University.

Kashioka, S., Ejiri, M., and Sakamoto, Y. 1976. A transistor wire-bonding system utilizing multiple local pattern matching techniques. *IEEE Transactions on Systems, Man, and Cybernetics* SMC–6(8):562–569.

Kelley, K. 1967. Early syntax acquisition. Rep. No. P–3719, Rand Corp., Santa Monica, Calif.

Kelly, M. D. 1970. Visual identification of people by computer. Memo AI–130, AI Project, Stanford University.

Kelly, M. D. 1971. Edge detection in pictures by computers using planning. In R. Meltzer and D. Michie (Eds.), *Machine intelligence 6.* New York: Elsevier, 379–409.

Kender, J. R. 1977. Instabilities in color transformations. *IEEE Conference on Pattern Recognition and Image Processing, Rensselaer Polytechnical Institute, Troy, N.Y.,* 266–274.

Kender, J. R. 1979. Shape from texture: An aggregation transform that maps a class of textures into surface orientation. *IJCAI 6*, 475–480.

Kender, J. R. 1980. *Shape from texture.* Doctoral dissertation, Computer Science Dept., Carnegie-Mellon University.

Kender, J. R., and Kanade, T. 1980. Mapping image properties into shape constraints: Skewed symmetry, affine transformable patterns, and the shape-from-texture paradigm. *AAAI 1*, 4–6.

Klein, S., and Kuppin, M. 1970. An interactive heuristic program for learning transformational grammars. *Computer Studies in the Humanities and Verbal Behavior* 3:144–162.

Kling, R. 1971. A paradigm for reasoning by analogy. *Artificial Intelligence* 2:147–178.

Klotz, I. M. 1980. The N-ray affair. *Scientific American* 242:168–176.

Knobe, B., and Knobe, K. 1977. A method for inferring context-free grammars. *Information and Control* 31:129–146.

Knuth, D. E., and Bendix, P. 1970. Simple word problems in universal algebras. In J. Leech (Ed.), *Computational problems in abstract algebra.* Oxford, England: Pergamon Press.

Kotovsky, K., and Simon, H. A. 1973. Empirical tests of a theory of human acquisition of concepts for sequential patterns. *Cognitive Psychology* 4:399–424.

Kowalski, R. 1974. Predicate logic as a programming language. In J. L. Rosenfeld (Ed.), *Information processing 74.* Amsterdam: North-Holland, 569–574.

Kowalski, R. 1979. *Logic for problem solving.* New York: American Elsevier.

Kowalski, R., and Kuchner, D. 1971. Linear resolution with selector function. *Artificial Intelligence* 2:227–260.

Kripke, S. A. 1971. Semantical considerations on modal logic. In L. Linsky (Ed.), *Reference and modality.* London: Oxford University Press, 63–72.

Langley, P. W. 1977. Rediscovering physics with BACON.3. *IJCAI 6,* 505–507.

Langley, P. W. 1980. Descriptive discovery processes: Experiments in Baconian science. Rep. No. CS–80–121, Computer Science Dept., Carnegie-Mellon University. (Doctoral dissertation.)

Lankford, D. S. 1975. Complete sets of reductions for computational logic. Memo ATP–25, Mathematics Dept., University of Texas, Austin.

Lankford, D. S., and Ballantyne, A. M. 1977. Decision procedures for simple equational theories with commutative axioms: Complete sets of commutative reductions. Memo ATP–35, Mathematics Dept., University of Texas, Austin.

Larson, J. 1977. Inductive inference in the variable valued predicate logic system VL21: Methodology and computer implementation. Rep. No. 869, Computer Science Dept., University of Illinois, Urbana.

Larson, J., and Michalski, R. S. 1977. Inductive inference of VL decision rules. *SIGART Newsletter* 63:38–44.

Leese, J. A., Novak, C. S., and Clark, B. B. 1971. An automated technique for obtaining cloud motion from geosynchronous satellite data using cross correlation. *Journal of Applied Meteorology* 10:118–132.

Lenat, D. B. 1976. AM: An artificial intelligence approach to discovery in mathematics as heuristic search. Rep. No. STAN–CS–76–570. Computer Science Dept., Stanford University. (Doctoral dissertation. Reprinted in R. Davis and D. B. Lenat. 1980. *Knowledge-based systems in artificial intelligence.* New York: McGraw-Hill.)

Lenat, D. B. 1977. On automated scientific theory formation: A case study using the AM program. In J. E. Hayes, D. Michie, and L. I. Mikulich (Eds.), *Machine intelligence 9.* New York: Halsted Press, 251–286.

Lenat, D. B. 1980. The nature of heuristics. Rep. No. HPP–80–26. Heuristic Programming Project, Computer Science Dept., Stanford University.

Lenat, D. B., Hayes-Roth, F., and Klahr, P. 1979. Cognitive economy in artificial intelligence systems. *IJCAI 6,* 531–536. (Extended version available as Rep. No. HPP–79–15, Heuristic Programming Project, Computer Science Dept., Stanford University.)

Lindsay, R. K., Buchanan, B. G., Feigenbaum, E. A., and Lederberg, J. 1980. *Applications of artificial intelligence for organic chemistry: The DENDRAL project.* New York: McGraw-Hill.

Loveland, D. 1978. *Automatic theorem proving: A logical basis.* Amsterdam: North-Holland.

Loveland, D., and Stickel, M. 1973. A hole in goal trees: Some guidance from resolution theory. *IJCAI 3,* 153-161.

Lucas, B. D., and Kanade, T. 1981. An iterative image registration technique with an application to stereo vision. *Proceedings of the Image Understanding Workshop,* 121–130.

Mackworth, A. K. 1973. Interpreting pictures of polyhedral scenes. *Artificial Intelligence* 4:121–137.

Mackworth, A. K. 1974. *On the interpretation of drawings as three-dimensional scenes.* Doctoral dissertation, Laboratory of Experimental Psychology, University of Sussex.

Mackworth, A. K. 1977a. Consistency in networks of relations. *Artificial Intelligence* 8:99–118.

Mackworth, A. K. 1977b. How to see a simple world: An exegis of some computer programs for scene analysis. In E. W. Elcock and D. Michie (Eds.), *Machine intelligence 8,* 510–537.

Mandler, G. 1975. *Mind and emotion.* New York: Wiley.

Marr, D. 1976. Early processing of visual information. *Philosophical Transactions of the Royal Society of London* (Series B) 275:483–524.

Marr, D. 1978. Representing visual information. In A. R. Hanson and E. M. Riseman (Eds.), *Computer vision systems.* New York: Academic Press, 61–80.

Marr, D., and Hildreth, E. 1980. Theory of edge detection. *Proceedings of the Royal Society of London* (Series B) 207:187–217.

Marr, D., and Nishihara, H. K. 1978. Representation and recognition of the spatial organisation of three-dimensional structure. *Proceedings of the Royal Society of London* (Series B) 200:269–294.

Marr, D., and Poggio, T. 1976. Cooperative computation of stereo disparity. *Science* 194:283–287.

Marr, D., and Poggio, T. 1977. A theory of human stereo vision. AI Memo 451, AI Laboratory, Massachusetts Institute of Technology.

Martelli, A. 1976. An application of heuristic search methods to edge and contour detection. *CACM* 19:73–83.

Maryanski, F. J. 1974. *Inference of probabilistic grammars.* Doctoral dissertation, Electrical Engineering and Computer Science Dept., University of Connecticut.

Maxam, A., and Gilbert, W. 1974. A new method for sequencing DNA. *Proceedings of the National Academy of Sciences* 74(2):560–564.

McCarthy, J. 1958. Programs with common sense. In *Proceedings of the Symposium on the Mechanization of Thought Processes, National Physical Laboratory* I:77–84. (Reprinted in M. L. Minsky (Ed.). 1968. *Semantic information processing.* Cambridge, Mass.: MIT Press, 403–409.)

McCarthy, J. 1963. A basis for a mathematical theory of computation. In P. Braffort and D. Hirschberg (Eds.), *Computer programming and formal systems.* Amsterdam: North-Holland.

McCarthy, J. 1968. Programs with common sense. In M. Minsky (Ed.), *Semantic information processing.* Cambridge, Mass.: MIT Press, 403–409.

McCarthy, J. 1980. Circumscription—A form of non-monotonic reasoning. *Artificial Intelligence* 13:27–39.

McCorduck, P. 1979. *Machines who think.* San Francisco: Freeman.

McDermott, D. 1978. Planning and acting. *Cognitive Science* 2:71–109.

McDermott, D. 1980. Non-monotonic logic II: Non-monotonic modal theories. Rep. No. 174, Computer Science Dept., Yale University.

McDermott, D., and Doyle, J. 1980. Non-monotonic logic I. *Artificial Intelligence* 13:41–72.

McKeown, D. M., and Kanade, T. 1981. Database support for automated photo interpretation. *Proceedings of the Image Understanding Workshop*, 7–13.

Mese, M., Miyatake, T., Kashioka, S., Ejiri, M., Yamazaki, I., and Hamada, T. 1977. An automatic position recognition technique for LSI assembly. *IJCAI 5*, 685–693.

Michalski, R. S. 1969. On the quasi-minimal solution of the general covering problem. *Proceedings of the Fifth International Federation on Automatic Control* 27:109–129.

Michalski, R. S. 1975. Variable-valued logic and its applications to pattern recognition and machine learning. In D. C. Rine (Ed.), *Computer science and multiple-valued logic theory and applications*. Amsterdam: North-Holland, 506–534.

Michalski, R. S. 1980. Pattern recognition as rule-guided inductive inference. *IEEE Transactions on Pattern Analysis and Machine Intelligence* PAMI–2:349–361.

Michalski, R. S., and Chilausky, R. L. 1980. Learning by being told and learning from examples: An experimental comparison of the two methods of knowledge acquisition in the context of developing an expert system for soybean disease diagnosis. *International Journal of Policy Analysis and Information Systems* 4:125–161.

Michalski, R. S., and Larson, J. B. 1978. Selection of most representative training examples and incremental generation of VL1 hypotheses: The underlying methodology and the description of programs ESEL and AQ11. Rep. No. 867. Computer Science Dept., University of Illinois, Urbana.

Milgram, D. L., and Kahl, D. J. 1979. Recursive region extraction. *Computer Graphics and Image Processing* 9:82–88.

Miller, G. A. 1956. The magical number seven, plus or minus two: Some limits of our capacity for processing information. *Psychological Review* 63:81–97.

Miller, G. A., Galanter, E., and Pribram, K. H. 1960. *Plans and the structure of behavior*. New York: Holt.

Miller, L. 1978. Has artificial intelligence contributed to an understanding of the human mind? A critique of arguments for and against. *Cognitive Science* 2:111–127.

Minsky, M. 1963. Steps toward artificial intelligence. In E. A. Feigenbaum, and J. Feldman (Eds.), *Computers and thought*. New York: McGraw-Hill, 406–450.

Minsky, M. L. (Ed.). 1968. *Semantic information processing*. Cambridge, Mass.: MIT Press.

Minsky, M. 1975. A framework for representing knowledge. In P. H. Winston (Ed.), *The psychology of computer vision*. New York: McGraw-Hill, 211–277.

Minsky, M. 1980. A framework for representing knowledge. In J. Haugeland (Ed.), *Mind design: Philosophy, psychology, and artificial intelligence*. Montgomery, Vt.: Bradford Books.

Minsky, M. L., and Papert, S. 1969. *Perceptrons; an introduction to computational geometry*. Cambridge, Mass.: MIT Press.

Mitchell, T. M. 1977. Version spaces: A candidate elmination approach to rule learning. *IJCAI 5*, 305–310.

Mitchell, T. M. 1978. Version spaces: An approach to concept learning. Rep. No. STAN–CS–78–711, Computer Science Dept., Stanford University. (Doctoral dissertation.)

Mitchell, T. M. 1979. An analysis of generalization as a search problem. *IJCAI 6*, 577–582.

Mitchell, T. M., Utgoff, P. E., and Banerji, R. B. In press. Learning problem-solving heuristics by experimentation. In R. S. Michalski, T. M Mitchell, and J. Carbonell (Eds.), *Machine learning*. Palo Alto, Calif.: Tioga.

Mitchell, T. M., Utgoff, P. E., Nudel, B., and Banerji, R. B. 1981. Learning problem-solving heuristics through practice. *IJCAI 7*, 127–134.

Montanari, U. 1971. On the optimal detection of curves in noisy pictures. *CACM* 14:335–345.

Moore, R. C. 1980a. *Reasoning from incomplete knowledge in a procedural deduction system*. New York: Garland.

Moore, R. C. 1980b. Reasoning about knowledge and action. Tech. Note 191, AI Center, SRI International, Inc., Menlo Park, Calif.

Moravec, H. P. 1979. Visual mapping by a robot rover. *IJCAI 6*, 598–600.

Moravec, H. P. 1980. Obstacle avoidance and navigation in the real world by a seeing robot rover. Tech. Rep. CMU–RI–TR–3, Robotics Institute, Carnegie-Mellon University.

Mori, K., Kidode, M., and Asada, H. 1973. An iterative prediction and correction method for automatic stereocomparison. *Computer Graphics and Image Processing* 2:393–401.

Mostow, D. J. 1981. Mechanical transformation of task heuristics into operational procedures. Rep. No. CS–81–113, Computer Science Dept., Carnegie-Mellon University. (Doctoral dissertation.)

Mostow, D. J. In press. Using the heuristic search method. In R. S. Michalski, T. M. Mitchell, and J. Carbonell (Eds.), *Machine learning*. Palo Alto, Calif.: Tioga.

Mostow, D. J., and Hayes-Roth, F. 1979a. Machine-aided heuristic programming: A paradigm for knowledge engineering. Rep. No. Rand N–1007–NSF, Rand Corp., Santa Monica, Calif.

Mostow, D. J., and Hayes-Roth, F. 1979b. Operationalizing heuristics: Some AI methods for assisting AI programming. *IJCAI 6*, 601–609.

Nagao, M., Matsuyama, T., and Ikeda, Y. 1978. Region extraction and shape analysis of aerial photographs. *IJCPR 4*, 620–628.

Nagao, M., Matsuyama, T., and Ikeda, Y. 1979. Structural analysis of complex aerial photographs. *IJCAI 6*, 610–616.

Nagin, P. A., Hanson, A. R., and Riseman, E. M. 1977. Region extraction and description through planning. COINS Tech. Rep. 77–8, Computer and Information Sciences Dept., University of Massachusetts, Amherst.

Naruse, M., Miyazaki, S., Yamada, T., and Igarashi, K. 1979. Fully automated integrated circuit wire bonding system. *Ninth International Symposium on Industrial Robots*, 87–97.

Neisser, U. 1976. *Cognition and reality*. San Francisco: Freeman.

Nelson, C. G., and Oppen, D. 1978. Efficient decision procedures based on congruence closure. Memo AIM–309 (CS–646), Computer Science Dept., Stanford University.

Nevatia, R. 1976. A color edge detector. *JCPR 3*, 829–832.

Nevatia, R., and Babu, K. R. 1981. Linear feature extraction and description. *IJCAI 6*, 639–641.

Nevatia, R., and Binford, T. O. 1973. Structured descriptions of complex objects. *IJCAI 3*, 641–647.

Nevins, A. J. 1974. A human oriented logic for automatic theorem proving. *J. ACM* 21:606–621.

Nevins, A. J. 1975. Plane geometry theorem proving using forward chaining. *Artificial Intelligence* 6:1–23.

Newell, A. 1970. Remarks on the relationship between artificial intelligence and cognitive psychology. In R. B. Banerji and M. D. Mearovic (Eds.), *Theoretical approaches to non-numerical problem solving*. Berlin: Springer-Verlag.

Newell, A., and Simon, H. A. 1956. The logic theory machine. *IRE Transactions on Information Theory* 2:61–79.

Newell, A., and Simon, H. A. 1963. Computers in psychology. In R. D. Luce, R. R. Bush, and E. Galanter (Eds.), *Handbook of mathematical psychology* (Vol. 1). New York: Wiley, 361–428.

Newell, A., and Simon, H. A. 1972. *Human problem solving*. Englewood Cliffs, N.J.: Prentice-Hall.

Nii, H. P., and Aiello, N. 1979. AGE (Attempt to Generalize): A knowledge-based program for building knowledge-based programs. *IJCAI 6*, 645–655.

Nii, H. P., and Feigenbaum, E. A. 1978. Rule-based understanding of signals. In D. A. Waterman and F. Hayes-Roth (Eds.), *Pattern-directed inference systems*. New York: Academic Press, 483–501.

Nilsson, N. J. 1965. *Learning machines*. New York: McGraw-Hill.

Nilsson, N. J. 1971. *Problem solving methods in artificial intelligence*. New York: McGraw-Hill.

Nilsson, N. J. 1980. *Principles of artificial intelligence*. Palo Alto, Calif.: Tioga.

Nitzan, D., Brain, A. E., and Duda, R. O. 1977. The measurement and use of registered reflectance and range data in scene analysis. *Proceedings of the IEEE* 65:2.

Norman, D. A. 1980. Twelve issues for cognitive science. *Cognitive Science* 4:1–32.

Norman, D. A., Rumelhart, D. E., and the LNR Research Group. 1975. *Explorations in cognition*. San Francisco: Freeman.

Ohlander, R. B. 1975. *Analysis of natural scenes*. Doctoral dissertation, Computer Science Dept., Carnegie-Mellon University.

Ohlander, R. B., Price, K., and Reddy, D. R. 1978. Picture segmentation using a recursive region splitting method. *Computer Graphics and Image Processing* 8:313–333. (Doctoral dissertation.)

Ohta, Y. 1980. *A region-oriented image-analysis system by computer*. Doctoral dissertation, Information Science Dept., Kyoto University.

Ohta, Y., Kanade, T., and Sakai, T. 1980. Color information for region segmentation. *Computer Graphics and Image Processing* 13:222–241.

O'Rourke, J. 1980. *Image analysis of human motion.* Doctoral dissertation, Moore School of Electrical Engineering, University of Pennsylvania.

Oshima, M., and Shirai, Y. 1979. A scene description method using three-dimensional information. *Pattern Recognition* 11:9–17.

Pao, T. W. 1969. A solution of the syntactical induction-inference problem for a non-trivial subset of context-free languages. Interim Rep. No. 69–19, Moore School of Electrical Engineering, University of Pennsylvania.

Pavlidis, T. 1977. *Structural pattern recognition.* Berlin: Springer-Verlag.

Peterson, G. E., and Stickel, M. 1977. Complete sets of reductions for equational theories with complete unification algorithms. Memo, Computer Sciences Dept., University of Arizona.

Pinker, S. 1979. Formal models of language learning. *Cognition* 7:217–283.

Polya, G. 1957. *How to solve it.* New York: Doubleday Anchor Books.

Popplestone, R. J., Brown, C. M., Ambler, A. P., and Crawford, G. F. 1975. Forming models of plane-and-cylinder faceted bodies from light stripes. *IJCAI 4.*

Pratt, W. K., Faugeras, O. D., and Gagalowicz, A. 1978. Visual discrimination of stochastic texture field. *IEEE Transactions on Systems, Man, and Cybernetics* SMC–8:796–804.

Presburger, M. 1930. Uber die Vollstandigkeit eins gewissen Systems der Arithmetik ganzer Zahlen in welchem die Addition als einzige Operation hervortritt. *Sprawozdanie z i kongresu matematykow krajow slowianskich, Warszawa (Comptes-rendus du I congrès des mathématiciens des pays slaves),* 92–101.

Prewitt, J. W. S. 1970. Object enhancement and extraction. In B. Lipkin and A. Rosenfeld (Eds.), *Picture processing and psychopictorics.* New York: Academic Press, 75–149.

Quillian, M. R. 1968. Semantic Memory. In M. Minsky (Ed.), *Semantic information processing.* Cambridge, Mass.: MIT Press, 216–270.

Quine, W. V., and Ullian, J. S. 1978. *The web of belief* (2nd ed.). New York: Random House.

Quinlan, J. R. 1979. Induction over large data bases. Rep. No. HPP–79–14, Heuristic Programming Project, Computer Science Dept., Stanford University.

Quinlan, J. R. In press. Inductive inference as a tool for the construction of high-performance programs. In R. S. Michalski, T. M. Mitchell, and J. Carbonell (Eds.), *Machine learning.* Palo Alto, Calif.: Tioga.

Reboh, R. 1981. Knowledge engineering techniques and tools in the PROSPECTOR environment. Rep. No. 243. AI Center, SRI International, Inc., Menlo Park, Calif.

Reeker, L. H. 1976. The computational study of language acquisition. In M. Rubinoff and M. C. Yovits (Eds.), *Advances in computers* (Vol. 15). New York: Academic Press, 181–237.

Reiter, R. 1976. A semantically guided deductive system for automatic theorem proving. *IEEE Transactions on Computers* C–25.

Reiter, R. 1980. A logic for default reasoning. *Artificial Intelligence* 13:81–132.

Risch, R. 1969. The problem of integration in finite terms. *Transactions of the AMS* 139:167–189.

Riseman, E. M., and Arbib, M. A. 1977. Segmentation of static scenes. *Computer Graphics and Image Processing* 6:221–276.

Rissland, E. L., and Soloway, E. M. 1980. Overview of an example generation system. *AAAI 1,* 256–258.

Roberts, L. 1965. Machine perception of three-dimensional solids. In J. Tippett (Ed.), *Optical and electro-optical information processing.* Cambridge, Mass.: MIT Press, 159–197.

Robertson, T. V., Swain, P. H., and Fu, K. S. 1973. Multispectral image partitioning. Tech. Rep. TR–EE–73–26, School of Electrical Engineering, Purdue University.

Robinson, G. A., and Wos, L. 1969. Paramodulation and theorem-proving in first order theories with equality. In D. Michie (Ed.), *Machine intelligence 4.* Edinburgh: Edinburgh University Press.

Robinson, J. A. 1965a. Automatic deduction with hyper-resolution. *International J. Computational Mathematics* 1:227–234.

Robinson, J. A. 1965b. A machine-oriented logic based on the resolution principle. *J. ACM* 12:23–41.

Robinson, J. A., and Sibert, E. E. 1980. Logic programming in LISP. School of Computer and Information Science, Syracuse University.

Roecker, F., and Kiessling, A. 1975. Methods for analyzing three dimensional scenes. *IJCAI 4.*

Rosenblatt, F. 1957. The perceptron: A perceiving and recognizing automaton. Rep. No. 85–460–1, Project PARA, Cornell Aeronautical Laboratory.

Rosenblatt, F. 1962. *Principles of neurodynamics: Perceptrons and the theory of brain mechanisms.* Washington, D.C.: Spartan Books.

Rosenfeld, A. 1969. *Picture processing by computer.* New York: Academic Press.

Rosenfeld, A. 1978. Some recent results using relaxation-like processes. *Proceedings of the Image Understanding Workshop,* 100–104.

Rosenfeld, A. 1979. *Picture languages: Formal models for picture recognition.* New York: Academic Press.

Rosenfeld, A., and Kak, A. C. 1976. *Digital picture processing.* New York: Academic Press.

Rosenfeld, A., and Lipkin, B. S. 1970. Texture synthesis. In B. C. Lipkin and A. Rosenfeld (Eds.), *Processing and psychopictorics.* New York: Academic Press, 309–345.

Rosenfeld, A., and Thurston, M. 1971. Edge and curve detection for visual scene analysis. *IEEE Transactions on Computers* C–20:562–569.

Rubin, S. 1978. *The ARGOS image understanding system.* Doctoral dissertation, Computer Science Dept., Carnegie-Mellon University.

Rumelhart, D. E., Lindsay, P. H., and Norman, D. A. 1972. A process model for long-term memory. In E. Tulving and W. Donaldson (Eds.), *Organization and memory.* New York: Academic Press, 198–246.

Sacerdoti, E. D. 1974. Planning in a hierarchy of abstraction spaces. *Artificial Intelligence* 5:115–135.

Sacerdoti, E. D. 1975. A structure for plans and behavior. Tech. Note 109, AI Center, SRI International, Inc., Menlo Park, Calif. (Doctoral dissertation.)

Sacerdoti, E. D. 1979. Problem solving tactics. Tech. Note 189, SRI International, Inc., Menlo Park, Calif.

Samuel, A. L. 1959. Some studies in machine learning using the game of checkers. *IBM J. Research and Development* 3:210–229. (Reprinted in E. A. Feigenbaum, and J. Feldman (Eds.). 1963. *Computers and thought.* New York: McGraw-Hill, 71–105.)

Samuel, A. L. 1967. Some studies in machine learning using the game of checkers. II—Recent progress. *IBM J. Research and Development* 11:601–617.

Schachter, G. J., Rosenfeld, A., and Davis, L. S. 1978. Random mosaic models for textures. *IEEE Transactions on Systems, Man, and Cybernetics* SMC–8:694–702.

Schank, R. C., and Abelson, R. P. 1977. *Scripts, plans, goals, and understanding.* Hillsdale, N.J.: Lawrence Erlbaum.

Schatz, B. R. 1977. Computation of immediate texture discrimination. *IJCAI 5,* 708.

Shafer, S. A. 1980. MOOSE: User's manual, implementation guide, evaluation. Tech. Rep. No. HH–B–70, Fachbereich Informatik, University of Hamburg.

Shannon, C. E., and Weaver, W. 1963. *The mathematical theory of communication.* Urbana: University of Illinois Press.

Shirai, Y. 1973. A context sensitive line finder for recognition of polyhedra. *Artificial Intelligence* 4:95–119.

Shirai, Y. 1978. Recognition of real-world objects using edge cues. In A. R. Hanson and E. M. Riseman (Eds.), *Computer vision systems.* New York: Academic Press, 353–362.

Shirai, Y., and Suwa, M. 1971. Recognition of polyhedrons with a rangefinder. *IJCAI 2,* 80–87.

Shortliffe, E. H. 1976. *Computer-based medical consultations: MYCIN.* New York: American Elsevier.

Shostak, R. S. 1975. On the completeness of the sup-inf method. SRI International, Inc., Menlo Park, Calif.

Simon, H. A. 1969. *Sciences of the artificial.* Cambridge, Mass.: MIT Press.

Simon, H. A. 1979a. Artificial intelligence research strategies in the light of AI models of scientific discovery. *IJCAI 6,* 1086–1094.

Simon, H. A. 1979b. *Models of thought.* New Haven, Conn.: Yale University Press.

Simon, H. A. In press. Why should machines learn? In R. S. Michalski, T. M. Mitchell, and J. Çarbonell (Eds.), *Machine learning.* Palo Alto, Calif.: Tioga.

Simon, H. A., and Feigenbaum, E. A. 1964. An information-processing theory of some effects of similarity, familiarization, and meaningfulness in verbal learning. *Journal of Verbal Learning and Verbal Behavior* 3:385–396.

Simon, H. A., and Lea, G. 1974. Problem solving and rule induction: A unified view. In L. Gregg (Ed.), *Knowledge and cognition.* Hillsdale, N.J.: Lawrence Erlbaum, 105–127.

Skinner, B. F. 1976. *About behaviorism.* New York: Vintage Books.

Skolem, T. 1967. The foundations of elementary arithmetic established by means of the recursive mode of thought, without the use of apparent variables ranging over infinite domains. In *From Frege to Goedel.* Cambridge, Mass.: Harvard University Press.

Smith, W., and Birnstein, M. 1976. A simple method for DNA restriction site mapping. *Nucleic Acids Research* 3:2387–2398.

Solomonoff, R. 1964. A formal theory of inductive inference. *Information and Control* 7:1–22, 224–254.

Soloway, E. 1978. Learning = interpretation + generalization: A case study in knowledge-directed learning. Rep. No. COINS–TR–78–13, Computer and Information Sciences Dept., University of Massachusetts, Amherst. (Doctoral dissertation.)

Soroka, B. I. 1980. Debugging manipulator programs with a simulator. *Autofact West Conference, Society of Manufacturing Engineers, Anaheim, Calif.*

Stefik, M. J. 1979. An examination of a frame-structured representation system. *IJCAI 6*, 845–852.

Stefik, M. J. 1980. Planning with constraints. Rep. No. 80–784, Computer Science Dept., Stanford University. (Doctoral dissertation.)

Sternberg, S. 1969. Memory-scanning: Mental processes revealed by reaction time experiments. *American Scientist* 57:421–457.

Stevens, K. 1980. Surface perception by local analysis of texture and contour. AI Memo 512, AI Laboratory, Massachusetts Institute of Technology.

Sugihara, K. 1979. Range-data analysis guided by a junction dictionary. *Artificial Intelligence* 12:41–69.

Sussman, G. J. 1973. A computational model of skill acquisition. AI Tech. Rep. 297, AI Laboratory, Massachusetts Institute of Technology. (Doctoral dissertation.)

Sussman, G. J. 1975. *A computer model of skill acquisition.* New York: American Elsevier.

Tamura, H., Mori, S., and Yamawaki, T. 1978. Textural features corresponding to visual perceptions. *IEEE Transactions on Systems, Man, and Cybernetics* SMC–8:460–473.

Tanimoto, S., and Klinger, A. (Eds.). 1980. *Structured computer vision: Machine perception through hierarchical computation structures.* New York: Academic Press.

Tanimoto, S., and Pavlidis, T. 1975. A hierarchical data structure for picture processing. *Computer Graphics and Image Processing* 4:104–119.

Tate, A. 1975a. Interacting goals and their use. *IJCAI 4*, 215–218.

Tate, A. 1975b. *Using goal structure to direct search in a problem solver.* Doctoral dissertation, University of Edinburgh.

Tate, A. 1976. Project planning using a hierarchic non linear planner. Rep. No. 25, AI Research Dept., University of Edinburgh.

Tenenbaum, J. M., and Barrow, H. G. 1976a. Experiments in interpretation-guided segmentation. *Artificial Intelligence* 8:241–274.

Tenenbaum, J. M., and Barrow, H. G. 1976b. IGS: A paradigm for integrating image segmentation and interpretations. *IJCPR 3*, 504–513.

Tenenbaum, J. M., Fischler, M. A., and Barrow, H. G. 1980. Scene modeling: A structural basis for image description. *Computer Graphics and Image Processing* 12:407–425.

Thompson, W. B. (Ed.). 1980. Machine perception. *Computer* 13:7–63.

Thorpe, C. E. 1981. Sonar image processing—An application of template matching through relaxation. Tech. Rep. CMU–RI–TR–81–6, Robotics Institute, Carnegie-Mellon University.

Tomita, F., and Tsuji, S. 1977. Extraction of multiple regions by smoothing in selected neighborhoods. *IEEE Transactions on Systems, Man, and Cybernetics* SMC-7:107–109.

Tomita, F., Yachida, M., and Tsuji, S. 1973. Detection of homogeneous regions by structural analysis. *IJCAI 3*, 564–571.

Tsuji, S., and Tomita, F. 1973. A structural analyzer for a class of textures. *Computer Graphics and Image Processing* 2:216–231.

Tsypkin, Y. Z. (Z. J. Nikolic, Trans.). 1973. *Foundations of the theory of learning systems*. New York: Academic Press.

Tukey, J. W. 1960. Conclusions vs. decisions. *Technometrics* 2:423–433.

Turner, K. J. 1974. *Computer perception of curved objects using a television camera.* Doctoral dissertation, School of Artificial Intelligence, Edinburgh University.

Tversky, A., and Kahneman, D. 1974. Judgement under uncertainty: Heuristics and biases. *Science* 185:1124–1131.

Ullman, J. D. 1980. *Principles of database systems.* Potomac, Md.: Computer Science Press.

Ullman, S. 1979. *The interpretation of visual motion.* Cambridge, Mass.: MIT Press.

Uno, T., Ejiri, M., and Tokunaga, T. 1976. A method of real-time recognition of moving objects and its application. *Pattern Recognition.*

Uno, T., Ikeda, S., Ueda, H., and Ejiri, M. 1979. An industrial eye that recognizes hole positions in a water pump testing process. G. G. Dodd and L. Rossol (Eds.), *Computer vision and sensor based robots.* New York: Plenum, 101–114.

van Melle, W. 1980. A domain-independent system that aids in constructing knowledge based consultation programs. Rep. No. 820, Computer Science Dept., Stanford University. (Doctoral dissertation.)

Vanderbrug, G. J., Albus, J. S., and Borkmeyer, E. 1979. A vision system for real-time control of robots. *Proceedings of the Ninth International Symposium and Exposition on Industrial Robots,* 213-231.

Vere, S. A. 1975. Induction of concepts in the predicate calculus. *IJCAI 4,* 281–287.

Vere, S. A. 1978. Inductive learning of relational productions. In D. A. Waterman and F. Hayes-Roth (Eds.), *Pattern-directed inference systems.* New York: Academic Press, 281–296.

Waldinger, R. 1977. Achieving several goals simultaneously. In E. W. Elcock and D. Michie (Eds.), *Machine intelligence 8.* New York: Halstead/Wiley.

Wallach, H., and O'Connell, D. N. 1953. The kinetic depth effect. *Journal of Experimental Psychology* 45:205–217.

Waltz, D. 1972. Generating semantic descriptions from drawings of scenes with shadows. AI-TR–271, Project MAC, Massachusetts Institute of Technology. (Reprinted in P. Winston (Ed.). 1975. *The psychology of computer vision.* McGraw-Hill, New York, 19–92.)

Wang, H. 1960. Toward mechanical mathematics. *IBM J. Research and Development* 4:2–22.

Warren, D. H. D. 1974. WARPLAN: A system for generating plans. Memo 76, Computational Logic Dept., School of Artificial Intelligence, University of Edinburgh.

Warren, D. H. D. 1981. Efficient processing of interactive relational database queries expressed in logic. *Proceedings of the Conference on Very Large Databases, Cannes, France,* 272–281.

Warren, D. H. D., Pereira, L. M., and Pereira, F. 1977. PROLOG—The language and its implementation compared with LISP. *Proceedings of the Symposium on Artificial Intelligence and Programming Languages (ACM); SIGPLAN Notices* 12(8); and *SIGART Newsletter* 64:109–115.

Wason, P. C., and Johnson-Laird, P. N. 1972. *Psychology of reasoning: Structure and content.* Cambridge, Mass.: Harvard University Press.

Waterman, D. A. 1968. Machine learning of heuristics. Rep. No. STAN–CS–68–118, Computer Science Dept., Stanford University. (Doctoral dissertation.)

Waterman, D. A. 1970. Generalization learning techniques for automating the learning of heuristics. *Artificial Intelligence* 1:121–170.

Wee, W. G., and Fu, K. S. 1969. A formulation of fuzzy automata and its application as a model of learning systems. *IEEE Transactions on System Science and Cybernetics* 5:215–223.

Weszka, J. S. 1978. A survey of threshold selection techniques. *Computer Graphics and Image Processing* 7:259–265.

Weszka, J. S., Dyer, C. R., and Rosenfeld, A. 1976. A comparative study of texture measures for terrain classification. *IEEE Transactions on Systems, Man, and Cybernetics* SMC–6:269–285.

Wexler, K. 1978. A review of John R. Anderson's language, memory, and thought. *Cognition* 6:327–351

Weyhrauch, R. W. 1980. Prolegomena to a theory of mechanized formal reasoning. *Artificial Intelligence* 13:133–170.

Widrow, B., and Hoff, M. E. 1960. Adaptive switching circuits. In *1960 IRE WESCON Convention Records* 4:96–104.

Wiederhold, G. 1977. *Database design.* New York: McGraw-Hill.

Winston, P. H. 1970. Learning structural descriptions from examples. Rep. No. TR–231, AI Laboratory, Massachusetts Institute of Technology. (Reprinted in P. H. Winston (Ed.). 1975. *The psychology of computer vision.* New York: McGraw-Hill, 157–209.)

Winston, P. H. (Ed.). 1975. *The psychology of computer vision.* New York: McGraw-Hill.

Winston, P. H. 1977. *Artificial intelligence.* New York: Addison-Wesley.

Witkin, A. P. 1980. A statistical technique for recovering surface orientation from texture in natural imagery. *AAAI 1,* 1–3.

Woodham, R. J. 1978. Reflectance map technique for analyzing surface defects in metal castings. AI Memo 457, AI Laboratory, Massachusetts Institute of Technology. (Doctoral dissertation.)

Wos, L., Robinson, G. A., and Carson, D. F. 1965. Efficiency and completeness of the set of support strategy in theorem proving. *J. ACM* 12:536–541.

Yachida, M., and Tsuji, S. 1971. Application of color information to recognition of 3-dimensional objects. *Pattern Recognition* 3(3):307–323.

Yakimovsky, Y., and Feldman, J. A. 1973. A semantics-based decision theory region analyzer. *IJCAI 3,* 580–588.

Yovits, M. C., Jacobi, G. T., and Goldstein, G. D. (Eds.). 1962. *Self-organizing systems 1962*. Washington, D.C.: Spartan Books.

Zadeh, L.A. 1979. Approximate reasoning based on fuzzy logic. *IJCAI 6*, 1004–1010.

Zucker, S. W. 1976a. Region growing: Childhood and adolescence. *Computer Graphics and Image Processing* 5:382–399.

Zucker, S. W. 1976b. Toward a model of texture. *Computer Graphics and Image Processing* 5:109–202.

Zucker, S. W., Hummel, R., and Rosenfeld, A. 1977. An application of relaxation labeling to line and curve enhancement. *IEEE Transactions on Computers* C–26(4):394–403.

Cumulative Indexes

NAME INDEX FOR VOLUMES I, II, AND III

Pages on which an author's work is discussed are italicized.

SUBJECT INDEX FOR VOLUMES I, II, AND III

601

ABOUT THIS BOOK

The Handbook of Artificial Intelligence was designed and edited by Dianne Kanerva, who also established the production procedures and managed the production team that typeset the volumes.

The *Handbook* is unusual in that, from the soliciting and writing of manuscripts through the production of camera-ready copy, it was prepared entirely through the facilities of the three computer systems (SUMEX, SCORE, and SAIL) available to the Heuristic Programming Project at Stanford University. Volumes II and III were typeset at the Department of Computer Science using Donald Knuth's Tau Epsilon Chi (TEX), a computer-based typesetting system designed for mathematical text. The text of the volumes is set in the Computer Modern family of fonts designed by Knuth with his META-FONT system. Intermediate copy was produced with a Xerox Dover laser printer; final camera-ready copy was produced with an Alphatype CRS photo-typesetter.

José L. González was responsible for tailoring and implementing a TEX macro package designed by Max Díaz to the requirements of the *Handbook*. González prepared the camera-ready copy of Volumes II and III of the *Handbook* and participated in editing. Dikran Karagueuzian prepared and typeset the bibliographies and name indexes of these last two volumes. The other individuals who participated in typesetting the *Handbook* were David Eppstein (especially the design of macros for the figures in Chap. XV and for the indexes), Jonni Kanerva (especially the layout and typesetting of Chap. XIII), and Janet Feigenbaum and Barbara Laddaga (especially the initial application of TEX to the task). Karagueuzian and Christopher Tucci operated the Alphatype CRS phototypesetter.

Printing, binding, jacket design, and artwork are by the publisher, William Kaufmann, Inc.

DUE

TDI

R

001.535   H236
                                           v.3

Mills College Library
Withdrawn

MILLS COLLEGE
LIBRARY

THE HANDBOOK OF ARTIFICIAL INTELLIGENCE

Volumes I and II by Avron Barr and Edward A. Feigenbaum

Volume III by Paul R. Cohen and Edward A. Feigenbaum